The
New International
Lesson Annual

2007-2008

September–August

Abingdon Press
Nashville

THE NEW INTERNATIONAL LESSON ANNUAL 2007–2008

Copyright © 2007 by Abingdon Press

This book is printed on acid-free paper.

Scripture quotations, unless otherwise noted, are from the *New Revised Standard Version of the Bible,* copyright 1989, Division of Christian Education of the National Council of the Churches of Christ in the United States of America. Used by permission. All rights reserved.

Scripture quotations marked (RSV) are taken from the *Revised Standard Version of the Bible,* copyright 1946, 1952, 1971 by the Division of Christian Education of the National Council of the Churches of Christ in the United States of America. Used by permission. All rights reserved.

Scripture quotations marked (NIV) are taken from the HOLY BIBLE, NEW INTERNATIONAL VERSION®. NIV®. Copyright © 1973, 1978, 1984 by International Bible Society. Used by permission of Zondervan Publishing House. All rights reserved.

Scripture quotations marked (KJV) are taken from the King James or Authorized Version of the Bible.

ISBN 978-0-687-49392-0

ISSN 1084-872X

07 08 09 10 11 12 13 14 15 16—10 9 8 7 6 5 4 3 2 1

MANUFACTURED IN THE UNITED STATES OF AMERICA

Preface

We are delighted to welcome you to the 2007–2008 study of God's creativity as recorded in Genesis; Christ's call as heard in the Gospel of Luke; God's covenantal relationship with the Israelites as documented in First and Second Chronicles, Daniel, Haggai, and Nehemiah; and images of Christ found in Hebrews, the Gospels, and the Letter of James. As you study each week, you will join countless Bible students around the world who use resources based on the work of the Committee on the Uniform Series, also known as the International Lessons.

Although adult learners often use *The New International Lesson Annual*, it is mainly designed for teachers of adults who want a solid biblical basis for each session and a teaching plan that will help them lead their classes. The following features are especially valuable for busy teachers who want to provide in-depth Bible study experiences for their students. Each lesson includes the following sections:

Previewing the Lesson highlights the background and lesson Scripture, focus of the lesson, three goals for the learners, a pronunciation guide in lessons where you may find unfamiliar words or names, and supplies you will need to teach.

Reading the Scripture includes the Scripture lesson printed in both the *New Revised Standard Version* and the *New International Version*. By printing these two highly respected translations in parallel columns, you can easily compare them for in-depth study. If your own Bible is another version, you will then have three translations to explore as you prepare each lesson.

Understanding the Scripture closely analyzes the background Scripture by looking at each verse. Here you will find help in understanding concepts, ideas, places, and persons pertinent to each week's lesson. You may also find explanations for Greek or Hebrew words that are essential for understanding the text.

Interpreting the Scripture looks at the lesson Scripture, delves into its meaning, and relates it to contemporary life.

Sharing the Scripture provides you with a detailed teaching plan. It is divided into two major sections: *Preparing to Teach* and *Leading the Class*.

In the *Preparing to Teach* section you will find a devotional reading related to the lesson for your own spiritual enrichment and a "to do list" to prepare your mind and classroom for the session.

The *Leading the Class* portion begins with "Gather to Learn" activities to welcome the students and draw them into the lesson. Here, the students' stories and experiences, or other contemporary stories, are highlighted as preparation for the Bible story. The next three headings of *Leading the Class* are the three main "Goals for the Learners." The first goal always focuses on the Bible story itself. The second goal relates the Bible story to the lives of the adults in your class. The third goal prompts the students to take action on what they have learned. You will find a variety of activities under each of these goals to help the learners fulfill them. The activities are diverse in nature and may include: listening, reading, writing, speaking, singing, drawing, interacting with others, and meditating. The lesson ends with "Continue the Journey," where you will find closing activities, preparation for the following week, and ideas for students to commit themselves to action during the week, based on what they have learned.

In addition to these weekly features, you will find:

- **Teacher enrichment article,** is intended to be useful throughout the year, so we hope you will read it immediately and refer to it often. The article in this volume, "Leading Effective Discussions for Spiritual Growth," will help you to discern when to use discussion, ways to overcome barriers, and ideas on framing questions. You will find the article immediately following the Contents.
- **List of Background Scriptures** is offered especially for those of you who keep back copies of *The New International Lesson Annual*. This feature, which follows the teacher enrichment article, will enable you to locate Bible background passages used during the current year. At some future date you may want to refer to these Scriptures.
- **Introduction to each quarter,** provides you with a quick survey of each lesson to be studied in the quarter. You will find the title, background Scripture, date, and a brief summary of each week's basic thrust. This feature begins on the first page of each quarter.
- **Meet Our Writer,** which follows each quarterly introduction, provides biographical information about each writer, including education, pastoral and academic teaching experience, previous publications, and family information.
- **The Big Picture,** written by the same writer who authored the quarter's lessons, is designed to give you a broader scope of the materials to be covered than is possible in each weekly lesson. You will find this background article immediately following the writer's biography in each quarter.
- **Close-up** give you focused information such as a time line, chart, overview, or list that you may choose to use anytime during the quarter, perhaps even repeatedly.
- **Faith in Action,** provides you will find ideas related to the broad sweep of the quarter that the students can use individually or as a class to act on what they have been studying. These ideas are intended for use beyond the classroom.

We love to hear from our readers! If you ever have any questions or comments, please write to me and include your e-mail address or phone number. I will respond as soon as your message reaches my home office in Maryland.

Dr. Nan Duerling
Abingdon Press
PO Box 801
Nashville, TN 37202

We thank you for choosing *The New International Lesson Annual*. God's grace and peace be with you as you study and lead others to a broader understanding of the Bible and a deeper relationship with our Lord Jesus Christ.

Nan Duerling, Ph.D.
Editor, *The New International Lesson Annual*

CONTENTS

List of Background Scriptures 10
Leading Effective Discussions for Spiritual Growth 11

FIRST QUARTER

God Created a People
September 2–November 25, 2007

Introduction: God Created a People 15
Meet Our Writer: Dr. Charles D. Yoost 16
The Big Picture: Telling the Story of God's Creation 17
Close-up: Abraham's Family Tree 21
Faith in Action: Creativity 22

UNIT 1: GOD CREATED A PEOPLE
(September 2-30)

LESSON		PAGE
1.	God Created the Heavens and the Earth 23	
	September 2—Genesis 1:1-6, 8, 10, 12-15, 19-20, 22-23, 25	
2.	God Created Humankind 31	
	September 9—Genesis 1:26-30	
3.	Abraham, Sarah, and Isaac 39	
	September 16—Genesis 15:5-6; 18:11-14a; 21:1-8	
4.	Abraham, Hagar, and Ishmael 47	
	September 23—Genesis 21:9-21	
5.	Isaac and Rebekah 55	
	September 30—Genesis 24:34-40, 42-45, 48	

UNIT 2: GOD'S PEOPLE INCREASED
(October 7-28)

6.	Esau and Jacob as Rivals 63
	October 7—Genesis 25:19-34
7.	Jacob's Dream at Bethel 71
	October 14—Genesis 28:10-22
8.	Jacob and Rachel 79
	October 21—Genesis 29:20-35
9.	Esau and Jacob Reconciled 87
	October 28—Genesis 33:1-11

UNIT 3: GOD'S PEOPLE RE-CREATED
(November 4-25)

10. Joseph's Dream 95
        November 4—Genesis 37:5-11, 19-21, 23-24a, 28
11. Joseph's Dream Began to Come True 103
        November 11—Genesis 41:25-40
12. God Preserved a Remnant 111
        November 18—Genesis 45:1-12
13. Jacob Blessed His Family 119
        November 25—Genesis 48:11-19

SECOND QUARTER

God's Call to the Christian Community
December 2, 2007–February 24, 2008

Introduction: God's Call to the Christian Community 127
Meet Our Writer: Dr. Michael Fink 128
The Big Picture: The Community Luke Envisioned 129
Close-up: The Gospel of Luke 133
Faith in Action: Responding to God's Call 134

UNIT 1: GOD'S CALL AT CHRISTMAS AND BEYOND
(December 2-30)

LESSON   PAGE
1. Called to Believe! 135
        December 2—Luke 1:8-23
2. Called to Be a Vessel 143
        December 9—Luke 1:26-38
3. Called to Proclaim! 151
        December 16—Luke 1:64, 67-80
4. Called to Rejoice! 159
        December 23—Luke 2:1-14
5. Called to Witness! 167
        December 30—Luke 2:22-35

UNIT 2: THE AWARENESS OF GOD'S INSTRUCTION
(January 6-27)

6. Inspired to Inquire! 175
        January 6—Luke 2:41-52
7. Inspired to Love! 183
        January 13—Luke 6:27-36
8. Inspired to Pray! 191
        January 20—Luke 11:5-13
9. Inspired to Trust! 199
        January 27—Luke 12:22-34

UNIT 3: GOD SUMMONS US TO RESPOND!
(February 3-24)

10.   Summoned to Labor! 207
         February 3—Luke 10:1-12, 17-20
11.   Summoned to Repent! 215
         February 10—Luke 13:1-9
12.   Summoned to Be Humble! 223
         February 17—Luke 14:1, 7-14
13.   Summoned to Be a Disciple! 231
         February 24—Luke 14:25-33

THIRD QUARTER

God, the People, and the Covenant
March 2–May 25, 2008

Introduction: God, the People, and the Covenant 239
Meet Our Writer: Rev. Janice Catron 240
The Big Picture: Covenantal Relationships 241
Close-up: The Chronicler and History 245
Faith in Action: Remembering and Caring 246

UNIT 1: SIGNS OF GOD'S COVENANT
(March 2-30)

LESSON   PAGE
1.   The Ark Comes to Jerusalem 247
         March 2—1 Chronicles 15:1-3, 14-16, 25-28
2.   God's Covenant with David 255
         March 9—1 Chronicles 17:1, 3-4, 6-15
3.   God Calls Solomon to Build the Temple 263
         March 16—1 Chronicles 28:5-10, 20-21
4.   Fulfillment of God's Promise 271
         March 23—2 Chronicles 6:10, 12-17; Luke 24:44-49
5.   Josiah Renews the Covenant 279
         March 30—2 Chronicles 34:15, 18-19, 25-27, 29, 31-33

UNIT 2: THE COVENANT IN EXILE
(April 6-27)

6.   Daniel Keeps Covenant in a Foreign Land 287
         April 6—Daniel 1:8-20
7.   Three Refuse to Break Covenant 295
         April 13—Daniel 3:10-13, 16-18, 21, 24-25
8.   Daniel's Life-and-Death Test 303
         April 20—Daniel 6:4-7, 10, 16, 19, 21, 25-26
9.   Daniel's Prayer for the People 311
         April 27—Daniel 9:1-7, 17-19

UNIT 3: RESTORATION AND COVENANT RENEWAL
(May 4-25)

10.   The Temple Rebuilt 319
        May 4—Haggai 1:1-4, 7-10, 12-15
11.   Rebuilding the Wall 327
        May 11—Nehemiah 2:1-8, 11, 17-18
12.   Up Against the Wall 335
        May 18—Nehemiah 4:1-3, 6-9, 13-15; 6:15
13.   Call to Renew the Covenant 343
        May 25—Nehemiah 8:1-3, 5-6, 13-14, 17-18

FOURTH QUARTER

Images of Christ
June 1–August 31, 2008

Introduction: Images of Christ 351
Meet Our Writer: Dr. John Indermark 352
The Big Picture: Images of Christ in Hebrews, the Gospels, and Us 353
Close up: Jesus in the Visual Arts 357
Faith in Action: Reflecting Christ's Image 358

UNIT 1: IMAGES OF CHRIST IN HEBREWS
(June 1-29)

LESSON   PAGE
1.   Jesus as God's Son 359
        June 1—Hebrews 1:1-4, 8-12
2.   Christ as Intercessor 367
        June 8—Hebrews 7:20-28
3.   Christ as Redeemer 375
        June 15—Hebrews 9:11-18; 10:12-14, 17-18
4.   Christ as Leader 383
        June 22—Hebrews 12:1-13
5.   The Eternal Christ 391
        June 29—Hebrews 13:1-16

UNIT 2: IMAGES OF CHRIST IN THE GOSPELS
(July 6-27)

6.   Christ as Teacher 399
        July 6—Luke 4:31-37; 20:1-8
7.   Christ as Healer 407
        July 13—Mark 1:29-45
8.   Christ as Servant 415
        July 20—John 13:1-8, 12-20
9.   Christ as Messiah 423
        July 27—Matthew 16:13-23

UNIT 3: IMAGES OF CHRIST IN US
(August 3-31)

10.   Doers of the Word 431
         August 3—James 1:17-27

11.   Impartial Disciples 439
         August 10—James 2:1-13

12.   Wise Speakers 447
         August 17—James 3:1-10, 13-18

13.   People of Godly Behavior 455
         August 24—James 4:1-12

14.   Prayerful Community 463
         August 31—James 5:13-18

List of Background Scriptures, 2007–2008

Old Testament

Genesis 1:1-25 . . . . September 2	1 Chronicles 15:1-28 . . . . March 2
Genesis 1:26–2:3 . . . . September 9	1 Chronicles 17:1-27 . . . . March 9
Genesis 15:1-6 . . . . September 16	1 Chronicles 28:1-21 . . . . March 16
Genesis 18:1-15 . . . . September 16	2 Chronicles 6 . . . . March 23
Genesis 21:1-8 . . . . September 16	2 Chronicles 34 . . . . March 30
Genesis 21:9-21 . . . . September 23	Ezra 5 . . . . May 4
Genesis 24 . . . . September 30	Nehemiah 1:1–2:20 . . . . May 11
Genesis 25:19-34 . . . . October 7	Nehemiah 4–6 . . . . May 18
Genesis 27:41–28:22 . . . . October 14	Nehemiah 8 . . . . May 25
Genesis 29 . . . . October 21	Daniel 1 . . . . April 6
Genesis 33 . . . . October 28	Daniel 3 . . . . April 13
Genesis 37 . . . . November 4	Daniel 6 . . . . April 20
Genesis 41:25-45 . . . . November 11	Daniel 9 . . . . April 27
Genesis 43:1–45:15 . . . . November 18	Haggai 1 . . . . May 4
Genesis 48:8-21 . . . . November 25	

New Testament

Matthew 16:13-23 . . . . July 27	Luke 14:25-33 . . . . February 24
Mark 1:29-45 . . . . July 13	Luke 20:1-8 . . . . July 6
Luke 1:5-25 . . . . December 2	Luke 24 . . . . March 23
Luke 1:26-38 . . . . December 9	John 13:1-20 . . . . July 20
Luke 1:57-80 . . . . December 16	Hebrews 1 . . . . June 1
Luke 2:1-20 . . . . December 23	Hebrews 7 . . . . June 8
Luke 2:22-38 . . . . December 30	Hebrews 9:11–10:18 . . . . June 15
Luke 2:41-52 . . . . January 6	Hebrews 12:1-13 . . . . June 22
Luke 4:31-37 . . . . July 6	Hebrews 13:1-16 . . . . June 29
Luke 6:27-36 . . . . January 13	James 1 . . . . August 3
Luke 11:5-13 . . . . January 20	James 2 . . . . August 10
Luke 12:22-34 . . . . January 27	James 3 . . . . August 17
Luke 10:1-12, 17-20 . . . . February 3	James 4 . . . . August 24
Luke 13:1-9 . . . . February 10	James 5 . . . . August 31
Luke 14:1, 7-14 . . . . February 17	

LEADING EFFECTIVE DISCUSSIONS FOR SPIRITUAL GROWTH

NAN DUERLING

Each teacher has methods that feel comfortable. Lecture is the preferred method for some teachers, and it certainly has its place, especially when you want to impart information that is likely unfamiliar to the class. However, once that information has been shared, students need an opportunity to interact with each other as they try to interpret that information and discern how it might apply to their lives. One very useful way to provide the environment for interaction is to lead a discussion. A class session can profitably include lecture *and* discussion. You do not have to choose one or the other; you can incorporate both. But you need to know when to select the discussion method, how to overcome the barriers to effective discussions, and how to ask questions that will evoke meaningful discussion.

Overcoming Barriers to Effective Discussions

Discussions can feel threatening to the leader. When you lecture, you control the information being shared. You do not have to worry about fielding a question or comment that you may not know how to answer. You do not have to be concerned about adults exploring questions whose answers are not carefully scripted. But is your purpose in leading the class to be seen as the "guru" who is always knowledgeable, or is it to help the students become spiritually formed in the likeness of Christ? Most assuredly, it is the latter. To assist others in the difficult work of spiritual formation, you need to be willing to take some risks. Ask yourself: What's the worst thing that will happen if I do not know an answer? In my experience, the answer is "absolutely nothing." Often I ask the student with the question to do some research and report back the following week. If possible, I give them some ideas as to where to look to find the information. This process empowers the adults to be better students of the Bible, to appreciate the scope of church history, and to recognize that committed Christians often disagree on answers. Sometimes I just affirm the validity of the question and note that even though people of faith have been wrestling with that very question for millennia, we still have no satisfactory answer because God moves in mysterious ways! If we only ask questions that have a specific answer, we probably are not asking the profound questions that will empower us to grow spiritually.

My class members do not want to talk. People attend classes for many reasons. Admittedly, some simply want to soak up any information you have to offer. Knowledge is important to our discipleship, but it is only one part of the spiritual growth equation. Making the knowledge one's own and integrating it into one's life are essential. We need to acknowledge that some adults are shy and choose not to share their ideas. Often, though, when students are reluctant to talk, the problem is that they fear looking "stupid" in front of their peers. As the teacher, you can allay that fear by the way you handle their questions. Encourage the class with comments such as, "There's no such thing as a stupid question," or "We're here to help each other learn, since none of us has all the answers." Affirm the importance of their questions. And when you are asking questions yourself, try to make them open-ended and non-threatening. (We'll talk more about framing types of questions later.) Recognize differences of opinion, but do not let the discussion turn into an opportunity for a dominant personality to convince everyone of the "correctness" of his or her opinion. Also, if students are willing to share personal information, agree together to keep sensitive information confidential.

Our class is much too large for a discussion. Some classes are huge, but meaningful discussion can go on in groups of three to five. Your main job as the leader in this situation is to provide the questions, not hear and adjudicate all the answers. Adult learners have life experiences and, in many cases, years of learning in the church. They can work in pairs or groups without needing a leader to say their answers are right or wrong. You will want to read aloud the questions, and if more than two questions are under consideration, post them on newsprint so that the groups can refer to them. When the groups come back together, you can ask them to report on their ideas; invite them to share a new insight, surprise, or puzzle that arose during the discussion; or just move on in the session without further comment. The groups do not need to rehash their entire conversation for the whole class.

Our classroom is oddly shaped or has poor acoustics. Again, smaller groups can go a long way toward overcoming this problem. Even if you meet in a sanctuary with fixed pews, two or three people in the same pew can talk together. Many people will be able to turn around to speak with others behind them. If you meet in a classroom and have access to tables, gather groups of four to six around each table. Or arrange chairs (and tables) in a U-shape so that people are looking at one another. If the acoustics are poor, having the students talk with people closer to them, and making sure that people can see each other, will enable everyone to hear better. If you are leading a discussion with the total group and find that people are not hearing each other, try asking the speaker to repeat a comment, or say it louder yourself so that everyone can hear it.

Discussions just pool everyone's ignorance. Here's where knowing when to lead a discussion is critical. Discussions are not appropriate for all situations. If you are trying, for example, to solicit information on the fall of Jerusalem in 587 B.C., you may find that the students do not have enough information to discuss that event. In this case, you may want to have a lecture prepared. Or you may want to provide research resources, such as commentaries, and devise specific questions for the students to answer using this expert help. Or, you may want to show a video in which a respected scholar speaks on the topic at hand. Once the students have credible information, then you will be able to discuss it.

Framing Questions for Information

Now that we've considered some barriers to discussion and ways to overcome them, let's look at some ways to frame effective discussion questions. As we consider the following examples, remember that different types of questions serve different purposes. Some questions elicit information. Others call forth imaginative responses to the information. One of the tricks to leading an effective discussion is to discern when one type of question will better serve the needs of the class than another type.

Yes or No Questions. The simplest—and least effective—questions elicit a yes or no answer. A yes or no question, such as "Do you think Sarah was happy to learn she was pregnant?" is closed because it does not really advance the discussion. Try rephrasing questions so that they are open-ended and will spark discussion: "Why do you think Sarah was happy to learn she was pregnant?" This question can encourage comments that can go in a number of different directions: pregnancy paves the way for God's promise of heirs to be fulfilled; pregnancy will take away the shame and isolation Sarah felt due to her barrenness; Sarah is thrilled to be able, at last, to give Abraham a child; Sarah has wanted to mother a child.

Factual Questions. Each of these questions has a specific, factual answer. Some easy questions that call for a factual response can help to "warm up" the class, but be careful about over-using them, especially for more difficult information that may not be common knowledge among the class members.

❖ "*Who* wrote the book of Revelation?"
❖ "*What* happened on the day of Pentecost?"
❖ "*Where* is Shechem?"
❖ "*When* did Nebuchadnezzar's troops sack Jerusalem and burn the temple?"
❖ "*How* did the Hebrews, led by Joshua, defeat Jericho?"

Analysis Questions. These questions help the students to probe deeper and re-group information in new ways.

❖ You might, for example, ask a question that calls for comparison and contrast: "How are the actions and attitudes of Elijah similar to and different from those of the priests of Baal on Mount Carmel, as described in 1 Kings 18:20-40?"
❖ Or you may try to seek a cause and effect: "What behaviors of the people, especially of the Israelite leaders, do Amos and Micah cite as reasons for impending punishment from God?"
❖ You may also ask the students to make some evaluations: "In John 4, Jesus and the woman of Samaria have a discussion. What effect did this discussion have on the woman? What effect did it appear to have on the disciples? Give reasons to support your answer."
❖ Consider asking the students to summarize material: "As you read accounts of Jesus' crucifixion in the four Gospels, which points are found in all of them?"
❖ Also think about raising questions that call for a definition. Generally, terms such as "grace," "salvation," or "born again," have different meanings for different people. Here's a sample question: "How would you define the way that Paul uses the word 'flesh' in his epistles?"

Framing Questions for Imagination

So far, we have been considering questions relating to thinking about specific information. They are very "left-brained" and, as educators would call them, "cognitive." They depend on knowledge, reason, and logic. But there are other types of questions that focus on the "right brain," our intuitive, creative, emotional side. For purposes of spiritual formation these "affective" questions are equally important, perhaps more so.

What If Questions. These questions challenge the students to think about how certain actions have affected the course of history. By focusing on specific actions the adults can conjecture what might have happened if. They can also recognize the importance of faithful response to God, even when the task seemed too challenging.

❖ "Despite being called from a burning bush, Moses had to be convinced to lead the Hebrews out of slavery. He did finally agree, but what might have happened if he had said no? What options did God have?"
❖ "Stephen preached an inspired sermon just before he was stoned to death as the first Christian martyr. What happened as a result of his death that aided the spread of the Christian faith? *(fact question)* What might have been the consequences had Stephen not been so bold and uncompromising in his witness?"

What Would You Have Done Questions. These speculative questions draw students into the Bible stories. Often we can see ourselves in the position of one of the Bible characters. We can more closely identify with how they might have felt. Spiritual growth can occur when our story intersects with the Bible story. The story is no longer "story" but has real meaning for our lives.

❖ "Suppose you had been in the crowd when Jesus broke a few loaves and fishes and fed a multitude—with leftovers. How would you have responded to Jesus?"

❖ "When Jesus called James and John, their father Zebedee and a hired man were left in the boat (Mark 1:20). What would you have said to your sons had you been Zebedee? What would you have said to Jesus?"

Sensory Questions. This type of question also draws the learner into the story. Even a new Christian, or one who is untutored in the Bible, is able to participate in discussions where sensory questions are asked. Often you will read a passage of Scripture, asking the students to be aware of what they can see, hear, taste, touch, or feel before you ask these questions.

❖ After reading Genesis 1:1–2:3 ask, "As the male and female created in the image of God first became aware of their surroundings, what might they have seen, heard, tasted, touched, or felt? How might they have responded to these sensations?"

❖ After reading the story of the transfiguration from Matthew 17:1-8, ask, "What sensory impressions might Peter, James, and John have experienced? Had you been with them, how do you think these experiences would have affected you?"

Retell the Story Questions. Consider challenging the students to use modern images to convey biblical teachings. Using these questions will prod the adults to think about what the story really means, as opposed to simply parroting what it says.

❖ "How could you retell the parable of the prodigal son, using contemporary images that a child can easily understand?"

❖ "Jesus said in Acts 1:8 that we are to be his witnesses 'to the ends of the earth.' Suppose you have an opportunity to share the good news of Jesus with someone who has never heard of him. What would you say?"

Putting It All Together

These examples will give you some ideas for constructing questions that will engage the students in meaningful discussion about the Bible stories and about how these stories impact their own faith journey. In addition to questions found in *The New International Lesson Annual* under Sharing the Scripture, you will want to construct questions that address the needs and concerns of your specific group. As you become more proficient in asking questions, you'll feel more comfortable about creating questions on the spot, often based on issues that the students themselves raise.

As you lead a discussion, you need to be aware of the group dynamics. Are some trying to impress others with their great storehouse of knowledge? Are some trying to sway opinion so that everyone believes as they do? Are some so enamored with the sound of their own voices that they try to dominate the discussion? As the leader you need to get control over these situations. Here are some methods that I have found useful that you may want to try.

• Have an understanding with the class that all points of view will be heard. Each adult may decide to agree or disagree, but he or she must be respectful of other opinions.

• Make the class feel successful. If you ask a question that drops with a thud to the floor, say something such as, "Gee, I think I had better rephrase that."

• Silence can truly be golden. Some people will have an immediate (often pat) answer for any question. Others will want to think more carefully before speaking. Allow time for the thinkers to respond.

• Relax! The world will not fall off of its axis just because you don't know a few answers or phrase a few questions poorly.

• Be encouraging, hospitable, and inviting. Let the students know that you genuinely want to hear their questions and answers.

First Quarter
God Created a People

SEPTEMBER 2, 2007—NOVEMBER 25, 2007

The 2007–2008 Sunday school year fittingly begins at the Bible's beginning with a study of Genesis. During this quarter we will trace the story of God's creative power from the creation of the universe through human creation to the creation of a covenant people. Although different circumstances, including barrenness, threatened the covenant family's existence more than once, God was always at hand to protect, preserve, and bless them.

Unit 1, "God Created a People," is a five-lesson exploration of Israel's earliest stories. "God Created the Heavens and the Earth," opens the unit on September 2 by examining the soaring poetic account of creation in Genesis 1:1-25. We move to Genesis 1:26–2:3 on September 9 to consider how "God Created Humankind" in the divine image. On September 16 we see the covenant family begin to form according to the stories in Genesis 15:1-6, 18:1-15, and 21:1-8 of "Abraham, Sarah, and Isaac." Genesis 21:9-21 explores the heart-wrenching relationship of "Abraham, Hagar, and Ishmael" on September 23. The unit concludes on September 30 as we see in Genesis 24 how God enables a servant to find a life-partner for Abraham's son in "Isaac and Rebekah."

The four sessions of Unit 2, "God's People Increased," examine the development of the covenant family through Jacob and his twin, Esau. Genesis 25:19-34 depicts "Esau and Jacob as Rivals" when this unit commences on October 7. "Jacob's Dream at Bethel," the session for October 14 from Genesis 27:41–28:22, confirms through the well-known dream of Jacob's "ladder" that the covenant people will continue through him. Intrigue abounds on October 21 with the story of "Jacob and Rachel," recounted in Genesis 29, as Jacob was tricked into first marrying Rachel's older sister, Leah. Despite years of separation after Jacob conned his brother out of his birthright, the restoration of a relationship is possible as we learn from "Esau and Jacob Reconciled," the lesson for October 28 rooted in Genesis 33.

Unit 3, "God's People Re-created," focuses on Joseph, Jacob's beloved son by Rachel—who had been barren for many years. As we begin on November 4, Genesis 37 describes "Joseph's Dream," which reveals his vocation—a disclosure that increases friction with his family. "Joseph's Dream Began to Come True," the lesson for November 11 from Genesis 41:25-45, affirms the plans and purpose God has for Joseph. In the midst of a widespread famine, "God Preserved a Remnant" through the work and careful stewardship of Joseph, as we shall see on November 18 in our study of Genesis 41:1–45:15. The fall quarter closes with a study of Genesis 48:8-21 on November 25 as Joseph takes his two sons, Ephraim and Manasseh, to his elderly father and "Jacob Blessed His Family."

MEET OUR WRITER

DR. CHARLES D. YOOST

Charles D. Yoost is the senior pastor of Church of the Saviour in Cleveland Heights, Ohio, where he has served since 1998. The congregation's worship services are broadcast locally on radio and television, and internationally by way of the Internet at www.wclv.com.

From 1992 to 1998, Yoost served as the Mansfield District Superintendent of the East Ohio Conference of The United Methodist Church. Prior to that, he was pastor at Church Hill United Methodist Church, Youngstown, and Northampton United Methodist Church, both in Ohio.

Yoost earned his bachelor of arts degree from the University of Akron. He received a master of theology and doctor of ministry degree from Boston University School of Theology.

In the East Ohio Conference, he currently chairs the Board of Congregational Development and is a frequent leader of workshops on discipleship and church growth. He also is a trustee of Ohio Northern University and the East Ohio Area Foundation of The United Methodist Church. Having served as a General Conference delegate in 1996, 2000, and 2004, Yoost was also a delegate to the World Methodist Conference in 1996. During the 2001-2004 quadrennium, he chaired the Legislation and Evaluation Committee of the General Board of Discipleship and was a member of the Steering Committee of the United Methodist Youth Organization. He has also served as the convener of the National Advisory Council for *Vision 2000*.

This is the third time Yoost has written for the *New International Lesson Annual*. He is also the author of five *Daily Bible Study* publications. He has written Sunday school lessons and daily devotions for *Mature Years* magazine, and for *Circuit Rider* magazine, a United Methodist publication for clergy.

Yoost is married and has two adult sons. His wife, Barbara, is a clinical nurse specialist, who teaches at the Kent State University College of Nursing. Son, Timothy and his wife, Jennie, are medial residents at the Medical University of South Carolina in Charleston. Son Stephen and his wife, Mary, practice law in Charlotte, North Carolina.

He enjoys participating in mission work trips with youth and adults. In his leisure time, Yoost plays the organ and piano.

THE BIG PICTURE: TELLING THE STORY OF GOD'S CREATION

The night air is cool. Although the desert sun has been beastly hot, once the sun goes down, a chill comes over the landscape. The surrounding area is eerily quiet. Danger lurks in the distance. Not only are hungry, wild beasts on the prowl but also gangs of robbers and thieves are known to lurk behind the rocks and in the caves. A fire gives light and warmth to the camp. Tired shepherds draw close to its gentle flames. A pot of stew is warming on the coals. Bread is unpacked from one of the knapsacks. Beverages are shared among the group.

Suppertime brings not only the nourishment of food but also the warmth and intellectual stimulation of conversation. With the size of the flock, each shepherd is often by himself for hours at a time. Now together for the evening meal and a night of rest, there will be some time for fellowship. After the food is shared, several find a comfortable spot just close enough to the fire to feel its warmth.

Andrew, one of the younger shepherds, asks Eli to tell a story. Eli is famous for his stories—famous, that is, among his colleagues and friends. He is a master storyteller. Even though the shepherds have heard his stories dozens of times before, they stop what they are doing, gather around, and become quiet as Eli begins.

"In the beginning," he says, clearing his throat and pausing for dramatic effect, "God created the heavens and the earth." For the next hour or so, Andrew and his fellow shepherds will sit spellbound. They will listen attentively as Eli tells them the story of creation, a story Eli heard his grandfather tell him, a story whose details are now so firmly etched in the minds and on the hearts of the shepherds that any one of them can correct him if he misplaces a detail. They can also prompt him should he hesitate. These are the stories of the clan. They give identity to the tribe—and meaning and purpose to life in this barren place.

For hundreds of years these stories were passed from generation to generation. When Israel became a nation, under the leadership of David, these stories were written on scrolls and came eventually to be known as Genesis, the first book of Moses. But for centuries the creation stories were part of an oral tradition that is practically as old as the race itself.

For Andrew and his fellow shepherds, the existence of God is assumed. In back of the created order is a Creator. No one could survive the heat of the desert sun and the loneliness of the desert nights without the presence and power of God.

Eli's story continues. He tells of the magnificent acts of God—separating the night from the day, water from the firmament, and fashioning of the sun and the moon. Andrew can almost see God taking a mass of hot, fiery substance and placing it in the sky, then reaching out and placing the moon out in the vast beyond as well. Finally, after God has designed the universe and has observed that it is good, at the center of the universe and at the apex of creation, God creates a person. Now Andrew and the others swell with pride, for Eli tells them that God created this person "in the image of God" (Genesis 1:27). That means the shepherds are special! Their daily existence may be monotonous and dreary, but they are not on this earth by accident, nor are they simply part of the natural order. They are children of God! As if that isn't enough, Eli reminds them that God said, "Be fruitful and multiply, and fill the earth and subdue it; and have dominion over the fish of the sea and over the birds of the air and over every living thing that moves upon the earth" (Genesis 1:28). How awesome to be part of God's creation! How special to be created by God! How humbling to be put in charge of every living thing! What a responsibility God has entrusted to us, thinks Andrew.

As one of the shepherds adds another coal to the fire to keep it burning through the night, Eli concludes his story with the creation of Eve. It will be several days until the shepherds return home to be reunited with their wives and families. Tonight the women will be with them only in their dreams. Eli's story will remind them of the fact that God knew it was not good for them to be alone. How thankful Andrew was that God had given him a partner in life. Naomi seemed to complement him so well. She was all the things that Andrew was not—gentle, attentive to detail, able to look at the big picture and plan for the future. How much Andrew loved her! As Eli finished his story, Andrew nodded off to sleep.

As the shepherds continued their search for pastures green enough to feed their growing flocks, Eli's stories continued each night. There were a number of versions of what had happened when the world was young, but all the Hebrew storytellers seemed to agree that their particular journey commenced with the calling of Abram.

Abram, too, was a shepherd, living a peaceful life in the country of Haran. God called him to leave his country, his kindred, and his father's house to go to a land that God did not identify. Trusting in God, Abram and his wife, Sarai, already senior citizens, packed their belongings and started a journey of faith.

Abram had been promised that he would be the father of many nations, yet Abram and Sarai were childless. God continued to promise, and Abram continued to trust God. Becoming a bit impatient, Sarai encouraged Abram to have a child with her slave girl, Hagar. The son born to them was named Ishmael. Sarai continued to be childless. God reiterated the covenant with Abram, changing both his and Sarai's names as a sign of God's claim upon their lives. Then one day Abraham and Sarah had three visitors come to their tent and tell them that Sarah would have a child. Sarah laughed in disbelief, just as Abraham had when God told him, but God had the last laugh, for Sarah bore a son: Isaac.

At this point in the story, Eli always became more animated. He told in some detail about the domestic problems between Sarah and Hagar, and of Sarah's growing resentment of Abraham's slave girl. Sarah became increasingly concerned about the inheritance that she wished to see Isaac receive. Ishmael, of course, was Abraham's firstborn son, which would entitle him to a double share of Abraham's estate.

In one of the sadder and more emotional chapters of the story, Abraham sends Hagar and Ishmael into the desert with barely enough provisions to make it down the road. Fearing death, Hagar braces for the worst. God hears her cry and provides for Hagar and her son. As part of God's promise to Abraham, eventually Ishmael became the father of a great nation and the progenitor of the Arabic people. What Eli would never know, but Bruce Feiler (*Abraham, A Journey to the Heart of Three Faiths*) tells us, is that early biographies of Muhammad "traced the lineage of the prophet's tribe back to Ishmael, and through him to Abraham, and thus back to Adam." Thus Abraham is the father, not only of the Jewish and Christian religion but of the followers of Islam as well. As Eli continues to tell his story, across the desert other shepherds are recounting the deeds of the travels of Ishmael and of Abraham, his father. Eli, however, is primarily interested in Isaac, from whom his family is descended.

Again, interest is high the night Eli tells the shepherds the romantic tale of Isaac and Rebekah. Not content to have his son marry one of the local women, Abraham sends Isaac back to Haran to find a wife. Stopping at the well outside the city, Isaac spots Rebekah, and it is love at first sight. Rebekah is willing to leave her family and becomes Isaac's wife, but alas, she, too, is barren. After Isaac prays to the Lord, Rebekah has twin boys, but the sibling rivalry begins while they are still in the womb! After a miserable pregnancy, Rebekah gives birth to Esau and Jacob, who are as different as day and night. Jacob is a gentle fellow, who likes domestic chores, while Esau is a rugged outdoorsman, preferring hunting to shepherding.

In a demonstration of the wit of his people, for which he takes considerable pride, Eli's voice gets stronger and more animated as he tells how Jacob tricked his brother and bought his birthright for a bowl of lentil stew! All the shepherds got a chuckle out of that one! But the chuckles are short-lived, for when he comes to his senses, Esau becomes enraged and plans to kill his brother. Jacob, getting wind of the impending danger, leaves home and heads for his Uncle Laban's home. On the way he has a dream. God assures Jacob that God is with him. God will fulfill the promise to make a great nation of Abraham and Isaac's descendants through Jacob. God can weave the human story into God's greater story and use all the characters in the story for God's purposes. The story of Jacob reminds the shepherds that God can use each of us, warts and all!

Now as Jacob nears the place where his Uncle Laban lives, he, too, stops at a well and meets Rachel, and again there is romance in the air! Jacob asks for Rachel's hand in marriage, and Laban agrees. However, the morning after the wedding, Jacob discovers that he has been tricked and finds Leah in his bed rather than her younger sister whom he loves. The trickster has been tricked! Defending his actions, because in their tradition the elder daughter must be married first, Laban promises Rachel's hand if Jacob will work another seven years. Smitten Jacob willingly agrees.

Now once again the issues of childbearing and resentment and family jealousy rear their ugly head. Leah has no problem having babies, but Rachel is barren and envious of her sister. Finally, Rachel is able to conceive and bear a son. When Joseph is born, he is the apple of his father's eye.

As a shepherd, Andrew can relate to Joseph's brothers. While they tended the sheep and traveled in much the same way that Andrew and his colleagues are used to doing, Joseph seemed to enjoy a carefree life by his father's side. Not only did Jacob send Joseph to spy on his brothers and report back to his doting father, the old man had made him a long robe with sleeves, as if Joseph were some kind of royalty!

Joseph, who enjoyed privileged status with his father, was also a prolific dreamer. Not only did he have wild dreams but he also felt compelled to share their content with his brothers. Always he was the star of the dream and his brothers were subservient to him. Eventually the dreams got so preposterous that even Joseph's father was taken aback.

One day when the brothers were at a considerable distance from home, they spotted Joseph on the horizon headed their way. They had had all they could take, and one of the brothers suggested killing him. But Reuben spoke up, "Let's not kill him, but throw him in that pit," he said, intending to rescue Joseph later on. The brothers put Joseph in the pit, but while they were discussing the whole matter, a caravan of traders came along, kidnapped Joseph, and took him with them to Egypt where they sold him as a slave.

Again, a sly smile came over the shepherds' faces as they mused over the fact that their ancestor Joseph always seemed to land on his feet. Joseph, the Hebrew slave, became a servant in Potiphar's house, a high-ranking official in the Egyptian government. Soon Joseph was put in charge of Potiphar's whole house. Again flirtation is part of the story. Joseph, a good-looking young man, catches the eye of Potiphar's wife, who desires to have sex with him. Joseph refuses, feeling that it would be disloyal to Potiphar. "Hell hath no fury like a woman scorned," so Potiphar's wife accuses Joseph of trying to rape her, and Joseph lands in prison.

While in prison, Joseph interprets two dreams. Both Pharaoh's chief baker and chief cupbearer have been put in prison. Joseph predicts that the chief cupbearer will be returned to his position, while the chief baker will be put to death. Both come to pass.

Alas, Pharaoh is haunted by dreams of his own. All of a sudden, the chief cupbearer remembers Joseph, who is wasting away in prison. (By this time Joseph has managed to become the person in charge of the prison, second in command to the chief jailer.) Joseph is summoned and interprets' Pharaoh's dreams. There will be seven years of plenty followed by seven years of lean, he tells Pharaoh. Joseph also recommends storing provisions for the coming famine. Pharaoh puts Joseph in charge of the entire operation and thus Egypt has grain when famine overcomes the whole land, just as Joseph predicted.

When the famine spreads, who should show up in Egypt needing food but the ten brothers. Joseph is happy to see them, but they do not recognize him, and that gives Joseph a window of opportunity to get even with them! He puts them through quite an ordeal before he reveals, "I am your brother, Joseph, whom you sold into Egypt" (Genesis 45:4). Fearful and apprehensive, the brothers are speechless. Yet Joseph reassures them that God's hand has been involved in the whole story. By coming to Egypt, Joseph is able to provide for his family's well-being. God has worked through Joseph to save not only his brothers and his beloved father, but also the whole human race.

Joseph invites his entire extended family to come to Egypt to live, and he promises to take care of them and provide for their well-being. The brothers go home and tell the news to Jacob, who is overjoyed that his son is alive and well.

When Joseph learns that his father is ill, he takes his two sons, Manasseh and Ephraim, to receive their grandfather's blessing. Jacob, who never thought he would see Joseph again, is thrilled to be able to place Joseph's sons on his lap and then give them his blessing. As he reaches out his hands to bless them, he uses his right hand to give the blessing to Ephraim, the younger brother. Joseph tries to correct his nearly blind father, but Jacob refuses to switch hands! History bears Joseph the fact that Ephraim will become the stronger tribe and predominate over the tribes of Manasseh. Andrew and the other shepherds nod their heads in agreement. The story concludes with the promise that Jacob's family will not always dwell in Egypt, but will eventually return to Canaan, the promised land.

As Andrew prepares his bedroll for another night's rest, he mulls over the stories he has heard. They have shaped his life. They have given him inspiration and encouragement on some dark days. They remind him of who he is and whose he is. He is grateful to Eli for his untiring willingness to share the stories of his people. Most of all, Abraham is grateful to God for God's creative, redemptive, and sustaining love, not only for Andrew and his family but also for all the peoples of the earth.

ABRAHAM'S FAMILY TREE

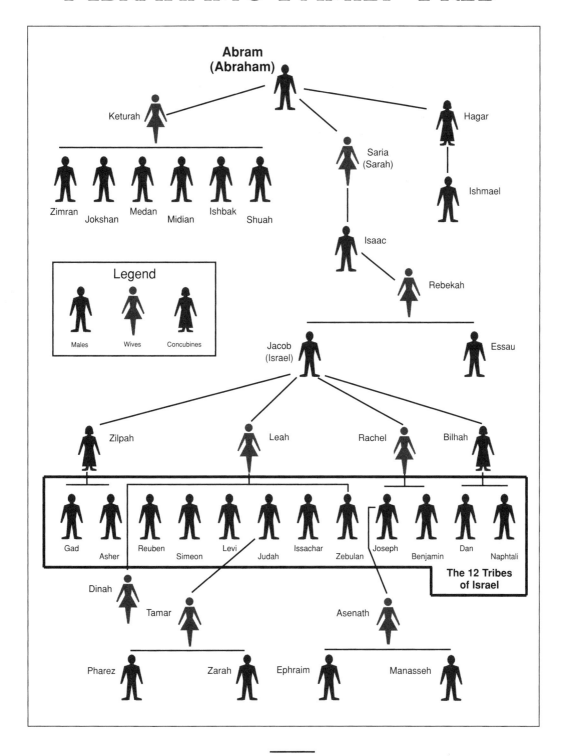

FAITH IN ACTION: CREATIVITY

During the fall quarter we are focusing on God's creative action: creating the universe, creating humanity, and creating a family of covenant people. We, too, can share in God's creativity in numerous ways. Help the adults to choose at least one idea from the list below that sparks their imagination. Suggest that they work individually, or with other members of the class, on the suggested project during times they schedule.

(1) Create a dish garden.
(2) Paint a picture that embodies some aspect of nature.
(3) Write a story about a family and its challenges.
(4) Use James Weldon Johnson's "The Creation" from *God's Trombones* and music of your choice as the setting for a modern dance.
(5) Arrange stones in a garden or patio as a sacred space, reminiscent of Jacob's stone pillow.
(6) Design and sew a quilt with symbols of your family or of your church's history.
(7) Carve an animal from wood and decorate it as you choose.
(8) Serve as a mediator to bring about reconciliation between two parties in conflict, possibly family members.
(9) Write a history of your family.
(10) Cook a special meal, perhaps including lentil soup.
(11) Make a collage depicting people of different ages, ethnic groups, races, and religions.
(12) Sing or play an instrument to praise God, using, if possible, words or music that you have written.
(13) Create a picture book for a child showing selected stories related to Abraham and his family.
(14) Make a scrapbook of events in your own family's life.
(15) Craft a candle, and light it during your personal devotional times.
(16) Brainstorm and implement ways that you can be a good steward of the resources entrusted to you.
(17) Write an autobiography of your relationship with God, including how your family's history has helped or hindered you in that relationship.
(18) Make a banner welcoming people to your Sunday school class.
(19) Build a diorama depicting Jacob's dream at Bethel with a "ladder" or staircase reaching toward heaven.
(20) Construct a chart of your family tree.
(21) Repair a home for a family in need.
(22) Use bits of colored paper, fabric, or tile to create a mosaic of a scene from this quarter's study.
(23) Construct a mobile that includes the sun, moon, and eleven stars Joseph saw in his dream (Genesis 37:9-11).
(24) Write a diary entry as if you were Sarah or Rebekah contemplating your barrenness.
(25) Make puppets from paper bags, fabric, or felt to tell stories of Jacob and Esau.
(26) Take photographs of the natural world. Put them together in an album or on a PowerPoint presentation with background music.
(27) Put together a crossword or word search puzzle using names and places we have studied during this quarter.
(28) Sculpt from clay a representation of a scene or character we have encountered this quarter.
(29) Use rhythm instruments to express emotions about different facets of creation, such as wind, fire, water, earth.
(30) Write a dialogue between Rachel and Leah.

SEPTEMBER 2

UNIT 1: GOD CREATED A PEOPLE

GOD CREATED THE HEAVENS AND THE EARTH

PREVIEWING THE LESSON

Lesson Scripture: Genesis 1:1-6, 8, 10, 12-15, 19-20, 22-23, 25
Background Scripture: Genesis 1:1-25
Key Verses: Genesis 1:1-2

Focus of the Lesson:
Without the earth and its ecosystems, human life would not be possible. How did creation come into being? In the Genesis 1 account, we learn that God chose to create life where none had existed and God provided means of support for that life.

Goals for the Learners:
(1) to explore the creation story as told in Genesis 1.
(2) to experience awe and wonder in the presence of creation.
(3) to make a commitment to accept stewardship responsibility for God's good creation.

Supplies:
Bibles, newsprint and marker, paper and pencils, hymnals, example of creation (such as a plant, rock, or animal)

READING THE SCRIPTURE

NRSV
Genesis 1:1-6, 8, 10, 12-15, 19-20, 22-23, 25

¹In the beginning when God created the heavens and the earth, ²the earth was a formless void and darkness covered the face of the deep, while a wind from God swept over the face of the waters. ³Then God said, "Let there be light"; and there was light. ⁴And God saw that the light was good; and God separated the light from the

NIV
Genesis 1:1-6, 8, 10, 12-15, 19-20, 22-23, 25

¹In the beginning God created the heavens and the earth. ²Now the earth was formless and empty, darkness was over the surface of the deep, and the Spirit of God was hovering over the waters.

³And God said, "Let there be light," and there was light. ⁴God saw that the light was good, and he separated the light from the

darkness. [5]God called the light Day, and the darkness he called Night. And there was evening and there was morning, the first day.

[6]And God said, "Let there be a dome in the midst of the waters, and let it separate the waters from the waters." . . . [8]God called the dome Sky. And there was evening and there was morning, the second day.

[10]God called the dry land Earth, and the waters that were gathered together he called Seas. And God saw that it was good. . . . [12]The earth brought forth vegetation: plants yielding seed of every kind, and trees of every kind bearing fruit with the seed in it. And God saw that it was good. [13]And there was evening and there was morning, the third day.

[14]And God said, "Let there be lights in the dome of the sky to separate the day from the night; and let them be for signs and for seasons and for days and years, [15]and let them be lights in the dome of the sky to give light upon the earth." And it was so. . . . [19]And there was evening and there was morning, the fourth day.

[20]And God said, "Let the waters bring forth swarms of living creatures, and let birds fly above the earth across the dome of the sky." . . . [22]God blessed them, saying, "Be fruitful and multiply and fill the waters in the seas, and let birds multiply on the earth." [23]And there was evening and there was morning, the fifth day.

[25]God made the wild animals of the earth of every kind, and the cattle of every kind, and everything that creeps upon the ground of every kind. And God saw that it was good.

darkness. [5]God called the light "day," and the darkness he called "night." And there was evening, and there was morning—the first day.

[6]And God said, "Let there be an expanse between the waters to separate water from water." . . . [8]God called the expanse "sky." And there was evening, and there was morning—the second day.

[10]God called the dry ground "land," and the gathered waters he called "seas." And God saw that it was good. . . . [12]The land produced vegetation: plants bearing seed according to their kinds and trees bearing fruit with seed in it according to their kinds. And God saw that it was good. [13]And there was evening, and there was morning—the third day.

[14]And God said, "Let there be lights in the expanse of the sky to separate the day from the night, and let them serve as signs to mark seasons and days and years, [15]and let them be lights in the expanse of the sky to give light on the earth." And it was so.

[19]And there was evening, and there was morning—the fourth day.

[20]And God said, "Let the water teem with living creatures, and let birds fly above the earth across the expanse of the sky." . . . [22]God blessed them and said, "Be fruitful and increase in number and fill the water in the seas, and let the birds increase on the earth." [23]And there was evening, and there was morning—the fifth day.

[25]God made the wild animals according to their kinds, the livestock according to their kinds, and all the creatures that move along the ground according to their kinds. And God saw that it was good.

UNDERSTANDING THE SCRIPTURE

Genesis 1:1-5. Creation bears evidence that there was a time when the world as we know it did not exist. From time immemorial, human beings have wanted to know how it all began. When and how did creation take place? The Bible addresses these questions by telling us that in the beginning, there was God. The Bible assumes God's presence and power from the dawn of creation.

In *The Storyteller's Companion to the Bible,* contemporary preacher and author Michael Williams states, "Before the beginning of the beginning of anything that ever was there was God and there was nothing. The emptiness was emptier than anyone could imagine, and the loneliness was lonelier than anyone could imagine. So God began to tell the story that became the universe, saying, 'Once upon a time there was light.' "

Most people today realize that the Bible is not a scientific textbook on creation. It is most fundamentally the product of a community of faith engaged in theological reflection on the creation. To claim that God created the world and all that exists is a matter of faith, grounded fundamentally in God's self-revelation. At the same time, in witnessing to God's creative activity the biblical writers made use of the available knowledge of the natural world. The creation stories presented in Genesis are pre-scientific in the sense that they predate modern science, but not in the sense that biblical people had no interest in those types of questions. Despite some modern claims to the contrary, the creation texts indicate that Israel's thinkers were very interested in questions of the "how" of creation as well as the questions of "who" and "why."

Described by many as a poem, the first verses of Genesis tell us that before God began creating, the earth was a "formless void"(1:2), something desolate and unproductive. Creation began when God brought order out of chaos. For biblical people, an ordered universe was conceivable only as a divine act of creation. God began the awesome process of bringing order out of chaos by calling light into existence.

God is the chief actor in the creation story. In fact, God is the only speaker. When God speaks, creation happens. The world as we know it comes into being in response to the sound of God's voice. Creation is good because creation comes from God.

How do we describe the beginning of it all, when God began the awesome work of creating? Some have called Genesis 1 a creation hymn. It sounds like poetry to our ears as God speaks sacred words and begins creating. The universe is vast, yet the author of Genesis makes the work so personal that we can almost hear God speaking the created order into being.

The most obvious sign of order is the gift of light and its daily separation from darkness. God's naming of all the works of creation reinforces God's power and dominion over creation.

Unlike our Western assumption, note that each day of creation begins with evening (see verses 5, 8, 13, 19, 23, and 31). Thus, each new day begins with rest.

Genesis 1:6-8. The Genesis story describes the sky as a translucent dome, a type of inverted basin placed in the midst of the waters. This God-given vault sets limits to the universe and provides focus for the story of humanity that will follow. God's speaking does not stand isolated from God's making. God does not create by merely speaking the created order into being, but by both speaking and doing. In like manner, existing in the image of God means having a vocation consisting of both word and deed.

Genesis 1:9-13. While not a scientific account of creation, the biblical narrative follows closely the sequence in which modern archeological research believes the world was formed. Modern science would concur with the biblical narrative that life began in the sea. Eventually dry land emerges, and plants grow on the dry ground. According to the biblical story, order has now replaced chaos to such an extent that the earth can produce vegetation.

Genesis 1:14-19. While light was created on the first day, time is now further ordered on Day Four. The luminaries that will preside over the day and the night are now created by God and put in place. Darkness is further restricted by the creation of the moon and the stars. Notice that neither the stars nor the planets have any divine character or potency. All power and authority is God's alone.

Genesis 1:20-23. The text makes it clear that everything that is created comes from God. The sea produces "swarms of living creatures"(1:20), including even the great sea monsters! Although frightening to some, these sea monsters are ultimately proclaimed good, for they were created by God's purposeful design.

When chaos is restricted, birds also emerge. To ensure the continuation of this good life, God endows each creature with reproductive functions.

Genesis 1:24-25. All the creatures that God created on the sixth day share the habitat of dry land. God continues to be pleased and feels that the creation is good. It is no accident that the words, "God saw that it was good," appear several times in the creation narrative (1:4, 10, 12, 18, 21, and 25). This affirmation of the created order is one of the strong themes of the story. Later in the narrative we will read about the sins of humankind and God's subsequent punishment. Before many chapters of Genesis are written, sin and death will become woven into the fabric of the story. Yet nothing in Genesis 3 changes the fact that human beings were created in the image of God and, as such, are part of God's good creation.

INTERPRETING THE SCRIPTURE

"He's Got the Whole World in His Hands"

Certainly the theme of this song expresses well the theological intent of the creation narrative. From Genesis to Revelation, this is God's story. God is the only speaker in the first chapter of Genesis. In the introduction to Genesis in his contemporary translation of the Bible known as *The Message,* pastor and teacher Eugene Peterson puts it well when he says, "God is the subject of life. God is foundational for living. If we don't have a sense of the primacy of God, we will never get it right, get life right, get our lives right. Not God at the margins; not God as an option; not God on the weekends. God at center and circumference; God first and last; God, God, God."

Peterson continues: "Genesis gets us off on the right foot. Genesis pulls us into a sense of reality that is God-shaped and God-filled. It gives us a vocabulary for speaking accurately and comprehensively about our lives, where we come from and where we are going, what we think and what we do, the people we live with and how to get along with them, the trouble we find ourselves in and the blessings that keep arriving."

There are times in our lives when music speaks in ways that words cannot. When the biblical writers wanted to describe the vastness and wonder of creation, they turned to the music of poetry and with word pictures attempted to describe the majesty and power of God. The four hymns I have chosen as subheadings help interpret the creation story for us today. Each hymn speaks to the awe and wonder of creation. With the writer of the Genesis story, each of these hymns affirms God at the center and circumference of our world.

"Morning Has Broken"

If you have ever been on an ocean beach or a mountain, (or at your kitchen table, for that matter), and have seen the sunrise, you know what an awe-inspiring sight that can be. The congregation I serve has the tradition of going to a cemetery on Easter morning. The worship service begins in darkness.

Slowly the area becomes lighter as the sun starts to rise. Soon the graveyard is ablaze with light. Light has overcome darkness once again! "Morning has broken like the first morning."

Peterson writes: "Earth was a soup of nothingness, a bottomless emptiness, an inky blackness. God's spirit brooded like a bird above the watery abyss.

"God spoke: 'Light! And light appeared.' "

My beloved Old Testament professor at Boston University School of Theology, Harrell F. Beck, as he interpreted these verses of Genesis said to our class, "I know what God was singing when God said, 'Let there be light!' God had a symphony orchestra playing Beethoven's *Fifth Symphony:* short, short, short, long. 'Let there be light! Let there be light!' " Dr. Beck sang.

How would *you* describe the dawn of creation, the separation of water from dry land, the formation of plants, the awesome act of bringing order out of chaos? The biblical writers used poetry and song to describe the indescribable, just as we do today. How do I describe my feelings for you? Let me sing you a song. How do I bring comfort to your troubled heart? Let me play you a tune. How do I communicate my conviction that God is at the center of the universe as well as at its periphery? Let the trumpet sound! Let the drum roll begin! The creative power of God is at work: "Praise for the singing! Praise for the morning!"

"God of the Sparrow, God of the Whale"

One of the more recent hymns cerebrating God's creative activity is "God of the Sparrow, God of the Whale." God has designed the world in such a way that all waters and plants, all fish and birds, all animals and all human beings have a place in God's created order.

Psalm 24:1 reminds us, "The earth is the LORD's and all that is in it, the world, and those who live in it." We do not own the creation; we are merely stewards of God's world. A steward is one who takes care of property for the owner. As I drive through deteriorating parts of our cities, and across country roads where abandoned buildings and junked cars abound, I am well aware that we have failed in our responsibility to be good stewards of God's creation. Air pollution, water pollution, noise pollution—all of these are contrary to the intention and purposes of God. Stewardship of the earth's resources is not just a social and political issue. Stewardship is fundamentally a theological issue. Nothing in the creation story gives us license to abuse God's world. We now know that many of the earth's resources (coal, oil, fresh water, to name a few) are finite. When our appetite for convenience and luxury leads us to consume a disproportionate share of God's resources, the whole of creation suffers. Future generations will pay a price for our lack of appreciation and respect for God's creation. In the words of the hymn, "How does the creature say Care/How does the creature say Life."

"How Great Thou Art"

"I see the stars, I hear the rolling thunder, thy power throughout the universe displayed." No wonder these words of Stuart Hines are the favorite of so many, for they describe the essence of God's creative activity in our midst.

The God who fashioned the world and hung the stars in their place did not stop creating when the six "days" of creation ended. Jews and Christians believe that the God who brought order out of chaos is still creating today. Every time a baby is born I marvel at God's creative activity in our midst. Because of God's creative activity men and women have made many wonderful inroads into the secrets of creation, thus opening new opportunities for each successive generation. Because of modern technology, we are able to communicate with people around the world. Lifesaving techniques and pharmaceutical products have been able not only to lengthen our life span but also to add quality and productivity to those added years.

Yet many issues loom before us. Does the possibility of cloning open new opportunities to enhance life, or are we in danger of "playing God"? Will our sophisticated military technology move us toward world peace or toward ongoing, possibly global, war? Will past abuse of the earth's resources lead us to better conservation policies and more responsible sharing with one another, or will human greed cause further shortages and more recklessness in the marketplace?

These questions and others need to be addressed in the light of the creation story. If these verses of Genesis are ignored by our generation, dire consequences will follow. Only by putting God at the center of our lives and acknowledging God's place at the center of the universe will we be able to live the full, free lives that God intends for us in harmony with one another. It is my prayer that each of us will reflect upon the meaning of the words we sing, for God is truly great!

SHARING THE SCRIPTURE

Preparing Our Hearts

Meditate on this week's devotional reading, found in Psalm 8. Here the psalmist offers praise to the sovereign name of God and comments on the place of humanity within God's creation. As you meditate on these words, consider how you see yourself in the scheme of God's creation. Write your own psalm of praise to God. Try to lift up someone who is feeling defeated with the assurance that he or she has dignity and honor before God and an important role to play as a steward of God's creation.

Pray that you and the adult learners will experience awe and majesty as you consider God's design for humanity.

Preparing Our Minds

Study the background from Genesis 1:1-25 and lesson Scripture, Genesis 1:1-6, 8, 10, 12-15, 19-20, 22-23, 25. As you prepare, explore your beliefs about how creation came into being.

Write on newsprint:
❑ information for next week's lesson, found under "Continue the Journey."
❑ activities for further spiritual growth in "Continue the Journey."

Read "Introduction" for this quarter," The "Big Picture," "Close-Up," and "Faith in Action." Decide how you will use these helps throughout the quarter. You may want to incorporate information from "Introduction" and/or "The Big Picture" into today's session.

Decide what you will bring to class as an example of creation. You may have a lovely plant, or a rock or seashell, or even an animal that could be safely brought and kept in the classroom during today's session. You may wish to contact several students to bring examples as well.

LEADING THE CLASS

(1) Gather to Learn

❖ Welcome the class members and introduce any guests.
❖ Pray that all who have gathered today will experience mystery and awe as they contemplate God's good creation.
❖ Select at least one of the following two options.

■ **Option 1:** Ask the students to observe nature as they take a stroll around the church property or immediate neighborhood. Invite them to report to the group on one or two findings that fascinated them the most.

- ■ **Option 2:** Encourage the class members to tell stories of memorable experiences they had in the midst of nature. Divide into groups or pairs so that more people will have a chance to participate.

❖ Read aloud today's focus statement: **Without the earth and its ecosystems, human life would not be possible. How did creation come into being? In the Genesis 1 account, we learn that God chose to create life where none had existed and God provided means of support for that life.**

(2) Explore the Creation Story as Told in Genesis 1

❖ Use "Introduction: God Created a People" to provide a survey of this quarter's sessions.

❖ **Option:** Read or comment on selected parts of "The Big Picture" article, "Telling the Story of God's Creation" to give the students a broader base from which to study this quarter's sessions.

❖ Assign the following verses from Genesis 1 to one or more readers: 1-6, 8, 10, 12-15, 19-20, 22-23, 25. Ask the students to listen for words or phrases that capture their attention as these verses are read.

❖ Invite the students to mention the words or phrases and state why they are of particular interest. Perhaps some students will report on a new insight gleaned from these words.

❖ Discuss these questions.
- (1) **What does this passage reveal to you about God?**
- (2) **What does this passage suggest about God's intentions for creation?**

❖ Read in unison from your hymnal one or more of the songs highlighted in Interpreting the Scripture. In conjunction with these hymns, use information from

this section to help the class understand and appreciate God's creative activity.

❖ **Option:** Read aloud "The Creation" from James Weldon Johnson's book *God's Trombones: Seven Negro Sermons in Verse.* (Although this book was originally published in 1927, you should be able to find it readily in a public library or bookstore.) Talk with the class about how Johnson's description of creation amplifies, modifies, and/or relates to the description in Genesis 1.

(3) Experience Awe and Wonder in the Presence of Creation

❖ Show to the class the plant, rock, seashell, animal, or whatever your brought as an example of God's good creation. Call upon any students who have also brought examples to show them now.

❖ Invite the students to comment on the intricacies of the example(s). Consider what this example reveals about God.

❖ Read aloud this quotation from Mary Webb (1881–1927) that describes the awe she experiences in the presence of creation: **Evening after evening in the summer, I have gone to see the white clover fall asleep in the meadow. Kneeling and looking very closely, one sees the two lower leaves on each stalk gently approach one another like little hands that were going to clap but thought better of it, and at last lie folded quietly as though for prayer. Then the upper leaf droops, as a child's face might, until it rests on the others. Everywhere in the dusk the white clover leaves are sleeping in an attitude of worship.**

❖ Encourage the students to comment on this quotation and to add other observations of how God's creation enables them to experience awe and wonder.

(4) Make a Commitment to Accept Stewardship Responsibility for God's Good Creation

❖ Challenge the students to make a list of any aspects of creation they can care for and record their suggestions on newsprint. Here are some ideas: *pets, gardens, water, air, houseplants, birds, wildlife, other people.*

❖ Ask the students to review the list and select one item they would like to work with. Now read the list aloud and those who are interested in a certain item should gather together. If the class is large, you may need several groups per item.

❖ Distribute newsprint and a marker to each group. Provide time for each group to brainstorm ways that they can be responsible for the facet of creation they have selected. Some of these ways include *direct action,* such as weeding a garden, picking up road litter, or exercising a dog. Other ways can include *advocacy,* such as writing letters to elected officials urging them to sponsor legislation that keeps air clean. Additional ways might be grouped under the heading of *education,* where, for example, experienced pet owners explain to new ones how to care for their pet's health and safety.

❖ Distribute paper and pencils. Ask each person to select and write one activity that he or she will commit to doing this week as a responsible steward of God's good creation. (Note that some groups may want to work together on a project.)

(5) Continue the Journey

❖ Pray that all who have come today will realize the preciousness of God's good creation and give thanks to God for it.

❖ Read aloud this preparation for next week's lesson. You may also want to post it on newsprint for the students to copy.
■ **Title: God Created Humankind**
■ **Background Scripture: Genesis 1:26–2:3**

■ **Lesson Scripture: Genesis 1:26-30**
■ **Focus of the Lesson: Human beings are amazing creatures, sharing much with other forms of life and yet distinctly different. Why was humanity created and placed on earth? The Israelites believed, as the Bible states in Genesis, that God created male and female in God's own image and entrusted them with the stewardship of all creation.**

❖ Challenge the students to complete one or more of these activities for further spiritual growth, which you will write on newsprint for the students to copy.

(1) **Find music (perhaps a hymn) or art that purports to depict creation. How does this artistic creation help you to appreciate nature?**

(2) **Locate pictures of the earth taken from space. What do these photos reveal about planet earth? What words would you use to describe these pictures? What emotions well up within you as you contemplate God's creation?**

(3) **Research points of view on evolution, creationism, and intelligent design. Formulate your own position, remembering that science and theology may interact in different ways for different people.**

❖ Sing or read aloud "Morning Has Broken."

❖ Conclude today's session by leading the class in this benediction, which is adapted from Genesis 14:19-20: **Blessed be you by God Most High, maker of heaven and earth; and blessed be God Most High.**

UNIT 1: GOD CREATED A PEOPLE
GOD CREATED HUMANKIND

PREVIEWING THE LESSON

Lesson Scripture: Genesis 1:26-30
Background Scripture: Genesis 1:26–2:3
Key Verse: Genesis 1:26

Focus of the Lesson:
Human beings are amazing creatures, sharing much with other forms of life and yet distinctly different. Why was humanity created and placed on earth? The Israelites believed, as the Bible states in Genesis, that God created male and female in God's own image and entrusted them with the stewardship of all creation.

Goals for the Learners:
(1) to examine the Genesis 1 account of the creation of humanity.
(2) to recognize and give thanks for God's role in the creation of humanity.
(3) to pledge to treat others with respect and dignity, for all are created in the image of God.

Supplies:
Bibles, newsprint and marker, paper and pencils, hymnals, pictures of human beings that reflect our diversity

---

READING THE SCRIPTURE

NRSV
Genesis 1:26-30

²⁶Then God said, "Let us make humankind in our image, according to our likeness; and let them have dominion over the fish of the sea, and over the birds of the air, and over the cattle, and over all the wild animals of the earth, and over every creeping thing that creeps upon the earth."
²⁷So God created humankind in his image,
    in the image of God he created them;
    male and female he created them.

NIV
Genesis 1:26-30

²⁶Then God said, "Let us make man in our image, in our likeness, and let them rule over the fish of the sea and the birds of the air, over the livestock, over all the earth, and over all the creatures that move along the ground."
²⁷So God created man in his own image,
    in the image of God he created him;
    male and female he created them.
²⁸God blessed them and said to them, "Be fruitful and increase in number; fill the earth

28God blessed them, and God said to them, "Be fruitful and multiply, and fill the earth and subdue it; and have dominion over the fish of the sea and over the birds of the air and over every living thing that moves upon the earth." 29God said, "See, I have given you every plant yielding seed that is upon the face of all the earth, and every tree with seed in its fruit; you shall have them for food. 30And to every beast of the earth, and to every bird of the air, and to everything that creeps on the earth, everything that has the breath of life, I have given every green plant for food." And it was so.

and subdue it. Rule over the fish of the sea and the birds of the air and over every living creature that moves on the ground."
29Then God said, "I give you every seed-bearing plant on the face of the whole earth and every tree that has fruit with seed in it. They will be yours for food. 30And to all the beasts of the earth and all the birds of the air and all the creatures that move on the ground—everything that has the breath of life in it—I give every green plant for food." And it was so.

UNDERSTANDING THE SCRIPTURE

Genesis 1:26. On the last half of the sixth day, God creates human beings. It may come as somewhat of a disappointment that we have to share this day with "living creatures of every kind: cattle and creeping things and wild animals of the earth of every kind" (1:25). Yet when God creates humanity, the tone changes, signaling the importance of this new development.

Who is God talking with when God says, "Let us make humankind in our image, according to our likeness" (1:26)? Scholars believe God is consulting other divine beings, members of the host of heaven. "Those who are not God are called to participate in this central act of creation," according to *The New Interpreter's Bible*. Terrence Fretheim continues by writing: "God is not in heaven alone, but is engaged in a relationship of mutuality within the divine realm, and chooses to share the creative process with others."

As the crowning glory of God's creative activity, humans are created in the image and likeness of God. In the ancient Near East the king was a representative of the gods, ruling on their behalf. Similarly, because human beings are created in the image of God, we are representatives of God in the

world as an extension of God's own dominion. Being created in the likeness of God, we are given the gifts needed to carry out the responsibilities specified in these verses.

When we hear the word "dominion," we tend to think of having power to control. In contrast, the Hebrew word translated as "dominion" describes this concept in terms of care-giving and nurturing, not exploitation or dominance. The model for how humans are to relate to non-humans is the way God relates to us. We are to rule living things on earth as God in turn rules us.

Genesis 1:27. God creates males and females as equal partners in the created order. They are both created in the divine image. Both are addressed in the commandment of Genesis 1:28.

Genesis 1:28. The ability to reproduce is seen as a blessing. Procreation is both God's gift and God's command. Human beings are to "be fruitful and multiply." God has brought the first creatures into existence; now the powers of propagating their own kind are given to them to continue God's act of creation. The writer is obviously concerned about populating the earth. The command to "subdue" the earth involves development of the created order. God intends that human beings bring the world to its fullest potential.

Genesis 1:29-30. As a sign of love and care for creation, God supplies vegetation as life-sustaining nourishment for both human beings and animals. Since no mention is made of eating meat, many readers deduce from this passage that human beings were intended to be vegetarians.

Genesis 1:31. The sixth day has been a busy one! God surveys the work of creation and is well pleased. The created order has come from God's hand precisely as intended, and thus it is very good. Chaos has been effectively restrained, and order prevails. The world is furnished and populated, and humanity has been brought into being to supervise God's created order.

Genesis 2:1-3. God takes delight in creation and, in sanctifying the seventh day, wills that humankind shall take similar delight. This rest is considered to be God's climactic work and humanity's highest good. The divine rest concludes creation. Thus, the Sabbath is part of the created order and, therefore, humans cannot mandate or abolish it. God's work of separating one day from the others stands parallel to God's other acts of separation (light from darkness, seas from the firmament, and so on) in the creation story. The work of bringing order out of chaos has reached its culmination in the creation of a day of rest for God and for the people God has created. The creative acts of these six days did not exhaust the divine creative power, however.

Although "the heavens and the earth were finished," God continues to create.

The Hebrew word translated "day" has caused much debate. A familiar explanation of the creation story is that God created the world in six days, but no one knows how long those days were. It is generally assumed by modern scholars that the "days" of Genesis, with their evening and morning rhythm are to be understood as twenty-four-hour days. Remember that the Genesis story is not intended as a twenty-first century science textbook explanation of creation. By interpreting the Bible's "days" as twenty-four-hour days we can more clearly see the analogy that just as God created the world in six days and then created a day of rest, so should we work six days and then spend the seventh day glorifying and praising God.

There are various interpretations of the significance of Sabbath observance in the Old Testament. In Isaiah 56:2-8, keeping the Sabbath is a sign that one keeps God's covenant. In Deuteronomy 5:12-15 the Sabbath is observed as a reminder of Israel's deliverance from Egypt. In this Genesis account, the author records God's rest as the climax of God's work of creation and God's blessing and hallowing of a day of rest.

Observing the Sabbath acknowledges that God is, indeed, the creator and provider of all things. When we set aside time for Sabbath rest, we participate in God's purposes, rather than giving priority to our own responsibilities and agendas.

INTERPRETING THE SCRIPTURE

Created in God's Image

In many communities today the battle is raging over how life began. Ever since Charles Darwin published his theory of evolution in *The Origin of Species* in 1859, there has been controversy surrounding the biblical explana-tion of creation. While the scientific community abandoned a six-day creation long ago, today many scientists are coming to see flaws in the theory of evolution.

We cannot view the Bible as a scientific textbook on creation. At the same time, science cannot address the question, "Why are we here?" Nor can people of faith leave God out of the equation, assuming that life simply evolved over time.

The theory that humankind descended from the apes has never been flattering. However, more than human pride is at stake! Philosophers as well as scientists acknowledge that there is a quantum leap between the most intelligent primate in the animal kingdom and the species known as "man." The Bible addresses that difference by declaring that we were created in the image of God.

To say that we are created in God's image makes an awesome statement, for the Judeo-Christian God is the epitome of truth, goodness, wisdom, inclusiveness, and love. One of the basic tenets of our faith is that each human being is of infinite worth because each is created in God's image. In Genesis, "image" refers to the entire human being, not just to some parts, such as the reason or the will.

Do we attempt to make God in our image? Biblical theology will not condone any idea other than the holiness and "otherness" of God. "Made in God's image" does not reveal as much about God as it does about us. Every person is valuable in God's eyes. Therefore, every person must be seen as valuable in our eyes as well, worthy of dignity and respect.

We have all heard of "self-made" men and women. In reality, that is a misnomer. No matter how strong and self-reliant we are, none of us can take credit for who we are. In the final analysis, all our resources and abilities are gifts from God.

Equal Partners

"So God created humankind in his image, in the image of God he created them, male and female he created them" (1:27). Later in Genesis 2 we will read another account of creation where God begins with the creation of 'adam. Then, after creating all the other plants and animals, seeing that the man lacks companionship, God creates a helper or partner for 'adam. "And the rib that the LORD God had taken from the man he made into a woman" (2:22). Through the years many have cited this passage as a reason why men should be dominant over women. There is nothing in the creation story that would justify that idea. I have heard it said that God did not take a bone from man's foot so that the woman would be subservient to him; God did not take a bone from his head so that the woman would be above him; God took a bone from his rib so that the two would work side by side.

There is no question in Genesis 1 that men and women were created to be partners. Not only are men and women created equal, but they are also given the same blessing and the same instruction: "Be fruitful and multiply, and fill the earth and subdue it" (1:28).

The Awesome Responsibility of Dominion

It is a fundamental Judeo-Christian belief that God has a purpose for every human life. Leon Yankwich is credited with saying, "There are no illegitimate children—only illegitimate parents." No one is on this earth by accident.

We learn in Genesis that human beings are to "have dominion over the fish of the sea and over the birds of the air and over every living thing that moves upon the earth" (1:28). What an awesome responsibility! Yet "dominion" does not mean domination! We have exploited the earth's resources to satisfy our insatiable appetite for possessions. We have paid little attention to the fact that we have upset the balance of nature due to our lust for more and more things. Sadly, some of the animals that God created have become extinct due to human carelessness and thoughtlessness. Some of the earth's resources have been depleted to an alarming degree.

God intends that we treat the earth with dignity, for it, too, is God's good creation. Many times people of faith have failed to remember "the earth is the LORD's" (Psalm 24:1).

If we manage God's creation wisely, as stewards are expected to do, God will provide all that we need for a full and abundant life. It is a sad commentary on modern life that we have the ability to provide enough food for all persons, yet thousands starve to death every day. Ours is a distribution problem, not a lack of resources. People are starving because as a world community we have not learned to share adequately with one another. God has given us dominion over every living thing. We must seek better ways to fulfill our calling as sons and daughters of God. The whole created order is depending on us!

God Takes a Day Off!

Growing up in the Midwest, I remember when Ohio's Blue Laws were strictly enforced. No retail establishments were open on Sunday, and restaurants were not permitted to sell alcoholic beverages on the "Sabbath."

How times have changed! I understand that Sunday is the biggest day of the week at some shopping malls. With the advent of the Internet, it is now possible to conduct business from banking to purchasing airline tickets to buying Christmas presents twenty-four hours a day, seven days a week.

I am fully appreciative of the argument that as Christians we should not impose our values and standards on a multicultural society. I do not believe that God intends us to legislate a Sabbath and force everyone to adhere to Christian customs. At the same time, secular studies indicate that the human body needs a rhythm of work, followed by rest.

I love the concept that God took time to enjoy and marvel at what God had created! We often complain that we don't have enough time to do the things we want to do. The truth is that time is a gift from God. It has been said that time is very democratic: God gives each of us twenty-four hours a day, seven days a week.

How can we justify working seven days a week when God completed the creation in six days and took the seventh as a day of rest? Working constantly demonstrates human arrogance and displays a lack of trust in God's benevolence. Furthermore, studies also show that if we ignore the rhythm that God has built into the created order, we do so at great risk to our physical, mental, and emotional health.

At the church I currently serve, we are talking about a Saturday night or Sunday night worship service. Our intention is to provide additional options for busy people. As we seek to accommodate our community's overscheduled lifestyle, I am realizing that we also need to address the need for Sabbath time: unscheduled, unstructured time when God can speak to us in the quiet of the moment without the television blaring or the cell phone ringing. God has designed the created order with a weekly cycle that includes twenty-four hours for rest and re-creation. How much time do you spend in Sabbath rest each week?

SHARING THE SCRIPTURE

Preparing Our Hearts

Meditate on this week's devotional reading, found in Isaiah 40:25-31. The prophet writes about God, "the Creator of the ends of the earth" (40:28), who "gives power to the faint and strengthens the powerless" (40:29). When you contemplate God's creation, especially humanity, what emotions and questions come to your mind? If someone were to ask, "Why are you here?," what would be your response?

Pray that you and the adult learners will give thanks and praise for life to the God who has created and continues to create.

Preparing Our Minds

Study the background, Genesis 1:26—2:3 and lesson Scripture, Genesis 1:26-30. As you read, think about why you believe humanity was created and placed on the earth.

Write on newsprint:
❑ steps under "Examine the Genesis 1 Account of the Creation of Humanity."
❑ information for next week's lesson, found under "Continue the Journey."
❑ activities for further spiritual growth in "Continue the Journey."

Collect pictures of males and females of all ages that reflect the diversity of humanity. If you are unable to do this, contact some class members early in the week and ask them to bring these pictures.

Option: Plan a lecture for "Examine the Genesis 1 Account of the Creation of Humanity."

LEADING THE CLASS

(1) Gather to Learn

❖ Welcome the class members and introduce any guests.

❖ Pray that all who have come to learn and fellowship together will be open to God's creative power in their lives.

❖ Show whatever pictures you have been able to collect of males and females of all ages that reflect our diversity.

❖ Invite the students to comment on the commonalities that humans share, even though we look different and speak a variety of languages.

❖ Ask: **Why do you think people exist on the earth?** (Be sure to avoid disputes about *how* we came to be.)

❖ Read aloud today's focus statement: **Human beings are amazing creatures, sharing much with other forms of life and yet distinctly different. Why was humanity created and placed on earth? The Israelites believed, as the Bible states in Genesis, that God created male and female in God's own image and entrusted them with the stewardship of all creation.**

(2) Examine the Genesis 1 Account of the Creation of Humanity

❖ Select a volunteer to read Genesis 1:26-30.

❖ Talk with the class about these three concepts that are prominent in the story: *image, dominion, blessed.* Use information from Understanding the Scripture, as well as "Created in God's Image" and "The Awesome Responsibility of Dominion" in Interpreting the Scripture, to help you lead a discussion or create an optional lecture. If you have access to *The New Interpreter's Study Bible,* include information in "Excursus: In God's Image" and "Excursus: Dominion or Dependence?" on pages 7-8. Discuss these questions.

(1) **If you believe that you are created in God's own image, what implications does that belief have for how you act?**
(2) **In what ways has humanity appropriately exercised dominion over every living thing? Give examples.**
(3) **What are some examples of ways that humanity has acted inappropriately in exercising dominion?**
(4) **In what ways do you feel blessed by God?** (Encourage the students to move beyond the notion of material blessings.)

❖ Divide the class into groups, distribute paper and pencils, and ask the adults to follow these steps, which you will post on newsprint:

■ **Step 1:** Make individual lists of ways that you are trying to be a good steward of creation.

■ **Step 2:** Discuss these ideas within your group and select together several ideas that seem particularly useful.

■ **Step 3:** Join the rest of the class to report on and hear the ideas from each group.

■ **Step 4:** Spend a few quiet moments considering how you might implement one or more of these ideas in your own life. Make a personal commitment to act and write it on your paper.

(3) Recognize and Give Thanks for God's Role in the Creation of Humanity

❖ Point out that different people explain how humans came to be created in different ways. Often, these ways clash in the school room. Debates about evolution and intelligent design have raged even into the twenty-first century. The problem in the schools is generally linked to what can be taught as science and what is a faith issue, which cannot be addressed in tax-supported schools.

❖ Read aloud these quotations regarding the creation of humanity.

■ **"A handful of earth to make God's image!"** (Elizabeth Barrett Browning, 1806–1861)

■ **"I repent me of the ignorance wherein I ever said that God made man out of nothing: there is no nothing out of which to make anything; God is all in all, and he made us out of himself. He who is parted from God has no original nothingness with which to take refuge."** (George MacDonald, 1824–1905)

■ **"Man is heaven's masterpiece."** (Francis Quarles, 1592–1644)

■ **"Whoever considers the study of anatomy, I believe, will never be an atheist."** (Edward Herbert, 1583–1648)

❖ Encourage the students to respond to any of the quotations. They may agree, disagree, or somehow modify the statements.

❖ Prompt the adults to state their own views about the creation of humanity, especially describing the role that they believe God played in this creation. (Recognize that the students' beliefs may vary widely.)

❖ Provide quiet time for the participants to meditate on God's role in their creation.

(4) Pledge to Treat Others with Respect and Dignity, for All Are Created in the Image of God

❖ Break the silence by looking once more at the pictures you brought to class. Note again that all humanity is created in God's image. The facts of our age, sex, race, culture, religion, historical period, and so on in no way change this belief.

❖ Encourage the adults to give examples of actions and attitudes that fly in the face of the belief that all humans are created in God's own image. You may want to talk about issues related to the sanctity of life for all people, such as abortion, capital punishment, war, or poverty.

❖ Ask: **How, then, do we treat all people with the respect and dignity that they deserve as those created in God's own image?**

(5) Continue the Journey

❖ Pray that each participant will feel affirmed knowing that they are created in the image of God and given responsibility to care for God's good creation.

❖ Read aloud this preparation for next week's lesson. You may also want to post it on newsprint for the students to copy.

■ **Title: Abraham, Sarah, and Isaac**

■ **Background Scripture: Genesis 15:1-6; 18:1-15; 21:1-8**

■ **Lesson Scripture: Genesis 15:5-6; 18:11-14a; 21:1-8**

■ **Focus of the Lesson: Family lines are so important that many people spend years tracing their genealogies. Why is the knowledge of a family tree so significant? For the numerous descendants of Abraham and Sarah, their family line was crucial because it was through this elderly couple and their son Isaac that God chose to create a covenant people.**

❖ Challenge the students to complete one or more of these activities for further spiritual growth, which you will write on newsprint for the students to copy.

(1) **Review Genesis 1:29, which is often interpreted as a biblical basis for vegetarianism. What is your view on this matter? Consider trying a vegetarian lifestyle for a day or two and see how you respond.**

(2) **Consider God's command in Genesis 1:28 and discern whether or not it is universally applicable today. What will you commit yourself to do to help those who suffer due to overpopulation, infertility, or unwanted pregnancy?**

(3) **Write in your spiritual journal about why you believe God created you. What gifts has God given you? What does God expect you to do with the rest of your life?**

❖ Sing or read aloud "I Sing the Almighty Power of God."

❖ Conclude today's session by leading the class in this benediction, which is adapted from Genesis 14:19-20: **Blessed be you by God Most High, maker of heaven and earth; and blessed be God Most High.**

UNIT 1: GOD CREATED A PEOPLE

ABRAHAM, SARAH, AND ISAAC

PREVIEWING THE LESSON

Lesson Scripture: Genesis 15:5-6; 18:11-14a; 21:1-8
Background Scripture: Genesis 15:1-6; 18:1-15; 21:1-8
Key Verse: Genesis 18:14a

Focus of the Lesson:
Family lines are so important that many people spend years tracing their genealogies. Why is the knowledge of a family tree so significant? For the numerous descendants of Abraham and Sarah, their family line was crucial because it was through this elderly couple and their son Isaac that God chose to create a covenant people.

Goals for the Learners:
(1) to tell the story of Isaac, the promised child of the covenant God made with Abraham and Sarah.
(2) to imagine the incredulity and joy that Abraham and Sarah might have felt when Isaac was born to them in their old age.
(3) to claim their place both within their human family and within God's covenantal family.

Pronunciation Guide:
Eliezer (el ee ee' zuhr)

Supplies:
Bibles, newsprint and marker, paper and pencils, hymnals

READING THE SCRIPTURE

NRSV
Genesis 15:5-6

⁵He brought him outside and said, "Look toward heaven and count the stars, if you are able to count them." Then he said to him, "So shall your descendants be."

⁶And he believed the LORD; and the LORD reckoned it to him as righteousness.

NIV
Genesis 15:5-6

⁵He took him outside and said, "Look up at the heavens and count the stars—if indeed you can count them." Then he said to him, "So shall your offspring be."

⁶Abram believed the LORD, and he credited it to him as righteousness.

Genesis 18:11-14a

¹¹Now Abraham and Sarah were old, advanced in age; it had ceased to be with Sarah after the manner of women. ¹²So Sarah laughed to herself, saying, "After I have grown old, and my husband is old, shall I have pleasure?" ¹³The LORD said to Abraham, "Why did Sarah laugh, and say, 'Shall I indeed bear a child, now that I am old? ¹⁴**Is anything too wonderful for the LORD?**

Genesis 21:1-8

¹The LORD dealt with Sarah as he had said, and the LORD did for Sarah as he had promised. ²Sarah conceived and bore Abraham a son in his old age, at the time of which God had spoken to him. ³Abraham gave the name Isaac to his son whom Sarah bore him. ⁴And Abraham circumcised his son Isaac when he was eight days old, as God had commanded him. ⁵Abraham was a hundred years old when his son Isaac was born to him. ⁶Now Sarah said, "God has brought laughter for me; everyone who hears will laugh with me." ⁷And she said, "Who would ever have said to Abraham that Sarah would nurse children? Yet I have borne him a son in his old age."

⁸The child grew, and was weaned; and Abraham made a great feast on the day that Isaac was weaned.

Genesis 18:11-14a

¹¹Abraham and Sarah were already old and well advanced in years, and Sarah was past the age of childbearing. ¹²So Sarah laughed to herself as she thought, "After I am worn out and my master is old, will I now have this pleasure?"

¹³Then the LORD said to Abraham, "Why did Sarah laugh and say, 'Will I really have a child, now that I am old?' ¹⁴**Is anything too hard for the LORD?**

Genesis 21:1-8

¹Now the LORD was gracious to Sarah as he had said, and the LORD did for Sarah what he had promised. ²Sarah became pregnant and bore a son to Abraham in his old age, at the very time God had promised him. ³Abraham gave the name Isaac to the son Sarah bore him. ⁴When his son Isaac was eight days old, Abraham circumcised him, as God commanded him. ⁵Abraham was a hundred years old when his son Isaac was born to him.

⁶Sarah said, "God has brought me laughter, and everyone who hears about this will laugh with me." ⁷And she added, "Who would have said to Abraham that Sarah would nurse children? Yet I have borne him a son in his old age."

⁸The child grew and was weaned, and on the day Isaac was weaned Abraham held a great feast.

UNDERSTANDING THE SCRIPTURE

Genesis 15:1. God has called Abraham and has promised to bless him and his descendants. God promises to reward Abraham for his faithfulness and counsels him to "not be afraid," words that appear often both in the Old and New Testaments.

Genesis 15:2-3. Abraham responds with a question about what God is going to "give" because the promise for an heir remains unfulfilled. Since Abraham has no children, following the Middle Eastern custom of a childless master adopting a slave to inherit his property, Eliezer of Damascus, a household slave, will be Abraham's heir.

Genesis 15:4. God has not given up on Abraham and Sarah, even if they have almost given up on God!

Genesis 15:5. God commands Abraham to look at the stars of the night. Then God assures the patriarch that his descendants will be as plentiful as the stars. Earlier (Genesis 13:16) God promised to make Abraham's children as plentiful as the "dust of the earth." In contrast to the ephemerality of dust, the star image suggests constancy and security.

Genesis 15:6. Abraham believes in the promises of God despite the lack of any real evidence. Such belief, says the narrator, is indeed righteousness, that is, a correct stance in relationship to God.

Genesis 18:1-2. When the text announces, "The LORD appeared to Abraham," a bit of dramatic irony enters the story, for the reader now knows more than Abraham does. In the heat of the day, when it is too hot to do anything but sit in the shade, Abraham is perhaps napping when seemingly out of nowhere three visitors appear. Remembering his manners, Abraham springs to his feet, runs to meet them, and bows down, a typical Middle Eastern greeting, not reserved for royalty, but customarily extended to any visitor.

Genesis 18:3-5. Abraham addresses the spokesman for the group and offers "a little water" to wash their feet and "a little bread" for refreshment. The strangers agree to accept Abraham's gracious hospitality.

Genesis 18:6-8. In typical Middle Eastern humility, Abraham has downplayed the worthiness of his gift of a meal and then proceeds to lay on a lavish feast. Although there is some disagreement about the modern equivalent of a "measure," some scholars suggest as much as seven quarts! To add to this generous portion of bread, Abraham "runs" to his herd, selects a "calf, tender and good," and gives it to a servant, who hurries to prepare it. He then takes curds and milk and the calf and sets them before the strangers, and stands near them under a tree while they eat.

Genesis 18:9-10. Having eaten, the strangers get on about the business of their mission. They ask for Sarah. (How did they know the name of Abraham's wife?) Sarah is eavesdropping, and overhears one of the visitors announce that in "due season" she will have a son.

Genesis 18:11. Once again to heighten the element of faith present in the story, the narrator points out that Abraham and Sarah are old, and that Sarah is well past childbearing age.

Genesis 18:12. Showing the same skepticism that her husband revealed earlier (Genesis 17:17), Sarah laughs at the news that she will become pregnant. The word "pleasure" may mean "fertility," in addition to "luxury" or "delight."

Genesis 18:13-14. We are unclear at what point in the story Abraham realizes that the visitors represent the Lord God. But by the time the child has been promised, Abraham recognizes the presence and the voice of the Lord. The divine visitor identifies Sarah's laughter as a sign of her disbelief, and asks rhetorically, "Is anything too hard for the LORD?" (NIV). The NRSV translates the same passage, "Is anything too wonderful for the LORD?" Is anything too incredulous for God? The unspoken answer that practically leaps from the page is a decisive "No. Of course not."

Genesis 18:15. Sarah denies that she laughed, as if any of us can hide any of our thoughts or actions from the Lord! God continues the conversation and makes no judgment, even when Sarah denies that she laughed.

Genesis 21:1-2. It is God who makes Isaac's birth possible. God follows through with the promises made to Abraham, and "Sarah conceived and bore Abraham a son in his old age." The particular promise referred to here is found in Genesis 18:9-15, but other promises to Abraham concerning an heir appear in Genesis 12:2; 13:16; 15:4-6; and 17:15-19.

Genesis 21:3. The name "Isaac" comes from the Hebrew word for "laugh." Isaac is born out of the laughter of disbelief. But now that the child is born, the laughter of skepticism turns into the laughter of unexpected joy.

Genesis 21:4. Abraham circumcises his son on the eighth day, according to the command given to him by God in Genesis 17:9-12, 19.

Genesis 21:5. The narrator continues to emphasize the advanced age of the patriarch. It has been twenty-five years since God called Abraham and promised that he would make of him "a great nation" (12:2). Abraham's patience has been tried, but his faith has endured.

Genesis 21:6-7. Those who were laughing *at* Sarah are now laughing with her! Sarah is overjoyed at the birth of Isaac; others who hear about the birth will rejoice *with* her. Verse 7 gives the reason: No one would have dreamed of announcing to Abraham that two such old people would become parents.

Genesis 21:8. As the child grows, Abraham continues to thank God for the blessing of Isaac's life. When Isaac is weaned, Abraham has a great celebration, marking one of the passages toward adulthood and the eventual material and spiritual inheritance that will be Isaac's.

INTERPRETING THE SCRIPTURE

God's Promises to Abram and Sarai

Abram and Sarai were already senior citizens when God called them to leave their comfortable surroundings and journey toward a new land. The Lord had promised to make of them "a great nation" (12:2), but it had been several years since they first heard that call. There is a sense of urgency that develops as we get older. My father-in-law used to say, "At my age, I don't even buy green bananas!" Abram's name means "exalted father." Yet there is a bit of irony that would have been obvious to Abram's relatives and friends: Abram and Sarai still have no children! Of course, Abram has a son born of Hagar, Sarai's Egyptian slave girl. But Abram and Sarai have been promised descendants, and they are becoming impatient. Frankly, the "exalted ancestor" is becoming the laughingstock of the region, for he and his wife have grown too old to have a family.

The narrator emphasizes the fact that "Abraham and Sarah were old, advanced in age" (18:11). To be sure that no one misses the point, he continues, "It had ceased to be with Sarah after the manner of women." It is going to take a miracle for Sarah to become pregnant. But that's just the point! The promised child and his resulting descendants (more than the number of stars in the sky) are a result of God's activity and God's design, not simply the result of the bodily union of Abraham and Sarah. Similarly, Christian baptism acknowledges that children are a gift from God.

Abram and Sarai's impatience is heightened as God changes their names in order to reflect more adequately the role in the history of salvation that this couple will play. Abram the "exalted father" becomes Abraham, "father of a multitude," and God reiterates that Sarah will have a son. Yet Sarah is not pregnant, and she knows all too well that what she is being promised is far-fetched at best.

We are told in the Psalms that a thousand years in God's eyes are the equivalent of a day in the life of us mortals (Psalm 90:4). Those words would have made Sarah and Abraham nervous! Yet Scripture points out to us that God's timing is not necessarily our timing. So often we are prevailed upon to wait, and most of us hate to wait. Our patience quickly wears thin.

Yet God is faithful. We who know the next chapter of the story realize that Abraham and Sarah simply had to adjust to God's timetable and not expect a son to be born on their terms. How hard it was for them! How difficult it is for us to be patient and to rely upon God!

The Perfect Host

The day started out like any other. Abraham and Sarah had no warning or no advanced knowledge that this day would be the day that God would visit them in a special way. As readers of the Holy Book, we know that the three strangers will represent God. Yet Abraham and Sarah are not privy to this knowledge.

In fine Middle Eastern style, Abraham offers the utmost in hospitality: water to wash the weary travelers' feet, and the shade of a tree where the strangers can rest. Moreover, he hastens to see to it that his guests have fresh baked goods, as well as meat, cheese, and milk.

How do we treat strangers who come to our door? What is our response to new people in our midst? The United Methodist Church is in the midst of a multi-million dollar "Igniting Ministry" Campaign, a denomination-wide effort to strengthen the hospitality ministries of our local churches. Hospitality is a key component of the teachings of both the Old and New Testaments. Abraham was not the only person to have divine visitors, for the Bible tells us that when we show hospitality to strangers, we may be entertaining angels without knowing it (Hebrews 13:2).

If we believe that every person is created by God, then shouldn't every person be treated with dignity and respect? As in the case of Abraham's visitors, it may not be immediately obvious that the visitors in our midst are heaven sent. But if we look closely, we will be able to see a spark of the divine in every person that we meet. No one is created outside the realm of God's love and intention and care.

"Is Anything Too Hard for the LORD?"

We live in an age of skepticism and disbelief. Any aura of mystery and mystique is strongly overshadowed by scientific formulas and mathematical probabilities. Due to the advance of modern technology, most couples know the gender of their babies several months before their children are born. Even in Bible times, there was no need for a pregnancy test in Abraham and Sarah's tent. Common sense told them that they were too old to have children.

What is a miracle? A miracle is not necessarily an act of God that defies the laws of nature, but an act of God that reveals a dimension of life that we did not previously see. I believe that miracles occur every day. The greatest miracle in Abraham and Sarah's life was not that they had a child at their advanced age, but that they continued to be open to God's will in every season of their lives, even when the outlook seemed bleak.

God continued to work in their lives, even though they were elderly. How many couples living around them had given up on God long ago? How many of us decide that we are too old to experience something new?

"Is anything too hard for the LORD?" The answer that the narrator wants to hear is this: "No, nothing is too difficult for God to accomplish." "For God all things are possible" (Matthew 19:26). How hard it is to affirm that teaching in our daily lives! The former Secretary General of the United Nations, Dag Hammarskjold (1905–1961), is quoted as having said, "For all that has been, thanks. For all that will be, yes!" Are we as open to God's blessings and God's promises as was this highly respected Christian? Will we let God use our lives to God's glory and for God's purposes?

Child of Blessing, Child of Promise

For over three years we had hoped and dreamed. For nine months we had eagerly anticipated the birth of a baby. The congregation I was serving at the time had been party to our anticipation. They had never had a baby in their parsonage before! One night my wife and I went to the hospital, and after some struggle a nine-pound-three-ounce baby was born. Excitedly, I went home and put these words on the church's outdoor sign: "It's a Boy!"

Is there anything more wonderful than the birth of a child? Does anything speak more clearly of the presence and power of God than does the miracle of birth? Abraham and Sarah were simply overjoyed with the gift of new life that had come to them in Isaac. The laughter of skepticism was suddenly replaced with the laughter of sheer joy!

The narrator reminds us once again that this child was born because God did "as he had promised" (Genesis 21:1). It is God who made Isaac's birth possible. We need to remember that all blessings come from God, who is the source of life itself.

SHARING THE SCRIPTURE

Preparing Our Hearts

Meditate on this week's devotional reading, found in Isaiah 51:1-5. The prophet calls us to look to our ancestors, Abraham and Sarah, for we are their descendants, just as surely as Isaac was. What comes to mind when you think of your own family origins? Do you know your ancestors and where they came from? Consider doing some genealogical research this week or talking with a family member who has done such research. What can you learn about your own roots?

Pray that you and the adult learners will be aware of your place in the family of God.

Preparing Our Minds

Study the background from Genesis 15:1-6, 18:1-15, and 21:1-8. The lesson Scripture is found in Genesis 15:5-6, 18:11-14a, and 21:1-8. As you review these passages, consider why a knowledge of one's family tree is so significant.

Write on newsprint:
❏ information for next week's lesson, found under "Continue the Journey."
❏ activities for further spiritual growth in "Continue the Journey."

❏ Invite a guest speaker early in the week if you plan to use that option for the "Gather to Learn" portion. Be sure to set a firm time limit with the guest when you extend the invitation.

LEADING THE CLASS

(1) Gather to Learn

❖ Welcome the class members and introduce any guests.

❖ Pray that those who have come today will recognize and give thanks for their valued place in God's good creation.

❖ Invite students to tell stories of tracing their family trees. What challenges, surprises, and serendipities did they experience along the way? Why did they become involved in genealogical research?

❖ **Option:** Invite a family genealogist, perhaps a member of the congregation, to talk with the class about why people find it important to trace their family trees.

❖ Read aloud today's focus statement: **Family lines are so important that many people spend years tracing their genealogies. Why is the knowledge of a family tree so significant? For the numerous descendants of Abraham and Sarah, their family line was crucial because it was** through this elderly couple and their son Isaac that God chose to create a covenant people.

(2) Tell the Story of Isaac, the Promised Child of the Covenant God Made with Abraham and Sarah

❖ Select a volunteer to read Genesis 15:5-6; 18:11-14a; 21:1-8.

❖ **Option:** Choose readers for the parts of a narrator, God, and Sarah. Ask them to present Genesis 15:5-6; 18:12-14a; 21:1-8 as a drama.

❖ Discuss these questions with the class. You may wish to list responses to questions 1, 2, and 3 on newsprint.

(1) **What does this passage tell you about God?**

(2) **What do you learn about Abraham?**

(3) **What do you learn about Sarah?**

(4) **In what ways can you identify with Abraham and Sarah?** (Many adults can relate to the joy of expecting a child.)

(5) **How would you have responded to the news that you would at last become a parent had you been Abraham or Sarah?** (Remember, these two are older adults!)

❖ Read or retell "God's Promises to Abram and Sarai" to help the class recall the urgency this elderly couple must have felt as the promise seemed to go unfulfilled.

❖ Ask the students to look in their Bibles at Genesis 18:13-14a and 21:6, which speak about Sarah and laughter. Also look at Genesis 17:17 where Abraham laughs. Talk about the meaning of the laughter in each of these cases. Note the difference between laughter of joy and laughter of skepticism. Also note that the name Isaac means "he laughed."

❖ Wrap up this section by encouraging the students to state how they see God at work in this story to establish the covenant.

(1) **How is what God is doing in keeping with their expectations of God?**

(2) **How is God's action surprising to them?**

(3) Imagine the Incredulity and Joy That Abraham and Sarah Might Have Felt When Isaac Was Born to Them in Their Old Age

❖ Distribute paper and pencils. Ask the students to write two short diary entries as if they were either Sarah or Abraham. One entry should discuss God's promise to them and how he or she felt about that. The other should express the emotions Abraham or Sarah felt at the birth of this child, including adjustments he or she had to make as a new—and elderly—parent.

❖ Provide time for each student to read one diary entry to a partner or small group.

❖ Invite the students to recall a similar joy in their own lives and share it with a partner or small group. Perhaps the joy was due to the birth of a child or grandchild, marriage, receiving a degree, landing a job, earning a promotion, or accepting Christ. Suggest that the students name the joy and state why it was so meaningful to them.

(4) Claim a Place Both within the Human Family and within God's Covenantal Family

❖ Suggest that the adults think about their places within their human families by identifying all the roles they play, such as son or daughter, spouse, parent, sibling, cousin, grandchild, niece or nephew, cousin.

❖ Encourage the students to talk about some of the privileges and responsibilities of each role they play. Also explore how they go about claiming each role.

❖ Suggest that the students now think about their place within the family of God.

(1) **What roles do they play there?**

(2) **How does it feel to be part of the family of God?**

❖ Work together as a class to trace the spiritual heritage of your congregation. Think about the impact that mission or outreach involvement has had on the church, as well as building projects, memorable programs, pastors who have really made a difference, and how the congregation has grown and been influential upon the community.

❖ **Option:** Create a timeline on newsprint of memorable instances of God acting within this community of faith. Think about pastors, lay members, mission trips, educational opportunities, building projects, ecumenical and community projects, or tragedies that had a profound effect on this congregation.

(5) Continue the Journey

❖ Pray that as the students depart they will remember that they are each special and unique persons within the family of God.

❖ Read aloud this preparation for next week's lesson. You may also want to post it on newsprint for the students to copy.

■ Title: Abraham, Hagar, and Ishmael
■ Background Scripture: Genesis 21:9-21
■ Lesson Scripture: Genesis 21:9-21
■ Focus of the Lesson: Seeds of dissension often continue to bear fruit long after the seeds have been sown. What contemporary exam-

ples can we find of long-standing dissension? The seeds of dissension begun in the Genesis story continue today between Muslims, who claim Ishmael as their ancestor, and Jews and Christians, who claim Isaac as their ancestor.

❖ Challenge the students to complete one or more of these activities for further spiritual growth, which you will write on newsprint for the students to copy.

(1) Talk with several family members to learn what they know about your family. You may want to begin to do some genealogical research.

(2) Spend time with a child this week. As you talk, play with, and care for this child think about the potential that he or she has. Do all in your power to nurture that promise.

(3) Recall the question from Genesis 18:14: "Is anything too wonderful for the LORD?" Turn over to God those problems that are besetting you and trust that no problem is too difficult for God to solve.

❖ Sing or read aloud "Our Parent, by Whose Name."

❖ Conclude today's session by leading the class in this benediction, which is adapted from Genesis 14:19-20: **Blessed be you by God Most High, maker of heaven and earth; and blessed be God Most High.**

UNIT 1: GOD CREATED A PEOPLE

ABRAHAM, HAGAR, AND ISHMAEL

PREVIEWING THE LESSON

Lesson Scripture: Genesis 21:9-21
Background Scripture: Genesis 21:9-21
Key Verse: Genesis 21:13

Focus of the Lesson:
Seeds of dissension often continue to bear fruit long after the seeds have been sown. What contemporary examples can we find of long-standing dissension? The seeds of dissension begun in the Genesis story continue today between Muslims, who claim Ishmael as their ancestor, and Jews and Christians, who claim Isaac as their ancestor.

Goals for the Learners:
(1) to examine God's care of and promise to Ishmael, the son of Abraham and Hagar.
(2) to reflect on God's continuing care for them.
(3) to become informed about the current state of Christian-Jewish-Muslim relationships and to do whatever possible to promote peace.

Pronunciation Guide:
Beersheba (bee uhr shee' buh)
Paran (pay' ruhn)

Supplies:
Bibles, newsprint and marker, paper and pencils, hymnals

READING THE SCRIPTURE

NRSV
Genesis 21:9-21

⁹But Sarah saw the son of Hagar the Egyptian, whom she had borne to Abraham, playing with her son Isaac. ¹⁰So she said to Abraham, "Cast out this slave woman with her son; for the son of this slave woman shall

NIV
Genesis 21:9-21

⁹But Sarah saw that the son whom Hagar the Egyptian had borne to Abraham was mocking, ¹⁰and she said to Abraham, "Get rid of that slave woman and her son, for that slave woman's son

not inherit along with my son Isaac." ¹¹The matter was very distressing to Abraham on account of his son. ¹²But God said to Abraham, "Do not be distressed because of the boy and because of your slave woman; whatever Sarah says to you, do as she tells you, for it is through Isaac that offspring shall be named for you. **¹³As for the son of the slave woman, I will make a nation of him also, because he is your offspring."** ¹⁴So Abraham rose early in the morning, and took bread and a skin of water, and gave it to Hagar, putting it on her shoulder, along with the child, and sent her away. And she departed, and wandered about in the wilderness of Beer-sheba.

¹⁵When the water in the skin was gone, she cast the child under one of the bushes. ¹⁶Then she went and sat down opposite him a good way off, about the distance of a bowshot; for she said, "Do not let me look on the death of the child." And as she sat opposite him, she lifted up her voice and wept. ¹⁷And God heard the voice of the boy; and the angel of God called to Hagar from heaven, and said to her, "What troubles you, Hagar? Do not be afraid; for God has heard the voice of the boy where he is. ¹⁸Come, lift up the boy and hold him fast with your hand, for I will make a great nation of him." ¹⁹Then God opened her eyes and she saw a well of water. She went, and filled the skin with water, and gave the boy a drink.

²⁰God was with the boy, and he grew up; he lived in the wilderness, and became an expert with the bow. ²¹He lived in the wilderness of Paran; and his mother got a wife for him from the land of Egypt.

will never share in the inheritance with my son Isaac."

¹¹The matter distressed Abraham greatly because it concerned his son. ¹²But God said to him, "Do not be so distressed about the boy and your maidservant. Listen to whatever Sarah tells you, because it is through Isaac that your offspring will be reckoned. **¹³I will make the son of the maidservant into a nation also, because he is your offspring."**

¹⁴Early the next morning Abraham took some food and a skin of water and gave them to Hagar. He set them on her shoulders and then sent her off with the boy. She went on her way and wandered in the desert of Beersheba.

¹⁵When the water in the skin was gone, she put the boy under one of the bushes. ¹⁶Then she went off and sat down nearby, about a bowshot away, for she thought, "I cannot watch the boy die." And as she sat there nearby, she began to sob.

¹⁷God heard the boy crying, and the angel of God called to Hagar from heaven and said to her, "What is the matter, Hagar? Do not be afraid; God has heard the boy crying as he lies there. ¹⁸Lift the boy up and take him by the hand, for I will make him into a great nation."

¹⁹Then God opened her eyes and she saw a well of water. So she went and filled the skin with water and gave the boy a drink.

²⁰God was with the boy as he grew up. He lived in the desert and became an archer. ²¹While he was living in the Desert of Paran, his mother got a wife for him from Egypt.

UNDERSTANDING THE SCRIPTURE

Genesis 21:9. A similar account of the story of the conflict between Sarah and Hagar is found in Genesis 16. The occasion of Isaac's weaning was a day of great celebration for the family of Abraham (21:8). As Isaac grew, however, the unresolved issue of the relationship between Abraham's two sons became more pronounced with each passing day. Even though Sarah had urged Abraham to take Hagar as his wife to try to produce an heir through this "slave woman," when Hagar becomes pregnant, Sarah becomes resentful. The custom of a wife handing over a slave woman to her husband to produce children was practiced in the Near East during this historical period. The product of such a union was considered to be the child of the lawful wife. At the feast celebrating Isaac's weaning, Sarah discovers Ishmael and Isaac playing together. The sight of this seeming equality of status between the two boys angers the jealous Sarah.

Genesis 21:10. Sarah does not confront Ishmael and his mother directly, but insists that Abraham "cast out this slave woman and her son." Sarah's repeated reference to "this slave woman," rather than calling Hagar by name is demeaning. Commentators note that Sarah refers to Ishmael as her (the slave woman's) son, rather than as Abraham's son, or as our son. She also expresses concern about the inheritance right of the two boys.

Genesis 21:11. Abraham is distressed at Sarah's request. His concern centers on Ishmael rather than Hagar because Sarah is in effect forcing him to choose between his two sons. "Distressed" about the situation, and torn between the demands of Sarah his wife and Ishmael his son, Abraham is unable to act.

Genesis 21:12-13. Much to the dismay of the modern reader, God appears to side with Sarah and tells Abraham to do what she says! The crux of the matter is that although both Isaac and Ishmael are Abraham's sons, it is through Isaac that the covenantal line will continue. Yet, God will not forget Ishmael; indeed, God "will make a great nation of him."

Thus God works through the jealous Sarah to accomplish the divine purpose, even though Sarah's strategy seems harsh. Here again, God chooses to work through imperfect people and difficult situations to achieve divine purposes. God does not wait until people are perfect in order to use them. Rather, God is able to weave impure motives and flawed human thinking into the tapestry that God is creating.

Genesis 21:14. Abraham arises "early in the morning" and without recorded comment does as Sarah (and God!) have instructed him. He sends Hagar and Ishmael into the wilderness of Beersheba, but does provide them with bread and water. By this action Abraham attempts to satisfy the angry command of his jealous wife, but also gives something of a chance for survival in the desert to his second wife and firstborn son. Hagar's wandering in the wilderness mirrors Israel's later experience. Commentators also point out the fact that in both cases there is the provision of water in the desert, supplied by the hand of a loving and benevolent God.

Genesis 21:15-16. The inadequacy of Abraham's meager gifts becomes clear all too soon, as the water runs out quickly. Hagar puts her child under a bush to give him what comfort she can from the merciless sun. Then she leaves him and goes "about the distance of a bowshot," because she cannot bear to watch her child die of exposure.

The text tells us "she lifted up her voice and wept." Hagar's plight is all the more tragic when we reflect upon the fact that the child born from her body was at the direct request of Sarah with the eager involvement of Abraham. How betrayed she must have felt!

Genesis 21:17-18. The narrator then tells us that God heard the voice of the boy. (The name "Ishmael" means "God hears.") God tells Hagar not to be afraid and reiterates the promise previously shared with Abraham: God has big plans for Ishmael and will make a great nation of him.

God's care for Hagar and Ishmael reveal to us the depth of God's concern for those who are not members of the covenantal family. God saves those who others view as outcasts or threats.

Genesis 21:19. "God opened her [Hagar's] eyes, and she saw a well of water." Notice that water did not appear miraculously. The implication is that the well was there all along. But when Hagar opened her ears to the voice of God, God caused her to see the provisions already made for her and her son. Hagar fills the skin and gives Ishmael a life-sustaining drink. Just as God will provide a ram for the sacrifice in the story of God's testing of Abraham in Genesis 22, thus sparing Isaac's life, in this moving story about Abraham's other son God provides water to save Ishmael's life. Both sons are vulnerable. Both sons could have died. In both cases, God acted to save them.

Genesis 21:20-21. Just as God has been with Abraham, and God will be with Isaac, so God is with Ishmael, and that bodes well for his future. In quick strokes, the narrator describes the growth of Ishmael, how he lives in the wilderness and becomes especially adept with the bow. Eventually, he becomes an expert hunter. Hagar exhibits no little strength in caring for Ishmael's needs. One commentator notes that Hagar's finding a wife for Ishmael among her own people in Egypt is the only time a mother does that in the Old Testament.

Thus, God is at work, making great nations both inside and outside the boundaries of Israel. Here in these early chapters of the Bible, the universality of God is being demonstrated to all readers and hearers of these great stories of the faith.

INTERPRETING THE SCRIPTURE

Conflict in the Family

A childless couple. Another woman. A jealous mother. The issue of fairness. Marital discord. It sounds more like a soap opera than a Bible story, but such is the saga of Abraham, Hagar, and Sarah. We must resist reading modern assumptions into these ancient characters. At the same time, these stories illustrate that jealousy, resentment, and family conflict are as old as the human race itself.

The liaison between Abraham and Hagar was originally Sarah's idea, and an accepted practice in her day. A barren wife could choose to make such an arrangement between her husband and a slave, knowing that she would have legal rights to the child. Yet, when Hagar became pregnant, Sarah became resentful of her "slave woman."

The resentment did not end when Sarah had a child of her own. In fact, the birth of Isaac seemed to have fueled the animosity between the two women. Whether a child is treated equally and fairly is always in the eye of the beholder. Isaac and Ishmael seemed to get along all right. But Sarah apparently kept careful score of how much attention her son was receiving from their father, Abraham.

Worried that Ishmael would get more attention than Isaac, and that Ishmael would be the recipient of the lion's share of Abraham's estate, since he was, after all, Abraham's firstborn son, Sarah goes to Abraham and demands that he throw Hagar and Ishmael out of the house.

Abraham Makes a Tough Decision

Imagine Abraham's predicament! Both Ishmael and Isaac were his sons. The text indicates that he loved both boys very much. To send Hagar and Ishmael into the desert was a death sentence. No one could survive the hot desert sun, the cold nights, and the lack of a source of food and water. If the elements did not kill the mother and her son, wild animals or bandits would.

Yet Abraham desperately wanted peace in the family, a peace that had not been present since Hagar first became pregnant. Perhaps Abraham thought that it would be best to do as Sarah demanded. While he was thinking about what course of action to take, God encourages him to follow Sarah's instruction. Abraham had heard God's voice before. God had vowed to cause a great nation to come from Abraham's offspring, and with the birth of Isaac, the promised child of the covenant, God's pledge was beginning to become reality. Well, Abraham thought, I'll just have to trust God once again. I'll just have to trust that Hagar and Ishmael will be all right, and that somehow God will provide for them.

Surely Abraham must have known that the flask of water and bread he packed for Hagar and Ishmael were no match for the deadly desert sun. It must have been a painful and emotional goodbye. Probably both Hagar and Abraham assumed that they would never see each other again. As the two of them looked at the Ishmael—well, his future was just too painful to think about. Yet God had promised that this boy would be the father of a great and mighty people. It was hard to keep believing that promise in light of the present circumstances.

Many times the future looks bleak for us and for those we love. I have counseled persons who have lost their jobs and those who have been diagnosed with life-threatening diseases. I have been with people as they have gone through divorce. I have prayed with those who have lost loved ones. It is extremely difficult to have faith and to be hopeful when life deals its crushing blows. Our faith teaches that God is always with us and makes a way when there seemingly is no way. Can we trust God when all the evidence indicates that there is no hope for us or for those we love? That is the challenge of faith that Abraham and Hagar confronted. That is the challenge we may face as well.

God Hears Hagar's Cry

When Hagar and Ishmael enter the desert, their meager provisions are quickly depleted. Hagar cannot bear to see her child die of dehydration, so she put him under a bush to protect him from the sun. From the description in Genesis 21, we assume that Ishmael is a young child. (He could have been as old as fourteen, though, since Abraham was eighty-six when Ishmael was born, according to Genesis 16:16, and one hundred when Isaac was born, per Genesis 21:5). After sheltering him, Hagar goes away and begins to weep, as the Psalmist will do when he is in despair and when Israel is in perilous times. The encouraging message for Hagar, for Ishmael, and for us is the wonderful news that God heard Hagar's cry and responded to her need even though she was not one of the covenant people. Indeed, many can identify with Hagar's plight. In hearing God's response to her, they can find help and hope for their own lives. Phyllis Trible puts it quite eloquently when she writes:

> Most especially, all sorts of rejected women find their stories in her. She is the faithful maid exploited, the black woman used by the male and abused by the female of the ruling class, the surrogate mother, the resident alien without legal recourse, the other woman, the runaway youth, the religious fleeing from affliction, the pregnant young woman alone, the expelled wife, the divorced mother with child, the shopping bag lady carrying bread and water, the homeless woman, the indigent relying upon handouts from the power structures, the welfare mother, and the self-effacing female whose own identity shrinks in service to others."

God hears the cry of the marginalized and the outcast of every nation. Do we?

God Provides for Hagar and Ishmael

God not only hears Hagar's cry, but also provides for Hagar and her son. While she had become convinced that they would die of thirst, she needed only to open her eyes to see a well of water that was nearby.

Not only did God provide for Hagar and Ishmael in the wilderness, but God also saw to it that the homeless pair continued to have their needs supplied. Indeed, the Bible tells us, "God was with the boy, and he grew up" (21:20). Ishmael became a skilled hunter, thus able to provide for himself and his mother. In time, he would marry and have a family, thus beginning to fulfill the promise that God would "make a great nation of him" (21:13).

Today the world is filled with descendants of Ishmael. More than one billion Muslims claim Ishmael as their father. Christians and Jews claim Isaac as their ancestor. All are children of Abraham. Sadly, seeds of dissension begun in the Genesis story continue today. Rarely does a day pass without a newspaper story or a television report of tension between Muslims, Christians, and Jews. Though worldwide conflict between ethnic and religious groups is as old as history itself, God works redemptively, even in the midst of family dissension. Moreover, even when we are the victims of cruelty and are treated unjustly, God hears our cries and responds to our concerns. God's care reaches us even in the wilderness areas of our lives. We are never beyond God's love and care.

God's love transcends interpersonal conflict. Rather than asking God to help *our* side, maybe we should examine our lives and ask ourselves whether we are on *God's* side. God's love and care extends to all persons. Like Hagar, we are called to open our eyes and see what God has provided. We are called to share God's love and God's provisions with all who are in need. In so doing, God will bless us and bless people everywhere.

SHARING THE SCRIPTURE

Preparing Our Hearts

Meditate on this week's devotional reading, found in Genesis 16. Here we find the story of the birth of Ishmael to Abram and Sarai's Egyptian slave, Hagar, who had no choice in the matter. This arrangement, which was quite acceptable in their cultural setting, caused heartache for Hagar, Ishmael, Sarai, and Abram. What has caused dissension and heartache within your family? How was the problem resolved? If the problem still looms large, what can you do to mend the family fences?

Pray that you and the adult learners will be sensitive to the needs of family members and do what you can to dispel dissension and bring about harmony.

Preparing Our Minds

Study the background and lesson Scripture, both of which are found in Genesis 21:9-21. As you study this lesson on conflict within Abram's family, think about contemporary examples of long-standing dissension.

Write on newsprint:
❏ chart for "Examine God's Care of and Promise to Ishmael, the Son of Abraham and Hagar."
❏ information for next week's lesson, found under "Continue the Journey."
❏ activities for further spiritual growth in "Continue the Journey."

Plan a lecture for "Examine God's Care of and Promise to Ishmael, the Son of Abraham and Hagar" if you choose to fill in the chart yourself.

Plan a lecture for "Become Informed about the Current State of Christian-Jewish-Muslim Relationships and Do Whatever Possible to Promote Peace" if you decide to do Option 1.

Collect news articles, books, or Internet reports concerning relationships among

Christians, Jews, and Muslims. Contact class members during the week who may be able to assist you in locating such information. Consider inviting a guest speaker who has expertise in this area. Be sure this person understands the context of the lecture and the time limit.

LEADING THE CLASS

(1) Gather to Learn

❖ Welcome the class members and introduce any guests.

❖ Pray that the adults who have gathered today will become aware of how God acts even in the midst of conflict.

❖ Invite the students to tell stories of their own families, or famous families, involving serious dissension and its aftershocks. Ask the students not to divulge names and to disguise details so as not to embarrass anyone. Serious dissension may end in a rupture of relationships, such as a divorce, family members refusing to contact one another, the need to relocate, or a decision to change jobs.

❖ Talk together about (1) how dissension begins and (2) its effects on the people involved.

❖ Read aloud today's focus statement: **Seeds of dissension often continue to bear fruit long after the seeds have been sown. What contemporary examples can we find of long-standing dissension? The seeds of dissension begun in the Genesis story continue today between Muslims, who claim Ishmael as their ancestor, and Jews, who claim Isaac as their ancestor.**

(2) Examine God's Care of and Promise to Ishmael, the Son of Abraham and Hagar

❖ Choose volunteers to read the parts of a narrator, Sarah, Hagar, and God in Genesis 21:9-21.

❖ Post this chart written on newsprint where everyone can see it. Work with the class to fill in the chart. Use as many lines as needed. As an option, fill it in yourself as you present a lecture.

Sarah's Concerns and Actions	Abraham's Concerns and Actions	Hagar's Concerns and Actions	God's Concerns and Actions

❖ Discuss these questions.
  (1) What do you learn about sources of family conflict from this story?
  (2) What do you learn about ways conflict is handled?
  (3) How would you have handled the conflict had you been involved?

❖ **Option:** Invite the students to turn to Galatians 4:21-31 to see how this story is used in the New Testament. Note that Paul's purpose here is to help the members of the church in Galatia recognize that they are descendants of Sarah. Consider how the telling of this story may promote continuing divisions among Abraham's children.

(3) Reflect on God's Continuing Care for the Learners

❖ Think about Hagar's position in the family by reading aloud the quote from Phyllis Trible found in "God Hears Hagar's Cry" in Interpreting the Scripture. Note that Hagar is oppressed and marginalized—and cared for by God.

❖ Brainstorm with the class ways that God cares for them. List these ideas on newsprint. Be sure to think beyond material care to physical, emotional, and spiritual care.

❖ Provide quiet time for the adults to give thanks for the care they receive from God.

❖ Talk about ways in which the class and/or congregation can help to provide care for the marginalized "Hagars" of your community. Such women may be single parents; they may have been victims of domestic violence; they may lack the education and skills to care financially for their family. Resolve to take any action on behalf of these "Hagars" that the class believes it can do.

(4) Become Informed about the Current State of Christian-Jewish-Muslim Relationships and Do Whatever Possible to Promote Peace

❖ Choose one of the following options to help the students become informed about relationships among Christians, Jews, and Muslims worldwide.

■ **Option 1:** Present a lecture on the information you have been able to locate. Be sure that you can present a balanced picture that fairly represents the situation.

■ **Option 2:** Distribute the materials you have located to groups of students. Distribute paper and pencils. Ask each group to take notes on the resource(s) they have been given and report back to the class.

■ **Option 3:** Introduce a guest speaker who has expertise in this area and allow time for a lecture.

❖ Ask this question: **What steps can we take to promote peace among the descendants of Abraham?** List ideas on newsprint and do whatever seems possible. Certainly, class members can pledge to pray for peace.

(5) Continue the Journey

❖ Pray that the class members will go forth realizing that God extends love to people who we may think are beyond the scope of God's care.

❖ Read aloud this preparation for next week's lesson. You may also want to post it on newsprint for the students to copy.

■ **Title: Isaac and Rebekah**
■ **Background Scripture: Genesis 24**
■ **Lesson Scripture: Genesis 24:34-40, 42-45, 48**

■ **Focus of the Lesson: Situations often seem challenging, but through God's creative power, the impossible becomes possible. What are some ordinary situations in which God acts? When Abraham's servant sought a wife for Isaac among family kin in Haran, he immediately recognized Rebekah as the right woman, and then blessed God for quickly leading him to her.**

❖ Challenge the students to complete one or more of these activities for further spiritual growth, which you will write on newsprint for the students to copy.

(1) **Look in a local phone book to see how many different religious faiths worship in your community. Consider visiting one or more of these houses of worship, especially one that is not Christian, to learn what the members there believe.**

(2) **Think about divisions in your own family. How might you go about bringing healing and reconciliation? Do whatever you can.**

(3) **Tell God in prayer what your needs are today and trust that God will provide a way for them to be met. Make a list of these needs in a spiritual journal or prayer book. Be sure to go back and note when and how each prayer is answered.**

❖ Sing or read aloud "God, Whose Love Is Reigning O'er Us."

❖ Conclude today's session by leading the class in this benediction, which is adapted from Genesis 14:19-20: **Blessed be you by God Most High, maker of heaven and earth; and blessed be God Most High.**

UNIT 1: GOD CREATED A PEOPLE
ISAAC AND REBEKAH

PREVIEWING THE LESSON

Lesson Scripture: Genesis 24:34-40, 42-45, 48
Background Scripture: Genesis 24
Key Verse: Genesis 24:48

Focus of the Lesson:
Situations often seem challenging, but through God's creative power, the impossible becomes possible. What are some ordinary situations in which God acts? When Abraham's servant sought a wife for Isaac among family kin in Haran, he immediately recognized Rebekah as the right woman, and then blessed God for quickly leading him to her.

Goals for the Learners:
(1) to unpack the story leading up to Isaac and Rebekah's marriage, which continued the hope of God's creating a people through the descendants of Abraham and Sarah.
(2) to recognize and affirm God's creative power at work in their lives.
(3) to seek God's guidance.

Pronunciation Guide:
Bethuel (bi thyoo' uhl)
Eliezer (el ee ee' zuhr)
Haran (hair' uhn)
Laban (lay' buhn)
Nahor (nay' hor)

Supplies:
Bibles, newsprint and marker, paper and pencils, hymnals

READING THE SCRIPTURE

NRSV
Genesis 24:34-40, 42-45, 48
    ³⁴So he said, "I am Abraham's servant. ³⁵The LORD has greatly blessed my master, and he has become wealthy; he has given

NIV
Genesis 24:34-40, 42-45, 48
    ³⁴So he said, "I am Abraham's servant. ³⁵The LORD has blessed my master abundantly, and he has become wealthy. He has

him flocks and herds, silver and gold, male and female slaves, camels and donkeys. ³⁶And Sarah my master's wife bore a son to my master when she was old; and he has given him all that he has. ³⁷My master made me swear, saying, 'You shall not take a wife for my son from the daughters of the Canaanites, in whose land I live; ³⁸but you shall go to my father's house, to my kindred, and get a wife for my son.' ³⁹I said to my master, 'Perhaps the woman will not follow me.' ⁴⁰But he said to me, 'The LORD, before whom I walk, will send his angel with you and make your way successful. You shall get a wife for my son from my kindred, from my father's house.'

⁴²"I came today to the spring, and said, 'O LORD, the God of my master Abraham, if now you will only make successful the way I am going! ⁴³I am standing here by the spring of water; let the young woman who comes out to draw, to whom I shall say, "Please give me a little water from your jar to drink," ⁴⁴and who will say to me, "Drink, and I will draw for your camels also"—let her be the woman whom the Lord has appointed for my master's son.'

⁴⁵"Before I had finished speaking in my heart, there was Rebekah coming out with her water jar on her shoulder; and she went down to the spring, and drew. I said to her, 'Please let me drink. . . . **⁴⁸Then I bowed my head and worshiped the LORD, and blessed the LORD, the God of my master Abraham, who had led me by the right way to obtain the daughter of my master's kinsman for his son.**

given him sheep and cattle, silver and gold, menservants and maidservants, and camels and donkeys. ³⁶My master's wife Sarah has borne him a son in her old age, and he has given him everything he owns. ³⁷And my master made me swear an oath, and said, 'You must not get a wife for my son from the daughters of the Canaanites, in whose land I live, ³⁸but go to my father's family and to my own clan, and get a wife for my son.'

³⁹"Then I asked my master, 'What if the woman will not come back with me?'

⁴⁰"He replied, 'The LORD, before whom I have walked, will send his angel with you and make your journey a success, so that you can get a wife for my son from my own clan and from my father's family.'

⁴²"When I came to the spring today, I said, 'O LORD, God of my master Abraham, if you will, please grant success to the journey on which I have come. ⁴³See, I am standing beside this spring; if a maiden comes out to draw water and I say to her, "Please let me drink a little water from your jar," ⁴⁴and if she says to me, "Drink, and I'll draw water for your camels too," let her be the one the LORD has chosen for my master's son.'

⁴⁵"Before I finished praying in my heart, Rebekah came out, with her jar on her shoulder. She went down to the spring and drew water, and I said to her, 'Please give me a drink.'

. . . . **⁴⁸and I bowed down and worshiped the LORD. I praised the LORD, the God of my master Abraham, who had led me on the right road to get the granddaughter of my master's brother for his son.**

UNDERSTANDING THE SCRIPTURE

Genesis 24:1. Abraham's final days provide an occasion to reflect upon how God has kept the promise and filled his life with blessings.

Genesis 24:2-4. Abraham's concern that

his son Isaac not marry a Canaanite woman but get a wife from "the old country" is more than a matter of oriental custom. Rather, it must be seen as the aged Abraham's final act of faith in God's promises. His demand for an oath likely indicates that he expects to die before his servant's return. The servant, who may have been Eliezer (15:2), is commanded to put his hand under Abraham's thigh, a clear reference to the genitals, the source of power and life. In Genesis 47:29-31 the dying Jacob commands his son Joseph to put his hand under his thigh and swear that he will not allow Jacob to remain buried in Egypt. Similarly, Abraham, near death, expresses his greatest wish that his son marry a woman of the clan, rather than one of the local Canaanite women, and insists his wish be sealed with an oath.

Genesis 24:5-9. The servant is at first reluctant to swear such an oath, fearing that a woman from Haran may be unwilling to return with him. He is further afraid that he will then have to take Isaac back to Mesopotamia, thus requiring a second long and dangerous journey. Abraham frees the anxious servant from such a requirement, assuring him that God will provide a wife. Further, "if the woman is not willing to follow you" (24:8), then the servant is free of the oath. With those stipulations clear, the servant "put his hand under the thigh of Abraham his master and swore to him concerning this matter" (24:9).

Genesis 24:10-14. Although the servant trusts God, he also knows that God works through human beings. Therefore he takes ten camels and "all kinds of choice gifts" (24:10) to help persuade a suitable bride to return with him. Upon arriving in Nahor, he goes right to the well of the city, the place where one may expect to find the women, since it was commonly their task to draw water for their respective households. The servant not only prays to the Lord for success in this venture, but like Gideon and his fleece (Judges 6:36-40) the servant sets a series of criteria by which he may know whether God is showing steadfast love by providing a woman for Isaac.

Genesis 24:15-27. The narrator's description of Rebekah enables the reader to know she will be Isaac's wife before the servant does. The narrator adds that she is both "very fair to look upon," and "a virgin, whom no man had known" (24:16). Upon learning who she is, the servant bows his head and worships the Lord, thankful for God's faithfulness.

Genesis 24:28-49. Rebekah runs quickly to her brother, Laban, who rushes out to meet Abraham's servant. Note that the first thing that attracts Laban's attention is the fine quality of the jewelry that the servant has given his sister. Laban's interest in money and fine things will play a significant role later in the unfolding story of God's plan for God's people. Laban readily invites the servant in for a meal, but the servant insists on telling of his errand in full before he eats, and this he proceeds to do in great detail! Finally, at the end of his long discourse, the servant issues a challenge to Laban and Bethuel, Rebekah's brother and father, respectively.

The servant asks Laban and Bethuel to give their sister/daughter to become Isaac's wife, imploring them to recognize the hand of God in all of this. Turning either to the right hand or to the left expresses an idiom captured well in the NIV's words, "so that I may know which way to turn" (24:49). What the servant does next depends on the response of these men. If Laban and Bethuel will not cooperate, the servant will be happy to take his jewels and go elsewhere to those who can see the hand of God at work.

Genesis 24:50-51. Bethuel and Laban are wise enough to see God's hand at work, and they readily agree to let Rebekah go to be the wife of Isaac.

Genesis 24:52-56. When he hears their response, the servant again bows his head and worships God. He does not answer in words, but distributes gifts (possibly a dowry) and eats with those who had accompanied him on his journey. After a night's sleep, the servant is eager to complete his mission. Oriental custom would call for a period of celebration of the betrothal before Rebekah's departure. His insistence on returning at once points up his fear that Abraham may not survive until the servant returns from his journey.

Genesis 24:57-61. Rebekah's family allows her to decide whether she will go with the servant immediately or observe the betrothal celebration. She agrees to go and leaves after her family bestows upon her a traditional blessing for children and triumph over foes. Rebekah is accompanied by her nurse Deborah (35:8) and other attendants.

Genesis 24:62-67. Isaac and Rebekah first meet while he is meditating in the field. He looks up and sees the camels coming home. Rebekah catches sight of Isaac and asks the servant who he is. The servant identifies Isaac as the "master," an indication of the transition from Abraham to Isaac. When she finds out that it is Isaac, her husband-to-be, Rebekah quickly veils her face in the typical Middle Eastern way.

Isaac brings Rebekah into his tent, and she becomes his wife. As Terrence Fretheim observes in *The New Interpreter's Bible*, Rebekah's "presence in Sarah's tent signifies her new role as matriarch of this family." The biblical narrator adds "he [Isaac] loved her" (24:67), signaling that what began as an arranged marriage was developing into a loving relationship. "Thus we know," as Michael Williams says in his *Storyteller's Companion to the Bible* "that the match of Isaac and Rebekah was one truly 'made in heaven,' or perhaps more accurately, one made by the guiding hand of God on earth."

INTERPRETING THE SCRIPTURE

An Arranged Marriage

The story of securing a bride for Isaac may sound strange to the ears of readers who have grown up with very different customs. In the United States, most of us are used to the cultural pattern of dating and falling in love with someone who will eventually become our spouse following mutual consent. Yet arranged marriages continue to be the order of the day in many Eastern countries, especially those less influenced by Western culture.

Psychologists tell us that the success rate for arranged marriages is roughly the same as that for "romantic" marriages. Presumably, the issue at stake is whether we decide we are going to love our spouses and make the marriage work. An Indian woman in my congregation told me that while she had never met her husband until the day of their marriage, "I have learned to love him." The story of Isaac and Rebekah begins as an arranged marriage, but grows into a loving relationship.

The issue at stake, of course, was that for Abraham's line to continue, Isaac needed to produce a male heir. Abraham had trusted God throughout his life, and God had never let him down. However, Abraham's patience had been tried on more than one occasion, and he preferred to die knowing that he had healthy grandchildren who would continue to fulfill God's promise that he would be "a great nation." His fondest wish was to see Isaac marry someone from his own clan, someone from Haran, the place from where he and Sarah migrated many years ago.

Families continue to play a major role not so much in the selection, but in the acceptance process and the integration of in-laws into the family. "Will he or she 'fit' in our family?" we ask. What is our responsibility as Christian people to provide a loving and accepting climate for the spouses of our relatives who may not be from "our country" and "our kindred"? What are the most important qualities for a husband or wife to possess? Surely skin color and nationality cannot be at the top of our list.

God Will Make a Way

When Abraham's servant heard his master's request, he was a bit reticent. After all, one of the "hometown girls" might not want to travel into the desert and follow Abraham and Isaac's nomadic journey.

Abraham is not put off. The God who took him from his father's house and promised that he would make of Abraham a great nation is not going to quit acting in human history just because there seem to be a few obstacles in the road. Surely the concern over whether one of the girls of Nahor would be willing to return with Abraham's servant must have seemed a small issue to Abraham. Remember this is the Abraham who had fathered a child at age one hundred when his wife Sarah was ninety! "Is anything too hard for the LORD?" (18:14) they had asked in those days. Now that Isaac is of marriageable age, the resounding "no" continues to ring throughout the prosperous camp of Abraham.

After we have seen God's hand at work, after something has occurred that has reassured us that God is still acting in human history, how quickly we return to doubt and anxiety! The Bible tells us over and over again that in spite of all the evidence we can cite to the contrary, God has a plan for our world in general and for our lives in particular. Fear and doubt have a way of paralyzing us. God calls us not to give in to anxiety and fear, but rather to trust and obey. While we are busy raising our concerns, God is already at work in ways that are more wonderful than we can imagine. God is able to make a way when there is no way. We simply need to trust God and pray that we will be able to discern God's hand at work in our life situations.

A Marriage Made in Heaven

Did God bring your parents together? If you are (or have been) married, did God cause you and your spouse to come together and fall in love, or is it merely human factors that guide the decision-making process where love and marriage are involved? In the story of Isaac and Rebekah, the narrator does not hide the fact that "choice gifts" were taken by Abraham's servant to influence the selection process. The weight (value) of the gold bracelets and rings are important. In like manner, the fact that Rebekah was "very fair to look upon" (24:16) has not been edited out of the story. To what extent is this a story of human attraction? To what extent is God involved?

I heard a sermon by Joe Harding, United Methodist pastor and co-founder of the Vision 2000 movement that swept the country a few years ago, in which he said: "Coincidences are God working incognito." As people of faith, we believe that things don't just "happen." In back of ordinary situations and seemingly common occurrences, God is acting to work out the divine plan. Believing that God is working out God's purposes does not imply a belief in predestination, that the course of events is already set by God and we can do nothing to alter it. That would deny human beings free will. The Genesis story does not support predestination, nor does it imply a kind of Deism that says God simply sets the world on its course and lets it operate on its own. Instead, God works through the creation and through human choice to guide the destiny of God's created order. By fervent prayer and careful discernment, it is possible to see God's hand at work and to cooperate with what God is doing in the world today. That is the calling that comes to every faithful believer.

Answered Prayer

The Bible tells us that Abraham had become extremely wealthy and well established. The servant with the most seniority in Abraham's house was the one called by Abraham to carry out the important duty of finding a bride for his son. Yet this well-respected and much-trusted spokesperson for Abraham did not take God's activity for granted. Before he began his mission in Nahor he prayed to God for guidance. When Rebekah unknowingly "passes the test" to become Isaac's bride, the servant bows his head and worships the Lord (24:48). Then, when Laban and Bethuel agreed to let her go back to join Abraham's family, the servant again "bowed himself to the ground before the LORD" (24:52).

We frequently turn to God in our time of need or want or when we are at our wit's end. But when the sun is shining and the climate is bright, we often forget about God and assume that the progress we have made is due to our own efforts and ingenuity. How easy it is to ignore the benevolent hand of God when things are going well! Does it take adversity in order to bring us to our knees? Abraham's servant gave thanks to God for his blessings all along the way. At every turn, he worshiped God. The mission he had to accomplish was important, and the servant recognized that it was only by God's hand that a bride for his master would be found. Do we entrust our most important decisions to God, and are we willing to follow where God leads? These questions are just as challenging for us today as they were for Abraham's servant in another culture in an earlier era. May we exhibit the same trust and devotion that Abraham's servant demonstrated all along the way!

SHARING THE SCRIPTURE

Preparing Our Hearts

Meditate on this week's devotional reading, found in Psalm 100. This very familiar passage reminds us that we are the people of God, who created us. Repeat this psalm of praise to God the Creator, extolling "his faithfulness to all generations" (100:5). Use words, music, art, or movement to offer praise to God in the way that is most meaningful to you.

Pray that you and the adult learners will continually give thanks for the God who created us and set us within families.

Preparing Our Minds

Study the background, which includes all of Genesis 24, and lesson Scripture, verses 34-40, 42-45, 48. As you ponder the Bible passage, think about some ordinary situations in which God acts.

Write on newsprint:

❏ information for next week's lesson, found under "Continue the Journey."
❏ activities for further spiritual growth in "Continue the Journey."

Plan a brief lecture to set the stage for "Unpack the Story Leading Up to Isaac and Rebekah's Marriage, which Continued the Hope of God's Creating a People through the Descendants of Abraham and Sarah."

LEADING THE CLASS

(1) Gather to Learn

❖ Welcome the class members and introduce any guests.
❖ Pray that the adults will be open to the leading of the Holy Spirit as they explore God's actions in the lives of Isaac and Rebekah and in their own lives.
❖ Briefly tell the story of C.S. Lewis' relationship with God. **Baptized as an infant in 1899 into the Church of Ireland,**

C.S. Lewis turned away from Christianity around 1913. After years of living as an atheist, Lewis returned first to a belief in God and then in 1931 reaffirmed Christianity. Describing his journey back to Christ in Surprised by Joy, he wrote: "Every step I had taken, from Absolute to 'Spirit' and from 'Spirit' to the 'God,' had been a step toward the more concrete, the more imminent, the more compulsive. . . . To accept the Incarnation was a further step in the same direction. It brings God nearer, or near in a new way. And this, I found, was something I had not wanted. . . . I know very well when, but hardly know how, the final step was taken. I was driven to Whipsnade one sunny morning. When we set out I did not believe that Jesus Christ is the Son of God, and when we reached the zoo I did."

❖ Discuss this question: **How do you see God at work in the midst of an ordinary activity in Lewis's life?**

❖ Read aloud today's focus statement: **Situations often seem challenging, but through God's creative power, the impossible becomes possible. What are some ordinary situations in which God acts? When Abraham's servant sought a wife for Isaac among family kin in Haran, he immediately recognized Rebekah as the right woman, and then blessed God for quickly leading him to her.**

(2) Unpack the Story Leading Up to Isaac and Rebekah's Marriage, which Continued the Hope of God's Creating a People through the Descendants of Abraham and Sarah

❖ Use information for verses 1, 2-4, 5-9, 10-14, and 15-27 in Understanding the Scripture to present a lecture that will set the stage for today's lesson.

❖ Choose a volunteer to read the story Abraham's servant tells to Laban, as found in Genesis 24:34-40, 42-45, 48.

❖ Discuss these questions.

(1) What do you learn about Abraham?
(2) What do you learn about Sarah?
(3) What do you learn about why the servant has come?
(4) What action told the servant that Rebekah was the woman who was to be Isaac's wife?

❖ Consider the role of prayer in the servant's finding Rebekah immediately by reading aloud "Answered Prayer" in Interpreting the Scripture. Be sure to point out that the servant worshipped God for leading him in the right direction, according to our key verse, Genesis 24:48.

(3) Recognize and Affirm God's Creative Power at Work in the Learners' Lives

❖ Note that sometimes we are unaware that God is working in our lives. Read aloud the second paragraph of "A Marriage Made in Heaven" in Interpreting the Scripture.

❖ Invite students to give examples, particularly from their own lives, to illustrate the saying that "coincidences are God working incognito." (To be sure everyone understands the term "in kag ne' to," you may want to define it as "concealing one's identity.") Some topics for these stories may include finding a spouse, landing a job, locating a new home, or discovering a community of faith where we feel like family.

❖ Conclude this portion of the lesson by asking the students if they can identify any patterns from their stories as to how God works in people's lives.

(4) Seek God's Guidance

❖ Recall that Abraham's servant prayed to God that he would know the woman who was to be Isaac's wife because she would offer water to him and his camels (Genesis 24:12-14). This sign was the servant's way of seeking God's guidance.

❖ Call on students to state ways that they seek God's guidance. You may want to list these ideas on newsprint.

❖ Distribute paper and pencils. Challenge each student to write a sentence or two about a dilemma or decision they currently face. Also ask them to write another sentence or two stating how they will seek God's guidance. Assure them that whatever they write will remain confidential.

❖ Ask the students to echo these words adapted from Isaiah 55:6: **We will seek the LORD while he may be found and call upon our God who is near us now.**

(5) Continue the Journey

❖ Pray that all who have participated today will be open to and thankful for God's creative power at work in their lives.

❖ Read aloud this preparation for next week's lesson. You may also want to post it on newsprint for the students to copy.

■ **Title: Esau and Jacob as Rivals**
■ **Background Scripture: Genesis 25:19-34**
■ **Lesson Scripture: Genesis 25:19-34**
■ **Focus of the Lesson: Siblings have clashed since the days of Cain and Abel. What are the roots of family conflict, especially hostility between** brothers or sisters? The story of Jacob and Esau reveals that a rivalry begun at birth continued into their adult years as Jacob persuaded Esau to sell his birthright.

❖ Challenge the students to complete one or more of these activities for further spiritual growth, which you will write on newsprint for the students to copy.

(1) Research marriage customs of a culture other than your own. Compare and contrast those customs with ones with which you are familiar.

(2) Be alert for instances when God is clearly ordering your steps this week. How do you know that God is leading you in a specific direction? Write about your experience in your spiritual journal.

(3) Make a list of the qualities you would like to see in a spouse. Which of these do you think are important to God? Why?

❖ Sing or read aloud "O Perfect Love."

❖ Conclude today's session by leading the class in this benediction, which is adapted from Genesis 14:19-20: **Blessed be you by God Most High, maker of heaven and earth; and blessed be God Most High.**

UNIT 2: GOD'S PEOPLE INCREASED
ESAU AND JACOB AS RIVALS

PREVIEWING THE LESSON

Lesson Scripture: Genesis 25:19-34
Background Scripture: Genesis 25:19-34
Key Verse: Genesis 25:23

Focus of the Lesson:
Siblings have clashed since the days of Cain and Abel. What are the roots of family conflict, especially hostility between brothers or sisters? The story of Jacob and Esau reveals that a rivalry begun at birth continued into their adult years as Jacob persuaded Esau to sell his birthright.

Goals for the Learners:
(1) to investigate two incidents of the rivalry between the twin sons of Isaac and Rebekah: Jacob, who became the patriarch of Israel, and Esau, who founded the line of Edomites.
(2) to reflect on the nature and effects of family conflict.
(3) to try to resolve conflicts with siblings or other family members.

Pronunciation Guide:
Aramean (air uh mee' uhn)
Bethuel (bi thyoo' uhl)   Edomite (ee' duh mit)
Laban (lay' buhn)   Paddan-aram (pad uhn air' uhm)
Seir (see' uhr)

Supplies:
Bibles, newsprint and marker, paper and pencils, hymnals; optional lentil soup, bowls, spoons, napkins

---

READING THE SCRIPTURE

NRSV
Genesis 25:19-34

¹⁹These are the descendants of Isaac, Abraham's son: Abraham was the father of Isaac, ²⁰and Isaac was forty years old when he married Rebekah, daughter of Bethuel

NIV
Genesis 25:19-34

¹⁹This is the account of Abraham's son Isaac.

Abraham became the father of Isaac, ²⁰and Isaac was forty years old when he the Aramean of Paddan-aram, sister of Laban the Aramean. ²¹Isaac prayed to the LORD for his wife, because she was barren; and the LORD granted his prayer, and his wife Rebekah conceived. ²²The children struggled together within her; and she said, "If it is to be this way, why do I live?" So she went to inquire of the LORD. ²³**And the LORD said to her,**

> **"Two nations are in your womb,**
> **and two peoples born of you shall be divided;**
> **the one shall be stronger than the other, the elder shall serve the younger."**

²⁴When her time to give birth was at hand, there were twins in her womb. ²⁵The first came out red, all his body like a hairy mantle; so they named him Esau. ²⁶Afterward his brother came out, with his hand gripping Esau's heel; so he was named Jacob. Isaac was sixty years old when she bore them.

²⁷When the boys grew up, Esau was a skillful hunter, a man of the field, while Jacob was a quiet man, living in tents. ²⁸Isaac loved Esau, because he was fond of game; but Rebekah loved Jacob.

²⁹Once when Jacob was cooking a stew, Esau came in from the field, and he was famished. ³⁰Esau said to Jacob, "Let me eat some of that red stuff, for I am famished!" (Therefore he was called Edom.) ³¹Jacob said, "First sell me your birthright." ³²Esau said, "I am about to die; of what use is a birthright to me?" ³³Jacob said, "Swear to me first." So he swore to him, and sold his birthright to Jacob. ³⁴Then Jacob gave Esau bread and lentil stew, and he ate and drank, and rose and went his way. Thus Esau despised his birthright.

married Rebekah daughter of Bethuel the Aramean from Paddan Aram and sister of Laban the Aramean.

²¹Isaac prayed to the LORD on behalf of his wife, because she was barren. The LORD answered his prayer, and his wife Rebekah became pregnant. ²²The babies jostled each other within her, and she said, "Why is this happening to me?" So she went to inquire of the LORD.

²³**The LORD said to her,**

> **"Two nations are in your womb,**
> **and two peoples from within you will be separated;**
> **one people will be stronger than the other,**
> **and the older will serve the younger."**

²⁴When the time came for her to give birth, there were twin boys in her womb. ²⁵The first to come out was red, and his whole body was like a hairy garment; so they named him Esau. ²⁶After this, his brother came out, with his hand grasping Esau's heel; so he was named Jacob. Isaac was sixty years old when Rebekah gave birth to them.

²⁷The boys grew up, and Esau became a skillful hunter, a man of the open country, while Jacob was a quiet man, staying among the tents. ²⁸Isaac, who had a taste for wild game, loved Esau, but Rebekah loved Jacob.

²⁹Once when Jacob was cooking some stew, Esau came in from the open country, famished. ³⁰He said to Jacob, "Quick, let me have some of that red stew! I'm famished!" (That is why he was also called Edom.)

³¹Jacob replied, "First sell me your birthright."

³²"Look, I am about to die," Esau said. "What good is the birthright to me?"

³³But Jacob said, "Swear to me first." So he swore an oath to him, selling his birthright to Jacob.

³⁴Then Jacob gave Esau some bread and some lentil stew. He ate and drank, and then got up and left.

So Esau despised his birthright.

UNDERSTANDING THE SCRIPTURE

Genesis 25:19-21. Our story begins with what is becoming a persistent theme in the patriarchal narratives: Rebekah, like her mother-in-law, Sarah, is barren. Tension immediately increases, for once again the infertility of a couple threatens the promise of "a great nation." "Isaac prayed to the LORD" concerning Rebekah's barrenness, and "the LORD granted his prayer." While the story moves quickly, the careful reader will note that Isaac was forty years old when he married Rebekah, and sixty when the twins were born. Thus it took God twenty years to grant Isaac's request.

Genesis 25:22. While Isaac was no doubt ecstatic over the news that Rebekah was pregnant, the reality for Rebekah was nine miserable months of suffering. Not understanding why she was in so much pain, Rebekah exclaimed, "If it is to be this way, why do I live?" Finding herself at a breaking point, Rebekah turns to the Lord. Her cry of despair, which suggests that she would rather be dead than to have to endure the difficulties of the pregnancy, also warns the reader that the story to follow will have more than its share of confusion and heartache.

Genesis 25:23. Rebekah receives an answer to her question. There is not one child in her womb, but two! Not only is Rebekah about to give birth to twins but also they are struggling with each other even before they are born! In a combination of dramatic foreshadowing and prophetic utterance, Rebekah is told "the elder shall serve the younger." Surely that word from the Lord influenced her attitude and actions toward her two sons throughout their formative years.

Genesis 25:24-26. Just as the Lord predicted, when Rebekah delivered, she gave birth to twins. The narrator misses no opportunity to tell us that they were by no means identical. In fact, the two boys were as different as day and night! The first was born with a ruddy complexion, and covered with hair. Because of his appearance, Isaac and Rebekah named this child Esau, or "red," a play on Edom, the nation of his descendants, and "hairy" a play on "Seir," the mountain range southeast of the Dead Sea where the Edomites lived.

The younger child is born with his hand gripping Esau's heel, so the Bible tells us he was named Jacob. The name "Jacob" in Hebrew is related to the noun "heel." According to commentators, the name may also mean "deceiver" or "supplanter," terms that certainly describe Jacob's later behavior.

Genesis 25:27-28. The narrator describes the young men by referring to their ways of life that often stood in tension. Esau becomes a skillful hunter, comfortable with those who are at home in the wild and on the move with animals, while Jacob identifies with those who live a more settled, pastoral way of life. The narrator does not hesitate to reveal the fact that each parent has a favorite child. Isaac's fondness for Esau seems to be based on their common love for the hunt and the savory food that comes from hunting. Rebekah, of course, believes that Jacob is the chosen one of God, and this, no doubt, has greatly influenced her favoring of the "quiet man." The theme of favorite children will recur in later stories.

Genesis 25:29-30. The story of the birthright no doubt delighted the descendants of Jacob with pride in the way their ancestor outwitted their Edomite ancestor, Esau. Not only has Jacob chosen to be the more domestic of the two boys but also has taken up cooking. Esau, coming in after a long day in the field, is famished. What the narrator tells us is "soup" or "lentil stew," Esau crudely refers to as "red stuff." Esau offers no greeting to his brother. He merely demands some of the "stuff." The portrait of Esau is less than flattering.

Genesis 25:31. Just as Esau reveals himself as crude, so also Jacob reveals himself as clever, always ready to take advantage of the situation. Jacob replies, "First sell me your birthright." While the precise meaning of the birthright is not clear from this passage, we can assume that the birthright of the eldest son is no small matter. Typically in the ancient Near East, the birthright of the eldest son entailed a leadership position in the family and a double share of the father's property.

Genesis 25:32. Not surprisingly, Esau exclaims, "I am about to die; of what use is a birthright to me?" "Esau, in an incredibly shortsighted act of stupidity," notes Michael Williams in his *Storyteller's Companion to the Bible,* "says that he will give up his right as eldest, his right of inheritance of property and blessing, all for some red stuff." Thus Esau is portrayed as insensitive and indifferent, easily outwitted regarding what is his, and more interested in his stomach than in his long-term future and well-being.

Genesis 25:33. The clever Jacob is careful to make the ridiculous agreement legal and binding. "Swear to me first," Jacob

demands. Unbelievable as it sounds, Esau agrees and sells his birthright to Jacob! While the narrator continues to show Esau in a negative light, Jacob is presented as a clever and opportunistic individual who knows what he wants. He takes advantage of his brother when Esau is vulnerable, and Jacob carefully covers the legal bases when the opening for advancement presents itself.

Genesis 25:34. In his *Storyteller's Companion to the Bible,* Michael Williams observes: "The picture of crudity continues as the famished and exhausted man of the field eats the food like some sort of animal, devouring it in hurried silence and rushing out without a word to his brother. The narrator concludes quite rightly, 'Thus he disdained his right as firstborn.'. . . Esau's folly and stupidity are evident. Yet Jacob's trickery and shady business practices are not themselves admirable." Can we see God's hand at work amidst the complicated stories of human life? That is one of the challenges that the book of Genesis puts before us.

INTERPRETING THE SCRIPTURE

Isaac's Prayer

God called Abraham and promised to make of him "a great nation" (Genesis 12:2). Already a senior citizen, Abraham left his country, his kindred, and his familiar surroundings and trusted God to provide for his needs. Nearly twenty-five years passed before Abraham was given the heir that would continue the promise of God to the next generation. Sarah's nervous laughter, when as an old woman she was promised a child, turned to joyous giggles when Isaac was born.

Now a generation has passed. Forty-year-old Isaac has been blessed with Rebekah, a beautiful girl from the country of Abraham's roots. Yet, like his mother, she is

barren. No doubt Isaac had heard many times the story of the three visitors to his father's tent who brought the promise that Abraham would at last have a child by Sarah. Was history repeating itself? If God was serious about this promise, why was it taking so long to be fulfilled?

Nowhere in the Bible is there a hint that Isaac questioned the promises of God. Yet when he prayed to the Lord that his wife would have a child, it was twenty years before "the LORD granted his prayer, and his wife Rebekah conceived" (25:21). Surely there is a lesson for us in the importance of persistence and patience in prayer!

We are reminded of Jesus' story of the persistent widow in Luke 18:1-8. We live in an age of instant breakfast, instant-on television, and e-mail messages that travel around the globe as fast as we can compose them. We often expect instant results from God as well. Did Isaac grow weary of praying for a child? Are we able to focus our thoughts and prayers and bring them consistently before our God? Are we willing and able to stay the course? Perhaps it would be good for each of us to ask ourselves what commitments we are willing to make for the long haul. Do we really believe that God will answer our prayers?

Rebekah's Prayer

Just as Isaac turned to God in his hour of need, so Rebekah did not hesitate to bring her concerns before the Almighty. No doubt thrilled to be carrying Isaac's child and thus helping to fulfill the promise that God had made with both her husband and father-in-law, Rebekah's joy was soon tempered by the difficulties of her pregnancy.

Just as God had answered Isaac's prayer, so God responded to Rebekah's concern. There is no indication that God took away her pain, but did offer her an explanation. She was going to have twins! No wonder she was so uncomfortable. The two boys she was carrying would be rivals throughout their lives. In fact, their struggle for power had already begun in her womb!

A Self-Fulfilling Prophecy

To what extent did God's message to Rebekah influence the way she raised her sons? God had indicated "the elder shall serve the younger" (25:23). Would it have been possible to treat both boys fairly when she believed that God's special blessing rested upon Jacob? There is no indication that Rebekah shared her thoughts with Isaac, but surely her favoritism was obvious. At the same time Rebekah was looking out for Jacob, Isaac was growing more and more partial to Esau. Thus the drama unfolded.

To what extent is sibling rivalry exacerbated by parental actions? We all know parents who deliberately humiliate a child because he or she does not fulfill the high standard of achievement set by a brother or sister. Instead of celebrating differences in giftedness, many times we belittle those who do not measure up.

Is it any wonder that Jacob and Esau continued their animosity into adult life? How do our actions influence those around us? Are we able to see the positive aspects of every person, or do we belittle those whose gifts are not in areas we value highly? May each of us reflect upon the high cost of playing favorites.

A Very Expensive Dinner!

Many times we judge a meal by its cost. Sometimes we are willing to pay a little more because of the quality or quantity of the food. No matter how much lentil stew Jacob served that night and how well it was seasoned, Esau paid too much for his dinner! Was the meal worth his birthright? No matter how hungry Esau thought he was, the obvious answer is "no."

Not only did Esau pay too much, but he also gave up something that he could not retrieve. Once he had forfeited his leadership role and his inheritance, these things could not be reestablished. In fact, so ludicrous was his agreement that Jacob made Esau take legal action to guarantee the permanence of the transaction.

Esau has been criticized for his shortsightedness and stupidity, while Jacob has often been lauded for being clever and calculating. Yet haven't all of us made decisions in the heat of the moment that we later regretted? And is it ever admirable to take advantage of another person's vulnerability?

I talked with a person recently who said, "I'd give anything to be able to go back and change fifteen minutes of my life five years ago." Many of us have not "sworn" by our decisions, but the choices that we have made have had far-reaching consequences, as was the case with Esau's decision. Sexual impropriety, questionable financial and business deals, decisions to indulge in excessive food and drink, decisions regarding the use of drugs—many times the implications of our choices, made in a few moments of time, haunt us for years to come.

Conversely, we are often encouraged and rewarded for our aggressive acts toward others. "It's a dog eat dog world," we are told. "Do unto others before they do unto you." Yet our faith teaches us that God is on the side of the least and the lost, and that when we take advantage of others, we become poorer for it. While we can admire Jacob for his ingenuity, as Christians we cannot in good conscience celebrate his tactics. The fact that he took advantage of Esau ultimately causes his stock to go down in our eyes. Instead of making his situation better, it made things worse for everyone involved causing continued tension and anxiety not only for him but also for his family and his descendants.

Esau is not the only one who has sold his birthright! How many of us have given up too quickly and conceded too soon? Have we sold out for a bowl of soup and sacrificed our integrity in the process? Not only individually, but also as communities we often give up too quickly. Many times a company comes to town with the promise of new jobs, and no one asks about the pollution and the deteriorating quality of life that is often an unspoken part of the deal. When we finally realize that we have sold our birthright, it is too late.

My children and grandchildren will not have the abundance of clean air and water that once was part of our world environment. Many of the "labor-saving" devices that purport to make our lives easier have caused additional stress and anxiety for us. Esau's dinner tasted good, but it was very expensive. How much are we willing to pay for a bowl of lentil stew? Sometimes the price is too high. May God help us to make wise choices.

SHARING THE SCRIPTURE

Preparing Our Hearts

Meditate on this week's devotional reading, found in 1 Corinthians 1:26-31. In this passage Paul writes that most of us are neither wise nor powerful nor born to nobility. Fortunately, none of that matters, for Jesus is our wisdom. One of the problems in the church in Corinth was rival factions. Left to our own devices, we can—and often do—set up rivalries based on traits that are of no importance to God. Some of these rivalries are even among brothers and sisters. Think about your own family. With whom do you have rivalries? What is the source of this competition? What steps can you take to end the rivalry?

Pray that you and the adult learners will be aware of rivalries and do all in your power to set them aside.

Preparing Our Minds

Study the background and lesson Scripture, both of which are found in Genesis 25:19-34. As you read, think about the roots of family conflict, especially hostility between brothers or sisters.

Write on newsprint:
❏ information for next week's lesson, found under "Continue the Journey."
❏ activities for further spiritual growth in "Continue the Journey."

Plan the lecture for "Gather to Learn" if you choose to use this option.

Gather lentil soup and serving supplies if you choose to do this optional activity.

Prepare brief lectures as suggested in "Investigate Two Incidents of the Rivalry between the Twin Sons of Isaac and

Rebekah: Jacob, Who Became the Patriarch of Israel, and Esau, Who Founded the Line of Edomites."

LEADING THE CLASS

(1) Gather to Learn

❖ Welcome the class members and introduce any guests.

❖ Pray that those who have gathered today will recognize conflicts and work to resolve them.

❖ Talk with the class about current conflicts in the news locally, nationally, or globally by discussing these questions.

   (1) **What appears to be the current conflict?**

   (2) **What do you know about the history of these parties that might have brought about the current clash?**

   (3) **From what you know about the situation, how do you think it can be resolved—or can it?**

❖ **Option:** Locate information on a conflict and prepare a lecture on it for the class.

❖ Read aloud today's focus statement: **Siblings have clashed since the days of Cain and Abel. What are the roots of family conflict, especially hostility between brothers or sisters? The story of Jacob and Esau reveals that a rivalry begun at birth continued into their adult years as Jacob persuaded Esau to sell his birthright.**

(2) Investigate Two Incidents of the Rivalry between the Twin Sons of Isaac and Rebekah: Jacob, Who Became the Patriarch of Israel, and Esau, Who Founded the Line of Edomites

❖ **Option:** Begin the Bible study by serving some lentil soup if that is possible in your space and with the size of your class. Let this be a reminder of the reason Esau was willing to give up his birthright.

❖ Choose one volunteer to read Genesis 25:19-28.

■ Use information from "Isaac's Prayer" in Interpreting the Scripture to discuss Isaac's persistence in praying for a child.

■ Present a brief lecture based on Genesis 25:22, 23, and 24-26 in Understanding the Scripture to explain Rebekah's concern and God's answer to her.

■ Note the tension between the boys' way of life as described in verses 27-28, as well as the parental favoritism.

❖ Select three readers for Genesis 25:29-34—a narrator, Jacob, and Esau.

■ Invite the class to comment on the character traits (flaws) they see in both Esau and Jacob.

■ Read aloud "A Very Expensive Dinner!" from Interpreting the Scripture.

■ Encourage the students to give examples of how people act like Esau or Jacob today. Consider the motivation for such behavior, which clearly leads to conflict and animosity.

(3) Reflect on the Nature and Effects of Family Conflict

❖ Brainstorm with the class issues or situations that may cause conflict within a family. These may include: *money, division of labor, adolescents pushing boundaries toward independence, problems with extended family, crises such as losing a job, time management, changes in family structure such as birth of a child or child leaving home.* List the ideas on newsprint.

❖ Brainstorm again, this time asking the students to identify how such conflicts affect the entire family and the individuals within it. (Think, for example, of how conflict affects adults at work, children at school, physical and emotional health, energy level, and marriage partners.)

(4) Try to Resolve Conflicts with Siblings or Other Family Members

❖ Choose volunteers to role-play family dissension in this scenario, which you will read aloud.

Jack and Annette's son Ron had moved back into his parents' home at the age of 32 after a failed marriage. His parents did not expect Ron to follow the rules of a teenager, but they did expect him to contribute to household expenditures, care for his own room and belongings, and live peaceably with them—none of which he chose to do. His presence created constant turmoil between him and his mom, him and his dad, and between his parents.

❖ Follow the role-play by discussing these questions.
    (1) What are the possible roots of these conflicts?
    (2) What are some ways that this conflict could be resolved?
    (3) Of the possible ways, which one(s) seem most Christ-like? Why?

❖ Distribute paper and pencils. Ask the students to write the name of a family member (or friend) with whom they are in a major or minor conflict. Suggest that they formulate in a short paragraph how they will go about trying to resolve this conflict, perhaps using approaches that have just been shared. Assure them that their plans are confidential.

❖ Ask the adults to repeat this sentence as you read it phrase by phrase: **Through prayer, and with God's guidance, I will take steps this week to resolve this conflict and reconcile our relationship.**

(5) Continue the Journey

❖ Pray that today's participants will recognize that conflict within the family is an old, old story that is continually repeated today, but can be resolved with God's help.
❖ Read aloud this preparation for next week's lesson. You may also want to post it on newsprint for the students to copy.
■ **Title: Jacob's Dream at Bethel**
■ **Background Scripture: Genesis 27:41–28:22**
■ **Lesson Scripture: Genesis 28:10-22**
■ **Focus of the Lesson: Humans dream, though we do not always remember or understand our dreams. What is the purpose of a dream? In the story of Jacob at Bethel, a dream reassured Jacob of God's continuing covenant with him.**

❖ Challenge the students to complete one or more of these activities for further spiritual growth, which you will write on newsprint for the students to copy.
    (1) Attend worship on this World Communion Sunday with thoughts in mind as to how this global service around the Lord's Table can be used as an occasion for reconciliation. Offer reconciliation to whomever you can.
    (2) Recall that Jacob took advantage of Esau's vulnerability. Be alert to situations this week where another person is vulnerable. Do all in your power to support this person and point out the consequences of poor choices.
    (3) Examine your own family tree, if you have one, or old photograph albums, or scrapbooks. Consider how someone's actions, perhaps an ancestor moving from one country to another, affected subsequent generations.

❖ Sing or read aloud "Help Us Accept Each Other."
❖ Conclude today's session by leading the class in this benediction, which is adapted from Genesis 14:19-20: **Blessed be you by God Most High, maker of heaven and earth; and blessed be God Most High.**

UNIT 2: GOD'S PEOPLE INCREASED
JACOB'S DREAM AT BETHEL

PREVIEWING THE LESSON

Lesson Scripture: Genesis 28:10-22
Background Scripture: Genesis 27:41–28:22
Key Verse: Genesis 28:15

Focus of the Lesson:
Humans dream, though we do not always remember or understand our dreams. What is the purpose of a dream? In the story of Jacob at Bethel, a dream reassured Jacob of God's continuing covenant with him.

Goals for the Learners:
(1) to explore the story of Jacob's dream at Bethel, its meaning, and its significance for God's covenant people.
(2) to recognize ways in which God communicates with them.
(3) to seek meaning from a dream.

Pronunciation Guide:
Beer-sheba (bee uhr shee' buh)   Bethel (beth' uhl)
Haran (hair' uhn)   Hittite (hit' tit)
Luz (luhz)   ziggurat (zig' oo rat)

Supplies:
Bibles, newsprint and marker, paper and pencils, hymnals

OCTOBER 14

READING THE SCRIPTURE

NRSV
Genesis 28:10-22

¹⁰Jacob left Beer-sheba and went toward Haran. ¹¹He came to a certain place and stayed there for the night, because the sun had set. Taking one of the stones of the place, he put it under his head and lay down in that place. ¹²And he dreamed that there was a ladder set up on the earth, the top of it

NIV
Genesis 28:10-22

¹⁰Jacob left Beersheba and set out for Haran. ¹¹When he reached a certain place, he stopped for the night because the sun had set. Taking one of the stones there, he put it under his head and lay down to sleep. ¹²He had a dream in which he saw a stairway resting on the earth, with its top reaching to

reaching to heaven; and the angels of God were ascending and descending on it. [13]And the LORD stood beside him and said, "I am the LORD, the God of Abraham your father and the God of Isaac; the land on which you lie I will give to you and to your offspring; [14]and your offspring shall be like the dust of the earth, and you shall spread abroad to the west and to the east and to the north and to the south; and all the families of the earth shall be blessed in you and in your offspring. [15]Know that I am with you and will keep you wherever you go, and will bring you back to this land; for I will not leave you until I have done what I have promised you." [16]Then Jacob woke from his sleep and said, "Surely the LORD is in this place—and I did not know it!" [17]And he was afraid, and said, "How awesome is this place! This is none other than the house of God, and this is the gate of heaven."

[18]So Jacob rose early in the morning, and he took the stone that he had put under his head and set it up for a pillar and poured oil on the top of it. [19]He called that place Bethel; but the name of the city was Luz at the first. [20]Then Jacob made a vow, saying, "If God will be with me, and will keep me in this way that I go, and will give me bread to eat and clothing to wear, [21]so that I come again to my father's house in peace, then the LORD shall be my God, [22]and this stone, which I have set up for a pillar, shall be God's house; and of all that you give me I will surely give one-tenth to you."

heaven, and the angels of God were ascending and descending on it. [13]There above it stood the LORD, and he said: "I am the LORD, the God of your father Abraham and the God of Isaac. I will give you and your descendants the land on which you are lying. [14]Your descendants will be like the dust of the earth, and you will spread out to the west and to the east, to the north and to the south. All peoples on earth will be blessed through you and your offspring. [15]I am with you and will watch over you wherever you go, and I will bring you back to this land. I will not leave you until I have done what I have promised you."

[16]When Jacob awoke from his sleep, he thought, "Surely the LORD is in this place, and I was not aware of it." [17]He was afraid and said, "How awesome is this place! This is none other than the house of God; this is the gate of heaven."

[18]Early the next morning Jacob took the stone he had placed under his head and set it up as a pillar and poured oil on top of it. [19]He called that place Bethel, though the city used to be called Luz.

[20]Then Jacob made a vow, saying, "If God will be with me and will watch over me on this journey I am taking and will give me food to eat and clothes to wear [21]so that I return safely to my father's house, then the LORD will be my God [22]and this stone that I have set up as a pillar will be God's house, and of all that you give me I will give you a tenth."

[handwritten margin note: Eben – Stone / Ebenezer – helping stone]

UNDERSTANDING THE SCRIPTURE

Genesis 27:41-45. Rebekah and Jacob have teamed up to deceive Isaac, who, aged and blind, gives the much-coveted blessing to Jacob. When Esau learns of the deception, he is furious and plots to kill Jacob. But Esau's vow to kill Jacob once Isaac has died threatens the future of God's promise. Again taking matters in her own hands,

when Rebekah learns of Esau's intent she devises a scheme to get Jacob safely out of the country.

Genesis 27:46. Rebekah makes no mention to Isaac of Esau's threat against Jacob. She would certainly not want Isaac to know that she had been involved in the plot. However, in an effort to get Jacob off the stage, she points out the bitterness for Isaac and herself that has resulted from Esau's marriage to two Hittite women (26:35) and strongly states her displeasure if Jacob should marry a woman "of the land" in which they lived.

Genesis 28:1-2. Isaac "takes the bait." He calls Jacob to his side and blesses him and instructs him to go to his grandfather Bethuel's house and marry one of the daughters of Laban, Rebekah's brother.

Genesis 28:3-5. In his *Storyteller's Companion to the Bible,* Michael Williams suggests that Isaac may only have appeared to be deceived. Perhaps that would explain the generous and extensive blessing that he now bestows upon Jacob before the young man leaves for Haran. After this blessing, there can be no doubt that Isaac has transferred the promised birthright to his younger son, Jacob.

Genesis 28:6-9. Esau witnesses his father give the blessing that should have been his to Jacob, and he hears Isaac instruct Jacob to avoid marrying a Canaanite (foreign) woman. Esau, who already had two Hittite wives (26:34-35), responds by hastily marrying an Israelite woman to regain his father's approval. This favorable portrayal of Esau appears similar to that given to Ishmael. Yet, like Ishmael, Esau continues to remain on the fringes of the family. Alas, his parents have invested their hopes almost exclusively in their younger, rascally son.

Genesis 28:10-11. Now Jacob flees from the hatred and threats of his brother, and comes to "a certain place," where he will spend an eventful night in the open air. He uses an ordinary stone to support his head.

Genesis 28:12. Jacob is able to sleep, but he has a dream that will affect the course of his future. He dreams that a ladder or stone stairway extends from earth to heaven. Commentators compare this stairway or ramp to those attached to temple towers (ziggurats) elsewhere in the ancient Near East. According to Terrence Fretheim, writing in *The New Interpreter's Bible,* these

stairways "were microcosms of the world, with the top of the towers representing heaven, the dwelling place of the gods. Such structures provided an avenue of approach from the human sphere to the divine realm. Priests or divine beings traversed up and down the stairway," thereby enabling communication between mortal human beings and the gods. The term "angels" can more correctly be translated "messengers," which is the true function of these beings.

Genesis 28:13-15. In Jacob's dream, the angels or messengers have no particular purpose; they are silent. God speaks to Jacob, promising to be with him.

First of all, God makes clear the continuity of God's promises to Jacob with those that God has made with Abraham and Isaac. This is the same God who has been with Jacob's ancestors. God's promise to Jacob fulfills Isaac's blessing in 28:3-4. Through the dream God makes it clear that Jacob has now received the same birthright and blessing that God had previously bestowed upon his father and grandfather.

God bestows many promises upon Jacob. As Fretheim points out, these include: "land; many descendants; dispersion of posterity throughout the land; . . . the extension of blessing to others through him; presence; keeping; and not leaving." The gift of land to Jacob is all-important. We might have anticipated that God would rebuke Jacob's conniving behavior. But instead, God promises Jacob the gift of the land. Then the familiar patriarchal blessing follows. Jacob, the one who has deceived and cheated his brother out of his birthright, is the one upon whom the hope of the world rests. The blessings that God promises are the most inclusive list that we have heard in the book of Genesis.

Genesis 28:16-19. As soon as he awakens, Jacob begins to realize how important his dream is and so interprets its meaning. First, Jacob is aware of new knowledge: "Surely the LORD is in this place—and I did not know it!" Jacob suddenly recognizes that

God has been and is present with him. He is awed by the fact that the God about whom his father talked has met him in such an ordinary place. In recognition of his encounter with God, Jacob takes his stone pillow and sets it up as a pillar. What had been quite ordinary now becomes a sacred symbol commemorating his experience. By anointing the stone with oil, Jacob consecrates it. Thus Jacob sets aside this site as a permanent worship center, which he called Bethel, meaning "house of God."

Genesis 28:20-22. Finally, Jacob responds to the incredible gifts that God has promised him. He reiterates what God has promised, adding food and clothing, but making conditional what God has already promised

unconditionally! If God will really do these things for Jacob, then God can be Jacob's God. As Williams observes, "This is Jacob after all. What else may we expect from him? His name is connected with deceit and cleverness; why should he treat God any differently from the way he treated his brother?"

What Jacob does not yet know but will learn is that God can be counted on to be faithful. Jacob need not be apprehensive nor worry about whether God will come through. Jacob vows to return a tenth of all that God promises to give. God will keep God's promises. Moreover, God will expect Jacob to keep his promises as well!

INTERPRETING THE SCRIPTURE

Jacob's Dream

Those who study sleep patterns tell us that all human beings dream several times each night. According to physicians, dreams are part of the way that the mind processes information. We have all had the experience of waking up with a start. Did we just have a dream or did the event actually take place? Sometimes it takes a while until we are sure.

In the Bible people took their dreams quite seriously. They were quite intent on discovering the meaning of what they had dreamed. In fact, prominent persons sought out those who could interpret dreams.

We are probably not too surprised to read that when he camped out for the night on his way to Haran to find a wife, Jacob had a dream. On the run to escape his brother's wrath after he had tricked him out of his leadership role and his inheritance, we might suspect that Jacob was in for a nightmare. But instead, he saw a ladder reaching to the heavens with angels ascending and descending upon it. Then Jacob saw God

standing beside him, and he heard God speak. If Jacob questioned the reality of God's presence he does not share it in the story. He simply took his dream at face value and listened to God's voice.

How do we know if God is trying to speak to us through our dreams? We can never guarantee that the voice we hear is the voice of God. Yet sometimes we become convinced that God is trying to tell us something. If God is everywhere and has created all things, it stands to reason that God can speak to us through our dreams. Perhaps if we have a dream that is especially compelling or if we have a recurring dream, we should share that dream with a trusted friend or counselor. God uses many methods to speak to people. Might God be trying to communicate with you through your dreams?

Of course, we also use the word "dream" to connote a lofty goal or an ideal situation. We may say that we dream of world peace or that humanity will solve the distribution problem and eliminate world hunger. One of the most famous dreams in our generation is that of Martin Luther King, Jr.

Certainly his "I Have a Dream" oration, which inspired and motivated millions of people, is a classic example of visionary leadership at its best.

What dreams has God placed deep within your heart? These, too, are worth sharing with colleagues and friends. I believe that God has placed far-reaching and lofty aspirations within our souls in order that we stretch and grow and become the people God knows we can be. May each of us pray fervently for discernment as we seek to interpret our dreams.

God's Promise

One of the questions I like to ask persons about their faith journey is this: When did God become more than a word to you? God became more than a word to Jacob at Bethel, when he slept under the stars with a stone pillow under his head. Before that night God was an abstract, theological concept. Now God was Jacob's companion on the journey of life.

While God's promises to Jacob seem detailed and extensive, did God promise Jacob more than God promises every faithful believer? First of all, God reassures Jacob that the One who speaks to him is the God of his ancestors. The same God who approached Abraham is also approaching Jacob. We believe that while our ideas of God change, God is consistent and unchanging.

God has given us the land to use as stewards. The human race has multiplied and through Jacob and his family the blessings of God continue to be known to people everywhere. Most important, God promises to be with Jacob wherever he goes. As the Psalmist states in Psalm 139, no matter who we are, no matter where we go, God is there, too. God has promised never to leave us nor forsake us. Jacob received that message at Bethel. May each of us receive that message and let its implications energize us and fill our lives with joy and hope this day!

"How Awesome Is This Place!"

Most of us have had mountaintop experiences, either literally or figuratively (or both), when we know beyond the shadow of a doubt that God is real and that God is with us. Jacob recognized God's presence at Bethel. When he awoke from his dream, Jacob exclaimed, "Surely the LORD is in this place—and I did not know it!" (Genesis 28:16). Sometimes we are so close to what is happening that it is only in retrospect that we realize the significance of what has taken place. Other times we are so preoccupied that we fail to see what should be obvious. What does it take for us to recognize the presence and power of God?

Jacob returned to Bethel later in his life (35:1-15). It was not that God could be found only in this place, but by returning to the place of Jacob's transformation he found strength to continue on. We, too, are influenced by the special places where God has been especially real to us. When we return to them, we find strength and encouragement. Have you returned to Bethel lately? Where are the "awesome places" where you were reassured that God was with you? God is everywhere. Yet God can be more easily perceived at certain moments in our lives. The Celts referred to these as the "thin places" where the veil between heaven and earth is especially porous and God's activity can thus be easily discerned. Bethel was a thin place—an "awesome place"—for Jacob. Where are the "awesome places" in your spiritual journey?

Jacob's Vow

As he is portrayed in Genesis, Jacob is certainly not a paragon of virtue. Dishonest, conniving, willing to take advantage of persons at their point of vulnerability, a man who would cheat his own brother and lie to his own father—why would God invest time and energy in Jacob?

The Bible does not sugarcoat the ambiguities of human nature. God saw leadership qualities in Jacob and used this man to further God's purposes in the world. For whatever reason, it is quite clear from Scripture that God picked Jacob over Esau to be the standard-bearer for the promises of God, and thus God blessed Jacob unconditionally.

It is quite ironic that Jacob turns around and tries to put conditions on God! If God will indeed do all the things that God has enumerated, plus a few more that Jacob adds, then Jacob will be quite happy to allow God to be his God. Are we, like Jacob, guilty of trying to place conditions on God? Do we attempt to bargain with God sometimes, even seek to "cut a deal" with the Almighty if we can?

Throughout the Bible we learn that God is the God of covenant promises: "Obey my voice, and I will be your God, and you shall be my people; and walk only in the way that I command you, so that it may be well with you" (Jeremiah 7:23). God always keeps God's side of the bargain. We are the ones who often fall short. Jacob did not have to worry about God's faithfulness. He needed to be concerned about his own willingness and ability to follow through.

The Scriptures make it clear that when we enter into an agreement with God, God expects us to fulfill our promises. The Bible tells us that while God is merciful and slow to anger, God also holds us accountable for our actions. We must not forget our promises to God, for every aspect of our lives is lived in God's presence.

SHARING THE SCRIPTURE

Preparing Our Hearts

Meditate on this week's devotional reading, found in Psalm 105:1-11. These verses remind us of God's covenant with Abraham, which extended to Isaac, Jacob, and succeeding generations. God's people increased because God was faithful to the covenant and continued to make the divine Self known to Abraham's descendants. How do you recognize God? Think about how God is revealed to you through other people, events, dreams, Scripture, or some other means. Record your thoughts in your spiritual journal.

Pray that you and the adult learners will be open to all means of recognizing God's presence in your life.

Preparing Our Minds

Study the background, Genesis 27:41–28:22, and lesson Scripture, 28:10-22. As you prepare, think about the purpose of dreams.

Write on newsprint:

❏ *Dreams are* for "Gather to Learn."

❏ information for next week's lesson, found under "Continue the Journey."
❏ activities for further spiritual growth in "Continue the Journey."

LEADING THE CLASS

(1) Gather to Learn

❖ Welcome the class members and introduce any guests.

❖ Pray that all who have gathered today will be aware of God's presence with them now—and always.

❖ Post a sheet of newsprint with these words: *Dreams are. . . .* Ask the students to add words or phrases to finish the sentence.

❖ Talk about the variety of ideas that have been generated. Ask the class if they can discern any trends here.

❖ **Option:** Read "Jacob's Dream" from Interpreting the Scripture to set the stage for today's lesson.

❖ Read aloud today's focus statement: **Humans dream, though we do not always** remember or understand our dreams. What is the purpose of a dream? In the story of Jacob at Bethel, a dream reassured Jacob of God's continuing covenant with him.

(2) Explore the Story of Jacob's Dream at Bethel, Its Meaning, and Its Significance for God's Covenant People

❖ Choose a volunteer to read Genesis 28:10-22.

❖ Divide into groups and give each group at least one sheet of newsprint and a marker. Follow these steps.

Step 1: Challenge the groups to list, in order, all that happened in these verses.

Step 2: Invite the groups to talk about and mark on newsprint the particular events in the story that:

(a) seemed most ordinary;

(b) seemed most unusual;

(c) showed God in action;

(d) showed Jacob's character.

Step 3: Option: Encourage each group to select one event and sketch it on newsprint.

Step 4: Bring the class back together and ask each group to report on the event(s) they found most intriguing. If groups did make sketches, allow them to show their work.

❖ Raise the following questions for class discussion.

(1) **What meaning do you think the story of Jacob's dream might have had for those who originally heard it?**

(2) **What meaning does this story have for the church today?**

(3) **What meaning does this story have for you personally?**

(3) Recognize Ways in which God Communicates with the Learners

❖ Read aloud the first paragraph of "How Awesome Is This Place" in Interpreting the Scripture.

❖ Invite class members to describe "mountaintop experiences" they have had with God. You may want to do this in pairs or small groups to give more people a chance to speak.

❖ Brainstorm ways in which God's presence is made known:

In the Bible: Possibilities include: *cloud, pillar of fire, dreams, prophets, angelic messengers, prayer, nature (whirlwind, earthquake, fire), Jesus, Holy Spirit.*

In our day: Possibilities include: *Bible, personal experience with Christ, friends, dreams, community of faith, written word, sermons, music, meditation, journaling, Holy Communion, circumstances of our lives.*

❖ **Option:** Read the following information and then talk with the class about Wesley's experience and how it might relate to their lives. **John Wesley, the founder of Methodism, had a very profound experience with God as he heard Luther's preface to Paul's Letter to the Romans read on May 24, 1738, at a Moravian meeting in London on Aldersgate Street. He wrote these now famous words in his journal: "About a quarter before nine, while he was describing the change which God works in the heart through faith in Christ, I felt my heart strangely warmed. I felt I did trust in Christ, Christ alone, for salvation; and an assurance was given me that He had taken away my sins, even mine, and saved me from the law of sin and death." Interestingly, earlier that day he had read these words from Mark 12:34 [KJV]: "Thou art not far from the kingdom of God."**

(4) Seek Meaning from a Dream

❖ Distribute paper and pencils. Invite each student to recall a dream that struck them as meaningful. Suggest that they meditate on this dream and write what they believe to be its meaning. Note that this con- tent of this exercise is not meant to be shared with anyone else. Also point out that multiple meanings are possible.

❖ Talk with the class in general terms about what they learned from this activity. Did God give them guidance about a decision? Was a challenge issued to take action? Was the dreamer given a key to "connect the dots" of prior events? Was the dreamer reassured about a situation or action?

❖ Ask: **What action will you take in response to this dream?** Provide moments of silence for the students to consider how they will respond to the presence of God in their lives through a dream.

(5) Continue the Journey

❖ Break the silence by praying that each participant will be aware of the many ways in which God communicates with humanity, open to receiving these communications, and ready to respond.

❖ Read aloud this preparation for next week's lesson. You may also want to post it on newsprint for the students to copy.

■ **Title: Jacob and Rachel**
■ **Background Scripture: Genesis 29**
■ **Lesson Scripture: Genesis 29:21-35**
■ **Focus of the Lesson: Hopes are sometimes dashed or temporarily put on hold. How do we respond when our fondest wishes remain unfulfilled? Jacob dearly loved Rachel but unexpectedly found after seven years of work that he must first marry her older sister Leah and then work seven more years for the woman of his heart.**

❖ Challenge the students to complete one or more of these activities for further spiritual growth, which you will write on newsprint for the students to copy.

(1) **Keep a notebook by your bedside and record any dreams you can remember as soon as you awaken. Do you believe that God is communicating with you through any of these dreams? If so, what is the message? How will you respond?**

(2) **Talk with someone about a time that you are absolutely positive that God was with you. How did you know God was present? How did God's presence make you feel?**

(3) **Research other dreams in the Bible. If you check a concordance for the root word "dream" and associated words (such as "dreamer," "dreamed"), you will find well over one hundred entries in the NRSV translation.**

❖ Sing or read aloud "We Are Climbing Jacob's Ladder."

❖ Conclude today's session by leading the class in this benediction, which is adapted from Genesis 14:19-20: **Blessed be you by God Most High, maker of heaven and earth; and blessed be God Most High.**

UNIT 2: GOD'S PEOPLE INCREASED
JACOB AND RACHEL

PREVIEWING THE LESSON

Lesson Scripture: Genesis 29:20-35
Background Scripture: Genesis 29
Key Verse: Genesis 29:20

Focus of the Lesson:
Hopes are sometimes dashed or temporarily put on hold. How do we respond when our fondest wishes remain unfulfilled? Jacob dearly loved Rachel but unexpectedly found after seven years of work that he must first marry her older sister Leah and then work seven more years for the woman of his heart.

Goals for the Learners:
(1) to delve into the story of Jacob's unwitting marriage to Leah and his promise to continue working for his father-in-law Laban so as to be able to marry Rachel also.
(2) to recognize that God works in their lives even in the midst of disappointing situations.
(3) to practice patience while waiting for God to work.

Pronunciation Guide:
Bilhah (bil' huh)   Issachar (is' uh kahr)
Laban (lay' buhn)   Levi (lee' vi)
Reuben (roo' bin)   Simeon (sim' ee uhn)
Zilpah (zil' puh)

Supplies:
Bibles, newsprint and marker, paper and pencils, hymnals

READING THE SCRIPTURE

NRSV
Genesis 29:20-35

²⁰So Jacob served seven years for Rachel, and they seemed to him but a few days because of the love he had for her.

²¹Then Jacob said to Laban, "Give me my

NIV
Genesis 29:20-35

²⁰So Jacob served seven years to get Rachel, but they seemed like only a few days to him because of his love for her.

²¹Then Jacob said to Laban, "Give me my

---

wife that I may go in to her, for my time is completed." [22]So Laban gathered together all the people of the place, and made a feast. [23]But in the evening he took his daughter Leah and brought her to Jacob; and he went in to her. [24](Laban gave his maid Zilpah to his daughter Leah to be her maid.) [25]When morning came, it was Leah! And Jacob said to Laban, "What is this you have done to me? Did I not serve with you for Rachel? Why then have you deceived me?" [26]Laban said, "This is not done in our country— giving the younger before the firstborn. [27]Complete the week of this one, and we will give you the other also in return for serving me another seven years." [28]Jacob did so, and completed her week; then Laban gave him his daughter Rachel as a wife. [29](Laban gave his maid Bilhah to his daughter Rachel to be her maid.) [30]So Jacob went in to Rachel also, and he loved Rachel more than Leah. He served Laban for another seven years.

[31]When the LORD saw that Leah was unloved, he opened her womb; but Rachel was barren. [32]Leah conceived and bore a son, and she named him Reuben; for she said, "Because the LORD has looked on my affliction; surely now my husband will love me." [33]She conceived again and bore a son, and said, "Because the LORD has heard that I am hated, he has given me this son also"; and she named him Simeon. [34]Again she conceived and bore a son, and said, "Now this time my husband will be joined to me, because I have borne him three sons"; therefore he was named Levi. [35]She conceived again and bore a son, and said, "This time I will praise the LORD"; therefore she named him Judah; then she ceased bearing.

wife. My time is completed, and I want to lie with her."

[22]So Laban brought together all the people of the place and gave a feast. [23]But when evening came, he took his daughter Leah and gave her to Jacob, and Jacob lay with her. [24]And Laban gave his servant girl Zilpah to his daughter as her maidservant.

[25]When morning came, there was Leah! So Jacob said to Laban, "What is this you have done to me? I served you for Rachel, didn't I? Why have you deceived me?"

[26]Laban replied, "It is not our custom here to give the younger daughter in marriage before the older one. [27]Finish this daughter's bridal week; then we will give you the younger one also, in return for another seven years of work."

[28]And Jacob did so. He finished the week with Leah, and then Laban gave him his daughter Rachel to be his wife. [29]Laban gave his servant girl Bilhah to his daughter Rachel as her maidservant. [30]Jacob lay with Rachel also, and he loved Rachel more than Leah. And he worked for Laban another seven years.

[31]When the LORD saw that Leah was not loved, he opened her womb, but Rachel was barren. [32]Leah became pregnant and gave birth to a son. She named him Reuben, for she said, "It is because the LORD has seen my misery. Surely my husband will love me now."

[33]She conceived again, and when she gave birth to a son she said, "Because the LORD heard that I am not loved, he gave me this one too." So she named him Simeon.

[34]Again she conceived, and when she gave birth to a son she said, "Now at last my husband will become attached to me, because I have borne him three sons." So he was named Levi.

[35]She conceived again, and when she gave birth to a son she said, "This time I will praise the LORD." So she named him Judah. Then she stopped having children.

UNDERSTANDING THE SCRIPTURE

Genesis 29:1. God has freely given the rascally Jacob the gift of the land, the promise of blessing, and the assurance of God's continuing presence. In response, Jacob has bargained with God (28:20-22) rather than offering God a gift of promise in return. Yet Jacob is the heir to the promises of Abraham. His journey takes him to "the land of the people of the east," the land of his relatives, the place where Abraham had once lived.

Genesis 29:2-3. Not surprisingly, Jacob goes to a well, always the center of community activity, where there are three flocks of sheep waiting for water. Apparently the stone covering the well is so heavy and large it takes several people to move it. The use of an unwieldy stone ensures that the various shepherds and their flocks will have fair and equal access to the precious, life-giving water.

Genesis 29:4-5. Jacob's questions establish that he has arrived at the right place. The shepherds are from Haran and they know his uncle Laban.

Genesis 29:6-8. When Jacob sees Laban's daughter Rachel, coming with her sheep, he suggests that the other shepherds get their water and move on, presumably so that he can be alone with Rachel. But the shepherds protest, no doubt remembering skirmishes in the past where the usual customs were not adhered to properly.

Genesis 29:9-12. The fact that Rachel is identified a second time may indicate that several versions of this story have been combined into the present narrative. It is love at first sight for Jacob! Not only does he greet the lovely Rachel with a kiss, but in a demonstration of physical prowess removes the massive stone from the well by himself and proceeds to water Rachel's flocks! Thus the story establishes Jacob as a kind of superhero, a strong and authoritative person who is not afraid to overstep the bounds of community customs.

The enterprising Jacob has no doubt noted that Rachel is not only beautiful but also represents great wealth. As he weeps tears of joy at the thought of being reunited with family, he tells Rachel that he is her father's kinsman. Rachel runs and tells her father that his sister's son has arrived.

Genesis 29:13-14. When Laban hears the news, he extends the typical Near Eastern hospitality, embracing Jacob and taking him to his home. Jacob brings Laban up to date on the family news, telling Laban "all these things." The family reunion lasts a whole month!

Genesis 29:15-20. Things continue on a harmonious note with Laban and his houseguest. Laban expresses concern for Jacob's welfare, in view of what will certainly be a lengthy stay. Jacob is invited to name his own wages.

At this point in the story, we are told for the first time that Laban actually has two daughters. Interest is heightened by the physical description of the two young women. Translators vary in their description of Leah's eyes. The NRSV says they are "lovely," while the NIV says they are "weak." Leah's name means "cow" or "weary one," whereas Rachel's name means "ewe." Rachel is described as "graceful and beautiful." Having just read the story of Jacob and Esau, the "older-younger" sibling issue is fresh on our minds.

Jacob suggests that he "serve" Laban for seven years in order to earn the hand of his beautiful daughter Rachel. Jacob receives what he interprets as an affirmation from the clever Laban: "It is better that I give her to you than that I should give her to any other man," he says (29:19).

Jacob's willingness to work for seven years reveals his deep love for Rachel. He apparently considers his service to Laban as a fitting dowry for her. Jacob considers his seven years of labor to be "but a few days."

Clearly, he is determined to have Rachel for his wife.

Genesis 29:21-25a. At the end of the seven years, Jacob asks for Rachel's hand in marriage, and Laban throws a great marriage feast. At the culmination of the feast, Laban takes the bride to the tent of her bridegroom. The marriage is consummated. But in the morning, when Jacob awakens, he discovers he has spent the night with Leah rather than Rachel!

Genesis 29:25b. The deceiver has been deceived! Jacob, who must suddenly have an idea of how his brother Esau felt when Jacob tricked him, confronts his uncle Laban. Jacob's whining about being tricked has a hollow ring to it as we remember that Jacob's whole life has been one long practice of deceit.

Genesis 29:26. Laban has a ready response, though one that has not been mentioned during Jacob's seven years of service: It is the custom in their country that the younger daughter cannot be given in marriage before the firstborn.

Genesis 29:27-30. We have seen that Jacob can drive a hard bargain, but he has met his match in Laban. If Jacob will complete the week of marital celebration with Leah, he can marry Rachel at the end of the week. He must also agree to work for Laban for another seven years. Because of his great love for Rachel, Jacob agrees without bargaining or argument. He married Rachel and "served Laban for another seven years." Yet the story does not hesitate to tell us Jacob "loved Rachel more than Leah." Once again, the subject of favorites looms large. The result will be heartache and pain for all involved.

Laban's scheme worked because of bridal veils that covered Leah and heavy drinking associated with the wedding celebration. However, his plot harms Rachel and Jacob and the love they share. It also abuses Leah, whose feelings are not taken into account, though she will soon express her pain and feelings of rejection.

Genesis 29:31-35. The competition and rivalry between Leah and Rachel provides the basic story line for the genealogy of the tribes of Israel. In the clash between Leah and Rachel we are reminded of the animosity between Sarah and Hagar, as well as the conflict between Jacob and his brother Esau. At this point Rachel is barren, while Leah gives birth to four sons—Reuben, Simeon, Levi, Judah—in rapid succession. Thinking that bearing children will cause Jacob to love her, Leah is disappointed. Each time she delivers a baby, Leah gets her hopes up, only to have Jacob turn away. Jacob is happy to have a growing family, but the gift of children does not cause him to love Leah and show affection to her.

INTERPRETING THE SCRIPTURE

A Labor of Love

No human emotion is denied or avoided in the biblical narrative. Even the patriarchs are portrayed with very realistic feelings. In a day of arranged marriages and politically motivated nuptials, the story of Jacob and Rachel is a story of romantic love at its best. When Jacob saw Rachel, it was love at first sight! He could not take his eyes off her. He proceeded to perform nearly superhuman feats for her benefit. He agreed to work long and hard for her hand. Even when he was tricked into marrying Leah, he was willing to work another seven years so that Rachel could become his wife. Thus, Genesis 29 is a love story par excellence.

The key verse of our lesson, "So Jacob

served seven years for Rachel, and they seemed to him but a few days because of the love he had for her"(29:20), reflects love in its early stages. When we first fall in love, the time we spend together goes by so quickly! The curfew comes so soon! Telephone conversations always seem shorter than they are. "When will the next time be that we get to see each other and talk?" we ask. When we are in love, activities that we plan are not nearly as important as just spending time together.

As love matures, some of the excitement and spark of romance may fade, but do our emotions change? Acts of love become the substance and bedrock of our relationships as the superficialities of physical appearance wane in their importance. Jacob's indentured service in order to earn the right to Rachel's hand reminds us of the Apostle Paul's description of love in 1 Corinthians where we are told: "Love is patient; love is kind. . . . [Love] bears all things, believes all things, hopes all things, endures all things" (1 Corinthians 13:4, 7). It is this type of love that makes Hollywood's storylines look cheap and even silly. True love, exemplified for us most dramatically in the love of Christ for the world, is a sacrificial love that does not keep score, but focuses on giving rather than receiving. This is mature love. It is the love that Jacob had for Rachel, a love that never ends.

The Trickster Is Tricked

There is something quite satisfying when Jacob, who has tricked Esau and has seemingly gotten away with it, now has a trick played on him. Unfortunately, as with all "reality" episodes, people's feelings are damaged in the process. Maybe Laban feared that Leah would never be married. The text doesn't say. However, his deceitful approach caused a lifetime of unhappiness for poor Leah, and made Jacob and Rachel's relationship more difficult.

The moral of the story for Jacob, though, is this: What goes around comes around. We cannot deceive people and take advantage of them at the points of their vulnerability without having dishonesty and duplicity catch up with us at some point along the way.

Yet there is an even deeper theme in the story of Jacob's marriages to these two sisters, a week apart. Through it all, God was at work! God did not approve of Jacob's behavior, or of Laban's. But God was able to work through those less than ideal human beings to carry on with the covenant purpose. As Terence Fretheim observes in *The New Interpreter's Bible:* "The community of faith is fortunate in having a God who does not insist on perfection before choosing to work in and through it." I had a seminary professor who used to say that the Bible is the record of what God can do with very poor material. Jacob and Laban were not paragons of virtue. However, God used them in order to further God's purposes. Even though our mistakes and our deliberate misdoings have a way of catching up with us, if we are willing to be used by God, God finds a way to weave our stories into the tapestry of God's larger story.

Jacob Shows Favoritism

My wife has a sister. I have two sisters and a brother. When we were growing up, both sets of parents bent over backward to be fair to each child. Yet from our childish perspective, each of us could point to times and places when it appeared that one sibling was favored over another. A television character used to say, "Mom always liked you best." Haven't most of us had similar feelings from time to time?

With Leah, it was more than a feeling. The Bible tells us plainly that Jacob "loved Rachel more than Leah" (29:30). In fact, we are told that Leah was "unloved" (29:31). My heart goes out to Leah. From all indications, she was not nearly as attractive as Rachel. Yet she had the same need to love and be loved as her "graceful and beautiful" sister (29:17). Her efforts to please Jacob got her nowhere. So Leah, doing what folks have done through the centuries, turned to the Lord in her frustration and despair. Not only did she cry out to the Lord, but the Lord also heard her cry. The story is almost pathetic as Leah gives birth to child after child believing that she would eventually find favor in Jacob's sight. "Now this time my husband will be joined to me," Leah hopes, "because I have borne him three sons" (29:34). Yet it was not to be.

Again human emotion is laid bare. Jacob was tricked into marrying Leah, but he cannot be forced to love her. Even though Leah is distraught, Jacob knows his heart. It belongs to Rachel. That is a fact Leah will have to accept.

Leah Seeks to Earn Jacob's Love

Leah would not take "no" for an answer. She continued to try to woo Jacob and to seek his favor, even though he clearly had no interest in her beyond having sexual relations. Leah did her best to earn Jacob's favor, but all for naught.

What do you do when your best is not enough, when you cannot reach your lofty goals? Are you able to persevere? Can you see the hand of God at work even in disappointing situations?

Leah never got Jacob's attention and never became the recipient of his love. In that sense, she remained a "desperate housewife" her whole life. Although she was the apple of no man's eye, Leah became the mother of half the tribes of Israel (Reuben, Simeon, Levi, Judah, Issachar, Zebulun), a vital link in the unfolding story of salvation. God worked through her and used her life to achieve something of great significance for the whole human race. Leah was not highly valued in Jacob's eyes, but in God's eyes Leah was a very significant person. Through her, God was able to accomplish great things. Leah's willingness to be used by God demonstrates that God can use each of us to accomplish great things for the glory of God.

SHARING THE SCRIPTURE

Preparing Our Hearts

Meditate on this week's devotional reading, found in Psalm 91. The psalmist assures us of God's protection, even when we are faced with incredible odds and terrifying possibilities. Under what circumstances have you needed to be assured of God's ability to safeguard you? How did the situation turn out in the end? How does God's "past performance" assure you that God will never forsake you?

Pray that you and the adult learners will trust God to take care of you, even when all seems lost.

Preparing Our Minds

Study the background from Genesis 29 and lesson Scripture, Genesis 29:20-35. As you review this passage recall how you might respond when your fondest wishes remain unfulfilled.

Write on newsprint:
❑ information for next week's lesson, found under "Continue the Journey."
❑ activities for further spiritual growth in "Continue the Journey."

LEADING THE CLASS

(1) Gather to Learn

❖ Welcome the class members and introduce any guests.

❖ Pray that all who attend today will recognize that God keeps promises even in the midst of disappointment and deceit.

❖ Invite the class members to tell stories of

wishes they had as children, perhaps for a special gift or opportunity to do something. Ask them to talk about how they felt when their wishes were fulfilled—or went unfulfilled.

❖ Read aloud today's focus statement: **Hopes are sometimes dashed or temporarily put on hold. How do we respond when our fondest wishes remain unfulfilled? Jacob dearly loved Rachel but unexpectedly found after seven years of work that he must first marry her older sister Leah and then work seven more years for the woman of his heart.**

(2) Delve into the Story of Jacob's Unwitting Marriage to Leah and His Promise to Continue Working for His Father-in-Law Laban so as to Be Able to Marry Rachel Also

❖ Choose volunteers to read the parts of the narrator, Jacob, Laban, and Leah in Genesis 29:21-35.

❖ Divide the students into groups of four. Each student will take the role of either Laban, Jacob, Rachel, or Leah. Encourage the group members to have a frank discussion about how they feel about the situation. The point here is to see the story from the perspective of different characters.

❖ Bring the class together. Ask: **As you heard this story from different viewpoints, what new insights did you glean?**

❖ Read or retell "The Trickster Is Tricked" in Interpreting the Scripture to illustrate how God was at work to fulfill God's purposes concerning the covenant. Note that God's people will continue to increase, despite the questionable behavior and tactics, especially of Jacob and Laban.

(3) Recognize That God Works in the Learners' Lives Even in the Midst of Disappointing Situations

❖ Read aloud this story of Luis Primitivo Marín García, now a coffee farmer: **"Following the triumph of the Sandinista Revolution in the 1980s, my family and I** began to experience painful difficulties because we were not in agreement with the political policies implemented by the Communist government. . . . I was a young man who was being pursued by the Sandinistas for obligatory military service, which led me to join the ranks of the Nicaraguan Democratic Resistance. When I was barely 15 years old, I had to leave my studies and my widowed mother and three little brothers. Two years later, my younger brother also had to join the Resistance after he was threatened by the Sandinistas because he had a brother in the counterrevolution: me."**

García went on to say how difficult life was for him and also for his family. He continued: "I left the Resistance and reentered civilian life. When I arrived in my community, the place where I was born, I had no hope for anything. I went to war with nothing and returned with nothing. Even worse, upon my return I found that some of my family members had already died with the unfulfilled hope that some day we would see each other again. They were my grandparents and some of my cousins—who had been killed for being sympathizers of the Resistance. This was an extremely difficult period of my life. I did not find work; people distrusted me. I was confronting the misery of poverty while I awaited the fulfillment of the promise achieved by the government of Doña Violeta de Chamorro."**

❖ Invite several volunteers to role-play the parts of Luis Primitivo Marín García and one (or more) interviewers who want to hear the story of his hopes and dreams and share with him how God has worked in their lives in situations when they felt deceived, disappointed, or as if their hopes had been dashed.

(4) Practice Patience while Waiting for God to Work

❖ Read this quotation from John Bunyan (1628–1688), author of *Pilgrim's Progress:*

Hope has a thick skin and will endure many a blow; it will put on patience as a vestment, it will wade through a sea of blood, it will endure all things if it be of the right kind, for the joy that is set before it. Hence patience is called "patience of hope," because it is hope that makes the soul exercise patience and long-suffering under the cross, until the time comes to enjoy the crown."

❖ Discuss these questions.
   (1) How do you think Jacob would respond to Bunyan's words?
   (2) What personal experiences have you had with the "patience of hope" that Bunyan writes about?
   (3) What situation(s) can we identify in our church or community where we are practicing "patience of hope" while we wait for God to work? (List these ideas on newsprint.)

❖ Select at least one of the situations the class has identified. Talk about how the adults can wait patiently for God to act, even if the situation is currently upsetting or disappointing to them. Note that, as we have seen with Jacob, patience and hopefulness do not preclude action.

❖ Ask students who are willing to commit themselves to practicing the "patience of hope" in this situation to raise their hands.

(5) Continue the Journey

❖ Pray that those who have come today will recognize God at work in all situations.

❖ Read aloud this preparation for next week's lesson. You may also want to post it on newsprint for the students to copy.

■ **Title: Esau and Jacob Reconciled**
■ **Background Scripture: Genesis 33**
■ **Lesson Scripture: Genesis 33:1-11**
■ **Focus of the Lesson: Relationships sometimes seem irreparably broken. What must happen for such damaged relationships to be restored? Esau, who had been wronged by his brother, willingly greeted Jacob and offered him hospitality and signs of reconciliation.**

❖ Challenge the students to complete one or more of these activities for further spiritual growth, which you will write on newsprint for the students to copy.
   (1) **Try to bolster someone who has worked hard to achieve dreams and yet feels disappointment.**
   (2) **Write in your spiritual journal about a disappointing situation in your life in which God worked to bring about good.**
   (3) **Compare your experience with a particular product or service with the media presentation of it. Do you feel deceived by the advertising? Why did this product fail to live up to your expectations? Call or write to the company in question to tell your story and explain reasons for your disappointment.**

❖ Sing or read aloud "Your Love, O God, Has Called Us Here."

❖ Conclude today's session by leading the class in this benediction, which is adapted from Genesis 14:19-20: **Blessed be you by God Most High, maker of heaven and earth; and blessed be God Most High.**

UNIT 2: GOD'S PEOPLE INCREASED

ESAU AND JACOB RECONCILED

PREVIEWING THE LESSON

Lesson Scripture: Genesis 33:1-11
Background Scripture: Genesis 33
Key Verse: Genesis 33:4

Focus of the Lesson:
Relationships sometimes seem irreparably broken. What must happen for such damaged relationships to be restored? Esau, who had been wronged by his brother, willingly greeted Jacob and offered him hospitality and signs of reconciliation.

Goals for the Learners:
(1) to present the story of the reunion between twin brothers, Esau and Jacob.
(2) to recall feelings associated with restoring relationships.
(3) to seek to restore a broken relationship.

Pronunciation Guide:
El-Elohe Israel (el el oh heh is' ray uhl)   Jabbok (jab' uhk)
Seir (see' uhr)   Shechem (shek' uhm)
Succoth (suhk' uhth)

Supplies:
Bibles, newsprint and marker, paper and pencils, hymnals

READING THE SCRIPTURE

NRSV
Genesis 33:1-11

¹Now Jacob looked up and saw Esau coming, and four hundred men with him. So he divided the children among Leah and Rachel and the two maids. ²He put the maids with their children in front, then Leah with her children, and Rachel and Joseph last of all. ³He himself went on ahead of

NIV
Genesis 33:1-11

¹Jacob looked up and there was Esau, coming with his four hundred men; so he divided the children among Leah, Rachel and the two maidservants. ²He put the maidservants and their children in front, Leah and her children next, and Rachel and Joseph in the rear. ³He himself went on

them, bowing himself to the ground seven times, until he came near his brother. **⁴But Esau ran to meet him, and embraced him, and fell on his neck and kissed him, and they wept.** ⁵When Esau looked up and saw the women and children, he said, "Who are these with you?" Jacob said, "The children whom God has graciously given your servant." ⁶Then the maids drew near, they and their children, and bowed down; ⁷Leah likewise and her children drew near and bowed down; and finally Joseph and Rachel drew near, and they bowed down. ⁸Esau said, "What do you mean by all this company that I met?" Jacob answered, "To find favor with my lord." ⁹But Esau said, "I have enough, my brother; keep what you have for yourself." ¹⁰Jacob said, "No, please; if I find favor with you, then accept my present from my hand; for truly to see your face is like seeing the face of God—since you have received me with such favor. ¹¹Please accept my gift that is brought to you, because God has dealt graciously with me, and because I have everything I want." So he urged him, and he took it.

ahead and bowed down to the ground seven times as he approached his brother. **⁴But Esau ran to meet Jacob and embraced him; he threw his arms around his neck and kissed him. And they wept.** ⁵Then Esau looked up and saw the women and children. "Who are these with you?" he asked.

Jacob answered, "They are the children God has graciously given your servant."

⁶Then the maidservants and their children approached and bowed down. ⁷Next, Leah and her children came and bowed down. Last of all came Joseph and Rachel, and they too bowed down.

⁸Esau asked, "What do you mean by all these droves I met?"

"To find favor in your eyes, my lord," he said.

⁹But Esau said, "I already have plenty, my brother. Keep what you have for yourself."

¹⁰"No, please!" said Jacob. "If I have found favor in your eyes, accept this gift from me. For to see your face is like seeing the face of God, now that you have received me favorably. ¹¹Please accept the present that was brought to you, for God has been gracious to me and I have all I need." And because Jacob insisted, Esau accepted it.

UNDERSTANDING THE SCRIPTURE

Genesis 33:1-3. The story begins on an anxious note. Jacob, who has spent the night wrestling with his conscience, now has his worst fears realized. The report he previously received of four hundred men coming with his brother Esau to meet him is accurate. They have been sighted on the horizon! The gifts that Jacob sent to appease his brother in Genesis 32:13-21 have arrived, but we have not heard Esau's response. The sight of Esau approaching with four hundred men would have indeed given Jacob reason to pause. Quickly he organizes his wives and children, arranging them in such

a way that his beloved Rachel and her son, Joseph, come last, and hence will be introduced last. Jacob can see only one course of action now: to throw himself on the mercy of his estranged brother, Esau. Jacob, who leads the entourage, bows seven times before Esau, just as a servant would bow before his lord as a sign of submission. Is Jacob acknowledging his previous wrongdoing? Jacob will refer to Esau as "lord" five times in this story, and will refer to himself as Esau's servant. Throughout the story Jacob expresses concern that he find favor in Esau's eyes. Clearly Jacob's demonstration of vulnerability as he limps toward Esau, bowing low to the ground, sets the stage for what happens next.

Genesis 33:4. Now comes the great surprise of the story: Esau "ran to meet him [Jacob], and embraced him, and fell on his neck and kissed him, and they wept." According to Terrence Fretheim, writing in *The New Interpreter's Bible*, "this impressive list of welcoming activities is unparalleled elsewhere in Genesis." Nothing in the story has prepared the reader for this astonishing scene! We have seen Esau only through the lens of the earlier story of Jacob's trickery and lately through the eyes of a fearful Jacob. The words of Esau indicate that he has completely forgiven his wretched brother! Esau's attitude is surprisingly magnanimous in contrast with his previous intentions to kill Jacob (see 27:41).

Genesis 33:5-7. At Esau's invitation, Jacob then introduces his wives and children. They follow Jacob's lead in bowing down, an action which the narrator repeats as each segment of the family is presented.

Genesis 33:8-9. After meeting Jacob's family, Esau asks Jacob why he has sent all those presents to him. Jacob says that he was trying "to find favor." But Esau cares nothing for the material goods, and comments, "I have enough, my brother."

Genesis 33:10. Hearing Esau's refusal, Jacob recognizes he is already in his brother's good graces. Now Jacob has another reason for offering gifts: gratitude. Fretheim writes, "The gift that was originally offered for purposes of appeasement (32:20) is, in fact, not necessary for reconciliation. Esau has forgiven Jacob quite apart from such an 'offering.' The 'sacrifice' can now function as a 'gift.'"

Michael Williams, in his *Storyteller's Companion to the Bible, Volume I,* notes: "Jacob urges Esau to accept his present because he says, 'Surely to see your face is like seeing the face of God' [33:10]. Here Jacob says far more than he knows. He thought that he had seen the face of God at the Jabbok river in the person of his wrestling partner. He had thought to appease the face of Esau by buying his favor, hoping that Esau would want to 'lift his face' in acceptance. But Jacob has been wrong all along about where one sees the face of God. In the open-hearted forgiveness of the old, brutish Esau, one can certainly and plainly see the face of God. Whoever would have thought that God would be revealed in Esau? But so it is in this wonderful story."

Genesis 33:11. In a tender moment in the story, Jacob entreats Esau to "please accept my gift," and Esau graciously takes what Jacob has offered him.

Genesis 33:12-17. Possibly desiring to merge the two families and live together in one place, Esau invites Jacob to accompany him to his home in Seir. Jacob says that he will, but that he must move slowly due to the size of his company. Taking Jacob's comment literally, Esau generously offers some of his own group to assist Jacob and his entourage. Jacob declines, saying in effect that although they have been reconciled, this is as far as the relationship should go. Jacob intends that the two families and their futures should remain separate. He tells Esau to go on ahead and he will follow. But he does not. Instead, he travels in another direction, and arrives at Succoth. Jacob and Esau have parted company. They will come together again only at their father's funeral (35:29). The story of Jacob and Esau's reconciliation concludes with the brothers going their separate ways, looking toward an open-ended future.

Genesis 33:18-20. Jacob now enters a new phase of life. Esau is out of the picture, as is Laban. No longer living on Laban's land, Jacob enters the land of promise, thereby fulfilling God's command (31:3, 13). Just as Abraham purchased a burial plot for Sarah in the promised land (Genesis 23), so Jacob purchases a plot near Shechem.

Jacob builds an altar and names it El-Elohe Israel, which means, "God, the God of Israel." Fretheim writes: "Inasmuch as El was the name of the Creator God worshiped at pre-Israelite Shechem, this act signals yet another claim: The God of this land is the God of Israel."

INTERPRETING THE SCRIPTURE

Jacob Fears the Worst

He had tricked his brother, deceived his father, and been on the run ever since. Now, after years of estrangement, avoidance, and being emotionally severed from his brother, Jacob is returning home. He is more than a little anxious. How will he be received?

Jacob receives word that Esau is coming to meet him with four hundred men! No wonder Jacob is "greatly afraid and distressed" (Genesis 32:7). Always resourceful, Jacob prepares an impressive gift, including "oxen, donkeys, flocks, (and) male and female slaves" (32:5). Surely these things will appease Esau, he reasons. Then, in an act of utter humility, Jacob makes himself vulnerable to the approaching Esau by going out ahead of his entourage, and bowing to the ground seven times in front of his brother. Jacob, who has lived by tricks and bribes and lies, fears that his brother will kill not only Jacob, but also his entire family.

It is amazing what the mind will do when communication breaks down. Since Jacob had had no contact with Esau for years, he assumed the worst. He assumed that Esau was still angry and vengeful. But lo and behold, Esau had experienced a change of heart. No longer angry and depressed over the poor choice he had made in selling his birthright for a pot of stew, he was ready to forgive and forget. It was Jacob who would need to catch up. Esau had already moved on!

What Is Most Important to You?

In one of his sermons, noted preacher Fred Craddock tells the story of Glenn Adsit, a schoolmate of his from years back. Adsit was under house arrest in China, where he ministered, when soldiers arrived and said, "You can return to America," and "you can take two hundred pounds with you."

Dr. Craddock continues by noting they had been there for years. Two hundred pounds certainly was not much. As soon as they got out the scales, the family arguments started! "Must have this vase." "Well, this is a new typewriter." "What about my books?" "What about this?" They weighed everything and finally got it exactly right: two hundred pounds.

"The soldiers asked, 'Ready to go?'"
"Yes."
"Did you weigh everything?"
"Yes."
"You weighed the kids?"
"No, we didn't."
"Weigh the kids."
"And in a moment, typewriter and vase and all became trash."

If you had to leave your home due to a hurricane or tornado or the threat of natural disaster or terrorist attack, what would you take with you? Many people in tropical areas have a "hurricane box" ready to take with them should they need to evacuate quickly. Faced with the possible annihilation of all that he had, Jacob decided to divide his household into two companies, thinking, "If Esau comes to the one company and destroys it, then the company that is left will escape" (32:8). Not willing to part with his wives or his children, though, Jacob kept them close to himself.

It is interesting how Jacob prioritized his family members. He put the maids and their children in front, then Leah and her children. He kept Rebekah and her son Joseph at the back to protect them. They were the closest to his heart.

In times of emergency, we quickly discover our true priorities. Why does it sometimes take calamity to remind us that the most important things in life are not *things,* but the relationships that we have with others? The threat of death caused Jacob to seek reconciliation with his brother and to get his priorities straight. What will motivate us to "get our act together"?

What a Reunion!

Is there a sentence more pleasant to our ears than, "I forgive you"? Is there any better news than to know that those we love have put the past behind and are willing to make a fresh start?

When Jacob and Esau, who hadn't seen each other for years, came together, there was tension in the air. Jacob, quite understandably, didn't know what to expect. But Esau's demeanor set the tone for the reconciliation that followed.

Forgetting about his dignity as a person of prominence in the Near East, Esau did not walk, but ran to meet Jacob! He not only ran, but he also embraced his brother. Then emotion overcame them both! We are reminded of the story of extravagance in Luke 15 where a loving father ran to meet his prodigal son and welcome him home with open arms.

Jacob rightly equates Esau's face with the face of God, for Esau's actions remind us of God's love and forgiveness. Moreover, the life one lives with God and the life one lives with other human beings are two sides of the same coin. If we are to accept God's forgiveness of us, we must be willing to forgive others. Remember the words of the Lord's Prayer: "Forgive us our debts, as we also have forgiven our debtors" (Matthew 6:12).

Life with God cannot be lived in isolation from our brothers and sisters without harming both relationships. Life with other humans cannot truly be lived in isolation from God if we are to become what God intends us to be.

Reconciliation Is Possible!

A man will go to the doctor, have his heart rate and blood pressure checked, have a stress test and all the rest, but ignore the fact that he has not been on speaking terms with members of his own family for years. The toll that is extracted from unresolved conflict is staggering. Yet reconciliation is possible! It was possible for Jacob and Esau. It is possible for you and me.

Conflict is normal and part of any human relationship. Yet the story of Jacob and Esau illustrates the point that no matter how serious the conflict or how deeply rooted in past history, reconciliation between family members is a possibility. And, since we are all part of the family of God, we really cannot justify the grudges and conflicts that keep us from being reconciled with one another and with God.

The story of Jacob and Esau reminds us that it is the one who has been sinned against who must offer forgiveness. Thus, in Esau Jacob sees the face of God. For Esau, like God, is gracious and willing to forgive. Jacob does not deserve the kindness that is shown to him by God and by Esau. It comes as a gift. Jacob is able to receive that gift, and because he is willing to receive that gift, it frees his life for a healthy future.

May we hear the words of forgiveness that are offered to us, and may we be reconciled both to God and to family members with whom we are estranged. Reconciliation is possible! The twin brothers, Jacob and Esau, have shown us the way.

SHARING THE SCRIPTURE

Preparing Our Hearts

Meditate on this week's devotional reading, found in Psalm 133. This psalm speaks of the joy that comes when family members live in unity. Brokenness is bound to occur in any human relationship, but it is especially painful within families. With whom do you need to be reconciled? What steps can you take right now to begin to mend fences? Do whatever is in your power to do, but remember that the other person may accept or reject your offer.

Pray that you and the adult learners will actively seek unity within your own families.

Preparing Our Minds

Study the background from Genesis 33 and lesson Scripture, verses 1-11. As you consider this passage, think about what must happen for damaged relationships to be restored.

Write on newsprint:
❑ information for next week's lesson, found under "Continue the Journey."
❑ activities for further spiritual growth in "Continue the Journey."

Plan the lecture for "Present the Story of the Reunion between Twin Brothers, Esau and Jacob" if you choose to do this option.

LEADING THE CLASS

(1) Gather to Learn

❖ Welcome the class members and introduce any guests.

❖ Pray that those who are present will be open to the leading of the Holy Spirit as you study and fellowship together.

❖ Read aloud this story adapted from the Internet: **As far back as I can remember, my older sister has always been the smarter one. She has been the one that gets** the good grades, knows all the right people, and says the right things at the right times. I have been the other kid. I'm the one that gets into trouble for opening my big mouth a little too wide. My grades have been consistently poor and all my teachers hated me. I walk in her shadow everyday because she excels at everything she tries, and I am just me. I was not about to try and follow in those gargantuan footsteps, at least, I'm not ready to try yet. She drives herself so hard because she feels that nothing she does is ever good enough and in this, she becomes her own worst enemy. Sibling rivalry dictates that I should resent the fact that she is so much better at doing what she does than I am, but I can't help but feel cheated by her sadness. She encourages me to find solace in the fact that she hates what she is doing with her life and wants to change it, even if she is frighteningly good at it. Sibling rivalry died the day she said that to me. Now I just love her.

❖ Talk with the class about this sibling relationship. Ask:
(1) **What are its strengths and weaknesses?**
(2) **How is this relationship like or unlike the relationship you have with your siblings?**

❖ Read aloud today's focus statement: **Relationships sometimes seem irreparably broken. What must happen for such damaged relationships to be restored? Esau, who had been wronged by his brother, willingly greeted Jacob and offered him hospitality and signs of reconciliation.**

(2) Present the Story of the Reunion between Twin Brothers, Esau and Jacob

❖ Select three volunteers—Jacob, Esau, and a narrator—to read Genesis 33:1-11.

❖ Encourage the students, as a class or in groups, to envision themselves as movie directors and answer these questions. If you work in groups, ask each group to report back to the class.

  (1) **Who would you cast as Jacob? Esau? Leah? Rachel?**

  (2) **What emotions would you see in the body language and faces of these characters?**

  (3) **What kind of music would you play as Esau ran to Jacob? As Esau talks with Jacob?**

  (4) **What would the background look like?**

  (5) **What special effects might you include?**

  (6) **What would be the title of this movie?**

❖ Wrap up this section by asking these questions in class, or by discussing the answers as a lecture.

  (1) **What lessons did Jacob and Esau learn from this reunion?**

  (2) **What lessons can you learn from these brothers?**

  (3) **How can this ancient story be applied to life in the twenty-first century?**

(3) Recall Feelings Associated with Restoring Relationships

❖ Lead the class in this guided imagery activity. Ask them to get in a comfortable position and close their eyes, if they wish. As you read, be sure to pause long enough to allow for reflection.

  ■ **Picture in your mind a sibling, other family member, or close friend with whom you have had a troubled relationship. Really notice this person, especially what is likeable about him or her.** (pause)

  ■ **Recall an argument or situation that caused a split in your relationship. Assess whether the situation seems as bad now as it did at the time.** (pause)

  ■ **Remember or imagine being reconciled with this person. What happened that enabled the two of you to move on? How did you feel?** (pause)

  ■ **Open your eyes when you are ready**.

❖ Invite volunteers to talk about the feelings they recalled when the relationship was restored. Preferably, they will not give details of the problem that created the rift.

(4) Seek to Restore a Broken Relationship

❖ Read or retell "Reconciliation Is Possible!" from Interpreting the Scripture as preparation for the following activities.

❖ Invite the students to explore feelings of childhood sibling rivalry within their own families by distributing paper and pencils and asking them to write about their relationship with a brother or sister, or other close relative if they have no siblings. Tell them they will not be asked to relate this information to the class.

❖ Brainstorm with the class reasons why adult siblings may continue to experience problems in their relationships. List the answers on newsprint. Ideas may include: *feeling left out when a sibling marries; having no time to spend with a sibling because of family, career, distance, or other time constraints; difficult decisions regarding care of elderly parents; not overcoming the role or label that parents assigned to each child in the family; inability to communicate with a sibling; personality clashes.*

❖ Point out these steps to restore a broken relationship that Rick Warren suggests in Chapter 20 of *The Purpose-Driven Life*. The class members may wish to comment on these ideas and add others.

  ■ "Talk to God before talking to the person."

  ■ "Always take the initiative."

  ■ "Sympathize with their feelings."

  ■ "Confess your part of the conflict."

- "Attack the problem, not the person."
- "Cooperate as much as possible."
- "Emphasize reconciliation, not resolution."

❖ Provide meditation time for the adults to consider how they may restore a broken relationship with a sibling or other family member. Ask them to write a commitment, between themselves and God, to do whatever is in their power to mend this fence and seek a closer relationship. Suggest that if the sibling in question has died that the class member write a letter to that sibling this week explaining the problem and what he or she would try to do if the sibling were alive. Such a letter will help to articulate problems and help the student move toward inner reconciliation.

(5) Continue the Journey

❖ Break the silence by praying that all who have come today will take whatever steps they can to bring about reconciliation in their families.

❖ Read aloud this preparation for next week's lesson. You may also want to post it on newsprint for the students to copy.
- **Title: Joseph's Dream**
- **Background Scripture: Genesis 37**
- **Lesson Scripture: Genesis 37:5-11, 19-21, 23-24a, 28**
- **Focus of the Lesson: Ordinary people are sometimes called to do extraordinary things. How do others feel when such people begin to reveal their sense of calling? Joseph** announced his dreams of greatness to his family and, understandably, he was met with anger and jealousy—a jealousy that led to Joseph's being taken to Egypt.

❖ Challenge the students to complete one or more of these activities for further spiritual growth, which you will write on newsprint for the students to copy.
(1) **Find a book on family conflict resolution that speaks to a problem within your own family, such as sibling rivalry or work and family conflicts. Read this book with discernment to see how it can help you. Journal about your feelings and any action you plan to take.**
(2) **Plan a reunion for your extended family. Depending upon how many people you wish to include, you may need several months of lead time to rent a meeting space and contact everyone. If someone in the family is a genealogist, ask this person to bring whatever information he or she has and possibly post a family tree.**
(3) **Call a sibling or other family member this week "just because."**

❖ Sing or read aloud "This Is a Day of New Beginnings."

❖ Conclude today's session by leading the class in this benediction, which is adapted from Genesis 14:19-20: **Blessed be you by God Most High, maker of heaven and earth; and blessed be God Most High.**

UNIT 3: GOD'S PEOPLE RE-CREATED
JOSEPH'S DREAM

PREVIEWING THE LESSON

Lesson Scripture: Genesis 37:5-11, 19-21, 23-24a, 28
Background Scripture: Genesis 37
Key Verse: Genesis 37:5

Focus of the Lesson:
Ordinary people are sometimes called to do extraordinary things. How do others feel when such people begin to reveal their sense of calling? Joseph announced his dreams of greatness to his family and, understandably, he was met with anger and jealousy— a jealousy that led to Joseph's being taken to Egypt.

Goals for the Learners:
(1) to examine the content of Joseph's dream and his family's response to it.
(2) to imagine the hopelessness of Joseph's situation and relate it to circumstances in their own lives.
(3) to recognize God's call, identify barriers to answering that call, and take steps to overcome the barriers.

Pronunciation Guide:
Dothan (doh' thuhn)   Ishmaelite (ish' may uh lit)
Midianite (mid' ee uh nit)   Potiphar (pot' uh fuhr)
Shechem (shek' uhm)   Sheol (shee' ohl)

Supplies:
Bibles, newsprint and marker, paper and pencils, hymnals, picture of Joseph in well, votive candles, matches

---

READING THE SCRIPTURE

NRSV
Genesis 37:5-11, 19-21, 23-24a, 28

5Once Joseph had a dream, and when he told it to his brothers, they hated him even more. 6He said to them, "Listen to this dream that I dreamed. 7There we were,

NIV
Genesis 37:5-11, 19-21, 23-24a, 28

5Joseph had a dream, and when he told it to his brothers, they hated him all the more. 6He said to them, "Listen to this dream I had: 7We were binding sheaves of binding sheaves in the field. Suddenly my sheaf rose and stood upright; then your sheaves gathered around it, and bowed down to my sheaf." [8]His brothers said to him, "Are you indeed to reign over us? Are you indeed to have dominion over us?" So they hated him even more because of his dreams and his words.

[9]He had another dream, and told it to his brothers, saying, "Look, I have had another dream: the sun, the moon, and eleven stars were bowing down to me." [10]But when he told it to his father and to his brothers, his father rebuked him, and said to him, "What kind of dream is this that you have had? Shall we indeed come, I and your mother and your brothers, and bow to the ground before you?" [11]So his brothers were jealous of him, but his father kept the matter in mind.

[19]They said to one another, "Here comes this dreamer. [20]Come now, let us kill him and throw him into one of the pits; then we shall say that a wild animal has devoured him, and we shall see what will become of his dreams." [21]But when Reuben heard it, he delivered him out of their hands, saying, "Let us not take his life.". . . [23]So when Joseph came to his brothers, they stripped him of his robe, the long robe with sleeves that he wore; [24]and they took him and threw him into a pit.

[28]When some Midianite traders passed by, they drew Joseph up, lifting him out of the pit, and sold him to the Ishmaelites for twenty pieces of silver. And they took Joseph to Egypt.

grain out in the field when suddenly my sheaf rose and stood upright, while your sheaves gathered around mine and bowed down to it."

[8]His brothers said to him, "Do you intend to reign over us? Will you actually rule us?" And they hated him all the more because of his dream and what he had said.

[9]Then he had another dream, and he told it to his brothers. "Listen," he said, "I had another dream, and this time the sun and moon and eleven stars were bowing down to me."

[10]When he told his father as well as his brothers, his father rebuked him and said, "What is this dream you had? Will your mother and I and your brothers actually come and bow down to the ground before you?" [11]His brothers were jealous of him, but his father kept the matter in mind.

[19]"Here comes that dreamer!" they said to each other. [20]"Come now, let's kill him and throw him into one of these cisterns and say that a ferocious animal devoured him. Then we'll see what comes of his dreams."

[21]When Reuben heard this, he tried to rescue him from their hands. "Let's not take his life," he said. . . .

[23]So when Joseph came to his brothers, they stripped him of his robe—the richly ornamented robe he was wearing—[24]and they took him and threw him into the cistern.

[28]So when the Midianite merchants came by, his brothers pulled Joseph up out of the cistern and sold him for twenty shekels of silver to the Ishmaelites, who took him to Egypt.

UNDERSTANDING THE SCRIPTURE

Genesis 37:1. Jacob and his family now live in the land of promise, the land chosen by God as the place from which the world's blessings will arise. Whereas Abraham and Isaac had lived in this promised land as "aliens," Jacob and his heirs will now settle there and it will be their home. Two themes will emerge in the story: the movement from Canaan to Egypt and the development of Israel's story, from one person to twelve tribes.

Genesis 37:2. Joseph quickly emerges as the focal point of the story. He is much younger than his brothers. As he is introduced, the narrator gives the first of three reasons that his brothers resent him: He is a tattletale bringing "bad reports" about the brothers to their father, Jacob.

Genesis 37:3. Joseph apparently has a relationship with his father that the other sons do not enjoy. As the child of Jacob's old age, it becomes obvious that Joseph is his father's pet. Thus he is given "a long robe with sleeves," because Jacob loves Joseph more than any of the other sons. The King James Version, following the Septuagint (early Greek translation of the Old Testament), has given us the common expression "coat of many colours." However, "long robe with sleeves" is a more accurate translation, and is in keeping with Joseph's privileged status, implying that he was excused from any manual labor. Laborers wore shorter garments to free their arms and legs for work. At any rate, Joseph's coat is a very distinctive and luxurious garment that sets him apart from the rest of the family. This preferential treatment was the second reason his brothers despised him.

Genesis 37:4. Because of the growing resentment among the brothers, communication broke down and they could no longer "speak peaceably" to their little brother. The Bible tells us plainly, "they hated him."

Genesis 37:5-8. Finally, the third reason for the resentment is reported. Joseph has a dream, which he shares with his brothers. This was not a benign dream; it indicates that Joseph will have preeminence over his brothers. Naturally, when Joseph reveals the content of his dream, his brothers "hated him even more." "Are you indeed to reign over us?" they ask in disgust. Little do they know!

Genesis 37:9-11. Joseph apparently does not grasp how deeply he is resented. He reports to his family on a second dream whose content is even more offensive. In this dream the sun, the moon, and eleven stars bow down to him. This dream is too much even for his doting father. Jacob rebukes Joseph, but keeps the matter in mind. Jacob does not appear gullible, nor does he reject the dream's potential significance. While he initially asks questions concerning the nature and the implications of the dreams, he takes these things and ponders them, revealing an openness to future possibilities.

Genesis 37:12-14. When the brothers are shepherding their father's flocks at Shechem, about fifty miles from Hebron, Jacob, apparently unaware of the animosity that has developed in his family, sends Joseph on what appears to be yet another spying mission.

Genesis 37:15-17. The delay heightens the drama. The brothers have moved north from Shechem to Dothan.

Genesis 37:18-20. Alas, the brothers have had enough of Joseph! When they see him approaching, they plot to kill him. Their motivation centers on Joseph's dreams as they exclaim, "Hear comes this dreamer." They assume that if they get rid of the dreamer, his dreams will evaporate and never become reality.

Genesis 37:21-22. In the midst of the plotting, Jacob's eldest son, Reuben, speaks up. Perhaps acting out of responsibility as the oldest brother, Reuben states that he does not want to see Joseph killed. In fact, the narrator tells us that he intends to rescue Joseph and take him back to their father.

Genesis 37:23-24. When Joseph arrives, the brothers strip him of his robe (and his status), and throw him into a dry cistern, which is a hole dug out to store rain water.

Genesis 37:25-28. After taking care of Joseph, the brothers sit down to eat a meal. When they spot a caravan headed toward Egypt, Judah intervenes. Appealing to their self-interest, Judah suggests they sell him to the Ishmaelites. "Why kill him when we can make a buck off him?" Judah in essence asks. His brothers agree.

According to the NRSV, while the brothers are busy talking, eating, and arguing, some Midianite traders kidnap Joseph and sell him to the Ishmaelites for the sum of twenty pieces of silver (see Leviticus 27:5). Suddenly

Joseph is headed for Egypt because "they drew Joseph up," where "they" apparently refers to the "Midianites" (NRSV, 37:28). According to the same verse in the NIV, however, Joseph is headed to Egypt because "his brothers pulled Joseph out of the cistern and sold him for twenty shekels."

Genesis 37:29-30. Reuben, the eldest brother who had suggested that Joseph be thrown into the pit, is so upset when he returns to find the pit empty that he tears his clothing, a traditional sign of mourning.

Genesis 37:31-35. Deprived of the profit from the sale of Joseph, the brothers still have his robe, the symbol of Joseph's preferential treatment. They dip it in animal blood and take it to their father for his identification, making no comment. Of course the elderly man immediately recognizes the torn and bloody robe, and believes that his beloved son has been dismembered and devoured by wild beasts. He begins a process of lifelong mourning. It is ironic that the brothers' effort to get rid of Joseph, the center of their father's affection, in effect causes Jacob to focus on his favorite son even more. Jacob finds no comfort in the thought of a reunion with Joseph in Sheol, the realm of the dead.

Genesis 37:36. Joseph, however, is far from dead! He has been sold, not to work in the quarries or on the great building projects, but as a household slave to a rich and powerful man, Potiphar, a captain of Pharaoh's personal bodyguard.

INTERPRETING THE SCRIPTURE

Dreams Have Consequences

Psychologists tell us that at various points in the sleep cycle, we are prone to dreaming. In fact, those who study sleep patterns tell us that we typically dream several times each night. Most dreams are unremembered, but a few dreams stay with us and sometimes surprise us with their content! While most of our dreams do not seem to make much sense, some dreams seem so real that they continue to haunt us for days and weeks to come.

In Bible times dreams were perceived much differently than they are today. With little understanding of the physiological components of dreaming, dreams were seen as vehicles of divine communication. When a person dreamed, the first question was, "What is God trying to say to me?" We have only to recall Jacob's dream to know that God can be involved in the process. Indeed, I would not want to rule out the dream as a possible method of divine communication in our day. I truly believe that God still uses dreams to influence human thinking and behavior. Yet, we would probably not look for a theological meaning to our dreams as quickly as did the Genesis dreamers.

Joseph was wise enough to look for the message of God in his dreams. The dreams concerning the sheaves of wheat seemed to indicate that Joseph was headed for a leadership position. However, in a society based on seniority, the fact that Joseph was the youngest son made this dream problematic at best. His brothers were clearly annoyed with his delusions of grandeur. But Joseph, being a bright and self-confident lad, recognized his dreams as more than just wishful thinking. He interpreted them as God's call upon his life.

The second dream was even more grandiose and more offensive to the members of Joseph's family. Many people are reluctant to share what they may perceive as God's call upon their lives. How do we know that the voices we have heard, the urgings we have felt, are of God? Joseph, however, without reservation tells his brothers the content of his second dream: The sun, the moon, and eleven stars bowed down to him! Even his father was outraged by this revelation. Yet we know that, as the result of a famine yet to come in the land, Joseph will someday have the whole world at his feet.

What impact did those early dreams have upon the faith formation and leadership development of Joseph? To what extent do we pay attention to our dreams, not only those dreams that wake us from sleep, but also the recurring thoughts that God may be placing upon our hearts concerning God's call and purpose for our lives? Have you heard God speak to you lately? Are you listening for God's voice? Do not dismiss your dreams too quickly or too lightly. They may be God's way of calling you to a specific path of service.

Tension in the Family

When anyone speaks to me about God's call upon his or her life, I always ask, "Have you shared this with your family?" For some, that is the most anxiety-provoking step in the process. "My sister, a minister?" "My son, a leader in the church?" Fortunate are those whose families are supportive of their calling. Many times people who feel God's call upon their lives find the greatest challenges to being accepted right in their own homes.

Joseph had more than the usual challenges. He was the obvious favorite of his father, Jacob. Not only did dad "like him best," but dad also demonstrated his partiality by showering Joseph with lavish gifts. To make matters worse, Joseph was a tattletale, bringing "bad reports" about his brothers to their father. In addition, Joseph freely shared the content of his dreams, which couldn't help but rub his brothers the wrong way. Did he not perceive that he would be "hated even more" (37:8) by telling the brothers what he had dreamed?

How do we take a different path from what our family has scripted us to follow? How do we become "our own person"? Most of us struggle with these questions throughout our lives. To break the mold, to dare to be different, to follow God's plan rather than the script that society or our parents or our peer group sets before us—this is the challenge that came not only to Joseph but also to every faithful believer. We might not appreciate Joseph's methodology, but we have to admire his integrity. The crowd did not influence him. He took the path less traveled.

The Dreamer Must Be Stopped!

The brothers must have recognized in Joseph leadership qualities that made his dreams seem especially threatening to them. When Joseph appeared on the horizon at Dothan, they were unable to get his dreams out of their minds and exclaimed, "Here comes this dreamer!" (37:19). Apparently they found Joseph's dreams ominous enough to want to kill him.

Who or what were the brothers trying to kill? Was it their obnoxious little brother, or was it his dream of preeminence and power? Why was this little twit so threatening to them? The Bible tells us that they were "jealous" (37:11). Jealousy can eat at us and destroy us. Pretty soon they hatched a plot to do away with Joseph and be done with the dreamer once and for all.

Throughout history people whose ideas differ significantly from the majority have been persecuted for their beliefs. In the early days of the church, faithful Christians were fed to the lions. Yet the faith did not die; rather, it grew and spread like wildfire.

What is of God cannot be squelched. Persecution and violence will never overcome the truth of God's love and forgiveness. The brothers sought to get rid of the dreamer. At the last minute, Reuben and then Judah intervened to save Joseph. Their merciful actions kept both the dream and the dreamer alive.

Stay Tuned!

A favorite strategy in a sequence of stories, be it a series of books or television shows, is to leave the audience in suspense. In fact, when a television program pauses for a commercial break, the talk show host will say, "Don't touch the remote! We'll be right back!"

Joseph being sold by the Midianite traders serves a similar function in the biblical narrative. For a brief while, it looked as if the brothers would kill Joseph and the story would be over. Then Reuben suggested he be put in a pit. While he was in the pit, Judah prevailed upon the brothers to sell Joseph to Ishmaelite traders who were passing that way. As they debated the merits of Judah's idea, some Midianite traders passed by, kidnapped Joseph, and sold him to the Ishmaelites themselves!

It may appear to the casual reader that Joseph is now off the stage and out of the story. After all, he no longer resides in the land of promise and is headed for Egypt. Yet those of us who know the story are aware that the saga of Joseph is not over. It is just beginning! Joseph is capable of much more than being a tattletale and a dreamer. He is destined for the greatness that his boyhood dreams indicated. He is being sold as a slave. But he will not perish in the quarries of Egypt or on one of Pharaoh's building projects. He will emerge as the number two leader in Egypt. The brothers may have thought they had seen the last of their arrogant sibling, but their relationship with him is by no means over. Stay tuned!

SHARING THE SCRIPTURE

Preparing Our Hearts

Meditate on this week's devotional reading, found in Psalm 70. This call for God to deliver the psalmist from enemies could have been the plea of Joseph, whose story we will begin to study today. When have you needed to be freed from people who wished you ill, if not bodily harm? How did your faith in God help you through this challenging situation? What advice would you give to someone who feels he or she must receive immediate help?

Pray that you and the adult learners will call upon God to help you find constructive ways to deal with an enemy.

Preparing Our Minds

Study the background, Genesis 37, and lesson Scripture, Genesis 37:5-11, 19-21, 23-24a, 28. As you delve into this reading, consider how others feel when ordinary people who are called to do extraordinary things reveal their sense of calling.

Write on newsprint:

❑ sheet for "Recognize God's Call, Identify Barriers to Answering That Call, and Take Steps to Overcome the Barriers."
❑ information for next week's lesson, found under "Continue the Journey."
❑ activities for further spiritual growth in "Continue the Journey."

Locate a picture depicting the brothers throwing Joseph into a well or his journey to Egypt. Check for "Joseph Cast into the Well" by Master of Jean de Mandeville at the Getty Museum (www.getty.edu/art/gettyguide/artObjectDetails?artobj=2901). Print the enlarged version. Or, locate other art in a book or online.

Bring enough votive candles for each participant. (Some churches keep a supply of these small candles.) Arrange them on a worship table prior to the session.

LEADING THE CLASS

(1) Gather to Learn

❖ Welcome the class members and introduce any guests.

❖ Pray that all who are present today will recognize God's voice speaking to them.

❖ Invite the students to tell stories of ordinary people doing extraordinary things. These people may now be well known, such as Rosa Parks or Coretta Scott King. Or they may be neighbors or church members whose acts of love, mercy, and compassion have made a real difference in people's lives. If you need a discussion starter, or prefer not to use students' stories, you may want to read the following aloud: **Franklin County Volunteers In Medicine was established by Dr. Phillip Stover to help care for the more than 1.4 million people of North Carolina who have no health insurance or are underinsured. Volunteers staff this clinic, which sees about two hundred chronically ill patients an evening. The Alliance Medical Ministry in Raleigh, headed by Dr. Susan Weaver, is a primary care facility that charges a small fee and has cared for about nine thousand people. In a blog by WRAL's Valonda Calloway, Dr. Weaver is quoted as saying, "It's the greatest gift I've ever been given. I tell people I don't think of it as a job."**

❖ Ask this question: **What do you think motivates people to step out and do something that most people cannot imagine?**

❖ Read aloud today's focus statement: **Ordinary people are sometimes called to do extraordinary things. How do others feel when such people begin to reveal their sense of calling? Joseph announced his dreams of greatness to his family and, understandably, he was met with anger and jealousy—a jealousy that led to Joseph's being taken to Egypt.**

(2) Examine the Content of Joseph's Dream and His Family's Response to It

❖ Choose someone to read Genesis 37:5-11.

■ Distribute paper and pencils. Ask the students to sketch either the symbols of the first dream or those of the second.

■ Talk with the class about how Joseph's brothers interpreted the first dream, and how his father interpreted the second dream.

■ Augment this discussion by reading the third and fourth paragraphs of "Dreams Have Consequences" in Interpreting the Scripture.

■ Ask these questions.
   (1) **Based on the biblical story, commentary, and the symbols depicted in your sketches, do you think the brothers and Jacob—Israel—responded fairly to Joseph? Why or why not?**
   (2) **What factors entered into their response?**

❖ Select a volunteer to read Genesis 37:19-21, 23-24a, 28.

■ Show the picture you have found of Joseph either in the well or on the way to Egypt. Talk with the class about what the body language and facial expressions of the characters involved, particularly Joseph, reveal. If you have a color picture, explore how the color affects the scene.

■ Discuss these questions.
   (1) **How would you describe the feelings of the brothers as depicted in the art and biblical text?**
   (2) **How would you describe Joseph's emotions?**
   (3) **What questions might Joseph want to ask his brothers?**

(3) Imagine the Hopelessness of Joseph's Situation and Relate It to Circumstances in the Learners' Lives

❖ Read or retell "The Dreamer Must Be Stopped!" in Interpreting the Scripture.

❖ Brainstorm situations in contemporary life that may cause people to despair. List ideas on newsprint.

❖ Provide meditation time for the adults to recall "Joseph situations" in their own lives, times when life took a direction far different than they had expected.

❖ Call the class back together. Encourage volunteers to tell about how their "Joseph situations" were resolved, enabling them to move forward in life or how they felt when they were able to overcome these situations.

(4) Recognize God's Call, Identify Barriers to Answering That Call, and Take Steps to Overcome the Barriers

❖ Read "Tension in the Family" in Interpreting the Scripture.

❖ Divide into groups. Post the following information and ask the group members to talk with one another about:

(a) **what they believe God is calling them to do now.**

(b) **barriers that impede them from answering the call. (For example, as with Joseph, family members may not support God's call on their life.)**

(c) **steps that can be taken to overcome the barriers. (For example, they may need to listen to the objections of a family member and see if action can be taken to overcome these concerns.)**

❖ Invite those who want to make a commitment to hearing and heeding God's call on their lives to light a votive candle on the worship table. Take a candle to anyone who would like to participate but cannot come to the table; let the student light the candle and then return it to the table. Leave the candles lit until the session ends.

(5) Continue the Journey

❖ Pray that all who have participated in today's session will be more open to hearing and responding to God's call on their lives.

❖ Read aloud this preparation for next week's lesson. You may also want to post it on newsprint for the students to copy.

■ **Title: Joseph's Dream Began to Come True**

■ **Background Scripture: Genesis 41:25-45**

■ **Lesson Scripture: Genesis 41:25-40**

■ **Focus of the Lesson: God's purposes are sometimes fulfilled in amazing ways. How, for example, did God work through Joseph to fulfill divine promises made to the covenant people? God gave Joseph the ability to interpret a dream for Pharaoh, who responded by elevating Joseph to a position of power, just as Joseph himself had dreamed.**

❖ Challenge the students to complete one or more of these activities for further spiritual growth, which you will write on newsprint for the students to copy.

(1) **Get in touch with God through prayer, meditation, journaling, walking a labyrinth, prayer walking, or whatever method works best for you. Focus on God's call at this point in your life. As you begin to discern or reaffirm this call, determine next steps in fulfilling that call.**

(2) **Explore possibilities for volunteer work that reflect your calling.**

(3) **Serve as a sounding board for a young person trying to perceive and follow God's call.**

❖ Sing or read aloud "Have Thine Own Way, Lord."

❖ Conclude today's session by leading the class in this benediction, which is adapted from Genesis 14:19-20: **Blessed be you by God Most High, maker of heaven and earth; and blessed be God Most High.**

UNIT 3: GOD'S PEOPLE RE-CREATED

JOSEPH'S DREAM BEGAN TO COME TRUE

PREVIEWING THE LESSON

Lesson Scripture: Genesis 41:25-40
Background Scripture: Genesis 41:25-45
Key Verse: Genesis 41:39

Focus of the Lesson:
God's purposes are sometimes fulfilled in amazing ways. How, for example, did God work through Joseph to fulfill divine promises made to the covenant people? God gave Joseph the ability to interpret a dream for Pharaoh, who responded by elevating Joseph to a position of power, just as Joseph himself had dreamed.

Goals for the Learners:
(1) to explore the story of Joseph's interpretation of Pharaoh's dream, and Pharaoh's response to Joseph.
(2) to affirm that God's promises cannot be thwarted.
(3) to look in unlikely places to see God at work in unlikely ways.

Pronunciation Guide:
Asenath (as' uh nath)   Dothan (doh' thuhn)
vizier (ve zir')   Zaphaneth-paneah (zaf uh nath-puh nee' uh)

Supplies:
Bibles, newsprint and marker, paper and pencils, hymnals, optional pictures of famine-stricken areas or shocks of dried corn or grain

---

READING THE SCRIPTURE

NRSV
Genesis 41:25-40

²⁵Then Joseph said to Pharaoh, "Pharaoh's dreams are one and the same; God has revealed to Pharaoh what he is about to do. ²⁶The seven good cows are seven years, and

NIV
Genesis 41:25-40

²⁵Then Joseph said to Pharaoh, "The dreams of Pharaoh are one and the same. God has revealed to Pharaoh what he is about to do. ²⁶The seven good cows are seven years,

the seven good ears are seven years; the dreams are one. ²⁷The seven lean and ugly cows that came up after them are seven years, as are the seven empty ears blighted by the east wind. They are seven years of famine. ²⁸It is as I told Pharaoh; God has shown to Pharaoh what he is about to do. ²⁹There will come seven years of great plenty throughout all the land of Egypt. ³⁰After them there will arise seven years of famine, and all the plenty will be forgotten in the land of Egypt; the famine will consume the land. ³¹The plenty will no longer be known in the land because of the famine that will follow, for it will be very grievous. ³²And the doubling of Pharaoh's dream means that the thing is fixed by God, and God will shortly bring it about. ³³Now therefore let Pharaoh select a man who is discerning and wise, and set him over the land of Egypt. ³⁴Let Pharaoh proceed to appoint overseers over the land, and take one-fifth of the produce of the land of Egypt during the seven plenteous years. ³⁵Let them gather all the food of these good years that are coming, and lay up grain under the authority of Pharaoh for food in the cities, and let them keep it. ³⁶That food shall be a reserve for the land against the seven years of famine that are to befall the land of Egypt, so that the land may not perish through the famine."

³⁷The proposal pleased Pharaoh and all his servants. ³⁸Pharaoh said to his servants, "Can we find anyone else like this—one in whom is the spirit of God?" ³⁹**So Pharaoh said to Joseph, "Since God has shown you all this, there is no one so discerning and wise as you.** ⁴⁰You shall be over my house, and all my people shall order themselves as you command; only with regard to the throne will I be greater than you."

and the seven good heads of grain are seven years; it is one and the same dream. ²⁷The seven lean, ugly cows that came up afterward are seven years, and so are the seven worthless heads of grain scorched by the east wind: They are seven years of famine.

²⁸"It is just as I said to Pharaoh: God has shown Pharaoh what he is about to do. ²⁹Seven years of great abundance are coming throughout the land of Egypt, ³⁰but seven years of famine will follow them. Then all the abundance in Egypt will be forgotten, and the famine will ravage the land. ³¹The abundance in the land will not be remembered, because the famine that follows it will be so severe. ³²The reason the dream was given to Pharaoh in two forms is that the matter has been firmly decided by God, and God will do it soon.

³³"And now let Pharaoh look for a discerning and wise man and put him in charge of the land of Egypt. ³⁴Let Pharaoh appoint commissioners over the land to take a fifth of the harvest of Egypt during the seven years of abundance. ³⁵They should collect all the food of these good years that are coming and store up the grain under the authority of Pharaoh, to be kept in the cities for food. ³⁶This food should be held in reserve for the country, to be used during the seven years of famine that will come upon Egypt, so that the country may not be ruined by the famine."

³⁷The plan seemed good to Pharaoh and to all his officials. ³⁸So Pharaoh asked them, "Can we find anyone like this man, one in whom is the spirit of God?"

³⁹**Then Pharaoh said to Joseph, "Since God has made all this known to you, there is no one so discerning and wise as you.** ⁴⁰You shall be in charge of my palace, and all my people are to submit to your orders. Only with respect to the throne will I be greater than you."

UNDERSTANDING THE SCRIPTURE

Genesis 41:25-31. After correctly interpreting the dreams of Pharaoh's imprisoned

cupbearer and baker, Joseph languished in prison for two more years before being called upon to interpret two disturbing dreams of Pharaoh. These dreams are actually mirror images of one another, both meaning the same thing. In the first dream Pharaoh saw "seven cows, fat and sleek" and seven other cows "poor, very ugly, and thin" (41:17-19). In the second dream Pharaoh saw seven full ears of grain and seven "withered" ones. Amazingly, in both dreams the seven decimated ones ate the seven healthy ones. Like Joseph himself, whose own dreams (Genesis 37:5-11) showed him in a position of authority over his older brothers, these dreams also depict the weaker dominating the strong.

To find out the meaning of these very troubling dreams, Pharaoh summons his court magicians and wise men who are trained in the interpretation of dreams, but, alas, none of them can help him. Pharaoh's chief cupbearer, suddenly recalls his encounter with "a young Hebrew" (41:12) whose interpretation of his dream and the dream of the baker turned out to be accurate predictions of the future.

Pharaoh has Joseph brought to him. Joseph makes no claim to dream interpretation, but says that God will provide the answers. Nevertheless, Joseph wastes no time in explaining the meaning of these dreams. The Egyptian magicians may not have been able to solve the mystery, but Joseph has no trouble at all. Seven—the number of cows and the number of ears of grain—refers to years of plenty and years of famine. Seven is also the number associated with completeness and perfection. As such, it was seen as a sacred number. The detail concerning the weaker cows or ears eating the stronger ones likely indicates that the seven years of famine would be so severe that they will "swallow up" any remembrance of the bountiful years.

Famine, caused by drought, locusts, or other reasons, was mentioned in biblical references of several historical periods, including during the time of Abram (Genesis 12:10), Isaac (Genesis 26:1), Ruth (Ruth 1:1), David (2 Samuel 21:1; 24:13), Elijah (1 Kings 18:2), and Elisha (2 Kings 4:38). However, unlike Palestine, where rainfall was insufficient in quantity and very sporadic, Egypt's land was watered by the Nile, which drew not only upon rainfall but also rivers of northeastern Africa. Since Egypt had a thriving agricultural economy, famine there would have been seen as an unusual, though not unheard of, occurrence.

Genesis 41:32. Joseph interprets the fact that Pharaoh has had two dreams with essentially the same content as a sign that the dreams are a message from God concerning what God will do. In addition, Joseph makes it clear that time is of the essence. God will act soon.

Genesis 41:33-36. Interpreting the dream is all that Joseph was asked to do. Yet without waiting for Pharaoh to respond, Joseph launches into a speech offering specific advice to the Egyptian ruler, the most powerful monarch on earth. Boldly, Joseph suggests that Pharaoh look around for a man who is "discerning and wise," who can prepare Egypt to deal with the coming calamity. Is there any doubt about who Joseph has in mind? Of course, Joseph means himself! His intention becomes even clearer when he enumerates what this wise and discerning man should do in this crisis. He suggests that Pharaoh appoint "overseers" who are responsible for stockpiling grain reserves so as to be ready for the coming disaster. Commentators note that public storing of grain was a common practice in Egypt from early times.

Genesis 41:37-38. Joseph has convinced Pharaoh that his suggested course of action is correct. Pharaoh recognizes that God has revealed these things to Joseph, and so Joseph must be the one on whom the spirit of God rests. Pharaoh addresses his rhetorical question to the court, thus drawing them into accepting his conclusion.

Genesis 41:39-40. Not only does Pharaoh believe Joseph's interpretation of his dream, but he also decides that Joseph is the "discerning and wise" one who should be vested with authority to act to minimize the turmoil that will be created by the coming famine. Therefore, Pharaoh elevates Joseph to second in command throughout Egypt; only Pharaoh himself has greater authority. In a matter of a few hours, Joseph has gone from forgotten foreign prisoner to an influential and powerful figure in the kingdom of Egypt. In Egyptian documents, such a position is referred to as "vizier."

Genesis 41:41-43. Pharaoh makes his decision official by holding an installation ceremony. First, Pharaoh takes off the signet ring, which bore his seal, and places it on Joseph's hand as a sign that he has the authority to act on the king's behalf. Next, Pharaoh puts "garments of fine linen" on Joseph, for high government officials generally wore linen. This change of clothing not only signifies Joseph's change in status but may also remind us of the special robe Jacob had made for his son. The third symbol of his new power is the gold chain, worn by those Pharaoh chooses to honor. Finally, Pharaoh announces that as Joseph rides in a chariot, heralds will precede him, crying out for people to pay homage to him by kneeling.

Genesis 41:44. Joseph's power is almost limitless. From verse 46 we learn that Joseph is only thirty years old when he is elevated to his new position. From Genesis 37:2, we learn that he was seventeen years old when he made the fateful trip to find his brothers at Dothan. Hence, within a span of only thirteen years, Joseph has risen to a prominent position, second only to Pharaoh himself.

Genesis 41:45. Pharaoh gives Joseph a new name in acknowledgment of his new status. The Egyptian name Zaphanethpaneah means, "God speaks and lives." God has spoken through Joseph and opened the door to life and prosperity for Egypt—and the Israelites. Pharaoh also gives Joseph a wife, Asenath, the daughter of a priest from the nobility of Egypt. ("Joseph and Aseneth," which can be found in English translation on the Internet, tells an extra-biblical story of their relationship.) Elevated to a high political status and now married, Joseph is thus becoming more and more at home in Egypt. His earlier dreams are beginning to come true.

INTERPRETING THE SCRIPTURE

Joseph Interprets Pharaoh's Dreams

In the past few years we have heard a great deal about sexual harassment. Most companies have seminars on ways of coping with unwanted flirtation and other inappropriate behavior. Sexual impropriety is not new to our generation, however. In the first book of the Bible, Joseph was "framed" after he rejected Potiphar's wife's advances towards him. When she accused Joseph of trying to seduce her, Potiphar had him thrown in prison. Although he rose to prominence even in jail, Joseph was left there, forgotten by Pharaoh's chief cupbearer, who had promised to secure Joseph's freedom.

Finally, when Pharaoh's dreams had the whole royal establishment in a tizzy, the chief cupbearer remembered Joseph, and Pharaoh had him brought forth. Not only had he interpreted the dreams of the chief baker and the cupbearer his but also interpretation of their dreams was one hundred percent accurate. What Joseph predicted had come true.

Many folks in our day spend money to gain financial advice. Others seek personal counseling and guidance on all manner of issues. While the interpretation of dreams may not be as prominent as some of the other avenues of analysis, discernment is a key word in our vocabulary these days. All of us seek to know what is best as we face an uncertain future.

Joseph obviously had a gift for reading

and understanding the signs of the times. Never one to take credit for his pronouncements, though, Joseph always credited his interpretations to God. He saw himself as merely the one through which God spoke.

Some people in our own culture and network of acquaintances have the gift of spiritual discernment. Those who desire clarity in their lives seek them out. Like Joseph, they listen to the thoughts and dreams of those who need advice and direction, and then share what they see. Their advice often contains both practical and spiritual components. In the story of Joseph, the fact that Pharaoh believed Joseph's interpretation of his dreams and heeded his advice enhanced not only the physical but also the spiritual well-being of the entire human race. Thus God worked through Pharaoh's dreams and Joseph's insightful mind to enhance the quality of life, not just for these two prominent persons, but for everyone. It is amazing what can happen when hearts are in tune with God!

Disasters Can Be Averted!

Most of us in the western world had never heard of a "tsunami." At Christmastime in 2004, "tsunami" suddenly became a household word. The southern United States will be recovering for years from hurricanes Katrina and Rita, which struck in August and September, 2005, respectively. A few weeks later in October, 2005, an earthquake in Pakistan killed thousands. It is human nature to ask why God allows these natural disasters to happen. Perhaps the power of God in nature is beyond our ability to discern. There are other lessons that come from encountering disasters, however. People often come together in amazing ways when tragedies occur. In a time of peril, our common humanity is underscored. Furthermore, it is inspiring to see the human spirit of perseverance prevail against all odds.

Sometimes we are able to see disaster brewing, and we are able to act to avert its worst effects. Such was the case in Egypt when Joseph, through the interpretation of Pharaoh's dreams, was able to see seven years of famine ahead. Joseph wisely realized that starvation could be averted if grain was stored during the "seven years of great plenty" (Genesis 41:29).

Pharaoh's dreams helped shape the future. God established the future to which the dreams pointed. At the same time, the full future that the dreams opened up depended on both God's involvement and wise decisions on the part of Pharaoh.

We always have a role in shaping the future. Even though our choices may be limited, God always gives us a part to play. That is the challenge of living responsibly in God's world!

God Works through Pharaoh

The Egyptian people worshiped Pharaoh, believing that he was divine. The Hebrews would have found this notion repugnant, for the God of Abraham was not a local deity, nor did the Jewish patriarchs ever claim that they were divine. Ironically, though, the biblical writers were able to see that God could work outside their religious sphere in economics and government to advance God's purposes. Sometimes God worked through secular rulers in ways that the rulers themselves did not recognize, including communicating with and through a dreamer!

God is not limited to one community or to our perception of how God works. The story of Joseph and the famine in Egypt testifies to the significant levels of divine activity outside the community of faith. When Pharaoh hears Joseph's interpretation, heeds his words, and begins saving grain for the lean years, he is acting to help God's chosen people survive and prosper, even though he had no knowledge of that when he made those decisions.

In retrospect, we can look back and see how God has worked in our lives and in the life of our community. God often works in unlikely places and uses the most unlikely people to accomplish divine purposes. Sometimes people are unaware that their actions benefit others. Yet God is able to use various people and situations to advance God's intentions for humanity.

God Works through Joseph

Joseph has come a long way since his tattletale days in Canaan. Since arriving in Egypt, he has demonstrated patience through numerous setbacks and deep suffering. He has remained loyal to God through many temptations, including the offer of Potiphar's wife to have a sexual liaison. His bold speech, especially in the presence of persons and systems of power, reveals his courage and his integrity. He acts wisely and in a discerning manner in all of his dealings with people and their problems. Joseph stands as a model of the godly life for persons living in a secular sphere.

Because Joseph is bold and assertive, he is able to rise politically with surprising rapidity. Thus he quickly finds himself in a place where God can use him to great advantage. Do we assert ourselves at appropriate times and places? Do we use our gifts and abilities to their fullest advantage? What does Joseph's story say to you and to me?

By the time Joseph was thirty years old, his dreams had come true. He was the number two man in Egypt, one of the most powerful rulers in the world of that day. Yet Joseph does not boast about what he has done or will do. Joseph does not take the credit for his interpretation of dreams or his wisdom. He always gives the credit to God.

Because Joseph is open to God's leadership and puts himself at God's disposal, God is able to use Joseph in a way that blesses the whole human race. When we seek God's will for our lives and consciously strive to follow the path where we believe God is calling us to walk, God will use us in ways that we do not initially envision. Thus Joseph is a role model for all of us—a role model not only of integrity, but an example of one who was willing to give his total self and his best energy to seeking God's will and following God's direction for his life.

SHARING THE SCRIPTURE

Preparing Our Hearts

Meditate on this week's devotional reading, found in Psalm 105:16-22. This passage within a psalm extolling God's faithfulness to Israel uses Joseph as an example of one through whom God fulfilled promises. Think about how you would have responded to the trials that Joseph underwent, as recorded by the psalmist. Could you "hang on" and await the fulfillment of divine promises? Write in your spiritual journal about how you perceive God at work in unlikely places and people, perhaps even yourself.

Pray that you and the adult learners will recognize that even though God sometimes works in apparently mysterious ways God's purposes are ultimately fulfilled.

Preparing Our Minds

Study the background, Genesis 41:25-45 and lesson Scripture, Genesis 41:25-40. As you read, consider how God sometimes works in amazing ways to fulfill promises.

Write on newsprint:
❏ information for next week's lesson, found under "Continue the Journey."
❏ activities for further spiritual growth in "Continue the Journey."

Option: Find pictures of famine-stricken areas in magazines or on the Internet. Post them in the classroom as a visible reminder of the disaster that will come upon Egypt in seven years. Or, set up one or more shocks of corn or grain that may be available in your area at this time.

Option: Prepare a lecture for "Explore the Story of Joseph's Interpretation of Pharaoh's Dream, and Pharaoh's Response to Joseph."

LEADING THE CLASS

(1) Gather to Learn

❖ Welcome the class members and introduce any guests.

❖ Pray that all who have gathered today will be open to God's re-creative power in their lives.

❖ Invite the students to talk with a partner or the class about a time when they saw God's purpose fulfilled or promise kept, perhaps in an unexpected way.

❖ Read aloud today's focus statement: **God's purposes are sometimes fulfilled in amazing ways. How, for example, did God work through Joseph to fulfill divine promises made to the covenant people? God gave Joseph the ability to interpret a dream for Pharaoh, who responded by elevating Joseph to a position of power, just as Joseph himself had dreamed.**

(2) Explore the Story of Joseph's Interpretation of Pharaoh's Dream, and Pharaoh's Response to Joseph

❖ Choose a volunteer to read the part of Joseph and one to read the words of Pharaoh in Genesis 41:25-40 as if they are holding a conversation. You may read verse 37, which is the narrator's only line. If you have brought pictures of famine or shocks of corn, ask the students to focus on these as the story is read.

❖ Discuss the following questions with the class, or prepare answers and present them in an optional lecture. Use information in Understanding the Scripture to assist you.

(1) **What is the significance of two dreams, one with the image of cattle and the other with the image of ears of grain?** (Genesis 41:32)

(2) **Since Joseph was asked only to interpret the dream, why do you think he advised Pharaoh as to how to handle the situation?** (Genesis 41:33-36)

(3) **How did Pharaoh respond to Joseph's ideas?** (Genesis 41:39-40)

(4) **Although this conversation turned out well for Joseph, what risks do you think he took in speaking so boldly before Pharaoh?**

(5) **In light of all that Joseph has endured, what words would you use to describe him?**

❖ Read aloud the third and fourth paragraphs of "God Works through Joseph" in Interpreting the Scripture.

❖ Invite the students to comment on how Joseph's openness to God and willingness to give God credit enabled his dreams to be fulfilled and God's will to be done.

❖ Ask: **How can Joseph be a role model for Christians today?**

❖ Conclude this portion of the lesson by reading in unison Genesis 41:39, today's key verse.

(3) Affirm That God's Promises Cannot Be Thwarted

❖ Point out that Joseph was the one through whom God would preserve the Hebrew people. Yet, Joseph found himself enslaved and imprisoned. It would appear that God's covenant promise would be thwarted, that Jacob and his family would die from starvation, but that did not prove to be the case.

❖ Invite the class to recall some of God's promises and discern whether they have been kept, kept despite obstacles, or somehow thwarted. Here are some promises you may want to use if you need to spark discussion.

■ Noah was assured by God that there would never again be a global flood (Genesis 9:8-17).

■ God promised Abraham a male heir, descendants as numerous as the stars, and a land (Genesis 15).

■ Through the prophet Nathan, God told David that his royal line would last forever (2 Samuel 7:16).

❖ Encourage the students to speak about any promises that they believe God has made to them and how these promises have been kept, kept despite obstacles, or thwarted.

❖ End this portion by reading these words of Colin Urquhart (1940—): **God is the God of promise. He keeps his word, even when that seems impossible; even when the circumstances seem to point to the opposite.**

❖ Invite the students who can affirm these words to say: **Amen and Amen.**

(4) Look in Unlikely Places to See God at Work in Unlikely Ways

❖ Divide the class into groups and give each group newsprint and a marker. Set a time limit and ask each group to list as many unlikely places as they can where they see God at work. Examples include: disaster sites, prisons, or countries where Christianity has been repressed.

❖ Ask each group to present their ideas to the class.

❖ Discern together if the class members can bring more of God's love and light to any of these situations, either in person or through gifts of goods or money.

❖ Talk about how recognizing God's presence and work in places where people feel hopeless can strengthen not only their faith but ours as well.

❖ Distribute paper and pencils. Encourage the adults to write a sentence or two concerning action they will take in light of this discussion.

(5) Continue the Journey

❖ Pray that the participants will go forth envisioning God's dreams for them and acting on what they believe God would have them to do.

❖ Read aloud this preparation for next week's lesson. You may also want to post it on newsprint for the students to copy.

■ **Title: God Preserved a Remnant**

■ **Background Scripture: Genesis 43:1–45:15**

■ **Lesson Scripture: Genesis 45:1-12**

■ **Focus of the Lesson: Often in retrospect, even the worst situation may have positive significance. How do we explain the good that comes out of such terrible circumstances? Joseph told his brothers that God had sent him to Egypt to preserve a remnant of the family of promise.**

❖ Challenge the students to complete one or more of these activities for further spiritual growth, which you will write on newsprint for the students to copy.

(1) **Visit a place that seems unlikely for God to be at work. Do what you can to bring the message of God's love to those in this place.**

(2) **Recall examples of dreams becoming reality in your life or in the life of someone significant to you. How did you see God at work here?**

(3) **Search your Bible and write in your journal at least one promise of God that is special to you. Claim this promise. Refer to it often as you watch how it is fulfilled in your life.**

❖ Sing or read aloud "Standing on the Promises."

❖ Conclude today's session by leading the class in this benediction, which is adapted from Genesis 14:19-20: **Blessed be you by God Most High, maker of heaven and earth; and blessed be God Most High.**

UNIT 3: GOD'S PEOPLE RE-CREATED
GOD PRESERVED A REMNANT

PREVIEWING THE LESSON

Lesson Scripture: Genesis 45:1-12
Background Scripture: Genesis 43:1–45:15
Key Verse: Genesis 45:7

Focus of the Lesson:
Often in retrospect, even the worst situation may have positive significance. How do we explain the good that comes out of such terrible circumstances? Joseph told his brothers that God had sent him to Egypt to preserve a remnant of the family of promise.

Goals for the Learners:
(1) to focus attention on the climax of the Joseph story.
(2) to identify times in their lives when God transformed bleak circumstances into positive outcomes.
(3) to give thanks for God's continuing presence in their lives.

Pronunciation Guide:
Asenath (as' uh nath)
Goshen (goh' shuhn)
Potiphar (pot' uh fuhr)

Supplies:
Bibles, newsprint and marker, paper and pencils, hymnals

READING THE SCRIPTURE

NRSV
Genesis 45:1-12

¹Then Joseph could no longer control himself before all those who stood by him, and he cried out, "Send everyone away from me." So no one stayed with him when Joseph made himself known to his brothers. ²And he wept so loudly that the Egyptians

NIV
Genesis 45:1-12

¹Then Joseph could no longer control himself before all his attendants, and he cried out, "Have everyone leave my presence!" So there was no one with Joseph when he made himself known to his brothers. ²And he wept so loudly that the

heard it, and the household of Pharaoh heard it. ³Joseph said to his brothers, "I am Joseph. Is my father still alive?" But his brothers could not answer him, so dismayed were they at his presence.

⁴Then Joseph said to his brothers, "Come closer to me." And they came closer. He said, "I am your brother, Joseph, whom you sold into Egypt. ⁵And now do not be distressed, or angry with yourselves, because you sold me here; for God sent me before you to preserve life. ⁶For the famine has been in the land these two years; and there are five more years in which there will be neither plowing nor harvest. ⁷**God sent me before you to preserve for you a remnant on earth, and to keep alive for you many survivors.** ⁸So it was not you who sent me here, but God; he has made me a father to Pharaoh, and lord of all his house and ruler over all the land of Egypt. ⁹Hurry and go up to my father and say to him, 'Thus says your son Joseph, God has made me lord of all Egypt; come down to me, do not delay. ¹⁰You shall settle in the land of Goshen, and you shall be near me, you and your children and your children's children, as well as your flocks, your herds, and all that you have. ¹¹I will provide for you there—since there are five more years of famine to come—so that you and your household, and all that you have, will not come to poverty.' ¹²And now your eyes and the eyes of my brother Benjamin see that it is my own mouth that speaks to you.

Egyptians heard him, and Pharaoh's household heard about it.

³Joseph said to his brothers, "I am Joseph! Is my father still living?" But his brothers were not able to answer him, because they were terrified at his presence.

⁴Then Joseph said to his brothers, "Come close to me." When they had done so, he said, "I am your brother Joseph, the one you sold into Egypt! ⁵And now, do not be distressed and do not be angry with yourselves for selling me here, because it was to save lives that God sent me ahead of you. ⁶For two years now there has been famine in the land, and for the next five years there will not be plowing and reaping. ⁷**But God sent me ahead of you to preserve for you a remnant on earth and to save your lives by a great deliverance.**

⁸"So then, it was not you who sent me here, but God. He made me father to Pharaoh, lord of his entire household and ruler of all Egypt. ⁹Now hurry back to my father and say to him, 'This is what your son Joseph says: God has made me lord of all Egypt. Come down to me; don't delay. ¹⁰You shall live in the region of Goshen and be near me—you, your children and grandchildren, your flocks and herds, and all you have. ¹¹I will provide for you there, because five years of famine are still to come. Otherwise you and your household and all who belong to you will become destitute.'

¹²"You can see for yourselves, and so can my brother Benjamin, that it is really I who am speaking to you.

UNDERSTANDING THE SCRIPTURE

Genesis 43:1-2. During the seven years of plenty, Joseph stockpiled grain against the evil days to come. As the famine spread, "all the world came to Joseph in Egypt to buy grain" (41:57). Because of the severity of the famine, Jacob again tells his

sons to go to Egypt for food, just as Joseph has anticipated.

Genesis 43:3-10. Judah reminds Jacob about the stern warning "the man" had given them about returning with Benjamin. (As the brothers leave Egypt after their first food-buying trip, Joseph insists that they bring Benjamin when they return, and then proceeds to hold Simeon hostage.) Jacob, or Israel as he is called in this story, wonders why his sons had even mentioned another brother. The ten brothers reply that it was in response to Joseph's questioning. Actually, the brothers volunteered this information, causing the reader to question whether the brothers are the "honest men" they purport to be (42:11). Judah's speech is highly persuasive, and Israel realizes that he must allow Benjamin to go.

Genesis 43:11-15. Reminiscent of his meeting with Esau, Israel sends an array of lavish gifts to "the man." The brothers are also to take double the money found in their grain sacks, and Benjamin will go too. Then Israel pronounces a benediction upon the success of the journey and resigns himself to whatever may come.

Genesis 43:16-25. The brothers follow their father's direction and proceed to Egypt. They are received cordially this time. Joseph invites them to dinner. They suspect a trap, and so take the initiative to tell the steward about the money that mysteriously appeared in their sacks of grain. They share with him that they are returning the money and have brought additional money for grain. Curiously, the steward says that God must have refilled the sacks for the money owed had been received. Simeon is returned, and the brothers prepare for dinner.

Genesis 43:26-28. When Joseph arrives, the brothers bow before him, reminding us of Joseph's dream (37:7). At the same time, the brothers' obeisance to Joseph indicates that their relationship with him remains formal and difficult, for they still do not recognize him.

Genesis 43:29-31. His encounter with Benjamin moves Joseph to the point that he excuses himself to weep in private.

Genesis 43:32-34. The meal is served separately to Joseph, to his brothers, and to the Egyptian members of Joseph's entourage. The brothers are seated according to age,

which astonishes them. Once again favorites are played. Benjamin's portion is five times what the others have to eat.

Genesis 44:1-5. Joseph does not desire to profit from his family's need for food. He ensures that his family has food by directing his steward to put food in the brothers' sacks for their return home to Canaan. The steward is also to include money. These directions sound like the ones Joseph gave for the first return trip (42:25), but this time his silver cup is also to be buried in Benjamin's sack. Joseph dispatches a steward to go after them soon after they leave. The steward accuses them of stealing Joseph's silver cup. Supposedly Joseph uses the cup for divinations, that is, seeking the meaning of events through observing patterns in the liquid at the bottom of the cup.

Genesis 44:6-13. Upon being accused, the brothers deny their guilt and cite the return of the money as evidence of their integrity. Why would they return the money, then steal it again? The steward agrees that the person found with the cup shall be enslaved while the rest can go free. When the cup is found in Benjamin's sack, the brothers are beside themselves. They tear their clothes in grief. Rather than going home to Canaan to face their father without Benjamin, they return to Egypt to confront Joseph.

Genesis 44:14-17. As the brothers lay prostrate before Joseph, he accuses them just as the steward had. Speaking on behalf of the group, Judah admits that they are completely under Joseph's authority. Joseph will allow all the brothers to return to their father, except the one who has the cup. That one will become his slave. Joseph knows, however, that Benjamin has the cup and that the brothers cannot return to their father without him. Will they treat Benjamin the way they once treated Joseph? Will they allow Benjamin to become a slave while they might go free?

Genesis 44:18-34. Judah makes an impassioned speech, "the longest in Genesis and a literary masterpiece," according to Terrence

Fretheim, writing in *The New Interpreter's Bible*. Unbeknownst to Judah, this speech reveals to Joseph Jacob's initial reaction and continued mourning for his beloved son. Judah offers to take Benjamin's place as a slave in Joseph's household if only his brother may be redeemed. Judah speaks straightforwardly and sincerely, explaining that the matter of Benjamin's return is a matter of life and death for Jacob. The effect of the speech on Joseph is overpowering, and the narrative moves swiftly to its conclusion.

Genesis 45:1-2. Joseph sends his servants away so that no one will hear when he reveals himself to his brothers. However, he weeps so loudly that the Egyptians hear him anyway.

Genesis 45:3. Joseph announces his identity, then in light of Judah's speech, asks if his father is still alive. The brothers are literally struck dumb by this revelation. They are fearful and taken aback.

Genesis 45:4. Joseph invites his brothers to come closer as he repeats, "I am your brother, Joseph, whom you sold into Egypt."

Genesis 45:5-8. Joseph is aware that his brothers are distressed and terrified. Since he has absolute power over them, Joseph could have taken many different kinds of actions to shame, blame, and punish his brothers. Instead, he tells them that everything has been in God's hands. The brothers are not absolved of their guilt, but they can rest assured that God has transformed their actions for God's own purposes. God has used the brothers' evil intent in sending Joseph to Egypt as a means of preserving life, rather than destroying it.

Genesis 45:9-15. Joseph wants to preserve his family's life. He tells his brothers to rush home, tell their father what has happened, and then return with the entire family and their possessions to settle near him in the land of Goshen. Joseph assures them that he will provide for all their needs during the continuing famine. The brothers now speak with Joseph, unlike the old days when they "could not speak peaceably to him" (37:4).

INTERPRETING THE SCRIPTURE

An Emotional Reunion

I love to watch the expression on people's faces as they come into the terminal after getting off an airplane. Some walk with a spring in their step, but most seem tired and weary. Then they spot the family members or friends who are waiting for them, and their whole demeanor changes. Suddenly their faces break into smiles, and their posture improves dramatically!

A flood of emotion must have come over Joseph when he saw his brothers after years of separation. Although Joseph had adopted the dress and style of the Egyptians, causing his brothers not to recognize him, he knew them instantly! They had not changed! They

were still doing their father's bidding, coming to Egypt to buy food for the clan.

Because Joseph's identity was not obvious to his brothers, he had some time to process his feelings. Even after years had passed, he could not "forgive and forget." Desiring some degree of revenge, he put the brothers through quite an ordeal.

But enough is enough! Eventually he could no longer contain his deep feelings for his family, and so he revealed his identity to them. In an unashamed display of emotion, Joseph "wept so loudly that the Egyptians heard it, and the household of Pharaoh heard it" (Genesis 45:2).

Joseph may have been ready to "bury the hatchet" and get on with his life but, alas, the news was so overwhelming to his brothers that they were speechless. They assumed Joseph had been taken to one of Pharaoh's construction sites never to be heard from again. Little did they expect to see him in Pharaoh's court! Moreover, as the number two man in all Egypt, they were beholden to him for their food and ultimately for their lives. Should he decide to throw them in prison or even execute them, they had little recourse. No wonder the NIV tells us that the brothers were "terrified at his presence" (45:3).

God's Ways Are Higher Than Our Ways

In Isaiah 55:9 we read, "For as the heavens are higher than the earth, so are my ways higher than your ways and my thoughts than your thoughts." Seeing the look of terror on the faces of his brothers, Joseph tries to reassure them. The brothers acted out of hatred and resentment by putting Joseph in the pit. Intending to sell him to the caravan of Ishmaelites who were on their way to Egypt, the Midianites beat them to the draw. At any rate, they intended to get Joseph out of their lives.

Joseph always managed to land on his feet! When he was sold into Egypt, he rose rapidly through the ranks to become the "chief of staff" of Potiphar's house. When he was sentenced to a jail term unjustly, he ascended to a position of prominence. Then when he was summoned to Pharaoh's court and was able to interpret Pharaoh's dreams, he again rose to a position of leadership, this time to be Pharaoh's right-hand man.

Never one to pat himself on the back, Joseph always gave the credit to God. He was always able to see God's hand at work, even in his times of seeming misfortune. According to Joseph, while the brothers thought they were getting rid of him, God was able to use this turn of events "to preserve life" (45:5). God used Joseph not only to keep his own family alive, but also to benefit the whole human race: "So it was

not you who sent me here, but God," Joseph exclaims (45:8). Joseph is more than the eternal optimist. He is a person of deep faith.

Many times we face bleak and discouraging circumstances in life. Earthquakes, hurricanes, and calamities of every type occur with shocking regularity. Disease seems beyond our ability to overcome or control. Violence and war take a toll on every country, and human relations are often strained to the breaking point. What are we to make of all this? I do not believe that God causes misfortune. But God can weave tragedy and difficult situations into God's life-giving purposes. Are we able to see God's hand at work, in spite of the evil that is so clearly identifiable?

Joseph Seeks Reconciliation

In spite of his antics when his brothers came to town, it is obvious that Joseph had "moved on" with his life. He had not spent his years in Egypt feeling sorry for himself and plotting ways to get even with his jealous brothers. When he reveals himself to them, Joseph is eager for reconciliation. To that end, he tries to reassure them that he has forgiven them and that he wants what is best for them.

The brothers are wary of Joseph at best. He has "jerked them around." They also remember the old days all too well. Now, ironically, Joseph's dreams have come true and they are before him on bended knee.

How hard it is to forgive and forget! Family grudges that go back years, even generations, continue to shape our behavior. How hard it is to let go! Yet we will never be free to live the life that God intends until we accept God's forgiveness and then, in turn, forgive our brothers and sisters for the times they have wronged us.

Joseph did not simply give lip service to his desire for reconciliation. He put "feet to his prayers." Not only did he give his brothers the food they needed, he invited them to "settle in the land of Goshen" (45:10). In this way, Joseph demonstrated that he genuinely cared about his family's welfare.

It must have taken incredible intestinal fortitude for the brothers to swallow their pride and move to Goshen. After all, they had gotten rid of their little brother because they were fed up with the way he lorded his delusions of grandeur over them. Now they had to eat humble pie if they wanted to eat at all!

My mother always says, "What goes around comes around." Many times our words and our actions come back to haunt us. We need to think before we speak and before we act. Joseph's brothers would attest to that.

The brothers did, in fact, "come around." To their credit, they were able to swallow their pride and accept the provisions of Egypt from the hand of their brother. Are we able to do what is best for our families and their future, or does our pride get in the way? The story of Joseph forces us to ask that question. The story also prompts us to consider how God works to bring good out of very difficult circumstances.

SHARING THE SCRIPTURE

Preparing Our Hearts

Meditate on this week's devotional reading, found in Psalm 85. Here the psalmist writes a lament on behalf of the community asking for divine favor to be restored to Israel. God has saved Israel in the past, and the psalmist believes that God is ready and willing to save them again. Note verses 10-13, considered to be one of the best examples of poetry in the Psalms. As you ponder Psalm 85, think about how God has looked upon you favorably, forgiven you, and restored you. Give thanks for God's steadfast love and mercy.

Pray that you and the adult learners will trust God to work in God's own time.

Preparing Our Minds

Study the background, Genesis 43:1–45:15, and lesson Scripture, Genesis 45:1-12. Think about how we explain the good that can come out of even the worst situation.

Write on newsprint:
❏ timeline of Joseph's life for "Focus Attention on the Climax of the Joseph Story."

❏ information for next week's lesson, found under "Continue the Journey."
❏ activities for further spiritual growth in "Continue the Journey."

LEADING THE CLASS

(1) Gather to Learn

❖ Welcome the class members and introduce any guests.

❖ Pray that today's participants will be open to the amazing works that God performs.

❖ Read aloud this excerpt from Rabbi Harold Kushner's *When Bad Things Happen to Good People.* **Martin Gray, a survivor of the Warsaw Ghetto and the Holocaust, writes of his life in a book called *For Those I Loved.* He tells how, after the Holocaust, he rebuilt his life, became successful, married, and raised a family. Life seemed good after the horrors of the concentration camp.**

Then one day, his wife and children were killed when a forest fire ravaged their home in the south of France. Gray was distraught, pushed almost to the breaking point by this added tragedy.

People urged him to demand an inquiry into what caused the fire, but instead he chose to put his resources into a movement to protect nature from future fires.

He explained that an inquiry, an investigation, would focus only on the past, on issues of pain and sorrow and blame. He wanted to focus on the future. An inquiry would set him against other people—"was someone negligent? whose fault was it?"—and being against other people, setting out to find a villain, accusing other people of being responsible for your misery, only makes a lonely person lonelier. Life, he concluded, has to be lived for something, not just against something.

We too need to get over the questions that focus on the past and on the pain—"why did this happen to me?"—and ask instead the question which opens doors to the future: "Now that this has happened, what shall I do about it?"

❖ Discuss these questions. **In the midst of a horrible situation Martin Gray chose to see what good could come out of it. Have you ever tried this strategy? What was the result?**

❖ Read aloud today's focus statement: **Often in retrospect, even the worst situation may have positive significance. How do we explain the good that comes out of such terrible circumstances? Joseph told his brothers that God had sent him to Egypt to preserve a remnant of the family of promise.**

(2) Focus Attention on the Climax of the Joseph Story

❖ Post this information on newsprint, or review it verbally, to highlight the events that have brought Joseph to the place where we meet him in today's lesson.

■ **Born first child of Rachel and eleventh child of Jacob (Genesis 30:22-24).**

■ **Father's favorite son; about age seventeen given a "long robe with sleeves"; tattletale who was hated by his brothers (Genesis 37:1-4).**

■ **Has dreams of power and preeminence (Genesis 37:5-11).**

■ **Put in a pit and sold by his brothers and taken to Egypt; brothers take his blood-stained coat to Jacob, who assumes Joseph is dead and mourns for his son (Genesis 37:12-36).**

■ **Bought by Potiphar and worked in his home; accused by Potiphar's wife of sexual advances; imprisoned (Genesis 39).**

■ **Interprets dreams of cupbearer and baker while in prison (Genesis 40).**

■ **Two years later called to interpret Pharaoh's dream regarding coming years of plenty and famine (Genesis 41:1-36).**

■ **Becomes second only to Pharaoh and in charge of stewardship of food at age thirty; given a wife named Asenath (Genesis 41:37-57).**

■ **Jacob sends brothers (except Benjamin) to get food in Egypt so they will survive famine; Joseph recognized brothers, but they did not recognize him; accused brothers of being spies; imprisoned them for three days; let them return home to get Benjamin but held Simeon hostage; once home, they realized money was in their sacks (Genesis 42).**

■ **Brothers return with Benjamin; return money but told no money was missing; fed dinner; Joseph plots to detain Benjamin; Judah makes an impassioned speech for Benjamin's release (Genesis 43–44).**

❖ Choose readers for the parts of Joseph and the narrator. Select other students to mime the parts of the brothers and Joseph using simple movements as the story is read from Genesis 45:1-12.

❖ Read aloud the third paragraph of "Joseph Seeks Reconciliation" in

Interpreting the Scripture. Allow time for students to comment on these ideas.

❖ Discuss these questions.

(1) **What evidence suggests that Joseph wanted to be reconciled with his brothers?**

(2) **How would you have felt had you been Reuben, who had suggested that Joseph be thrown into a pit rather than killed?**

(3) **How would you have felt if you had been Judah, who hatched the plan of selling him to traders?**

(3) Identify Times in the Learner's Lives When God Transformed Bleak Circumstances into Positive Outcomes

❖ Recall the story of Martin Gray that we looked at in the "Gather to Learn" portion.

❖ Divide the students into small groups. Ask each person to tell the group about a time when God transformed bleak circumstances of their lives into positive outcomes. (Be aware that some students may not feel they have such stories to tell. Others may find memories too painful to share. Remind them that not all events are as dramatic as Martin Gray's.)

❖ Bring the class together and ask: **What impact do such experiences have on our relationship with God?**

(4) Give Thanks for God's Continuing Presence in the Learners' Lives

❖ Read the third paragraph of "God's Ways Are Higher Than Our Ways" in Interpreting the Scripture, which highlights Joseph's sense of God's continuing presence.

❖ Distribute paper and pencils. Encourage the students to write a psalm or prayer or hymn of thanks for God's continuing presence and power that can bring good out of terrible situations.

(5) Continue the Journey

❖ Pray that everyone who has come will recognize how God can transform bad things into good outcomes.

❖ Read aloud this preparation for next week's lesson. You may also want to post it on newsprint for the students to copy.

■ Title: Jacob Blessed His Family
■ Background Scripture: Genesis 48:8-21
■ Lesson Scripture: Genesis 48:11-19
■ Focus of the Lesson: One generation dies and another is born. What legacies do older generations want to leave for younger ones? Jacob moved to Egypt and lived out his last days; he blessed his grandsons, assured that they would continue to grow into a multitude, just as God had promised Abraham and Sarah.

❖ Challenge the students to complete one or more of these activities for further spiritual growth, which you will write on newsprint for the students to copy.

(1) **Talk with one or more recent immigrants to learn why they came to your country and community and how they adjusted to a new culture.**

(2) **Recall an incident in your own life that seemed like a calamity at the time but could later be interpreted as a blessing in disguise. Journal about how you did show—or could have shown—trust in God during this difficult time.**

(3) **Do whatever is in your power to restore a relationship with someone who has hurt or betrayed you.**

❖ Sing or read aloud "Blessed Be the Name."

❖ Conclude today's session by leading the class in this benediction, which is adapted from Genesis 14:19-20: **Blessed be you by God Most High, maker of heaven and earth; and blessed be God Most High.**

UNIT 3: GOD'S PEOPLE RE-CREATED
JACOB BLESSED HIS FAMILY

PREVIEWING THE LESSON

Lesson Scripture: Genesis 48:11-19
Background Scripture: Genesis 48:8-21
Key Verse: Genesis 48:11

Focus of the Lesson:
One generation dies and another is born. What legacies do older generations want to leave for younger ones? Jacob moved to Egypt and lived out his last days; he blessed his grandsons, assured that they would continue to grow into a multitude, just as God had promised Abraham and Sarah.

Goals for the Learners:
(1) to examine the story of Jacob's blessing of Joseph's sons, Ephraim and Manasseh.
(2) to feel more closely connected to their own heirs and ancestors.
(3) to make a commitment to live so as to leave a legacy of Christ-like character.

Pronunciation Guide:
Ephraim (ee' fray im)
Manasseh (muh nas' uh)
Shechem (shek' uhm)

Supplies:
Bibles, newsprint and marker, paper and pencils, hymnals, current world map, small sticky notes

---

READING THE SCRIPTURE

NRSV
Genesis 48:11-19

¹¹Israel said to Joseph, "I did not expect to see your face; and here God has let me see your children also." ¹²Then Joseph removed them from his father's knees, and he bowed himself with his face to the earth. ¹³Joseph took them both, Ephraim in his

NIV
Genesis 48:11-19

¹¹Israel said to Joseph, "I never expected to see your face again, and now God has allowed me to see your children too."

¹²Then Joseph removed them from Israel's knees and bowed down with his face to the ground. ¹³And Joseph took both of

right hand toward Israel's left, and Manasseh in his left hand toward Israel's right, and brought them near him. ¹⁴But Israel stretched out his right hand and laid it on the head of Ephraim, who was the younger, and his left hand on the head of Manasseh, crossing his hands, for Manasseh was the firstborn. ¹⁵He blessed Joseph, and said,

"The God before whom my ancestors Abraham and Isaac walked,

the God who has been my shepherd all my life to this day,

¹⁶the angel who has redeemed me from all harm, bless the boys;

and in them let my name be perpetuated, and the name of my ancestors Abraham and Isaac;

and let them grow into a multitude on the earth."

¹⁷When Joseph saw that his father laid his right hand on the head of Ephraim, it displeased him; so he took his father's hand, to remove it from Ephraim's head to Manasseh's head. ¹⁸Joseph said to his father, "Not so, my father! Since this one is the firstborn, put your right hand on his head." ¹⁹But his father refused, and said, "I know, my son, I know; he also shall become a people, and he also shall be great. Nevertheless his younger brother shall be greater than he, and his offspring shall become a multitude of nations."

them, Ephraim on his right toward Israel's left hand and Manasseh on his left toward Israel's right hand, and brought them close to him. ¹⁴But Israel reached out his right hand and put it on Ephraim's head, though he was the younger, and crossing his arms, he put his left hand on Manasseh's head, even though Manasseh was the firstborn.

¹⁵Then he blessed Joseph and said,

"May the God before whom my fathers
　　Abraham and Isaac walked,

the God who has been my shepherd
　　all my life to this day,

¹⁶the Angel who has delivered me from all
　　harm

—may he bless these boys.

　　May they be called by my name

　　and the names of my fathers Abraham
　　　　and Isaac,

　　and may they increase greatly

　　upon the earth."

¹⁷When Joseph saw his father placing his right hand on Ephraim's head he was displeased; so he took hold of his father's hand to move it from Ephraim's head to Manasseh's head. ¹⁸Joseph said to him, "No, my father, this one is the firstborn; put your right hand on his head."

¹⁹But his father refused and said, "I know, my son, I know. He too will become a people, and he too will become great. Nevertheless, his younger brother will be greater than he, and his descendants will become a group of nations."

UNDERSTANDING THE SCRIPTURE

Genesis 48:8. When Joseph learns that his father Jacob (often referred to here as Israel, see Genesis 35:10) is gravely ill, he takes his two sons, Manasseh and Ephraim, to their grandfather. Although the sons were born of an Egyptian mother, Jacob adopts them as his own sons, "just as Reuben and Simeon are" (48:5), in a legal act, which was accompanied by a ceremony apparently so well

known as to require no description. A ritual of blessing concludes the adoption ceremony. Although one could imply from Jacob's question "Who are these?" that he is meeting his grandsons for the first time, in actuality the children's identity must be verified as part of the blessing ritual.

Genesis 48:9. Joseph considers that his sons are God's gift to him.

Genesis 48:10-11. Because he has trouble seeing, Jacob asks that the boys be brought closer to him so he can bless them. After kissing them and embracing them, Jacob exclaims that he never expected to see Joseph alive again after the incident with the brothers many years ago. Yet now he is privileged not only to see Joseph, but to live long enough to see Joseph's sons as well!

Genesis 48:12. By placing the boys on his knees, Jacob symbolically legitimizes the status of Manasseh and Ephraim as sons. Joseph takes the boys from his father's lap. Then Joseph bows his face to the earth, a gesture of honor.

Genesis 48:13. Joseph takes each boy by the hand, carefully placing Ephraim on Joseph's right side toward his father's left hand and Manasseh on Joseph's left side toward his father's right hand so that with his poor eyesight Israel will not have trouble distinguishing the older from the younger.

Genesis 48:14. Apparently Israel can see better than his son thinks he can! He takes his right hand and places it on Ephraim's head, and then reaches across and places his left hand on the head of Manasseh. The person who receives the blessing from the person's right hand has the more favored status, and so the placement of Israel's hands is highly significant.

Genesis 48:15-16. As he bestows the blessing, Jacob's words appear to treat equally Ephraim and Manasseh, who he has just adopted. He begins a three-part invocation in liturgical language similar to Aaron's benediction in Numbers 6:24-26.

(1) God is the one before whom Abraham and Isaac have walked. God's action preceded their response. Their faithfulness provides a backdrop for what Jacob now has to say to his son and his grandsons.

(2) God is the one who has been Jacob's shepherd all the days of his life. The image of God as shepherd includes the ideas of guidance, protection, and the provision of sustenance for the journey. No doubt Jacob draws this image of God from his own experience as a shepherd.

(3) Finally, God is the one who has redeemed Jacob from all harm. Jacob's reference to the godly work of angels recalls his dream in Genesis 28:10-17. In this dream, God promised to be with Jacob and not leave him.

Genesis 48:17-19. When he sees that Jacob has crossed his hands, Joseph interrupts the ritual, thinking of Jacob's failing sight. Joseph tries to switch Jacob's hands, but Jacob calmly resists, knowing full well what he is doing. Is Jacob remembering his own story, when his father (also nearly blind) gave him the blessing originally meant for his older brother? He explains that both sons will become great leaders and have large families and many offspring. However, Ephraim's descendants will truly be preeminent, so prominent that "Ephraim" will become another name for the entire northern kingdom. According to commentators, Israelites believed that Jacob's act of putting Ephraim ahead of Manasseh accounted, in part, for the later history of these tribes. While both tribes were powerful during the early years, Ephraim became the more powerful by the time of King David.

Genesis 48:20. Jacob now gives the second blessing to each son. Again we are to assume that the words are the same. However, Jacob puts "Ephraim ahead of Manasseh." The sons' names can be invoked when the people of Israel bless others: "God bless you as God has blessed Ephraim and Manasseh." What God has done for the sons of Joseph will be an ongoing example of divine blessing.

Genesis 48:21. Even though Joseph's sons have been adopted and received a blessing from Jacob—Israel—it is clear from these verses that Joseph has not been swept off the stage but rather remains an heir. In essence, Joseph has superceded his brothers as the firstborn son and through his own sons will receive the double share of the inheritance that normally is given to the firstborn. By placing this story concerning the bestowing of blessings upon Joseph's offspring before the blessing of all the sons of Israel (Genesis 49), the narrator underscores the importance of Joseph.

In these verses Jacob speaks more directly to Joseph than in the previous narrative. Jacob has included Joseph in the blessings of his sons up to this point. God will be with them. This promise, usually associated with a journey, looks ahead to the exodus. God will also bring the people back to the land of promise. With God's help, Joseph has cared for his family. Now Jacob reassures his son that God will continue to care for their growing clan.

INTERPRETING THE SCRIPTURE

Unexpected Blessings

As a pastor, I frequently visit those who are unable to get out and about. At the end of a visit, the person usually thanks me for coming. Usually I want to thank them! Typically, through sharing their stories of faith and perseverance, sometimes in the face of tremendous odds, I have received more than I have given. In like manner, Sunday school teachers and Bible study leaders often say that they learn more than their students. Was Jesus reflecting on similar circumstances when he said, "It is more blessed to give than to receive"? (Acts 20:35).

Nearing the end of Jacob's long and colorful life, Joseph brings his two sons to see their grandfather and to receive his blessing, which involved both physical as well as spiritual benefits. After greeting the boys warmly, Jacob exclaims to Joseph, "I did not expect to see your face; and here God has let me see your children also!" (Genesis 48:11, today's key verse).

When his sons returned from Shechem with Joseph's bloodstained robe, Jacob concluded that a wild animal had devoured his favorite, and Jacob would never see his son again. What glad news it was when his sons returned from Egypt to tell their aging father that Joseph was alive!

Many parents and grandparents fear the worst when their children leave home for military service, especially when they are assigned to a combat unit. What a glad day it is when the soldiers' tour of duty is over and they return home! Is there anything more painful than losing a child? Is there any reunion more joyful than being reunited with those who are our own flesh and blood?

Jacob is prepared to give his blessing to Manasseh and Ephraim. But just seeing these two lads is a blessing for him! He who is willing to share is also the recipient of God's grace. How good it is to spend time with those that we love!

From Generation to Generation

How will you pass on your most valuable treasures to those who mean the most to you? We are advised to have a will and to update it frequently. Some people give heirlooms to their children and grandchildren before they die.

More important than the china or the silver or the furniture, though, is the faith that many of us learned through our parents and our grandparents, the faith that we desire to see passed on to our children and grandchildren. When I was a District Superintendent in The United Methodist Church, I frequently conducted meetings in churches where there were few children, youth, or young adults. After the meeting at one church, I was invited to stay for a birthday party for one of the women who was eighty years old. Other than me, she was the youngest person present! How will our churches survive if we do not pass on the good news?

How do we instill the values of the faith in the minds and hearts of the next generation? Jacob began by reminding his grandsons that *his* father and grandfather had walked with God (see 48:15). God had been Jacob's shepherd, guiding and protecting him. Now Jacob prayed that his grandsons would allow God to be *their* shepherd and would walk with God as their family had done for four generations. He taught them by the example of his life that God would always be faithful and would always see them through. God had promised to make their clan a great nation. According to their grandfather, God could be trusted. Ephraim and Manasseh could count on God to see them through.

In who or what do we put our trust? The Bible story and our own experiences declare that God is faithful. We can trust God's love and care through all generations.

The Younger Son Is Favored!

From many perspectives, it appears that life is not fair. As early as grade school, children recognize that some students are more intelligent and some are better looking than others. We soon see that wealth is far from evenly distributed in this world. Some people seem to have all the "luck." Sometimes it appears that even God plays favorites!

When Manasseh and Ephraim came before Jacob, Jacob seemed to sense that although Ephraim was younger, he had more ability and would become more prominent in adulthood than his older brother. It would not be the first time a younger brother received the more generous blessing traditionally reserved for the eldest son! Due to Jacob's own aggressive nature, he had tricked his brother Esau into selling his birthright for a pot of lentil stew. Now, two generations later, Jacob intention-

ally gives his blessing to Ephraim, giving him the advantage and the upper hand as the brothers seek their fortune.

How do we respond when we are treated unfairly? It is awkward for both the favored child as well as those who are not given their "fair" share. Even when parents seek to be meticulous in their attempt at fairness and equity, sibling rivalry and jealousy still often cause problems in families.

Is it possible to be fair in family relationships? Rather than using seniority, the patriarchs often made decisions based on the strengths and weaknesses of their children. There is no evidence that Manasseh objected to his grandfather's choice of Ephraim over him. Maybe there is a lesson here for families in all generations. Rather than to allow jealousy and resentment to eat us up, maybe we should accept life with its inequities, and simply attempt to bloom where we are planted.

Passing On the Legacy of Faith

In the final analysis, the most valuable thing that Jacob passed on to his children and grandchildren was neither his property nor his wealth, but his faith. It was a faith that had been known in previous generations, but it was a faith in danger of dying if it were not passed on to the next generation. Someone has said, "God has no grandchildren." The faith is always one generation from extinction.

In spite of the fact that for economic reasons, Jacob and his extended family were forced to leave Canaan and move to Egypt, Jacob trusted God and assured Joseph that "God will be with you and will bring you again to the land of your ancestors" (48:21). At the time of Jacob's death, it looked as if the Israelites would no longer be residents of Canaan. Yet God had promised this land to Abraham, Isaac, and Jacob!

Notice that Jacob is not distraught, but calm in his remarks. He does not doubt the providence of God. For a while, the people may have to live in a foreign land. But ultimately, God will see to it that they are in the place where God intends them to be.

Many things in life seem to be adverse to the life of faith. Much of what we hope for and dream about does not seem to come to pass. Yet God is working God's purposes out in spite of all the evidence to the contrary.

Are we able to trust God, even when it would appear that the forces of evil are having their way? Can we see the hand of God, even in detours and setbacks? Jacob trusted that his people would ultimately reside in the promised land of Canaan, even though he died a resident of Egypt. His faith inspired the people to believe that God would keep God's promise. We can pass on no greater legacy than the faith and confidence in God that Jacob exemplified. May our trust in God be so evident that it inspires and energizes the next generation to follow where God leads!

SHARING THE SCRIPTURE

Preparing Our Hearts

Meditate on this week's devotional reading, found in Psalm 145:1-13a. In verse 4 the psalmist writes, "One generation shall laud your works to another." We do leave a legacy of our spiritual beliefs, attitudes, and actions, as well as our material resources. What kind of legacy are you leaving for the children, grandchildren, or other members of the next generation? How are you communicating this legacy? Ponder whether there are things that you would like to change about your legacy and act accordingly.

Pray that you and the adult learners will be mindful of the legacy that you are leaving for the generations that follow you.

Preparing Our Minds

Study the background from Genesis 48:8-21 and lesson Scripture, verses 11-19. As you read think about the legacy that an older generation would like to leave for a younger one.

Write on newsprint:
❑ information for next week's lesson, found under "Continue the Journey."
❑ activities for further spiritual growth in "Continue the Journey."
Option: Research Ephraim to see how

this tribe named after Joseph's younger son fulfilled Jacob's prophecy in Genesis 48:19. Plan to use this information in the "Examine the Story of Jacob's Blessing of Joseph's Sons, Ephraim and Manasseh" portion.

Be prepared to post a large, current world map where the students can stand in front of it.

LEADING THE CLASS

(1) Gather to Learn

❖ Welcome the class members and introduce any guests.

❖ Pray that those who have come will open their hearts and minds to the word that God has for them today.

❖ Invite students, as a class or in groups, to tell stories of a beloved family member, perhaps a parent or grandparent, who made a deep and lasting impression. What was so special about this person? How has his or her legacy affected the course of your life?

❖ Read aloud today's focus statement: **One generation dies and another is born. What legacies do older generations want to leave for younger ones? Jacob moved to Egypt and lived out his last days; he blessed his grandsons, assured that they would continue to grow into a multitude, just as God had promised Abraham and Sarah.**

(2) Examine the Story of Jacob's Blessing of Joseph's Sons, Ephraim and Manasseh

❖ Choose a volunteer to read Genesis 48:11-19. Suggest that as this person reads, the rest of the class close their eyes and try to enter into the scene.

❖ **Option:** Select a volunteer to read Genesis 48:11-19 as four people mime the actions of Joseph, Jacob, Ephraim, and Manasseh.

❖ Talk about what the adults could see, hear, or feel as this scene was read.

❖ Ask these questions.

(1) **Why was Joseph "displeased" when he saw that Jacob had placed his right hand on Ephraim's head (48:17)?** (See "The Younger Son Is Favored! in Interpreting the Scripture.)

(2) **What might you imagine that Joseph was thinking as he witnessed his father give the blessing of the firstborn to his younger son?**

(3) **What reason(s) did Jacob give for placing his right hand on Ephraim?** (See 48:19. If you did any research on Ephraim, present a brief lecture.)

❖ Invite the students to read from several translations the blessing in verses 15-16. Discern with them what Jacob expected to happen as he blessed Ephraim and Manasseh. (See Genesis 48:15-16 in Understanding the Scripture.)

❖ Note that the blessing in verse 20 is still invoked today by Jewish parents upon their children.

(3) Feel More Closely Connected to One's Heirs and/or Ancestors

❖ Post a large, current world map. Distribute small sticky notes and pencils. Ask each participant to write the first name of a parent or child or sibling, one name per note. Invite the adults to affix each note to its appropriate place on the map to show where that person now lives. (If you do not have sticky notes, use slips of regular paper and tacks or tape.)

❖ Look at the map and ask: **How are we able to stay connected to our families when many of us are so geographically distant?**

❖ Note that some families stay connected by holding family reunions. These may take the form of a day-long event, a cruise, camping, a week at the beach, or some other special way of staying in touch. Some family reunions include worship services to remind each member of the legacy of faith they have inherited and have the privilege of passing on.

❖ Prompt the class members to tell about family reunions they have attended. Perhaps some students will have stories to tell of relationships broken by distance, divorce, military service, or for some other reason that were reconnected many years after folks had lost touch with one another.

❖ **Option:** Use this true story as a discussion starter. **"Marian," the youngest of seven siblings, was sent to live with family friends when her mother became unable to care for her. The siblings had yearned to see their sister, who was only a year old when she left them, but because she had not been legally adopted it was difficult to find her. After losing contact for forty-one years, the siblings finally located "Marian" and had a wonderful reunion with her. They said that they feel like a "complete family again" now that their missing baby sister has been reunited with them.**

(4) Make a Commitment to Live So As to Leave a Legacy of Christ-like Character

❖ Encourage the adults, as a class or in groups, to tell stories of blessings they have received from parents or grandparents or other significant members of prior generations.

❖ Brainstorm with the class what they believe to be the marks of someone with Christ-like character. List these ideas on newsprint.

❖ Distribute paper and pencils. Ask the students to select from this list the five characteristics they believe are most important. As they write each one on their paper, they are to describe how they currently embody this trait or what they need to do to be more faithfully conformed to the image of Christ as it relates to this trait.

❖ Provide time for silent meditation so that the adults may consider how they can model and pass these traits on to coming generations.

(5) Continue the Journey

❖ Break the silence by praying that all who have gathered for class today will recall the blessings they have received from prior generations and do all they can to bless the generations to follow.

❖ Read aloud this preparation for next week's lesson. You may also want to post it on newsprint for the students to copy.

■ **Title: Called to Believe!**

■ **Background Scripture: Luke 1:5-25**

■ **Lesson Scripture: Luke 1:8-23**

■ **Focus of the Lesson: People find it hard to believe that the miraculous**

could happen to them. What evidence do we have that miracles can happen in our lives? God promised Elizabeth and Zechariah a miracle, and God fulfilled that promise.

❖ Challenge the students to complete one or more of these activities for further spiritual growth, which you will write on newsprint for the students to copy.

(1) **Write in your spiritual journal about what you wish your family will inherit from you in terms of a legacy of faith. List several concrete actions that you will take to turn that wish into a reality.**

(2) **Review any legal or financial documents to ensure that your estate will go to the people and organizations (including the church) you want to receive it.**

(3) **Contact a family member you have not been in touch with for some time. Talk with this person and see about meeting with one another to reconnect.**

❖ Sing or read aloud "Forward Through the Ages."

❖ Conclude today's session by leading the class in this benediction, which is adapted from Genesis 14:19-20: **Blessed be you by God Most High, maker of heaven and earth; and blessed be God Most High.**

SECOND QUARTER
God's Call to the Christian Community

DECEMBER 2, 2007–FEBRUARY 24, 2008

Our study during December, January, and February explores the Gospel of Luke to discern ways in which God calls the community of faith—the church—to live out the purpose for which it was created.

The five sessions in Unit 1, "God's Call at Christmas and Beyond," explore how God's call was heard and responded to by Elizabeth and Zechariah, Mary the mother of Jesus, the shepherds, and Simeon. "Called to Believe!"—the lesson for December 2 from Luke 1:5-25—examines Gabriel's astounding message to Zechariah that he and Elizabeth would have a long-awaited child in their old age. On December 9 in the lesson "Called to Be a Vessel!" from Luke 1:26-38, Gabriel again appears, this time to Mary, to tell her that she will bear "the Son of the Most High," and she readily agrees to be God's servant. Zechariah proclaims a vision for his newborn son, John, in "Called to Proclaim!"—the lesson for December 16—based on Luke 1:57-80. On December 23, "Called to Rejoice!" tells the Christmas story as recorded in Luke 2:1-20. The first unit concludes on December 30 as Simeon recognizes the infant Jesus, "the consolation of Israel," in "Called to Witness!"—rooted in Luke 2:22-38.

Unit 2, "The Awareness of God's Instruction," examines the inspiration that comes to us through God's call that enables us to learn, love, pray, and trust. The unit opens on January 6 with "Inspired to Inquire!" where we see the account in Luke 2:41-52 of Jesus as a boy of twelve conversing with the "amazed" temple rabbis. Luke 6:27-36—the Scripture for "Inspired to Love!" on January 13—delves into Jesus' teachings on how his followers are to respond to others, especially their enemies. On January 20 we move to Luke 11:5-13 to encounter Jesus' teachings on prayer in "Inspired to Pray!" This unit ends on January 27 with "Inspired to Trust!" which investigates Jesus' teachings in Luke 12:22-34 on overcoming anxiety and worry.

Unit 3, "God Summons Us to Respond!" considers how we cooperate with God by responding to the call to labor in building the community of faith, to repent when we have failed or fallen short, to serve God with humility, and to be dedicated disciples. The lesson for February 3, "Summoned to Labor!" analyzes Luke 10:1-12, 17-20, in which Jesus sends workers into the harvest field, two by two, to witness. Luke 13:1-9, the basis for "Summoned to Repent!" on February 10, takes an in-depth look at the concept of repentance. "Summoned to Be Humble!"—the session for February 17 from Luke 14:1, 7-14—uses Jesus' parable of guests choosing seats at a wedding banquet to teach the value of humility. The unit comes to a close on February 24 with a study of Luke 14:25-33, "Summoned to Be a Disciple!"—where Jesus sets forth the sacrifices expected of those who will be his disciples.

MEET OUR WRITER

DR. MICHAEL FINK

Michael Fink moved to the beautiful mountains and lakes near Dandridge, Tennessee, in 2003, to take early retirement. Born in Sylacauga, Alabama, and reared in a Birmingham suburb, Mike was schooled in Alabama, Georgia, and Kentucky. He served churches in Kentucky, Indiana, and North Carolina; taught in colleges in North Carolina and Tennessee; and served for twenty-five years in various editorial, management, and staff capacities with a Christian publisher.

Dr. Fink has led Christian education conferences, consulted on Christian publishing, and ministered in twenty-three states in the United States as well as in ten foreign countries. He has coauthored one book, has contributed to five others, and has published Bible studies, sermons, poetry, and articles in numerous publications. With two master's degrees and a doctorate in New Testament, he especially enjoys exposition of the Gospels, such as this quarter's study in the Gospel of Luke.

Since retiring, Mike has been an adjunct professor at Carson-Newman College in Jefferson City, Tennessee, and has worked part-time at a classic small-town hardware store—a great way, he thinks, to get to know people in a new location. A college major in mathematics has blossomed into a lifelong attachment to computers with a special focus on screening stocks and developing investment strategies. He manages several portfolios for family members.

Mike's wife, Evelyn, is a preschool specialist who loves gardening, music, and shepherding their family of three daughters, two sons-in-law, and four grandchildren. Together Mike and Evelyn enjoy entertaining friends and boating in their pontoon boat on Douglas Lake. They like to travel and almost always have a book on cassette or CD playing as they drive. Since retiring, they have been in an almost continuous project of remodeling and upgrading their home. They are active members of First Baptist Church in Jefferson City, Tennessee.

THE BIG PICTURE: THE COMMUNITY LUKE ENVISIONED

Because the Gospel of Luke and the book of Acts are the two parts of Luke's effort to trace the beginnings of the early church, they play a unique role in the life of the church today. Both are addressed to Theophilus, who may be an actual person, but could be any reader who is a "friend of God" (the literal meaning of "Theophilus").

We know that Luke was associated with Paul (Colossians 4:14; 2 Timothy 4:11; Philemon 24), and many assume that Luke's purpose in his writing is to support Paul's mission to the Gentiles. Some view that mission as a displacement of Israel as God's chosen people by a new community of believers who were freed from the bonds of the Old Testament law and were to live entirely under God's grace.

The Tension Between the Old and the New

Luke seems to have a wider vision for the Christian community that Jesus founded. His purpose can be illustrated by comparing how Matthew, Mark, and Luke each recorded the conclusion of a parable Jesus used to contrast the old with the new. The parable first speaks of an old garment being patched by new cloth. Then the parable speaks of new wine being put in old or fresh wineskins. This contrast between old and new is widely recognized as dealing with the tension between the old forms of Judaism and the emergence of a new Christian community (see Luke 5:33, 37-39).

The Gospel of Mark, written about the time of the Jewish Revolt against Rome (A.D. 66–70), reflects a time when the old ways of Judaism were strained by the new spirit in the Christian community (Mark 2:21-22). Mark emphasized "the new" pulling away from "the old." The power of the new wine would destroy the old wineskins. Mark concluded that new wine required fresh wineskins so that the new wine would not be lost. He envisioned a Christian community that needed to break away from the institutions and practices of Judaism in order to preserve its charter from Christ. Remaining in the Jewish community would bring more division and the ultimate destruction for both. The new Christian community needed new forms to express its character and mission.

Matthew, recognized as the most Jewish of the Gospels, reached a similar conclusion. Matthew, however, expressed greater concern about the preservation of the old and urged the preservation of both (Matthew 9:16-17). He saw the same results as Mark when trying to keep the old and new together, but he removed the emphasis on the new tearing away from the old and the new wine being the force that bursts the wineskins. He concluded, "So both are preserved," as a reconciling gesture for old and new living side by side but separate.

Luke recognized the distinctiveness of the old and the new ways (Luke 5:36-39). He knew that the new community would be damaged if part of it were torn away in an attempt to repair the old. "The new will not match the old" (5:36). The new wine will burst the old wineskins; the new wine will be spilled; and the old wineskins will be destroyed. He then proposed fresh wineskins for the new wine, conceding a break between the old forms and the new community. As a conclusion, however, Luke, the only Gentile writer of a New

Testament Gospel, stated, "No one after drinking old wine desires new wine, but says, 'The old is good'"(5:39). Having acknowledged the necessary break between the old and the new, Luke commends the old. Why would he do that? To answer that question, we need to look at Paul's mission as he described and practiced it.

Paul's Mission Strategy

The best description of Paul's mission strategy comes from Paul's Letter to the Romans in which he articulated extensively the relationship between Judaism (the old) and Christianity (the new). The best description of Paul's practice of that missionary strategy comes in the Acts of the Apostles, the second of the two New Testament volumes written by Luke. Drawing from these sources, let us note four emphases.

First, Paul articulated a strategy based on the gospel coming first to the Jews and then to the Gentiles. In Romans, Paul repeated this principle three times in the first two chapters, "the Jew first and also to the Greek" (1:16; 2:9, 10). This strategy was based on historical reality—God sent Jesus as a Jew to live among the Jews. The good news Jesus himself proclaimed was focused on the Jews (Matthew 15:24), though the final commission he gave his disciples focused on all nations (Matthew 28:19-20).

Second, Luke recorded that Paul followed this principle in his missionary work. Whenever he took the gospel to a new town, he first went to the synagogue (Acts 9:20; 13:5, 14; 14:1; 17:1-2) or found the Jews who lived in that town (Acts 16:3) and proclaimed the gospel to them. Though "an apostle to the Gentiles" (Romans 11:13), Paul first offered the gospel to the Jews.

Third, only after the gospel had been offered to the Jews did Paul turn and offer it to the Gentiles (see Acts 13:46). Often the focus on the Gentiles grew out of the rejection of Paul's message by some of the Jews. As Paul's ministry widened, opponents from the Jewish community began to counter his message and attack him as the messenger. The heightened tension with the synagogues contrasted with the openness to the gospel among many Gentiles. Therefore, Paul intensified his focus on the Gentiles to whom he felt Christ had sent him.

Fourth, Paul never gave up on the Jews. He saw his work among the Gentiles as a result of the stumbling of those Jews who held on to works as a means of salvation rather than accepting God's grace (Romans 11:1-11). In fact, the acceptance of the gospel by the Gentiles would make the Jews jealous and would prompt them to accept the gospel (11:11-12). The Gentiles who were being saved actually were being grafted onto the true Israel (11:17). Their inclusion was not a cause for boasting, but rather an occasion for hope that all Israel would accept God's grace (11:18-24).

In light of these understandings, we can begin to grasp what Luke was about in his Gospel and why he commended the old and stated that "after drinking old wine" no one "desires new wine" (Luke 5:39).

The Roots of the Gospel in Pious Judaism

Luke roots his Gospel in the goodness of pious Judaism. We will especially see this focus in the first unit of this study, "God's Call at Christmas and Beyond." The gospel indeed came first to the Jews, and the roots of that gospel had been sunk deep in the faith of a people who claimed their heritage from Abraham. Through the patriarchs, the prophets, the kings, and a remnant of faithful people through the centuries, God had been in the good news business.

Luke started his Gospel by recounting the stories of people such as Zechariah, Elizabeth, Mary, Joseph, Simeon, and Anna. Each of these stories is an expression of the pious Judaism from which Jesus emerged. These were men and women of faith, obedience, devotion, and hope. They lived by the commandments, worshiped at the temple, and studied the Scriptures in the synagogue. Their piety did not rest on some strict standard of legal observance or some claim of works righteousness. They were indeed true children of Abraham, children of the promise, and children of God (Romans 9:7-8). Luke found and celebrated this goodness in the old.

Jesus was born surrounded by this kind of Jewish piety. The announcement of his birth claimed his unique status as the Son of God and the promised heir to King David's throne (Luke 1:32). He was "a Savior, who is the Messiah, the Lord" (2:11). All of these tied Jesus to the promises and the hopes of Judaism. Luke affirmed these important roots as good.

Although the Gospels focus on significant tension between Jesus and some Jewish leaders, we should not overlook the ongoing rootage of Jesus' ministry in Judaism. He attended and taught in synagogues. His twelve closest disciples were from a widely representative Jewish background. He focused his teaching and ministry primarily on Jewish people, and many of them responded positively. He interacted socially with Pharisees (7:36; 11:37; 14:1); and Pharisees even warned him of Herod's evil intents toward him (13:31).

Luke continued this emphasis even after Jesus' death and resurrection. Devout Jews were center stage at Pentecost (Acts 2:5), were the first converts (2:37-42), and responded by the thousands to the apostles' message (4:4). A prominent member of the Sanhedrin urged caution in opposing the apostles (5:33-39). A large number of "priests became obedient to the faith" (6:7). Even at the end of Acts, some Jewish leaders visited Paul during his house arrest and were convinced by what he said (28:17-24).

Thus, Luke embraced the both-and rather than the either-or view of the Christian community. He was unwilling to see the new and dynamic spirit torn out of the new community of faith so that the old and the new could exist together. He affirmed the need for the new community to define its own parameters and forms. Yet, he did not abandon the faith and devotion that formed the core of the true Israel. That was the trunk of the olive tree onto which the new branches were grafted and from which the wild olive shoots would forever draw their nourishment and strength (Romans 11:17). At the end, all God's faithful would have the right to the tree of life (Revelation 22:14).

Jesus and the New Community

Though rooted in pious Judaism, the community that Jesus formed had a spirit and power so strong that Jesus defined his ministry this way: "The Spirit of the Lord is upon me, because he has anointed me to bring good news to the poor. He has sent me to proclaim release to the captives and recovery of sight to the blind, to let the oppressed go free, to proclaim the year of the Lord's favor" (Luke 4:18-19).

Luke caught Jesus' vision of a new community that was not composed of people who were better, more pious, or more spiritual than those who had gone before. Instead, the new community was to be composed of the poor, the captives, the blind, and the oppressed. Those who were shunned because of diseases, physical infirmities, or political loyalties (5:12-28) were welcomed. The poor, hungry, bereaved, and despised were recipients of Jesus' blessings (6:20-23). In compassion, Jesus healed the sick (7:1-10), raised the dead (7:11-15), forgave the sinful (7:36-50), and drove out demons (8:26-33). The power at work in Jesus was spiritual power that transformed, empowered, enlightened, and set free all who would come to him.

Jesus himself was the focal point of this new community. He was the physician for those who were sick (5:31-32). He was the "lord of the sabbath" (6:5) who shifted the significance of the law from obedience toward doing good and saving life (6:6-10). His teachings were the foundation for life that enjoined hearers to put his words into action (6:46-49). He disclosed the secrets of the kingdom of God (8:10).

Although Jesus sought those who would "hear the word of God and do it" (8:21), he sought more than those who would merely observe his teachings. He sought faith (7:9, 50;

8:48) and called people to follow him (5:27). Following him, however, would not bring political power, public acclaim, or social position. Rather, following Jesus involved self-denial, taking up a cross, and losing life (9:23-24).

Luke 9:51 provides a pivotal point in the Gospel. Jesus "set his face to go to Jerusalem" knowing that "the days drew near for him to be taken up." That decision also provided a pivotal point for Jesus' disciples. Would-be followers could offer no "I will follow you but . . ." excuses (9:57-62). Jesus' "follow me" became more persistent and excluded all compromise.

The New Community Takes Shape

The Gospel of Luke ends with the death and resurrection of Jesus in Jerusalem. The cross to which he called others was a cross he chose to bear. The Messiah had to suffer these things (24:26), but God's plan was not finished. The Messiah would enter his glory (24:26), and "repentance and forgiveness of sins" would be "proclaimed in his name to all nations" (24:47). Empowered by the Holy Spirit, the disciples would be "witnesses of these things" (24:48).

In the Acts of the Apostles, Luke sketched out how the followers of Jesus became a new community of "witnesses in Jerusalem, in all Judea and Samaria, and to the ends of the earth" (Acts 1:8). The numberless multitudes that had followed Jesus earlier had been reduced to about one hundred twenty people who were praying fervently and waiting for the promised baptism of the Holy Spirit (1:4-5, 14-15).

The coming of the Holy Spirit upon the disciples on the day of Pentecost (2:3-4) set in motion a dramatic expansion and reshaping of this new community of believers. First, three thousand devout Jews repented and were baptized (2:5, 37-41). This group devoted itself to the apostles' teaching and fellowship (2:42), and more believers joined in this community so that soon the number of followers reached five thousand (4:4).

The expansion of the church took many turns, but important breakthroughs began to accelerate the expansion beyond the Jewish community in Jerusalem. Philip received a responsive acceptance among the Samaritans—distant relatives from the northern kingdom of Israel who had intermarried with the native population and had created their own forms of worship (8:4-14). An Ethiopian eunuch who probably would have been classified as a "god-fearer" (one attracted to Judaism but not a full convert) accepted Philip's message (8:26-38). Saul, a strong Jewish opponent of the early Christians who later was to be called Paul, was converted (9:1-19).

The turning point in these breakthroughs came in the conversion of the Gentile centurion Cornelius, along with his relatives and close friends (10:1-48). Although it was unlawful for a Jew to associate with or to visit a Gentile (10:28), Peter followed the vision he received and presented the gospel to Cornelius. This conversion of a Gentile and the subsequent endorsement of Peter's actions by the church in Jerusalem (11:1-18) opened the way for the new Christian community to break down all barriers and present the gospel to all people.

Luke concluded Acts with the gospel being proclaimed "without hindrance" in Rome (28:31), symbolizing the spread of the Christian mission to the very center of the Roman Empire, which itself stretched to the ends of the earth.

The Christian community that Luke envisioned, therefore, was a fellowship that spanned the religious, social, racial, and geographic barriers that divided humanity. The dividing wall of hostility between people was broken down by Jesus' sacrifice, and through Christ one new humanity has been created, reconciled to God and to one another (Ephesians 2:11-22).

God calls us to be disciples of Christ, and as disciples we become part of a new community of believers drawn into oneness from among all humanity. The call still goes out, and the vision is not yet fulfilled. We are yet summoned to respond—to repent, to submit, to obey, and to follow in the Master's footsteps.

Close-Up:
The Gospel of Luke

Since all of this quarter's lessons are taken from Luke, you may find it helpful to have some background about this Gospel. For a really in-depth look, see *The New Interpreter's Bible,* vol. IX, where you will find Luke discussed in great detail by R. Alan Culpepper, Dean of the School of Theology of Mercer University in Atlanta, Georgia.

Writer

According to tradition that extends back to the second century, Luke was a physician and a traveling companion of Paul. However, neither Luke's occupation nor his association with the apostle can be verified. His knowledge of medicine is not that deep, and his writings about travels with Paul could have been borrowed from other sources. Hence, many scholars contend that the writer of this Gospel, who also wrote Acts, is anonymous.

Date

Although most scholars agree that this Gospel was likely written between A.D. 80–85, the earliest manuscripts that we have date from A.D. 175–225. By this time, the title *Gospel of Luke* appeared on these incomplete portions of the Gospel manuscripts.

Basic Structure of Luke According to Culpepper

(Lessons in our study related to each section are noted.)

Luke 1:1-4	The Prologue
Luke 1:5–2:52	The Infancy Narrative
	Lessons 1, 2, 3, 4, 5, 6
Luke 3:1–4:13	Preparation for the Ministry of Jesus
Luke 4:14–9:50	The Ministry in Galilee
	Lesson 7
Luke 9:51–19:27	The Journey to Jerusalem
	Lessons 8, 9, 10, 11, 12, 13
Luke 19:28–21:38	The Ministry in Jerusalem
Luke 22:1–24:53	The Passion and Resurrection Narratives

Emphasis of Luke's Gospel

God's Messiah has come into the midst of human history for the purpose of salvation for all people. In this Gospel, written for a Gentile audience, we see a compassionate Jesus who befriends those on the margins of society. We often see him eating with people who the religious leaders and well-to-do people of his day had scorned or ignored. Luke portrays Jesus as especially concerned with the poor, while also warning the rich of the hazard of their wealth. Obedient to God, Jesus serves as a model for those who answer the call to discipleship. His disciples are expected to witness for him as they are empowered and directed by the Holy Spirit.

FAITH IN ACTION: RESPONDING TO GOD'S CALL

Our lessons during this winter focus on "God's Call to the Christian Community." As we study the Gospel of Luke, we will see how God calls individuals, creates communities, and calls these communities to live out the purposes for which they were created.

Plan time either as part of a Sunday session or at a different time to do this discernment activity with the class. Or, write this information on newsprint, ask the adults to copy it, and suggest that they work on it at home. Set a date for everyone to report back on how they feel led to respond to God's call in their lives.

God Calls/Disciples Respond

God calls us in many ways: through prayer; Bible study; meditation; a sermon; the words of one who has discerned something about us; an awareness of our spiritual gifts, which are given to build up the body of Christ; an encounter with nature; a serendipity that puts us in the right place at the right time; the still, small voice of the Holy Spirit within, leading us; a passion that prompts us to act as a witness or servant for God.

How can you begin to answer that call? Here are some action steps that you can take to respond faithfully to God's call.

Look at what you are already doing. Make a list of the ministries in which you already participate. Which ones make good use of your talents? Which ones allow you to follow your passions for ministry? Which ones are you ready to jettison because you no longer feel called to do them? Sometimes we hang on to tasks that we are no longer called to do because we feel no one else will volunteer if we step back. Others in the congregation do have gifts, and if God wants a particular ministry to continue, the right person will be called and will step forward.

Consider all the ministries your church supports. Do any of these that you are not currently involved with match your gifts, passions, and available time? If so, talk with the contact person to see if you can make a contribution to a particular ministry.

Redesign one of the current ministries around your call. Formulate a plan for change in a current ministry and present it to the appropriate body for approval. A new twist on an old theme can bring greater energy to that activity. For example, your congregation may be doing something for one age group that you have the gifts and passion to expand to another age group or make into an intergenerational activity.

Envision a new ministry to meet needs that are not currently being met. Meditate, start a journal, and dream about how you could begin such a ministry. Think about who could join you. Find out what steps you need to take to have this program officially approved. Take steps to transform your vision into a reality.

UNIT 1: GOD'S CALL AT CHRISTMAS AND BEYOND
CALLED TO BELIEVE!

PREVIEWING THE LESSON

Lesson Scripture: Luke 1:8-23
Background Scripture: Luke 1:5-25
Key Verse: Luke 1:20

Focus of the Lesson:
People find it hard to believe that the miraculous could happen to them. What evidence do we have that miracles can happen in our lives? God promised Elizabeth and Zechariah a miracle, and God fulfilled that promise.

Goals for the Learners:
(1) to consider the story of God's miraculous gift to Elizabeth and Zechariah.
(2) to identify experiences in their own lives when God was unmistakably at work.
(3) to challenge others to believe God's promises.

Pronunciation Guide:
Abijah (uh bi' juh)

Supplies:
Bibles, newsprint and marker, paper and pencils, hymnals

READING THE SCRIPTURE

NRSV
Luke 1:8-23

⁸Once when he was serving as priest before God and his section was on duty, ⁹he was chosen by lot, according to the custom of the priesthood, to enter the sanctuary of the Lord and offer incense. ¹⁰Now at the time of the incense offering, the whole assembly of the people was praying outside. ¹¹Then there appeared to him an angel of the Lord, standing at the right side of the altar of incense. ¹²When Zechariah saw him, he was

NIV
Luke 1:8-23

⁸Once when Zechariah's division was on duty and he was serving as priest before God, ⁹he was chosen by lot, according to the custom of the priesthood, to go into the temple of the Lord and burn incense. ¹⁰And when the time for the burning of incense came, all the assembled worshipers were praying outside.

¹¹Then an angel of the Lord appeared to

terrified; and fear overwhelmed him. ¹³But the angel said to him, "Do not be afraid, Zechariah, for your prayer has been heard. Your wife Elizabeth will bear you a son, and you will name him John. ¹⁴You will have joy and gladness, and many will rejoice at his birth, ¹⁵for he will be great in the sight of the Lord. He must never drink wine or strong drink; even before his birth he will be filled with the Holy Spirit. ¹⁶He will turn many of the people of Israel to the Lord their God. ¹⁷With the spirit and power of Elijah he will go before him, to turn the hearts of parents to their children, and the disobedient to the wisdom of the righteous, to make ready a people prepared for the Lord." ¹⁸Zechariah said to the angel, "How will I know that this is so? For I am an old man, and my wife is getting on in years." ¹⁹The angel replied, "I am Gabriel. I stand in the presence of God, and I have been sent to speak to you and to bring you this good news. ²⁰But now, because you did not believe my words, which will be fulfilled in their time, you will become mute, unable to speak, until the day these things occur."

²¹Meanwhile the people were waiting for Zechariah, and wondered at his delay in the sanctuary. ²²When he did come out, he could not speak to them, and they realized that he had seen a vision in the sanctuary. He kept motioning to them and remained unable to speak. ²³When his time of service was ended, he went to his home.

him, standing at the right side of the altar of incense. ¹²When Zechariah saw him, he was startled and was gripped with fear. ¹³But the angel said to him: "Do not be afraid, Zechariah; your prayer has been heard. Your wife Elizabeth will bear you a son, and you are to give him the name John. ¹⁴He will be a joy and delight to you, and many will rejoice because of his birth, ¹⁵for he will be great in the sight of the Lord. He is never to take wine or other fermented drink, and he will be filled with the Holy Spirit even from birth. ¹⁶Many of the people of Israel will he bring back to the Lord their God. ¹⁷And he will go on before the Lord, in the spirit and power of Elijah, to turn the hearts of the fathers to their children and the disobedient to the wisdom of the righteous—to make ready a people prepared for the Lord."

¹⁸Zechariah asked the angel, "How can I be sure of this? I am an old man and my wife is well along in years."

¹⁹The angel answered, "I am Gabriel. I stand in the presence of God, and I have been sent to speak to you and to tell you this good news. ²⁰And now you will be silent and not able to speak until the day this happens, because you did not believe my words, which will come true at their proper time."

²¹Meanwhile, the people were waiting for Zechariah and wondering why he stayed so long in the temple. ²²When he came out, he could not speak to them. They realized he had seen a vision in the temple, for he kept making signs to them but remained unable to speak.

²³When his time of service was completed, he returned home.

UNDERSTANDING THE SCRIPTURE

Luke 1:5-7. Luke began his "orderly account" (Luke 1:1) of Jesus' story with a focus rooted in poor, pious, priestly Judaism. Poverty is emphasized most clearly in the temple sacrifice of "a pair of turtledoves or two young pigeons" by Mary and Joseph (2:24), a sacrifice prescribed for those who could not afford a sheep (Leviticus 12:6). Piety is emphasized in Zechariah and Elizabeth, both of whom were "righteous before God, living blamelessly according to all the commandments and regulations of the Lord" (Luke 1:6). Piety also is seen in the subsequent examples of Mary, Joseph, Simeon, and Anna.

The priestly aspect of Jesus' heritage often is overshadowed by his messianic roots as a son of David. Old Testament regulations required that a priest such as Zechariah (who "belonged to the priestly order of Abijah," Luke 1:5) marry from among his own kin (Leviticus 21:13-15). If Elizabeth were of a priestly family and was also a "relative" of Mary (Luke 1:36), Mary herself likely had some sort of priestly lineage. Other New Testament writings picked up this priestly role of Jesus as the perfect and great High Priest who offered himself as a sacrifice and a ransom for many. The genealogies of Jesus in Matthew 1:1-16 and Luke 3:23-38 are traced through Joseph, however, and do not reflect a priestly heritage.

Luke also set his account in the context of Herod's reign in Judea. This king is Herod I, also known as Herod the Great, who first served under Roman authority as governor of Galilee (47 B.C.). His authority quickly expanded. With the support of Mark Anthony and Octavius Caesar, the Roman senate confirmed Herod as king of Judea around 40 B.C. He died in 4 B.C.

The political intrigue, treachery, and brutality that marked Herod's reign sharply contrast with the plight of humble Zechariah and Elizabeth. "Getting on in years," they had no children (Luke 1:7). Such barrenness often was viewed as a specific act of God (Genesis 20:18; 1 Samuel 1:5) that brought reproach or "disgrace" on the woman (Luke 1:25). Busybodies often assumed that such women brought disgrace upon themselves because of some fault or flaw of character.

Luke 1:8-10. Zechariah bore a name that occurred frequently in the Old Testament.

The name, which meant "the Lord has remembered," had particular significance for those looking for the fulfillment of God's promises. For long years, Zechariah probably wondered, "Has the Lord remembered?"

Priests were members of the tribe of Levi, who lived and served among the other tribes. The priests themselves descended from Aaron, the brother of Moses, and thus were a subset of the tribe. They were organized into twenty-four divisions (1 Chronicles 24), and each division took its turn serving for a week at a time in the temple in Jerusalem.

Incense was burned twice each day on an altar located before the curtain that set apart the Holy of Holies in the temple (Exodus 30:1-9). A priest from the serving division was chosen by lot to make this incense offering. Faithful believers gathered outside the temple to pray during these times.

Luke 1:11-17. An angel appeared to Zechariah when he entered the temple. The word *angel* means "messenger," "envoy," or "one who is sent." Not only was the angel "of the Lord" but also the angel stood to the right of the altar, a position signifying power and authority.

Fear mixed with awe was a natural response to such a heavenly visitor. "Do not be afraid" is the recurring response to recipients of these visits in Luke's Gospel (1:13, 30; 2:10). Following that encouragement, the angel in each case also proclaimed good news. In the case of Zechariah, the news was that his prayer had been answered. Although verse 7 stated Zechariah and Elizabeth's situation, this is the first hint of how they were responding to their childlessness. They had been praying—and evidently praying fervently—for a child.

The angel prophesied about the child's birth, his future, his dedication to the Lord, his role in God's plan, and his impact on the nation. In the spirit and power of the Old Testament prophet Elijah, this child would "make ready a people prepared for the Lord" (1:17). The Old Testament ends with the hope that God would send just such a prophet (Malachi 4:5-6).

The angel instructed Zechariah to name his son *John*. The Hebrew equivalent of this most appropriate name means "the Lord has been gracious."

Luke 1:18-20. Zechariah knew his situation well. He was "an old man" (1:18) and Elizabeth was "getting on in years" (1:7). Although he did not come right out and state his doubt that this prophecy could be fulfilled, he certainly expressed his skepticism by asking the angel for some kind of sign.

The angel responded to his skeptical attitude directly. First, he disclosed his name, Gabriel. Zechariah would have known immediately that this was one of the chief angels mentioned in the Hebrew Scriptures (Daniel 8:16; 9:21) and other Jewish writings. Second, Gabriel affirmed his position as one who stood in the very presence of God and had been sent at God's direction. Finally, Gabriel gave Zechariah an immediate sign for which he would not have wished: Zechariah would be unable to speak from that moment until the day the prophecy was fulfilled.

Luke 1:21-23. The people waiting outside the temple became concerned about Zechariah's delay. Perhaps they feared that the old priest had died in the midst of what was probably a once-in-a-lifetime experience of serving in the holy place.

When Zechariah emerged from the temple and could not speak, the people concluded that he had seen a vision. They knew that something significant had happened. Trying his best with hand motions, Zechariah could not communicate about his encounter without the words that now were bottled up inside of him.

After the week of his division's service concluded, Zechariah returned to his home in the Judean hill country (Luke 1:39-40).

Luke 1:24-25. After Zechariah returned home, Elizabeth did conceive as the angel had promised. She remained in seclusion for five months, perhaps fearing that at her age the pregnancy would not be carried full term. When she went public, she did so with praise to God, giving God credit for looking favorably on her and granting her prayer. She also was vindicated among her people, who had viewed her childlessness as a disgrace.

INTERPRETING THE SCRIPTURE

The Miraculous and the Mundane

The popular understanding of miracles seems to require some suspension or contradiction of known scientific law. Something often is considered a miracle only if no other plausible explanation can be given for the event or action. When we have exhausted our reasoning and scientific knowledge, we then seem content to attribute the unexplainable to an act of God.

For well over a century, theologians have struggled with this "God in the gap" approach. We recognize that actions or events that could not be explained a hundred years ago often are easily explained today with our current scientific understandings. As the gaps in our scientific knowledge grow smaller, some wonder whether God's active role in human life will not also seem to shrink and God will grow smaller in our understanding. If science continues to shrink the gaps in our understanding, will God eventually go out of business?

Maybe we sell God short by assuming that God always must work in some big, spectacular way. Does every miracle require the suspension of natural law or the contradiction of scientific understanding? I think not, and Zechariah may be an example in point.

We know a lot today about infertility and how the human body works in the whole reproductive process. Of course, we do not know and understand everything. Some of our efforts likely will look primitive in light of future understandings, and we probably should move cautiously in manipulating factors that we do not fully understand.

Yet remarkably, the story of Zechariah and Elizabeth is not filled with evidence of manipulation. Zechariah supplied the sperm. Elizabeth supplied the ovum. The conception was by natural means. Sure, the age of the couple was unusual; but such things happen from time to time. The miraculous in this story is found not in the spectacular breaking of natural law but rather in a confluence of rather mundane circumstances. Those circumstances converge around the people, prayer, priority, prediction, possibility, and purpose woven into the event. Zechariah and Elizabeth prayed fervently that God would fulfill a purpose in them. Gabriel represented God in affirming the possibility and predicting the outcome in God's time.

What happened to Zechariah and Elizabeth could be explained as an unusual but not unheard of occurrence. Yet in the eyes of their faith, God had done something spectacular for them.

Perhaps we miss the miraculous in our lives because we fail to see in the convergence of mundane circumstances the presence of God at work, bringing about the divine purpose for us, in us, and through us.

Ask, and It Will Be Given You

Although Zechariah and Elizabeth certainly had prayed for years that God would give them a child, note that Gabriel says, "your prayer has been heard" (Luke 1:13). The word translated as *prayer* is singular both in the Greek text and in the English translation.

Most people pray for many things through the years, but the persistent prayers of Zechariah and Elizabeth for a child were so focused that they all could be categorized as one prayer. Could such focus, passion, and determination be better breeding grounds for miracles than the haphazard, spur-of-the-moment, hit-and-miss prayers that characterize so much modern prayer?

Luke records a parable of Jesus that illustrates persistent prayer (Luke 18:1-8). A widow repeatedly petitioned an unjust judge to intervene on her behalf. Because of her doggedness, the judge decided to grant her justice so that he could get her off his back. Jesus was not comparing God to the unjust judge in this parable. Indeed, his point is more like saying, "If an unjust judge will intervene justly on your behalf, how much more will a loving God do for you when you pray always and do not lose heart?"

Sometimes our petitions need to be tested over time. Things that seem of supreme importance today can easily evaporate into insignificance after a few days, weeks, months, or years. When we look back over our lives, we often will thank God that some of our zealous prayers of the moment went unanswered.

The sons of Zebedee asked fervently for a special place in Christ's kingdom; but Jesus told them that they were so short-sighted, they didn't know what they were asking for (Mark 10:35-40). Fervency and sincerity alone are not the answer.

James wrote, "The prayer of the righteous is powerful and effective" (James 5:16). Luke employed the same term, "righteous" (Luke 1:6), to describe Zechariah and Elizabeth. This term implies relationship with God, faithfulness to God's will, and commitment to God's purposes.

Jesus' promise, "Ask, and it will be given you" (Luke 11:9), is a simple promise; but we best understand that promise in the context of a relationship with God that embodies faith, commitment, persistence, humility, and hope. Our prayers will be more powerful and effective if we follow the example of faithful believers such as Zechariah and Elizabeth.

Critical Moments of Divine Encounter

Even in our most intimate moments with God, most of us have not seen angels, much less conversed with them. We may think that such encounters do not occur these days; or we may assume that we simply are not spiritual enough to have these kinds of intimate spiritual experiences.

I like to ask people I meet to tell me about the time in life when they most sensed the presence of God. I have found that most people can name at least one experience when they somehow sensed God's presence. Surprisingly, even the most secular agnostics will identify such experiences. Often the described experience involves the death of a loved one, but the experiences are as varied as are the people I have queried. I have concluded that God is not without witness in our world.

Unfortunately, most of us do not nurture these experiences and reflect upon them. We enjoy the warm fuzzy feeling of God's presence and comfort, but we think the encounter is for our benefit. God comforts us momentarily; but when the passage of time distances us from the painful moment or the time of loss, we no longer need that comfort. The divine encounter slips into the past as little more than a flicker of remembrance.

Most of us do not have frequent moments of divine encounter. Like Zechariah, we may only have one significant moment in our lifetime. What we do with that moment can make an enormous difference. Will we dismiss it? Will we (like Zechariah) greet the moment with skepticism? Or will it become a moment of conception for us when new life begins to take shape within us and the divine encounter begins to shape all that we are and all that the future holds?

God had a purpose that was larger than Zechariah and Elizabeth's desire to have a child. In contrast to Zechariah, Elizabeth rejoiced in "what the Lord has done for me" (Luke 1:25). God was at work, and John was to play a significant role in fulfilling God's purposes in God's time. Luke 1:16-17 ties this child of praying parents into God's plan for ushering in a new age of God's self-revelation in human form. Our critical moments of divine encounter also can tie us into God's plan for the ages and offer us surprising opportunities.

SHARING THE SCRIPTURE

Preparing Our Hearts

Meditate on this week's devotional reading, found in Psalm 66:1-4, 16-20. In these passages the psalmist sings praise and calls on everyone who fears the Lord to listen as he tells what God has done for him. What words of witness to God's mighty deeds in your life have you shared—or could you share—with others? Tell others this good news, which may lead your hearers to come to God through Jesus.

Pray that you and the adult learners will be aware of the "everyday" miracles that God is performing in your lives.

Preparing Our Minds

Study the background, Luke 1:5-25, and lesson Scripture, Luke 1:8-23. As you consider this reading think about any evidence you have that miracles can and do happen in our lives.

Write on newsprint:
❑ information for next week's lesson, found under "Continue the Journey."
❑ activities for further spiritual growth found in "Continue the Journey."

Read the "Introduction" for this quarter, "The Big Picture," "Close-up," and "Faith in Action." Decide how you will use these helps. You may want to incorporate information from the "Introduction" and "The Big Picture" into today's session.

LEADING THE CLASS

(1) Gather to Learn

❖ Welcome the class members and introduce any guests.

❖ Pray that all who have come on this first Sunday of Advent will prepare their hearts to receive the good news of Jesus' coming as God-with-us.

❖ Discuss this question with the class. Write their ideas on newsprint: **How would you define the word** *miracle*?

❖ **Option:** Read these quotations concerning miracles and ask the class to comment on them.

■ **Every believer is God's miracle.** (Philip James Bailey, 1816–1902)

■ **Miracles are not contrary to nature but only contrary to what we know about nature.** (Saint Augustine of Hippo, 354–430)

■ **The miracles of Jesus were the ordinary works of his Father, wrought small and swift that we might take them in.** (George Macdonald, 1824–1905)

❖ Read aloud today's focus statement: **People find it hard to believe that the miraculous could happen to them. What evidence do we have that miracles can happen in our lives? God promised Elizabeth and Zechariah a miracle, and God fulfilled that promise.**

(2) Consider the Story of God's Miraculous Gift to Elizabeth and Zechariah

❖ Use the "Introduction" to the winter quarter to provide a survey of this quarter's sessions.

❖ Consider reading or commenting on selected parts of "The Big Picture: The Community Luke Envisioned" to give the students a broader base from which to study this quarter's sessions.

❖ Use information for Luke 1:5-7 in Understanding the Scripture to set the stage for today's lesson.

❖ Choose volunteers for the parts of a narrator, Gabriel, and Zechariah to read Luke 1:8-23 as a drama.

❖ Ask the class members to put themselves in Zechariah's place. **What questions would you have wanted to ask Gabriel?**

❖ Encourage the students to look at the story from the vantage point of the people waiting for Zechariah to come out of the sanctuary. **What questions would you have wanted to ask Zechariah?**

❖ **Option:** Distribute paper and pencils. Invite the students to write a journal entry as if they were either Zechariah or one of the people who awaited him. Ask them to consider questions they have about the events that have transpired. Also ask them to include their emotional response to this amazing day. Provide an opportunity for volunteers to share their journal entries with a small team or the whole class.

(3) Identify Experiences in the Learners' Lives When God Was Unmistakably at Work

❖ Discuss these questions with the class.

  (1) What miracles have you witnessed in your own life, in the life of someone you know or have heard about, or in your church?

  (2) With whom have you shared your story concerning these miracles? How did these people react?

  (3) How would you respond to people who say they do not believe in miracles?

❖ **Option:** Invite volunteers to role-play this scene, which you will need to read aloud: **As one who believes in miracles, you are talking to a friend who claims that miracles are impossible, that there is a rational explanation for everything that happens. State some miracles from your**

experience (or from the Bible) and, without arguing, try to persuade your friend that miracles can and do occur, perhaps more often than we know.

❖ Debrief this role-play by encouraging the adults to talk about ways they have found to share their faith with people who must have a solid explanation for everything that happens.

(4) Challenge Others to Believe God's Promises

❖ Distribute paper and pencils if you have not already done so. Ask the students to search their Bibles for promises that God has made and ways that those promises have been fulfilled. List these promises on the paper. Some students may know the chapter and verse, whereas others will be able to quote or paraphrase the promise. Here are several covenantal promises if the class needs some starters: Genesis 6:18 (Noah); 9:11 (Noah); 12:2, 3, 7 (Abraham); Deuteronomy 28:1-68 (Moses and the Israelites); 2 Samuel 7:16 (David); Jeremiah 31:31-34 (promise of a new covenant).

❖ Divide the students into groups and ask them to tell one another a promise that is especially meaningful to them. The students should state why the promise is so important to them.

❖ Talk about how belief in God's promises—even when those promises seemingly require a miracle to fulfill—enable people to answer God's call.

❖ Conclude the session by challenging the learners to share their promises with others and give testimony as to why they find it crucial to believe and respond to God's promises.

(5) Continue the Journey

❖ Pray that all who have participated in today's session will hear and respond to God's call on their lives.

❖ Read aloud this preparation for next week's lesson. You may also want to post it on newsprint for the students to copy.

■ **Title: Called to Be a Vessel!**
■ **Background Scripture: Luke 1:26-38**
■ **Lesson Scripture: Luke 1:26-38**
■ **Focus of the Lesson: We want to know that we are significant to someone and that our lives count for something. How does God address these needs by calling us to serve? Mary is an example of how God can call us to significance and purpose.**

❖ Challenge the students to complete one or more of these activities for further spiritual growth, which you will write on newsprint for the students to copy.

(1) **Page through your Bible looking for examples of miracles. Write a few words about each one in your journal. Who experienced this miracle, why, and how did they respond?**

(2) **Do some research on Gabriel. What can you learn about this archangel? Where else does he appear in the Scriptures?**

(3) **Remember that Zechariah was called to believe, but he found it difficult to accept Gabriel's words of promise. What is God calling you to believe that may also be difficult to accept? Pray that God will strengthen and guide you.**

❖ Sing or read aloud "Come, Thou Long-Expected Jesus."

❖ Conclude today's session by leading the class in this benediction, which is taken from Ephesians 6:23-24: **Peace be to the whole community, and love with faith, from God the Father and the Lord Jesus Christ. Grace be with all who have an undying love for our Lord Jesus Christ. Amen.**

UNIT 1: GOD'S CALL AT CHRISTMAS AND BEYOND
CALLED TO BE A VESSEL!

PREVIEWING THE LESSON

Lesson Scripture: Luke 1:26-38
Background Scripture: Luke 1:26-38
Key Verse: Luke 1:38

Focus of the Lesson:
We want to know that we are significant to someone and that our lives count for something. How does God address these needs by calling us to serve? Mary is an example of how God can call us to significance and purpose.

Goals for the Learners:
(1) to encounter the powerful narrative in which Mary is called to be the mother of God's Son.
(2) to recognize their significance and purpose in God's kingdom.
(3) to respond as Mary did by saying yes to God's plan for them.

Pronunciation Guide:
Annunciation (uh nuhn see ay' shuhn)
Josephus (jo see' fus)
Midrash (mi' drash)
Talmud (tal' mood)

Supplies:
Bibles, newsprint and marker, paper and pencils, hymnals, picture depicting the Annunciation

READING THE SCRIPTURE

NRSV
Luke 1:26-38

²⁶In the sixth month the angel Gabriel was sent by God to a town in Galilee called Nazareth, ²⁷to a virgin engaged to a man whose name was Joseph, of the house of David. The virgin's name was Mary. ²⁸And

NIV
Luke 1:26-38

²⁶In the sixth month, God sent the angel Gabriel to Nazareth, a town in Galilee, ²⁷to a virgin pledged to be married to a man named Joseph, a descendant of David. The virgin's name was Mary. ²⁸The angel went

he came to her and said, "Greetings, favored one! The Lord is with you." ²⁹But she was much perplexed by his words and pondered what sort of greeting this might be. ³⁰The angel said to her, "Do not be afraid, Mary, for you have found favor with God. ³¹And now, you will conceive in your womb and bear a son, and you will name him Jesus. ³²He will be great, and will be called the Son of the Most High, and the Lord God will give to him the throne of his ancestor David. ³³He will reign over the house of Jacob forever, and of his kingdom there will be no end." ³⁴Mary said to the angel, "How can this be, since I am a virgin?" ³⁵The angel said to her, "The Holy Spirit will come upon you, and the power of the Most High will overshadow you; therefore the child to be born will be holy; he will be called Son of God. ³⁶And now, your relative Elizabeth in her old age has also conceived a son; and this is the sixth month for her who was said to be barren. ³⁷For nothing will be impossible with God." **³⁸Then Mary said, "Here am I, the servant of the Lord; let it be with me according to your word." Then the angel departed from her.**

to her and said, "Greetings, you who are highly favored! The Lord is with you."

²⁹Mary was greatly troubled at his words and wondered what kind of greeting this might be. ³⁰But the angel said to her, "Do not be afraid, Mary, you have found favor with God. ³¹You will be with child and give birth to a son, and you are to give him the name Jesus. ³²He will be great and will be called the Son of the Most High. The Lord God will give him the throne of his father David, ³³and he will reign over the house of Jacob forever; his kingdom will never end."

³⁴"How will this be," Mary asked the angel, "since I am a virgin?"

³⁵The angel answered, "The Holy Spirit will come upon you, and the power of the Most High will overshadow you. So the holy one to be born will be called the Son of God. ³⁶Even Elizabeth your relative is going to have a child in her old age, and she who was said to be barren is in her sixth month. ³⁷For nothing is impossible with God."

³⁸"I am the Lord's servant," Mary answered. "May it be to me as you have said." Then the angel left her.

UNDERSTANDING THE SCRIPTURE

Luke 1:26-27. Luke split the account of Gabriel's announcement of the coming birth of a son to Zechariah and Elizabeth from the account of John's actual birth. Intervening is what often is called the *Annunciation,* a term derived from the Latin word for "announcement." This announcement holds special significance. It involved a second appearance of the angel Gabriel in Luke's Gospel as well as the declaration to Mary that she would be the mother of Jesus. The Roman tradition celebrates a feast commemorating this "Annunciation" on March 25 each year.

Nazareth was a relatively unknown town that was not mentioned in the Old Testament, in the Midrash (the rabbis'

comments on and explanations of the Old Testament), in the Talmud (the collection of writing containing Jewish civil and religious law), or in the writing of the first-century Jewish historian Josephus. Luke probably referenced the better-known district of Galilee in the northern part of Palestine to assist his readers in locating the small town. Galilee was known as a Gentile region (Isaiah 9:1; Matthew 4:15). Luke's reference here foreshadows the scope of Christ's ministry to the people of all nations—something that becomes more evident as Luke's Gospel unfolds.

Mary and Joseph are introduced with only one descriptor each. Mary was a virgin. Joseph, "of the house of David," was a descendant of Israel's idealized king. Their betrothal was a more formal matter than current engagements. It involved agreements and pledges between the two families that required the equivalent of a divorce to nullify. Joseph and Mary both possessed familiar biblical names. His parallels the Old Testament patriarch Joseph, and her name in Greek literally corresponds with the name of Moses' sister, Miriam.

Luke 1:28-30. Gabriel's greeting of Mary as "favored one" recalls Elizabeth's conclusion that the Lord had looked "favorably" on her (1:25). The root word is found in verse 30 where Gabriel says that Mary has found grace or "favor" with God. The verb form in verse 28 was used in New Testament times only to speak of divine grace and thus could be translated as "one who has been blessed with God's grace."

When combined with the assurance that "the Lord is with you," Gabriel's announcement was intended to reassure Mary. Instead, it produced bewilderment. In pondering "what sort of greeting this might be," perhaps Mary recalled the Old Testament account of angels who took wives for themselves from among the daughters of humanity and bore children with them (Genesis 6:1-4). Gabriel quickly put such notions aside by affirming that she had found favor "with God." She had no cause to be afraid.

Luke 1:31-33. Gabriel's announcement to Mary covered three significant stages in the birth of a child: conception, birth, and naming. Mary would conceive in her womb—the child would be her own offspring. The child would be a son. The child would be named Jesus. Jesus was a name commonly found among the Jews in biblical times and was a Greek form of the Hebrew name Joshua. Its root meaning is "God is salvation." Matthew recorded a later angelic visit to Joseph in a dream with similar instructions about naming the child (Matthew 1:20-21).

Gabriel then disclosed the true significance of the coming child. In a prophecy filled with messianic imagery, Gabriel tied the child to God ("Son of the Most High"), to David ("the throne of his ancestor"), to the nation ("reign over the house of Jacob"), and to eternity ("of his kingdom there will be no end"). We have difficulty recognizing the revolutionary nature of this prophecy. From an obscure place and with a relatively unknown couple, God was about to launch something that was historic, universal, and eternal.

Luke 1:34-37. Interestingly, Mary questioned the first of Gabriel's statements (the conception) without being staggered and overwhelmed by the rest of the prophecy. She knew she was a virgin. She seems to have assumed that if the physical issues of conception could be overcome, the spiritual issues would fall into place. She did not doubt Gabriel's statement; she merely questioned the *how* of it.

Mary did not fall back on the most natural explanation: She and her espoused husband would marry and have a child who would fulfill Gabriel's prophecies. She recognized an immediacy in Gabriel's announcement that meant such extraordinary outcomes would not follow ordinary processes.

Gabriel confirmed Mary's insight. Rather than focusing on the *how* of the conception, however, Gabriel focused on the *who*. The Holy Spirit would come upon Mary, and the power of God Almighty would overshadow or cover her like a cloud—an image we find in other biblical accounts that focus on the presence of God (see Exodus 40:35; Matthew 17:5; Mark 9:7; Luke 9:34). The child to be born would be holy or set apart as specially dedicated to God. He would be called God's Son.

In case Mary still had questions or misgivings, Gabriel gave her a sign that would confirm his revelations to her. Her relative Elizabeth, who had been barren, had conceived and was in the sixth month of her pregnancy. "Nothing will be impossible with God," whether a child for an elderly woman who had been barren or a child born of the Holy Spirit to a virgin.

Luke 1:38. Mary's response to this overwhelming announcement by Gabriel was simple and to the point. "Here am I" translates a word that means "to look, behold, or see." It is derived from an imperative form, however, and thus issues a command that could be understood as "Behold me, the servant of the Lord" or "See me as the servant of the Lord."

The word *servant* is the same word in

Greek as *slave*. It can speak of low status and forced subjection, but it certainly carries more meaning here. Like the son who would be born to her, Mary did not count status as something to be grasped; but rather, taking the role of a slave, she humbled herself and became obedient to God's call (compare Philippians 2:6-8). Gabriel's words to her became the call of God to service—not merely for a moment or for nine months, but for a lifetime.

INTERPRETING THE SCRIPTURE

The Humble Roots of Great Events

Because of our familiarity with this Bible story, we may overlook the task Luke faced. He took what otherwise would be an insignificant event involving unknown people from an inconspicuous place and elevated it to a supremely important event in salvation history. Nazareth was such an out-of-the-way village that Luke had to place it "in Galilee" to help his readers locate it. In comparison with the famous, the prominent, and the powerful of the day, Mary and Joseph were unknowns. The popular expectations for the Messiah were for a powerful military ruler who would throw off oppression and defeat the nation's enemies. Surely such a one would be born in the king's palace in Jerusalem.

God often does not work in ways we expect. Too often we look for great signs, powerful testimony, or spectacular results. As Paul observed in 1 Corinthians 1, however, God did not choose the wise, the powerful, or the blue bloods of this world to demonstrate the power of salvation. Instead, God chose the foolish, the weak, the humble, and the despised. God did not use a military conqueror to establish the kingdom. God chose instead an executioner's cross as the instrument of redemption for all who believe.

God is likely working in our lives today in unexpected ways. Unexpected people in unexpected places can be instruments of God's grace. The wise, the strong, the confident, and the popular often tickle our ears with words that seem right by earthly standards. Our spiritual ears, however, must be attuned to the voices of those the world considers foolish, weak, humble, and despised. Of course, our ears should be open to hearing every voice; but we must guard our hearts with spiritual discernment to weed out the worldly and to nurture the spiritual no matter how unlikely the source, how unrealistic the message, or how improbable the task.

We also must not overlook the possibility that we ourselves might be chosen channels through which God will do something significant and unexpected in our time. No matter how preposterous that might sound, such a possibility bestows significance and purpose on each of us. Whether our calling is to tasks great or small, God has ways of using the talents, gifts, and lives of any who say, "Here am I, the servant of the Lord" (Luke 1:38). Such commitment is the humble root of every great spiritual harvest.

Active Engagement in God's Will

In 1966 John Lennon, group member of the British rock band the Beatles, offended many American Christians by stating that the Beatles were "more popular than Jesus." Despite this audacity, one of the Beatles' most famous songs was based on the declaration of Mary in Luke 1:38, "Let it be."

The difference between what the Beatles and Mary meant by "let it be" is considerable, however. The Beatles advocated passive resignation to life's circumstances, being at peace with whatever happens because you cannot control it. When times of trouble, hours of darkness, or stormy nights come, let it be. When you are brokenhearted, let it be. Everything will turn out all right in the end if you just passively accept whatever comes.

Sometimes we hear Christians talk about surrendering to God's will. Such talk seems to imply that God gradually removes all other choices and options and thereby forces us to accept the divine will. In such a view, God's will is so overpowering, all we can do is throw in the towel, lay down our arms, and passively submit.

Mary's acceptance of God's plan was not such a passive resignation. Neither was it total surrender because God had overpowered her and left her no other way out. Rather, her "let it be" was a decision to become actively engaged in God's will. We may not be able to imagine what other options she had or what consequences would have resulted if she had chosen differently, but Mary chose all of the opportunities and all of the consequences of God's plan revealed to her by Gabriel.

How did she do this? Mary first committed herself to being "the servant [or slave] of the Lord," a rich biblical expression used of apostles, prophets, and others who were committed to God, body and soul. Like Isaiah, Mary offered herself to God, "Here am I" (Isaiah 6:8). And certainly foreshadowing her son in the Garden of Gethsemane, she affirmed to God, "not my will but yours be done" (Luke 22:42).

If God were to choose you and me to do something special in our time, what kind of response would we make? Would our words be, "Let it be according to your will"? In reality, God already has chosen us. Second Timothy 1:9 reminds us that God not only saved us, but God also "called us with a holy calling, not according to our works but according to his own purpose and grace." Maybe we should change the first sentence in this paragraph to acknowledge God's call: Since God has chosen you and me to do something special in our time, what kind of response will we make?

The Physical as Foundation for the Spiritual

When told by Gabriel that she would bear a son, Mary focused on the physical barriers that hindered the accomplishment of God's spiritual purposes. Whereas the spiritual realities that God would accomplish through Mary's son were enormous, Mary rightly saw that the physical barrier of a virgin conceiving was a significant hurdle to accomplishing the spiritual purposes.

We would be wrong to think that God accomplishes spiritual objectives today without any physical means and resources. The church of Jesus Christ often faces physical barriers that hinder the church's accomplishment of God's spiritual intentions. Churches cannot fully achieve their objectives without people, places, programs, and financial resources. When churches lack the necessary physical resources, spiritual achievement most often will founder.

Gabriel responded to Mary's concern about the physical barriers by focusing on the *who* rather than on the *how*. Although God continues to be the great Who in supplying resources for people, in reality we are the major physical resource for carrying out God's purposes. We are the people. Our church facilities are the places. Our worship, study, and ministries are the programs. Our tithes and offerings are the financial resources.

Of course, we often face the danger of making the physical resources rather than the spiritual goals our chief objectives. Churches can place too much emphasis on recruiting workers, constructing buildings, inventing programs, and raising funds. We can focus so strongly on the physical barriers to ministry that we lose sight of the fact that God is the power behind our efforts.

Though Mary was concerned about the physical barriers, remember that she alone could not break them down. As in the case of Mary, the work of the Holy Spirit in our midst and the overshadowing presence of God's power is the precursor of overcoming even the physical barriers that stand between the church and its mission objectives. Like Mary, we are called to be the vessels of God, and like her we can trust God to remove all barriers if we but say yes to God.

SHARING THE SCRIPTURE

Preparing Our Hearts

Meditate on this week's devotional reading found in Psalm 40:1-5. The psalmist sings a song of thanksgiving for God's deliverance from "the desolate pit" and "miry bog" (40:2). Why would God do such a thing? Could it be that God has a purpose for each of our lives that is not to be thwarted? Think about times when you have needed help and God responded. Did you feel that you had significance before God? What purpose, perhaps even new purpose, did you feel called to fulfill? Write about such an experience in your spiritual journal.

Pray that you and the adult learners will praise God for divine intervention in your lives and respond by saying yes to whatever plans God has for you.

Preparing Our Minds

Study the background and lesson Scripture, both of which are found in Luke 1:26-38. Think about how God addresses our need to have our lives count for something by calling us to serve.

Write on newsprint:
❑ information for next week's lesson, found under "Continue the Journey."

❑ activities for further spiritual growth in "Continue the Journey."

Locate a picture of the Annunciation on the Internet or in a book that you can bring to class. Artists who have depicted this famous scene include Botticelli (1445–1510), Fra Filippo Lippi (1457–1504), Melchoir Broederlam (active 1381–1409), Caravaggio (1571–1610), Dante Gabriel Rossetti (painting, 1850).

Option: Prepare one or more lectures for "Encounter the Powerful Narrative in which Mary Is Called to Be the Mother of God's Son."

LEADING THE CLASS

(1) Gather to Learn

❖ Welcome the class members and introduce any guests.

❖ Pray that all who have come today will be open to God's call on their lives.

❖ Spend a few moments reviewing the familiar calls of Moses and Jeremiah, found in Exodus 3:1-6 and Jeremiah 1:5, 9-10, respectively.

❖ Ask the class to remember how these remarkable leaders responded to God's call. Note that Moses had all kinds of excuses for not serving, according to Exodus 3 and 4: people will want to know who sent him;

people may not believe him; he is not a good speaker; God should send someone else. Jeremiah claimed to be "only a boy" and unable to speak (Jeremiah 1:6).

❖ Point out that in contrast Isaiah gave an immediate, positive response: "Here am I; send me!" (Isaiah 6:8).

❖ Note that in the end, all three of these spiritual giants answered God's call. We remember them because they made significant contributions to the kingdom of God.

❖ Read aloud today's focus statement: **We want to know that we are significant to someone and that our lives count for something. How does God address these needs by calling us to serve? Mary is an example of how God can call us to significance and purpose.**

(2) Encounter the Powerful Narrative in which Mary Is Called to Be the Mother of God's Son

❖ Show the picture(s) of the Annunciation that you have brought. Invite the students to tell the story as it seems to appear in this picture. Ask them to note specific images or symbols and tell how the picture is enriched by their use. (If you have a large class, you may want to locate more than one picture and divide into groups to do this activity.)

❖ Invite three volunteers to read the parts of the narrator, Mary, and Gabriel from Luke 1:26-38.

❖ Encourage the students to discuss what they learn about the coming Jesus, Mary, and Joseph from this passage. Augment their discussion with information from "Understanding the Scripture," either informally or in a prepared lecture.

❖ Focus on Mary's acceptance of God's will for her life. Read or retell the third, fourth, and fifth paragraphs from "Active Engagement in God's Will" in Interpreting the Scripture. Discuss these questions, or answer them yourself in an optional lecture.

(1) Our writer states: Mary's "'let it be' was a decision to become actively engaged in God's will." What do you think might have led Mary to agree to God's will?

(2) What commitments did Mary apparently make in order to become actively engaged in God's will?

(3) What are the risks and rewards that she likely encountered?

(4) What would you have done had you been Mary? Why?

(3) Recognize the Learners' Significance and Purpose in God's Kingdom

❖ Distribute paper and pencils. Encourage the students to list high points on their spiritual journey to date. Ask them to review their lists to see what they reveal about God's purpose for their lives.

❖ Invite the students to talk with a small group about their findings. If the adults know one another well, they may be able to add ideas and help one another to identify their life purposes.

❖ Point out that *Christian vocation* is a term often used to refer to the work that God calls each of us to do, the purpose for our lives. Read these words found in *Wishful Thinking: A Seeker's ABC* by Frederick Buechner as he writes about how we can discern our vocation, our purpose: **"The kind of work God usually calls you to is the kind of work (a) that you need most to do and (b) that the world most needs to have done. . . . The place God calls you to is the place where your deep gladness and the world's deep hunger meet."**

❖ Provide quiet time for the students to once again review their lists. Suggest that they consider these questions.

(1) Do your purposes reflect the kind of work you need to do and the world needs to have done?

(2) If not, what changes can you make so that what you do better reflects who God calls you to be?

(4) Respond as Mary Did by Saying Yes to God's Plan

❖ Break the silence by inviting the students to listen to you read paragraphs two through four of "The Humble Roots of Great Events" in Interpreting the Scripture.

❖ Solicit comments from the students about times when they have said yes to God. How did they feel about making such a commitment? How did the situation work out?

❖ Ask the students to read in unison today's key verse, Luke 1:38, ending with "word."

(5) Continue the Journey

❖ Pray that today's participants will recognize and fulfill the purpose that God has for their lives.

❖ Read aloud this preparation for next week's lesson. You may also want to post it on newsprint for the students to copy.
■ **Title: Called to Proclaim!**
■ **Background Scripture: Luke 1:57-80**
■ **Lesson Scripture: Luke 1:64, 67-80**
■ **Focus of the Lesson: We often talk about experiences that change us. What difference do these transforming events make in how we live? At John's birth, Zechariah proclaimed the vision of God's future for his son John, who would prepare people for the coming of the Messiah.**

■ Challenge the students to complete one or more of these activities for further spiritual growth, which you will write on newsprint for the students to copy.
   (1) Look for descriptions of Mary in hymns or carols. How do these poetic descriptions square with or diverge from your understanding of Mary as recorded in the Bible?
   (2) Be alert for opportunities to act as "a servant of the Lord" this week. Perhaps God will lead you to perform an act of kindness for a stranger.
   (3) Spend extra time in prayer, meditation, and devotional Bible reading this week as you prepare during the Advent season to recall Jesus' birth and look ahead to his second coming.

❖ Sing or read aloud "To a Maid Engaged to Joseph."

❖ Conclude today's session by leading the class in this benediction, which is taken from Ephesians 6:23-24: **Peace be to the whole community, and love with faith, from God the Father and the Lord Jesus Christ. Grace be with all who have an undying love for our Lord Jesus Christ. Amen.**

UNIT 1: GOD'S CALL AT CHRISTMAS AND BEYOND
CALLED TO PROCLAIM!

PREVIEWING THE LESSON

Lesson Scripture: Luke 1:67-80
Background Scripture: Luke 1:57-80
Key Verse: Luke 1:64

Focus of the Lesson:
We often talk about experiences that change us. What difference do these transforming events make in how we live? At John's birth, Zechariah proclaimed the vision of God's future for his son John, who would prepare people for the coming of the Messiah.

Goals for the Learners:
(1) to recognize how Zechariah's behavior changed as a result of the fulfillment of God's promise in John's birth.
(2) to review their life-changing events.
(3) to tell others how believing in Jesus changes their lives.

Supplies:
Bibles, newsprint and marker, paper and pencils, hymnals

READING THE SCRIPTURE

NRSV
Luke 1:64, 67-80

⁶⁴Immediately his [Zechariah's] mouth was opened and his tongue freed, and he began to speak, praising God.

⁶⁷Then his father Zechariah was filled with the Holy Spirit and spoke this prophecy:
⁶⁸ "Blessed be the Lord God of Israel,
for he has looked favorably on his people and redeemed them.
⁶⁹ He has raised up a mighty savior for us in the house of his servant David,

NIV
Luke 1:64, 67-80

⁶⁴Immediately his [Zechariah's] mouth was opened and his tongue was loosed, and he began to speak, praising God.

⁶⁷His father Zechariah was filled with the Holy Spirit and prophesied:
⁶⁸ "Praise be to the Lord, the God of Israel,
because he has come and has redeemed his people.
⁶⁹ He has raised up a horn of salvation for us in the house of his servant David
⁷⁰ (as he said through his holy prophets of long ago),

70 as he spoke through the mouth of his holy
      prophets from of old,
71   that we would be saved from our
      enemies and from the hand of all who
      hate us.
72 Thus he has shown the mercy promised to
      our ancestors,
      and has remembered his holy covenant,
73 the oath that he swore to our ancestor
      Abraham,
      to grant us 74that we, being rescued
      from the hands of our enemies,
   might serve him without fear,
75 in holiness and righteousness
      before him all our days.
76 And you, child, will be called the prophet
      of the Most High;
      for you will go before the Lord to pre-
      pare his ways,
77 to give knowledge of salvation to his
      people
      by the forgiveness of their sins.
78 By the tender mercy of our God,
      the dawn from on high will break upon
      us,
79 to give light to those who sit in darkness
      and in the shadow of death,
      to guide our feet into the way of peace."
80 The child grew and became strong in
spirit, and he was in the wilderness until the
day he appeared publicly to Israel.

71 salvation from our enemies
      and from the hand of all who hate us—
72 to show mercy to our fathers
      and to remember his holy covenant,
73 the oath he swore to our father Abraham:
74 to rescue us from the hand of our enemies,
      and to enable us to serve him without
      fear
75 in holiness and righteousness before him
      all our days.
76 And you, my child, will be called a
      prophet of the Most High;
      for you will go on before the Lord to
      prepare the way for him,
77 to give his people the knowledge of sal-
      vation
      through the forgiveness of their sins,
78 because of the tender mercy of our God,
      by which the rising sun will come to us
      from heaven
79 to shine on those living in darkness
      and in the shadow of death,
   to guide our feet into the path of peace."
80And the child grew and became strong
in spirit; and he lived in the desert until he
appeared publicly to Israel.

UNDERSTANDING THE SCRIPTURE

Luke 1:57-58. After Mary returned home (Luke 1:56), Elizabeth and Zechariah experienced the fulfillment of Gabriel's prophecy (1:13). The prophecy spoke of the birth and naming of the child. Luke's account spanned John's conception (1:24), birth (1:57), and naming (1:59-63). This same focus on significant events was seen with Mary in verse 31.

The joy that Elizabeth expressed in her pregnancy (1:25) was completed by the birth of her son. Even the neighbors and relatives who once had viewed her childlessness as a disgrace rejoiced with her. All the neighbors and relatives joined in this rejoicing. They recognized that the Lord had shown great mercy to Elizabeth. Luke also used a stronger Greek word for God's *mercy* than he had employed in verse 25 to speak of God's looking favorably on Elizabeth.

Luke 1:59-66. Since the time that God had established the covenant with Abraham, the covenant symbol of circumcision had been administered to male children when they were eight days old (Genesis 17:9-13). As devout believers "living blamelessly according to all the commandments and regulations of the Lord" (Luke 1:6), Zechariah and Elizabeth followed this practice.

The eighth day also was the day on which a child customarily was named (compare Luke 2:21). Because Zechariah had been unable to speak since his encounter with Gabriel in the temple (1:20), his brothers or other male relatives likely assumed the duty of naming the child. Naming children after significant relatives was a common practice. Because of Zechariah's advanced age (1:18), they probably thought they could honor Zechariah most by naming the child after him.

Elizabeth intervened, however, and insisted that the child be named John (meaning "the Lord has been gracious"). Luke does not explain how Elizabeth knew about Gabriel's instructions on naming the child (1:13); but when the relatives gestured to Zechariah about his wishes, Zechariah requested a tablet and confirmed in writing Elizabeth's spoken choice. Not only did this concurrence amaze the relatives, but at that moment Zechariah regained his ability to speak. Gabriel's prophecy (1:20) had been fulfilled in every respect.

The results of these events were amazement, fear, and reflection. The news spread quickly into the entire region as people learned the whole story from Zechariah's encounter in the temple to the birth of this special child of his old age. People recognized that God was at work in the birth of this child, and they rightly wondered what purpose God was planning for him.

Luke 1:67-75. When Zechariah regained his speech, he spoke first in praise (1:64) and then in prophecy (1:68-79). His words of praise grew out of his experience with God in the temple. His words of prophecy came from an infilling of the Holy Spirit.

The prophecy began with a blessing for God's wonderful deeds. In this case, the focus is on the fulfillment of the nation's messianic hope.

Whereas many think of prophecy as foretelling the future, Zechariah's blessing reveals another important aspect of prophecy. He announced the fulfillment of the nation's hopes in advance, and he did so by declaring the work as already accomplished.

Some of the prophecy could indeed be considered accomplished. God had redeemed the chosen people (1:68) on many occasions. God had spoken through many prophets (1:70). God had shown mercy and remembered the covenant (1:72) many times. Essential elements of the prophecy, however, were unfulfilled. The "mighty savior" had not yet been raised up (1:69). The Jews were living under the domination of Roman power and had not been saved from their enemies (1:71, 73). These unfulfilled expectations were part of the people's messianic hope.

We would expect verses 68-75 to be filled with verbs in the future tense to point to these unfulfilled expectations. Instead, every verb form in verses 68-75 except one is in the Greek aorist tense. The aorist tense is like a snapshot, denoting action at a particular point of time in the past. Zechariah's prophetic power comes in his certainty in asserting that the future purposes of God are so established and unalterable that we can view them as already accomplished. The coming of the mighty savior from the house of David who would save the people from their enemies was so certain that Zechariah said it was already done!

The only exception to the Greek aorist verbs in this section is the verb *serve* in verse 74. This verb is in the present tense and speaks of the current purpose of God's people—to serve God "without fear, in holiness and righteousness" (1:74-75).

Luke 1:76-79. Zechariah turned from his praise of God to address his newborn son. This too is prophetic. Zechariah shifted into the future tense as he peered into God's purposes for the life and ministry of John the Baptist. One day this newborn would be recognized as a prophet of the Most High preparing the way (Isaiah 40:3; Malachi 3:1) for "the Son of the Most High" (Luke 1:32).

The mercy God had shown Elizabeth (1:58) would be multiplied exponentially as the promised "dawn from on high" (1:78) would come and break the bondage of captivity that had held the people in darkness and in the shadow of death (Malachi 4:2; Psalm 107:10; Isaiah 9:2). The net result could be described as living in "peace," that Old Testament *shalom* of spiritual well-being based in covenant with God and reflected in all dimensions of life.

Luke 1:80. Luke concluded with a broad summary statement about John. He grew, became strong, and lived in the wilderness until his public appearance. All of these events and circumstances led to Luke's conclusion that the hand of the Lord was with John from before his birth (Luke 1:66). Luke prepared his readers to look carefully at the role John would play in the gospel and to listen attentively to his words of testimony about Jesus (see especially Luke 3).

INTERPRETING THE SCRIPTURE

Changing Faithfulness into Fulfillment

Both John the Baptist and Jesus made repentance central in their proclamations (Matthew 3:2; 4:17). The word *repent* means to change one's mind or to turn around and change direction. Change is at the heart of our responses to the gospel.

Many of the analogies that we use to describe conversion and Christian experience focus on change. Once I was blind, but now I see. Once I was dead in sin, but now I am alive in Christ. Once I was lost, but now I am found. Such essential changes result when we acknowledge our sin, confess it to God, and through faith accept God's offer of forgiveness and salvation.

When God breaks through into our lives, changes take place at many levels. For Zechariah, the changes may not have been as dramatic as for a drug dealer turning from a life of blatant sin to faith and obedience. But Zechariah's changes were just as important and may bear more similarity to our experiences.

Zechariah was a good and moral person. He tried to do what was right and just. He was respected by his friends. He did important work for God and God's people. He had been faithful to God through many decades. But at the center of his life, something was awry. God was in his head, but something was missing in his heart. His religion was practiced, formal, and essentially sincere, but it was incomplete. He was disappointed in God and in himself. The one thing he thought central to the purpose of his life—fathering a child—was unfinished. He faithfully continued his routines; but time was running out, and he was about prayed-out.

Too many people in the church have given up on faithfulness. We are impatient and impulsive; and when things do not go as we expect, we give up on God rather than maintain our faithfulness. We try to fill the emptiness with activity or diversions. We try to drown the emptiness with drugs, alcohol, or other risky behaviors. We try to compensate for our sense of incompleteness by hard work, achievement, and symbols of success.

Of course, the desires of our hearts are not always the desires of God's heart for us. In Zechariah's case, the two corresponded. In ours, they may not. Zechariah lacked the spark that came when an intimate encounter with God confirmed God's will for him. God honored his faithfulness, and God will do the same with us.

When we encounter God, we may have to change our priorities, our directions, our hopes, and our dreams. God has the best plan, the right direction, and the greatest dream for us. When we are faithful in seeking God, God will be faithful in turning our faithfulness into fulfillment. Gratitude, rejoicing, blessing, and praise flow from knowing we are in God's will and are fulfilling God's purposes. If we are faithful in asking, seeking, and knocking, God will fill our lives with purpose and meaning.

Changing Disgrace into Joy

Most of us face the judgment of other people. Elizabeth's failure to meet the expectations of her friends and neighbors caused her to feel a sense of disgrace. Barrenness is not a one-person issue. Couples react differently to it and to the judgments of others. We have no indication that Zechariah felt *disgraced* by their childlessness, but he certainly wanted a child, as evidenced by the angel's assurance that his prayer had been heard and that Elizabeth would bear a son. Elizabeth, however, would have felt greatly disgraced because in her culture barrenness was viewed as a sign of God's disfavor upon the woman. Although the expressions of their disappointment, emptiness, and despair were different, a new perspective was needed by both of them.

Too many of us audaciously assume that we know more about what is best for others than they know themselves. We set high standards for others, load them down with expectations, and then lash out when they fail to measure up. We do this to our spouses, children, and friends. We do it to our leaders in churches, schools, and government. We have even been known to do it to foreign nations.

Equally as often, we are on the receiving end of such expectations. As a result, our failure to measure up and meet the standards set by others fills us with a sense of failure, disgrace, and even self-disgust. To compensate, we try to make ourselves more attractive by changing our wardrobes, our appearances, and our bodies. We try to convey success with larger homes, more powerful cars, and expensive hobbies. We try to improve our self-image with meditation, medication, and therapy.

Our problem is that we are trying to change ourselves rather than changing the standards, expectations, and goals that drive us. Elizabeth only made progress when she recognized that God was the one who was working to make her life full and abundant. God was the one who showed mercy to her.

Grace and mercy are expressions of unmerited love. They come regardless of appearance, status, wealth, or achievement. They come because God wants for us the most full and abundant life possible. Grace transforms disgrace into joy as it transforms us into the people God intends for us to be. Such transformation comes by the renewing of our minds as we discern the good, acceptable, and perfect will of God (Romans 12:2).

Changing Despair into Purpose

For a nation with barely two hundred years of national history, we have a difficult time understanding the despair experienced by God's people who lived for more than half a millennium under foreign domination. From the fall of Jerusalem to the Babylonians in 587 B.C. through control by the Romans, the Jews had only brief spells of semi-independence through New Testament times.

The messages of their prophets had pictured a different scenario. God had promised a Messiah, an anointed king from the lineage of King David, who would overthrow the oppressors and would lead the people to worldwide prestige and power.

Keeping alive the flame of messianic hope was difficult when foreigners or their puppet representatives ruled the land, when the holy temple had been desecrated, when taxes were siphoned off to foreign capitals, and when foreign soldiers regularly pressed people into menial service. Occasionally the flames of hope were revived as one or another messianic pretender rallied fighters to overthrow the oppressors, but each failed in turn.

Like Mary in the previous lesson, Zechariah nursed the hope. Inspired by the Holy Spirit, he anticipated the future fulfillment and treated it as having already happened.

Hope without some tangible experience is difficult to sustain. Zechariah's prophecy gave God's people a purpose to fulfill while they waited for fulfillment. The purpose is to "serve [God] without fear, in holiness and righteousness . . . all our days" (Luke 1:74-75).

Despair fades when we face it courageously. No matter how dismal the circumstances or bleak the future may appear, God calls us to fearless purpose and devotion. John Bunyan in his classic *Pilgrim's Progress* has Christian pass through many treacherous trials. When imprisoned in Doubting Castle, Christian passionately states, "What a fool I am, to lie this way in a stinking dungeon when I may as well walk at liberty! I have a key in my bosom called Promise, and I am persuaded that it will open any lock in Doubting Castle."

Such promise banishes fear and enables us to serve God faithfully and proclaim good news even in despairing circumstances. Such promise undergirds holiness and righteousness until we reach the Celestial City.

SHARING THE SCRIPTURE

Preparing Our Hearts

Meditate on this week's devotional reading, found in Malachi 3:1-4. The prophet introduces the messenger who will prepare the way of the Lord. Christians believe this messenger is John the Baptist, whose long-anticipated birth is the focus of today's lesson. What do you know about John? What attributes link him with the messenger who Malachi and Isaiah (40:3) point toward?

Pray that you and the adult learners will be open to people and situations that move you closer to God.

Preparing Our Minds

Study the background, Luke 1:57-80, and the lesson Scripture, Luke 1:67-80. As you ponder this material think about how events that change us make a difference in the way we live.

Write on newsprint:
- ❑ information for next week's lesson, found under "Continue the Journey."
- ❑ activities for further spiritual growth in "Continue the Journey."

LEADING THE CLASS

(1) Gather to Learn

❖ Welcome the class members and introduce any guests.

❖ Pray that all who have come to this session will recognize God's transforming power in their lives.

❖ Encourage the students to talk about the changes they see, hear, taste, touch, and smell around them as they and others prepare to celebrate Christmas. Invite them to talk about how their homes, churches, and other places they go seem different with the scents, sights, and sounds of the approaching holiday. Ask them to describe how these changes may affect their attitudes and behaviors.

❖ Read aloud today's focus statement: **We often talk about experiences that change us. What difference do these transforming events make in how we live? At John's birth, Zechariah proclaimed the vision of God's future for his son John, who would prepare people for the coming of the Messiah.**

(2) Recognize How Zechariah's Behavior Changed as a Result of the Fulfillment of God's Promise in John's Birth

❖ Use information for verses 57-66 in Understanding the Scripture to set the stage for today's lesson by recounting the story of the birth and naming of John the Baptizer.

❖ Read aloud Luke 1:67-80 by dividing the class in half. Assign half the class the odd-numbered verses, beginning with verse 69. The other half will read the even-numbered verses, beginning with verse 68. You will read verses 67 and 80. Note that verses 68-79 are often called the Latin word *Benedictus*.

❖ **Option:** Use "Canticle of Zechariah" if you have access to *The United Methodist Hymnal* (page 208). You will need to read the first and last verses from Luke, but the class can read verses 68-79 responsively. Use the sung response.

❖ Encourage the class to identify the following information, as contained in verses 68-79, and list it on newsprint.

■ God's actions in the past.
■ John the Baptizer's actions in the future, as prophesied by his father, Zechariah.
■ God's future actions, as prophesied by Zechariah.

❖ Go beyond today's Scriptures by talking with the adults about how they understand Zechariah's prophecies about John to have been fulfilled during his ministry.

❖ Focus on Zechariah by comparing and contrasting his behavior in this passage with his behavior in Luke 1:8-23, which we studied on December 2. **How would you account for the changes that are evident in Zechariah's behavior?**

(3) Review the Learners' Life-Changing Events

❖ Distribute paper and pencils. Invite the students to draw a line across the bottom of the paper and label it "Life-changing Events." Then, ask them to draw straight lines upward, perpendicular to the bottom line. On each line the students will write the approximate date, a brief description of a transformational event, and how that event changed their lives. Major spiritual experiences, marriage, or the birth of a child would be good examples of transforming events.

❖ Encourage the adults to look over what they have written. Read these questions, pausing after each one for silent consideration:

■ **Are there one or two events that were more life-changing than any of the others? Why?**
■ **Were some changes for the better, whereas others were changes for the worse? What made the difference in your assessment?**
■ **Did any changes seem to make life better (or worse) only to later turn out to make things worse (or better)?**
■ **Where did you see God at work in any of these events?**

❖ Suggest that the students talk with small groups about their findings. Perhaps they will learn that others have had similar experiences at roughly the same time in their lives. See what bridges they can build to one another based on their transformational events.

❖ Discuss this question: **How did any of these significant events positively or negatively affect your relationship with God?**

❖ Conclude this portion of the lesson by reading aloud the last paragraph under "Changing Faithfulness into Fulfillment" in Interpreting the Scripture. Invite volunteers to comment on these observations in relation to their own experiences.

(4) Tell Others How Believing in Jesus Changes Their Lives

❖ Point out that for many people the most significant transformational event in their lives is the decision to follow Christ as a disciple.

❖ Distribute hymnals. Divide the class into teams of three or four. Ask each team to page through the hymnal looking for hymns that proclaim one's desire to follow Jesus. Note those hymn numbers on the back of the paper they have already received. Write a few words about why this hymn is meaningful in terms of a decision to follow Jesus.

❖ Bring the class back together to report on their findings. They may notice that some of the music speaks clearly about change. In "Amazing Grace," for example, we read: "I once was lost, but now am found; was blind, but now I see." Lost/found; blindness/sight. These constitute profound changes. Similarly, Brian Wren's hymn "This Is a Day of New Beginnings" also challenges us to remember the past but also "move on" to a changed life.

❖ **Option:** If you have an able accompanist or song leader, invite the students to sing several favorite hymns from the lists.

(5) Continue the Journey

❖ Pray that each person who has come today will be more keenly aware of how God is working in his or her life, especially as we draw closer to Christmas.

❖ Read aloud this preparation for next week's lesson. You may also want to post it on newsprint for the students to copy.

- **Title: Called to Rejoice!**
- **Background Scripture: Luke 2:1-20**
- **Lesson Scripture: Luke 2:1-14**
- **Focus of the Lesson: Everyone looks for reasons to rejoice. How can we rejoice in the midst of all life brings? The shepherds, whose lives were hard and often disparaged, received the announcement of God's fulfilled promise of the Messiah and declared their joy to all.**

❖ Challenge the students to complete one or more of these activities for further spiritual growth, which you will write on newsprint for the students to copy.

(1) **Talk with a child about his or her relationship with God. Tell a personal story to illustrate how important that relationship is to you.**

(2) **Be available to a parent with a young child to help mentor this parent and child in the faith.**

(3) **Spend time in prayer and meditation recalling how God has worked in your life. Give thanks. Ponder ways that you can pass on this good news to others, and make every effort to do so.**

❖ Sing or read aloud "Blessed Be the God of Israel."

❖ Conclude today's session by leading the class in this benediction, which is taken from Ephesians 6:23-24: **Peace be to the whole community, and love with faith, from God the Father and the Lord Jesus Christ. Grace be with all who have an undying love for our Lord Jesus Christ. Amen.**

UNIT 1: GOD'S CALL AT CHRISTMAS AND BEYOND
CALLED TO REJOICE!

PREVIEWING THE LESSON

Lesson Scripture: Luke 2:1-14
Background Scripture: Luke 2:1-20
Key Verse: Luke 2:11

Focus of the Lesson:
Everyone looks for reasons to rejoice. How can we rejoice in the midst of all life brings? The shepherds, whose lives were hard and often disparaged, received the announcement of God's fulfilled promise of the Messiah and declared their joy to all.

Goals for the Learners:
(1) to explore the circumstances around Jesus' birth and people's responses to it.
(2) to express joy at the good news of God's fulfilled promise.
(3) to tell someone the good news of God's gift of the Messiah.

Pronunciation Guide:
Gaius Octavianus (gay' uhs ock tavy ee an us)
Quirinius (kwi rin' ee uhs)

Supplies:
Bibles, newsprint and marker, paper and pencils, hymnals, optional nativity scene with moveable figures, optional art supplies for making Christmas cards, refreshments, Christmas music on CD or tape and appropriate player

---

READING THE SCRIPTURE

NRSV
Luke 2:1-14

¹In those days a decree went out from Emperor Augustus that all the world should be registered. ²This was the first registration and was taken while Quirinius was governor of Syria. ³All went to their own towns to be registered. ⁴Joseph also went from the town of Nazareth in Galilee to Judea, to the

NIV
Luke 2:1-14

¹In those days Caesar Augustus issued a decree that a census should be taken of the entire Roman world. ²(This was the first census that took place while Quirinius was governor of Syria.) ³And everyone went to his own town to register.

⁴So Joseph also went up from the town of

city of David called Bethlehem, because he was descended from the house and family of David. [5]He went to be registered with Mary, to whom he was engaged and who was expecting a child. [6]While they were there, the time came for her to deliver her child. [7]And she gave birth to her firstborn son and wrapped him in bands of cloth, and laid him in a manger, because there was no place for them in the inn.

[8]In that region there were shepherds living in the fields, keeping watch over their flock by night. [9]Then an angel of the Lord stood before them, and the glory of the Lord shone around them, and they were terrified. [10]But the angel said to them, "Do not be afraid; for see—I am bringing you good news of great joy for all the people: [11]**to you is born this day in the city of David a Savior, who is the Messiah, the Lord.** [12]This will be a sign for you: you will find a child wrapped in bands of cloth and lying in a manger." [13]And suddenly there was with the angel a multitude of the heavenly host, praising God and saying,

[14]Glory to God in the highest heaven,
    and on earth peace among those whom he favors!"

Nazareth in Galilee to Judea, to Bethlehem the town of David, because he belonged to the house and line of David. [5]He went there to register with Mary, who was pledged to be married to him and was expecting a child. [6]While they were there, the time came for the baby to be born, [7]and she gave birth to her firstborn, a son. She wrapped him in cloths and placed him in a manger, because there was no room for them in the inn.

[8]And there were shepherds living out in the fields nearby, keeping watch over their flocks at night. [9]An angel of the Lord appeared to them, and the glory of the Lord shone around them, and they were terrified. [10]But the angel said to them, "Do not be afraid. I bring you good news of great joy that will be for all the people. [11]**Today in the town of David a Savior has been born to you; he is Christ the Lord.** [12]This will be a sign to you: You will find a baby wrapped in cloths and lying in a manger."

[13]Suddenly a great company of the heavenly host appeared with the angel, praising God and saying,

[14]"Glory to God in the highest,
    and on earth peace to men on whom his favor rests."

UNDERSTANDING THE SCRIPTURE

Luke 2:1-2. The birth of Jesus is the second birth described by Luke, and Luke obviously intended to associate the two. Both were preannounced by the angel Gabriel. Both were unexpected occurrences given the circumstances of the mothers-to-be. The first birth narrative anticipates the second by assigning John the Baptist a role in preparing for the coming of the Messiah. The birth of Jesus focuses on the fulfillment of the messianic expectations.

Luke also set these two births in contrast, subtly highlighting the different consequences of the two events. John's birth is localized, set in the context of a regional monarch, King Herod of Judea (Luke 1:5). It focuses on the Jewish temple (1:8-22), an undisclosed "Judean town in the hill county" (1:39), and a wilderness provenance for John's upbringing (1:80). Whereas we may think of the Jerusalem temple as being a place of glorious renown, we must remember that at the time of John's birth the temple was about a third of the way through a vast rebuilding project that went on for more than forty-six years (John 2:20).

By contrast, the birth of Jesus, who is called Savior, Messiah, and Lord (Luke

2:11), is set in the context of the most powerful ruler of that day. "Emperor Augustus" (2:1) was the title bestowed in 27 B.C. by the Roman Senate on Gaius Julius Caesar Octavianus, the founder of the Roman Empire. The title meant "worthy of reverence" and in Greek bore implications of divinity. So powerful was his rule that "all the world" fell under the authority of his decree.

The historical dating of Jesus' birth is complicated by the available data related to the rule of Herod (died in 4 B.C.; see Matthew 2:1-19), the service of Quirinius (began 6 B.C.), and the registration ordered by Augustus. Only a little evidence is found outside the New Testament for the latter. By tying Jesus' birth to this "all the world" perspective, Luke underscored the universal significance of the event.

Luke 2:3-7. The registration ordered by Augustus required a return to the ancestral home. Because Joseph descended from the family of David, he went from his home in Nazareth to Bethlehem, the city of David. By the most direct route through Samaria, this journey of less than one hundred miles would have passed near such historic Old Testament locations as Shechem, Shiloh, Bethel, and Jerusalem. Many devout Jews of that time, however, avoided Samaria by taking a longer route along the eastern side of the Jordan River.

The fact that Mary accompanied Joseph to Bethlehem underscores the unusual circumstances of their situation. Though formally betrothed, Mary under normal circumstances would not have accompanied Joseph prior to the finalization of their marriage. Because she was expecting a child, Mary and Joseph must have decided together that the circumstances required her to travel with him.

The Scriptures do not reveal how advanced Mary's pregnancy was when they traveled or how long they stayed in Bethlehem prior to the birth of Jesus. We only are told that the time of her delivery arrived while they were in Bethlehem, and she bore a son. "Inn" should be understood as a *guest room*, though not the private accommodations to which we are accustomed. This room, possibly in the home of family or friends, would have been overcrowded with Davidic descendants who flooded Bethlehem. Peasant homes had different levels for family and animals. Perhaps the place affording Mary the most privacy for childbirth was the level where the animals slept. In stark contrast to the universal significance of the events, the new baby was laid in a feeding trough in the stable area of the house.

Luke 2:8-14. The introduction of shepherds in verse 8 is another startling contrast. Earlier in Israel's history when the people were more nomadic, shepherds were esteemed members of the clan. As cities were built and the people settled in their tribal regions, however, shepherds began to be viewed as transients and vagabonds. Because they moved from place to place in search for grazing lands for their sheep, shepherds sometimes were considered untrustworthy and their testimony was received with suspicion. In spite of that potential problem, Luke elevated this band of unnamed shepherds to a role of prominence in first hearing and then spreading the good news of Jesus' birth.

Like Zechariah (1:12) and Mary (1:30) before them, the shepherds responded to the appearance of an angel with terror. Although the angel is not named here, Luke emphasizes that this is an angel "of the Lord."

The announcement to the shepherds is filled with words of messianic hope: good news, great joy, David, Savior, Messiah, and Lord. The long-awaited announcement was good news "for all the people"; yet the Savior was born "to you." The hope of the nation for generations had found fulfillment in the immediate experience of this band of shepherds, who like all humanity stood in need of a Savior.

The angel assumed the shepherds would seek and "find" this promised one and thus gave the shepherds a confirming sign: The child would be wrapped in bands of cloth and would be lying in a manger. If the shepherds were puzzled by this unusual sign, the appearance of a multitude of heavenly hosts swept all questions aside. The host (literally "army") of angels praised God and called for peace for those receiving God's favor.

Luke 2:15-20. After the angels departed, the shepherds decided to go to Bethlehem to see firsthand the situation disclosed to them by the Lord through the angels. They found Mary and Joseph; and just as the angel had promised, they found "the child lying in a manger."

The confirmation of the angel's sign prompted the shepherds to tell others about the child, and the shepherds' story amazed all who heard the story, just as it has amazed subsequent generations.

Whereas Mary pondered these events personally, the shepherds openly declared the story of the angel, the sign, and the fulfillment of the sign in a Bethlehem stable. They praised God for what they had heard and seen. What had been told them in advance had been fulfilled, and they testified to the truth they had experienced.

INTERPRETING THE SCRIPTURE

The Promise and the Unexpected

In the movie *Liar Liar*, Jim Carrey played a fast-track lawyer who failed to keep the promises he made to his son. When his son's birthday wish (that his dad would go twenty-four hours without lying) comes true, the lawyer discovers how much he depends on lying and the consequences of telling the truth. From the son's perspective, of course, the issue is one of depending on the truth and the consequences of lying.

Promises are powerful forces in life. Marriages, jobs, relationships, business transactions, and legal systems depend on the integrity of promises. When promises are made, they provide high expectations. When promises are kept, they sustain bonds of faithfulness, trust, and integrity.

The messianic promises of the Old Testament held varying influences among the Jewish people through centuries of bondage, oppression, and foreign domination. At times the visions of peace, prosperity, and justice were their only sources of hope. At other times the nation grasped at would-be messiahs who promised a mighty deliverance from God and then failed when the only power they possessed was their own.

Luke's testimony is that God keeps promises. God kept them immediately in the revelations given to the shepherds, but behind the immediate was an eternal promise that God would rescue people from their bondage to sin and death. Luke drew out the eternal promise with references to David, Savior, Messiah, and Lord. He affirmed that the promised Messiah was born on a particular day in a particular place. God was keeping the promises made to prophets, kings, and priests centuries ago.

With that affirmation, however, Luke gave the promises a twist. The recipients of the promises had visions of a powerful ruler who would ascend David's throne and throw off all foreign domination. He would establish peace and prosperity for the people. All nations would flock to Jerusalem to pay homage to Israel's king and Israel's God.

Luke's twist is an unexpected one. The Messiah would not be born in a palace but in a stable. The sign that he was the Messiah would not be a crown but a feeding trough. The focus would not be on an earthly kingdom but on the glory of God who reigns in the highest heaven. The consequences would not be solely for the Jews but would be for those on whom God showers his favor.

Sometimes we hear what we want to hear. We interpret the promises that others make in terms of what we want to achieve rather than in terms of the promise itself. God's promises are not always what they seem to us. They have an unexpected twist that forces us to focus on the faithfulness, trust, and integrity of God to accomplish what God intends in God's time, in God's place, and through God's unexpected servants.

The Low and the Mighty

Most of us do not achieve fame and prominence. Even people who have their five minutes in the spotlight quickly fade in the corporate mind and disappear from society's radar screen. People who knew great prominence in one generation are relatively unknown in the next. The high and the mighty rarely maintain their status for long.

Luke's story of Jesus is filled with some of the high and mighty. Emperor Augustus likely was the most widely known person in his generation. Coins all over the Roman Empire bore his image, and the length of his reign and the scope of his influence can hardly be appreciated today. From the perspective of Judea, Herod the Great held a prominent position. His prominence may have been more notoriety than esteem, but the salacious aspects of his reign would have been feast for the gossips.

Whereas people like John the Baptist, Mary, Joseph, and the shepherds were not the kinds of people to attract society's note, we probably could say that the emperors and the kings of that day are known more widely today because of their association with the Christmas story than because of their own status. How ironic that the only lasting memory of the powerful grows out of the long-term significance in God's economy of the powerless and lowly.

Luke's Gospel focuses on the poor and outcasts. The main characters of his Gospel are more a part of those groups than they are part of the high and mighty of their day.

Why does God work mostly in unexpected ways among the least esteemed segments of society? Could the reason be that the lowly exhibit more openness, sincerity, and responsiveness than do those focused on wealth, status, and power? Could availability, receptivity, and vulnerability provide a more fertile soil for seeds of faith to grow? Could praise and adoration come more easily from lives that have been touched by God's unmerited grace?

The Local and the Universal

Sometimes experts advise the church to think globally and act locally. This advice rests on the power of a global mission to motivate the church. Something powerful happens when God's people view themselves as part of a great cloud of witnesses who through long centuries have praised God, supported one another in good times and bad, and served humanity with love and compassion. We are part of something big. The God who chose Abraham, who inspired the prophets through the centuries, who sent his only Son to redeem humanity, and who stands alongside us in our daily walk is an awesome God. When we celebrate something that happened more than two thousand years ago, we join a mighty chorus in praising the God from whom all blessings flow.

The experts' advice also recognizes that a church cannot do everything. Its resources are focused locally because its members, facilities, and opportunities are greatest in their own community. Thinking globally is not the end. Vision without action never accomplishes anything. Our faithfulness to the global vision is lived out each day as we work, worship, witness, and serve.

Luke related the local dimensions of his story about Jesus to the universal. We have seen how God takes ordinary people like us, works through them in a particular setting, and accomplishes something of universal consequence. We have witnessed the stories of simple believers such as Zechariah and Elizabeth, faithful folk such as Mary and Joseph, unique characters such as John the Baptist, and people on the edges of society like the shepherds. Behind all these stories the transcendent is invading the ordinary. Luke presents this transcendence as angelic beings and heavenly hosts. We know it all is evidence of God at work among humanity in ways familiar since Old Testament times and yet ways as unique as God's one and only Son.

We learn that God is in our midst, but God is more likely to be found in unexpected places and circumstances than in the programmed efforts we use to invoke him. People of prominence and special status often miss God, whereas those with open hearts are filled by God's love.

As we gather to study the Christmas story, to sing praises, to ponder the events in our hearts, and to declare the coming of the Christ, let us open our hearts to the transcendent Presence. Let God penetrate our doubts and fears, our pain and suffering, our hopelessness and despair, our secularity and jadedness, our pride and privilege. Let the simple story of simple folk call us to a singleness of heart as we join the angelic hosts in praising God and offering God's peace to all who will receive God's gracious love.

SHARING THE SCRIPTURE

Preparing Our Hearts

Meditate on this week's devotional reading, found in Psalm 96:1-6. Listen and hear the psalmist praise the Creator God's glory and salvation. As Christmas is rapidly approaching, write your own song or poem of praise to God for the gift of Jesus. Declare God's glory to others. What new song can you sing?

Pray that you and the adult learners will prepare your hearts and minds to welcome Bethlehem's babe.

Preparing Our Minds

Study the background from Luke 2:1-20 and lesson Scripture, verses 1-14. Think about how you can rejoice in the midst of all that life brings.

Write on newsprint:

❑ information for next week's lesson, found under "Continue the Journey."
❑ activities for further spiritual growth in "Continue the Journey."

Option: Bring, or ask a class member to bring, a nativity scene that has moveable characters. Prepare a table where the scene will be set up during the session.

Option: Gather whatever art supplies you will use if you choose to make Christmas cards. If you will be giving these cards to a particular children's class, talk with the teacher to make sure that the adults will make enough cards for each child.

Bring refreshments for a time of celebration. You may want to contact some of the students and ask them to contribute cookies, punch, fruit, or whatever else the group prefers.

Set up the player for any Christmas music that you chose to bring.

LEADING THE CLASS

(1) Gather to Learn

❖ Welcome the class members and introduce any guests.

❖ Pray that all who participate today will experience joy and celebration as they contemplate the birth of Jesus.

❖ Ask each person to name one reason he or she has to rejoice this Christmas. People may repeat answers that others have already given. These reasons may relate directly to Christmas and/or have a decidedly personal slant. For example, one person may comment on the meaning of her relationship with Christ, whereas another is thrilled that his son, daughter-in-law, and new grandchild will be visiting during the holidays. If someone feels that he or she has no reason to rejoice, do not press the issue.

❖ Read aloud today's focus statement: **Everyone looks for reasons to rejoice. How can we rejoice in the midst of all life brings? The shepherds, whose lives were hard and often disparaged, received the announcement of God's fulfilled promise of the Messiah and declared their joy to all.**

(2) Explore the Circumstances Around Jesus' Birth and People's Responses to It

❖ Ask two volunteers to read the story from Luke's Gospel, one from Luke 2:1-7 and the other from verses 8-13. The class will read verse 14 in unison, though words will vary if they use different translations.

❖ **Option:** If you brought a nativity set, line the figures up where they are easily accessible to the students. Invite volunteers to pick up a figure, bring it to the table where you have set the stable, place the figure, and tell the part of the story related to this figure as they arrange it. What the students are doing is retelling the story in their own words. (Be sure to exclude the Magi

and star, as these are found in Matthew's Gospel but not in Luke's.)

❖ Focus on Luke 2:10-11. Discuss with the class or in small groups what it means to claim that Jesus is Savior, Messiah, and Lord. What difference do these understandings make in the students lives, particularly as they consider their relationship with Jesus? Also discuss their responses to the idea that this holy child is born "to you."

(3) Express Joy at the Good News of God's Fulfilled Promise

❖ Read the fourth paragraph of "The Promise and the Unexpected."

❖ Invite the adults to call out promises they find in the Old Testament that are related to the Savior and that they believe are fulfilled in Jesus. Here are some Scriptures to consider if you need discussion starters.
   ■ Isaiah 9:1-7
   ■ Micah 5:2-5a
   ■ Zechariah 9:9-10

❖ Note that many of the promises refer to a royal ruler who would be like his ancestor David. Jesus was indeed a ruler, but not the one people had expected. He had no interest in military might. Instead, he had come to announce the reign of God.

❖ Discuss these questions.
   (1) What do fulfilled promises reveal to you about God?
   (2) How do you perceive that Jesus fulfilled the promises that the class identified?
   (3) In what ways do you express your joy that God has sent the promised Messiah?

(4) Tell Someone the Good News of God's Gift of the Messiah

❖ Encourage the adults to summarize what they believe to be the good news of Christmas.

❖ **Option:** Distribute art supplies that

you have brought. These could include old Christmas cards, construction paper, markers, scissors, glitter, yarn, and any other items you think would be helpful. Provide time for each student, or a pair of students, to create a card. The card should include words that proclaim the good news of Christmas, the reason why we rejoice. Consider creating these cards for one or more of the church's children's classes, or for the adults to give to significant children in their own lives.

❖ Conclude this time with some informal sharing and celebration. Set out whatever refreshments have been brought. Play any Christmas music that you have brought. Make these closing minutes a time of rejoicing!

(5) Continue the Journey

❖ Pray that the students will experience new meaning as they celebrate and rejoice in the Savior's birth.

❖ Read aloud this preparation for next week's lesson. You may also want to post it on newsprint for the students to copy.

■ **Title: Called to Witness!**
■ **Background Scripture: Luke 2:22-38**
■ **Lesson Scripture: Luke 2:22-35**
■ **Focus of the Lesson: We like to hear and tell good news. How do we respond to the good news of Christmas? Simeon responded to the birth of Jesus the Messiah by** declaring that God was keeping the promise of salvation.

❖ Challenge the students to complete one or more of these activities for further spiritual growth, which you will write on newsprint for the students to copy.

(1) **Visit someone for whom the holidays are not a time of rejoicing, perhaps because of illness, loneliness, or a crisis. In a subdued way, showing care and respect for the challenges this person faces, state why you rejoice in the Savior's birth.**

(2) **Buy and/or collect gifts for a family and/or children in need. Be humble in your generosity. Let these people know that Jesus has come to be their Messiah.**

(3) **Attend any special services and programs your church might offer this season. Use every opportunity to gather with God's people and rejoice in the Savior's birth.**

❖ Sing or read aloud "Sing We Now of Christmas."

❖ Conclude today's session by leading the class in this benediction, which is taken from Ephesians 6:23-24: **Peace be to the whole community, and love with faith, from God the Father and the Lord Jesus Christ. Grace be with all who have an undying love for our Lord Jesus Christ. Amen.**

UNIT 1: GOD'S CALL AT CHRISTMAS AND BEYOND
CALLED TO WITNESS!

PREVIEWING THE LESSON

Lesson Scripture: Luke 2:22-35
Background Scripture: Luke 2:22-38
Key Verse: Luke 2:34

Focus of the Lesson:
We like to hear and tell good news. How do we respond to the good news of Christmas? Simeon responded to the birth of Jesus the Messiah by declaring that God was keeping the promise of salvation.

Goals for the Learners:
(1) to explore Simeon's response to the birth of the Messiah.
(2) to recognize the work of the Holy Spirit in their lives.
(3) to challenge each other to witness to the promises that God fulfills in their lives.

Pronunciation Guide:
Asher (ash' uhr)   Essene (es' een)
levirate (lev' uh rite)   Nunc Dimittis (noonk di mit' is)
Paraclete (pair' uh kleet)   Phanuel (fuh nyoo' uhl)
Sanhedrin (san hee' druhn)   Sicarii (si kahr' ee i)
Simeon (sim' ee uhn)   Zilpah (zil' puh)

Supplies:
Bibles, newsprint and marker, paper and pencils, hymnals

READING THE SCRIPTURE

NRSV
Luke 2:22-35

²²When the time came for their purification according to the law of Moses, they brought him up to Jerusalem to present him to the Lord ²³(as it is written in the law of the Lord, "Every firstborn male shall be

NIV
Luke 2:22-35

²²When the time of their purification according to the Law of Moses had been completed, Joseph and Mary took him to Jerusalem to present him to the Lord ²³(as it is written in the Law of the Lord, "Every

designated as holy to the Lord"), [24]and they offered a sacrifice according to what is stated in the law of the Lord, "a pair of turtledoves or two young pigeons."

[25]Now there was a man in Jerusalem whose name was Simeon; this man was righteous and devout, looking forward to the consolation of Israel, and the Holy Spirit rested on him. [26]It had been revealed to him by the Holy Spirit that he would not see death before he had seen the Lord's Messiah. [27]Guided by the Spirit, Simeon came into the temple; and when the parents brought in the child Jesus, to do for him what was customary under the law, [28]Simeon took him in his arms and praised God, saying,

[29] "Master, now you are dismissing your
    servant in peace,
    according to your word;
[30] for my eyes have seen your salvation,
[31] which you have prepared in the presence
    of all peoples,
[32] a light for revelation to the Gentiles
    and for glory to your people Israel."

[33]And the child's father and mother were amazed at what was being said about him. [34]Then Simeon blessed them and said to his mother Mary, "This child is destined for the falling and the rising of many in Israel, and to be a sign that will be opposed [35]so that the inner thoughts of many will be revealed—and a sword will pierce your own soul too."

firstborn male is to be consecrated to the Lord"), [24]and to offer a sacrifice in keeping with what is said in the Law of the Lord: "a pair of doves or two young pigeons."

[25]Now there was a man in Jerusalem called Simeon, who was righteous and devout. He was waiting for the consolation of Israel, and the Holy Spirit was upon him. [26]It had been revealed to him by the Holy Spirit that he would not die before he had seen the Lord's Christ. [27]Moved by the Spirit, he went into the temple courts. When the parents brought in the child Jesus to do for him what the custom of the Law required, [28]Simeon took him in his arms and praised God, saying:

[29] "Sovereign Lord, as you have promised,
    you now dismiss your servant in peace.
[30] For my eyes have seen your salvation,
[31] which you have prepared in the sight of
    all people,
[32] a light for revelation to the Gentiles
    and for glory to your people Israel."

[33]The child's father and mother marveled at what was said about him. [34]Then Simeon blessed them and said to Mary, his mother: "This child is destined to cause the falling and rising of many in Israel, and to be a sign that will be spoken against, [35]so that the thoughts of many hearts will be revealed. And a sword will pierce your own soul too."

UNDERSTANDING THE SCRIPTURE

Luke 2:22-24. Like Zechariah and Elizabeth (1:6, 59), Joseph and Mary reflected the genuine piety of grassroots Judaism in the first century. Although much was corrupt and twisted in the religious politics of the day, and though religious factions struggled for supremacy over the institutions of the faith, many Jews remained faithful to the commands of God.

Following the stipulation of the Old

Testament covenant, Jesus was circumcised on the eighth day (2:21; see Genesis 17:10-14). Following the divine directions communicated through Gabriel (Luke 1:31), the child was named Jesus. The circumcision and naming are recorded in verse 21.

After observing the forty days of ceremonial purification that the law required following the birth of a male child (Leviticus 12:1-4), Mary and Joseph took Jesus to the temple in Jerusalem to present him to the priest and to offer the prescribed sacrifice that removed the mother's ceremonial uncleanness (Leviticus 12:6-8). Since Jesus was a firstborn male child, Luke also tied these events to the consecration of the first-born prescribed in Exodus 13:11-16 as an act of remembrance of God's deliverance of the firstborn in the escape from Egypt (13:14-16). Significantly, Mary offered the sacrifice prescribed for the poor who could not afford a sheep (Leviticus 12:8).

Luke 2:25-32. In addition to the preparations that God had made for the coming of the Messiah, already detailed by Luke, two other individuals were being prepared for their role in the dedication of the child. These two, Simeon and Anna, were elderly people of great piety and devotion through whom the Holy Spirit already was at work in confirming that God's promises about the Messiah were being fulfilled. Almost half of Luke's references to "the Holy Spirit" are messianic preparations found in 1:1–2:26.

Simeon, a "righteous and devout" man who lived in Jerusalem, was a Spirit-empowered individual. Luke notes that the Holy Spirit rested on him (2:25), revealed truth to him (2:26), and guided him (2:27). The focus of Simeon's attention was "looking forward to the consolation of Israel" (2:25). The word *consolation* is the root word from which early translators of the Bible in English derived the word *Paraclete*. The word speaks of encouragement, exhortation, and comfort. In terms of Jewish views of the future, the "consolation of Israel" was a time when God would comfort oppressed people by delivering them through the Messiah. Later Jewish references actually speak of the Messiah as "comforter."

The Holy Spirit had revealed to Simeon that he would not die before he saw the Lord's Messiah. Led by the Spirit to the temple at the time of Jesus' dedication, Simeon recognized Jesus as the promised "consolation." He broke into a song of praise that shifted the focus of that consolation. The

salvation brought by the Messiah was prepared in the presence of all people, not just the Jews. Christ would be both a light for revelation to the Gentiles as well as for the glory of Israel. The scope of the gospel for all people was underscored again by Luke. Having seen the fulfillment of God's promise to him, Simeon was ready to die in peace.

Luke 2:33-35. Joseph and Mary were amazed by Simeon's words about Jesus. Perhaps Simeon's words brought into sharper focus what Gabriel previously had said to Mary about her son. Interestingly, Luke refers to Joseph as "the child's [Jesus'] father." Although not biologically true, Joseph obviously was acting already as a father in the upbringing of the child. In listing the ancestors of Jesus, Luke stated that Jesus "was the son (as was thought) of Joseph" (3:23).

Simeon blessed the family and then spoke prophetically and somewhat obscurely to Mary. He pointed to the role that Jesus would play as a decisive sign in revealing the inner thoughts of the people. Some in Israel would rise and others would fall because of the manner in which they accepted or rejected him. So sharp would be the division that even Mary would suffer at the outcome. This is Luke's first indication that the promised Messiah would not win the support of the entire nation. Luke hints at the passion of the Christ, which will be a growing theme as the Gospel builds toward its climax.

Luke 2:36-38. Anna was the second person the Spirit had prepared to play a role in the dedication of Jesus at the temple. Luke identifies her as "a prophet" (2:36), "a widow" (2:37), and a devotee of the temple (2:37).

In addition, Luke gives her Jewish family background, naming her father, Phanuel, rather than her deceased husband (to whom she was married for seven years) as her family origins. Apparently after her husband's death she had moved back into her birth family rather than being accepted and maintained by her husband's family, as was often the custom. Luke also notes that she was of the tribe of Asher. Although this maintained her Jewish heritage, Asher was not among the most notable tribes. Asher himself was the second son of Jacob borne by Zilpah, the handmaid of Jacob's less favored wife, Leah (Genesis 30:9-12).

Luke's statement in verse 37 that Anna "never left the temple" raises some practical questions. Some interpreters view this as hyperbole and point to a similar comment Luke makes that the disciples "were continually in the temple blessing God" (24:53). Luke intentionally depicted Anna as a woman of unusual piety and faithfulness to God. Her presence in the temple, her many years of worshiping there, and the practices of fasting and prayer underscored his point. The Greek verb translated "left" in 2:37 also can mean that she never deserted the temple or never fell away from her devotion to it. Since fasting night and day for such a long period of time is unlikely, Luke may be speaking of her devotion rather than her continuous presence in the temple.

Like Simeon, Anna also praised God at seeing the child; and she began to speak about the child to all of those who were looking for the deliverance of the Messiah.

INTERPRETING THE SCRIPTURE

The Faithfulness of God's People

We live amid religious tumult. Religious traditions of families are strained by physical distances, social changes, and the melding of other cultures, races, and religious ideas into the melting pot of American religion. New generations cast off the practices, values, and standards of the past. Traditions are questioned; practices are discarded; and the new, the fresh, the different are welcomed for the vitality they offer.

At the same time, some religious groups react violently to the threats of change. Differences even within common traditions set Sunnis against Shiites in the Middle East, Hindus against Buddhists in India, Catholics against Protestants in Ireland, and fundamentalists against liberals within Christian denominations.

With these differences, political influences enter into religious decision-making as special-interest groups, power blocks, propaganda, and electioneering dominate the way churches do their work. Many feel uncomfortable about the whole situation, but most have no sense of how to address— much less overcome—the problems.

In many respects, Judaism in the first century was similar. The Pharisees, who controlled the synagogue and enjoyed broad lay support, were squared off against the Sadducees, who controlled the temple, the Sanhedrin, and the high priesthood. Roman and Greek practices, as well as religious and philosophical perspectives, were making headway in Jewish society.

Radical elements in the society adopted violent means to achieve sacred objectives. The Zealots and the more radical Sicarii employed murder and intrigue in their zeal to overthrow their Roman oppressors. Some, such as the Essenes, withdrew into strict communities trying to escape the creeping paganism of secular society.

Somehow God saw in this confusion "the fullness of time" and chose this moment to send "his Son, born of a woman . . . to redeem" humanity so that "we might receive adoption as children" of God (Galatians 4:4-5).

Luke reminds us that the fullness of time was possible because humble believers were not swayed from the foundational principles and practices of their faith. They remained faithful in the midst of turmoil and confusion. They held to the traditions that expressed God's will for his people. They were faithful in prayer and worship; they were steadfast in their devotion to God; and they were open to God's doing something new and unexpected in their midst.

The Guidance of God's People

The Holy Spirit is a controversial subject in the church. Many Christians around the world equate the Holy Spirit with an emotional, high-pitched, ecstatic kind of religious experience manifesting itself in supernatural gifts such as healings, miracles, tongues, and prophecy.

Others in the church virtually ignore the idea of the Holy Spirit. Because they assume that the work of the Holy Spirit is a personal experience that differs between individuals, they conclude that we cannot distinguish between the Holy Spirit and an individual's personal preferences. If two people holding opposite views can claim to be inspired by the Holy Spirit, the church needs something more objective and concrete on which to base its life and practices. For many, this objective and concrete foundation is the Bible. Of course, when different interpretations of the Bible emerge, "my interpretation" is the right one!

Simeon can guide us in considering the role of the Holy Spirit in our lives and in the life of the church. First, Luke states that the Holy Spirit "rested" (Luke 2:25) on Simeon. Actually the Greek text simply states that the Holy Spirit was "on" Simeon. The word *on* conveys the idea of motion that has reached its goal. This implies that the Spirit of God is always moving toward us, but we do not always allow the Spirit to reach its goal of abiding in us.

The Holy Spirit is not merely a resource in dire need. The Spirit is not God's instant aid in getting out of trouble, helping through grief, or providing direction at important decision points. The Holy Spirit is a presence that is nurtured in life. Luke's statement that Simeon was "righteous and devout" (2:25) indicates Simeon had long nurtured the presence of the Spirit by the way he lived and the way he related to God.

Second, Luke states in verse 26 that the Holy Spirit "revealed" to Simeon. The Spirit gave Simeon perspective, insight, and purpose. Simeon lived with a Spirit-directed goal in life, and he had assurance that the goal would be fulfilled. The goal related to God's larger plan and purpose, however, not to Simeon's profit, happiness, or pleasure.

Most people would love to have revelations from the Spirit; but they are more interested in revelations about who they should marry, which jobs they should take, which stocks they should buy, or which schools are best for their children. Because we are self-centered, should we be surprised how easily "the Spirit" guides us toward things that we either consciously or unconsciously have already decided are best?

Third, because Simeon nurtured the presence of the Spirit and focused on God's purpose, he was guided by the Spirit. He was able to be where God wanted him to be, to recognize what God was about in Jesus, and to testify about what God had in store for his people. Maybe if we could look at Christmas through the eyes of the Spirit, we too could see clearly what God was about in Jesus, how we fit into God's plan, and how we can tell others the good news of God's love and redemption through Jesus Christ.

The Consolation of God's People

We stand on the verge of a new year with concern about the future. Even as we focus on the good news of Christmas, wars, economic uncertainties, family problems, vocational concerns, loneliness, and health issues cast a pall of gloom over the future. We look at our world and see hunger, injustice, exploitation, violence, and disease. We could easily give up hope in the face of these and other mounting problems.

Like Simeon, we should look for the "consolation" of God's people. But where is our comfort? What is the source of our encouragement? Who will exhort us to reach for spiritual armor to fortify us for troubled times?

Now early in Luke's Gospel, we are at a stage of rejoicing over the good news of what God did in Jesus. But Luke's Gospel does not end in chapter 2. Ahead are days mixed with success and failure, popularity and contempt, new life and brutal death, despair and hope.

Simeon looked at the future of this baby being dedicated by his parents in the temple, and he saw hope. Yes, he also saw ominous signs of divisiveness and pain; but mostly he saw that God was consoling his people by entering into human affairs and bringing salvation through the Son. Simeon saw the future, and he praised God. Simeon felt the danger, and he blessed this new family who would face uncertain days ahead. Simeon glimpsed the purposes of God and declared that all people, Jews and Gentiles, would see God's salvation.

In Christmas, we too catch a glimpse of the purposes of God. Though the future is hazy, the purpose is clear. God is at work in our midst. God is guiding through the Holy Spirit. The revelation of God's future establishes our direction. Because we know God is in control, we are consoled. We are hopeful and filled with purpose. We can testify that God's light is shining on us and guiding us to a future built on God's will.

SHARING THE SCRIPTURE

Preparing Our Hearts

Meditate on this week's devotional reading, found in Isaiah 49:5-6. These two verses are part of Isaiah's Second Servant Song, found in verses 1-6. What does the prophet say about the identity and purpose of this Servant? What connections, if any, can you make between the prophet's description and Jesus? Select a word or phrase and continue to call it to mind during the week. What fresh insights can you gain from this familiar passage?

Pray that you and the adult learners will listen and tell the good news of God's Servant.

Preparing Our Minds

Study the background, Luke 2:22-38, and lesson Scripture, verses 22-35. As you meditate on this passage, think about how you and others respond to the good news of Christmas.

Write on newsprint:
❏ information for next week's lesson, found under "Continue the Journey."
❏ activities for further spiritual growth in "Continue the Journey."

LEADING THE CLASS

(1) Gather to Learn

❖ Welcome the class members and introduce any guests.

❖ Pray that all who have come to study and fellowship today will be open to the leading of God's Spirit.

❖ Note many families contact or see one another during the holidays. This is a time for sharing memories and news of the year in words and pictures. Invite the students to tell the class or a partner some good news of their own family.

❖ Read aloud today's focus statement: **We like to hear and tell good news. How do we respond to the good news of Christmas? Simeon responded to the birth of Jesus the Messiah by declaring that God was keeping the promise of salvation.**

(2) Explore Simeon's Response to the Birth of the Messiah

❖ Select a volunteer to read Luke 2:22-24.

◼ Point out that Mary, Joseph, and the infant Jesus came to the temple for two rights: purification of the mother (Leviticus 12:1-8) and dedication of the firstborn son to God (Exodus 13:2, 12-16).

◼ Choose someone to read the passage from Leviticus 12. Note that the woman who bears a son is "ceremonially unclean seven days," and for thirty-three more days she is not allowed to enter the sanctuary or "touch any holy thing." Also see if the class can discern that Mary and Joseph must have been people of modest means because they brought "a pair of turtledoves or two young pigeons" (Luke 2:24), which Leviticus 12:8 states is the acceptable sacrifice for a woman who "cannot afford a sheep."

◼ Ask another adult to read Exodus 13:2, 12-16. Note the context of God's deliverance of the people from Egypt.

❖ Select two readers, one to read Simeon's words in Luke 2:29-32, 34b-35 and the other to read Luke 2:25-28, 33-34a.

◼ Point out that Simeon's speech in verses 29-32 is known as the Nunc Dimittis, which is Latin for "now you are dismissing."

◼ Note that Simeon's words in these four verses are clearly rooted in Isaiah. Ask volunteers to read aloud Isaiah 40:5; 42:6; 46:13; 49:6; 52:9-10 in order to hear the prophet's words.

◼ Discuss these questions with the class. You may want to list responses in a chart on newsprint.

(1) **What does this passage tell you about Simeon?** (Look carefully at the words used to describe him. Although Luke does not call him a prophet, Simeon has the characteristics of one who is called to be a messenger of God. He is clearly guided by the Holy Spirit.)

(2) **What does it tell you about Jesus and his mission?**

(3) **What do you learn about the nature of salvation?** (Notice that salvation is for both Jews and Gentiles. Hence, Paul's mission to the Gentiles was not an afterthought but part of God's plan from the beginning.)

(4) **Although verse 33 says that Jesus' parents were "amazed," no response is noted concerning Simeon's words to Mary in verses 34-35. How do you imagine that Mary interpreted his words?**

(5) **How do you believe that Simeon's prophecy was fulfilled?**

◼ Look especially at today's key verse, Luke 2:34, ending with "in Israel." Encourage the students to explain what they understand this verse to mean. (The idea here is that Jesus will bring not only salvation but also judgment. "Falling and rising" are not sequential actions but rather refer to the fate of two different groups.)

(3) Recognize the Work of the Holy Spirit in the Learners' Lives

❖ Note that Simeon was able to discern who Jesus was and bear witness to him because "the Holy Spirit rested" on this "righteous and devout" man (Luke 2:25).

❖ Read "The Guidance of God's People" in Interpreting the Scripture.

❖ Prompt the students to comment on their understanding of the person and work of the Holy Spirit. (Be aware that the responses may vary widely.)

❖ Personalize the discussion by inviting the students to talk with a partner or small group about experiences they have had with the Spirit. Perhaps they will have some current examples to share.

(4) Challenge Each Other to Witness to God's Salvation in Christ

❖ Read or retell "The Consolation of God's People" in Interpreting the Scripture.

❖ Ask: **How is Jesus the fulfillment of God's promise of "the consolation of Israel" (Luke 2:25)?**

❖ Distribute paper and pencils. Provide time for silent contemplation and written reflection on this idea: **What difference does it make in my life that God took on human form and lived among us as Jesus?**

❖ Encourage volunteers to read what they have written. Affirm each student's witness.

❖ Conclude this portion of the lesson by challenging the students to go forth to witness to the salvation that God has prepared for each of them and for all people. Make clear that witnessing includes both words and deeds.

(5) Continue the Journey

❖ Pray that the participants will be alert for opportunities to be witnesses for Christ this week.

❖ Read aloud this preparation for next week's lesson. You may also want to post it on newsprint for the students to copy.

■ **Title: Inspired to Inquire!**
■ **Background Scripture: Luke 2:41-52**
■ **Lesson Scripture: Luke 2:41-52**
■ **Focus of the Lesson: We have questions for which we seek answers. How does inquiry within the community of faith lead to maturity? Entering into dialogue in the temple, Jesus grew in faith and wisdom.**

❖ Challenge the students to complete one or more of these activities for further spiritual growth, which you will write on newsprint for the students to copy.

  (1) Talk with at least one person this week about your relationship with Jesus. Encourage that person to consider how Jesus can make a difference in his or her life.

  (2) Ponder any predictions that were made when you were young, or that were made to you as a parent regarding your own child. Have any of these predictions come true? Has the prediction in any way shaped your life or the life of your child? If so, how?

  (3) Recall that Simeon and Anna were devoted servants of God. Take action this week to witness to your faithfulness as a servant of Christ.

❖ Sing or read aloud "My Master, See, the Time Has Come."

❖ Conclude today's session by leading the class in this benediction, which is taken from Ephesians 6:23-24: **Peace be to the whole community, and love with faith, from God the Father and the Lord Jesus Christ. Grace be with all who have an undying love for our Lord Jesus Christ. Amen.**

UNIT 2: THE AWARENESS OF GOD'S INSTRUCTION
INSPIRED TO INQUIRE!

PREVIEWING THE LESSON

Lesson Scripture: Luke 2:41-52
Background Scripture: Luke 2:41-52
Key Verse: Luke 2:49

Focus of the Lesson:
We have questions for which we seek answers. How does inquiry within the community of faith lead to maturity? Entering into dialogue in the temple, Jesus grew in faith and wisdom.

Goals for the Learners:
(1) to explore the story of Jesus' learning in the temple.
(2) to recognize the relationship between inquiry and spiritual growth.
(3) to make a commitment to lifelong learning in the community of faith.

Supplies:
Bibles, newsprint and marker, paper and pencils, hymnals, picture of boy Jesus in the temple

---
READING THE SCRIPTURE

NRSV
Luke 2:41-52

⁴¹Now every year his parents went to Jerusalem for the festival of the Passover. ⁴²And when he was twelve years old, they went up as usual for the festival. ⁴³When the festival was ended and they started to return, the boy Jesus stayed behind in Jerusalem, but his parents did not know it. ⁴⁴Assuming that he was in the group of travelers, they went a day's journey. Then they started to look for him among their relatives and friends. ⁴⁵When they did not find him, they returned to Jerusalem to search for him.

NIV
Luke 2:41-52

⁴¹Every year his parents went to Jerusalem for the Feast of the Passover. ⁴²When he was twelve years old, they went up to the Feast, according to the custom. ⁴³After the Feast was over, while his parents were returning home, the boy Jesus stayed behind in Jerusalem, but they were unaware of it. ⁴⁴Thinking he was in their company, they traveled on for a day. Then they began looking for him among their relatives and friends. ⁴⁵When they did not find him, they went back to Jerusalem to look for him.

⁴⁶After three days they found him in the temple, sitting among the teachers, listening to them and asking them questions. ⁴⁷And all who heard him were amazed at his understanding and his answers. ⁴⁸When his parents saw him they were astonished; and his mother said to him, "Child, why have you treated us like this? Look, your father and I have been searching for you in great anxiety." ⁴⁹**He said to them, "Why were you searching for me? Did you not know that I must be in my Father's house?"** ⁵⁰But they did not understand what he said to them. ⁵¹Then he went down with them and came to Nazareth, and was obedient to them. His mother treasured all these things in her heart.
⁵²And Jesus increased in wisdom and in years, and in divine and human favor.

⁴⁶After three days they found him in the temple courts, sitting among the teachers, listening to them and asking them questions. ⁴⁷Everyone who heard him was amazed at his understanding and his answers. ⁴⁸When his parents saw him, they were astonished. His mother said to him, "Son, why have you treated us like this? Your father and I have been anxiously searching for you."
⁴⁹**"Why were you searching for me?" he asked. "Didn't you know I had to be in my Father's house?"** ⁵⁰But they did not understand what he was saying to them.
⁵¹Then he went down to Nazareth with them and was obedient to them. But his mother treasured all these things in her heart. ⁵²And Jesus grew in wisdom and stature, and in favor with God and men.

UNDERSTANDING THE SCRIPTURE

Luke 2:41-42. Passover was one of three annual pilgrim festivals in the Jewish calendar. It began as a family observance commemorating the sparing of Israel's firstborn when God graciously passed over them near the end of the Egyptian captivity (Exodus 11:1–12:32). Passover was observed on the fifteenth day of the first month of the year. The Jewish calendar was based on a lunar cycle; and the first month, called Nissan, corresponded roughly with our March/April.

As time passed, the family observance was combined with the Feast of Unleavened Bread, a seven-day festival commemorating the hasty departure from Egypt. From the time of Josiah's reformation around 621 B.C., the observance of Passover and the Feast of Unleavened Bread focused on the temple in Jerusalem (see 2 Chronicles 35). Faithful Jews traveled to Jerusalem each year for the observance, singing "pilgrim psalms" such as Psalms 84 and 122 along the way.

Joseph and Mary had adopted this annual practice. In the year when Jesus was twelve, he accompanied them. Although thirteen is the age in contemporary Judaism when a son becomes accountable for keeping the law (*bar mitzvah*), that understanding developed after New Testament times. The earliest traditions, however, do associate the beginning signs of puberty as the time of a son assuming full accountability for keeping the commandments.

Luke 2:43-45. Travel in New Testament times could be dangerous. The parable of the good Samaritan (Luke 10:25-37) was realistic to its hearers because robbers did in fact attack travelers. To counteract this danger, relatives and friends often traveled together. In the safety of numbers, Mary and Joseph could allow Jesus the freedom to move in and out among the company of fellow travelers.

Jesus decided to stay behind in Jerusalem without asking or receiving the permission of his parents. Because he was an obedient, responsible, and trustworthy child, his parents did not worry about him. They probably missed him only when he failed to appear for supper.

We can only estimate how far "a day's journey" would have been. If the traveling group was large, the progress would have been slower. Mostly walking in mountainous terrain and carrying their own supplies, they probably would be able to travel fifteen to twenty miles a day.

When Jesus was missed, Joseph and Mary searched among their traveling party. Unable to locate him, they returned to Jerusalem. They likely searched along the return route as well as in Jerusalem.

Luke 2:46-49. When his parents found him after a three-day search, Jesus was in the precincts of the temple. The Jewish historian, Josephus, gives rather full descriptions of Herod's temple. The temple itself was about one hundred fifty feet on all sides, but it was surrounded by courtyards designed for increasingly restricted entry. The largest and outermost courtyard was the Court of the Gentiles. This area was greatly expanded by Herod, and the whole area was surrounded by a colonnade.

The colonnade was where merchants sold animals used in sacrifices, where moneychangers exchanged forbidden foreign currency for coins that could be offered in the temple, and where teachers (rabbis) gathered to discuss the law. During the years of his ministry, Jesus often taught in the temple, and the colonnade was the likely location. The eastern portion of the colonnade was called Solomon's Portico (see John 10:23; Acts 3:11; 5:12).

Teachers generally sat to teach (see Matthew 5:1); but the surprising element here is that Jesus was sitting, as the original Greek states, "in the middle of" them. This would have been considered a rather audacious act were it not for the responses of the observers. Those who heard him were amazed. The word translated "amazed" has a rather unique usage in the New Testament. It can convey astonishment mingled with fear because the event is miraculous, extraordinary, or difficult to understand. We might say they were amazed, awestruck, and dumbfounded. Another Greek word describes his parents' reaction. They too were amazed or astonished, but the roots of the word graphically depict them as "knocked out."

In Jesus' interchange with the teachers, Luke mentions two aspects of their conversations. First, Jesus was "listening to" the teachers. This term implies hearing, learning, and understanding. Second, Jesus was questioning them. This implies asking questions and inquiring about or investigating a matter. Luke also mentions two aspects of Jesus' participation that impressed those who heard him. First, he mentions Jesus' "understanding." The Greek term implies comprehension, intelligence, shrewdness, and insight. The word often implied that the understanding comes from God. Second, Luke mentions Jesus' "answers." The teachers were questioning Jesus back. The twelve-year-old was holding his own with the scholars.

After the anxiety of the search, Mary was focused on the concern that she and Joseph had for Jesus' welfare. Calling Jesus "child," she tried to draw him back toward his parents and their authority. Jesus, however, had his focus on another kind of relationship—one with his heavenly Father. He called Mary to remember who he was and who he was becoming. Though the time of his leaving home had not yet arrived, Jesus showed that he already was relating with one whom he would call, "Abba, Father."

The Greek text is not clear about the focus of Jesus' statement related to his Father's "house" (NRSV), "business" (KJV), or "interests" (NRSV note). Pressing the literal meaning, his answer to Mary is something like, "Did you not already know that it was a divine destiny for me to be among those of my Father?"

Reaction to Jesus

Luke 2:50-52. You can see why Mary and Joseph did not understand what Jesus meant. They knew from the beginning what Jesus was to be. They were aware of the divine necessity that was central to his coming. They just were not expecting this understanding from him at the age of twelve.

Jesus returned home to Nazareth with Joseph and Mary. He continued as an obedient son. Mary continued to treasure these things in her heart (compare 2:19). And Jesus, already wise beyond his years, continued to grow in wisdom, in age, as well as in goodwill with God and people.

INTERPRETING THE SCRIPTURE

Strength in Numbers

Living in community provides safety and strength for community members. As Jewish travelers in New Testament times joined together for safety and mutual protection on their pilgrimages to Jerusalem, so too can believers today draw strength from being part of a community of faith.

If you have lived even briefly in a foreign country, you probably have experienced how citizens of one country are drawn together in other societies. Being with people who speak your language, share many of your values, and enjoy a common heritage provides a sense of comfort, support, and belonging in a foreign culture. Look at people in your community who have come from other countries. You likely will have noticed that they have formed a subculture. They may live close to each other. They socialize with each other. They aid and assist each other in adapting to a foreign environment.

People naturally act this way, not because they don't like being where they are or because they are rejecting their new culture. They find that being part of a community with common experiences, values, and goals strengthens their identity, aids them in adapting to new circumstances, and provides support and encouragement in living a happy life.

Many believers have spoken of the Christian experience as a pilgrimage. Most of us who are part of a church community have found that the community provides strength for us in our faith journey. Sometimes we find that community in a Bible study group, a prayer group, or a group engaged in mission or ministry. Sometimes we find it in a men's prayer breakfast, a lunch-hour Bible study group, or a group on a prayer retreat.

Our support group doesn't have to be large. Jesus said that two or three gathered in his name would find him in the midst of them. The dangers to our faith come when we become Lone Rangers. Our morals, motivation, integrity, and identity are strengthened by walking together in the Christian life. When members of our company are found missing, we must seek them out and call them back to the family of faith.

Growing in Wisdom

Although wisdom cannot be equated with education, its development certainly can be fostered through education. Although true wisdom ultimately is a gift from God, we can grow in wisdom through thoughtful reflection on the experiences of daily life. Even though wisdom generally is an individual characteristic, it often is strengthened in the give and take with others.

That formula for growing in wisdom—education, reflection, and interaction—certainly sounds like many Bible study groups of which I have been a part. Bible study based on sound educational principles that call us to reflect on the message and meaning of God's word and that allow for sharing insights and experiences with others can play a significant role in developing wisdom.

Many in our society seem to value education solely for its vocational opportunities. In the midst of hectic lifestyles with ever increasing demands, many seem unable to find the time for thoughtful reflection. Too many of us only want to be with people who think, act, and vote the way we do. Our society desperately needs more of what Bible study groups offer.

Jesus' experience in the temple as a twelve-year-old boy gives some insights into how we gain wisdom through our interactions with others. First, notice that Jesus sought the company of established teachers. Whereas we discover later in the Gospels that Jesus had many differences with these teachers, he began his search for wisdom with those who by training, experience, and commitment had the most to offer. He put himself in the midst of those from whom he could learn the most.

Second, Jesus listened to what the teachers had to say. Too many today begin with the assumption that they already know best and that they have little to learn from their teachers. Listening without prejudging is a skill we ought to develop.

Third, Jesus asked questions. Questions are our way of developing clarity, delving deeper, and drawing out the implications of what we are learning. Questions can focus on the superficial level of facts, but wisdom comes in probing the how and why questions.

Finally, note that the interaction with the teachers involved the give and take of asking and answering questions. These teachers were not lecturers only. They questioned Jesus, probably with the same intensity with which they had been questioned; and Jesus' answers were surprising to all who heard him.

All of us could apply these good principles in our attempts to grow in knowledge, understanding, and wisdom.

Treasures in the Heart

Mary's response to the events with Jesus in the temple prompted Luke for the second time to mention that she "treasured all these things in her heart" (2:51; compare 2:19). In Jewish thought, the heart was considered the seat of physical, mental, and spiritual life. Although we tend to focus scientifically on the physical life represented in the heart, we still maintain phrases that parallel the pre-scientific ideas. Memories are such important parts of our lives, and we know they aren't actually kept in the heart. But we still understand the meaning of keeping treasures in our hearts.

Much of our health and well-being depends on what we do with the images, thoughts, feelings, and memories that inhabit our conscious and subconscious minds. This is especially true of the emotion-laden experiences that have brought us either great joy or great pain. Good memories can sustain us in the hardest times. Bad memories can plague us even when almost everything seems right with the world.

How do we handle the treasures and the baggage in our minds? Mary "pondered" these matters in her heart (2:19). She considered them, weighed them, and evaluated them. She treasured those that gave meaning and understanding to what she was experiencing. I suspect that these same treasures sustained her years later when her son was crucified.

Mary held on to some memories that she didn't fully understand, hoping that one day new insight would come to explain them. She also probably discarded some images, thoughts, and feelings as unnecessary baggage that was too burdensome to bear alone.

Some parents would have been incensed by Jesus' actions. They would have resented the lack of respect and consideration shown. They would have fussed about the inconvenience they had suffered. They would have fretted about having to travel home on the dangerous highways without their relatives and friends to protect them. They would have reproached the child and shamed him publicly for his actions. They would have punished their child severely to ensure that he never did anything like that again.

Mary didn't have all of the pieces of the puzzle yet, but she had been pondering the pieces she had. The treasures she already had stored away prepared her to respond to Jesus with patience, gentleness, love, and forgiveness. Those are pretty good ways for us to handle the good and the bad in our lives. Treasure the good. Get rid of the bad by practicing patience, gentleness, love, and forgiveness. Hold on to the rest in the expectation that God still has more to teach us.

SHARING THE SCRIPTURE

In the Temple

Preparing Our Hearts

Meditate on this week's devotional reading, found in Psalm 148:7-14. In this hymn, the psalmist calls all of creation to praise God's glory. We finish the Christmas season and its festivities on January 5, also known as Twelfth Night. In many Christian churches January 6 is designated as Epiphany, the day when Jesus was "made known" or "revealed" to the Magi. These Gentiles had come from afar to worship and praise him. What words of praise and worship will you offer to the Christ today?

Pray that you and the adult learners will offer praise even as you ask questions about your faith in order to grow toward spiritual maturity.

Preparing Our Minds

Study the background and lesson Scripture, both of which are taken from Luke 2:41-52. As you delve into this passage think about how inquiry within the community of faith leads to spiritual maturity.

Write on newsprint:
❏ information for next week's lesson, found under "Continue the Journey."
❏ activities for further spiritual growth in "Continue the Journey."

Search the Internet or a library to find at least one picture of the boy Jesus in the temple and/or being reunited with his parents that you can bring to class.

Prepare a lecture using the information from Understanding the Scripture. Select facts or ideas that you think may be unfamiliar to the class.

LEADING THE CLASS

(1) Gather to Learn

❖ Welcome the class members and introduce any guests.

❖ Pray that all who attend today will experience God's presence and grace.

❖ Divide the class into small groups. Within the groups ask the adults to talk about the kinds of spiritual questions that were important to them when they were in their early teens. Also ask them to identify who answered those questions and what wisdom they gained from these persons.

❖ Come back together. Invite any group that wants to tell a brief story or two to do so.

❖ Read aloud today's focus statement: **We have questions for which we seek answers. How does inquiry within the community of faith lead to maturity?**

Entering into dialogue in the temple, Jesus grew in faith and wisdom.

(2) Explore the Story of Jesus' Learning in the Temple

❖ Choose a volunteer to read Luke 2:41-52.

❖ Present a brief lecture from Understanding the Scripture to help the class members understand what is happening and why.

❖ Ask the students to imagine that they were Joseph or Mary. Discuss how they might have felt when they realized that Jesus was not with their company as they returned to Jerusalem. List some possible emotions on newsprint.

❖ Encourage the adults to imagine themselves as the twelve-year-old Jesus. List some possible emotions he may have been feeling while he was separated from his parents and then reunited.

❖ Suggest that the students imagine themselves as the learned rabbis. Talk together about what they might have been thinking or feeling as they interacted with Jesus.

❖ Show the picture(s) you located of the boy Jesus in the temple and/or being reunited with his parents. Invite the class to talk about how this picture depicts the emotions they have identified, or perhaps other emotions they have not yet mentioned.

❖ Discuss these questions.

(1) **What does this story reveal about Jesus' relationship with Mary and Joseph?** (Note that in verses 48-49 Mary and Jesus clearly have different understandings as to who his father is.)

(2) **Had you been Mary, what might you have "treasured" in your heart?**

(3) **What do you learn about Jesus' understanding of who he is?**

(4) **If you could ask any character in this story just one question, what would it be?**

(3) Recognize the Relationship between Inquiry and Spiritual Growth

❖ Read paragraphs four through seven of "Growing in Wisdom" in Interpreting the Scripture. See if the students have other ideas to add to the four that are discussed.

❖ Look again at the Bible story, asking the students to recall how they began to learn the stories of faith and grow "in wisdom" (2:52). Be sensitive to the fact that some class members may have started their walk with Christ very early in life, others around the time of confirmation, and still others at a much later age.

❖ Observe that some adults believe they have learned the Bible stories as children and, therefore, have no need to continue to study and ask questions. Role-play a conversation between someone who believes that all she or he ever needed to know about Christianity was learned in third grade and someone who believes that on-going study and inquiry are necessary for spiritual growth.

❖ Debrief the role-play by inviting the observers to comment on their understanding of how spiritual formation and growth occur.

(4) Make a Commitment to Lifelong Learning in the Community of Faith

❖ Ask the students why they attend Sunday school. Be aware that you will likely get a variety of answers—*spouse or friend attends; enjoy fellowship; feel obligated to do so; children are in Sunday school, so I'm here anyway; enjoy studying; interested in how my faith relates to current events; want to grow in the faith*—and that many people have more than one reason for attending.

❖ Observe that Sunday school is an important venue for learning and growth. Invite students to list other venues, which may include: *weekday classes, covenant groups, mission work teams, Bible study groups.*

❖ Distribute paper and pencils. Suggest

that those who are willing write a covenant between themselves and God, indicating their intention to continue to keep growing and learning throughout life. Students may want to state what they intend to do to continue learning.

❖ **Option:** Invite volunteers to read their covenants. Students may express similar ideas in different words.

(5) Continue the Journey

❖ Pray that everyone who has participated in today's session will be inspired to continue their lifelong inquiry into spiritual matters in order to grow in their relationship with Christ.

❖ Read aloud this preparation for next week's lesson. You may also want to post it on newsprint for the students to copy.

■ **Title: Inspired to Love!**
■ **Background Scripture: Luke 6:27-36**
■ **Lesson Scripture: Luke 6:27-36**
■ **Focus of the Lesson: Every person needs to learn how to express love to others. What does Jesus teach us about loving our enemies? Jesus taught his disciples to love their enemies, do good to those who hate them, and do to others as they would have others do to them.**

❖ Challenge the students to complete one or more of these activities for further spiritual growth, which you will write on newsprint for the students to copy.

(1) **Make a list of three to five questions related to the Bible or spirituality. Do whatever study or research necessary to find possible answers. Remember that some matters of faith are a mystery!**

(2) **Act as a mentor or spiritual friend to someone who wants to grow in the faith. Books are available to help you develop these skills.**

(3) **Ponder how parents and/or other significant adults in your life led you in the faith. If possible, thank at least one of these people. Follow their example by helping others.**

❖ Sing or read aloud "Our Parent, by Whose Name."

❖ Conclude today's session by leading the class in this benediction, which is taken from Ephesians 6:23-24: **Peace be to the whole community, and love with faith, from God the Father and the Lord Jesus Christ. Grace be with all who have an undying love for our Lord Jesus Christ. Amen.**

UNIT 2: THE AWARENESS OF GOD'S INSTRUCTION
INSPIRED TO LOVE!

PREVIEWING THE LESSON

Lesson Scripture: Luke 6:27-36
Background Scripture: Luke 6:27-36
Key Verse: Luke 6:35

Focus of the Lesson:
Every person needs to learn how to express love to others. What does Jesus teach us about loving our enemies? Jesus taught his disciples to love their enemies, do good to those who hate them, and do to others as they would have others do to them.

Goals for the Learners:
(1) to explore the meaning of the love that Jesus taught.
(2) to realize that Jesus expects us to love all people, including those we do not like.
(3) to agree to do something for someone that they would like to have done for them.

Supplies:
Bibles, newsprint and marker, paper and pencils, hymnals

READING THE SCRIPTURE

NRSV
Luke 6:27-36

27"But I say to you that listen, Love your enemies, do good to those who hate you, 28bless those who curse you, pray for those who abuse you. 29If anyone strikes you on the cheek, offer the other also; and from anyone who takes away your coat do not withhold even your shirt. 30Give to everyone who begs from you; and if anyone takes away your goods, do not ask for them again. 31Do to others as you would have them do to you.

32"If you love those who love you, what credit is that to you? For even sinners love

NIV
Luke 6:27-36

27"But I tell you who hear me: Love your enemies, do good to those who hate you, 28bless those who curse you, pray for those who mistreat you. 29If someone strikes you on one cheek, turn to him the other also. If someone takes your cloak, do not stop him from taking your tunic. 30Give to everyone who asks you, and if anyone takes what belongs to you, do not demand it back. 31Do to others as you would have them do to you.

32"If you love those who love you, what credit is that to you? Even 'sinners' love those who love them. 33And if you do good those who love them. ³³If you do good to those who do good to you, what credit is that to you? For even sinners do the same. ³⁴If you lend to those from whom you hope to receive, what credit is that to you? Even sinners lend to sinners, to receive as much again. **³⁵But love your enemies, do good, and lend, expecting nothing in return.** Your reward will be great, and you will be children of the Most High; for he is kind to the ungrateful and the wicked. ³⁶Be merciful, just as your Father is merciful.

to those who are good to you, what credit is that to you? Even 'sinners' do that. ³⁴And if you lend to those from whom you expect repayment, what credit is that to you? Even 'sinners' lend to 'sinners,' expecting to be repaid in full. **³⁵But love your enemies, do good to them, and lend to them without expecting to get anything back.** Then your reward will be great, and you will be sons of the Most High, because he is kind to the ungrateful and wicked. ³⁶Be merciful, just as your Father is merciful.

UNDERSTANDING THE SCRIPTURE

Introduction. After a night of prayer on a mountain, Jesus called his disciples to him. He chose twelve from among them to be apostles. He and his disciples then went down to a level place where they were joined by a large crowd (6:12-20). There Jesus taught his disciples some of the foundational issues that define what an obedient follower of the Lord is like (6:46-49).

Most of what Luke records of Jesus' teaching on this occasion is found in the Gospel of Matthew. Much is paralleled in the Sermon on the Mount (Matthew 5–7). A small portion is unique to Luke's Gospel (Luke 6:24-26).

Matthew and Luke record in slightly different ways a summarization of the Old Testament law to love God and to love your neighbor as yourself (Matthew 22:34-40; Luke 10:25-28). In Jesus' teaching on this occasion, he focused on the love your neighbor part of that summary. The focus had a sharper edge, however; for rather than addressing relationships with friendly neighbors, Jesus raised the standard by focusing on loving your enemies.

Luke 6:27-31. Jesus offered two sweeping principles (6:27-28 and 6:31) and then spoke of how to put those principles into practice (6:29-30 and 6:32-34). Together

these principles, when put into practice, define what Jesus meant by love.

The first principle that Jesus presented was, "Love your enemies" (6:27). Starting with, "But I say to you," Jesus states this principle as a contrast ("but") to what generally is believed to be practical. He also bases it on his own authority, not on the authority of law or reason. This command is so counter to the normal way of thinking (that is, love your family and friends, but distance and protect yourself from your enemies) that Jesus realized people really had to "listen" in order to grasp the importance of the principle.

The imperative verb for "love" here is familiar in its noun form to most Bible students. The noun is the Greek word *agape*. This kind of love is not a passion that is attracted by the beauty or worthiness of the person loved. Rather it is a spirit of patience, mercy, and generosity that is bestowed by the lover.

Jesus explained this kind of love through a series of practices that give evidence of *agape*. Those practices are do good (6:27), bless (6:28), pray (6:28), offer (6:29), do not withhold (6:29), give (6:30), and forgive [do not ask] (6:30). Together these practices demonstrate a spirit that guides disciples in relating to those who hate, curse, abuse, strike, take, and beg. The hostility of the enemy spans the range of emotion (hate), verbal abuse (curse), physical attack (strike on the cheek), and taking by force (take your coat). Jesus also included begging (wanting what is yours without earning it) and borrowing (taking what is not yours and using it as your own).

The responses that Jesus proposed are not passive. He did not call his disciples merely to bear the brunt of mistreatment. Rather, he called them to react back, but exactly in the opposite way that an enemy would expect. Rather than defensiveness, anger, threat, retaliation, meekness, or self-pity, he taught vulnerability, kindness in words and deeds, and giving more than what was demanded.

The second principle that Jesus taught often has been called the Golden Rule. Similar teachings can be found in other religions, but almost always the principle has been applied as a restraint: "Do not do to others what you do not want them to do to you."

In the Greek text of the Golden Rule, the principle begins with "just as you want men to do to you" rather than the command, "do to them likewise." This may seem a subtle difference from the English translations, but it is significant. The first principle, "Love you enemies," is a straightforward command. This second principle begins by engaging the disciple's imagination. Think how you like to be treated by others. Think of the respect, dignity, understanding, and compassion with which you want to be treated. Now apply those same expectations to others, and act toward them in that manner. The command grows out of the disciple's own standards for just treatment. It is not imposed abstractly.

Luke 6:32-34. Verses 32-34 draw out the implications of both principles. The implications are based on three actions: "love" (6:32), "do good" (6:33), and "lend" (6:34). "Love" is drawn directly from the first

principle, but it is also an expectation we have for the ways others treat us in the second principle. "Do good" and "lend" were applications of the first principle and are given expectations of the second.

The common element that runs through these three implications is risk. Disciples face no risk in loving those who will return their love. They face no risk in doing good to those who will do good back. No risk comes in lending to those who they are confident will repay them. Significant risk comes, however, in loving those who might not love in return and especially those who hate. Doing good to others opens disciples to the risk of misunderstanding, suspicion, and rejection. Doing good to those who have treated them badly causes disciples to appear weak or makes them vulnerable to further abuse. Lending with no expectation of return exposes disciples to loss and risks future exploitation or ongoing dependency.

Luke 6:35-36. Verse 35 summarizes the two principles and their implications by reiterating three ideas: "love your enemies," "do good," and "lend, expecting nothing in return." Jesus underscored that the risk involved in following these actions would bring a great reward—not from the enemy, the recipient of good deeds, or the person receiving the loan/gift but from God. By following the principles the followers would not only indicate that they were disciples of Jesus but would show that they were children of God. Their family resemblance would be seen in following the Father's example. God is kind to the ungrateful and the wicked. God is merciful.

Jesus asserted that to love, to put in action toward others the best a disciple can imagine for self, and to risk with no reward in sight are really all following the example in how the loving Father has related to humanity historically and continues to relate to disciples today.

INTERPRETING THE SCRIPTURE

Listen

I once heard an educator talk about communication in terms of colors. She said, "As I teach, think of my message as being blue. The student hears the message in yellow. The communication ends up being green." Her point was that sometimes our communications are jumbled because a teacher has an unidentified point of view and students have experiences and prejudices that affect what is heard.

"Listen" and "hear" are rather frequent commands in the Gospels. On occasion Jesus stated that some who heard his parables would not listen (Matthew 13:13) or understand them (Luke 8:10). Listening is more than an auditory experience. It is more than sound waves striking the eardrums. It is even more than the impulses from the sound waves reaching the brain. Really listening requires attention, discrimination, thought, reflection, and response.

Some of Jesus' teachings are hard sayings. They go against conventional wisdom. They challenge our regular patterns of thinking and behaving. They require an unaccustomed point of view. They demand eyes that see spiritual dimensions and ears that hear cryptic messages with open, unhindered, and impartial minds. When we have really listened, our lives will reflect it.

When we encounter the hard sayings of Jesus, let's truly listen. Let's strive to ensure that the conclusion will not be that of G. K. Chesterton: "The Christian ideal has not been tried and found wanting. It has been found difficult and left untried."

Love

The shift from legalistically adhering to laws of prohibition ("Thou shalt not") to lovingly doing good toward others ("Love your enemies, do good," and "lend") may be the most central aspect of Jesus' ethic. Discarding explicit restrictions is never easy. Demerits imposed for infractions are always easier to administer than are merits that require subjective evaluation.

The hard part of loving came when Jesus extended "be merciful" to include mercy toward Samaritans, tax collectors, prostitutes, Gentiles, and enemies. All of these and others Jesus lumped under the term "sinners" (Luke 6:32-34). He used that term, not as Paul did in speaking of those who miss the mark, but in the pejorative sense widely applied to the irreligious people of his day who did not observe the law.

His command to love challenged long years of prejudice toward the Samaritans, despised because these once pure Jewish people who lived in the north of Israel had intermarried with non-Jews. It challenged the anger and bitterness toward collaborators with the occupying Roman forces. It challenged the disgust toward the moral degenerates in their midst. It challenged the fear and antipathy toward foreign people and their practices. It challenged the resentment and desire for vengeance against those who caused anguish, pain, and suffering.

Overcoming these challenges is never easy. Jesus recognized that suppressing the bad feelings was not enough. Something positive was required. Disciples cannot always control what others do to them, but they can control how they react. Jesus did not call for payback time. Instead he advocated overcoming evil with good (Romans 12:21) through an *agape* kind of love.

It's easy to affirm that love is the answer to all the world's problems. It's also easy to find love too difficult when we try to apply it to specific situations in life. That often makes it too easy to leave it untried.

Lend

The United States has always been a nation in debt. According to the Bureau of Public Debt (www.publicdebt.treas.gov/opd/opd.htm), the first reported debt in 1791 was $75 million. The debt rose from over $90 million in 1861 to over $524 million in 1862. By July 1865, because of the Civil War, the debt surpassed $2.5 billion. The debt almost tripled in the first year of World War I, and almost doubled again the second year, reaching over $27 billion. During World War II, the debt went from almost $49 billion to $269 billion. The national debt surpassed $1 trillion in 1981. In 2005, the debt was on the verge of $8 trillion, about $27,000 per person in this country. The closest the nation ever came to being out of debt was 1835, when the public debt was $33,733.

All this debt is owed to someone, but the underlying reality of this debt is that the debt holders are counting on being able to get their investment back with interest.

The International Monetary Fund has been under pressure to write off the debts of the most underdeveloped countries. Many see this as a humane thing to do with IMF money. But would anyone strongly advocate forgiving this debt if the money were coming directly out of their own pockets? Who among us would be willing (and able) to chip in $27,000 per member of our household to pay off the debt of the United States?

Jesus' instruction to lend expecting nothing in return is about that radical. The idea goes against basic principles and values of a capitalistic, free-market society where risks are rewarded, hard work and merit are valued, ingenuity and determination are recognized, and self-reliance is promoted.

In our give-and-take society we have too much take and not enough give. Too many hearts are closed to the poor, the disadvantaged, the hungry, the naked, the sick, the imprisoned—oops, I slipped into Matthew 25:31-46 there. And there's the rub. When we see the least of these and minister to them, we are ministering to Jesus. And when those to whom we minister see us, they see the Father whose children are following his example.

Likeness

Old Testament writers and prophets recognized the centrality of God's love for the chosen people. Although recognizing that the people fell short of deserving that love, they never quite grasped the obligation placed on recipients of grace. Jesus' commandments to love capture the significance of grace and the obligations that grace places upon its recipients to show mercy toward others. The parable of the unforgiving servant (Matthew 18:23-35) dramatically makes that point. The king in the parable, upon confronting the unforgiving servant, says, "Should you not have had mercy on your fellow slave, as I had mercy on you?" (18:33).

If we are acknowledged recipients of grace, we will follow God's example. If we do not follow that example, we have not been sincere in acknowledging our need for grace or in fully receiving God's mercy.

Although Jesus promised great rewards for those who love, do good, and lend with no hope of return, surely the greatest reward is being identified as "children of the Most High" (Luke 6:35). In the early nineteenth century, the word *spit* was used to mean "an exact likeness or counterpart of a person." That meaning evolved through folk culture into the expression, "He's the spittin' image of his father."

Paul tells us that Jesus "is the image of the invisible God" (Colossians 1:15). When we know Christ, we know the Father (John 8:19). As adopted children, we may never be a "spittin' image" of our heavenly Father; yet Jesus reminds us to strive to be like God. When we live in God's likeness, follow God's example, and show mercy to others, we indeed show that we are children of God. As such, we try to love as Jesus taught us that God loves.

SHARING THE SCRIPTURE

Preparing Our Hearts

Meditate on this week's devotional reading, found in Psalm 37:1-11. This song teaches us not to worry—"do not fret" (37:1, 7, 8). Instead, we are to put our trust in God, who will reward us with fulfilled promises. Read this psalm alongside of today's lesson Scripture. What similarities and/or differences do you see?

Pray that you and the adult learners will be open to God's instruction at all times, especially concerning how we are to love others—even our enemies.

Preparing Our Minds

Study the background and lesson Scripture, found in Luke 6:27-36. As you meditate on this passage ponder what Jesus said about loving enemies.

Write on newsprint:
❑ information for next week's lesson, found under "Continue the Journey."
❑ activities for further spiritual growth in "Continue the Journey."

Plan a brief lecture as suggested for "Explore the Meaning of the Love That Jesus Taught."

Prepare the chart for "Explore the Meaning of the Love That Jesus Taught." Fill in the headings and verse numbers in advance.

LEADING THE CLASS

(1) Gather to Learn

❖ Welcome the class members and introduce any guests.

❖ Pray that those who have come today will hear the good news of God's love for all.

❖ Tell this true story: **A Christian, who we'll call Martha, was being harassed by a co-worker. Martha wanted to pray that her** co-worker would just leave her alone, but the Holy Spirit convinced her to pray for God's mercy in this co-worker's life. Martha began to grow spiritually and eventually left her job to move into full-time ministry. She taught her son to pray for his enemies as well. The classmate who was bullying him is now a close friend.

❖ Ask: **What conclusions can you draw from Martha's experience concerning the power of love?**

❖ Read aloud today's focus statement: **Every person needs to learn how to express love to others. What does Jesus teach us about loving our enemies? Jesus taught his disciples to love their enemies, do good to those who hate them, and do to others as they would have others do to them.**

(2) Explore the Meaning of the Love That Jesus Taught

❖ Set the stage for today's lesson by lecturing briefly on the Introduction found in Understanding the Scripture.

❖ Choose a volunteer to read Luke 6:27-36 as if Jesus were speaking directly to the class.

❖ Look at the behaviors, both positive and negative, listed in verses 27-30. Create a chart and ask the class to fill it in, or fill it in yourself as you speak about each item. Information under Luke 6:27-30 in Understanding the Scripture will help you.

Verses in Luke 6	Positive Behaviors Jesus' Followers Are to Practice	To Counteract Negative Behaviors of Enemies
27	love . . . do good	hatred
28	bless	curse
28	pray	abuse
29	offer	strike
29	do not withhold	take away (steal)
30	give	beg
30	forgive (do not ask)	take away (steal)

❖ Ask the class to read in unison Luke 6:31. Encourage them to comment on how this Golden Rule shapes their own behavior.

❖ Observe that verses 32-34 are basically "if. . .then" statements. Point out that the "if" portion assumes you are taking certain actions, while the "then" portion raises question about how valuable these actions really are.

❖ Direct the students' attention to verses 35-36. Instead of loving and lending as "sinners" do, Jesus calls his followers to include enemies among those they love, and to be willing to lend without expectation of return.

❖ Read aloud "Love" from Interpreting the Scripture. Ask the students to imagine themselves as faithful Jews listening to Jesus. Discuss how they might have responded to his message. Now ask them to imagine themselves as those who are on the margins. Discuss how they might have responded.

❖ Conclude this segment by encouraging the students to state which of Jesus' teachings contained in today's lesson spoke most clearly to them, and why.

(3) Realize That Jesus Calls Us to Love All People, Including Those We Do Not Like

❖ Invite students to tell stories of how their attempts to love their enemies yielded fruit. They may speak with a small group or the whole class. Suggest that they mention challenges to loving their enemies and how they overcame them.

❖ Read aloud this scenario and invite the students to suggest how Maureen could respond in a loving manner. **Maureen is in a quandary. A former friend, Reba, called and wanted to have lunch. Maureen knows that Reba has been spreading hurtful gossip about her, which is why she has been avoiding Reba. Yet, Maureen feels that she should talk with Reba face to face about the reason for this rift. Maureen recognizes that she cannot undo the damage caused by the gossip, but she does want to live faithfully for Christ and, therefore, must love this woman she perceives to be an enemy. What advice can you give Maureen for dealing with this situation?**

❖ **Option:** Solicit two students to role-play a meeting between Reba and Maureen. Ask the class to "rate" Maureen on how well she handled this situation.

❖ Encourage the students to state any new insights they have gleaned from today's lesson concerning how to love their enemies.

(4) Agree to Do Something for Someone That the Learners Would Like to Have Done for Them

❖ Distribute slips of paper and pencils. Ask each person to write one act of kindness that is free or very low-cost that someone else in the class could do for them. Have them put their name and phone number on the paper.

❖ Collect the papers and start reading the requests (though not the names), one by one. After each one, ask if there is someone who would be willing to undertake this kindness. Give the paper to that person.

❖ Provide time for the "giver" and "receiver" to make arrangements as to time and place for the activity.

(5) Continue the Journey

❖ Pray that those who have come today will recognize the importance of loving those who oppose them.

❖ Read aloud this preparation for next week's lesson. You may also want to post it on newsprint for the students to copy.
- ■ Title: Inspired to Pray!
- ■ Background Scripture: Luke 11:5-13
- ■ Lesson Scripture: Luke 11:5-13
- ■ Focus of the Lesson: We long for a relationship with someone who cares enough to listen to and respond to our needs. To whom can

we go? Jesus taught that we have a loving heavenly parent to whom we can persistently bring our needs and the desires of our heart.

❖ Challenge the students to complete one or more of these activities for further spiritual growth, which you will write on newsprint for the students to copy.

(1) Read *Strength to Love,* a collection of sermons by Martin Luther King, which includes "Loving Your Enemies."

(2) Pray, contribute, and do whatever else you can for people who are victims of hatred, injustice, and oppression. Pray especially for those who are victimizing them that they may be transformed.

(3) Forgive an enemy this week. Do something tangible, such as treat to lunch, to indicate your sincerity about mending the relationship.

❖ Sing or read aloud "Breathe on Me, Breath of God."

❖ Conclude today's session by leading the class in this benediction, which is taken from Ephesians 6:23-24: **Peace be to the whole community, and love with faith, from God the Father and the Lord Jesus Christ. Grace be with all who have an undying love for our Lord Jesus Christ. Amen.**

UNIT 2: THE AWARENESS OF GOD'S INSTRUCTION
INSPIRED TO PRAY!

PREVIEWING THE LESSON

Lesson Scripture: Luke 11:5-13
Background Scripture: Luke 11:5-13
Key Verse: Luke 11:9

Focus of the Lesson:
We long for a relationship with someone who cares enough to listen to and respond to our needs. To whom can we go? Jesus taught that we have a loving heavenly parent to whom we can persistently bring our needs and the desires of our heart.

Goals for the Learners:
(1) to explore Jesus' teachings on being persistent in taking our needs to God.
(2) to experience the trust and security of praying to God.
(3) to approach God with perseverance, trusting God to respond.

Supplies:
Bibles, newsprint and marker, paper and pencils, hymnals, colored pencils or markers, optional commentaries, optional meditative music on CD or tape and appropriate player

---

READING THE SCRIPTURE

NRSV
Luke 11:5-13

⁵And he said to them, "Suppose one of you has a friend, and you go to him at midnight and say to him, 'Friend, lend me three loaves of bread; ⁶for a friend of mine has arrived, and I have nothing to set before him.' ⁷And he answers from within, 'Do not bother me; the door has already been locked, and my children are with me in bed; I cannot get up and give you anything.' ⁸I tell you, even though he will not get up and give him anything because he is his friend, at least

NIV
Luke 11:5-13

⁵Then he said to them, "Suppose one of you has a friend, and he goes to him at midnight and says, 'Friend, lend me three loaves of bread, ⁶because a friend of mine on a journey has come to me, and I have nothing to set before him.'

⁷"Then the one inside answers, 'Don't bother me. The door is already locked, and my children are with me in bed. I can't get up and give you anything.' ⁸I tell you, though he will not get up and give him the

because of his persistence he will get up and give him whatever he needs.

⁹"So I say to you, Ask, and it will be given you; search, and you will find; knock, and the door will be opened for you. ¹⁰For everyone who asks receives, and everyone who searches finds, and for everyone who knocks, the door will be opened. ¹¹Is there anyone among you who, if your child asks for a fish, will give a snake instead of a fish? ¹²Or if the child asks for an egg, will give a scorpion? ¹³If you then, who are evil, know how to give good gifts to your children, how much more will the heavenly Father give the Holy Spirit to those who ask him!"

bread because he is his friend, yet because of the man's boldness he will get up and give him as much as he needs.

⁹"So I say to you: Ask and it will be given to you; seek and you will find; knock and the door will be opened to you. ¹⁰For everyone who asks receives; he who seeks finds; and to him who knocks, the door will be opened.

¹¹"Which of you fathers, if your son asks for a fish, will give him a snake instead? ¹²Or if he asks for an egg, will give him a scorpion? ¹³If you then, though you are evil, know how to give good gifts to your children, how much more will your Father in heaven give the Holy Spirit to those who ask him!"

UNDERSTANDING THE SCRIPTURE

Introduction. Jesus lived in a time and place where people knew about prayer. Reared in a family that faithfully followed the Jewish laws and traditions (Luke 2:21-24), Jesus certainly was exposed to the tradition of reciting the Shema (Deuteronomy 6:4) daily in the morning and in the evening. He would have known and likely practiced the Jewish custom of praying three times a day (Daniel 6:10; compare Acts 3:1; 10:3).

Luke in particular among the Gospels gives great attention to Jesus' practice of prayer. Jesus prayed after his baptism (3:21). He often withdrew to a private place to pray (5:16). He prayed before choosing the Twelve (6:12). He prayed with his disciples (9:18, 28). He prayed for Peter (22:31-32). He prayed on the Mount of Olives as the time for his crucifixion approached (22:39-46).

Jesus also was aware of the abuses that accompanied the traditional practice of prayer. He saw the hypocrisy, grandstanding, and pride of the pseudo-pious (Matthew 6:5; Luke 18:9-14; 20:47). He criticized the distracting commercialization that interrupted prayer in the temple (19:45-46).

He noted the empty babbling of Gentile prayers (Matthew 6:7).

Given this background, we should not be surprised that Jesus taught his disciples about prayer. In fact, Luke notes that after observing Jesus at prayer, the disciples asked him to teach them to pray (Luke 11:1). After giving the disciples a model prayer (11:2-4), Jesus expanded on his teaching by use of a series of vivid illustrations that foster an understanding of prayer.

Luke 11:5-8. The first illustration is actually a story told to underscore a point. Jesus posed a hypothetical situation. By starting with "Suppose one of you," Jesus engaged his listeners by inviting them to place themselves in the situation.

The situation was an extreme demand placed on the traditional Jewish practice of hospitality. When a guest arrived, whether announced or unannounced, good hospitality demanded the offering of food and lodging. To fail to show proper hospitality would be a great loss of face and loss of standing in the eyes of the community.

The situation in this passage was

complicated by two factors. First, the guest was a "friend," not just a stranger passing through town. Although hospitality was demanded for both kinds of visitors, to disappoint a friend would be a severe lapse in the fundamental rules of etiquette. Second, the host had nothing on hand to serve the guest. This condition was more common than the exception for most people in Jesus' time. Most earned only enough each day to make it until the next day. Generally only enough food was prepared to suffice that day's needs. If the guest had arrived before supper, the family would have stretched what they had for themselves to include the guest. At midnight, however, little was available, nothing was prepared, and the options available were few.

In such a situation, most people would turn to a friend who had the resources they need. At midnight, however, the host had to inconvenience one friend in order to be hospitable to another. The neighbor's door would have been locked, the lamp would have been trimmed, and the family would have been in bed long before the guest arrived.

Jesus concluded that even though friendship with a neighbor would not be enough motivation to get out of bed and give the neighbor what he needed, persistence would prompt him to act. Who wants someone pounding on the door all night asking for help? Just to get rid of the persistent neighbor, most people would get up, help him out, and then get back to bed.

The Greek word translated "persistence" (11:8) seems key to understanding the illustration. Because this is the only occurrence of the word in the New Testament, other sources must be employed to determine the meaning. Literally the word means "shamelessness" and has aspects of boldness as well as impudence in its background. It pictures a person who is unabashed, who is not easily shamed or made uneasy, or who cannot be disconcerted.

Luke 11:9-10. The relationship between these verses and the preceding illustration has been interpreted differently. Some interpreters see them as calling disciples to the kind of persistence illustrated in prior verses. As with the parable of the widow and the unjust judge (18:1-8), persistence pays off. If you pester God continuously, you will eventually get your request answered. This is supported by the use of the Greek imperatives in the present tense, which imply, "continue asking," "continue searching," and "continue knocking."

Other interpreters think these verses are intended as a contrast to the previous illustration. They point to the verses that follow (11:11-13) for support. Their contention is that God is not a reluctant neighbor or an unjust judge. Instead, God is a heavenly parent who knows how to give good gifts to his children. Rather than focusing on the imperatives in verse 9, they focus on the promises in verse 10. Those promises are for "everyone," and they assure that all who are asking, searching, and knocking will have their prayers answered.

Luke 11:11-13. Jesus concluded these teachings on prayer with another example that drew the listener into the deliberations by addressing "anyone among you." Using a simple parent-child analogy, Jesus posed two questions that showed the reasonableness of a parent acting for the benefit of the child. The first question is based on the child's request for a fish. The second is a request for an egg. In both cases Jesus assumed that any parent would meet these basic requests because the child asked and the request was not unreasonable. How unimaginable it would be for a parent to give a child a snake rather than the requested fish or a scorpion rather than the requested egg.

From the parent-child analogy, Jesus moved to the way in which the heavenly Father relates to his children. If human parents know how to give good gifts to their children, how much more will the heavenly Father know how to bless his children who pray to him! The reference to "you . . . who are evil" is a contrast designed to heighten the goodness of God.

In Matthew's version of this same teaching (Matthew 7:7-11), the Father gives "good things to those who ask him" (7:11). Luke writes, "will . . . give the Holy Spirit to those who ask him!" The Holy Spirit is a particular interest of Luke, and he may be emphasizing that the heavenly Father will give the greatest of all gifts—God's own self as an ever-present Spirit—"to those who ask."

INTERPRETING THE SCRIPTURE

Power of Prayer

The story is told of a backwoodsman who heard that a hardware store in town was selling a chain saw guaranteed to cut five cords of wood in an hour. Having several trees recently felled by a storm, he decided to test the guarantee and bought one.

A week later he returned to the store demanding his money back. "I used that saw for five days and didn't cut even one cord," he exclaimed.

"Let's see that saw," the clerk replied defensively. Taking the saw, he pulled the starter cord; and the engine turned over instantly, "W-w-w-h-h-h-r-r."

The startled customer jumped back, shouting, "What's that noise?"

The power of a chain saw is not in owning a saw. If we fail to start the engine, the saw will be virtually useless. Likewise, the power of prayer is not merely in the act of praying. Although prayer is verbal (asking), it is also spatial (searching, seeking, questing, journeying) and relational (knocking, gaining access, entering). We often neglect these latter two aspects, especially the relational.

Do you have neighbors who only stop by to see you when they want to borrow something? Do you have co-workers who only come by when they have something they need for you to do for them? Most friendships with neighbors and co-workers will go only so far. In Jesus' story, loaning three loaves of bread to a friend likely would not have been a problem at any other time of day. Disturbing a friend's rest when a hard day of work lay ahead, however, and rousing the family from sleep in the middle of the night and then having to get them settled back down again—these hardly justified helping out a neighbor who was unprepared for guests when you were asleep. Persistent nagging may be the only way to get a response.

Now change the relationship to that with a loving parent who is deeply committed to doing good for the child. Like a loving parent, God is far more likely to say, "[Child], you are always with me, and all that is mine is yours" (Luke 15:31), when we are with God in body, soul, mind, and spirit. That kind of relationship empowers us. James observed, "The prayer of the righteous is powerful and effective" (James 5:16).

Persistence in Prayer

A lot of people are aware of the promises made about prayer. They even try prayer out for a few days. But they never discover the power in prayer. They go to God and ask for something; and when nothing happens, they go away empty-handed. They search for God in times of stress or difficulty; and when they don't find God, they go away disillusioned. They knock; but when the door is not answered immediately, they walk away assuming that no one is at home.

Most often we are not persistent in prayer because our concerns are immediate, selfish, short-sighted, and fickle. Few prayer concerns last more than several days. Even if God were to address those concerns and provide some answer, we would be unaware of it because we have moved on to other concerns.

In recent years, experiencing God has been a popular idea in many Christian circles. All of us on some level want to know God and understand God's will. The Scriptures are full of examples of people who experienced God. Most of those examples, however, are experiences initiated by God. Far more frequently the Scriptures advise us to seek God. We prefer to experience something immediately and dramatically, however, rather than to do the hard work of searching.

Persistence in prayer is not merely persistence in asking, searching, and knocking. It is also persistence in listening to God. The answer to every prayer is heard by listening to God—not by praying, not by talking, not by asking, not by demanding answers, not by expecting a posthaste response, but by listening. A friend once remarked, "To sit in the presence of a king, a pope, or a president of the United States is a great honor, even if one says not a word. How much greater to sit quietly in the presence of the King of Kings!"

Through persistent prayer we discover what is important, valuable, good, and most fulfilling. Through persistent prayer we are conformed to God's purpose, will, and intention for us. As we are shaped by prayer, the answers to prayer become more obvious.

Promise of Prayer

Many interpreters think that "how much more" (Luke 11:13) is the key to understanding many of Jesus' parables. A parable lays two realities alongside each other. The first reality is the daily experience of life that most people can understand. The second reality is a spiritual reality that we cannot see, measure, manipulate, or control on a human plane. Drawing on the human experience, a connection is made to the spiritual reality; but the spiritual reality is always so much more than human experience can describe.

Jesus promised his disciples that prayer would work. If they were persistent; if they continued asking, searching, and knocking; and if they cherished the special relationship they enjoyed with a loving heavenly Father, then they would find that prayer would change things.

Too much religious thought today focuses on the promise of prayer as a guarantee of success, riches, and happiness. Too many think that God's main desire is to bless us, enlarge our influence, empower our work, and protect us from harm. Too many think it's all about us rather than all about God.

We have forgotten that God's blessing is for the poor, hungry, and weeping (Luke 6:20-21). We have overlooked that God's Son "came to . . . his own, and his own people did not accept him" (John 1:11). We have rejected the idea that faithfulness leads to a cross rather than a crown.

We need to grasp a more important perspective. In effect, God says, "If you will trust me and entrust yourself to me, I will give you what you really need. I don't promise what you value from a worldly perspective, but I will fill your spirit with all you need to live a life of blessed joy." The gift of the Holy Spirit—that ever-present companion in life who walks with us through struggle, pain, hardship, rejection, and loss—is the greatest promise of all. We can count on God to listen to us; all we need to do is pray.

SHARING THE SCRIPTURE

Preparing Our Hearts

Meditate on this week's devotional reading, found in Psalm 28:6-9. After praying for help, the psalmist writes in verse 6, "Blessed be the LORD, for he has heard the sound of my pleadings." How do you experience the psalmist's assurance that God has indeed listened and heard? Do you pray for what you need? Do you believe that God answers you, even if the answers are not always what you might want? Spend some time in prayer seeking God and praying for your needs and the needs of others.

Pray that you and the adult learners will be persistent in prayer, trusting that God is listening and will answer.

Preparing Our Minds

Study the background and lesson Scripture, Luke 11:5-13. Ponder who you can go to when you need someone who cares enough to listen and respond to your needs.

Write on newsprint:
❏ information for next week's lesson, found under "Continue the Journey."
❏ activities for further spiritual growth in "Continue the Journey."

Gather art supplies, including plain paper or newsprint, colored pencils or markers, which the students will need to draw a picture.

Option: Bring meditative music and appropriate player to class.

Collect commentaries if you choose to use that option.

Prepare a lecture from Understanding the Scripture for "Explore Jesus' Teachings on Being Persistent in Taking Our Needs to God."

Option: Plan a lecture to answer the three questions in the section "Explore Jesus' Teachings on Being Persistent in Taking Our Needs to God."

LEADING THE CLASS

(1) Gather to Learn

❖ Welcome the class members and introduce any guests.

❖ Pray that everyone who has gathered today will move toward a deeper relationship with God as you study and pray together.

❖ Read this testimony to answered prayer: **A woman prayed for more than two years for her grandson, who was deeply depressed and abusing drugs and alcohol. He had left home and was living in his car. His family was finally able to enroll him in a high school for troubled boys, which he graduated from two years later. He returned home, and is a much more mature person with a job and goals. The grandmother writes that she will be forever grateful for this answer to prayer.**

❖ Ask: **How would you describe this grandmother's prayer life and its effect on her grandson?**

❖ Read aloud today's focus statement: **We long for a relationship with someone who cares enough to listen to and respond to our needs. To whom can we go? Jesus taught that we have a loving heavenly parent to whom we can persistently bring our needs and the desires of our heart.**

(2) Explore Jesus' Teachings on Being Persistent in Taking Our Needs to God

❖ Choose three volunteers, one to read Luke 11:5-8, one to read verses 9-10, and the other to read verses 11-13. Note that these verses follow Luke's version of The Lord's Prayer.

❖ Use information under Luke 11:5-8 in Understanding the Scripture to explain in a lecture the issues involved in these verses. Do the same for verses 9-10 and 11-13. Point out that even though these three sections can be seen as separate parts, together they offer Jesus' teaching on persistence in prayer.

❖ **Option:** Divide the class into groups and give each group at least one commentary. Assign either verses 5-8, 9-10, or 11-13 to each group, though be aware that some commentaries will not have the information subdivided this way. Ask each group to create their own commentary on their assigned verses. Provide time for the groups to report back to the class. Discuss any new insights and questions that arose.

❖ Discuss these questions, or answer them yourself in a brief lecture.

(1) **What do you learn about prayer from Jesus' teachings here?**

(2) **What do you learn about God, particularly as related to prayer?** (Be sure to include the idea of God's goodness and willingness to answer all who ask. Note that this goodness far exceeds that of the human parent discussed in verses 11-13.)

(3) **What other teachings of Jesus can you recall concerning prayer?** (Note that Jesus taught not only through words but also by example. A few examples are given in the second and third paragraphs under Introduction in Understanding the Scripture.)

(3) Experience the Trust and Security of Praying to God

❖ Retell the first paragraph under "Persistence in Prayer" in Interpreting the Scripture.

❖ Read aloud this excerpt from the beginning of chapter 3 of Mark Twain's *Huckleberry Finn* as an example of someone who felt nothing happened and walked away from God: **"Then Miss Watson took me in the closet and prayed, but nothing come of it. She told me to pray every day, and whatever I asked for I would get it.**

But it warn't so. I tried it. Once I got a fish-line, but no hooks. It warn't any good to me without hooks. I tried for the hooks three or four times, but somehow I couldn't make it work. By and by, one day, I asked Miss Watson to try for me, but she said I was a fool. She never told me why, and I couldn't make it out no way."

❖ Discuss these questions with the class.

(1) **What seems to be Huck's attitude toward prayer?**

(2) **Why does he apparently hold this attitude?**

(3) **Why does Miss Watson tell him he is a fool?**

(4) **How is Huck's experience similar to or different from your own?**

(5) **If you could speak to Huck, what personal testimony could you give about trusting God to answer prayer?**

(4) Approach God with Perseverance, Trusting God to Respond

❖ Read aloud Luke 11:9, today's key verse. Prompt the students to consider how this verse might affect their faith development if they really took it seriously.

❖ **Option:** Play some meditative music softly in the background throughout this portion of the lesson.

❖ Distribute unlined paper or newsprint and colored pencils or markers. Encourage the students to draw a symbol or picture that captures the essence of today's lesson, particularly as expressed in the key verse. Some may be able to draw a person knocking on a door, whereas others may choose to show a hand rapping, or simply a door knocker or other symbol.

❖ Divide the class into small groups. Invite students who wish to do so to show their drawings (others may prefer not to show them but simply describe their work) and explain how this picture or symbol speaks to them about approaching God with perseverance.

❖ Provide quiet time for the students to offer silent prayer.

(5) Continue the Journey

❖ Conclude the silent prayer by praying that all who participated today will go forth with renewed inspiration to pray confidently and persistently, trusting that God will hear and respond.

❖ Read aloud this preparation for next week's lesson. You may also want to post it on newsprint for the students to copy.

■ **Title: Inspired to Trust!**
■ **Background Scripture: Luke 12:22-34**
■ **Lesson Scripture: Luke 12:22-34**
■ **Focus of the Lesson: We all face pressure and may experience anxiety. What can we do to combat anxiety and worry? Jesus says that when we trust in God we have no need to worry.**

❖ Challenge the students to complete one or more of these activities for further spiritual growth, which you will write on newsprint for the students to copy.

(1) **Keep a list of prayer requests that you receive this week. Pray for each person or situation at least twice daily. By the end of the week, note any change. Choose one need and make a commitment to pray persistently until the situation is resolved.**

(2) **Read a book about prayer. Underline or take notes on points that will enable you to be a more effective pray-er.**

(3) **Memorize today's key verse, Luke 11:9. Whenever you face an obstacle, recite this verse.**

❖ Sing or read aloud "Canticle of Prayer," found on page 406 of *The United Methodist Hymnal* and based in part on Luke 11:9-10. Or, sing or read another hymn on prayer.

❖ Conclude today's session by leading the class in this benediction, which is taken from Ephesians 6:23-24: **Peace be to the whole community, and love with faith, from God the Father and the Lord Jesus Christ. Grace be with all who have an undying love for our Lord Jesus Christ. Amen.**

UNIT 2: THE AWARENESS OF GOD'S INSTRUCTION
INSPIRED TO TRUST!

PREVIEWING THE LESSON

Lesson Scripture: Luke 12:22-34
Background Scripture: Luke 12:22-34
Key Verse: Luke 12:22

Focus of the Lesson:
We all face pressure and may experience anxiety. What can we do to combat anxiety and worry? Jesus says that when we trust in God we have no need to worry.

Goals for the Learners:
(1) to explore Jesus' teaching on trusting God.
(2) to turn over to God anxiety and worry.
(3) to make a commitment to pursue a relationship with God that will alleviate their worry and anxiety.

Supplies:
Bibles, newsprint and marker, paper and pencils, hymnals, paper bag

---

READING THE SCRIPTURE

NRSV
Luke 12:22-34

22He said to his disciples, "Therefore I tell you, do not worry about your life, what you will eat, or about your body, what you will wear. 23For life is more than food, and the body more than clothing. 24Consider the ravens: they neither sow nor reap, they have neither storehouse nor barn, and yet God feeds them. Of how much more value are you than the birds! 25And can any of you by worrying add a single hour to your span of life? 26If then you are not able to do so small a thing as that, why do you worry about the rest? 27Consider the lilies, how they grow: they neither toil nor spin; yet I tell you, even

NIV
Luke 12:22-34

22Then Jesus said to his disciples: "Therefore I tell you, do not worry about your life, what you will eat; or about your body, what you will wear. 23Life is more than food, and the body more than clothes. 24Consider the ravens: They do not sow or reap, they have no storeroom or barn; yet God feeds them. And how much more valuable you are than birds! 25Who of you by worrying can add a single hour to his life? 26Since you cannot do this very little thing, why do you worry about the rest?

27"Consider how the lilies grow. They do

Solomon in all his glory was not clothed like one of these. ²⁸But if God so clothes the grass of the field, which is alive today and tomorrow is thrown into the oven, how much more will he clothe you—you of little faith! ²⁹And do not keep striving for what you are to eat and what you are to drink, and do not keep worrying. ³⁰For it is the nations of the world that strive after all these things, and your Father knows that you need them. ³¹Instead, strive for his kingdom, and these things will be given to you as well.

³²"Do not be afraid, little flock, for it is your Father's good pleasure to give you the kingdom. ³³Sell your possessions, and give alms. Make purses for yourselves that do not wear out, an unfailing treasure in heaven, where no thief comes near and no moth destroys. ³⁴For where your treasure is, there your heart will be also.

not labor or spin. Yet I tell you, not even Solomon in all his splendor was dressed like one of these. ²⁸If that is how God clothes the grass of the field, which is here today, and tomorrow is thrown into the fire, how much more will he clothe you, O you of little faith! ²⁹And do not set your heart on what you will eat or drink; do not worry about it. ³⁰For the pagan world runs after all such things, and your Father knows that you need them. ³¹But seek his kingdom, and these things will be given to you as well.

³²"Do not be afraid, little flock, for your Father has been pleased to give you the kingdom. ³³Sell your possessions and give to the poor. Provide purses for yourselves that will not wear out, a treasure in heaven that will not be exhausted, where no thief comes near and no moth destroys. ³⁴For where your treasure is, there your heart will be also.

UNDERSTANDING THE SCRIPTURE

Introduction. Because Matthew and Luke included a sizable body of Jesus' teachings that are very similar, scholars think that the two drew from a common source of teaching tradition. Luke explicitly states that he investigated carefully the oral and written traditions about Jesus and put them in an orderly account (Luke 1:1-4).

Matthew presented a good portion of these common teachings in the Sermon on the Mount (Matthew 5–7). Luke dispersed the material throughout his Gospel. Luke 12:22-34 is very similar to Matthew 6:25-33 and 6:19-21, differing slightly in the order of the material. Other differences may reflect an Aramaic origin for the common tradition that was translated into Greek differently by the two Gospel writers. Aramaic was probably the native language Jesus spoke.

Both Matthew and Luke record that these teachings were given to Jesus' disciples but in the presence of a crowd of people

(Matthew 5:1; 7:28-29; Luke 12:1). Luke prepares for the teachings with warnings about hypocrisy, possible persecution, and greed. Immediately preceding today's Scripture lesson is the parable of a rich man who focused on material security and neglected his relationship with God (Luke 12:16-21).

Luke 12:22-24. After telling the parable, Jesus addressed his disciples and focused on the human tendency to trust in material possessions. "Therefore" (12:22) indicates that what follows is an extension or application of the parable. "I tell you" is an expression of Jesus' authority as teacher. In contrast to the typical rabbi of his day, Jesus did not recite rabbinic precedents as his authority. The fresh independence of Jesus' teaching frequently astonished those who heard him (Matthew 7:28-29).

Jesus associated the drive for material possessions and the tendency to trust in them with "worry about your life" (Luke

12:22). The Greek verb for "worry" comes from a compound that literally means "to have a divided mind." It denotes anxiety or undue concern. "Life" is a term that can apply either to physical, earthly life or to the soul of a person (the inner life with its feelings and emotions that can transcend the earthly). Sometimes the word speaks of both. Here Jesus drew on the dual meaning. The anxiety about life relates to food and clothing, but "life" is much more than physical nourishment and apparel. Barns full of goods do not mean one can relax (12:18-20).

To illustrate the undue concern often felt about food, Jesus pointed to the ravens or crows. These "unclean" birds, which were forbidden as food in the Old Testament (Leviticus 11:13-15; Deuteronomy 14:11-14), did not sow or reap in order to store up food for the future; yet God feeds them. If God cares for unclean birds, how much more will he take care of those created in God's image!

Luke 12:25-28. Jesus also addressed worry by focusing on the relative powerlessness that people face in dealing with significant issues in life. Worry and fretting cannot add a single hour to a person's life—in fact, worry likely shortens life. If a person cannot add an hour to life, why worry about the other issues that so often occupy human thought and effort?

In verses 22-23 Jesus identified both food and clothing as objects of human anxiety and concern. After addressing food in verse 24, he returned to the concern for clothing in verses 27-28 and reiterated the premise that the body is more than clothing.

The type of flower translated "lilies" (12:27) is generic. It probably refers to the wonderful variety of flowers that adorned the fields of Galilee following the "later" or spring rain (Deuteronomy 11:14; compare Jeremiah 5:24). The beauty of these flowers, which surpasses the splendor of King Solomon's fabled wardrobe, is achieved without sweat and toil or aching bodies wracked with pain. It doesn't require planting, harvesting, ginning, spinning, or weaving.

The "grass of the field" (12:28) is more likely wild grass than cultivated grass. It was cut for hay or straw. In addition to being feed for animals, it was burned for heat and cooking and also was used as an inferior building material (1 Corinthians 3:12). In extreme contrast to grass's short lifespan and mundane usage stands the care of God in providing for the needs of his human creation—even those with only a little faith!

Luke 12:29-31. "Striving" and "worrying" are central in these verses. Interestingly, in Greek "striving" is the exact same word used in Luke 11:9 in Jesus command to "search." Here as there the force is on "keep striving" or "continue searching."

Striving or searching itself is not the issue. The issue is the object of the striving or searching. Striving for things to satisfy the human appetites is a characteristic of the heathen nations of the world. Disciples will make the kingdom of God the object of their search.

The word translated "keep worrying" (12:29) is used only here in the New Testament. The root idea is to hover between hope and fear, to be restless or anxious. John reminds us that "there is no fear in love" (1 John 4:18). When we love God with all our hearts, souls, minds, and strength, fear will be turned into hope. Knowing that God loves us, we can be assured that God knows all that we need and will supply those needs.

Luke 12:32-34. Not only will God supply the needs of the disciples but God will also give them the kingdom. If we understand the kingdom as the reign of God in the hearts of people, this gift of the kingdom is God assuming the throne in the hearts of those who have relinquished control to God. The assurance of God's reign relieves the fears of the flock of the Good Shepherd because they are confident that the Shepherd takes delight in giving such a gift. "Good pleasure" (12:32) employs the same verb used in Mark 1:11 of the Father's being "well pleased" in Jesus when he was baptized.

A disciple's focus on the kingdom of God has consequences for the way we live on earth. When trust is in God and anxiety for temporal physiological needs is abated, the disciple has the freedom to focus on "unfailing treasure in heaven" (12:33). When the emotions and concerns of the heart for earthly security are replaced by faith and hope in God, the locus of our treasure will be heaven. Jesus heightened the shift of priorities by calling for disciples to sell their possession and give alms to the poor. Rather than stashing valuables in our purses and wallets where they are in danger of loss by wear, robbery, or theft, Jesus called for storing treasure in heaven.

INTERPRETING THE SCRIPTURE

The Value of Life

Values permeate all aspects of life. For some people value is wrapped up in dollar signs. For others it is measured by time. Some measure value by the skills that are exhibited or the amount that can be accomplished in a workday. Some value insight; others value know-how. Some value independence whereas others value relationships.

Often our values are in conflict. A parent has to balance the demands of spouse, child, extended family, job, church, and social and recreational interests. At the same time concerns arise over keeping food on the table and a roof overhead, as well as having reliable transportation, adequate protection from sickness and hazards and loss, as well as saving for retirement. Although spouses or children might value a relationship based on time spent together, they may receive gifts based on monetary value as a substitute for personal presence.

Values also conflict when stated values differ from the values actually lived. Many who say, "God first, family second, and job third," reflect a different set of values when their calendars or checkbooks are examined. With all of these values in conflict, many people are stressed out, anxious, overworked, and testy.

Jesus offers some clues for getting our values in perspective. First, he emphasizes that we are persons of value ("of how much more value are you," 12:24). Our value in God's eyes is a gift of grace. It is not based on bank balances, position, rank, achievement, appearances, education, or skills. It is based solely on who we are as people of faith created in God's image. When the basic issues of being loved and accepted unconditionally are resolved in our lives, we will strive for different things. We will have only One whom we will strive to please, and that One is well pleased when we live with God as king.

Second, Jesus emphasized that life is a unity of body and soul. If we focus solely on the physical life and neglect the spiritual life, we have only a half-life. Jesus didn't follow the ascetics and call us to mortify the body so that the spirit might soar. Instead, he called us to recognize that life is more than either one separately and is whole only when it is lived as body and soul together.

When we are centered in God's unconditional love and balance life as body and soul together, our values will become kingdom values.

The Control of Life

In 1967, Dr. Thomas Holmes and Dr. Richard Rahe developed a Social Readjustment Rating Scale that was based on "Life Change Units." They contended that certain kinds of changes in life create stress, and too many changes in a year's time raise the possibility of illness. Events like the death of a spouse, divorce, a child going away to college, or losing a job create high levels of stress that can predispose one to illness or accident.

Most of us like to be in control. We don't like to leave things to chance. We plan for various aspects of our lives; but the more we plan, the more we find that trying to maintain control is extremely stressful.

Life is unpredictable. Things happen for which we didn't plan and over which we have no control. A hurricane strikes; and in the aftermath tempers flare, accusations fly, and bureaucrats squabble. Over a hundred police officers quit and a couple committed suicide because of the unrelenting stress. People who are accustomed to getting and keeping things under control fold.

At one point or another in our lives, most of us will recognize that we are finite. We have neither the ability nor the power to alter some of the circumstances that swirl out of control. We can't add a day to our lives or an inch to our height. At some point we have to trust that some power greater than we are has the ability to bring order out of chaos. How much more comforting it will be when we recognize that the unknown power is not unknown at all—but is the loving God and Father of our Lord Jesus Christ!

Perhaps a portion of my poetic paraphrase of Psalm 46, which is used here with permission, says this best: *Though all the things we count as sure / Are changing, failing, insecure, / And though the world on any day / Could at His voice just melt away, / We know the Lord is with us here, / A fortress mighty, steadfast, near.*

The Treasure of Life

A frequently heard joke affirms that the person who dies with the most toys wins. The consumer-oriented societies in which the wealth of our world resides seem to live by that maxim. Life is much more than food and clothing. Real life is a Lexus in the garage, a Rolex on the wrist, and a vacation home in Aspen. Real clothing is an Armani outfit with a Coach handbag and Gucci shoes. Real food is caviar, truffles, and five-dollar cups of cappuccino.

We don't call people "consumers" in our society for no reason. With about 5 percent of the world's population, the United States consumes over 26 percent of the world's annual oil usage. A rapidly increasing trade deficit and growing national debt demonstrate that we Americans consume more than we produce and borrow to make up the difference.

In the midst of this obvious wealth, we must note that in 2004 over 13 percent of the population of the United States was living in poverty. And the almost $15,000 annual income that marks the poverty line in the United States for a family of three looks like wealth for many of the poorest in our world whose annual incomes amount to only a few hundred dollars a year.

Our greatest fear seems to be that someone will take our toys away. We stand ready to defend what we feel is ours by right against all aggressors. Homeland security and national defense have become synonymous with protecting our toys. No wonder the stock market gyrates on every piece of news that might affect the security of our toys. No wonder we have facial tics, acid reflux, and mental breakdowns.

Maybe we are striving for the wrong things. Maybe our anxieties are misplaced. Maybe God is saying to us (compare 12:20-21), "You fools! Your life will be demanded of you soon. And the toys you have gained, whose will they be?" So it is with those who store up treasures for themselves but are not rich toward God.

Maybe the only way to free ourselves from this deep-seated materialism is to sell our possessions and give to the poor. Maybe when our hearts are free from earthly treasures we will be able to trust fully in God and find the unfailing treasure in heaven.

SHARING THE SCRIPTURE

Preparing Our Hearts

Meditate on this week's devotional reading, found in Psalm 31:1-5. The psalmist declares that God is his "rock" (31:3) and "refuge" (31:4). Can you say amen to that? Before you answer, think about whatever load of anxiety you carry around. Are you really trusting God to take care of you, to be your refuge even in time of trouble? List whatever worries you and pray about each item. As you pray, turn each one over to God and rely on God to take care of it.

Pray that you and the adult learners will set aside your anxieties by learning to trust in God.

Preparing Our Minds

Study the background and lesson Scripture in Luke 12:22-34. As you read, ponder what you do to combat worry and anxiety.

Write on newsprint:

❏ information for next week's lesson, found under "Continue the Journey."

❏ activities for further spiritual growth in "Continue the Journey."

Locate the "Holmes-Rahe Social Readjustment Rating Scale" cited under "The Control of Life." This list is found in many psychology textbooks and can also be found at Internet sites including: http://www.cop.ufl.edu/safezone/doty/dotyhome/wellness/HolRah.html.

Bring to class one or more paper bags, which will be used to collect shredded paper.

LEADING THE CLASS

(1) Gather to Learn

❖ Welcome the class members and introduce any guests.

❖ Pray that the students will increase their trust in God's willingness and ability to care for them in all circumstances.

❖ Read aloud several items from the "Holmes-Rahe Social Readjustment Rating Scale." See if the value that Doctors Holmes and Rahe assign to particular stresses "ring true" for the students.

❖ You may wish to mention that since 1967 when this scale was developed other researchers have noted that some events carry a different weight than previously assumed, but the events themselves are still stressful. Point out that the scale has been used to determine the probability of illness resulting from too much stress.

❖ Invite the students to talk about ways people use to reduce stress and worry. The class members may suggest all sorts of ways, some of which are positive—prayer, meditation, exercise, becoming educated about the problem that is causing the anxiety, for example—and some of which are negative—overeating, fretting, drug abuse, for example. Try to affirm and encourage use of positive methods.

❖ Read aloud today's focus statement: **We all face pressure and may experience anxiety. What can we do to combat anxiety and worry? Jesus says that when we trust in God we have no need to worry.**

(2) Explore Jesus' Teaching on Trusting God

❖ Choose a volunteer to read aloud Luke 12:22-34 as if this person were Jesus speaking to his disciples. Suggest that the adults leave their Bibles closed and listen intently.

❖ Ask the class to call out words or phrases that they found especially meaningful. List these ideas on newsprint.

❖ Discuss these questions.

    (1) How would you summarize Jesus' teaching in this passage in one sentence?

(2) What has been your experience in terms of God caring for you?

(3) In what ways does this passage challenge the realities you experience and/or see around you? (Some students may raise the issue of poverty, hunger, homelessness among many people, including among those who profess Christ.)

(4) What do you think God expects you to do to help those in need? (Challenge the class to think not only of short-term ways of assisting, such as collecting food for a pantry, but also of long-term ways to ameliorate the problem, such as enacting legislation to help those in need.)

❖ Direct the students' attention to verse 34. Talk with them about how they keep their heart and treasure focused in the same direction and on God.

❖ **Option:** Discuss how people who live in a society where most of us must buy our food, clothing, and shelter, rather than grow or create them ourselves, can live according to Jesus' teachings. Is this possible? What adaptations might we need to make to the teaching?

(3) Turn Over to God Anxiety and Worry

❖ Distribute paper and pencils. Ask each student to make a confidential list of worries that are now besetting them.

❖ Encourage the students to review their lists and place an asterisk next to any worries that are related to money and material goods.

❖ Talk with the class in general terms about how our society's emphasis on "having" and "owning" create many of our financial problems.

❖ Read or retell "The Treasure of Life" in Interpreting the Scripture. Reread the last paragraph and invite the class to comment on the feasibility of Jesus' teaching to sell our possessions and give to the poor.

❖ Prompt the students to symbolically

turn over their worries to God by tearing up their papers into small shreds. Pass around a paper bag (or several bags if the class is large) so that everyone can rid themselves of the worries they have listed.

(4) Challenge the Learners to Pursue a Relationship with God That Will Alleviate Their Worry and Anxiety

❖ Read the fourth paragraph of "The Control of Life," found in Interpreting the Scripture.

❖ Invite the students to tell stories of times when they realized that they were finite, that control over one's life is truly an illusion. Such times particularly occur when we or a loved one face serious illness, we experience the devastation of a natural disaster, or a loved one dies.

❖ Ask: **How did this knowledge of your inability to control your life change your relationship with God?**

❖ Conclude this portion of the lesson by reading Michael Fink's paraphrase of Psalm 46, which is the last paragraph of "The Control of Life."

(5) Continue the Journey

❖ Pray that those who have participated today will alleviate anxiety by living in a close, personal relationship with Jesus Christ.

❖ Read aloud this preparation for next week's lesson. You may also want to post it on newsprint for the students to copy.

■ **Title: Summoned to Labor!**

■ **Background Scripture: Luke 10:1-12, 17-20**

■ **Lesson Scripture: Luke 10:1-12, 17-20**

■ **Focus of the Lesson: We are often summoned to struggle for purposes greater than ourselves. How do we respond to the summons? When Jesus appointed seventy disciples to prepare his way, they obeyed** despite the probability of hardship and rejection.

❖ Challenge the students to complete one or more of these activities for further spiritual growth, which you will write on newsprint for the students to copy.

(1) Give 10 percent of your paycheck to the church this week as a sign of trusting God. If you cannot give 10 percent, or if you are already a tither, try to increase your gift so that you are stretching yourself. Recognizing that we are but stewards of our money empowers us to trust God more fully.

(2) Donate money and/or do hands-on work with your church or another group that serves the poor, hungry, or homeless.

(3) Write today's key verse, Luke 12:22, on an index card. Post it in a place where you will see it often and be reminded that you can trust in God for all things.

❖ Sing or read aloud "Seek Ye First."

❖ Conclude today's session by leading the class in this benediction, which is taken from Ephesians 6:23-24: **Peace be to the whole community, and love with faith, from God the Father and the Lord Jesus Christ. Grace be with all who have an undying love for our Lord Jesus Christ. Amen.**

UNIT 3: GOD SUMMONS US TO RESPOND!
SUMMONED TO LABOR!

PREVIEWING THE LESSON

Lesson Scripture: Luke 10:1-12, 17-20
Background Scripture: Luke 10:1-12, 17-20
Key Verse: Luke 10:2

Focus of the Lesson:
We are often summoned to struggle for purposes greater than ourselves. How do we respond to the summons? When Jesus appointed seventy disciples to prepare his way, they obeyed despite the probability of hardship and rejection.

Goals for the Learners:
(1) to explore Jesus' call to labor for the kingdom.
(2) to identify challenges they face in working for God's kingdom.
(3) to respond obediently to God's call to work for the kingdom.

Supplies:
Bibles, newsprint and marker, paper and pencils, hymnals

READING THE SCRIPTURE

NRSV
Luke 10:1-12, 17-20

¹After this the Lord appointed seventy others and sent them on ahead of him in pairs to every town and place where he himself intended to go. **²He said to them, "The harvest is plentiful, but the laborers are few; therefore ask the Lord of the harvest to send out laborers into his harvest.** ³Go on your way. See, I am sending you out like lambs into the midst of wolves. ⁴Carry no purse, no bag, no sandals; and greet no one on the road. ⁵Whatever house you enter, first say, 'Peace to this house!' ⁶And if anyone is there who shares in peace, your peace

NIV
Luke 10:1-12, 17-20

¹After this the Lord appointed seventy-two others and sent them two by two ahead of him to every town and place where he was about to go. **²He told them, "The harvest is plentiful, but the workers are few. Ask the Lord of the harvest, therefore, to send out workers into his harvest field.** ³Go! I am sending you out like lambs among wolves. ⁴Do not take a purse or bag or sandals; and do not greet anyone on the road.

⁵"When you enter a house, first say, 'Peace to this house.' ⁶If a man of peace is there, your peace will rest on him; if not, it

will rest on that person; but if not, it will return to you. ⁷Remain in the same house, eating and drinking whatever they provide, for the laborer deserves to be paid. Do not move about from house to house. ⁸Whenever you enter a town and its people welcome you, eat what is set before you; ⁹cure the sick who are there, and say to them, 'The kingdom of God has come near to you.' ¹⁰But whenever you enter a town and they do not welcome you, go out into its streets and say, ¹¹'Even the dust of your town that clings to our feet, we wipe off in protest against you. Yet know this: the kingdom of God has come near.' ¹²I tell you, on that day it will be more tolerable for Sodom than for that town.

¹⁷The seventy returned with joy, saying, "Lord, in your name even the demons submit to us!" ¹⁸He said to them, "I watched Satan fall from heaven like a flash of lightning. ¹⁹See, I have given you authority to tread on snakes and scorpions, and over all the power of the enemy; and nothing will hurt you. ²⁰Nevertheless, do not rejoice at this, that the spirits submit to you, but rejoice that your names are written in heaven."

will return to you. ⁷Stay in that house, eating and drinking whatever they give you, for the worker deserves his wages. Do not move around from house to house.

⁸"When you enter a town and are welcomed, eat what is set before you. ⁹Heal the sick who are there and tell them, 'The kingdom of God is near you.' ¹⁰But when you enter a town and are not welcomed, go into its streets and say, ¹¹'Even the dust of your town that sticks to our feet we wipe off against you. Yet be sure of this: The kingdom of God is near.' ¹²I tell you, it will be more bearable on that day for Sodom than for that town.

¹⁷The seventy-two returned with joy and said, "Lord, even the demons submit to us in your name."

¹⁸He replied, "I saw Satan fall like lightning from heaven. ¹⁹I have given you authority to trample on snakes and scorpions and to overcome all the power of the enemy; nothing will harm you. ²⁰However, do not rejoice that the spirits submit to you, but rejoice that your names are written in heaven."

UNDERSTANDING THE SCRIPTURE

Luke 10:1-7. "After this" refers to Luke 9:57-62, where Jesus described the dedication required of those who would be his disciples. Those who had heard Jesus were volunteering to follow him, but Jesus raised high standards for them. He called for commitment that required sacrifice, breaking with the past, and single-minded focus on the kingdom of God.

Despite those high standards, the number of disciples was expanding. Luke 9:1 references twelve disciples. A comparison of the *New Revised Standard Version* and the *New International Version* shows that seventy or seventy-two others were ready to be put

into service at the beginning of chapter 10. The difference between those latter numbers arises because the oldest Greek manuscripts of the Gospel of Luke differ. Most manuscripts record seventy, but a few important early manuscripts have seventy-two. Most interpreters prefer the number seventy because of its special significance as a multiple of the sacred number seven and because of its long history from Old Testament times, beginning with the seventy elders appointed to assist Moses in Numbers 11:10-24.

Jesus' strategy was to divide the seventy into pairs and to use each pair as an advance team that would go to the places he planned to visit and make arrangements for his coming. Their presence signified that "the kingdom of God has come near to you" (Luke 10:9; compare 10:11).

Another part of Jesus' strategy was to multiply laborers for the abundant harvest that lay before them. The seventy represented the first phase of that multiplication; but as the pairs spread into the towns and places ahead of Jesus, they too would be asking the Lord of the harvest to send out more laborers.

Jesus sent the disciples out with a warning and some instructions to guide their work. He warned them about their vulnerability in the face of the dangerous forces they would face. They were like lambs in the midst of wolves. The word used for lamb means a young sheep and represents the main animal used in the sacrifices of the Old Testament. Sheep are rather helpless animals when lacking the supervision of a shepherd. A young lamb is especially vulnerable to predators. Wolves were viewed as especially "ravenous" (Matthew 7:15) and "savage" (Acts 20:29) predators.

Rather than arming the disciples with powerful forces that would prevail over the opposition, Jesus instructed the disciples in a way that would heighten their vulnerability and increase their dependence on the Lord of the harvest for their care. "No purse, no bag, no sandals" represented a self-imposed poverty (10:4; compare Luke 9:58). "Greet no one on the road" represented a devoted purpose and goal from which nothing should detract them (10:4; compare 9:59-62). The disciples were to depend upon the hospitality of people of peace for their housing and food. They were to remain under the care of such households, accepting whatever hospitality was offered.

"Peace to this house" (10:5) was a greeting akin to the greetings in 1 Samuel 25:6, Luke 7:50, and John 20:19, 21. With the greeting came a blessing of peace that invited from God security, health, wholeness, and

spiritual completeness for the recipient of the blessing.

Luke 10:8-12. The disciples were not only to seek hospitable households that would welcome them but they also were to seek towns that welcomed them. Since the disciples were preparing places for Jesus to visit, perhaps these instructions are an extension of Luke 9:48. Those towns that welcomed the disciples were by proxy welcoming Jesus and the One who sent him.

When the disciples found a community that welcomed them, they were to accept its hospitality. They also were to cure those who were sick in that town and declare this healing as evidence of the nearness of the kingdom of God. Such a testimony about the kingdom recalls the answer Jesus gave to the disciples of John the Baptist in Luke 7:18-23.

If the disciples found a town that did not welcome them, they were to completely dissociate themselves from it. In a kind of prophetic act, they were to wipe the dust of that town from their feet. Because of the town's lack of hospitality and receptivity, they would face a fate worse than the Old Testament city of Sodom. The seriousness of rejecting the kingdom was greater than arguably the most egregious example of inhospitality and depravity in the Old Testament, which resulted in the destruction of Sodom (Genesis 19:1-29).

Luke 10:17-20. When the seventy returned from their reconnaissance, they were filled with joy. They found that working in the name of Jesus brought results that exceeded their expectations. Even demons submitted to them. From the beginnings of his ministry (Luke 4:31-37), Jesus had rebuked the spiritual forces of evil that held humanity captive. Very likely these same disciples had witnessed Jesus' power over the demonic following the transfiguration (Luke 9:37-43). Now they had experienced that power firsthand.

The fall of Satan from heaven has a dual focus. In the Old Testament, Isaiah prophetically announced the fall of the king of Babylon (called "Day Star," but in the King James Version called "Lucifer"), who had sought to exalt himself to divine status (Isaiah 14:12-20). Later traditions combined the serpent in the Garden of Eden (Genesis 3), the ringleader of the "sons of God" who consorted with women (6:1-4), Lucifer, and the accuser, Satan, into a rebellious angel who was cast out of heaven. The disciples' power over the demons similarly recalled Satan's fall.

The second focus points to Revelation 12:7-9 and the beginning of the final defeat of Satan at the end of time. Satan and his angels will be thrown down to earth in anticipation of their final defeat. The disciples' power over Satan is a glimpse of the future victory Christ will win over all evil.

The power to defeat demons is only part of the protection Jesus offered the seventy. "Nothing will hurt" them, whether snakes, scorpions, or enemies. Yet Jesus cautioned that the most important matter is to have one's name written in heaven. Security in eternity is of greater consequence than security from earthly dangers.

INTERPRETING THE SCRIPTURE

Harvest Time

Prior to the industrial age, most people would have been intimately acquainted with Jesus' comparison of the kingdom of God to a time of harvest. Much of the cycle of every year played out a pattern of tilling the soil, planting the seed, weeding the fields, harvesting the crop, and threshing the grain. The future for each family depended on the success of this enterprise. Not only would their appetites be satisfied during the following year by the results of the harvest but the produce also would be used in exchange for other necessities of life.

Because of its significance, everything was riding on the harvest. All the efforts of the year came into focus. If the natural forces of rain and sunshine cooperated, a good harvest would be an occasion of great joy. If drought, frost, or flood disrupted the processes, the days ahead would be filled with want and worry.

Though most of us are insulated from the day-to-day concerns of the farmer, we can occasionally glimpse the results of a poor or a bountiful harvest. The prices of orange juice, coffee, cocoa, and many other commodities in our grocery stores can be influenced by events at harvest time in places near and far.

The harvest is an especially appropriate symbol for kingdom concerns. It can be a time of joy or sorrow, opportunity or defeat. It is the result of long anticipation and of forces that often are beyond our control. Harvesting itself is a time-sensitive enterprise. It cannot be started before the crop is ready, nor can it be delayed beyond the opportune season. Life itself hangs in the balance.

The kingdom of God demands not only preparation and readiness but also dependence and vulnerability. Acceptance of the kingdom may well be a time-sensitive matter for us. If we delay, postpone, or dally, we may lose our opportunity. Eternity itself may hang in the balance.

Harvest Workers

Mechanical threshing machines have sharply reduced the need for farm labor with many crops today, but most of us are aware of the significant role that farm workers and migrant workers play in harvesting much of the produce in our country. The reality is that if sufficient laborers are not available, fruit and vegetables will spoil and rot in the fields; and the crop will be lost. And the more abundant the crop, the greater will be the loss.

Think for a moment about a can of green beans that you can buy in the grocery for less than a dollar. Obviously you will see represented there the farmer who grew the beans. But have you thought of how many others have contributed to making that can of beans possible? Let your imagination run. The farmer has farm equipment made by someone else, transported and distributed by others, and sold and serviced by still others. Someone produced the fertilizer used in his farming. The ingredients of iron, rubber, plastics, and chemicals that went into the equipment and fertilizer were produced by a host of other people. What about the can itself? What about its label? Add to that the factory workers who canned the beans, those who transported the cans, those who stocked it on the shelves, and those who check customers out at the cash register. Then think of the management and corporate functions that made all these enterprises possible. That one can of beans represents far more than the labor of one farmer. It represents the integration of farming, manufacturing, energy, mining, paper, printing, shipping, computer, and many other industries. Tens and tens of thousands of people have a hand in the process. If you think hard enough, you might even be able to connect your own work in some way to that can of green beans.

What happens to this great enterprise if no laborers show up to pick the plentiful harvest? What happens if too few show up? In some places in our world where the economy depends heavily on agriculture, critical times during the harvest season cause schools, offices, and factories to close down so that everyone can help bring in the harvest.

The crucial role that laborers play in the harvest parallels the crucial role that committed disciples play in the kingdom of God. When we are summoned by God to be part of the kingdom, we are not called to sit in the stands and cheer the team on. We are not called merely to stand on the sidelines sending in plays for the team on the field. When the laborers are few—as they always are in the kingdom—God calls each of us to the fields that are ready for harvesting.

Harvest Hope

Hope is a fragile thing. It is such an important aspect of maintaining a sense of meaning and purpose in life. When hope fades and dies, life can become empty, hollow, and desperate.

At one time or another in life, all of us will struggle with the loss of hope. Sometimes hope fades when a loved one dies, a relationship fails, a job turns sour, a child disappoints, a disaster strikes, or a terminal disease threatens. Sometimes we feel as if our hearts have been wrenched from our bodies, and all purpose and meaning in life are gone.

The prospect of a plentiful harvest is a solid foundation for hope. The assurance that the kingdom of God has come near to you is a source of strength. How do we tap into these underlying sources of hope and assurance?

First, we have the assurance that the harvest is God's, not ours. Our emotions and states of mind may swing from great highs to deep lows, but God's harvest is sure and unchanging. Joy lies at the end of the harvest if we are patient and ready to join the laborers in the harvest.

Second, God provides companions for us along the way. Whether we are working in pairs or are part of the two or three who gather together in God's name, we know that we are strengthened by others who enter the harvest with us. The way may be difficult. The threats may be real. The opposition may be great. But we benefit from the strength we draw from our fellow disciples.

Third, God will provide for our needs.

We may be humbled into deep dependence on God and others, but people of peace will be found along our way who will sustain us when we have no other resources.

Fourth, God will protect us. In Christ's name, we will see even the demons submit to us. We will be protected from the threat of enemies.

Fifth, we will become wounded healers who in Christ's authority restore health to those whose lives we touch. We will sense the nearness of God's kingdom as God works in, around, and through us to bring salvation to others.

Finally, our greatest joy and hope will be found in the comforting knowledge that our names are written in heaven. As Paul reminds us, "I am convinced that neither death, nor life, nor angels, nor rulers, nor things present, nor things to come, nor powers, nor height, nor depth, nor anything else in all creation, will be able to separate us from the love of God in Christ Jesus our Lord" (Romans 8:38-39).

SHARING THE SCRIPTURE

PREPARING OUR HEARTS

Meditate on this week's devotional reading, found in Psalm 78:1-4. What does this psalm convey about the importance of teaching the next generation about "the glorious deeds" and "might" (78:4) of God? How are you responding to this summons to tell others, particularly younger people, about God?

Pray that you and the adult learners will respond to this command by teaching younger generations about God, both in word and in deed.

Preparing Our Minds

Study the background and lesson Scripture, both of which are taken from Luke 10:1-12, 17-20. Think about how you respond to a summons to struggle for a purpose greater than yourself.

Write on newsprint:
❑ list of biblical characters and verses for "Respond Obediently to God's Call to Work for the Kingdom."
❑ information for next week's lesson, found under "Continue the Journey."
❑ activities for further spiritual growth in "Continue the Journey."

Plan a brief lecture from Understanding the Scripture for "Explore Jesus' Call to Labor for the Kingdom."

Prepare an optional lecture for "Respond Obediently to God's Call to Work for the Kingdom."

LEADING THE CLASS

(1) Gather to Learn

❖ Welcome the class members and introduce any guests.

❖ Pray that all who have gathered today will listen to and obey God's voice.

❖ Encourage the students to tell stories of their participation in groups that struggle for purposes greater than themselves. Perhaps they work for legislation to help the poor; or build homes for Habitat for Humanity; or participate in mission trips to help build/rebuild not only structures but also lives. Ask the adults to discuss why they respond to needs.

❖ Read aloud today's focus statement: **We are often summoned to struggle for purposes greater than ourselves. How do we respond to the summons? When Jesus appointed seventy disciples to prepare his way, they obeyed despite the probability of hardship and rejection.**

*(2) Explore Jesus' Call to Labor
for the Kingdom*

❖ Choose one person to read Luke 10:1-12.

■ Discuss these questions.

(1) How might you have responded if Jesus had selected you to go as one of the seventy to prepare the way for him as he traveled from town to town?

(2) Why do you suppose Jesus sent each one with a partner? (Recall that Jewish law, found in Deuteronomy 17:6 and 19:15, required two witnesses to testify to facts.)

(3) What might you have thought about the "luggage restrictions" he placed on you in verse 4?

(4) What concerns might you have had about the accommodations?

(5) What is your main mission in each town?

(6) How are you to act in towns that don't want to hear what you have to say? Why?

■ Follow the discussion with a brief lecture from Understanding the Scripture from Luke 10:1-7 and 8-12.

❖ Select a volunteer to conclude the story by reading verses 17-20. Underscore the following points.

■ The seventy returned joyous, having accomplished work to an extent that far exceeded their expectations.

■ The seventy had used their spiritual power to overcome demons—a sign that Satan would be defeated at the end of time.

■ Authority over snakes and scorpions is to be understood metaphorically; that is, as authority over evil.

■ The seventy are told to rejoice not just because Satan's power has been shattered, but more importantly because their names are written in the heavenly book of life.

■ The joy the seventy experienced is prompted not only by overcoming evil but also because their lives are properly ordered in relationship to God.

(3) Identify Challenges the Learners Face in Working for God's Kingdom

❖ Brainstorm with the class answers to this question: **What challenges do you encounter as you try to work for God's kingdom?** List answers on newsprint.

❖ See if the class can categorize these challenges. For example, some may have to do with perceived personal limitations; others with restrictions in the workplace on talking about God; others with family members nixing plans for kingdom work; and still others with laws or regulations that make it difficult to proclaim one's faith.

❖ Divide the class into several groups and assign a category to each one. Ask the groups to discern ways that people can overcome the challenges the class has identified.

❖ Provide an opportunity for the groups to report to the class and for all students to add their comments.

(4) Respond Obediently to God's Call to Work for the Kingdom

❖ Do a Bible study of people who have responded to God's call to work in the kingdom with "here am I." Ask different students to look up and read these verses, which you will list on newsprint prior to class.

■ Abraham—Genesis 22:1, 11
■ Jacob—Genesis 31:11
■ Jacob—Genesis 46:2
■ Moses—Exodus 3:4
■ Samuel—1 Samuel 3:5, 6, 8
■ psalmist—Psalm 40:7
■ Isaiah—Isaiah 6:8
■ Mary—Luke 1:38
■ Paul—2 Corinthians 12:14

❖ Talk with the students about these characters by asking these questions.

(1) **What do you know about this person that would help you to understand why he or she said "Here I am" to God?**

(2) **What difference did this person's willingness to work obediently make in the kingdom of God?**

❖ **Option:** Prepare information on the selected verses and characters prior to class and present it in a lecture.

❖ Work with the class to create a litany to which they can respond, "Here I am, Lord." Brainstorm with them ideas for such a litany, and list those ideas on newsprint. You may want to use biblical images, such as an abundant crop waiting to be harvested. You may consider ideas that class members could implement, such as working in a mission field; leading God's people in some way; proclaiming the good news of Jesus Christ in both word and deed.

❖ Conclude this portion of the lesson by reading together the litany the class has written.

(5) Continue the Journey

❖ Pray that today's participants will go forth obediently to labor for the kingdom of God.

❖ Read aloud this preparation for next week's lesson. You may also want to post it on newsprint for the students to copy.

■ **Title: Summoned to Repent!**
■ **Background Scripture: Luke 13:1-9**

■ **Lesson Scripture: Luke 13:1-9**
■ **Focus of the Lesson: As we look at our lives, we see things about us that we would like to change. How do we change our behavior so that we are better people? Jesus called people to repent and to allow God to transform their lives.**

❖ Challenge the students to complete one or more of these activities for further spiritual growth, which you will write on newsprint for the students to copy.

(1) **Take action this week, preferably with a spiritual partner, to labor for God's kingdom.**

(2) **Read a book on gifts discovery, such as Charles V. Bryant's *Rediscovering Our Spiritual Gifts.* Complete the gifts inventory in this book (or elsewhere). Discern how you can best use your gifts to build up God's kingdom. Make a commitment to use your gifts.**

(3) **Offer hospitality to someone who is laboring for the kingdom, such as a lay witness team or choir.**

❖ Sing or read aloud "Here I Am, Lord."

❖ Conclude today's session by leading the class in this benediction, which is taken from Ephesians 6:23-24: **Peace be to the whole community, and love with faith, from God the Father and the Lord Jesus Christ. Grace be with all who have an undying love for our Lord Jesus Christ. Amen.**

UNIT 3: GOD SUMMONS US TO RESPOND!
SUMMONED TO REPENT!

PREVIEWING THE LESSON

Lesson Scripture: Luke 13:1-9
Background Scripture: Luke 13:1-9
Key Verse: Luke 13:3

Focus of the Lesson:
As we look at our lives, we see things about us that we would like to change. How do we change our behavior so that we are better people? Jesus called people to repent and to allow God to transform their lives.

Goals for the Learners:
(1) to investigate the biblical concept of repentance.
(2) to examine areas of their lives in which they need to make changes.
(3) to repent and allow God to transform their lives.

Pronunciation Guide:
Gihon (gi' hon)
Shelah (shee' luh)
Siloam (si loh' uhm)

Supplies:
Bibles, newsprint and marker, unlined paper and pencils, hymnals, Bible dictionary, candle and matches, optional meditative music and appropriate player

---

READING THE SCRIPTURE

NRSV
Luke 13:1-9

¹At that very time there were some present who told him about the Galileans whose blood Pilate had mingled with their sacrifices. ²He asked them, "Do you think that because these Galileans suffered in this way they were worse sinners than all other Galileans?

NIV
Luke 13:1-9

¹Now there were some present at that time who told Jesus about the Galileans whose blood Pilate had mixed with their sacrifices. ²Jesus answered, "Do you think that these Galileans were worse sinners than all the other Galileans because they suffered

3No, I tell you; but unless you repent, you will all perish as they did. 4Or those eighteen who were killed when the tower of Siloam fell on them—do you think that they were worse offenders than all the others living in Jerusalem? 5No, I tell you; but unless you repent, you will all perish just as they did."

6Then he told this parable: "A man had a fig tree planted in his vineyard; and he came looking for fruit on it and found none. 7So he said to the gardener, 'See here! For three years I have come looking for fruit on this fig tree, and still I find none. Cut it down! Why should it be wasting the soil?' 8He replied, 'Sir, let it alone for one more year, until I dig around it and put manure on it. 9If it bears fruit next year, well and good; but if not, you can cut it down.' "

this way? **3I tell you, no! But unless you repent, you too will all perish.** 4Or those eighteen who died when the tower in Siloam fell on them—do you think they were more guilty than all the others living in Jerusalem? 5I tell you, no! But unless you repent, you too will all perish."

6Then he told this parable: "A man had a fig tree, planted in his vineyard, and he went to look for fruit on it, but did not find any. 7So he said to the man who took care of the vineyard, 'For three years now I've been coming to look for fruit on this fig tree and haven't found any. Cut it down! Why should it use up the soil?'

8" 'Sir,' the man replied, 'leave it alone for one more year, and I'll dig around it and fertilize it. 9If it bears fruit next year, fine! If not, then cut it down.' "

UNDERSTANDING THE SCRIPTURE

Luke 13:1-3. This portion of Luke's Gospel tells of events that only Luke among the Gospel writers records. The immediacy and sequencing of the expressions "at that very time" (13:1) and "then" (13:6) convey a sense of an eyewitness who was present in the crowd (12:1) closely following the events.

"Pilate" (13:1) is Pontius Pilate, the Roman procurator of Judea from A.D. 26–36. Procurators were civil officers whose chief responsibility was overseeing government revenues. They also were responsible for maintaining order and pacifying subjected people.

Little is known of Pilate historically. Early Jewish writers viewed him negatively and ascribed to him rape, murder, blasphemy, and injustice. Legends developed about him in the centuries following Christ that range from Pilate having committed suicide to both Pilate and his wife becoming Christians. The length of his service argues for his having been an able administrator.

Galilee was a region where many Gentiles or foreigners lived. The region's background was in the Israelite tribes of Asher, Zebulun, Issachar, and Naphtali. After the death of Herod the Great in 4 B.C., Galilee became a separate district ruled by his descendants (see Luke 23:6-12).

Galileans generally stood outside the mainstream of the traditional Jewish parties. Because they were not meticulous in observing all the rules and regulations of Judaism, Galileans were considered unrefined and overly secular. In other ways they were more conservative and argumentative than the mainstream parties.

Nothing is known of the occasion when Pilate mingled the blood of Galileans with their sacrifices. Since sacrifices were offered in Jerusalem (where Pilate was responsible for peace and order), we can speculate that some Galileans caused a ruckus in the temple and Pilate forcefully restored order.

In spite of much biblical evidence to the

contrary, popular theology in Jesus' time assumed that God blessed the righteous and caused the wicked to suffer. Jesus rejected such thinking. Those who had suffered under Pilate's heavy hand were not necessarily receiving just desserts for their sins.

Luke 13:4-5. "Siloam" was a pool of water within the walled city of Jerusalem fed by a spring called Gihon. The spring originally was located outside the city's wall. Its water was collected in a reservoir and ran through an underground aqueduct to the Pool of Shelah (called the King's Pool in Nehemiah 2:14). Under the threat of an Assyrian invasion in the days of Hezekiah (715–687 B.C.), another aqueduct was dug between Gihon and Siloam.

Nothing is known of a "tower" at Siloam, but this might have been a temporary edifice used in refurbishing the pool. The eighteen who were killed could have been workers engaged in the refurbishing or people from Jerusalem who were drawing water from the pool when the tower collapsed.

The Greek word translated "offenders" (Luke 13:4) literally means a debtor. In its expanded meaning, it also applied to one who was obligated, culpable, or guilty. Its meaning approaches "sinner" when the debt is toward God.

With the exception of one word in the Greek text, verse 5 exactly replicates verse 3. The difference lies in two adverbs that mean "in the same way" or "similarly."

"Repent" is a rich word in biblical vocabulary. The word in the Hebrew Old Testament comes from a root that means "to sigh or breathe strongly" and by implication means "to be sorry." The Greek word used in Luke means "to change one's mind" or "to think differently." Although carrying some sense of remorse, it focuses strongly on a change of direction, a turning away from one thing and a turning toward another. Whereas Luke used the word previously in quoting Jesus (10:13 and 11:32), Matthew and Mark introduced the word

early in their accounts of Jesus' preaching (Matthew 3:2; 4:17; Mark 1:15). Their focus was on turning toward God's kingdom and the gospel.

The meaning of "perish" is difficult to translate in English. The root idea is to ruin, destroy, or lose. Greek has a middle voice in its verbs that is different from the English active voice (where the subject initiates the action—"you will destroy") and the English passive voice (where the subject is acted on by another—"you will be destroyed by God"). The middle voice calls attention back to the action of the subject. Compare this with what a basketball coach might say when his team has the ball with the score tied and five seconds left in the game. "It is all in your hands. No one can beat you but yourselves." We might paraphrase Jesus, "If you don't change direction, you will bring destruction upon yourselves."

Luke 13:6-9. The parable of the barren fig tree draws on a popular agricultural product of the Middle East. From Genesis 3:7, where fig leaves were sewn together as clothing for Adam and Eve, to Revelation 6:13, where stars falling from the sky are compared to the fig tree dropping its fruit, frequent references are made to the tree and its sweet fruit.

The fig tree also served as an image for Israel among the prophets in the Old Testament. Looking for its fruit symbolized God's search for a faithful people (Jeremiah 8:13; Hosea 9:10; Micah 7:1-2) and frequently pointed to impending national distress (Jeremiah 5:17; Hosea 2:12; Joel 1:7, 12; Amos 4:9).

Those familiar with the Old Testament prophets would immediately recognize Luke 13:6 as representing God's search for a faithful people. They also would have recognized an impending judgment for the unfaithful nation.

The Gospels frequently reflect the practice of landowners or masters of households using servants or slaves to take care of their property. Jesus used this relationship often in his teaching (Luke 12:39; 14:21; and 22:11). The man who owned the vineyard in this case employed a gardener to oversee his vineyard as well as the fruit trees he had planted.

Fig trees usually are propagated by cuttings. Regular fertilizing and mulching were needed in the dry and sandy soil found in much of Palestine. Since the crop is borne on the terminals of the previous year's growth, the third year is the natural time to begin expecting a crop.

The gardener's advice to wait one more year is both an offer of grace and recognition that judgment is imminent. The central message is that God was giving the chosen people one more opportunity to bear the fruit of repentance. If they failed to respond, judgment would come and they would perish.

INTERPRETING THE SCRIPTURE

The Difficulty of Change

Adolescence is a time of significant change in human development. Rapid changes take place in the physical, mental, emotional, and social dimensions of life. A false assumption is that once adolescence is past, change ceases. In reality, though the rate of change may slow, adults experience more change between their twenties and their seventies than do adolescents.

Because adulthood changes generally occur slowly and often represent decline in physical, mental, and social ability, adults tend to eschew change, try to postpone it, and fight to preserve the status quo. The idea of making significant changes likely will be exciting to youth, accepted as necessary by younger adults, but avoided like the plague by many older adults.

A gospel that has change at its heart is difficult for many adults. Many youth embrace spiritual redirection. Most adults have grown so accustomed to the status quo that they can hardly imagine the need for much spiritual change. Many churches experience "culture wars" if they try to incorporate new approaches in their planning or their practices. One side in the war declares, "Thou shalt not change anything."

Repentance is not easy because too many do not see the need for change. We prefer to be comfortable rather than conflicted about our relationship with God. We would rather justify our behavior and continue our old habits than to admit that we might be wrong. We are more often stubborn than we are sorry. Our course has been so set and our momentum has become so strong that changing directions requires a greater effort than we are willing to make.

Unfortunately, too many do not see sin as a problem. Too many of us do not see the prospect of perishing spiritually and eternally as the end of our current course. We assume that we are as good as or better than the next person, and that is good enough for us. Because we assume that we are okay, we will not be ready when the knockout comes. We need to hear with our hearts, "Unless you repent, unless you turn around and change the direction of your lives, you will all perish."

The Hand of God in Disasters

When a tornado struck a seminary campus, one brash student announced that God had declared judgment on the seminary. When the tsunamis struck Southeast Asia, prominent televangelists declared them as God's judgment on nations that were allowing Christians to be persecuted. When hurricanes struck New Orleans, some voices were heard asserting that God was judging the godlessness of that city.

When humanity fell into deep depravity, God sent a flood to destroy all except Noah and his family (Genesis 6–8). When Pharaoh refused to release the Israelites from their captivity, God sent a series of plagues on the Egyptians (Exodus 7–12). When the Assyrian king Sennacherib and his army threatened Jerusalem, God sent an angel who destroyed 185,000 of the enemy (2 Kings 18–20). When Jesus and his disciples were caught in a sudden storm on the Sea of Galilee, Jesus rebuked the wind and stilled the storm. His disciples remarked, "Who then is this, that even the wind and the sea obey him?" (Mark 4:35-41).

So, which is it? Are natural disasters direct interventions of God to judge sinners and save the righteous? If a tornado destroys one home but leaves the one next door intact, is God punishing one and rewarding another? If one city is decimated by a hurricane while another is spared, is God saying something to both cities?

These difficult questions require careful reflection. My thinking goes along these lines: God, the creator of all that is, certainly has the authority, power, and ability to alter the course of natural processes in order to achieve the purpose and goal that God desires. We, on the other hand, are too quick to assume that we know the mind of God and can read God's purpose in any isolated event. Although the power and ability certainly are God's, direct divine interventions probably are a lot less frequent than we may think.

Jesus affirmed that God "makes his sun rise on the evil and on the good, and sends rain on the righteous and on the unrighteous" (Matthew 5:45). Most natural disasters are status neutral. They affect people regardless of their economic, educational, employment, religious, or moral status. The impact may not be quite the same for each person, but the differences are more the consequence of individual circumstances than status.

Too often the unaffected assume they are the chosen and protected and must therefore be morally superior to the affected. Jesus quashed that idea. He reminds us that all of us fall short of God's expectations. There is no such thing as better or worse sinners. We all are sinners; and unless we reorient our lives toward the kingdom of God and its offer of grace for all, we shall bring destruction upon ourselves.

The Grace of a Second Chance

Many people look contemptuously at others and decide that these unworthy souls are "wasting the soil" from which they were made. Their contempt may not be readily evident, but you can sometimes see it in eyes that glaze over when looking at those who are different in their status, achievement, rank, or skin color. Unlike Jesus, they do not view the crowds with compassion or see them as "harassed and helpless, like sheep without a shepherd" (Matthew 9:36).

Sometimes you hear the contempt in snide remarks about others, jokes about the exaggerated differences others exhibit, or racial epithets. Perpetrators fail to realize that "by your words you will be justified, and by your words you will be condemned" (Matthew 12:37).

The gardener's statement to the landowner in Luke 13:9 is ironic, "If it bears fruit next year, well and good; but if not, you can cut it down." By any degree of the imagination, the landowner had the right to cut the tree down whenever he pleased. He was not obligated to follow the gardener's suggestions. But here is where grace enters in the parable and in the divine-human relationship.

Jesus taught that God is a God of one more chance. If Jesus taught Peter that forgiveness should be extended seventy-seven times (or "seventy times seven," KJV; see Matthew 18:21-22), how much more patient must God be with those who sin against him.

Jesus did not dodge the inevitable judgment (and he taught that the judgment might be closer than we think), but the prospect of judgment was a compassionate warning and a concerned call to repentance rather than a threat designed to coerce a response. It was an invitation to redirect life in a radical way, rather than a gloat over the prospect that sinners are going to get their due.

God gives us second chances, but some day the second chances will end. The last chance may be years away, or it may be today in an unexpected disaster. For all of us the truth remains, "Unless you repent, you will all perish" (Luke 13:3).

SHARING THE SCRIPTURE

Preparing Our Hearts

Meditate on this week's devotional reading, found in Psalm 63:1-6. Read this psalm slowly and prayerfully. Can you really say that you are seeking and thirsting after God? Or are other priorities crowding God out? If so, what do you need to do to repent and seek the Lord? Write in your spiritual journal about any specific changes that you need to make.

Pray that you and the adult learners will turn from whatever inhibits you from continually seeking God's presence.

Preparing Our Minds

Study the background and lesson Scripture, both found in Luke 13:1-9. As you consider this passage, think about how we can change our behavior so as to be better people.

Write on newsprint:
❑ information for next week's lesson, found under "Continue the Journey."
❑ activities for further spiritual growth in "Continue the Journey."
Prepare two brief lectures from Understanding the Scripture for "Investigate the Biblical Concept of Repentance."

Select meditative music and an appropriate player. You will want to choose either quiet instrumental music or a recording of soothing nature sounds.

Option: Locate further information about the spiritual practice of *Examen* either in books or on the Internet. We will use this prayer form in "Repent and Allow God to Transform the Learners' Lives."

LEADING THE CLASS

(1) Gather to Learn

❖ Welcome the class members and introduce any guests.
❖ Pray that all who have come today will be open to new directions in their lives.
❖ Divide the class into groups and give each group newsprint and a marker. Set a time limit for the groups to brainstorm answers to these questions: **If you could change two things to make the world better, what would they be? Why do they need to be changed? How would you change them?**
❖ Call the groups back together and hear their ideas. Perhaps the class will choose one or two "best ideas."
❖ Read aloud today's focus statement: **As we look at our lives, we see things about us that we would like to change. How do we change our behavior so that we are better people? Jesus called people to repent and to allow God to transform their lives.**

(2) Investigate the Biblical Concept of Repentance

❖ Select a volunteer to read Luke 13:1-5.
■ Use information for these verses

from Understanding the Scripture to help the students understand what is known about the events referenced in this passage.

■ Distribute one, preferably several, Bible dictionaries and have one or more students look up and read the definition of "repent."

■ **Option:** Help the class to write their definition if you have located several meanings.

❖ Choose someone to read Luke 13:6-9.

■ Use information for these verses from Understanding the Scripture to explain Jesus' use of the fig tree and gardening practices associated with raising fig trees.

■ Be sure to point out that fig trees reach maturity in three years. If they have not produced fruit by then, they probably will not. Hence, the gardener was giving the tree a second chance.

■ Consider these questions:

(1) **What relationship do you see between Jesus' teachings in verses 1-5 and his parable of the fig tree in verses 6-9?** (Here you will want to focus on the idea that we believe God patiently gives us a second chance—a chance to repent. If we choose not to accept that opportunity, we will perish, or be cut down just as the fig tree, because God will eventually render judgment.)

(2) **How do Jesus' teachings in verses 1-9 help you to understand how one becomes a disciple?**

(3) Examine Areas of the Learners' Lives in which They Need to Make Changes

❖ Distribute unlined paper and pencils. Encourage the students to draw one or more symbols that represent at least one area in their lives where change is needed. Artistic talent is not important, as the adults will not be asked to share this work. The symbols may be very basic; for example, a stick figure may represent a relationship that has soured, or a dollar sign may remind the students that they need to be better stewards of their finances. If you have brought meditative music, play it as the class members work.

❖ Challenge the students to work this week on at least one item they have identified.

(4) Repent and Allow God to Transform the Learners' Lives

❖ Tell the class that they will devote time to an ancient form of prayer, developed by Saint Ignatius of Loyola (1491–1556), the founder of the Society of Jesus (Jesuits). This prayer, known as *Examen*, was designed to help people serve God better by walking closely with Christ and being aware of one's spiritual state. Note that many practitioners of *Examen* do this twice a day, spending about fifteen minutes each time.

❖ Ask the students to get into a relaxed position as you lead them through the five steps of this traditional prayer. You may wish to light a candle as a point of focus.

■ **Step 1:** Recall you are in the presence of the triune God—Father, Son, and Holy Spirit.

■ **Step 2:** Look at your day with gratitude by giving thanks to God for the gifts of this day. Look at each event, including the simple pleasures, such as the smile of a child or purring of a kitten.

■ **Step 3:** Ask the Holy Spirit to help you look at your actions and motivations as you have responded to God's gifts.

■ **Step 4:** Review your day, as if watching a movie. Ask yourself these questions.

■ When did I fail?
■ When did I show love?

■ What habits and life patterns do I discern today?

■ How has Jesus helped me this day, both to do something positive and avoid something negative?

■ Where have I seen God, perhaps in other people or the Scriptures?

■ **Step 5:** Reconcile and resolve is a talk with Jesus in which you share your thoughts and feelings. This is an appropriate time to repent and to ask that you become more Christ-like each day.

■ Conclude by leading the students in the Lord's Prayer.

❖ Invite any volunteers to talk about how the experience of this time-tested prayer touched them.

(5) Continue the Journey

❖ Pray that all who have come today will be aware of reasons that they need to repent and take time each day to do so.

❖ Read aloud this preparation for next week's lesson. You may also want to post it on newsprint for the students to copy.

■ **Title: Summoned to Be Humble!**

■ **Background Scripture: Luke 14:1, 7-14**

■ **Lesson Scripture: Luke 14:1, 7-14**

■ **Focus of the Lesson: Our society values and rewards people who put themselves first. What is a better way to live? At a meal where people are clamoring for the best seats, Jesus tells a parable about humility.**

❖ Challenge the students to complete one or more of these activities for further spiritual growth, which you will write on newsprint for the students to copy.

(1) Try *Examen* as a spiritual discipline of prayer. Check books and/or the Internet for additional information on the use of this practice.

(2) Take special care of a plant that is fragile or unproductive. Let this plant serve as a reminder of God's willingness to give second chances to those who repent.

(3) Take action to make a positive change in your life.

❖ Sing or read aloud "Just as I Am, Without One Plea."

❖ Conclude today's session by leading the class in this benediction, which is taken from Ephesians 6:23-24: **Peace be to the whole community, and love with faith, from God the Father and the Lord Jesus Christ. Grace be with all who have an undying love for our Lord Jesus Christ. Amen.**

UNIT 3: GOD SUMMONS US TO RESPOND!
SUMMONED TO BE HUMBLE!

PREVIEWING THE LESSON

Lesson Scripture: Luke 14:1, 7-14
Background Scripture: Luke 14:1, 7-14
Key Verse: Luke 14:11

Focus of the Lesson:
Our society values and rewards people who put themselves first. What is a better way to live? At a meal where people are clamoring for the best seats, Jesus tells a parable about humility.

Goals for the Learners:
(1) to explore humility as Jesus depicted it in a parable.
(2) to probe their feelings about being intentionally humble.
(3) to make a commitment to build up other people.

Supplies:
Bibles, newsprint and marker, paper and pencils, hymnals

READING THE SCRIPTURE

NRSV
Luke 14:1, 7-14

¹On one occasion when Jesus was going to the house of a leader of the Pharisees to eat a meal on the sabbath, they were watching him closely.

⁷When he noticed how the guests chose the places of honor, he told them a parable. ⁸"When you are invited by someone to a wedding banquet, do not sit down at the place of honor, in case someone more distinguished than you has been invited by your host; ⁹and the host who invited both of you may come and say to you, 'Give this person

NIV
Luke 14:1, 7-14

¹One Sabbath, when Jesus went to eat in the house of a prominent Pharisee, he was being carefully watched.

⁷When he noticed how the guests picked the places of honor at the table, he told them this parable: ⁸"When someone invites you to a wedding feast, do not take the place of honor, for a person more distinguished than you may have been invited. ⁹If so, the host who invited both of you will come and say to you, 'Give this man your seat.' Then, humiliated, you will have to take the least

your place,' and then in disgrace you would start to take the lowest place. [10]But when you are invited, go and sit down at the lowest place, so that when your host comes, he may say to you, 'Friend, move up higher'; then you will be honored in the presence of all who sit at the table with you. **[11]For all who exalt themselves will be humbled, and those who humble themselves will be exalted."**

[12]He said also to the one who had invited him, "When you give a luncheon or a dinner, do not invite your friends or your brothers or your relatives or rich neighbors, in case they may invite you in return, and you would be repaid. [13]But when you give a banquet, invite the poor, the crippled, the lame, and the blind. [14]And you will be blessed, because they cannot repay you, for you will be repaid at the resurrection of the righteous."

important place. [10]But when you are invited, take the lowest place, so that when your host comes, he will say to you, 'Friend, move up to a better place.' Then you will be honored in the presence of all your fellow guests. **[11]For everyone who exalts himself will be humbled, and he who humbles himself will be exalted."**

[12]Then Jesus said to his host, "When you give a luncheon or dinner, do not invite your friends, your brothers or relatives, or your rich neighbors; if you do, they may invite you back and so you will be repaid. [13]But when you give a banquet, invite the poor, the crippled, the lame, the blind, [14]and you will be blessed. Although they cannot repay you, you will be repaid at the resurrection of the righteous."

UNDERSTANDING THE SCRIPTURE

Luke 14:1. The religious associations of Jews in the first century were more like American political parties than contemporary religious denominations. Although some people were closely tied to the parties' core beliefs and objectives, most were influenced by the persuasiveness of the parties' arguments and how the parties' ideas impacted their lives. Few were "card-carrying" members of a party.

The Pharisees generally were the party of the people. Whereas the Sadducees held significant influence in larger cities among the privileged and well-connected, the Pharisees drew grass-root support from hardworking, pious, tradition-bound people. The Sadducees generally controlled the temple and the high judicial functions of the nation. The power of the Pharisees lay in the synagogues where the Scripture was studied and its practice encouraged.

Although we often think of the Pharisees

as enemies of Jesus, the invitation to dine in the home of a leader of the Pharisees shows that some Pharisees were open to interaction and dialogue with Jesus.

Overall, the Pharisees were exacting and meticulous in their demands and tended toward legalism. They thought that the sins of the nation delayed the coming of God's kingdom. They were committed to wiping out the sin that held back the kingdom. Jesus, on the other hand, focused on grace and God's will and purpose. He saw the kingdom as already present, growing in small and sometimes hidden ways. These differences led many Pharisees to be suspicious of Jesus and to question his commitment to observing the Old Testament laws.

When Jesus visited the home of the Pharisee leader on a Sabbath, the very occasion raised tension. How to observe the Sabbath was a sensitive point of the Pharisees' disagreement with Jesus. Verses

3-6 show that Jesus did not hesitate to challenge the Pharisees' views about the Sabbath.

Luke 14:7-9. Although focused on the meticulous observance of the Old Testament laws, the Pharisees were not immune to an ostentatious display of piety. They often enlarged their phylacteries (receptacles containing verses of Scripture worn on the forehead and arm during prayer; Matthew 23:5), lengthened the fringes on their prayer shawls (23:5), and relished the deference shown them by others (23:7). Jesus observed that they loved "to have the place of honor at banquets and the best seats in the synagogues," (23:6). Their piety became a point of pride and distinction that elevated them above the less observant and less pious.

Noting these Pharisaic tendencies, Jesus told the guests a "parable" (Luke 14:7). Unlike many of Jesus' parables, this one did not involve much imagery that required interpretation. Instead, it directly addressed the current meal by laying it alongside a wedding banquet. The parable involved direct instruction in what kind of behavior every person should display, no matter their rank or status.

The risk in seeking places of honor, distinction, and prominence is the loss of face and esteem that comes when such places are lost. The pride and ego that are obsessed with such places are crushed when others gain more honor and higher status. The sense of embarrassment is great when a host publicly demotes one guest in favor of one more distinguished. Jesus warned that seeking to elevate self above others is foolhardy and invites disappointment (see Proverbs 25:6-7).

Luke 14:10-11. The antidote to foolish pride is humility. The humble assume the lowest place. This is not a strategy designed to gain advantage but is rather a recognition of how far short they fall from the glory of God. Rather than trying to exalt themselves, they leave all judgment to God. They allow the host of the banquet to judge the honor that each guest deserves, recognizing that whatever they receive is a gift of grace. Expecting nothing, they can never be disappointed. Being honored by another, they gain what they could not have achieved through their own pride.

Humility is a characteristic that Jesus himself claimed (Matthew 11:29) and exhibited (Philippians 2:8). It is a characteristic that God values (Matthew 18:4 and Luke 1:48, 52). The humiliation of those who exalt themselves and the exaltation of those who are humble have a long history in biblical thought. Jesus repeatedly uses this reversal with reference to the Pharisees (Matthew 23:12; Luke 18:14). James 4:6 and 1 Peter 5:5 reflect the same principle.

Luke 14:12-14. Next Jesus turned his attention to his host, a leader of the Pharisees. Jesus noted that the other guests were very much like their host. They were his friends, his relatives, and his rich and prominent neighbors. Like most people, the host enjoyed being surrounded by people like himself.

Jesus went straight to the motive for the meal. The guest list had been selected because each offered the prospect for giving something back to the host. Each guest offered the host acceptance, affirmation, support, encouragement, friendship, and esteem. The cost of entertaining would be repaid liberally. The more prominent guests were included to help advance the host's status. Jesus may have been in this category. A leader who could make peace with a critic really would show his leadership skills.

Although the host's behavior was not as obvious and callous as the actions of the guests who were wrangling for places of prominence, the objective was the same: self-advancement. Jesus advocated a different standard. Rather than entertaining for self-advancement, entertain by self-giving. Seek those for whom a meal makes a difference—not because it meets a social need, but because it meets a basic need to sustain life. The poor, the crippled, the blind, and the lame represented the disabled, the disadvantaged, and the dismissed in society who, like Lazarus (Luke 16:19-21), sit unnoticed at the gate longing for the crumbs that fall from the table of the rich.

The poor cannot repay the kindness shown to them, but a reversal is in store just the same. Those who humbly minister to the needy will experience the blessings of God, who will repay them abundantly in the final judgment. They are the true "righteous," not those who are good because they hope to gain some earthly advantage for their hospitality.

INTERPRETING THE SCRIPTURE

We're Number One!

American society is schooled in the notion that anything less than the best is mediocrity. Being "number one" is synonymous with success. Hardly anyone remembers who came in second, much less who came in last. We assume that the number one team is the best in sports, the best-selling book is by the best writer, the richest American is the highest achiever, the top vote-getter is the best candidate, and the most-watched TV show is the best entertainment. We give trophies, Oscars, crowns, titles, awards, and other recognitions to the top in almost every category. Occasionally a number two might say they try harder; but if that is true, why are they still number two?

The "number one" syndrome often is carried to extremes in sports. Parents start toddlers on the course to be the next world champion gymnast. Junior high/middle school kids take steroids to enhance their athletic performance. Students neglect their studies to focus on winning sports scholarships or pro contracts. Professional athletes risk long-term physical consequences by shielding injuries to get through the season.

In business, the entire work ethic is based on the idea that the best will rise to the top and should be rewarded. Our system of compensation communicates that the number one guy is worth hundreds or thousands of times more than the worker bees. We work long hours, sacrifice time with family and friends, skip sleep, and take pills to keep ourselves one step ahead of the competition. Incentives are based on results for the corporation without regard to the cost to the employees.

Even churches are not immune to "the biggest is the best" fallacy. Gimmicks are used to boost attendance. Worship tends toward entertainment. Large, beautiful, and expensive buildings convey an image of success whereas the needs of the poor and needy often are neglected. Big-name pastors and media ministries set the standard for ministerial success. Budgets focus on keeping the local church machine well-greased and functioning whereas mission and ministry enterprises often get second-class status.

Disciples of Jesus need to hear his words and his example, "The greatest among you will be your servant" (Matthew 23:11).

The Best or My Best?

Competitiveness generally begins with discipline and determination to be my best. Striving to be my best is healthy as long as achievement is measured in terms of my capabilities and potential. A new dynamic sets in, however, when I begin to define my best in terms of my competitors' achievements. The destructive influence of comparison with others begins to twist "my best" into a hunger to be "the best."

As competition intensifies, healthy discipline and determination are distorted. Many will do almost anything to boost their performance; and if that is not enough to get to the top, they begin to focus on status and play the game of one-upmanship.

One distortion from intense competitiveness is stepping on others in order to get to the top. Whenever you see people striving for the top without sensitivity to the feelings of others or without concern for the consequences of their actions, you can be sure that getting to the top is more important to them than the destruction they leave in their wake. Covering up our own weaknesses and mistakes, hiding or changing the record, complaining about unfair competition, or excessive boastfulness are other ways we step on others to get a boost up.

Another distortion is tearing down others so that my best is protected as the best. Whenever you hear someone belittling another person, poking fun at their accomplishments, spreading ugly rumors about them, or plotting to exploit their weaknesses, you can be sure that their only way to being the best is by undermining those who are better than they are. When we have different standards of expectation for ourselves than we have for others, when we criticize or denigrate others, when we accuse others of having an unfair advantage, or when we discount their achievements and accomplishments, our competitiveness has turned mean.

If being *the* best is a source of unhealthy competitiveness, being *my* best is a matter of stewardship. A considerable difference exists between the two. Contrary to some misunderstandings, Christians are not called to be low achievers, mealy-mouthed do-nothings, or placid workers. Christ inspires us to be people of passion, commitment, determination, and faithfulness.

We are called to use all of our talents, abilities, and gifts for the sake of God's kingdom, but not for our own advancement. As Christ's disciples, we are called to deny ourselves (Luke 9:23), to regard others as better than ourselves (Philippians 2:3), to focus on the interests of others (2:4), and not

to think more highly of ourselves than we ought to think (Romans 12:3). These commands will crucify our competitive spirits. At the same time, however, we are to become living sacrifices unto God (Romans 12:1), be good stewards of God's grace (1 Peter 4:10), and develop the gifts that are within us (1 Timothy 4:14).

I'm Proud That I'm So Humble

You probably are familiar with the story of the man who sincerely sought to be humble. As he succeeded, however, he discovered that he was becoming proud of his humility. Shocked by that contradiction, he genuinely repented of his pride for his humility. So deep was his repentance that he soon discovered that he now was proud of his repentance for his pride at being so humble. And so the story goes.

In reality, humility is a complicated character trait. It is a characteristic easily feigned and often walks hand-in-hand with hypocrisy. Humility can be noticed by others, but its genuineness cannot be determined. Indeed, in merely being noticed, humility loses some of its essential nature and becomes suspect. This means that each of us must evaluate this characteristic for ourselves. How do we do that?

First, humility always relates to motive; and we can evaluate our motives. Any effort at self-advancement, any attempt to gain advantage over others, or any action that puts others down will make humility suspect. Anything that we do primarily for the purpose of enhancing our position, status, power, influence, or reputation questions the legitimacy of our humility. When ego drives our actions, efforts, goals, and relationships, humility has departed from us. Pride stands at the opposite end of the scale from humility. Jesus encouraged his host to question his motive in such a mundane thing as the guest list. So must we. Humility brings no rewards except at "the resurrection of the righteous" (Luke 14:14).

Second, although Paul doesn't list humility as a fruit of the spirit (Galatians 5:22-23), humility almost always is joined with other characteristics like those. Ephesians 4:1-3, Colossians 3:12-14, and 1 Peter 3:8 join humility with a variety of Christian virtues such as gentleness, patience, love, unity of spirit, peace, compassion, kindness, meekness, forgiveness, harmony, and sympathy. Whereas humility is an inner virtue that cannot be accurately measured, most of these describe manners of relating to other people that can be observed. Where these characteristics are missing, or where their opposites are evident, we can be sure that humility is absent.

Paul reminds us that Christ is our primary example of humility (Philippians 2:8) and points to evidences of humility that will flow from Christ-like humility (2:1-4).

SHARING THE SCRIPTURE

Preparing Our Hearts

Meditate on this week's devotional reading, found in Psalm 25:1-10. Verse 9 reminds us that God "leads the humble in what is right, and teaches the humble his way." What comes to mind when you think of "humility"? Even though this is a trait that God calls us to have, most of us really don't want to be humble. We want to be the "top dog," not the doormat. But is this what humility is really about? Ponder the meaning and purpose of humility.

Pray that you and the adult learners will be open to possible new understandings about humility and willingly commit yourselves to live as God's humble people.

Preparing Our Minds

Study the background and lesson Scripture, both of which are found in Luke 14:1, 7-14. As you read, think about how our society rewards those who put themselves first, and then ask yourself if there is a better way—a way more pleasing to God—to live.

Write on newsprint:
❏ words "When I hear the word *humility* I think of . . ." for "Probe the Learners' Feelings about Being Intentionally Humble."
❏ information for next week's lesson, found under "Continue the Journey."
❏ activities for further spiritual growth in "Continue the Journey."

Prepare a brief lecture on Luke 14:1 from Understanding the Scripture for "Explore Humility as Jesus Depicted It in a Parable."

Plan the lecture on Luke 7–14 from Understanding the Scripture for "Explore Humility as Jesus Depicted It in a Parable."

LEADING THE CLASS

(1) Gather to Learn

❖ Welcome the class members and introduce any guests.

❖ Pray that each one who has come today will recognize who they are in relation to Christ and to other people.

❖ Read the first paragraph of "I'm So Proud That I'm Humble" in Interpreting the Scripture and invite the class to comment. Does this ring true?

❖ Mention Mac Davis's familiar hit song that includes these two lines:
"Oh Lord it's hard to be humble
when you're perfect in every way."

❖ See if the class can recall anything the singer says that indicates how proud he really is. He mentions his good looks, his popularity with women, how much he enjoys his own company, that some people claim he's egotistical, that to know him is to love him, and that he is doing the best he can to be humble.

❖ Note that even though we may laugh about these lyrics, many people think (at least in their hearts) that they are so good that humility is beneath them. Ask: **How does our society value and encourage people who put themselves first and seemingly have no concept of humility?**

❖ Read aloud today's focus statement: **Our society values and rewards people who put themselves first. What is a better way to live? At a meal where people are clamoring for the best seats, Jesus tells a parable about humility.**

(2) Explore Humility as Jesus Depicted It in a Parable

❖ Read aloud Luke 14:1. Use information in Understanding the Scripture to set the scene for the class.

❖ Select a volunteer to read Luke 14:7-14 and discuss these questions.

    (1) What lesson did Jesus want to teach the guests at the Sabbath meal?

    (2) What lesson did he want to teach the host?

    (3) How do these lessons apply to your life?

❖ Present a brief lecture based on Understanding the Scripture from Luke 14:7-14. This information will help the adults to better understand the background for Jesus' points.

❖ **Option:** Lead the students in looking at Proverbs 19:17 (which relates to being kind to the poor) and Proverbs 25:6-7 (which speaks about one's position in relation to the king). Ask them to connect these verses with their reading from Luke 14.

(3) Probe the Learners' Feelings about Being Intentionally Humble

❖ Invite the students to complete this sentence, which you will write on newsprint: **When I hear the word** *humility* **I think of . . . .** List their ideas on the newsprint.

❖ Sort through this list by asking the students to discern items that seem like positive traits and put a + by those. (Examples include: *being a servant-leader, someone who works quietly behind the scenes; an individual who shares credit with others*.) Go through the list again, this time putting a − by those items that seem like negative traits. (Examples include: *being a doormat; having a very low opinion of myself; someone who is chosen last*.)

❖ Read paragraphs two through five of "I'm Proud That I'm So Humble" in Interpreting the Scripture.

❖ Talk with the class about how the ideas they listed and the ideas you just read are similar or different.

❖ Distribute paper and pencils. Invite the students to complete this sentence independently: **True humility that Jesus teaches about . . . .**

❖ Encourage them to share their sentences with a partner or small group.

❖ Conclude this portion of the lesson by reading in unison today's key verse, Luke 14:11.

(4) Make a Commitment to Build Up Other People

❖ Observe that Jesus teaches his host to be hospitable to people who have no social standing or means to repay his hospitality. Jesus particularly notes "the poor, the crippled, the lame, and the blind" in verse 13.

❖ Ask the class to think of groups of people they to whom they could offer hospitality who likewise would be unable to repay them.

❖ Challenge the class to make a commitment to offer such hospitality. The adults may choose to do this individually or as a group. Perhaps an event will take place in the home(s) of the class, or at a place where those in need live or meet, or at the church.

If you will work together on this project, set up a task force to plan the event. Be sure to provide time during a future session for the task force to report back and solicit participation.

(5) Continue the Journey

❖ Pray that today's participants will find joy in living humbly.

❖ Read aloud this preparation for next week's lesson. You may also want to post it on newsprint for the students to copy.

- ■ **Title: Summoned to Be a Disciple!**
- ■ **Background Scripture: Luke 14:25-33**
- ■ **Lesson Scripture: Luke 14:25-33**
- ■ **Focus of the Lesson: People look for a cause or a purpose that they can passionately support. What is worth giving up everything for? Jesus challenged the crowd to leave everything behind and become his disciples.**

❖ Challenge the students to complete one or more of these activities for further spiritual growth, which you will write on newsprint for the students to copy.

(1) **Recall a time when you made a conscious decision to be last, per-** haps in some sport or other activity. **Why did you make this decision? Did your actions lead to the consequences you intended? Would you make this decision again? Why or why not?**

(2) **Be alert for encounters this week with someone who finds it difficult to be humble. What, specifically, makes you uncomfortable about being around this individual? Try to see beyond outward appearances and hear the cry of this person's heart. Offer a silent prayer as you interact with this person.**

(3) **Show your humility by doing an act of kindness for someone (or a group) that cannot repay you.**

❖ Sing or read aloud "Humble Thyself in the Sight of the Lord," found in *The Faith We Sing.*

❖ Conclude today's session by leading the class in this benediction, which is taken from Ephesians 6:23-24: **Peace be to the whole community, and love with faith, from God the Father and the Lord Jesus Christ. Grace be with all who have an undying love for our Lord Jesus Christ. Amen.**

UNIT 3: GOD SUMMONS US TO RESPOND!

SUMMONED TO BE A DISCIPLE!

PREVIEWING THE LESSON

Lesson Scripture: Luke 14:25-33
Background Scripture: Luke 14:25-33
Key Verse: Luke 14:27

Focus of the Lesson:
People look for a cause or a purpose that they can passionately support. What is worth giving up everything for? Jesus challenged the crowd to leave everything behind and become his disciples.

Goals for the Learners:
(1) to discern the meaning of being a disciple of Jesus.
(2) to reflect on the sacrifice Jesus expects of them.
(3) to examine and reorder their priorities in light of Jesus' call to take up their cross and follow him.

Supplies:
Bibles, newsprint and marker, paper and pencils, hymnals

READING THE SCRIPTURE

NRSV
Luke 14:25-33

25Now large crowds were traveling with him; and he turned and said to them, 26"Whoever comes to me and does not hate father and mother, wife and children, brothers and sisters, yes, and even life itself, cannot be my disciple. **27Whoever does not carry the cross and follow me cannot be my disciple.** 28For which of you, intending to build a tower, does not first sit down and estimate the cost, to see whether he has enough to complete it? 29Otherwise, when he has laid a foundation and is not able to

NIV
Luke 14:25-33

25Large crowds were traveling with Jesus, and turning to them he said: 26"If anyone comes to me and does not hate his father and mother, his wife and children, his brothers and sisters—yes, even his own life—he cannot be my disciple. **27And anyone who does not carry his cross and follow me cannot be my disciple.**

28"Suppose one of you wants to build a tower. Will he not first sit down and estimate the cost to see if he has enough money to complete it? 29For if he lays the foundation finish, all who see it will begin to ridicule him, [30]saying, 'This fellow began to build and was not able to finish.' [31]Or what king, going out to wage war against another king, will not sit down first and consider whether he is able with ten thousand to oppose the one who comes against him with twenty thousand? [32]If he cannot, then, while the other is still far away, he sends a delegation and asks for the terms of peace. [33]So therefore, none of you can become my disciple if you do not give up all your possessions."

and is not able to finish it, everyone who sees it will ridicule him, [30]saying, 'This fellow began to build and was not able to finish.' [31]"Or suppose a king is about to go to war against another king. Will he not first sit down and consider whether he is able with ten thousand men to oppose the one coming against him with twenty thousand? [32]If he is not able, he will send a delegation while the other is still a long way off and will ask for terms of peace. [33]In the same way, any of you who does not give up everything he has cannot be my disciple."

UNDERSTANDING THE SCRIPTURE

Luke 14:25-27. Jesus did not view the support of large crowds as a sign of success. He recognized popularity as a failure of the multitudes to hear and understand the serious nature of his call to discipleship.

These crowds were not disinterested followers. They had listened to Jesus teach. They had heard him forgive the sinful and warmed to his talk of God's love and grace. They had seen him heal the sick, raise the dead, calm the storm, drive out demons, and feed the multitudes; and they were drawn to his benevolent power. They had heard his criticisms of the religious establishment and were enlivened by the fresh movement of the Spirit that turned their dead traditions into living promise. And they were traveling with him, even though he had "set his face to go to Jerusalem" (Luke 9:51) because the days drew near for him to die.

So, Jesus turned, faced the crowds, and upped the ante. Anyone who wanted to come to him and be his disciple had hard choices to make. The choices were broad and deep. They involved shifting commitments, changing priorities, and discarding all else that was precious. Father and mother, brothers and sisters, wife and children—even life itself—had to be evaluated

in light of the supreme importance and exclusive demands of discipleship.

The verb "hate" in verse 26 literally means to hate, persecute in hatred, detest, or abhor. The word is used often in the New Testament to describe an attitude of the secular world and of believers before they became followers of Christ (Luke 1:71; John 7:7; 15:18-19, 23-25; 17:14; Titus 3:3; 1 John 3:13, 15). Disciples are to respond to such hatred with love (Matthew 5:43-44; Luke 6:22, 27). Hatred toward others contradicts a Christian's profession (1 John 2:9, 11; 3:15; 4:20) and indicates that he or she has fallen away (Matthew 24:10).

In spite of that broad usage, Jesus' teaching here aligns more with a forced choice between loyalties such as we find in Matthew 6:24. The strong incompatibility of embracing two options forces a person to heartily embrace one and strongly reject the other.

The most intimate relationships in life, and indeed life itself, must not divide the loyalties of the disciple. Carrying the cross and following Jesus describe the profound difficulty disciples face in turning from the easy way toward the hard road that leads to life (Matthew 7:13-14).

Luke 14:28-30. Jesus used two examples to describe the dynamics involved in making this hard choice. The first example invited the listener to reflect on discipleship by asking, "Which of you?" Such an invitation drew on the daily experience of the listeners. Although "tower" (Luke 14:28) could refer to public projects such as castles, the listeners likely would have associated Jesus' question with towers built in vineyards (Matthew 21:33; Mark 12:1) or farm buildings.

Some people start out on a building project without plans or preparation, but doing so risks the ridicule of others who see an unfinished project as testimony to the builder's lack of foresight, planning, and resources. Having to stop with only a foundation because resources to finish the project were not available from the beginning is a cause of embarrassment.

The prudent person begins with the intent to build, draws up plans, estimates the cost, and then decides whether the resources are available to finish the project. If not, the project will be abandoned or adjusted to fit the means and circumstances.

Through this example, Jesus urged followers to consider their choices in a prudent manner. A would-be disciple who turns back when the choices become difficult may be worse off than one who never began the journey at all. Failure and its associated embarrassment often discourage a second attempt and close the door to future possibilities. The landscapes are full of unfinished lives that started the journey when the way appeared easy but fell back when times became hard. Not every seed brings a bountiful return (Luke 8:4-15), and not every traveler on the road with Jesus becomes a disciple.

Luke 14:31-32. The second example advised careful and prudent consideration before making consequential decisions. It posed an issue of kings contemplating war. Although Palestine historically was a region often torn by war, the situation at the time of Jesus was somewhat different. Rome had established its authority over the entire region. Although Rome had left a few puppet kings in place, it would not have tolerated

these kings waging war against one another, much less against Rome itself. Such actions would have been dealt with harshly. Instead, the first century was a time of political intrigue, currying Roman appointments, eliminating competitors, and brokering deals.

Though a hypothetical rather than a historical example, Jesus' listeners had knowledge of warring kings from their past. As people who had been on the losing end of most wars since the fall of Jerusalem to Babylon in 587 B.C., the people understood the advisability of weighing options before entering into war.

Two other aspects in verse 31 support this oppressed nation perspective. First, the opposing king "comes against" the king, implying a defensive position against an invading army. Israel had not been an aggressor nation for centuries and, indeed, spent most of its efforts opposing occupying forces. Second, the opposing army greatly outnumbered the king's army. The question the king faced was whether he was able to "oppose" the superior numbers of the enemy.

Asking for terms of peace often involved surrender with dignity and the payment of tribute; but if done while the enemy was still far away, it increased the likelihood of humane treatment and avoided the death and destruction that war involves.

Luke 14:33. Two transitional words point to what Jesus said previously. "Therefore" is the customary way of summing up a point and drawing a conclusion. "So" means "in the same manner" and called the crowds to consider their choices with the same prudence that the builder of the tower and the king used in considering their situations.

Jesus raised the bar for disciples. The listeners had been thinking of breaking family ties and giving their lives—ideas pretty easily entertained in the abstract. The cross (Luke 14:27) was in the future and did not yet convey vivid imagery about the consequences of discipleship. When Jesus interpreted hating life itself (14:26) in terms of giving up everything, the reality suddenly struck home. We can think of life without some relationships. We can fantasize about being a martyr for an important cause. But bidding farewell, renouncing, or saying goodbye to everything is the ultimate hard choice. "All your possessions" (NRSV) makes us think about the consequences, but even that translation falls short of Jesus' meaning—"everything!" (NIV). The only thing left is a Teacher, a Leader, a Master who demands all of our loyalties.

INTERPRETING THE SCRIPTURE

Tough Choices

Most of us tend to be "both/and" rather than "either/or" kinds of people. We want open roads ahead with the widest variety of choices. We like to keep our options open— to choose what we want, when we want it, and where we want it. Strictures from any quarter make us uncomfortable.

Even when we should know better, we try to have it all. We try to separate good health from what we eat or drink, how much we sleep or exercise, and the risky behaviors in which we engage. We try to separate sex from love and intimacy. We want to act responsibly on Sunday and live our alter ego the rest of the week. We insist that work must be fun, worship must be entertaining, and citizenship must not be taxing.

We want to vote a split ticket, straddle every fence, and adopt every idea that sounds good to us. We want to taste it all, embrace it all, and conform to it all, maintaining room to maneuver based on the circumstances.

What we don't want are tough choices. Our courage is not strong enough, our commitments are not deep enough, and our endurance is not lasting enough to make a choice and stick with it. We prefer escape clauses, golden parachutes, pressure release valves, and clear exits in the event of an emergency. We want to hedge our bets, insure our potential liabilities, and hold puts and calls to protect us against swings in popular sentiment.

In the face of all this, Jesus bluntly says, "Get real. By trying to have it all, you have nothing. By trying to insure it all, you feed your insecurities and starve your faith. By trying not to choose, you choose destruction."

We are faced with incompatible choices. We cannot serve two masters; we cannot be two selves; we cannot walk two paths. We must choose one or the other. Failing to choose is the same as making the wrong choice. The only real option is to give up everything for the supreme privilege of following as a disciple of Jesus. Every other choice fails.

Abstract Illusions

Inside most of us is a world where life is wonderful. In that world each of us is good. Our motives are pure, our achievements are great, and our causes are right. In that world we make the right decisions, we make significant contributions, and we sense the esteem that comes from knowing that we are wise, benevolent, and appreciated.

Though such illusions are important to our sense of worth, well-being, and happiness, even the most notorious criminals follow the same course of self-justification that sometimes borders on self-delusion. We think we know more about ourselves than anyone else, but modern psychiatry teaches us that we code painful realities in order to make them more palatable to our sensitive egos.

Illusions become destructive when they are segregated from reality. When our actions and our perceptions of them are divorced, we become defensive, angry, and retaliatory toward those who challenge our views and understandings. Fortunately only a few of us reach the point where we cannot separate illusion from reality.

Jesus often confronted people whose illusions diverged from the reality revealed in their actions. When James and John held illusions about their pivotal places in his kingdom, Jesus asked them, "Are you able to drink the cup that I am about to drink?" (Matthew 20:22). When Peter asserted that he was ready to go to prison or even die with Jesus, Jesus yanked Peter back from his illusions with a prediction of his denials (Luke 22:31-34).

Illusions can infect our discipleship. We can think abstractly that we are willing to forsake relationships with family and friends for the cause of Christ. We can think that we would lay down our lives as martyrs for Christ's causes of justice and righteousness. Too often our illusions are far from the reality revealed in our actions. My Boy Scout leader taught me, "What you do speaks so loudly that I cannot hear what you say." We might paraphrase Jesus, "What you say means little if you do not support your words with your actions. Cast aside your illusions, and put your faith into practice."

Easy Compromises

Some of Jesus' teachings have been called "hard sayings." The sayings are hard because the demands are extreme, the expectations are stratospheric, the implications are mind-boggling, and the applications are absolute. What we really think when we encounter these sayings is that the demands are excessive, the expectations are unreasonable, the implications are too far-reaching, and the applications are impractical.

A reasonable understanding of these sayings demands that we see them as hyperbole, so we set them aside as nice ideas that really cannot be taken literally or applied seriously. These overstatements must be designed to get our attention and challenge us to move a little in their direction. If every Christian were to take these sayings literally, all of us would end up as penniless orphans ready to be crucified. Thus begins the endless compromises that we make with the demands of the gospel.

One of my seminary professors spoke of the gospel as both gift and demand. The gift in the gospel is the love and grace of God offered to us in Jesus Christ. The demand is the call of God to follow Jesus as Master and Lord of our lives. The demand without the gift leads to legalism. The gift without the demand leads to libertinism. The gift of the gospel fosters mercy. The demand of the gospel fosters justice.

One common human quality is the desire to have mercy for ourselves and justice for others. God is loving and merciful, and we certainly deserve the gift of grace. But other people ought to abide by the law, be morally correct, and face God's wrath when they sin.

These attitudes lead us to soften God's demands, make easy compromises with God's absolutes, and absolve ourselves from any shortcomings. The hard sayings are for others, not for us. These attitudes also incline us to be unmerciful with others, judgmental toward their failures, and vindictive toward any injury we experience as a result of their actions.

Some followers, when faced with the uncompromising claims of Christ find his teachings difficult (John 6:60), turn back, and no longer follow him (6:66). Many try to live in grace while blinking at the demands, making easy compromises whenever the demands seem too great. Some find the grace so overwhelming that they can do nothing less than embrace the demands as well.

What kind of disciple are you?

SHARING THE SCRIPTURE

Preparing Our Hearts

Meditate on this week's devotional reading, found in Psalm 139:1-6. The psalmist makes clear that we cannot escape the God who searches us and knows our every movement. How does this knowledge make you feel? Are you comforted, terrified, or indifferent about being hemmed in by God? Talk with God about your feelings.

Pray that you and the adult learners will give thanks for God's constant presence in your lives.

Preparing Our Minds

Study the background and lesson Scripture, found in Luke 14:25-33. Think about causes that you can so passionately support that you would be willing to give up everything for them.

Write on newsprint:

❑ information for next week's lesson, found under "Continue the Journey."

❑ activities for further spiritual growth in "Continue the Journey."

Plan a lecture from Understanding the Scripture for "Discern the Meaning of Being a Disciple of Jesus."

LEADING THE CLASS

(1) Gather to Learn

❖ Welcome the class members and introduce any guests.

❖ Pray that those who have come together today will give serious attention to the demands of discipleship.

❖ Observe that we are often bombarded by causes—charitable, political, social, medical, religious—seeking our time, talent, and financial support. Challenge the class to come up with at least twenty causes that have sought their support in recent months.

You may wish to list these ideas on newsprint.

❖ Ask these questions.

(1) **What criteria do you use to determine whether or not you will support this cause?** (List these criteria on newsprint.)

(2) **If you agree to support a certain cause, what criteria determine how much time, talent, and money you are willing to invest in it?**

(3) **Are there any causes you would be willing to give up everything, perhaps even your life, to support? If so, what draws you so single-mindedly to this cause?**

❖ Read aloud today's focus statement: **People look for a cause or a purpose that they can passionately support. What is worth giving up everything for? Jesus challenged the crowd to leave everything behind and become his disciples.**

(2) Discern the Meaning of Being a Disciple of Jesus

❖ Choose a volunteer to read today's Scripture lesson from Luke 14:25-33.

❖ Make a list on newsprint of what Jesus expects of those who are truly his disciples. (Include: *loyalty to Jesus that supercedes even loyalty to one's family; carrying the cross; following him; giving up all possessions.*) Note that to be a disciple requires one to count the cost first, before "signing on."

❖ Invite the students to comment on this list and raise questions.

❖ Follow-up by presenting a lecture on information you select from Understanding the Scripture. Be sure to explain the meaning of "hate" in verse 26, as well as the two examples—building a tower and fighting a war.

❖ Challenge the class to suggest other examples related to counting the cost. One modern example is whistle-blowers who when they spot a serious problem are willing to risk their jobs and face harassment in order to call attention to the problem. Another is citizens willing to challenge political authority, knowing that reprisals might result.

❖ Conclude this section by asking the class to comment on the difference between those who simply "tag along" with Jesus and those who follow him faithfully as true disciples.

(3) Reflect on the Sacrifice Jesus Expects of the Learners

❖ Direct the students' attention again to the list of Jesus' expectations.
  (1) Why is each one so difficult for most of us?
  (2) Which one is the most challenging for you personally? Why?
❖ Read these quotations, pausing after each one to invite the students to comment on how the author's understanding intersects with or challenges their own ideas on cross-bearing.
  ■ **The believer's cross is no longer any and every kind of suffering, sickness, or tension, the bearing of which is demanded. The believer's cross must be, like his Lord's, the price of his social non-conformity. It is not, like sickness or catastrophe, an inexplicable, unpredictable suffering; it is the end of a path freely chosen after counting the cost. . . . It is the social reality of representing in an unwilling world the Order to come.** (John Howard Yoder, 1927–)
  ■ **To take up the cross means that you take your stand for the Lord Jesus no matter what it costs.** (Billy Graham, 1918–)
  ■ **The man with a cross no longer controls his destiny; he lost control when he picked up his cross. That**

cross immediately became to him an all-absorbing interest, an overwhelming interference. No matter what he may desire to do, there is but one thing he can do; that is, move on toward the place of crucifixion. (A. W. Tozer, 1897–1963)

(4) Examine and Reorder Priorities in Light of Jesus' Call to Take Up One's Cross and Follow Him

❖ Distribute paper and pencils. Ask the students to write on the sheets their priorities in life. This list may include family, career, personal interests/hobbies (which may be listed separately), volunteer work, and anything else that each individual feels is important.
❖ Ask the students to rank these priorities with one (1) being the most important.
❖ Invite them to re-rank, if necessary, these priorities based on their recollection of the way in which they spent their time and money over the last two weeks.
❖ Draw attention one last time to the list of Jesus' expectations written earlier in the session. Challenge the adults to look at their own list as Jesus would and meditate on this question: **What changes do I need to make to bring my priorities into line with Jesus' call to take up my cross and follow him?**
❖ Close this portion of the lesson by inviting the students to write one sentence as to how they will begin to reorder their priorities, if need be, during the week ahead. Suggest that they put this paper in their Bible and refer to it often.

(5) Continue the Journey

❖ Pray that today's participants will commit themselves to taking up their cross and following Jesus more closely.
❖ Read aloud this preparation for next week's lesson. You may also want to post it on newsprint for the students to copy.

■ **Title: The Ark Comes to Jerusalem**

■ **Background Scripture: 1 Chronicles 15:1-28**

■ **Lesson Scripture: 1 Chronicles 15:1-3, 14-16, 25-28**

■ **Focus of the Lesson: Families, groups, and nations all have symbols of their belonging to one another, their history together. What symbols really matter in our lives? David brought the ark of God, a symbol of the covenant, back to the people of Israel and reminded them of their covenant relationship with God.**

❖ Challenge the students to complete one or more of these activities for further spiritual growth, which you will write on newsprint for the students to copy.

(1) Read German theologian Dietrich Bonhoeffer's *The Cost of Discipleship,* based in large part on the Sermon on the Mount. Discern how his understanding can inform your own practice of discipleship.

(2) Take some sacrificial action this week, perhaps giving money that you would normally spend for something else, or using your time to help someone in need.

(3) Write several personal examples of "cross carrying" in your spiritual journal. How does it feel to carry the cross? Is it truly a burden, or does it somehow make you feel more connected to Christ?

❖ Sing or read aloud "Take Up Thy Cross."

❖ Conclude today's session by leading the class in this benediction, which is taken from Ephesians 6:23-24: **Peace be to the whole community, and love with faith, from God the Father and the Lord Jesus Christ. Grace be with all who have an undying love for our Lord Jesus Christ. Amen.**

THIRD QUARTER
God, the People, and the Covenant

MARCH 2, 2008–MAY 25, 2008

During the spring quarter we will focus on God's covenant relationship with the people of Israel. Through the years, the people's faithfulness to the covenant wavered, but God remained steadfastly committed during the monarchy, the exile, and the restoration of the people to Jerusalem. Various prophets and kings led the way in restoring the Israelites' covenant relationship with God. The ark, the temple, the ritual of the Festival of Booths, and prayers speak of the covenant.

Unit 1, "Signs of God's Covenant," includes five sessions from 1 and 2 Chronicles. The unit opens on March 2 with "The Ark Comes to Jerusalem," a session from 1 Chronicles 15:1-28 that considers the celebration with which David had the ark of the covenant delivered to Jerusalem. "God's Covenant with David," the session for March 9 rooted in 1 Chronicles 17:1-27, explores what it means to be in a covenant relationship with God. On March 16 we turn to 1 Chronicles 28:1-21 to study how "God Calls Solomon to Build the Temple." The unit continues with an Easter lesson on March 23 that examines 2 Chronicles 6 and Luke 24, "Fulfillment of God's Promise." Here we see God's promises fulfilled in the dedication of the temple and also in Jesus' resurrection. "Josiah Renews the Covenant" concludes the unit on March 30 with a look at how the people's broken relationship with God can be mended according to 2 Chronicles 34.

The first of four sessions in Unit 2, "The Covenant in Exile," begins on April 6 with a study of Daniel 1 to see how "Daniel Keeps Covenant in a Foreign Land" where values and practices differed greatly from his own. The lesson for April 13, "Three Refuse to Break Covenant," examines the familiar story of Shadrach, Meshach, and Abednego in the fiery furnace as recorded in Daniel 3. Another well-known story, Daniel in the lions' den, is the basis for "Daniel's Life-and-Death Test," the session from Daniel 6 on April 20. "Daniel's Prayer for the People," found in Daniel 9, delves into Daniel's communal confession and intercessory prayer in the lesson for April 27.

Unit 3, "Restoration and Covenant Renewal," spotlights the period after the exiles had begun to return to Israel. Haggai 1 and Ezra 5 focus on the priority of rebuilding the temple, as we will learn on May 4 in "The Temple Rebuilt." Nehemiah 1:1–2:20, the background of our study for May 11, recounts the story of a visionary leader who encourages the people in "Rebuilding the Wall." Internal and external threats to the completion of the wall are examined on May 18 in "Up Against the Wall," which is based on Nehemiah 4–6. The unit closes on May 25 with a lesson on Nehemiah 8 in which Ezra reads from the book of the law of Moses and issues a "Call to Renew the Covenant" to which the people respond with a celebration of the Festival of Booths.

MEET OUR WRITER

THE REVEREND JANICE CATRON

Janice Catron is a Christian educator and ordained minister in the Presbyterian Church (USA) currently pastoring at John Knox Presbyterian Church in Louisville, Kentucky. Prior to moving to this congregation, she served on the national staff of the Presbyterian Church (USA) for fourteen years in various positions related to education and publication. In conjunction with her publishing work, Rev. Catron was a member of the Committee of the Uniform Series. She also taught as adjunct faculty at Louisville Presbyterian Theological Seminary.

A native of Mississippi, Rev. Catron received her B.S. from Millsaps College, her M.A. from Emory University, her M.Div. from Louisville Presbyterian Theological Seminary, and did her doctoral work at the University of Chicago. In addition to writing for *The New International Lesson Annual,* Janice is the author of *Job: Faith Remains When Understanding Fails* and *God's Vision, Our Calling: Hope and Responsibility in the Christian Life.*

Janice and her husband, Gordon Berg, live in Louisville, where he provides information technology support for a nonprofit educational and counseling facility for emotionally challenged teenage girls. When not working, Janice and Gordon enjoy watching movies together, playing on the computer, and spoiling their cat.

THE BIG PICTURE: COVENANTAL RELATIONSHIPS

The general title for this quarter—"God, the People, and the Covenant"—points us theologically to one of the most intimate expressions of relationships that we know as people of faith. The connections formed through covenant promises and agreements are not like any other: They involve one's total self in full commitment, and they bind a community through its willing participation in working toward the best possible life for all.

Our relationship to our God and to one another as defined by covenant is both sacred and unique. As we will see through these thirteen lessons drawn primarily from several biblical books (1 and 2 Chronicles, Daniel, Nehemiah, Ezra, and Haggai), God's faithfulness remains constant, even when ours does not. In the stories of the Hebrews' life before, during, and after the exile, we see that God's covenant love is not bound to one place or time and that it transcends the harshest of circumstances. In the Christian interpretation of God's promise to David, we celebrate the eternal covenant God has made with humanity through Jesus Christ. So, at the heart of this quarter, we find much that speaks to our role as people of faith today.

The question of what it means to be in covenant relationship with God and one another runs like a thread through every lesson. Accordingly, it will be helpful to explore that concept more fully here. What did the Jewish readers of these texts, including Jesus himself, assume about the covenant relationships being described? What is the connection between the "old" covenant and the "new"? How do we live faithfully in covenant today? These are the topics we will explore.

Covenant in the Old Testament

The Hebrew word for "covenant" is *berith,* which you will find translated several different ways in modern Bibles. In each case, the translators are doing their best to express one key meaning of the word out of several possibilities. So, for example, you may see:

- *agreement*—used in the sense of two parties working together to find mutual understanding.
- *contract*—used in the sense of a legally binding agreement.
- *testament*—used in the sense of a "last will and testament."
- *promise*—used to emphasize one's trustworthiness in following through on an agreement.
- *vow*—used to indicate an oath that is both legal and sacred.
- *treaty*—normally used to indicate an agreement between two formerly hostile groups.
- *alliance*—normally used to indicate an agreement between two formerly neutral groups.
- *partnership*—used to emphasize the equality and mutual responsibility of both parties.

In the Old Testament, there are two primary types of covenant that we see: those that exist among humans, and those that exist between humans and God. The former instances of *berith* are most often translated as "treaty," while the latter are most often translated as "covenant." Of course, both forms of covenant involve God at some level. In the human-to-human covenants, God is invoked as a witness and a guardian to ensure the agreement will be maintained. In the human-divine covenants, God is an active partner who always initiates the relationship.

Following the pattern of historical treaties, the covenants with God tend to begin with a brief call to pay attention (the preamble), followed by a prologue that recounts what God has done with and for the people. This history is what gives human beings the courage and the faith to enter into partnership with God. The history reassures us of who God is and how God operates. Because it grounds the covenant on what God has already done, we can trust the covenant promises made to us.

Next come the stipulations of the covenant. On the divine side, God promises to be steadfast and faithful in bringing the faith community into abundant blessings. Furthermore, God often indicates that these blessings will not be limited to the faith community alone, but will extend through it into the world. On the human side, the faith community is given laws to guide their way of relating to God and to others. In the traditional understanding of covenant, these laws are understood as an extension of God's love and grace; they are a type of "blueprint" by which God tries to show people how to begin building the heavenly realm on earth.

Like the ancient treaties, God's covenants can also stipulate where a text will be kept and when it will be read to the people. For example, shortly before his death, Moses had the people renew their covenant with God. At that time he also wrote down the law (that is, the terms of the covenant) and instructed the priests to read it aloud every seven years in the presence of all the people (Deuteronomy 31:10-13). The purpose of these public readings was twofold: (1) so that those who knew the covenant would not forget it but recommit to it, and (2) so that those who were unaware of the covenant or who had not heard its terms would have a chance to accept the blessings it offered.

Some of the covenants between God and people also include a list of witnesses. Of course, when God is one of the covenant partners, it's a little hard to call on God to be witness to that same treaty. So the list of witnesses on those occasions is usually drawn from the created order: mountains, hills, streams, and so on (see, for example, Deuteronomy 30:19). After all, what better testament to God's faithfulness as a partner is there than the world God has already given us?

Finally, many of the divine covenants in the Bible include a detailed description of the blessings and curses that will follow, depending on whether the faith community keeps the covenant. These often emphasize the life that comes in keeping God's covenant and the death that comes outside of it (see, for example, Deuteronomy 28).

The "Old" Covenant and the "New"

When we move into the New Testament, there is a shift in the way covenant relationships are described. The Greek language did not have a word that was an exact equivalent of *berith,* so Greek-speaking writers used the closest parallel they could find in legal terminology: *diatheke.* This term originally referred to any legally binding arrangement of one's affairs, especially as it related to the disposition of one's property after death. In its most general secular usage, *diatheke* might be translated as "pact." Most often, however, it was used in the legal sense of "will" or "testament." That English translation for *diatheke* still lives on whenever we refer to either the Old or New Testament today.

Despite the difference in the Hebrew and Greek terms, however, the "old" and "new" covenants are more connected than one might think. God accomplished something unique in Christ, yet the Christ event is set fully in the context of God's prior relation with the world—and with the Hebrew people in particular. Thus Jesus was a Jewish man from a Jewish family, and he lived for the most part in a Jewish community. He grew up with Jewish Scripture, and he worshiped the Jewish God. He also placed himself squarely within the Old Testament concept of covenant, and he tried to teach the people what it truly meant.

In that sense, Jesus was in a long tradition of Jewish prophets who emphasized the covenant relationship as an attitude, not just external obedience to a set of laws. The core of their message was that the covenant relationship was to be in, of, and from the heart—and that one's actions then followed accordingly (see Deuteronomy 30:6 and Jeremiah 31:31, 33-34, for example). Jesus reclaimed this prophetic message and gave it concrete expression in his own person. Through his teachings, we get the sense that the former covenant is still in force, but now under far better terms. As Jesus said, "Do not think that I have come to abolish the law or the prophets; I have come not to abolish but to fulfill" (Matthew 5:17).

Moreover, Jesus' teachings often illustrated the loving and reconciling aspect of the covenant relationships to which we are called. The importance of an intact, unbroken relationship with God and others was so important, in fact, that when asked to cite the greatest commandment, Jesus replied: "'You shall love the Lord your God with all your heart, and with all your soul, and with all your mind.' This is the greatest and first commandment. And a second is like it: 'You shall love your neighbor as yourself.' On these two commandments hang all the law and the prophets" (Matthew 22:34-40; see also Mark 12:28-34; Luke 10:25-28).

The word for *love* Jesus used in these commandments is *agape*, the Greek equivalent to the steadfast covenant love (*hesed*) described in the Old Testament. Whatever points theologians and Bible scholars may debate regarding how the "old" and "new" covenants relate to one another, one aspect is indisputable: All covenants with God are fulfilled through relationships that reflect the divine love God has for us.

God's love is best seen, of course, in Jesus' life, death, and resurrection—and in those momentous events, God accomplished something that had never been achieved before. God in Christ broke down all the barriers that kept people from living fully into their covenant relationships, opening new ways to approach God and to relate to one another. Thus, 1 Timothy 2:5 speaks of Jesus as a "mediator between God and humankind." The Greek word translated here as "mediator" refers to a person who arbitrates between two parties to negotiate a pact or ratify a covenant. It can also refer to one who creates or restores harmony or friendship. Accordingly, the writer of the Letter to the Hebrews uses this same term to speak of Christ as one who has negotiated a covenant between us and God that is not only "new" (Hebrews 9:15; 12:24) but "better" (8:6).

The New Covenant in Christ

When speaking of the new covenant we have in Christ, the New Testament writers often selected certain elements of Old Testament covenant theology and gave them new emphasis in light of the Christ event. Four aspects of the new covenant in Christ that directly relate to our Christian life together are remembrance, freedom, hospitality, and belonging.

(1) *Remembrance.* This is a key concept in both testaments. After all, we can keep the covenant only insofar as we remember its terms and continue to honor them. What's more, part of our covenantal relationship with others involves remembering them—keeping them in mind, staying aware of them, and lifting them up as a priority in our lives. This holds true for our relationship with God as well.

Forms of the verb "remember" run throughout many books of the Bible. For example, during the time of Israel's suffering as slaves in Egypt, God "remembered" the covenant with their ancestors (Exodus 2:24) and then brought about their deliverance. Throughout later generations, as the people of Israel celebrated the Passover event, they did so to "remember" what God did for them—to keep the original event fresh in people's minds so they could claim the story as their own. That is the same reason Jesus said at the Last Supper, "Do this in "remembrance" of me" (Luke 22:19; 1 Corinthians 11:24).

"Remembering" both roots us in the past and points us toward a future, and the result directly affects our relationships in the present. In looking back, we are reminded of God's great love for the world, shown in Jesus' death and resurrection. In looking ahead, we see the wholeness that God intends for all the peoples of the world. Our calling in the present is to shape our relationships with God and others in such a way as to reflect the divine love we remember and the glory we anticipate.

(2) *Freedom.* One of the things Jesus accomplished theologically for us is a new exodus. The parallels between the exodus account and the Gospel descriptions of the life, death, and resurrection of Jesus—particularly in the celebration of that Passover meal that we know as the Last Supper—are deliberate. We are supposed to hear the echoes of the former event in the latter.

The New Testament often speaks of Christ's accomplishment in terms of our freedom from the bondage of sin and death. Another way to word this is to say that in Christ we have been set free to wholeness and life. We have been freed to enter and maintain the *agape* relationships to which we are called.

(3) *Hospitality.* In the earliest days of Israel's celebration of covenant meals, sitting together at table was important as a concrete symbol of the new relationship in which both parties now became like family to one another. People did not sit down to eat together unless (1) a host was offering hospitality to a guest, who was then honor-bound not to harm the host; (2) two allies were sharing a meal; or (3) it was a family mealtime.

More than that, sharing a meal with someone, even a passing stranger, obligated one as host to extend protection to the person. Sitting at the meal together when ratifying a covenant was a solid sign and seal of the new relationship being established. Through that act, one party said to the other, "I will trust you. I will agree to protect you and to be there for you in the way that family is."

We understand Christ to be our host at the table, to which we come by his invitation. This act of divine hospitality then becomes the model by which we are to welcome others, both at the table and away from it. The wonderful, grace-filled surprise is that the more we open ourselves to receive the hospitality that God in Christ offers us, the easier it becomes for us to extend that same hospitality to others.

(4) *Belonging.* As hinted at above, a covenant establishes a relationship that amounts to a new family system. In Christ, God brings us into the divine family in a way that makes us siblings and co-heirs with Christ! We move from being a nameless people to being children of God. We are claimed and named by God, who gives us a new identity as individuals and as a community.

The stories we will study this quarter have much to say about who we are and whose we are. We learn about our identity by studying how God relates to us as covenant people. We see in the Old Testament accounts the strengths and foibles of the Israelites and recognize that we too can be either faithful or unfaithful. We also recognize that God is always faithful. God keeps covenant with us as Christians through our Lord Jesus Christ, who came to be the mediator who enables us to claim our heritage as sons and daughters of God. Thanks be to God!

CLOSE-UP:
THE CHRONICLER AND
HISTORY

The Chronicler's history—1 and 2 Chronicles—basically parallels the work of the Deuteronomic Historian (Deuteronomy, Joshua, Judges, 1 and 2 Samuel, 1 and 2 Kings). Why, then, do we need both of these historical accounts in the Bible? The main difference is that the Chronicler focuses on Israel's worship traditions, institutions, and worship leaders. Although Chronicles includes history from Adam through Cyrus the Great (539 B.C.), the focus on the temple is not surprising because, modern commentators argue, Chronicles was written during the Persian period of Judah's history (539–332 B.C.). Some scholars limit the date to the latter half of that period, 450–332 B.C. Previously, the books of Ezra and Nehemiah were included in the Chronicler's history, but more recent scholarship suggests that Chronicles was likely written later than these other two books. One reason for this shift is that the Chronicler envisions the people of God as being united. In contrast, Ezra and Nehemiah argue for a separate community of Judeans who have returned to their homeland from exile.

Biblical readers throughout the centuries have noted that the Chronicler's history is based on the same basic storyline as Samuel and Kings. At one time, Chronicles was seen as more or less a supplement to Samuel and Kings. In fact, the Greek translation of the Hebrew Bible, known as the Septuagint, names this book *Paraleipomena*, which means "the things left out." Current scholars see Chronicles as far more than an addendum. While there are many similarities, there are also differences. The Chronicler omits some of the source material, such as stories that cast his hero David in a negative light. This writer adds other information that he has either written himself or found in other places, such as Ezra, Nehemiah, Zechariah 1–8, Psalms, Jeremiah, and the Pentateuch (Genesis through Deuteronomy) as it appears in its final edited form. Thus, although the Chronicler draws heavily upon Samuel and Kings, he employs other sources and weaves a story that emphasizes both the exile of the people of Judah and their restoration. He seeks to show that the rise and fall of the community of faith depends upon its spiritual relationship with God.

Since 1 and 2 Chronicles were certainly meant to be a continuous story, it is appropriate to see how these two books flow together. Whereas a variety of schemata may be found, the one presented here is based on Leslie C. Allen's helpful work in *The New Interpreter's Bible, Volume 3*. In the first of the four blocks, 1 Chronicles 1:1–9:34, we see Israel's election and a broad sweep of history before the exile, as well as the possibility of restoration. The second section, 1 Chronicles 9:35–2 Chronicles 9:31 depicts the reigns of David and Solomon. An important focus is the placement, construction, and dedication of the temple. The third division, 2 Chronicles 10:1–28:27, looks at the divided kingdom. Finally, 2 Chronicles 29:1–36:23 considers the reunited kingdom.

Faith in Action: Remembering and Caring

During this quarter we have explored Israelite history, especially as it concerns the temple. We have also seen how leaders have inspired people to rebuild/restore their place of worship. We, too, need to remember our church's stories and pass them on to others. Likewise, we need to maintain our physical facilities so that generations to come can worship in the space that is so dear to us. Here are some ideas for remembering and caring.

(1) Write a church history if you do not already have one that is up to date. Work with a team to interview long-time members who can recall their own experiences in this congregation, as well as stories that have been handed down to them. If the church has kept good records, you should be able to find information about people and programs. Ask members of the congregation to share pictures they have. Be sure to include elderly members who are no longer able to attend church regularly. They will likely have many memories and pictures to share.

(2) Publish your church history. If the budget allows, you could give a copy to each church member and visitor. Or, you could sell the history for a nominal fee over cost and use the proceeds as a fundraiser for a designated project.

(3) Enter your work in a church history contest. Some denominations run such contests. Check with your conference or local judicatory to see what opportunities are available.

(4) Use the church history as a teaching tool for newer members, children, and youth. Perhaps you could visit classes and tell at least parts of the history. A new members' class would be an ideal forum, as would a confirmation class.

(5) Create a "church history day." Attractively arrange displays, pictures, artifacts, news articles, and whatever else you can find. Use video and/or audio presentations, if possible. Consider using such an event in conjunction with a capital fundraising drive. Remind people where your congregation has been so that they will want to help it move forward into the decades to come.

(6) Use snippets from your church history in a regular column or article for a local newspaper. Some community members may be interested enough to visit.

(7) Make videos of current activities so that future members will have an opportunity to see and hear your generation's contribution.

(8) Work with the trustees to do upkeep and repairs as your skills and talents allow.

(9) Use your creative gifts to add something special to the church facilities, such as a flower bed, mural, banner, or labyrinth.

(10) Survey your facilities to see if they are accessible to people with disabilities. Consider not only people with mobility challenges but also those who are hearing or sight impaired. Be aware that people of all ages may need to have special accommodations made for them to be able to fully participate. Send your findings to trustees who could take action to make the building more welcoming for all people.

UNIT 1: SIGNS OF GOD'S COVENANT

THE ARK COMES TO JERUSALEM

PREVIEWING THE LESSON

Lesson Scripture: 1 Chronicles 15:1-3, 14-16, 25-28
Background Scripture: 1 Chronicles 15:1-28
Key Verse: 1 Chronicles 15:3

Focus of the Lesson:
Families, groups, and nations all have symbols of their belonging to one another, their history together. What symbols really matter in our lives? David brought the ark of God, a symbol of the covenant, back to the people of Israel and reminded them of their covenant relationship with God.

Goals for the Learners:
(1) to understand the importance of the ark of the covenant to the people of Israel.
(2) to identify worship symbols that remind them of their relationship with God and with one another.
(3) to participate in worship.

Pronunciation Guide:
Chenaniah/Kenaniah (ken uh ni' uh)   ephod (ee' fod)
Levite (lee' vite)   Obed-edom (oh bid ee' duhm)
Uzzah (uhz' uh)

Supplies:
Bibles, newsprint and marker, paper and pencils, hymnals, worship table and appropriate symbols such as cross, Bible, and candles and matches; optional picture of the ark of the covenant

---

READING THE SCRIPTURE

NRSV
1 Chronicles 15:1-3, 14-16, 25-28
    [1]David built houses for himself in the city of David, and he prepared a place for the ark

NIV
1 Chronicles 15:1-3, 14-16, 25-28
    [1]After David had constructed buildings for himself in the City of David, he prepared

---

of God and pitched a tent for it. ²Then David commanded that no one but the Levites were to carry the ark of God, for the LORD had chosen them to carry the ark of the LORD and to minister to him forever. **³David assembled all Israel in Jerusalem to bring up the ark of the LORD to its place, which he had prepared for it.**

¹⁴So the priests and the Levites sanctified themselves to bring up the ark of the LORD, the God of Israel. ¹⁵And the Levites carried the ark of God on their shoulders with the poles, as Moses had commanded according to the word of the LORD.

¹⁶David also commanded the chiefs of the Levites to appoint their kindred as the singers to play on musical instruments, on harps and lyres and cymbals, to raise loud sounds of joy.

²⁵So David and the elders of Israel, and the commanders of the thousands, went to bring up the ark of the covenant of the LORD from the house of Obed-edom with rejoicing. ²⁶And because God helped the Levites who were carrying the ark of the covenant of the LORD, they sacrificed seven bulls and seven rams. ²⁷David was clothed with a robe of fine linen, as also were all the Levites who were carrying the ark, and the singers, and Chenaniah the leader of the music of the singers; and David wore a linen ephod. ²⁸So all Israel brought up the ark of the covenant of the LORD with shouting, to the sound of the horn, trumpets, and cymbals, and made loud music on harps and lyres.

a place for the ark of God and pitched a tent for it. ²Then David said, "No one but the Levites may carry the ark of God, because the LORD chose them to carry the ark of the LORD and to minister before him forever." **³David assembled all Israel in Jerusalem to bring up the ark of the LORD to the place he had prepared for it.**

¹⁴So the priests and Levites consecrated themselves in order to bring up the ark of the LORD, the God of Israel. ¹⁵And the Levites carried the ark of God with the poles on their shoulders, as Moses had commanded in accordance with the word of the LORD.

¹⁶David told the leaders of the Levites to appoint their brothers as singers to sing joyful songs, accompanied by musical instruments: lyres, harps and cymbals.

²⁵So David and the elders of Israel and the commanders of units of a thousand went to bring up the ark of the covenant of the LORD from the house of Obed-Edom, with rejoicing. ²⁶Because God had helped the Levites who were carrying the ark of the covenant of the LORD, seven bulls and seven rams were sacrificed. ²⁷Now David was clothed in a robe of fine linen, as were all the Levites who were carrying the ark, and as were the singers, and Kenaniah, who was in charge of the singing of the choirs. David also wore a linen ephod. ²⁸So all Israel brought up the ark of the covenant of the LORD with shouts, with the sounding of rams' horns and trumpets, and of cymbals, and the playing of lyres and harps.

UNDERSTANDING THE SCRIPTURE

Overview. First and Second Chronicles were initially one book, written to tell the history of the people of Israel from creation to the start of the Persian Empire. The first nine chapters (1 Chronicles 1–9) record the genealogy from Adam to David, and the rest of 1 Chronicles deals exclusively with the reign of David. Second Chronicles tells the story of Solomon, who like David is presented as an idealized king (2 Chronicles 1-9), and the book then presents the history of the divided kingdom down to the fall of Judah. It ends with the command of Cyrus of Persia to rebuild Jerusalem and allow the exiles to return home (2 Chronicles 36:22-23).

The Chronicler drew from numerous accounts, including several books of the Bible, in composing his own record of Israel's history. One can see the writer's familiarity with the Pentateuch (Genesis–Deuteronomy), 1 and 2 Samuel, and 1 and 2 Kings, for example. Because the Chronicler wanted to make a particular theological point, however—notably that the reigns of David and Solomon represented a Golden Age in which the kingdom was faithfully in relationship with God—he was highly selective in choosing which stories to include in his history. Thus, 1 and 2 Chronicles contain none of the more sordid accounts related to the "ideal" kings, such as David's murderous desire for Bathsheba (2 Samuel 11) or Solomon's eventual worship of other gods (1 Kings 11:4-8).

First Chronicles 15:1-28 continues a story that began in 1 Chronicles 13. There we read of David's first attempt to move the ark to Jerusalem and the tragedy that ensued. A well-meaning man, Uzzah, put out his hand to steady the ark, and God immediately struck him dead. Angry and then fearful, David left the ark in the household of a man named Obed-edom.

First Chronicles 15 picks up three months later. David has built a home for the ark in Jerusalem, a tent to be used until the temple is built. He is ready to try again, and this time he knows to warn people that God will only allow Levites, using poles, to transport the holy ark.

1 Chronicles 15:1-2. David has been busy constructing his palace (14:1), and now he establishes a place for the ark. In chapter 15, verses 1, 3, and 12 all underscore that it was the king himself who prepared this site, a point that stands in stark contrast to Saul's neglect (13:3). Some commentators see a further sign of David's zeal in that the Chronicler does not place the king in the palace until 17:1, *after* the ark has been brought to its own home.

Verse 2 clearly shows respect for the ark as the symbol of God's presence. It is holy, and therefore not to be touched except by those who are dedicated to God's service—the priests. The regrettable death of Uzzah (13:10) is now seen, in retrospect, as a just and necessary response to the unintentional defilement of God's property (and therefore God's own Self).

1 Chronicles 15:3-15. David assembles "all Israel" to join in bringing the ark to Jerusalem. He then gathers all the priests and addresses their leaders, giving them the instruction to carry the ark to Jerusalem. Although the Chronicler uses the term "Levites" throughout these verses, these religious leaders did not exist as a special class in David's time. Thus, David probably addressed a more generic priestly group. We also read that the priests carried the ark on poles that rested on their shoulders, as Moses commanded. In this last detail, the Chronicler wants to show further how the second attempt to move the ark was far better grounded in scriptural instruction than the first attempt had been.

1 Chronicles 15:16-24. These verses continue the picture of David as the one who established and oversaw the worship practices that would one day extend to the temple. Under his instruction, the head priests appoint musicians from among their tribe to provide choral music for the upcoming event.

1 Chronicles 15:25-28. At last we see the big event. David, the elders of the people, and the commanders of the army (15:25) go to celebrate along the way as the priests bring the ark up from the house of Obed-edom. The list of personnel is deliberate. The Chronicler has already shown that the religious leaders agreed to and participated in moving the ark. Now we see that the political leaders, represented by the heads of the tribal families and the leaders of the army, did so as well. Through this inclusive list, the Chronicler underscores that bringing the ark to Jerusalem was the will of all the people.

The Chronicler also makes clear that this is the will of God. Certainly the priests recognize that. In thanks to God for allowing them to carry the ark, they offer a sacrifice of seven bulls and seven rams (15:26). Seven is a holy number indicating completeness, and perhaps here it serves as a signal that God's will for the ark (and the people) is about to be completed at last. This fits theologically with another literary point: Beginning in these verses, the writer refers to the ark as "the ark of the covenant of the LORD. " Most scholars think this shift in language represents the writer's belief that God's covenant was about to be fulfilled in a new way in David's reign.

To add to this picture, in this section we see David embodied as the head of both the religious and political sides of the kingdom. We know he is the political head, by virtue of being king, but the Chronicler takes pains to show him as the religious head as well. David dresses in the traditional linen robe of the priests, and he also wears an ephod, a religious garment associated with the high priest (15:27).

INTERPRETING THE SCRIPTURE

A Congregation's Symbol

The small church where I serve as pastor will soon be celebrating its fortieth anniversary. As various founding members of the congregation have gathered to share stories and to reminisce, those of us who are newer to the church's life have learned much about the items around us.

For example, there is a rather large, plain metal cross mounted on one wall of the educational wing that appears to have been put up in lieu of any nicer decoration. In fact, that cross represents a significant stage in the congregation's development. Another church gave it as a gift to the newly formed congregation forty years ago, and various members faithfully carried it each week to the school in which they met for Sunday services. After the sanctuary was built, the metal cross hung in a place of honor. Years later, when the new educational wing was dedicated, the cross was moved there as a visual symbol of the church's humble beginnings and of God's faithful and ongoing work in the life of the congregation.

For those who know its history, that plain metal cross remains rich in memories and meaning. Likewise, most of us can think of items from our family or church life that carry great significance. These items may not look special to anyone else, but to members of the family or the congregation, they are treasures that trace a history together and affirm our belonging to one another.

A Theological History

For the Hebrews, the ark of the covenant was the key symbol of their identity as the people of God. According to tradition, the ark was a gold-plated wooden box carried on long poles and built during Moses' time as a container for the Ten Commandments (Deuteronomy 10:2, 5; Exodus 25:10-22). Christians later maintained that manna from the wilderness and Aaron's staff were also stored there (Hebrews 9:4; compare Exodus 16:33-34; Numbers 17:10). In terms of the items it housed, the ark was a symbol of God's lordship, providence, and grace.

Practically speaking, the ark was also seen as a sort of portable throne for God, symbolizing the ongoing presence of God among the people. In biblical times, this was a radical and new concept. Most theologies of the ancient Near East held that deities were tied to a particular place, a region over which they had total control. For lesser deities, this might be a small area, such as a river ford or a mountain ridge. For greater deities, the scope could be as large as a country's borders. If a deity somehow left the area with which it was associated, its divine power was diminished.

The ark represents one step in the evolution of the people's understanding of God. They now knew that God was not confined to Sinai; God could leave the mountain and still have full divine power. Yet the people continued to view God as needing a particular place in which to manifest the divine presence. In this regard, the ark served as a replacement for the mountain. What a revolutionary thought this represented, though: God could travel with the people anywhere. Moreover, God actually *chose* to be in the midst of the people wherever they were!

The Ark as Symbol

The ark served as a powerful reminder of all that God had done for the people from the exodus through the wilderness wanderings to establishing a home in the promised land. Thus it is no wonder that the ceremony to bring the ark to rest in Jerusalem at last was surrounded by acts of worship, joy, and praise.

It is hard for us to completely understand what David and the people felt. We belong to a culture where visual images bombard us daily. Icons are merely common tools for starting a computer program or navigating the Internet. Trademarks and logos have commercialized the notion of *symbol* to the point that the concept has little to do with true power anymore.

One of the challenges for the church today is reclaiming the depth of meaning a symbol can convey. We should be able to look at the key symbols of our faith and be moved to a visceral reaction by what they represent: the very power and grace of God.

That is what the Hebrews felt when they looked at the ark, the "throne of God." They knew that God was not limited to the ark's physical locale, but they also knew that the ark represented the solemn promise of the God of all space and time to be uniquely present with them always. At the start of a new life as a united kingdom—Israel and Judah under one king—this was a powerful image indeed. No wonder they greeted the entry of the ark into Jerusalem with such worshipful joy and celebration!

Our Lenten Symbols

It will soon be Holy Week, and most of our churches will celebrate some form of the Lord's Supper on Maundy Thursday. There we will use symbols of our own to celebrate God's presence in our midst. In our worship and ritual, we will affirm once again, as Christians have through the ages, that at the table we meet God in the risen Christ through the power of the Holy Spirit.

The communion service itself is multilayered in meaning, as was the ark. There are the symbols of bread and wine (or juice), reminding us that God chooses to work through the ordinary elements of everyday life. Then the words of institution are spoken, the bread is broken, and the wine is poured. The actions themselves become symbols— Christ's body is broken anew before our eyes, and we see and hear his blood poured out for the forgiveness of our sins.

In that moment, the entire sacrament becomes a symbol that transcends the centuries. It connects us back to the first disciples, sitting at the meal with Jesus. It also thrusts us forward to a mystical participation in the heavenly feast that is to come. It certainly celebrates the living presence in our midst—of the Messiah, Immanuel, God-with-us.

An Exercise in Imagination

Imagine, if you will, that your church has just received an amazing bit of news. A few weeks ago, biblical archeologists uncovered the actual plate and cup used by Jesus at the Last Supper. The authentication is beyond doubt.

Now you learn that, because of family connections one of the archeologists has to your congregation, the cup and plate will be used in your Maundy Thursday celebration of the Eucharist. You will touch the plate that Jesus held and drink from the cup he used. How much more meaningful would the sacrament be? Would you be unaffected by the fundamental power of symbols at that moment?

If you can imagine how you might feel on that night, then you can understand the immeasurable joy and solemn gratitude that the Hebrews felt on seeing the ark enter their city. Like David and his people, we too need to hold fast to our symbols—the water, the bread and wine, the cross, and others—because these are our most sacred reminders of God's faithfulness.

SHARING THE SCRIPTURE

Preparing Our Hearts

Read aloud this week's devotional reading, found in Psalm 150. Count the number of times "praise" is mentioned in these six verses. Who is to praise God? Why are we to offer praise? How do we praise? Notice that this hymn neither asks anything from God nor mentions any specific benefits from God. Offer your own praise to God, perhaps by using a musical instrument.

Pray that you and the adult learners will always have a song of praise in your heart for God, whose greatness surpasses all.

Preparing Our Minds

Study the background from 1 Chronicles 15:1-28. The lesson Scripture will focus on verses 1-3, 14-16, 25-28. As you prepare, think about the symbols that really matter in your life.

Write on newsprint:
❏ information for next week's lesson, found under "Continue the Journey."
❏ activities for further spiritual growth in "Continue the Journey."

Read the introduction to the quarter entitled "God, the People, and the Covenant," "The Big Picture: Covenantal Relationships," "Close-Up: The Chronicler and History," and "Faith in Action: Remembering and Caring." Decide how you will use these helps. You may want to incorporate information from the quarterly introduction and "The Big Picture" into today's session.

Prepare to read aloud Exodus 25:10-22 for "Understand the Importance of the Ark of the Covenant to the People of Israel."

Gather a cross, Bible, candles, matches, and any other symbols the class would find helpful for a worship table.

Option: Locate a picture of the ark of the covenant.

LEADING THE CLASS

(1) Gather to Learn

❖ Welcome the class members and introduce any guests.

❖ Pray that everyone who has gathered today will be aware of God's abiding presence.

❖ Read aloud this list of symbols, one by one. Invite the students to call out whatever comes to mind when they think of this symbol. Note that symbols may mean different things to different people, so there is no one "correct" answer.

■ flag
■ cross
■ ring
■ coat of arms
■ rainbow

- chalice
- donkey
- elephant
- four-leaf clover
- V (made with index and middle fingers)

❖ Invite class members to name other symbols that are meaningful to them.

❖ Read aloud today's focus statement: **Families, groups, and nations all have symbols of their belonging to one another, their history together. What symbols really matter in our lives? David brought the ark of God, a symbol of the covenant, back to the people of Israel and reminded them of their covenant relationship with God.**

(2) Understand the Importance of the Ark of the Covenant to the People of Israel

❖ Use the introduction entitled "God, the People, and the Covenant" to provide a survey of this quarter's sessions.

❖ Consider reading or commenting on selected parts of "The Big Picture: Covenantal Relationships" to give the students a broader base from which to study this quarter's sessions.

❖ Help the class to envision and understand the importance of the ark of the covenant by reading aloud Exodus 25:10-22, which describes the ark. Observe that the "covenant" (or "testimony") referred to in verse 16 is the stone tablets inscribed with the Ten Commandments. For the Israelites, the ark of the covenant was the primary symbol of God's presence with them.

❖ **Option:** Show the class one or more pictures of the ark of the covenant. Since this sacred object has been lost, you will find various representations of it, all based on the description in Exodus 25.

❖ Select a volunteer to read the story of the ark of the covenant being brought to Jerusalem from 1 Chronicles 15:1-3, 14-16, 25-28.

❖ Discuss these questions.

(1) **What do you know about where the ark of the covenant was housed?** (See Understanding the Scripture, 1 Chronicles 15:1-2.)

(2) **Why was it so important that the Levites, and only the Levites, carry the ark?** (Note the final two paragraphs under "Overview" in Understanding the Scripture. Verses 9-14 of 1 Chronicles 13 are also pertinent. Also point out in 15:14 that the Levites "sanctified themselves" in preparation for this sacred task.)

(3) **What do you learn from 15:16, 25-28 about the way the ark of the covenant was received by the people?** (Observe that this was an occasion of joyous worship that included all Israel.)

(4) **Suppose you had been in the crowd. How might you have felt when you saw the ark of the covenant, the symbol of God's presence, pass before you?**

(5) **What religious symbols give you the same feeling of God's immediate presence?**

(3) Identify Worship Symbols That Remind the Learners of Their Relationship with God and with One Another

❖ Read "A Congregation's Symbol" from Interpreting the Scripture.

❖ Brainstorm with the class any symbols in your church building that are especially meaningful. Talk about why they evoke such cherished memories. This discussion will provide a wonderful opportunity for long-standing members to acquaint newer students with the history of your church.

❖ **Option:** Walk to wherever these symbols are located so that everyone may see them, if the adults are physically able to do so and will not disturb other classes.

(4) Participate in Worship

❖ Encourage the students to list worship components that are essential for them. Write their ideas on newsprint. Different adults, depending on their traditions, will have different answers, but likely your list will include: *music (instrumental/sung), reading from the Scriptures, sermon, prayers.* The students may want to add some other components, such as creeds and sacraments.

❖ Distribute paper and pencils. Encourage each student to list at least one example of a specific song, Scripture, prayer, and so on from the items on the list that he or she finds especially meaningful. (They may also want to list sermon topics that draw them closer to God.)

❖ Hear the students' suggestions. Help the class to select from these ideas and put together a brief worship service (without a sermon or sacrament), based on the class members' ideas. Write what the group plans to do in order on newsprint.

❖ Choose several students to take leadership roles for this worship service. These roles may include song leader, Scripture reader, person to offer a prayer, someone to lead a creed, and so on.

❖ Ask several students to arrange on a worship table whatever symbols you have brought. While they are doing this, be sure to distribute hymnals.

❖ Invite the leaders to gather at the worship table, if possible, and guide the class through the brief worship service that they have constructed.

(5) Continue the Journey

❖ Pray that today's participants will identify and continue to remember a symbol of God's presence that has meaning for them.

❖ Read aloud this preparation for next week's lesson. You may also want to post it on newsprint for the students to copy.

■ **Title: God's Covenant with David**
■ **Background Scripture: 1 Chronicles 17:1-27**
■ **Lesson Scripture: 1 Chronicles 17:1, 3-4, 6-15**
■ **Focus of the Lesson: People make personal covenants with others. Who can you trust to keep covenant with you? God made a lasting covenant with David through the prophet Nathan.**

❖ Challenge the students to complete one or more of these activities for further spiritual growth, which you will write on newsprint for the students to copy.

(1) **Write an account of a time when God's presence was especially real to you. Where were you? What was happening? Why do you think that you felt God so strongly with you at this time?**

(2) **Be alert for sacred and secular symbols this week. To which group of people is each symbol significant? What makes each symbol special?**

(3) **Create a symbol that has meaning for you. For example, perhaps you will fashion a cross from beads or draw a picture of a descending dove.**

❖ Sing or read aloud "Surely the Presence of the Lord."

❖ Conclude today's session by leading the class in this benediction, based on 2 Chronicles 34:31: **We renew our covenant to follow the LORD, keeping his commandments, with all our heart and all our soul, to perform the words of the covenant.**

UNIT 1: SIGNS OF GOD'S COVENANT
GOD'S COVENANT WITH DAVID

PREVIEWING THE LESSON

Lesson Scripture: 1 Chronicles 17:1, 3-4, 6-15
Background Scripture: 1 Chronicles 17:1-27
Key Verses: 1 Chronicles 17:7c-8

Focus of the Lesson:
People make personal covenants with others. Who can you trust to keep covenant with you? God made a lasting covenant with David through the prophet Nathan.

Goals for the Learners:
(1) to explore God's covenant with David.
(2) to recognize covenants made in their lives with others and with God.
(3) to commit themselves to a covenant relationship with God.

Pronunciation Guide:
hesed (kheh' sed)

Supplies:
Bibles, newsprint and marker, paper and pencils, hymnals, optional water, pitcher, and basin

---

READING THE SCRIPTURE

NRSV
1 Chronicles 17:1, 3-4, 6-15

¹Now when David settled in his house, David said to the prophet Nathan, "I am living in a house of cedar, but the ark of the covenant of the LORD is under a tent."

³But that same night the word of the LORD came to Nathan, saying: ⁴Go and tell my servant David: Thus says the LORD: You shall not build me a house to live in. . . . ⁶Wherever I have moved about among all Israel, did I ever speak a word with any of

NIV
1 Chronicles 17:1, 3-4, 6-15

¹After David was settled in his palace, he said to Nathan the prophet, "Here I am, living in a palace of cedar, while the ark of the covenant of the LORD is under a tent."

³That night the word of God came to Nathan, saying:

⁴"Go and tell my servant David, 'This is what the LORD says: You are not the one to build me a house to dwell in. . . . ⁶Wherever I have moved with all

the judges of Israel, whom I commanded to shepherd my people, saying, Why have you not built me a house of cedar? [7]Now therefore thus you shall say to my servant David: Thus says the LORD of hosts: **I took you from the pasture, from following the sheep, to be ruler over my people Israel; [8]and I have been with you wherever you went, and have cut off all your enemies before you; and I will make for you a name, like the name of the great ones of the earth.** [9]I will appoint a place for my people Israel, and will plant them, so that they may live in their own place, and be disturbed no more; and evildoers shall wear them down no more, as they did formerly, [10]from the time that I appointed judges over my people Israel; and I will subdue all your enemies.

Moreover I declare to you that the LORD will build you a house. [11]When your days are fulfilled to go to be with your ancestors, I will raise up your offspring after you, one of your own sons, and I will establish his kingdom. [12]He shall build a house for me, and I will establish his throne forever. [13]I will be a father to him, and he shall be a son to me. I will not take my steadfast love from him, as I took it from him who was before you, [14]but I will confirm him in my house and in my kingdom forever, and his throne shall be established forever. [15]In accordance with all these words and all this vision, Nathan spoke to David.

the Israelites, did I ever say to any of their leaders whom I commanded to shepherd my people, "Why have you not built me a house of cedar?"'

[7]"Now then, tell my servant David, 'This is what the LORD Almighty says: **I took you from the pasture and from following the flock, to be ruler over my people Israel. [8]I have been with you wherever you have gone, and I have cut off all your enemies from before you. Now I will make your name like the names of the greatest men of the earth.** [9]And I will provide a place for my people Israel and will plant them so that they can have a home of their own and no longer be disturbed. Wicked people will not oppress them anymore, as they did at the beginning [10]and have done ever since the time I appointed leaders over my people Israel. I will also subdue all your enemies.

"'I declare to you that the LORD will build a house for you: [11]When your days are over and you go to be with your fathers, I will raise up your offspring to succeed you, one of your own sons, and I will establish his kingdom. [12]He is the one who will build a house for me, and I will establish his throne forever. [13]I will be his father, and he will be my son. I will never take my love away from him, as I took it away from your predecessor. [14]I will set him over my house and my kingdom forever; his throne will be established forever.'"

[15]Nathan reported to David all the words of this entire revelation.

UNDERSTANDING THE SCRIPTURE

Overview. This chapter in 1 Chronicles follows its source, 2 Samuel 7, very closely. The overall purpose of the chapter is to explain why David did not build the temple. As in the 2 Samuel account, the narrative relies heavily on a word play that translates easily into English: the various meanings of the word "house."

In this account, we see the certain threads of the Chronicler's theology repeated.

Remember that the Chronicler wrote between 400 and 250 B.C., at least 160 years after the Babylonian exile ended as a result of Cyrus's decree. A remnant had returned home, but Israel, the city of Jerusalem, and the temple were a shambles, and the people were still falling away from Yahweh. The Chronicler responded to the situation by rewriting the history of Israel to confirm God's sovereignty. Thus the book of Chronicles describes God's miraculous efforts to save the chosen people time after time. In this interpretation of history, it does not matter that Judah is not an independent state in the Chronicler's day—the region and its capital city, Jerusalem, are nonetheless holy congregations. The God of history is still working out an all-encompassing divine plan for the people. The Chronicler details the outline of that plan in God's promise to David.

1 Chronicles 17:1-2. David is now living in the completed palace. He expresses a concern to the prophet Nathan, however, that the ark is still housed in a tent. The implication is that David is eager to begin work on the temple. The Chronicler wanted to show that David, despite his own physical comfort, would not rest easy until the symbol of God's presence with the people had also received a suitable dwelling place in Jerusalem.

Moreover, the Chronicler wanted to show David's continued piety in another way as well. As king, David could simply order the construction of the temple. By going to Nathan, however, he is implicitly asking the prophet for feedback—in other words, he is seeking God's guidance and permission. Nathan responds exactly as we, the readers, would expect at this point in the story. He tells David to proceed with his plan because God is on the king's side.

1 Chronicles 17:3-10a. In a startling turn of events, we learn that on "that same night" (17:3) God came to Nathan with another plan. The prophet is to tell David that, according to the Lord, the king is not to build a place for God to dwell (that is, the

temple). The rationale is that God has never had a single, stationary home before nor had God asked for one.

Lest David see this as a form of divine rejection, however, God says more. First, God reviews certain divine dealings from the past and the present. Nathan is to remind David of the king's chosen status as the shepherd of God's people and of the way God has been present with David ever since. Following this reminder, God then points to the future and a glorious promise. Rather than David building a house for God, God is going to build a name for David and a home for the people. It is hard to imagine a better promise for a king: David will receive fame and, even better, his people will receive permanence, safety, and peace.

1 Chronicles 17:10b-15. These next verses continue the words that Nathan is to say to David. Skillfully twisting the meaning of the word "house," the prophetic message proclaims that it is God who will build a "house" (dynasty) for the king, rather than David building a "house" (temple) for the Lord. The Chronicler sets the stage for his later description of Solomon's reign (2 Chronicles 1–9) by speaking now of a son of David whom God will "raise up" and "establish" (17:11). This child of David's will be the one to build the temple, and God in turn will "establish his throne forever" (17:12). It should be noted that the Hebrew term translated "forever" (17:12, 14) literally means something like "an incomprehensibly long time"—not what we specifically mean with our word "eternity." Verse 15 records succinctly that Nathan delivered the message in full to David.

1 Chronicles 17:16-22. Verse 16 begins, "David went in and sat before the LORD." Wanting to address God directly, rather than through an intermediary like Nathan, David apparently goes to the tent that housed the ark. There he sits before the ark itself, which symbolizes the presence of God, and offers a prayer of praise and thanksgiving. Looking to all that God has already done for him, David acknowledges that nothing on his own part (or on the part of his family) deserves such regard. Then David speaks, one assumes with humility and awe, of the promise God has made to bless the royal family even more in the future. In verses 19-22, David praises God for past mighty deeds on behalf of Israel that have culminated in the relationship described so beautifully in verse 22: "And you made your people Israel to be your people forever; and you, O LORD, became their God."

1 Chronicles 17:23-27. Finally David turns to the prophecy concerning himself and his dynasty. In what amounts to a hearty amen, David asks God to fulfill the divine promise. The Chronicler immediately follows these words with others that show David's true motives. As the historian writes it, the king was not making a demand of God for his own benefit but was encouraging God to take an action through which the divine name will be "magnified forever" (17:24). Verse 25 adds to the picture of David's humility when the king says that he only dared pray to God (presumably about the issue at hand) because God had already revealed the divine plans for a Davidic dynasty. The final two verses seem to describe the promises of both God and David as a "done deal" when David states as fact that God *has blessed forever* and *is blessed forever.*

INTERPRETING THE SCRIPTURE

God's Covenant with David

This lesson highlights the ongoing covenant that God made with David. The king has successfully brought the ark to Jerusalem, but now he longs to build a permanent structure for it. David shares his desire with the prophet Nathan, who subsequently has a dream in which God delivers a message for the king. The words of the prophet are a surprise and, initially, a disappointment: David is not to be the one who will build God's temple. The good news, however, is that God will instead build a "house" (that is, a dynasty) for David.

To those of us who know how this story ends, it may be difficult to put ourselves in David's place. For the king, this is an extravagant promise, rich with grace and unmerited favor. After all, God had reluctantly granted the people a king in the first place only because they would not quit begging for one. There was no promise initially of a dynasty. Now, however, God tells David:

"I will raise up your offspring after you, one of your own sons, and I will establish his kingdom. He shall build a house for me, and I will establish his throne forever" (17:11-12).

Given that most covenant agreements set stipulations for both parties, God's covenant with David seems to be a little one-sided. There is a long list of things that God promises to do for David, while David is asked . . . what? Not to build the temple?

In reality, the language of what God has already done for David—taking him from the pasture and setting him as king over Israel—defines David's responsibility in this relationship. He is to be the shepherd-king that God anointed him to be. He is to care for God's people with the same passionate intensity and selfless giving that God does. Of course, as we mentioned earlier, David did not always live up to this goal. God kept the covenant in place, however, which means that God never stopped asking David to strive to fill the role that God created for him.

Covenant Love

At the heart of every covenant God originates is a single goal: "I will be your God, and you shall be my people" (Jeremiah 7:23; see also Exodus 6:7; Jeremiah 11:4; 30:22; Ezekiel 36:28). Certainly God's covenant with David grew out of the relationship that already existed between the two of them and took it to a new level. Moreover, because David was the king, he represented all of Israel and Judah; in this regard, the covenant with David was, by extension, a covenant made on behalf of all the people he ruled.

As those who follow in the footsteps of the Old Testament people of faith, we need to ask what this passage has to teach us about God's dealings with the church today. For starters, we see unchanging good news. After all this time, God's covenants still offer order, safety, and peace in a world full of caprice, uncertainty, and animosity. After all, God has a purpose: to set us into a right relationship with our Creator and with one another. God's covenants are all designed to help us achieve this end.

There is a special Hebrew word used to describe the love that drives and defines such covenants. The word is *hesed*, and it is often translated as "steadfast love" (as in 17:13). *Hesed* is the kind of love that remains true and unchanging forever. It is faithful love that endures even in the face of scorn and infidelity on the part of the recipient. It is the love exemplified by Jesus on the cross.

The trustworthiness of God's promise to David rests in this love. God will be true to the divine word, no matter what. Later David will fail in his role as the shepherd-king by taking a woman named Bathsheba while she was the wife of another man—and then having that man killed to conceal the crime. God's promise will still stand, however, and David's dynasty will come to pass. In an act of either ultimate grace or divine irony, the promise will even be fulfilled through a child born to Bathsheba after she becomes David's wife.

Our Covenants

Time and again, both the biblical texts and our own experience witness to the fact that we are created for relationship with other people and with God. The need to know others, interact with them, and be accepted by them runs so deeply in the human psyche that it directly affects our mental, emotional, and physical well-being. Moreover, there is growing scientific evidence that we are equally designed to yearn for a spiritual connection to something greater than ourselves. The need for such relationships is, in essence, encoded in our gene pool.

We also recognize that we are created with a desire for security. We not only need relationships, we desperately need to know that we can trust those with whom we interact. The closer we are to people and the more they mean to us, the more we count on their faithfulness and continued commitment to the relationship we have established—and the more they count on us to provide the same.

The Bible interprets our need for connectedness and security as a call to *covenant*. There are many examples of covenant relationships in our life together as families and congregations. One might think of the commitments made by married couples, the promises made by the congregation at a baptism, or the vows made by ordained people and the congregations they serve. Certainly there is an implied covenant agreement in each congregation by which members mutually agree to participate actively and responsibly in the worship and mission of the church. When the individuals within the congregations live into this covenant agreement, they present a clear witness to the love of God, who remains in an everlasting covenant with us.

Covenant Living Today

In our own calling as Christians, there are certain covenant responsibilities to which

God calls us; and, as with David, God never stops asking us to try to achieve these. If we focus on covenant living as revealed in Jesus Christ, we can see three relationship goals that God sets for us.

1. We are to strive for loving relationships. Jesus' teaching on the greatest commandments makes clear that we are to love God, neighbor, and self. We are to have not just any love, however, but a love that grows out of and reflects the same steadfast, unwavering, and unconditional love that God always has for us.

2. We are to strive for responsible relationships. Divine love demands that we speak against destructive behavior in others and work for wholeness on their behalf. We are also, of course, called to act responsibly by monitoring our own behavior as well.

3. We are to strive for transforming relationships. If God is at the heart of all our relationships, then we should expect change for the better, both in ourselves and in others.

The covenant made between God and David was, and is, an everlasting covenant. In a world far removed from ancient biblical times, nothing has changed. The words still ring out: "I will raise up your offspring after you . . . and I will establish his throne forever" (17:11-12). As heirs in Christ to that promise, may our response always be, as David's was in essence, "We are your people forever!"

SHARING THE SCRIPTURE

Preparing Our Hearts

Meditate on this week's devotional reading, found in Psalm 78:67-72. These verses, which are part of a psalm that contrasts God's goodness with Israel's ungratefulness, speak about God's choice of David as the shepherd of God's flock. Note that David cares for the people "with upright heart" (78:72). Think about people in your own life who care for and guide you. Give thanks to them and to God for allowing you to be in a relationship with them.

Pray that you and the adult learners will choose to live in faithful covenant relationships with God and with each other.

Preparing Our Minds

Study the background in 1 Chronicles 17:1-27 and lesson Scripture, verses 1, 3-4, 6-15. Think about who you can trust to keep a covenant with you.

Write on newsprint:
❑ information for next week's lesson, found under "Continue the Journey."
❑ activities for further spiritual growth in "Continue the Journey."

Create a brief lecture for "Commit to a Covenant Relationship with God" if you choose to present the suggested information yourself.

Decide whether you will include the optional reaffirmation of the baptismal covenant of your denomination. Check with your pastor about the role he or she wants/needs to play, depending on the rules of your church. Gather supplies, including water, pitcher, and basin. (If you are United Methodist, note "The Baptismal Covenant IV," pages 50-53 in *The United Methodist Hymnal*.)

LEADING THE CLASS

(1) Gather to Learn

❖ Welcome the class members and introduce any guests.

❖ Pray that all who have gathered today will feel trust and caring within the group.

❖ Observe: **When people join any kind**

of organization—a church, civic association, service club, gang, social club, and so on—they are expected to abide by the purposes and rules of the group.

❖ Ask: **What are some characteristics of people who keep their promises to the group?**

❖ Read aloud today's focus statement: **People make personal covenants with others. Who can you trust to keep covenant with you? God made a lasting covenant with David through the prophet Nathan.**

(2) Explore God's Covenant with David

❖ Choose three volunteers to read 1 Chronicles 17:1, 3-4, and 6-15, respectively.

❖ Examine with the class the particular statements regarding the covenant that God makes to David through Nathan in verses 6-15. List these ideas on newsprint. Be sure to include the following ideas, which are listed in the order they appear in the text.

■ God did not request that a temple be built.

■ God chose David to be a shepherd-king over the people of Israel.

■ God has been with David constantly.

■ God has protected David from enemies.

■ God will make David's name great.

■ God will create a safe space for the Israelites to live in.

■ God will subdue Israel's enemies.

■ God will build a house (dynasty) for David by raising up one of David's sons and establishing his kingdom.

■ God will allow the son to build God's house.

■ God will establish the son's throne forever.

■ God will be as a father to David's son.

■ God will never remove steadfast love from this son, and his throne will be established permanently.

❖ Ask:

(1) Based on Nathan's words, what covenantal responsibilities does God expect David to fulfill? (Note the final two paragraphs of "God's Covenant with David" in Interpreting the Scripture.)

(2) What would you say is the basis for God's covenant with David? (*Hesed*, or steadfast love, is the root of this covenant. If time permits, you may wish to read "Covenant Love" in Interpreting the Scripture.)

(3) Recognize Covenants Made in the Learners' Lives with Others and with God

❖ Read aloud "Covenant Living Today" from Interpreting the Scripture. You may want to list the three italicized points on newsprint.

❖ Encourage the students to brainstorm types of covenant relationships they have with others and with God. Examples include marriage, church membership, and baptism. List their ideas on newsprint.

❖ Distribute paper and pencils. Provide quiet time for the students to reflect on at least one of the covenant relationships that exists in their own lives. Tell them they will not be asked to share their reflections, but encourage them to honestly rate themselves on their faithfulness to this relationship. Suggest that they consider changes they need to make to create a stronger relationship.

(4) Commit to a Covenant Relationship with God

❖ Ask the students to recall covenant relationships that God has made with humanity. Here is a list. Depending on the time, you may want to have several students look up these references and read them aloud or retell the gist of the content. Or, you may wish to provide this information in a brief lecture.

■ Covenant with Noah (Genesis 9:1-17)

■ Covenant with Abraham (Genesis 12:1-4; 13:14-17; 15:1-7; 17:1-14)

■ Covenant with Moses (Exodus 20:1–31:18)

■ Covenant of the Land (Deuteronomy 30:1-10)

■ Covenant with David (2 Samuel 7:4-16; 1 Chronicles 17:3-15)

■ The New Covenant (Jeremiah 31:31-37)

❖ Encourage the students to talk about the covenant that they believe God made with them at their baptism. What responsibilities do they have for this covenant, which in many denominations would have been publicly expressed at one's confirmation?

❖ Invite any who chooses to do so to commit/recommit themselves to a covenant relationship with God by giving thanks for God's faithful relationship with them. Do this by opening the floor to brief expressions of thanksgiving from each student. End this activity by inviting the students to repeat these words from the covenant renewal ceremony recorded in Joshua 24:15: **Choose this day whom you will serve . . . but as for me and my household, we will serve the LORD.**

❖ **Option:** If you have access to your denomination's reaffirmation of the baptismal covenant, plan to do this reaffirmation. If your pastor needs to be present, schedule this event at a time in the class period when he or she can attend.

(5) Continue the Journey

❖ Pray that all who have come today will be faithful to their covenant relationship with God.

❖ Read aloud this preparation for next week's lesson. You may also want to post it on newsprint for the students to copy.

■ **Title: God Calls Solomon to Build the Temple**

■ **Background Scripture: 1 Chronicles 28:1-21**

■ **Lesson Scripture: 1 Chronicles 28:5-10, 20-21**

■ **Focus of the Lesson: People long to know that the tasks they do have meaning. How can we know our tasks are meaningful? David affirmed that God had chosen Solomon for a specific task, that of building a sanctuary for the worship of God.**

❖ Challenge the students to complete one or more of these activities for further spiritual growth, which you will write on newsprint for the students to copy.

(1) **Page through the Psalms. List ones that focus on our trust in God and on God's trustworthiness. Over the next few weeks, plan to read carefully the psalms you have identified.**

(2) **Recall that Nathan clarified God's will to David. Can you think of instances when someone helped to clarify God's will for you? Did you accept what this person said? How did this clarification help you to grow spiritually?**

(3) **Look for opportunities this week to give priority to your covenant with God. Are there ways you can serve people? In what ways are you worshiping God? How do who you are and what you do reflect your covenant relationship with God?**

❖ Sing or read aloud "We, Thy People, Praise Thee."

❖ Conclude today's session by leading the class in this benediction, based on 2 Chronicles 34:31: **We renew our covenant to follow the LORD, keeping his commandments, with all our heart and all our soul, to perform the words of the covenant.**

UNIT 1: SIGNS OF GOD'S COVENANT
GOD CALLS SOLOMON TO BUILD THE TEMPLE

PREVIEWING THE LESSON

Lesson Scripture: 1 Chronicles 28:5-10, 20-21
Background Scripture: 1 Chronicles 28:1-21
Key Verse: 1 Chronicles 28:10

Focus of the Lesson:
People long to know that the tasks they do have meaning. How can we know our tasks are meaningful? David affirmed that God had chosen Solomon for a specific task, that of building a sanctuary for the worship of God.

Goals for the Learners:
(1) to hear David's plan for his son Solomon to build the temple.
(2) to realize that God calls them to accept specific responsibilities.
(3) to identify and begin to work on a task that God has called them to do.

Pronunciation Guide:
Uriah (yoo ri' uh)

Supplies:
Bibles, newsprint and marker, paper and pencils, hymnals

READING THE SCRIPTURE

NRSV
1 Chronicles 28:5-10, 20-21

⁵"And of all my sons, for the LORD has given me many, he has chosen my son Solomon to sit upon the throne of the kingdom of the LORD over Israel. ⁶He said to me, 'It is your son Solomon who shall build my house and my courts, for I have chosen him to be a son to me, and I will be a father to him. ⁷I will establish his kingdom forever if

NIV
1 Chronicles 28:5-10, 20-21

⁵"Of all my sons—and the LORD has given me many—he has chosen my son Solomon to sit on the throne of the kingdom of the LORD over Israel. ⁶He said to me: 'Solomon your son is the one who will build my house and my courts, for I have chosen him to be my son, and I will be his father. ⁷I will establish his kingdom forever if he is unswerving

he continues resolute in keeping my commandments and my ordinances, as he is today.' [8]Now therefore in the sight of all Israel, the assembly of the LORD, and in the hearing of our God, observe and search out all the commandments of the LORD your God; that you may possess this good land, and leave it for an inheritance to your children after you forever.

[9]"And you, my son Solomon, know the God of your father, and serve him with single mind and willing heart; for the LORD searches every mind, and understands every plan and thought. If you seek him, he will be found by you; but if you forsake him, he will abandon you forever. [10]**Take heed now, for the LORD has chosen you to build a house as the sanctuary; be strong, and act."**

[20]David said further to his son Solomon, "Be strong and of good courage, and act. Do not be afraid or dismayed; for the LORD God, my God, is with you. He will not fail you or forsake you, until all the work for the service of the house of the LORD is finished. [21]Here are the divisions of the priests and the Levites for all the service of the house of God; and with you in all the work will be every volunteer who has skill for any kind of service; also the officers and all the people will be wholly at your command."

in carrying out my commands and laws, as is being done at this time.'

[8]"So now I charge you in the sight of all Israel and of the assembly of the LORD, and in the hearing of our God: Be careful to follow all the commands of the LORD your God, that you may possess this good land and pass it on as an inheritance to your descendants forever.

[9]"And you, my son Solomon, acknowledge the God of your father, and serve him with wholehearted devotion and with a willing mind, for the LORD searches every heart and understands every motive behind the thoughts. If you seek him, he will be found by you; but if you forsake him, he will reject you forever. [10]**Consider now, for the LORD has chosen you to build a temple as a sanctuary. Be strong and do the work."**

[20]David also said to Solomon his son, "Be strong and courageous, and do the work. Do not be afraid or discouraged, for the LORD God, my God, is with you. He will not fail you or forsake you until all the work for the service of the temple of the LORD is finished. [21]The divisions of the priests and Levites are ready for all the work on the temple of God, and every willing man skilled in any craft will help you in all the work. The officials and all the people will obey your every command."

UNDERSTANDING THE SCRIPTURE

Overview. Earlier, in 1 Chronicles 22:2-19, David began assembling plans and materials for the temple because, according to the text, Solomon was too young and inexperienced to handle such a massive and detailed building project on his own. This perspective only appears in the Chronicler's version of history, however (compare 1 Kings 5–7). Here it was important to show David as the one who actually made all the arrangements for the temple because, for the Chronicler, Israel's most significant king must be linked to its most significant institution.

First Chronicles 23:1 records the passing of the kingship to Solomon during David's old age. In chapter 28, following a public announcement that God has chosen Solomon to build the temple, David hands over the building plans to his son at last.

Students of history will notice that David's description of how Solomon came to the throne is idealized here. As Paul K. Hooker notes in *First and Second Chronicles, Westminster Bible Companion:*

> Readers who know the story of 2 Samuel know that the process by which Solomon came to succeed his father was a torturous and bloody one, moved along by the deaths of one after another of David's other sons and characterized by intrigue and deception. The question thus naturally arises: Is the Chronicler unaware of all this, or has he chosen to ignore it? The answer is, in all likelihood, "no" to both. The Chronicler is fully aware of the story of Solomon's succession; he has on more than one occasion cited texts from the middle of that story. But the 2 Samuel story is the story of the historical-political process by which Solomon achieved his father's throne, and that is not the focus for the Chronicler. Rather, his interest is in a theological reading of the result of that process: that God has guided events so that a will set in motion long before Solomon or David or even Israel itself would come to fruition in Solomon's accession and the construction of the Temple. The Chronicler has no need to recount the very human story of that accession, but only to state clearly the divine intention that has brought it to pass.

1 Chronicles 28:1. Chapter 27 gave a detailed description of David's royal administration, including the military and civil leadership positions he developed. The first verse of chapter 28 shows all those leaders now assembled to hear David's final instructions concerning the temple's construction. The only ones notably missing are the priests—presumably because their tasks will come later, once the temple is complete.

1 Chronicles 28:2-8. David addresses the assembled leaders and charges them to help Solomon in the task of constructing the temple. In verses that recall the divine message carried to David by Nathan in chapter 17, the king explains that God commanded him not to build the temple himself. In verse 3, David adds a reason for God's denial: As a warrior, David has shed blood and therefore cannot build God's holy dwelling place (see also 22:8). These verses are an interesting twist on Solomon's words in 1 Kings 5:3, in which he says his father could not build the temple because he was always having to engage in "the warfare with which his enemies surrounded him."

The king follows this disappointing news about God's message with a statement of affirmation concerning the divine regard for David and his family. God "took delight in making [David] king over all Israel" (1 Chronicles 28:4), and now God has chosen Solomon to succeed David as king and to be the one entrusted to build the temple. Those who support Solomon and his endeavor will be able to partake of the eternal blessing that God has granted the kingdom through the divinely chosen family.

1 Chronicles 28:9-10. David gives a personal charge to Solomon. Rather than beginning with political injunctions, the king lists spiritual responsibilities first: Know God; serve God single-mindedly and wholeheartedly; seek God. David's only other charge to his son is to "be strong, and act" (28:10) in building the temple.

1 Chronicles 28:11-19. At last David hands over his plans for the temple to Solomon. The Chronicler includes a great deal of detail to show that it was all David's work and not Solomon's. According to Steven S. Tuell, writing in *First and Second Chronicles* of the Interpretation series, the detail served another purpose as well:

> The point is clear. God's temple demands and deserves the best and the most that human beings can supply. . . . Contemporary readers may well be offended by this extravagance. Shouldn't our resources rather be used to combat injustice, to feed the hungry and clothe the naked? Perhaps we

should recall Jesus' words when his followers were offended by an alabaster jar broken, its precious contents wasted (Matt. 26:6-13; Mark 14:3-9). While we are always and everywhere called to use our resources to aid the needy, our highest calling, in the words of the Westminster Catechism, is "to glorify God and to enjoy him forever." Extravagance in the service of God's glory is no waste!

Note that the plans David passed along were actually of divine origin, transmitted by God to the beloved king. Verse 19 establishes that David received the plans for the temple in much the same way that Moses received the plans for the tabernacle (see Exodus 25–30): "All this, in writing at the LORD's direction, he made clear to me—the plan of all the works." It is unclear, however, whether the writing refers to something transcribed by God or by David.

1 Chronicles 28:20-21. Once again David encourages Solomon to be strong and to act. Lest the task appear too daunting and therefore frightening, the king reassures his son that God will be with him. David then hands over a list of the organizational structure of the priests and Levites, completing everything that Solomon needs for worship to begin in the new temple. Finally, David reminds Solomon that he can call on any skilled volunteer, any leader, or indeed any person in the kingdom for help if needed.

INTERPRETING THE SCRIPTURE

Insights from David

This week's passage contains a significant speech by David to his son Solomon. Here we see David confirm Solomon as his heir to the throne and also as the one designated by God to build the temple. It is difficult to imagine two more meaningful tasks than ruling God's people and building God's house, and we can only assume that Solomon felt humbly awed as he undertook them both.

David's speech to Solomon provides a few clues as to how we are empowered to accomplish the tasks to which God calls us. The promise is that if we genuinely strive to do what God asks, even in the most ordinary actions, then God will see to our success. In that moment, we can find real fulfillment and a sense of worth in what we do.

There are three points that David highlights. First, we need to keep our minds on a single goal—serving God—and we need to embrace that goal with willing hearts (28:9). If we see every task we undertake in that light, then our satisfaction will come not from the task itself, but from the sheer joy of pleasing our Lord.

Second, we need to "be strong, and act" (28:10). Sometimes we take on a task unwillingly, only to find to our surprise that it is a source of joy. An adult may agree under pressure to lead the weekly youth group, for example, and then discover deep joy in the relationships that are formed during that time of fellowship. Teaching a class, visiting those who are homebound, working on a home for Habitat for Humanity, volunteering time to plant a food garden in a needy neighborhood—the opportunities are endless to get involved and find personal satisfaction in doing God's work in the world.

Finally, David points out that Solomon's task will be accomplished through the help of trained professionals and volunteers with "skill for any kind of service" (28:21). What a wonderful reminder that the greatest tasks the church undertakes are never meant for one person alone. God graces us with a multitude of gifts and talents through the members and staffs of our congregations, and together we can accomplish the work that

God sets for us. In working together, we also find an extra bonus: Not only is there meaning in the task itself but there is a rich and abiding nourishment that grows from the fellowship we share in working together as brothers and sisters in Christ.

What About the Ordinary?

It's easy enough to see how Solomon's tasks were meaningful. After all, he was going to rule a holy nation and build a glorious and expensive house of worship for his God. For most of us, however, the tasks to which we are called are far more mundane—and certainly not glamorous. How are we to see meaning in them day in and day out?

Perhaps it helps to remember the example set by our Lord on this day in the church year. Many Christian churches are celebrating Palm Sunday today in commemoration of Jesus' triumphal entry into Jerusalem. The crowds that day saw a king riding toward an eventual coronation. We know that, in fact, it was the Messiah heading to the cross.

When we take up our cross and follow Jesus along the path of servanthood, then we find that even the most ordinary tasks can be invested with a holy joy. Preparing a child's lunch for school, reading the newspaper to a neighbor whose sight is dimmed, sweating in a soup kitchen, or washing the communion ware at church can all become means by which we invite the presence of God into our lives at that moment. Whatever the activity, when we dedicate our action to the glory of God and we invite God to bless the moment, then the task we are performing truly becomes a moment of wonder and joy.

Reassurance Regarding Special Tasks

While the ordinary tasks of each day are always present, there are also special times in the life of congregations when we are called to unique projects or roles in the community. Here the challenge is not to find meaning, but to find the courage and energy to proceed. As with building the temple, no one questions the importance of these undertakings, but it is easy to feel inadequately prepared.

Thank goodness we have the same reassurance that David gave Solomon. In all that God calls us to do, no matter how huge the endeavor, we need not be afraid or dismayed, because God is with us (28:20). Generations later, the apostle Paul would put it this way: "Not that we are competent of ourselves to claim anything as coming from us; our competence is from God" (2 Corinthians 3:5).

If we review David and Solomon's story to this point, we can see four points of reassurance regarding our ability to take on the larger tasks to which God calls us.

(1) We don't have to be perfect for God to use our gifts. Time and again, the Bible shows us God working through imperfect people. David himself is an example. His early career has been interpreted by most biblical scholars as being a bit thuggish, he was a hothead (see 1 Samuel 25), and his dealings with Bathsheba and Uriah were far from godly (see 2 Samuel 11). In his later years, Solomon was not much better. First Kings 11:1-13 describes how he began to actively follow the gods of his foreign wives. If God can work through David and Solomon, surely God can work through us.

(2) God will not let our imperfections interfere with reaching the divine goal. God will keep working through us in spite of ourselves. Romans 8:28 captures this sense when it says, "We know that all things work together for good for those who love God, who are called according to his purpose." As long as we are sincerely seeking to serve God—and sometimes even when we are not!—God will work through us to achieve divine purposes.

(3) We each have gifts, and the community needs them all. The affirmation that all are

gifted has significant implications for the church and for how individual members perceive their roles within Christ's body. It serves as a challenge to each of us to seek God's gifts in ourselves and others, and it holds us all accountable for bringing those gifts to bear in God's service. We have no excuse on this front. God has given us gifts for the church, and God expects us to use them.

(4) It is in the whole community that we find all the gifts we need, not just in any one person.

Each of us stands in the midst of a community of people who are brothers and sisters, our family in Christ, who are also gifted in some way. Together as a whole, we can do the tasks God sets for us. This is part of God's grace at work. God tells us, in essence, "Only do what you can and that's enough—because if everyone does what he or she can, it will be more than enough." The evidence of this is in the ministries of the church itself, both large and small.

SHARING THE SCRIPTURE

Preparing Our Hearts

Meditate on this week's devotional reading, found in Psalm 132. Here we see a psalm concerning the divine right that David and his house have to be the rulers of God's people in Zion. Verses 11-12 specifically mention God's oath to David that one of his sons will be forever on his throne. Clearly, God has chosen David and his descendants for the specific task of leadership. What tasks has God called you to do? Are you doing them?

Pray that you and the adult learners will be alert for opportunities to accomplish significant tasks for God.

Preparing Our Minds

Study the background from 1 Chronicles 28:1-21 and lesson Scripture, verses 5-10, 20-21. Ponder how you know that the tasks you do are meaningful.

Write on newsprint:
❑ information for next week's lesson, found under "Continue the Journey."
❑ activities for further spiritual growth in "Continue the Journey."

Plan a brief lecture to introduce Bible information for "Hear David's Plan for His Son Solomon to Build the Temple."

LEADING THE CLASS

(1) Gather to Learn

❖ Welcome the class members and introduce any guests.

❖ Pray that the adults will be aware of God's call on their lives.

❖ Encourage the adults to talk with the class or in a small group about where they find meaning in the work they do. For some, meaning will be found within the context of their paid employment. Others will find meaning outside their jobs, perhaps as volunteers. Still others will find meaning as they work to raise children and/or care for other family members.

❖ Ask: **What criteria do you use to decide if a task is meaningful?**

❖ Read aloud today's focus statement: **People long to know that the tasks they do have meaning. How can we know our tasks are meaningful? David affirmed that God had chosen Solomon for a specific task, that of building a sanctuary for the worship of God.**

(2) Hear David's Plan for His Son Solomon to Build the Temple

❖ Use information from the Overview and verses 1, 2-8 in Understanding the Scripture to set the scene for the class.

❖ Choose a volunteer to read 1 Chronicles 28:5-8.

■ Invite the students to comment on the important points in this passage. Be sure they include these ideas.

• Solomon is seen here as the son of David who was chosen to sit on the throne.

• God promises to be a father to Solomon.

• God promises that Solomon's kingdom will be forever, but only if Solomon obeys God's laws.

• The Chronicler apparently believes that obedience is humanly possible (compare Deuteronomy 30:11-14).

• In verse 8, David addresses the assembled Israelite leaders and charges them to be obedient to God's commands so that they and their descendants might possess the land forever.

■ Encourage the students to envision themselves as the Israelite leaders. Invite them to say how they might receive these words from David concerning Solomon and concerning their own future. What questions might they want to raise with David?

❖ Select someone to read David's words to Solomon from 1 Chronicles 28:9-10, 20-21 and

■ Ask these questions.

(1) **What commands and warnings does David give to Solomon?**

(2) **What promises does David give to Solomon concerning God, based on his own experiences with God?**

(3) **What can Solomon expect from the leaders in terms of building the temple? (See verse 21.)**

■ Note the three points that David makes to Solomon by reading or retelling "Insights from David" in Interpreting the Scripture.

(3) Realize That God Calls the Learners to Accept Specific Responsibilities

❖ Retell or read aloud "What About the Ordinary?" in Interpreting the Scripture to help the learners see that they may be called to significant tasks, even though they are far more mundane than Solomon's mandate to rule a holy nation and build a temple.

❖ Brainstorm answers to this question: **What kinds of responsibilities are we as Christians called to shoulder?** List these ideas on newsprint. Note that they may be things that individuals can do, or they may be things that require teamwork and the use of everyone's talents.

❖ Look at the list with the class. Encourage them to talk candidly about how they see their congregation carrying out these responsibilities. Here are some questions you may want to raise.

(1) **How are our members using their God-given gifts to fulfill God's purposes?**

(2) **Approximately how many (or what percentage) of our church members are truly using their gifts?**

(3) **If we were all to use our gifts to fulfill God's purposes, how would our church be different?**

(4) Identify and Begin to Work on a Task That God Has Called the Learners to Do

❖ Lead the class in reading in unison today's key verse, 1 Chronicles 28:10.

❖ Distribute paper and pencils. Ask the adults to rewrite this key verse by deleting the words "build a house as the sanctuary" and adding words that describe a task they feel called to do. Be sure to give the students adequate time to reflect on this task.

❖ Invite each person to read the verse, as personalized, to the class or a small group.

❖ Prompt the class or group to respond after each person has read by stating how they may be able to help this individual to do the task. Perhaps the adults can even recommend someone else in the class or congregation who could be the "volunteer who has skill" (28:21) for this type of work.

❖ Conclude this portion of the lesson by reading the four points listed under "Reassurance Regarding Special Tasks" to bolster the confidence of the class as they take on tasks to which God has called them.

(5) Continue the Journey

❖ Pray that all who have come today will realize that just as God called Solomon to build the temple, God also calls them to fulfill specific tasks.

❖ Read aloud this preparation for next week's lesson. You may also want to post it on newsprint for the students to copy.

- **Title: Fulfillment of God's Promise**
- **Background Scripture: 2 Chronicles 6; Luke 24**
- **Lesson Scripture: 2 Chronicles 6:10, 12-17; Luke 24:44-49**
- **Focus of the Lesson: Promises are to be kept, but many never come to fulfillment. Whose promises can we trust? God is faithful in keeping promises, as Solomon recognized and declared to the Israelites, and as Jesus' resurrection demonstrated.**

❖ Challenge the students to complete one or more of these activities for further spiritual growth, which you will write on newsprint for the students to copy.

(1) **Write in your spiritual journal about an influential mentor in any area of your life. Why was this person so helpful to you? What difference did his or her mentoring make in your life?**

(2) **Think back to goals you had for your life when you were in high school or college. How have these goals changed? In what ways has God directed you that you may not have planned for yourself?**

(3) **Identify someone who clearly has been called by God for a specific task. This work may be in the church or may be in the home, the community, or elsewhere. Do what you can to encourage this individual and help him or her to be successful in this endeavor.**

❖ Sing or read aloud "Take My Life, and Let It Be."

❖ Conclude today's session by leading the class in this benediction, based on 2 Chronicles 34:31: **We renew our covenant to follow the LORD, keeping his commandments, with all our heart and all our soul, to perform the words of the covenant.**

UNIT 1: SIGNS OF GOD'S COVENANT

FULFILLMENT OF GOD'S PROMISE

PREVIEWING THE LESSON

Lesson Scripture: 2 Chronicles 6:10, 12-17; Luke 24:44-49
Background Scripture: 2 Chronicles 6; Luke 24
Key Verse: 2 Chronicles 6:10

Focus of the Lesson:
Promises are to be kept, but many never come to fulfillment. Whose promises can we trust? God is faithful in keeping promises, as Solomon recognized and declared to the Israelites, and as Jesus' resurrection demonstrated.

Goals for the Learners:
(1) to explore how the dedication of the temple and Jesus' death and resurrection fulfill God's promises.
(2) to recall promises that God has made and kept in their lives.
(3) to evaluate their dependability in making and keeping promises.

Supplies:
Bibles, newsprint and marker, paper and pencils, hymnals

READING THE SCRIPTURE

NRSV
2 Chronicles 6:10, 12-17

[10]Now the LORD has fulfilled his promise that he made; for I have succeeded my father David, and sit on the throne of Israel, as the LORD promised, and have built the house for the name of the LORD, the God of Israel.

[12]Then Solomon stood before the altar of the LORD in the presence of the whole assembly of Israel, and spread out his hands.

NIV
2 Chronicles 6:10, 12-17

[10]"The LORD has kept the promise he made. I have succeeded David my father and now I sit on the throne of Israel, just as the LORD promised, and I have built the temple for the Name of the LORD, the God of Israel."

[12]Then Solomon stood before the altar of the LORD in front of the whole assembly of Israel and spread out his hands. [13]Now he

[13]Solomon had made a bronze platform five cubits long, five cubits wide, and three cubits high, and had set it in the court; and he stood on it. Then he knelt on his knees in the presence of the whole assembly of Israel, and spread out his hands toward heaven. [14]He said, "O LORD, God of Israel, there is no God like you, in heaven or on earth, keeping covenant in steadfast love with your servants who walk before you with all their heart— [15]you who have kept for your servant, my father David, what you promised to him. Indeed, you promised with your mouth and this day have fulfilled with your hand. [16]Therefore, O LORD, God of Israel, keep for your servant, my father David, that which you promised him, saying, 'There shall never fail you a successor before me to sit on the throne of Israel, if only your children keep to their way, to walk in my law as you have walked before me.' [17]Therefore, O LORD, God of Israel, let your word be confirmed, which you promised to your servant David."

Luke 24:44-49

[44]Then he said to them, "These are my words that I spoke to you while I was still with you—that everything written about me in the law of Moses, the prophets, and the psalms must be fulfilled." [45]Then he opened their minds to understand the scriptures, [46]and he said to them, "Thus it is written, that the Messiah is to suffer and to rise from the dead on the third day, [47]and that repentance and forgiveness of sins is to be proclaimed in his name to all nations, beginning from Jerusalem. [48]You are witnesses of these things. [49]And see, I am sending upon you what my Father promised; so stay here in the city until you have been clothed with power from on high."

had made a bronze platform, five cubits long, five cubits wide and three cubits high, and had placed it in the center of the outer court. He stood on the platform and then knelt down before the whole assembly of Israel and spread out his hands toward heaven. [14]He said:

"O LORD, God of Israel, there is no God like you in heaven or on earth—you who keep your covenant of love with your servants who continue wholeheartedly in your way. [15]You have kept your promise to your servant David my father; with your mouth you have promised and with your hand you have fulfilled it—as it is today.

[16]"Now LORD, God of Israel, keep for your servant David my father the promises you made to him when you said, 'You shall never fail to have a man to sit before me on the throne of Israel, if only your sons are careful in all they do to walk before me according to my law, as you have done.' [17]And now, O LORD, God of Israel, let your word that you promised your servant David come true."

Luke 24:44-49

[44]He said to them, "This is what I told you while I was still with you: Everything must be fulfilled that is written about me in the Law of Moses, the Prophets and the Psalms."

[45]Then he opened their minds so they could understand the Scriptures. [46]He told them, "This is what is written: The Christ will suffer and rise from the dead on the third day, [47]and repentance and forgiveness of sins will be preached in his name to all nations, beginning at Jerusalem. [48]You are witnesses of these things. [49]I am going to send you what my Father has promised; but stay in the city until you have been clothed with power from on high."

UNDERSTANDING THE SCRIPTURE

Overview of 2 Chronicles 6. Second Chronicles 5–6 picks up the story of the now-completed temple. In chapter 5, Solomon assembled all the people for a joyous festival during which the ark was finally installed in the inner sanctuary of the temple, the holy of holies. The close of that chapter records that a cloud filled the temple and "the glory of the LORD filled the house of God" (5:14). This is the context for Solomon's address to the people and his prayer of dedication, which we read in chapter 6. For the most part, verses 1-40 are taken almost verbatim from 1 Kings 8:12-53. The only new material is found in 2 Chronicles 6:13 and 41-42. Note that this ending in verses 41-42, which quotes Psalm 132:8-10, focuses on David and the ark, whereas 1 Kings 8:51-53 is concerned with Moses and the exodus.

2 Chronicles 6:1-11. These verses record Solomon's address to the people. The opening line may seem a bit odd at first, because it describes God as living in "thick darkness." The reference is to the holy of holies, which had no windows. The only source of light came on the rare occasions when the door was opened to the outer sanctuary.

Going back to the exodus event, Solomon briefly retells the history of Israel in a way designed to highlight the divine selection of Jerusalem as God's special place and David as God's special ruler over the people. The king then states that this day marks the fulfillment of God's promise to David that Solomon would succeed him and build the temple. For his part, Solomon has fulfilled David's promises to God not only by building the temple but also by bringing the ark to rest in it.

2 Chronicles 6:12-42. These verses record Solomon's prayer of dedication. Standing before the altar, "in the presence of the whole assembly of Israel" (6:12), Solomon spreads his hands for the prayer. Verse 13 then adds two details not found 1 Kings 8. Here we read that the king was on a special bronze platform and that he knelt to pray. By the Chronicler's time only priests could stand on the floor directly before the altar to pray, and kneeling for prayer was considered an appropriate form of humility before God. Accordingly, most commentators think the historian introduced the platform and the body posture to make Solomon fit the piety of a later generation.

The prayer itself begins in verse 14. Solomon starts by praising God for mighty deeds of the past and asking that God fulfill the rest of the divine promise to David. The king then acknowledges that no place can contain God, so the prayer is that God will stay ever mindful of the temple and pay particular attention to the prayers directed there. In *First and Second Chronicles* in the Westminster Bible Companion series, Paul K. Hooker states:

> One comes to the Temple not to meet God—God can be and is met anywhere in the world over which God is sovereign Lord—but to offer prayer and worship, to seek God's mercy and forgiveness, and to avail oneself of the grace and goodness promised by God. . . . Above all else, the Temple is the place toward which the divine eye is always trained and the divine ear forever attentive, ready to hear the prayers of the penitent and worshipful, ready to forgive and restore.

Verses 22-31 and 34-39 concern the prayers of the Israelites: Solomon asks that God respond as appropriate to those prayers with justice, vindication, forgiveness, support, and/or redemption. As an interesting contrast, when Solomon turns in verses 32-33 to the prayers of foreigners, he merely asks that God grant whatever they ask, so that "all the peoples of the earth may know your name and fear you" (6:33).

The last two verses of this chapter are from Psalm 132:8-10. By putting the words of the psalm in Solomon's mouth, the Chronicler serves two purposes: He establishes Solomon as a devout follower of God, while at the same time reminding us that David is the more important figure. The phrase "anointed one" from the psalm here refers to the current king, Solomon.

Overview of Luke 24. This chapter of the Gospel contains Luke's account of the resurrection and post-resurrection appearances of Jesus.

Luke 24:1-12. The women who had followed Jesus from Galilee (see 23:55) come to the tomb on Sunday morning, bearing burial spices. At the empty tomb, "two men in dazzling clothes" (24:4) miraculously appear and announce that Jesus has risen. The women carry this news to the eleven and "all the rest" (24:9), but the group does not believe them. Peter alone goes to the tomb to see for himself, and he returns home amazed.

Luke 24:13-35. The risen Jesus appears to "two of them" (24:13) who were on their way home from Jerusalem to Emmaus. Along the way, he interprets the Scriptures that relate to the Messiah. They invite Jesus to dinner and then recognize him at last in the breaking and blessing of the bread. Jesus immediately vanishes, and the two return quickly to Jerusalem. Once there, they seek out "the eleven and their companions" (24:33) to share the good news that they had seen the risen Lord.

Luke 24:36-53. Jesus appears in the room with the assembled group and offers a blessing of peace. At first they believe him to be a ghost, but Jesus reassures them otherwise. He points to his hands and feet as a sign that he is truly the one who was crucified, and then invites them to touch him so they can see he is not a ghost. As a final sign that he is truly alive, Jesus eats a piece of fish.

Jesus then teaches the group so they can understand how Scripture has pointed to all that happened. He also asks them to stay in the city until God clothes them "with power from on high" (24:49). After this last speech, Jesus leads them from the city to Bethany, where he blesses them. During the blessing, he ascends into heaven. The group worships him and then returns in joy to Jerusalem, where "they were continually in the temple blessing God" (24:53).

INTERPRETING THE SCRIPTURE

Solomon's Prayer

Last week we looked at the instructions that David gave Solomon for building the temple. Now we skip ahead to the completion of the construction and Solomon's prayer at the dedication ceremony.

The core of Solomon's prayer is praise for God's steadfast love, especially as witnessed in the events that led to this moment. At the heart of 2 Chronicles 6:3-11 is an amazing affirmation of the Davidic line and of the temple itself. Since the exodus, God has not deigned to choose a city in which to dwell or a king through whom to rule—until now. The sense of election and purpose is unmistakable, as is the affirmation that God's promise has been kept so far.

Solomon then prays that God's promise will be kept in the future as well. Today, on Easter Sunday, we Christians celebrate that God did indeed keep the promise to David in the life, death, and resurrection of Jesus. Moreover, we celebrate God's permanent dwelling with us through the living Christ and through the "new temple" of ourselves.

God's Holy Dwelling Place

The Gospel of John says that in Jesus, "the Word was made flesh, and dwelt among us" (1:14, KJV). The Greek word translated "dwelt" here is literally "tabernacled." In the same way that God's glory and presence filled the tabernacle in the wilderness, making that tent the place where God truly dwelt among the people, so God was present in Jesus Christ. Later, John also describes Jesus' body as being the real temple in which God was present with the people (John 2:21).

This concept of Jesus as the dwelling place of God underlies the name Emmanuel, God-with-us. It was also part of what led to the charges against Jesus in Jerusalem: The religious leaders reacted to his claim that if the temple were destroyed he would raise it again in three days (Matthew 26:61; John 2:19). Specifically, Jesus is quoted as saying, "I will destroy this temple that is made with hands, and in three days I will build another, not made with hands" (Mark 14:58). There is no mistaking the contrast between the temple made by humans and the house made by God.

As Christians, we believe that we are set apart (or consecrated) as the body of Christ to be a designated place where God's presence comes into the world. We are God's temple, both as individuals (1 Corinthians 6:19) and as a community (2 Corinthians 6:16). Through our union with Christ, the writer of Ephesians says, "the whole structure is joined together and grows into a holy temple in the Lord; in whom you also are built together spiritually into a dwelling place for God" (Ephesians 2:21-22). What's more, we are "built upon the foundation of the apostles and prophets, with Christ Jesus himself as the cornerstone" (Ephesians 2:20). Christ is the one who holds the whole building together and makes it grow into a sacred temple dedicated to the Lord.

Living in Easter Hope

We have been raised with Christ. What, then, does it mean to live the resurrection life?

Our Scripture passages for today suggest at least two things. First is that believers are to trust what God has already done in Christ and trust that the rest of God's promises will come to fulfillment in due time. In the events of Easter morning, God showed the world an unmistakable blueprint for the future. Christ has been raised from the dead and placed over all creation to ensure that we will truly inherit the fullness of God's promises. Our discipleship takes place in this context of waiting for that day to arrive.

In the meantime, we affirm the astounding good news that by the power of God there is life and hope in the very place and time where we experience only death and hopelessness. An old cliché says that where there is life, there is also hope. Many have come to distrust that promise. There is simply too much evidence to the contrary. Neither a starving child locked into the cycle of poverty nor a wealthy person locked into a lonely and empty lifestyle would say that they have reason to hope merely because they are alive. Our world is filled with examples of life without hope. What is undeniably true from the perspective of the gospel is that *where there is hope in Christ, there is always life.* Hope for eternal life enlivens and invigorates life now. It gives purpose and direction for both the present and the future.

Thus we who believe today are heirs to the promise, and that is our hope. When tempted to despair or to become discouraged, we can persevere in the service of work and prayer and worship. We can be the ambassadors of hope to those whose lives appear hopeless. To the extent that we are able to communicate hope and a reason to trust God's promises, we become channels of life.

The Steadfast Spirit

Solomon's prayer celebrates God's faithfulness to the covenant promise, a faithfulness that grows out of God's own steadfast love. In a way, Jesus' parting words to the disciples echo that same theology. God has been faithful in fulfilling promises through the Messiah, and God will continue to be faithful in the days ahead. The proof of God's ongoing steadfast love is the gift of the Holy Spirit (Luke 24:49).

The risen Christ continues to speak to believers today in a myriad of ways—through the Scriptures, through the community of faith, through our relationships and experiences, even through the natural order of life. In these and other ways the Spirit guides us into further understanding of the life God wants us to live. This is the promise of Jesus himself (see John 14:15-17, 26).

The promises of Scripture are validated again and again by human experience. We see and hear reason to trust these promises in the lives of countless people who live with courage and confidence, despite difficult days and unhappy prospects. We see it in the faces of people who suffer illness or disability, and yet who are able to ask of themselves, "How do I meet this moment and these circumstances in faith and hope?" Ultimately we find the best reasons to trust God's promises in the lives of Easter people like the disciples and Mary Magdalene—and ourselves.

Luke closes his Gospel where Solomon's prayer begins—in the temple. We read in Luke 24:52-53 that the disciples "returned to Jerusalem with great joy; and they were continually in the temple blessing God." With those first disciples who witnessed the resurrected Christ, the church proclaims with inexpressible joy this Easter Day, "Jesus Christ is risen! Alleluia!" We also echo the words of Solomon from so long ago: "O LORD, God of Israel, there is no God like you, in heaven or on earth, keeping covenant in steadfast love with your servants who walk before you with all their heart. . . . Indeed, you promised with your mouth and this day have fulfilled with your hand" (2 Chronicles 6:14-15). Thanks be to God! Amen!

SHARING THE SCRIPTURE

Preparing Our Hearts

Meditate on this week's devotional reading, found in Psalm 135:1-5. The psalmist calls the servants of God to sing praise. He speaks about the greatness of the Lord, the Creator. As you read this psalm, meditate on how you perceive God to be great. For you, what characteristics make God the One who "is above all gods" (135:5)? Offer praise to God in word, song, art, or dance.

Pray that you and the adult learners will be continually aware of who our great God is.

Preparing Our Minds

Study the background from 2 Chronicles 6, Luke 24, and lesson Scripture for this Easter Sunday, 2 Chronicles 6:10, 12-17 and Luke 24:44-49. As you read, ask yourself: Whose promises can we trust?

Write on newsprint:
❑ information for next week's lesson, found under "Continue the Journey."
❑ activities for further spiritual growth in "Continue the Journey."

Be careful about timing the activities this Easter Sunday. Some class members may need to be excused for part of the session due to choir or other activities. The lesson focus is on the fulfillment of God's promises, but we are trying to meld together the promise concerning the temple and the promise that Jesus would be resurrected from the dead. Be intentional about including material from both 2 Chronicles 6 and Luke 24.

LEADING THE CLASS

(1) Gather to Learn

❖ Welcome the class members and introduce any guests.

❖ Pray that those who have come today will be led by God's Spirit to celebrate God's fulfilled promises.

❖ Read aloud this adage: **The big print giveth and the small print taketh away.**

❖ Talk with the students about promises that have been made to them, perhaps concerning products or services. Encourage them to cite examples from their own experience that support this adage or prove it false.

❖ Read aloud today's focus statement: **Promises are to be kept, but many never come to fulfillment. Whose promises can we trust? God is faithful in keeping promises, as Solomon recognized and declared to the Israelites, and as Jesus' resurrection demonstrated.**

(2) Explore How the Dedication of the Temple and Jesus' Death and Resurrection Fulfill God's Promises

❖ Select someone to read 2 Chronicles 6:12-17, which is part of Solomon's prayer as the temple is dedicated.

■ **Option:** Invite those who are able to make motions at appropriate places as the passage is read or reread:
- standing and spreading hands (6:12);
- kneeling for prayer and spreading hands (6:13);
- walking before God (6:14);
- opening mouth and raising hands with palms up (6:15);
- walking (6:16).

■ Discuss these questions.
  - **(1) What does Solomon say to and about God?**
  - **(2) What promises has God made to David?**

(3) Has God's promise been fulfilled? How do you know?

❖ Choose a volunteer to read Luke 24:44-49.

■ Put these verses in context for the class by noting verse 13: These events are occurring in the evening on Easter.

■ Ask the adults to envision themselves with the other disciples when the resurrected Christ suddenly appears and begins teaching. Ask: **What do you suppose Jesus might have said to the disciples in order to open their minds? What questions would you have wanted him to answer?**

❖ Read or retell "Solomon's Prayer" in Interpreting the Scripture to help the students relate a promise of 2 Chronicles 6 to its fulfillment in Christ Jesus.

❖ Read these words from "Living in Easter Hope" in Interpreting the Scripture: **Our Scripture passages for today suggest at least two things. First is that believers are to trust what God has already done in Christ and trust that the rest of God's promises will come to fulfillment in due time. . . . In the meantime, we affirm the astounding good news that by the power of God there is life and hope in the very place and time where we experience only death and hopelessness.** Invite the class to comment on these two points in light of their own relationship with God through Christ.

(3) Recall Promises That God Has Made and Kept in the Learners' Lives

❖ Distribute hymnals and ask the students to turn to "Standing on the Promises." Either sing or read this hymn together. Ask the students to consider the benefits, according to this song, of standing on divine promises.

❖ Post a sheet of newsprint. Invite the adults to call out favorite promises from the

Bible. Some learners may be able to quote the passage directly and even give chapter and verse. Others will just know the gist of the promise. Write whatever they can remember.

❖ Divide the class into small groups, keeping the newsprint in view. Suggest that the adults talk in their groups about how they have witnessed God as a keeper of the promises they have listed (and others). They may tell stories of God's work in their lives or the lives of others.

❖ Culminate this activity by asking the class this question: **Based on the biblical record and your own experience, what observations can you make concerning God as a promise-keeper?**

(4) Evaluate the Learners' Dependability in Making and Keeping Promises

❖ Distribute paper and pencils. Be sure to note that what the students write will remain confidential. Prompt them to list at least two promises they have made in recent months. If possible, one should be to a person and another to the church or another organization. Ask them to evaluate how well they have kept these promises. Perhaps they have completely fulfilled the promise; maybe they are taking steps to keep it; or maybe they have made no effort to address it.

❖ Suggest that the students now write or think about how they measure up as promise-keepers. What strengths can they rely on and build upon as they seek to fulfill new promises? What weaknesses need to be overcome?

❖ Close by suggesting that the students put their papers in their Bibles and refer to them often this week.

(5) Continue the Journey

❖ Pray that those who have come today will be filled with Easter hope as they recall how God has already kept promises and can be trusted to do so in the future.

❖ Read aloud this preparation for next week's lesson. You may also want to post it on newsprint for the students to copy.

- ■ **Title: Josiah Renews the Covenant**
- ■ **Background Scripture: 2 Chronicles 34**
- ■ **Lesson Scripture: 2 Chronicles 34:15, 18-19, 25-27, 29, 31-33**
- ■ **Focus of the Lesson: Broken covenants are difficult to restore. What does it take for relationships to be reestablished? Josiah was grieved by the people's broken covenant with God and in humility took steps to restore their relationship with God.**

❖ Challenge the students to complete one or more of these activities for further spiritual growth, which you will write on newsprint for the students to copy.

(1) **Talk with someone this week about how God fulfilled the promise to raise Christ up, and what his resurrection means for our lives.**

(2) **Take steps this week to fulfill a promise that you have made to someone. Notice how you feel about being true to your word. Also observe how the other person (or organization) responds to your faithfulness.**

(3) **Read the Gospel accounts from Matthew 28:1-15; Mark 16:1-11; Luke 24:1-12; and John 20:1-18. Note similarities and differences. Consider why each Gospel writer tells the story in his particular way. Ponder what this pivotal story says to you concerning God's willingness and ability to keep promises.**

❖ Sing or read aloud "Cristo Vive (Christ Is Risen)."

❖ Conclude today's session by leading the class in this benediction, based on 2 Chronicles 34:31: **We renew our covenant to follow the LORD, keeping his commandments, with all our heart and all our soul, to perform the words of the covenant.**

UNIT 1: SIGNS OF GOD'S COVENANT

JOSIAH RENEWS THE COVENANT

PREVIEWING THE LESSON

Lesson Scripture: 2 Chronicles 34:15, 18-19, 25-27, 29, 31-33
Background Scripture: 2 Chronicles 34
Key Verse: 2 Chronicles 34:31

Focus of the Lesson:
Broken covenants are difficult to restore. What does it take for relationships to be reestablished? Josiah was grieved by the people's broken covenant with God and in humility took steps to restore their relationship with God.

Goals for the Learners:
(1) to delve into the story of the recovery of a book of the law during temple renovations.
(2) to recognize that Scripture presents standards by which they measure their faithfulness to the covenant.
(3) to renew a commitment to God as a group.

Pronunciation Guide:
Amon (am' uhn)
Huldah (huhl' duh)
Manasseh (muh nas' uh)
Shaphan (shay' fuhn)

Hilkiah (hil ki' uh)
Josiah (joh si' uh)
Nebuchadnezzar (neb uh kuhd nez' uhr)
Tyre (tir)

Supplies:
Bibles, newsprint and marker, paper and pencils, hymnals, expendable pottery or china and glue, optional hammer

---

READING THE SCRIPTURE

NRSV
2 Chronicles 34:15, 18-19, 25-27, 29, 31-33
    [15]Hilkiah said to the secretary Shaphan, "I have found the book of the law in the house

NIV
2 Chronicles 34:15, 18-19, 25-27, 29, 31-33
    [15]Hilkiah said to Shaphan the secretary, "I have found the Book of the Law in the

of the LORD"; and Hilkiah gave the book to Shaphan. . . . [18]The secretary Shaphan informed the king, "The priest Hilkiah has given me a book." Shaphan then read it aloud to the king.

[19]When the king heard the words of the law he tore his clothes.

[25]Because they have forsaken me and have made offerings to other gods, so that they have provoked me to anger with all the works of their hands, my wrath will be poured out on this place and will not be quenched. [26]But as to the king of Judah, who sent you to inquire of the LORD, thus shall you say to him: Thus says the LORD, the God of Israel: Regarding the words that you have heard, [27]because your heart was penitent and you humbled yourself before God when you heard his words against this place and its inhabitants, and you have humbled yourself before me, and have torn your clothes and wept before me, I also have heard you, says the LORD.

[29]Then the king sent word and gathered together all the elders of Judah and Jerusalem. . . . **[31]The king stood in his place and made a covenant before the LORD, to follow the LORD, keeping his commandments, his decrees, and his statutes, with all his heart and all his soul, to perform the words of the covenant that were written in this book.** [32]Then he made all who were present in Jerusalem and in Benjamin pledge themselves to it. And the inhabitants of Jerusalem acted according to the covenant of God, the God of their ancestors. [33]Josiah took away all the abominations from all the territory that belonged to the people of Israel, and made all who were in Israel worship the LORD their God. All his days they did not turn away from following the LORD the God of their ancestors.

temple of the LORD." He gave it to Shaphan.

[18]Then Shaphan the secretary informed the king, "Hilkiah the priest has given me a book." And Shaphan read from it in the presence of the king.

[19]When the king heard the words of the Law, he tore his robes.

[25]" 'Because they have forsaken me and burned incense to other gods and provoked me to anger by all that their hands have made, my anger will be poured out on this place and will not be quenched.' [26]Tell the king of Judah, who sent you to inquire of the LORD, 'This is what the LORD, the God of Israel, says concerning the words you heard: [27]'Because your heart was responsive and you humbled yourself before God when you heard what he spoke against this place and its people, and because you humbled yourself before me and tore your robes and wept in my presence, I have heard you, declares the LORD.' "

[29]Then the king called together all the elders of Judah and Jerusalem. . . . **[31]The king stood by his pillar and renewed the covenant in the presence of the LORD—to follow the LORD and keep his commands, regulations and decrees with all his heart and all his soul, and to obey the words of the covenant written in this book.**

[32]Then he had everyone in Jerusalem and Benjamin pledge themselves to it; the people of Jerusalem did this in accordance with the covenant of God, the God of their fathers.

[33]Josiah removed all the detestable idols from all the territory belonging to the Israelites, and he had all who were present in Israel serve the LORD their God. As long as he lived, they did not fail to follow the LORD, the God of their fathers.

UNDERSTANDING THE SCRIPTURE

Overview. The Chronicler is near the end of his history, and for the first time in this study we enter the period of the divided kingdom. This chapter records the reign of Josiah, who is remembered as a great religious reformer in the southern kingdom of Judah (see also 2 Kings 22:1–23:30). For the Chronicler, however, Josiah was also notable for his reinstitution of the Passover, which is described in greater detail in 2 Chronicles 35:1-19 than in 2 Kings 23:21-23.

2 Chronicles 34:1-7. Josiah begins his thirty-one-year reign at the age of eight. The Chronicler is quick to note that he did what was right in God's eyes and "walked in the ways of his ancestor David" (34:2). Of all the kings of Judah before now, only Josiah's great-grandfather Hezekiah had been favorably compared to the ideal king, David (see 29:2). At sixteen, Josiah actively begins to seek after the God of David. According to the Chronicler, Josiah begins a sweeping religious reform at twenty (the age of legal responsibility) that includes the elimination of all idols and worship of other deities. Second Kings 23:4-20 says this reform took place after the finding of the book of the law (see below) in Josiah's "eighteenth year" (2 Kings 22:3).

2 Chronicles 34:8-13. Prior to Josiah's time, less diligent kings had allowed the temple to fall into ruin. In the eighteenth year of Josiah's rule, when he is twenty-six, the king orders repairs to begin. The work is to be financed from a collection that the priests took from the people. These verses record some of the detail of the work. As is common with the Chronicler, this section includes more information on the Levites and the musicians than does the parallel account in 2 Kings 22:3-7. Interestingly, the Chronicler also gives more credit to the help supplied by members of the former northern kingdom than does the author of 2 Kings (see 2 Chronicles 34:9).

2 Chronicles 34:14-18. This account of the finding of the book of the law closely follows its source, 2 Kings 22:8-10. While bringing out the collection money, the priest Hilkiah finds "the book of the law of the LORD given through Moses" (2 Chronicles 34:14). He gives the scroll to the secretary Shaphan, who then takes the scroll to the king and reads it to him.

It is unclear where and how this scroll actually was found. Was it in the collection box, stored with the money somewhere, or just lying amid the ruins of the temple? Or could there have been even more to the story? Many scholars suggest that perhaps the scroll's discovery was not much of an accident after all—that Hilkiah either possessed the scroll or knew where it was, and the priest finally felt the time was right under Josiah to make it public. As for the content of the scroll, most scholars think it contained one of the earliest forms of Deuteronomy.

2 Chronicles 34:19-21. Josiah's response to hearing the scroll is not a happy one. He tears his clothes in grief when he realizes how far the people have strayed from God's law and what the subsequent punishment will be. In the ancient Near East, tearing one's clothes was a common practice when responding to news of a death or other tragedy. Based on this reaction, it is possible that Josiah heard words similar to those found in Deuteronomy 6:13-17 and 28:15-24.

The king's next action is to appoint a group to check with a prophet (2 Chronicles 34:20-21). Josiah needs to know if the scroll is real and the words are valid. We know from other texts that it was not uncommon to "inquire of the LORD" through a prophet in emergencies (see 1 Kings 22:5, for example). For someone as devoted as Josiah, it is no less than we would expect.

2 Chronicles 34:22-28. Hilkiah and the others go to Huldah to seek an answer for the king. Their choice of prophet is significant because it affirms, along with other texts like Exodus 15:20 and Judges 4:4, that women were recognized and honored as prophets. Indeed, Huldah herself must have been remarkable at discerning the word of the Lord. There were many prophets in Jerusalem during Josiah's time, including Jeremiah (Jeremiah 1:1-2), yet it was Huldah whom the men sought out to answer the king's most urgent question.

Huldah validates the scroll as genuine and warns that the punishments mentioned there will come to pass. She also relays a message of divine grace to the king. Because of Josiah's faithfulness and penitence, God will keep peace in his lifetime and not bring disaster until after his death. The men return with this message to Josiah.

Huldah's words concerning Josiah did not come to pass. Rather than dying in peace, he fell in battle (35:24). This may raise questions for us about the nature of prophecy in biblical times. It helps to see that this was not the first time that the divine plan adapted as events unfolded. The prophet Jonah declared to the city of Nineveh that it would be destroyed in forty days (Jonah 3:4), yet God decided to spare the city after the inhabitants repented. Ezekiel once prophesied that Nebuchadnezzar would destroy Tyre (Ezekiel 26:1-7). When the Babylonian king was unable to defeat the city, Ezekiel then said that God would give him Egypt instead (29:17-20). Despite these instances, Hebrew tradition regarded both Jonah and Ezekiel as true prophets. Clearly the Chronicler thought of Huldah the same way.

2 Chronicles 34:29-33. In response to God's word, Josiah gathers at the temple all the leaders and "all the people both great and small" (34:30). The writer makes one small but consistent change in the list of those who were assembled: Where 2 Kings 23:2 includes "the prophets" on the list, the Chronicler replaces this with "the Levites."

After reading the scroll aloud to everyone, Josiah then makes a covenant to follow the laws it contains, and he has the people pledge to this as well. The rest of the verses record how the people kept this covenant as long as Josiah was alive.

INTERPRETING THE SCRIPTURE

Josiah and His Ancestors

Josiah's grandfather, King Manasseh, ruled for fifty-five years (2 Kings 21:1), longer than any previous king in Israel or Judah. Although his reign was peaceful, Manasseh is not remembered well because of certain religious and political decisions. He rebuilt altars to pagan gods, shed innocent blood, and courted an alliance with Assyria. As a result, biblical historians considered him to be one of the worst kings Judah ever had.

Manasseh was succeeded by his son Amon, who continued his father's foreign policies. The people were no longer tolerant of a pro-Assyrian policy, however, and members of Amon's own royal court assassinated him after only two years. These same insurgents were then killed, and the people put Amon's eight-year-old son Josiah on the throne.

Somehow, Josiah avoided the religious pitfalls and palace intrigues that had preceded his reign. As a teenager, he began a series of reforms and religious restorations that led to a critical discovery. During long-overdue temple repairs, a priest came forward with a scroll—"the book of the law" (2 Chronicles 34:15)—that he claimed to have found. The contents of this scroll changed everything.

The Words of the Book

What was this book of the law? A few scholars have suggested that it included portions of Exodus or some other ancient holiness code. Based on Josiah's subsequent reforms, however, most think the text contained a version of Deuteronomy, especially chapters 12–26, with some additions.

When we look at the specific reforms Josiah initiated, it is easy to see how far Israel had drifted from the relationship that God wanted them to have with the Holy One and with one another. Second Chronicles 34–35 and 2 Kings 22–23 outline some of the major areas of change that Josiah addressed. Among Josiah's efforts were reforms on topics discussed in Deuteronomy and related to:

- immediate cessation of all pagan worship practices and centralization of worship (Deuteronomy 7:1-6; 12:1–13:18; 17:2-7; 23:17-18).
- clean and unclean foods (14:3-21).
- tithing (14:22-29).
- debtors, the poor, and slaves (15:1-18).
- major religious festivals (16:1-17).
- duties of Israel's leaders (16:18–18:22).
- punishment for particular crimes (19:1-21).
- rules for waging war (20:1-20).
- marriage and sexual purity (22:13-30).

There were many other reforms as well, all of which relate to some portion of Deuteronomy.

The Call to Covenant

Josiah's first reaction on hearing the law was to despair. He recognized how greatly the people had strayed from a right relationship with God, and he knew that he was helpless to change their past. Somehow, however, he saw the hope of reestablishing a proper relationship within the very guidelines of the book itself. Josiah did not waste any time: He read the book to the people and their leaders, and then he invited them

to join him in renewing their covenant with God. It was a chance to start over, a chance to make things right with God and one another—and the people took it.

The call to covenant renewal forced the people to make the choice to change. In order to follow God with all our heart and with all our soul, we too may have to make changes in our lives. For most of us, the most difficult change is making time to reconnect with God on a regular basis—to be still and know that God is God. All too often we become swept up in the busyness and chaos of our lives. Sometimes, as with the folk in Judah, our spiritual lives get sidetracked until a crisis occurs. Then we stop and wonder how we could have gotten so far off balance. We find that we have lost our sense of who God is and, accordingly, who we are. This is when it is most important to stop and seek God.

The Call to Holiness

In many ways, Josiah's call to recommit to God and the covenant was a call to holiness. In Hebrew, the word we translate as "holy" literally means to be "separate" or "set apart." This provides a critical insight into the Hebrew understanding of the nature of God. The holy God is a God who is separate from everything else; God is set apart from the created world and all that is in it. This does not mean that God is not involved in the world—far from it! It does mean that God alone is totally righteous and pure, divinely sacred. Unlike any created being, God is "majestic in holiness, awesome in splendor, doing wonders" (Exodus 15:11). The proper response to God's majestic holiness can only be awe and wonder, mixed with a healthy amount of respect.

To the Hebrews, God's people were also considered holy, because they were separated unto God. Israel was not holy because of any virtue the people possessed or because it was impressive in any way (see

Deuteronomy 7:7). Rather, Israel's holiness was the result of God's loving action, and it was the expression of a covenant relationship with the holy God.

As God's chosen ones, the people of Israel were to demonstrate their holiness by being set apart from the rest of the world. They were not to worship other gods. They were not to follow foreign ways. In contrast to other people, they were to love God and neighbor without fail (Deuteronomy 6:5; Leviticus 19:18). Holiness began as a condition—being called into covenant relationship with God—but it was received through loving hearts. Holiness was lived out in faithful relationships with God and others.

The clearest example we have of holiness is in the person of Jesus Christ. Jesus shows us what holiness truly is. Every aspect of his life demonstrates God's divine holiness to us. When we look at Jesus, we see a model of human holiness as well.

Because Jesus is one with God, he is holy in his own right. The same cannot be said for the rest of humanity. Our sinful nature keeps us from being perfect. The New Testament agrees with the Old Testament:

We cannot be holy by our own power. What, then, are we to do?

The good news of the New Testament is that we do not need to do anything. God has already acted on our behalf. Jesus, through his holy life and sacrificial death, has done it all. Through the death and resurrection of Jesus, we have been restored to a right relationship with God, the cosmos, and one another. We have been reestablished into full partnership in the divine covenant through Christ's action on our behalf, and God now counts us as holy.

The book of the law showed Josiah and the people how grievously they had shattered the covenant. They immediately wondered what, if anything, they could do to restore that broken relationship. Happily, they found the answer in that same book.

We have found our answer in Jesus Christ, but that in turn leads to a new question. Given that God in Christ has done for us what we could not do for ourselves—that is, restore us to the covenant relationship in full—what will we do to keep that relationship intact?

SHARING THE SCRIPTURE

Preparing Our Hearts

Meditate on this week's devotional reading, found in Psalm 119:25-40. In verse 30, the psalmist writes, "I have chosen the way of faithfulness." To live faithfully, he seeks to know and enact God's word, to "enlarge [his] understanding" (119:32). How can the psalmist's words be a model for you as you seek to live in a covenantal relationship with God?

Pray that you and the adult learners will be so aware of your relationship with God that any estrangement will be immediately recognized so that the relationship can be restored.

Preparing Our Minds

Study the background, which includes all of 2 Chronicles 34, and lesson Scripture, verses 15, 18-19, 25-27, 29, 31-33. As you get ready to teach this lesson, ask yourself what it takes for broken relationships to be reestablished.

Write on newsprint:
❏ list of Josiah's reforms (and related Scripture passages) as found under "The Words of the Book" in Interpreting the Scripture.
❏ information for next week's lesson, found under "Continue the Journey."
❏ activities for further spiritual growth in "Continue the Journey."

Find a piece of pottery or china that can be broken during class. Also find glue that will put whatever you have broken back together again. Prior to class, place the object where all can see it, being sure to have paper under it and a hammer nearby.

LEADING THE CLASS

(1) Gather to Learn

❖ Welcome the class members and introduce any guests.

❖ Pray that those who have gathered will renew their relationship with one another and with God.

❖ Direct attention to the piece of pottery or china you have brought. Hold it up. Ask the class to comment on its appearance. Then, strike one blow with a hammer so that it breaks but does not shatter into too many pieces. (Be sure that you and the students are far enough away to prevent injury.)

❖ Ask for one or more volunteers to come forward and glue the object back together.

❖ Hold up the object (if possible) or invite the students to walk by it. Again, ask them to comment on its appearance. Encourage them to draw conclusions about restoring things to wholeness—to their "pre-broken" state.

❖ Read aloud today's focus statement: **Broken covenants are difficult to restore. What does it take for relationships to be reestablished? Josiah was grieved by the people's broken covenant with God and in humility took steps to restore their relationship with God.**

(2) Delve into the Story of the Recovery of a Book of the Law During Temple Renovations

❖ Help the class to understand why reforms were needed in the days of King Josiah (640–609 B.C.) by reading "Josiah and His Ancestors" from Interpreting the Scripture.

❖ Choose one or more volunteers to read 2 Chronicles 34:15, 18-19, 25-27, 29, 31-33.

❖ Ask these questions.

(1) What were the problems that Josiah identified after hearing words from "the book of the law" read? (Note that this "book" was likely a portion of Deuteronomy.)

(2) What steps did he take to bring about reforms?

(3) What do Josiah's actions reveal to you about the importance of leadership when it comes to making changes?

❖ Post the newsprint on which you have written the kinds of reforms that Josiah tried to make, along with the Scripture references from Deuteronomy.

❖ Divide into groups and assign each group at least one passage to read and discuss.

❖ Bring the class back together and ask a spokesperson for each group to comment on important findings.

(3) Recognize That Scripture Presents Standards by Which the Learners Measure Their Faithfulness to the Covenant

❖ Point out that the group has already investigated the scriptural standards that prompted Josiah to act.

❖ Work in the same groups (or different ones, if you choose) to have the students identify issues and Scripture passages from the Old or New Testament that state standards by which we are to live faithfully in covenant with God. Provide each group with newsprint and a marker to list their findings. (If they need help getting started, suggest Acts 2:43-47, which shows the covenant community of the New Testament in its earliest days, or 1 Peter 2, which speaks about how we are to live as chosen people and servants of God.)

❖ Call the class together again. Ask each group, in turn, to report on their findings.

Or, if you have space, post their newsprint sheets and encourage class members to mill around and read what each group has written.

❖ Talk with the class about what the church would look and act like if we truly "mended our fences" with God and neighbor and lived faithfully as covenant-keeping people.

(4) Renew a Commitment to God as a Group

❖ Invite the class to imagine that Josiah has come into their midst. Recall that the Israelites had been unfaithful to God and, therefore, Josiah's reforms were essentially a call to the community to recommit itself to holiness. Suppose Josiah were to come to your church (or denomination or community of faith in your nation). Ask: **What kinds of reforms might he call us to undertake? Why?**

❖ **Option:** If you think the class may need help in understanding the concept of "holiness," read or retell "The Call to Holiness" in Interpreting the Scripture and then ask the prior question.

❖ Talk with the class about how they might lead and/or participate in the reforms they have suggested. You may wish to distribute paper or pencils first and have the students jot down their ideas before you begin a discussion.

❖ Invite those students who are willing to commit themselves to being the holy people that God calls us to be to read in unison today's key verse, 2 Chronicles 34:31.

(5) Continue the Journey

❖ Pray that today's participants will continually renew their covenant to live as God's holy people.

❖ Read aloud this preparation for next week's lesson. You may also want to post it on newsprint for the students to copy.

■ **Title: Daniel Keeps Covenant in a Foreign Land**
■ **Background Scripture: Daniel 1**
■ **Lesson Scripture: Daniel 1:8-20**
■ **Focus of the Lesson: When persons are thrust into situations foreign to their values and convictions, they often face the pressure to conform. How can they keep true to who they are? Daniel and his friends offer examples of persistence in keeping true to their convictions while adapting to a foreign land.**

❖ Challenge the students to complete one or more of these activities for further spiritual growth, which you will write on newsprint for the students to copy.

(1) **Read Robert Frost's poem "Mending Wall." As you think about relationships in your own life that may need mending, consider who you are "walling in or walling out." What do you need to do to fix a relationship?**

(2) **Ponder your relationship with God. How would you rate it? How do you think God rates it? What evidence can you give to support these ratings? If you are not satisfied with them, what steps will you take to improve them?**

(3) **Go to someone from whom you have been estranged, regardless of who caused the rift. Do whatever is in your power to heal this breach.**

❖ Sing or read aloud "Let There Be Peace on Earth."

❖ Conclude today's session by leading the class in this benediction, based on 2 Chronicles 34:31: **We renew our covenant to follow the LORD, keeping his commandments, with all our heart and all our soul, to perform the words of the covenant.**

UNIT 2: THE COVENANT IN EXILE

DANIEL KEEPS COVENANT IN A FOREIGN LAND

PREVIEWING THE LESSON

Lesson Scripture: Daniel 1:8-20
Background Scripture: Daniel 1
Key Verse: Daniel 1:8

Focus of the Lesson:

When persons are thrust into situations foreign to their values and convictions, they often face the pressure to conform. How can they keep true to who they are? Daniel and his friends offer examples of persistence in keeping true to their convictions while adapting to a foreign land.

Goals for the Learners:

(1) to explore the pressures to conform that Daniel and his friends faced in the court of Babylonian King Nebuchadnezzar.
(2) to identify pressures to conform in different arenas of their lives.
(3) to stand firm under pressure and refuse to compromise cherished convictions.

Pronunciation Guide:

Azariah (az uh ri' uh)   Hananiah (han uh ni' uh)
Jehoiakim (ji hoi' uh kim)   Mishael (mish' ay uhl)
Nebuchadnezzar (neb uh kuhd nez' uhr) Shinar (shi' nahr)

Supplies:

Bibles, newsprint and marker, paper and pencils, hymnals

READING THE SCRIPTURE

NRSV
Daniel 1:8-20

8But Daniel resolved that he would not defile himself with the royal rations of food and wine; so he asked the palace master to allow him not to defile himself. 9Now

NIV
Daniel 1:8-20

8But Daniel resolved not to defile himself with the royal food and wine, and he asked the chief official for permission not to defile himself this way. 9Now God had

God allowed Daniel to receive favor and compassion from the palace master. [10]The palace master said to Daniel, "I am afraid of my lord the king; he has appointed your food and your drink. If he should see you in poorer condition than the other young men of your own age, you would endanger my head with the king." [11]Then Daniel asked the guard whom the palace master had appointed over Daniel, Hananiah, Mishael, and Azariah: [12]"Please test your servants for ten days. Let us be given vegetables to eat and water to drink. [13]You can then compare our appearance with the appearance of the young men who eat the royal rations, and deal with your servants according to what you observe." [14]So he agreed to this proposal and tested them for ten days. [15]At the end of ten days it was observed that they appeared better and fatter than all the young men who had been eating the royal rations. [16]So the guard continued to withdraw their royal rations and the wine they were to drink, and gave them vegetables. [17]To these four young men God gave knowledge and skill in every aspect of literature and wisdom; Daniel also had insight into all visions and dreams.

[18]At the end of the time that the king had set for them to be brought in, the palace master brought them into the presence of Nebuchadnezzar, [19]and the king spoke with them. And among them all, no one was found to compare with Daniel, Hananiah, Mishael, and Azariah; therefore they were stationed in the king's court. [20]In every matter of wisdom and understanding concerning which the king inquired of them, he found them ten times better than all the magicians and enchanters in his whole kingdom.

caused the official to show favor and sympathy to Daniel, [10]but the official told Daniel, "I am afraid of my lord the king, who has assigned your food and drink. Why should he see you looking worse than the other young men your age? The king would then have my head because of you."

[11]Daniel then said to the guard whom the chief official had appointed over Daniel, Hananiah, Mishael and Azariah, [12]"Please test your servants for ten days: Give us nothing but vegetables to eat and water to drink. [13]Then compare our appearance with that of the young men who eat the royal food, and treat your servants in accordance with what you see." [14]So he agreed to this and tested them for ten days.

[15]At the end of the ten days they looked healthier and better nourished than any of the young men who ate the royal food. [16]So the guard took away their choice food and the wine they were to drink and gave them vegetables instead.

[17]To these four young men God gave knowledge and understanding of all kinds of literature and learning. And Daniel could understand visions and dreams of all kinds.

[18]At the end of the time set by the king to bring them in, the chief official presented them to Nebuchadnezzar. [19]The king talked with them, and he found none equal to Daniel, Hananiah, Mishael and Azariah; so they entered the king's service. [20]In every matter of wisdom and understanding about which the king questioned them, he found them ten times better than all the magicians and enchanters in his whole kingdom.

UNDERSTANDING THE SCRIPTURE

Overview. The book of Daniel has some of the characteristics of wisdom literature. These writings attempt to show how following certain wise precepts ordained by God (and discernible by common sense) can help one prosper in the world. While wisdom writings often take the form of proverbs or parables, they also include certain longer prose forms. These "wisdom tales" usually recount the development of a young person in a foreign court who grows in wisdom under some form of testing—and subsequently rises to favor and power. Scholars frequently place the stories of Daniel and his friends in this genre, along with the stories of Joseph (Genesis 37–50) and Esther.

There is much more to the book of Daniel than a tie to wisdom literature, however. Like the New Testament book we call Revelation, Daniel also belongs to a type of literature known as "apocalyptic." The word "apocalypse" comes from the Greek word for "unveiling" or "revelation." Accordingly, apocalyptic writings use coded imagery and numerology to interpret current persecutions or traumas as "birth-pangs" that, when rightly understood, reveal the imminent approach of an end-time when a new divine order will hold sway. Thus, such works provide a sneak preview of a glorious age to come, a future in which all the wrongs of this world will be made right.

Apocalyptic literature first appeared around 300 B.C., with many Jewish and Christian apocalypses written between 300 B.C. and A.D. 200. It has several characteristics, including the following:

- belief that all will be judged in the future life, with each person receiving reward or punishment as he or she deserves.
- a belief in a cosmic struggle between Good and Evil, which Good will ultimately win.
- a belief in two creations: the current one, which is under Evil's domination, and the future new one, which represents a return to paradise-like conditions.

The goal of all apocalyptic writings is to encourage believers to hold fast during difficult times and to reassure them that better days lie ahead.

Many scholars speculate that the author of Daniel was a person of faith who wanted to lend strength to other Jews who were suffering under the severe persecutions of Antiochus Epiphanes (175–164 B.C.). To this end, he retold six traditional stories that would have been familiar to his audience. These tales are set in Babylon, and all of them take place just before or just after the Persian conquest. The stories show the pressure that foreign rulers placed on the Jews to abandon their religious practices and how God helped the Jews who remained faithful to triumph. To help encourage the intended readers, the author also added four visions designed to interpret the present persecutions and to affirm the coming of a future day when faithful Jews of the current crisis would celebrate an ultimate victory.

Daniel 1:1-2. The opening verses of the book establish the supposed historical setting. We are told that in the third year of the reign of King Jehoiakim of Judah (that is, 606 B.C.), King Nebuchadnezzar of Babylon besieged Jerusalem and subsequently carried off Jehoiakim and several of the temple vessels to Babylon. There is no other record of a siege on the city at this time, so this detail is probably a fiction invented to supply a context for the main part of the story. The name Nebuchadnezzar is a Hebraized version of Nabuchadrezzar, the name of the king who carried away captives and the temple treasure to Babylon in 597 B.C. (see 2 Kings 24:10-16). Babylon itself is called by the more ancient name Shinar in verse 2 (see also Genesis 10:10; Isaiah 11:11).

Daniel 1:3-7. The next few verses advance the story by rehearsing a common strategy employed by conquering nations in the ancient Near East. Kings took promising young men of royal and noble families to the foreign court for education and indoctrination into the ways of their new overlords. These young men were treated well and taught carefully, so that they would be very supportive of the conquering nation by the time they were old enough to achieve a position of power within their own political structure. To further their association with their new ruling country, the foreign king often gave the young men new names in his own tongue. This helped to mark them as citizens of his realm and not of the one in which they had been born. The entire process was a device that had been used with great success for hundreds of years. Note, however, that the narrative continues to call Daniel by his Hebrew name, representing his resistance to accept Babylonian ways.

In addition to this historical background, the author adds a new detail. In Daniel 1:4 we read a list of extraordinary criteria for the young men to be selected: handsome and without physical defect, well educated in the area of the wisdom tradition, insightful as well as knowledgeable, and competent to serve in a king's palace. This idealized description helps to introduce the four young men who will serve as our main characters before we even know their names.

Daniel 1:8-17. These verses record the determination of Daniel and his three friends to remain faithful to the laws of their religion. With the palace master's permission, they alone avoid the palace rations for a kosher diet. In addition, these verses also establish God's role in the events. God moves the palace master to have compassion for Daniel (1:9), and God graces the four young men with wisdom and knowledge (1:17). God even graces Daniel with "insight into all visions and dreams" (1:17). The "ten days" of the test may represent a literary device marking the time as significant because Hebrew theology considered ten to be a number of completeness and wholeness.

Daniel 1:18-21. Vindication for following God's law comes when the king recognizes the superior wisdom and knowledge of Daniel and his friends, which we know to be God-given, and stations them in the king's court. Indeed, the king finds them "ten times" (see above) wiser and more learned than any of the official sages, here called "magicians and enchanters." Daniel continues serving in the court until "the first year of King Cyrus" (538 B.C.), almost seventy years after the story begins.

INTERPRETING THE SCRIPTURE

Understanding the Book's Purpose

"The Covenant in Exile" serves as the guiding theme for these next four lessons, which are drawn from the book of Daniel. The first three lessons highlight the problems faced by a people trying to maintain their religious and cultural integrity in the midst of a foreign land, while the fourth contains a beautiful and heartfelt prayer of Daniel.

As you read through these stories from Daniel, keep in mind the circumstances under which the book likely was composed. Although the story is set in the period of the exile in Babylon, most scholars think it was written over 400 years later as a response to the Jewish persecutions under Antiochus IV (also called Antiochus Epiphanes). Every faithful act of Daniel and his friends, along with every miraculous rescue and reward from God, was meant to inspire a suffering Jewish population to stay true to their own covenant with God.

Life under Antiochus was tragic for faithful Jews. The emperor loved Greek culture with a passion, and he took on himself that same dream that had been Alexander the Great's: to spread Greek culture throughout the world. Like Alexander, Antiochus genuinely believed that Greek learning was superior to any other. The only way a people could be truly civilized was to embrace Greek art, manners, and academia.

One can see the problem. Antiochus wanted more than to expose other nations to the Greek language and lifestyle; he wanted the whole world to *become* Greek. To accomplish this, he had to stop people from pursuing their former practices, both secular and religious.

Not surprisingly, the Jews were a constant source of irritation to Antiochus. He became determined to force their conversion. Now it was not enough that they adopt Greek ways and speak the language. Antiochus decided to completely eradicate their religion, so he outlawed all Jewish practices. He destroyed the interior of the temple, rebuilt it with the trappings of Greek religion, and rededicated it to Zeus Olympios. He set up a statue in the temple and demanded that the Jews bow down to it as a god. He even sacrificed a pig on the temple's altar.

It is no wonder that the writer of Daniel was outraged and repulsed. He decided to fight Antiochus the only way he could: with words. So the writer presented Daniel and his friends as models of faithfulness. He wanted to show how Jews in the past also faced pressure to conform to a pagan culture and religion but chose to remain true instead. They counted on God's own faithfulness to them and they were not disappointed. One way or another, the writer wanted to say, God will deliver the faithful from persecution because—despite how it may seem—God remains sovereign over history.

Daniel's First Test

The story for this week comes from the first chapter of Daniel. Here we see Daniel, along with all the other special young men chosen to be groomed for service in the Babylonian king's court, offered food and wine from the king's own kitchens. Daniel and his three friends choose to follow the Jewish dietary laws instead, however, and they prosper as a result. In light of Antiochus's persecutions, Daniel's refusal of the royal rations becomes a symbol of allegiance to the Torah over the emperor's regulations.

As the chapter closes, God blesses the young men who held to their convictions—so much so that none can compare with them (1:19). Indeed, Nebuchadnezzar finds them "ten times better than all the magicians and enchanters in his whole kingdom" (1:20). To Daniel in particular God gives insight into visions and dreams (1:17), an ability that will be significant in chapter 2.

A Message for Us

As with Daniel and the exile (or the Jews under Antiochus), we sometimes feel swept into a situation for which we are not ready. When this change also involves grief or suffering, we can feel buried by a sense of helplessness and despair over our inability to control what's happening. At their worst, such circumstances can tempt us to look for comfort wherever we can find it—no matter how far that solution takes us from God.

Certainly that was the case for the Jews who suffered during the rule of Antiochus. They were still living in their homeland, but they lost the freedom to practice their religion. They saw sacred rites, ancient traditions, and treasured family customs all forbidden on pain of death. They must have been tempted to give up, to quit waiting on God to bring relief. After all, they only had to conform to the laws of the emperor, and they could have safe and prosperous lives.

The book's message to those persecuted people is also a message for us. In every generation, there are things that happen beyond our control. As long as the church lives in the world, there will always be the tension between how we do things and what others value. Nevertheless, like Daniel and his friends, we can choose how we will respond within the limits that are set for us. Like the Jews in the second century B.C., we can hold fast to the truth that, while we may not be in control, ultimately God is. The Lord of history is also the Lord of our lives, and the divine faithfulness to us demands an equally radical faithfulness in return.

The Challenge to Hold True

In many ways, Christians, like Daniel, are "aliens in a foreign land." In North America, we live in a post-Christian era: that is to say, our culture is no longer defined by Christian values. So we live in a world where secular values contradict biblical values, popular lifestyles devalue spirituality, and organized religion has no appeal to many. Certain cultural studies show that increasing numbers of people are unwilling to make commitments to organizations, especially those that take time or money. Congregations routinely accommodate the community calendar rather than compete with soccer practice or other secular demands. As the church, we find ourselves constantly challenged to maintain a

private world of faithfulness and love in the midst of an outer world of chaos and selfishness.

So how can we stay true to our role as the people of God? First, we have to recognize that choosing God over culture takes great courage—such as the courage to refuse the king's rations, knowing that such defiance could be punished by death. Courageously choosing God sometimes means admitting doubts. Sometimes it means questioning popular beliefs and cultural norms. Sometimes it means taking an unpopular stance. Always it means saying no to the things that "defile" us, and saying yes to God.

Moreover, Daniel shows us that our personal relationship with God must be the base on which we build our lives. Without that base, our careers, our lives, and our accumulated cultural honors and material wealth are meaningless. With that base, however, we are able—indeed, compelled—to live lives that reflect and magnify God's grace. We can remain focused on God, not on culture. With that base, we do not let the world distort our understanding of right and wrong, nor do we let the world dictate our priorities. With that base, like Daniel, we are able to live into God's promise of a transformed life—a life of being blessed and of blessing others.

SHARING THE SCRIPTURE

Preparing Our Hearts

Meditate on this week's devotional reading, found in Psalm 141:1-4. In this psalm, the writer prays to be preserved from evil. He wants God to help him guard his tongue, a theme found both in Old Testament wisdom literature and James 3. Verse 4 specifically mentions eating the "delicacies" of evildoers—a point that relates to today's lesson. Be aware this week of times when you are tempted to speak or

act in ways unbefitting a Christian. Ask God to keep you from such behaviors.

Pray that you and the adult learners will seek God and avoid evil.

Preparing Our Minds

Study the background from Daniel 1 and lesson Scripture, verses 8-20. Think about how you can remain true to who you are even when pressured to conform to foreign values.

Write on newsprint:

❑ information for next week's lesson, found under "Continue the Journey."

❑ activities for further spiritual growth in "Continue the Journey."

Plan a lecture of background material for "Explore the Pressures to Conform That Daniel and His Friends Faced in the Court of Babylonian King Nebuchadnezzar."

LEADING THE CLASS

(1) Gather to Learn

❖ Welcome the class members and introduce any guests.

❖ Pray that those who gather will listen for God's voice and follow it, despite other voices that try to drown it out.

❖ Remind the class of the cliché: **When in Rome, do as the Romans do.** Invite the students to talk, with the class or in groups, about what that means. Ask: **How should we respond in situations that challenge our convictions and urge us to act in ways that undermine our beliefs?**

❖ Read aloud today's focus statement: **When persons are thrust into situations foreign to their values and convictions, they often face the pressure to conform. How can they keep true to who they are? Daniel and his friends offer examples of persistence in keeping true to their convictions while adapting to a foreign land.** ✓

(2) Explore the Pressures to Conform That Daniel and His Friends Faced in the Court of Babylonian King Nebuchadnezzar

❖ Use information from "Overview" and verses 1-2 and 3-7 in Understanding the Scripture to introduce today's lesson in a lecture.

❖ Select someone to read Daniel 1:8-20.

❖ Work with the students to fill in this chart by identifying the problem Daniel faced, possible solutions, and the outcome.

Problem	Possible Solutions	Outcome
As part of their indoctrination into King Nebuchadnezzar's court, Daniel and his three friends were to eat royal rations.	(1) Daniel could have accepted the royal food. (2) Daniel could have gone on a hunger strike. (3) Daniel could suggest an alternative menu in keeping with his Jewish dietary code.	(1) Daniel chose the third solution and convinced the guard to allow a ten-day trial of food acceptable to the Jewish youth. (2) The guard agreed to Daniel's idea. (3) The king declared Daniel and his friends to be ten times better than the royal sages.

(3) Identify Pressures to Conform in Different Arenas of the Learners' Lives

❖ Read or retell "The Challenge to Hold True" from Interpreting the Scripture.

❖ Distribute paper and pencils. Invite the students to list pressures they experience to conform that are in conflict with their Christian beliefs and values.

❖ Divide into groups and ask the students to consider strategies they can use to hold fast to their beliefs rather than cave in to pressure.

❖ Bring the groups together and ask them to highlight helpful ideas that came out in the discussion.

(4) Stand Firm Under Pressure and Refuse to Compromise Cherished Convictions

❖ Read aloud this Jataka tale, abbreviated from the Buddhist tradition.

Once upon a time, a flock of quail were feeding in the grass at the edge of a meadow, scratching, and pecking for survival. A hunter came and trapped the quail. The hunter was also a merchant, so he put the quail into a cage. They tried to fly, but hit

the ceiling. They tried to peck, finding only hard wood. They lowered their heads and walked around the cage in a circle, crying, except for one bird who stood in a corner, her eyes fixed on a piece of sky.

The merchant came and stuck his arm down into the cage and felt the quail. "Too thin," he frowned, and threw seeds and grain down. The quail crowded, furiously pecking, pushing, each desperate to get their share. All but the one bird, who seemed to live on sky and sunlight.

Every day the merchant would come and reach his arm into the cage, frown, and throw more seeds down. Until one day the hunter said, "Ah ready for market." But then he spied the Blue Sky Bird. "What is this? All bones!" He reached for Blue Sky Bird, and pulled her out, opening his hand to examine her. Seizing the moment, Blue Sky Bird flew to the safety of a nearby branch, just out of reach.

The other quail looked up at her and cooed softly, "How?"

Blue Sky Bird cooed sadly back, "You ate your captor's food, and now you will die. I refused my captor's food, and now I am free." And away she flew.

❖ Discuss these questions.

(1) What common themes do you see in this story and today's lesson from Daniel?

(2) How can this story and Daniel's story be models for you in terms of standing fast in your convictions, especially when tempted to do otherwise?

❖ Provide quiet time for the students to reflect on these stories and affirm their own commitment to stand firm in their own convictions.

(5) Continue the Journey

❖ Break the silence by praying that all who have come today will resolve to stand firm in those Christian convictions that are essential for them.

❖ Read aloud this preparation for next week's lesson. You may also want to post it on newsprint for the students to copy.

■ **Title: Three Refuse to Break Covenant**

■ **Background Scripture: Daniel 3**

■ **Lesson Scripture: Daniel 3:10-13, 16-18, 21, 24-25**

■ **Focus of the Lesson: Many people are willing to take risks when they hold firm convictions. What is worth dying for? Three Hebrews held captive in King Nebuchadnezzar's court risked their lives by refusing to bow down and worship anything but the Lord God.**

❖ Challenge the students to complete one or more of these activities for further spiritual growth, which you will write on newsprint for the students to copy.

(1) Write in your spiritual journal about two convictions that are non-negotiable for you. Where do you find biblical support for these? How do you hold fast to these convictions in situations where others do not espouse them?

(2) Research the genre of apocalyptic literature. What attracts or repels you about this genre? How can it help you in your own spiritual journey?

(3) Encourage someone who feels pressured to follow the crowd to hold fast to his or her Christian convictions.

❖ Sing or read aloud "I Want a Principle Within."

❖ Conclude today's session by leading the class in this benediction, based on 2 Chronicles 34:31: **We renew our covenant to follow the LORD, keeping his commandments, with all our heart and all our soul, to perform the words of the covenant.**

UNIT 2: THE COVENANT IN EXILE
THREE REFUSE TO BREAK COVENANT

PREVIEWING THE LESSON

Lesson Scripture: Daniel 3:10-13, 16-18, 21, 24-25
Background Scripture: Daniel 3
Key Verses: Daniel 3:17-18

Focus of the Lesson:
Many people are willing to take risks when they hold firm convictions. What is worth dying for? Three Hebrews held captive in King Nebuchadnezzar's court risked their lives by refusing to bow down and worship anything but the Lord God.

Goals for the Learners:
(1) to examine the story of the three Hebrew captives who risked their lives rather than break their covenant with God.
(2) to analyze reasons why some people risk everything to remain true to their religious beliefs.
(3) to find ways to support those who are being persecuted for their faith.

Pronunciation Guide:
Abednego (uh bed' ni goh)   Chaldean (kal dee' uhn)
Dura (door' uh)   Meshach (mee' shak)
Nebuchadnezzar (neb uh kuhd nez' uhr)   Shadrach (shad' rak)
trigon (tri' gon)   xenophobia (ze ne fo' be a)

Supplies:
Bibles, newsprint and marker, paper and pencils, hymnals

READING THE SCRIPTURE

NRSV
Daniel 3:10-13, 16-18, 21, 24-25
10"You, O king, have made a decree, that everyone who hears the sound of the horn, pipe, lyre, trigon, harp, drum, and entire

NIV
Daniel 3:10-13, 16-18, 21, 24-25
10 "You have issued a decree, O king, that everyone who hears the sound of the horn, flute, zither, lyre, harp, pipes and all kinds of

musical ensemble, shall fall down and worship the golden statue, [11]and whoever does not fall down and worship shall be thrown into a furnace of blazing fire. [12]There are certain Jews whom you have appointed over the affairs of the province of Babylon: Shadrach, Meshach, and Abednego. These pay no heed to you, O King. They do not serve your gods and they do not worship the golden statue that you have set up."

[13]Then Nebuchadnezzar in furious rage commanded that Shadrach, Meshach, and Abednego be brought in; so they brought those men before the king.

[16]Shadrach, Meshach, and Abednego answered the king, "O Nebuchadnezzar, we have no need to present a defense to you in this matter. [17]**If our God whom we serve is able to deliver us from the furnace of blazing fire and out of your hand, O king, let him deliver us. [18]But if not, be it known to you, O king, that we will not serve your gods and we will not worship the golden statue that you have set up."**

[21]So the men were bound, still wearing their tunics, their trousers, their hats, and their other garments, and they were thrown into the furnace of blazing fire.

[24]Then King Nebuchadnezzar was astonished and rose up quickly. He said to his counselors, "Was it not three men that we threw bound into the fire?" They answered the king, "True, O king." [25]He replied, "But I see four men unbound, walking in the middle of the fire, and they are not hurt; and the fourth has the appearance of a god."

music must fall down and worship the image of gold, [11]and that whoever does not fall down and worship will be thrown into a blazing furnace. [12]But there are some Jews whom you have set over the affairs of the province of Babylon—Shadrach, Meshach and Abednego—who pay no attention to you, O king. They neither serve your gods nor worship the image of gold you have set up."

[13]Furious with rage, Nebuchadnezzar summoned Shadrach, Meshach and Abednego. So these men were brought before the king.

[16]Shadrach, Meshach and Abednego replied to the king, "O Nebuchadnezzar, we do not need to defend ourselves before you in this matter. [17]**If we are thrown into the blazing furnace, the God we serve is able to save us from it, and he will rescue us from your hand, O king. [18]But even if he does not, we want you to know, O king, that we will not serve your gods or worship the image of gold you have set up."**

[21]So these men, wearing their robes, trousers, turbans and other clothes, were bound and thrown into the blazing furnace.

[24]Then King Nebuchadnezzar leaped to his feet in amazement and asked his advisers, "Weren't there three men that we tied up and threw into the fire?"

They replied, "Certainly, O king."

[25]He said, "Look! I see four men walking around in the fire, unbound and unharmed, and the fourth looks like a son of the gods."

UNDERSTANDING THE SCRIPTURE

Overview. Daniel 3 tells the story of Shadrach, Meshach, and Abednego in the fiery furnace. The tale makes several points, all designed to bolster the author's audience in the midst of their own persecution. First, there is the affirmation that God has the power to deliver the faithful and sometimes chooses to work miracles on their behalf. Those moments are not to be taken for granted, however, nor is our faithfulness to be based on the expectation of such miracles. Second, God joins the faithful in their suffering, as symbolized by the fourth man in the furnace (3:25). Most of all, however, the story teaches that it is better to die as a martyr than to dishonor God by worshiping an idol.

Daniel 3:1-7. Nebuchadnezzar commissions the creation of a giant statue to be set up on the plain of Dura. The location of the plain is unknown, as is the exact design of the statue. The dimensions are sixty cubits by six cubits (3:1), which roughly translates to ninety feet tall and nine feet wide. The oddness of these dimensions has prompted scholars to propose that the "statue" actually describes an obelisk or a monolith carved at the top or perhaps a very tall pedestal with a statue at the top. Structures of all three types were common throughout the ancient Near East.

Verses 2-7 describe a ceremony of dedication, and certain features call to mind similar ceremonies related to the temple in Jerusalem (1 Kings 8; 2 Chronicles 7) and the wall of Jerusalem (Nehemiah 12). First, the king required officials from throughout the kingdom to attend so that all the people would be represented symbolically, regardless of nationality or language. In addition, the ceremony included choral music supported by wind instruments (horn and pipe), stringed instruments (lyre, trigon, and harp), and percussion (drum). Both details fit the traditional way that dedication ceremonies took place on a national level.

The story adds a unique twist to this ceremony, however—whoever does not comply with the king's command will be "thrown into a furnace of blazing fire" (3:6). While burning alive was used as a punishment in Old Testament times (see Genesis 38:24; Joshua 7:15), it was not a common feature at a dedication ceremony! The furnace in this case was a type of kiln common in the ancient Near East, with an opening in the side to allow the placing of objects and an opening in the top to allow for smoke ventilation.

Daniel 3:8-12. "Certain Chaldeans" (3:8) come forward to accuse the three Jewish

men of treason and sedition in refusing to bow down to the statue. They refer to the three as "certain Jews" (3:12), a parallelism of language that intentionally heightens our sense of tension between these two groups.

"Chaldean" can refer to the ethnic identity of the Babylonians (see Daniel 9:1; Jeremiah 24:5; 25:12; Ezekiel 1:3) or to the profession of divination as it was practiced in Babylon (Daniel 2:4-10; 4:7; 5:7). If the former meaning applies, then the accusation seems to stem from racism and/or xenophobia (a fear of strangers). Certainly there is some indication that while three men are singled out, the accusers are implicating all Jews in general. If the latter meaning is meant, then the accusation could well grow from professional jealousy and from anger that these three men received positions of honor while the accusers did not.

Of course, there is always the possibility that the writer intends the word to carry *both* the ethnic and the professional meanings, which would intensify the level of hatred and maliciousness being projected by the accusers. Lest we think this was a well-intentioned act of patriotism on their part, the writer uses a peculiar idiom in verse 8. Where the NRSV translates that the Chaldeans "denounced" the Jews, the literal sense is that they "ate pieces of" them. The viciousness of the attack is clear.

Daniel 3:13-15. The accusation is enough to send the king into a furious rage. On his command, the three men are brought before him. The king then insists that they make a choice: to bow down to the statue at the next sounding of the music or be thrown into the furnace. He ends his angry ultimatum with an intended rhetorical question: "Who is the god that will deliver you out of my hands?" (3:15). That question, as we will see, is the crux of the story.

Daniel 3:16-18. The three men do not hear the question as a satiric gibe that all salvation will be beyond them; rather, they hear it as a call to defend God—which they refuse to do on the basis that such a defense is irrelevant. God may save them or God may not, but that revelation can only come after their moment of decision. They must choose for or against God with no certainty, or even probability, of a miracle. This is the true measure of faith, that they do indeed choose God anyway.

Daniel 3:19-23. In anger at the men's defiance, the king orders the furnace heated seven times more than usual. The number seven is used here as a literary device to indicate "as much as possible." When the furnace is ready, the three men are bound and thrown in through the top opening with all their clothes on. (Normally victims of this kind of punishment were stripped before being fed to the fire.) The heat is so intense that those who toss them into the blaze are killed.

Daniel 3:24-30. Watching through the bottom opening of the furnace, the king sees four men, unbound and unhurt, walking around in the fire. The fourth man has the appearance of a god (literally, "a son of a god"). The king calls to Shadrach, Meshach, and Abednego and asks them to come out of the furnace, which they do. Now the extent of the miracle is apparent; not only are the men unharmed, but even their clothes were untouched—"and not even the smell of fire came from them" (3:27). In recognition of the power demonstrated by their God, the king promotes the three men and makes a decree guaranteeing their protection against future accusations or slander.

INTERPRETING THE SCRIPTURE

A Bit of Background

Daniel 3 provides the third of six stories told about Daniel and his friends, although this is the only story in which Daniel does not appear. The problem is straightforward: Nebuchadnezzar required everyone to worship a golden statue or die. The three young Hebrews had no intention of worshiping anyone—or anything—other than God.

The chapter before this one tells more about what happened to Daniel and his friends prior to this event. In Daniel 2, Daniel interprets a dream for Nebuchadnezzar when no one else can. The king is so amazed and grateful that he immediately falls on his face to "worship" Daniel. Then, in a move that foreshadows the future triumph of the Jews, the king promotes Daniel to a position of highest authority and, at Daniel's request, promotes his friends as well.

There is also a dark side to this story, however. While the king verbally gives credit to Daniel's God as "God of gods and Lord of kings and a revealer of mysteries" (2:47), the author intends for us to see him as a man of limited understanding and easy idolatry. The actions with which the king honors Daniel—bowing before him with face to the ground and commanding for him offerings of grain and incense—are all actions that one should reserve for a deity. The fact that the king is willing to treat Daniel as a god on this occasion sets us up for the events in chapter 3, in which the king demands that others worship a golden statue.

While the narrative does not describe the form of the statue with any precision, it does state several times that it was made of gold. Whether it was made completely of gold or only gold-plated is unclear—and also a bit irrelevant. What matters is that the king has spent a fortune of gold on a statue that is intended to serve as an idol. Perhaps the listeners to this text were supposed to hear an echo of another idol of gold that God's people were tempted to worship: the golden calf that Aaron made during the time of the Hebrews' wilderness wanderings (Exodus 32).

The Why and the How

The three faithful believers in this story quickly had to face the question of whether they were willing to die for their faith. Their situation, however, mirrored an important theological concept in Judaism—one that we see running throughout certain biblical historical books such as Deuteronomy and 1–2 Kings. This theology held that every human choice is one for God or one for death. The three men faced a physical death in the fiery furnace, but they also faced a spiritual death if they did not remain true to God. As models of faith, they proclaimed the latter to be an intolerable option.

Shadrach, Meshach, and Abednego found the courage to stay true to God despite the very real threat of a fiery death. Their story challenges us to ask both *why* and *how* they did so. *Why* is it that some people risk everything to remain true to their personal beliefs, and *how* do they find the inner resources to do so?

The answer to both questions must lie in the depth of their personal relationship with God. Somehow, when God is the center of our lives and we live in the constant awareness of the Holy One we worship, then our choices are driven by awe, gratitude, and a desire to honor God in all we say and do. Moreover, that same relationship fuels our commitment and gives us the power we need to act on the choices we know are right. As Christians, we do not need an angel to walk with us, as happened for the three men in the furnace, because we have Christ himself beside us.

What Is Worth Dying For?

Daniel was written to Jews in the early centuries before Christ who were going through a lot of persecution. It was intended to help them feel better and to hold on to their faith in the midst of mass persecution. Just a few generations later, letters like those of Peter and John would be written to give similar support to Christians undergoing persecution of their own.

The significance of this really came home to me a few years ago when my husband and I had the privilege of spending some time in Greece and Turkey. While we were in Turkey, we went to a central region called Cappadocia, where we visited one entire underground city. The city was many stories deep, sort of like a high-rise in reverse. We started on the top floor and worked our way down.

Although we were in a cave, we had the distinct feel of being in a town. We walked down city streets with doorways opening off to either side. The doorways themselves provided entry into individual homes with carved-out shelves, benches, and niches. There were places to put pots or oil lamps and spaces clearly designed to hold a bed. In almost every dwelling, a carved-out window looked onto the street so one could watch the neighbors pass by. After the residential levels, we came to the common area shared by the community as a whole. There was a common kitchen area, a winery, a stable, and a school.

This had been a whole city full of ten thousand people—and the reason they were underground is that they were Christians hiding from persecution. We got to walk through the underground city with electric lights and a lot of fresh air. The original inhabitants had enhanced the natural venting that was part of the cave system so they could breathe easily at all levels of the city, and we were very comfortable breathing air that came through their engineering skill. Large traces of smoke on the walls, however, attest that life was not always that pleasant underground. Most of the time the people lived there, they plugged the vents so that escaping smoke would not give away their location. They lived with light from oil lamps in the midst of greasy smoke that was rarely allowed to vent. No doubt it hung in the air, everywhere, coating everything they touched and dimming the little light there was. The smell would have been constant. They lived in the dark because that is the only way they could live. They raised their children there, educated them there, and taught them the faith there.

For the first time, it became real to me that people have died so that I might be a Christian. I know Christ died for me, but we do not talk a lot about those people from the early Christian church who, from generation to generation, really suffered and endured amazing things because of their faith in God and in Jesus Christ. It is because of them that we are here. We stand in that tradition of faith. They are the ones who teach us that the answer to the question for this lesson—What is worth dying for?—actually lies in the question of *who* is worth dying for. Their response? Why, the God who died for us, of course!

SHARING THE SCRIPTURE

Preparing Our Hearts

Meditate on this week's devotional reading, found in Psalm 121. Pilgrims on their way to Zion sang this song, which assured them of God's continuing protection. Try to memorize these eight short verses. Recite this psalm in situations where you feel uneasy or uncertain. Let this psalm remind you that at all times and in all places you can count on God to be your guard and guide.

Pray that you and the adult learners will hold fast to your faith, knowing that God can always be relied on to care for you.

Preparing Our Minds

Study the background from Daniel 3 and lesson Scripture, verses 10-13, 16-18, 21, 24-25. Consider what you are willing to risk dying for.

Write on newsprint:

❑ sentence for "Gather to Learn": I feel so passionately committed to . . . that I would be willing to risk my life for it.
❑ information for next week's lesson, found under "Continue the Journey."
❑ activities for further spiritual growth in "Continue the Journey."

Check the Internet or a library for illustrations of Shadrach, Meshach, and Abednego in the fiery furnace. Bring at least one picture to class. Many artists have worked with this subject, so you should have no difficulty in locating a picture.

Research the issue of persecution of Christians and bring some current examples to class. Check with your pastor to see if your denomination has any specific programs to support such persons. If so, find out whatever you can about these programs.

Prepare the suggested lecture to introduce "Examine the Story of the Three Hebrew Captives Who Risked Their Lives Rather Than Break Their Covenant with God."

LEADING THE CLASS

(1) Gather to Learn

❖ Welcome the class members and introduce any guests.
❖ Pray that the adults who have gathered will be strong in their faith.
❖ Post these words written on newsprint and ask the adults to call out ideas to complete the sentence: **I feel so passionately committed to . . . that I would be willing to risk my life for it.**

❖ Talk with the group about the kinds of things they have identified, perhaps family, nation, certain causes, particular ideas. Ask: **What criteria determine your willingness to die for a person, cause, or conviction?** List these ideas on newsprint.

❖ Read aloud today's focus statement: **Many people are willing to take risks when they hold firm convictions. What is worth dying for? Three Hebrews held captive in King Nebuchadnezzar's court risked their lives by refusing to bow down and worship anything but the Lord God.**

(2) Examine the Story of the Three Hebrew Captives Who Risked Their Lives Rather Than Break Their Covenant with God

❖ Introduce today's lesson with a brief lecture on background from the Overview and Daniel 3:1-7 in Understanding the Scripture and "A Bit of Background" in Interpreting the Scripture.

❖ Select one or more volunteers to read Daniel 3:10-13, 16-18, 21, 24-25.

❖ Read the first and second paragraph of "The Why and the How" from Interpreting the Scripture. Allow time for the students to answer the questions at the end of the second paragraph. Read the third paragraph as a conclusion.

❖ Show the picture(s) you have brought of the three men in the fiery furnace. Invite the adults to comment on how the artist views this scene. How are the men depicted? What emotions do they seem to be feeling? What about the emotions of the other characters who are shown?

❖ Encourage the class to read in unison the key verses from Daniel 3:17-18 and discuss these questions.

    (1) What does the three men's comment to the king, who held power of life and death, reveal about their relationship with God?

    (2) How is this relationship different from that of people who give up when God does not act in ways they want God to act?

    (3) How can Shadrach, Meshach, and Abednego serve as role models for us?

(3) Analyze Reasons Why Some People Risk Everything to Remain True to Their Religious Beliefs

❖ Read aloud "What Is Worth Dying For?" in Interpreting the Scripture. Ask the students to close their eyes and imagine themselves in this underground city. Encourage the students to talk about what they see, hear, taste, touch, and smell here.

❖ Read aloud this summary of a news article concerning a brutal attack on Christians in Vietnam: **Christians in Vietnam appear to be facing increasing persecution. In May 2006, the home and adjacent chapel of Mennonite Pastor Nguyen Hong Quang was attacked by security forces of the Vietnamese government. Pastor Quang, known as a voice for human and religious rights, was "badly beaten" and some church members were seriously injured after being pushed to a concrete floor from a height of about sixteen feet. Others, including infants, were clubbed with nightsticks or electric cattle prods. The reason for the raid, according to authorities, was that the church construction exceeded the bounds of a building permit, but Christians believe that the animosity of local officials toward the church precipitated the assault. By the time the violence ended, Pastor Quang's church and home had been completely destroyed. He plans to bring a lawsuit against the Vietnamese government before an international court.**

❖ Discuss these questions.

    (1) Pastor Quang is quoted as saying "I vow to fight back and die right here." Given what has happened to him and members of his church, what do you believe motivates him to take such a strong stand?

(2) Suppose you had been Pastor Quang or a church member injured in this attack. What would your attitude be toward your persecutors? Why? How will this attitude bolster the cause of Christ?

(4) Find Ways to Support Those Who Are Being Persecuted for Their Faith

❖ Present to the class any information you have found about people around the globe who are currently being persecuted for their faith.

❖ Brainstorm with the class ways that they can support people who are being persecuted for their faith. Some ways include prayer, financial support through appropriate agencies, inviting spokespeople to address your church on this issue and to name ways you can help.

❖ Conclude the session by reading aloud Matthew 5:10-11 as a reminder that those who are persecuted are cared for by God, just as Shadrach, Meshach, and Abednego were.

(5) Continue the Journey

❖ Pray that today's participants will hold fast to their own faith and help others who are being persecuted for the sake of Jesus Christ.

❖ Read aloud this preparation for next week's lesson. You may also want to post it on newsprint for the students to copy.
   ■ Title: Daniel's Life-and-Death Test
   ■ Background Scripture: Daniel 6
   ■ Lesson Scripture: Daniel 6:4-7, 10, 16, 19, 21, 25-26

■ Focus of the Lesson: People may be tempted to compromise their convictions in seemingly small ways. What does it matter if you compromise your convictions? When the order was made not to pray to anyone but the king for thirty days, Daniel refused to quit his three daily times of prayer to God or to hide his actions.

❖ Challenge the students to complete one or more of these activities for further spiritual growth, which you will write on newsprint for the students to copy.
   (1) Research current persecution of Christians around the world. Try to discern why Christians are being persecuted. Consider action that you can take to help those who face harassment.
   (2) Recall that the three Hebrew friends refused to worship the golden statue because they knew who they were and Whose they were. Make a list of characteristics that identify you as a Christian. Which traits enable you to defend your faith, to death if necessary?
   (3) Encourage your church to take risks, perhaps by undertaking new, cutting-edge projects, so as to draw others to Christ.

❖ Sing or read aloud "Stand By Me."

❖ Conclude today's session by leading the class in this benediction, based on 2 Chronicles 34:31: We renew our covenant to follow the LORD, keeping his commandments, with all our heart and all our soul, to perform the words of the covenant.

UNIT 2: THE COVENANT IN EXILE
DANIEL'S LIFE-AND-DEATH TEST

PREVIEWING THE LESSON

Lesson Scripture: Daniel 6:4-7, 10, 16, 19, 21, 25-26
Background Scripture: Daniel 6
Key Verse: Daniel 6:10

Focus of the Lesson:
People may be tempted to compromise their convictions in seemingly small ways. What does it matter if you compromise your convictions? When the order was made not to pray to anyone but the king for thirty days, Daniel refused to quit his three daily times of prayer to God or to hide his actions.

Goals for the Learners:
(1) to survey the events leading up to and following Daniel's night in the lions' den.
(2) to recognize that prayer empowers people to withstand challenges to their faith.
(3) to make a commitment to include prayer and other spiritual disciplines as a regular part of life.

Pronunciation Guide:
Aramaic (air uh may' ik)   Belshazzar (bel shaz' uhr)
Darius (dah ri' uhs)   satrap (say' trap)

Supplies:
Bibles, newsprint and marker, paper and pencils, hymnals

READING THE SCRIPTURE

NRSV
Daniel 6:4-7, 10, 16, 19, 21, 25-26

⁴So the presidents and the satraps tried to find grounds for complaint against Daniel in connection with the kingdom. But they could find no grounds for complaint or any corruption, because he was faithful, and no

NIV
Daniel 6:4-7, 10, 16, 19, 21, 25-26

⁴At this, the administrators and the satraps tried to find grounds for charges against Daniel in his conduct of government affairs, but they were unable to do so. They could find no corruption in him, because he

negligence or corruption could be found in him. [5]The men said, "We shall not find any ground for complaint against this Daniel unless we find it in connection with the law of his God."

[6]So the presidents and satraps conspired and came to the king and said to him, "O King Darius, live forever! [7]All the presidents of the kingdom, the prefects and the satraps, the counselors and the governors are agreed that the king should establish an ordinance and enforce an interdict, that whoever prays to anyone, divine or human, for thirty days, except to you, O king, shall be thrown into a den of lions."

[10]**Although Daniel knew that the document had been signed, he continued to go to his house, which had windows in its upper room open toward Jerusalem, and to get down on his knees three times a day to pray to his God and praise him, just as he had done previously.**

[16]Then the king gave the command, and Daniel was brought and thrown into the den of lions. The king said to Daniel, "May your God, whom you faithfully serve, deliver you!"

[19]Then, at break of day, the king got up and hurried to the den of lions. . . . [21]Daniel then said to the king, "O king, live forever!"

[25]Then King Darius wrote to all peoples and nations of every language throughout the whole world: "May you have abundant prosperity! [26]I make a decree, that in all my royal dominion people should tremble and fear before the God of Daniel:

For he is the living God,
enduring forever."

was trustworthy and neither corrupt nor negligent. [5]Finally these men said, "We will never find any basis for charges against this man Daniel unless it has something to do with the law of his God."

[6]So the administrators and the satraps went as a group to the king and said: "O King Darius, live forever! [7]The royal administrators, prefects, satraps, advisers and governors have all agreed that the king should issue an edict and enforce the decree that anyone who prays to any god or man during the next thirty days, except to you, O king, shall be thrown into the lions' den."

[10]**Now when Daniel learned that the decree had been published, he went home to his upstairs room where the windows opened toward Jerusalem. Three times a day he got down on his knees and prayed, giving thanks to his God, just as he had done before.**

[16]So the king gave the order, and they brought Daniel and threw him into the lions' den. The king said to Daniel, "May your God, whom you serve continually, rescue you!"

[19]At the first light of dawn, the king got up and hurried to the lions' den.

[21]Daniel answered, "O king, live forever!"

[25]Then King Darius wrote to all the peoples, nations and men of every language throughout the land:

"May you prosper greatly!

[26]"I issue a decree that in every part of my kingdom people must fear and reverence the God of Daniel.

"For he is the living God
and he endures forever."

UNDERSTANDING THE SCRIPTURE

Overview. Daniel 5 records the account of Daniel's translation and interpretation of writing on the wall that mysteriously appears at a feast hosted by King Belshazzar. The chapter ends with Belshazzar's death, the fall of the Neo-Babylonian empire and the rise of the Medes, and by the end of chapter 6, the Persians have appeared.

As we will quickly see, however, the

change in ruling empire does not change much for the people of faith. There are new challenges that arise from edicts of the new king and new tests of faith to be met. Thus we have the groundwork for the account of Daniel in the lions' den.

One additional thing to note: Starting with Daniel 2:4b and going through 7:28, the text is written not in Hebrew but in Aramaic. Scholars speculate that this entire block of text represents an earlier collection of stories that circulated independently and was written down in the late fourth or early third centuries B.C. The Scripture readings for this lesson and the one before both come from the Aramaic section of Daniel.

Daniel 6:1-5. While these verses reflect some of the organizational structure of the Persian Empire, much seems to be a fictional creation. The Persian government did use satraps (literally, "protectors of the kingdom" or "protectors of kingship") to oversee designated regions, but the number given in the first verse—120—is exaggerated. In addition, there is no record of any triumvirate of presidents (literally, "heads") within the Persian governmental structure.

There is also some question as to the identity of the king. History records no "Darius the Mede" (5:31), although there were three Persian kings named Darius. None of these overthrew the Neo-Babylonian Empire, however—that was done by Cyrus of Persia. The only hint of a historical connection lies in the age of Darius mentioned in 5:31. One of Cyrus's generals, Gobyras, was about sixty-two at the time of the Babylonian conquest. Nevertheless, the writer clearly thinks of this Darius as preceding Cyrus (see 6:28).

Daniel 6:6-9. The NRSV says that the presidents and satraps "conspired and came" to the king (6:6). The two verbs in English translate a single Aramaic verb that implies both "acting together" and "agitating." The intent is to show that the men all committed to the common cause of agitating the king against Daniel, although this agenda was hidden

from the king himself. Once the law was in place, their plan could proceed because not even the king could change it at that point. For other examples of irrevocable Persian laws, see Esther 1:19 and 8:8.

Daniel 6:10-13. People familiar with the Hebrew Scriptures would know that there was no set time of day to pray nor set number of prayers to be made. Some prayed at morning and at night (1 Chronicles 23:30), some prayed seven times a day (Psalm 119:164), and others followed other patterns. In addition, there was no set prayer posture. One could stand (1 Samuel 1:26; 1 Kings 8:22; Psalm 106:30), kneel (1 Kings 8:54; 2 Chronicles 6:13; Ezra 9:5), or lie prostrate (Numbers 16:45; Joshua 7:6; 1 Kings 18:42). Rather than being tempted to use this lack of specificity regarding prayer as an "out" to change his patterns and become inconspicuous in his devotion, however, Daniel chooses to stick to his private routine—and thereby make a public statement about his loyalty to God.

Daniel 6:14-15. When the king hears of the charge against Daniel, he is very distressed. This might be because he simply does not want to lose Daniel, or it may also indicate that he realized he had been duped. In any event, the king tried desperately until sunset to save Daniel. Given that each day started at sunset in the Near Eastern culture, this is the equivalent of saying that a modern-day king worked up to the last moment of a scheduled dawn execution.

Daniel 6:16-18. At the king's reluctant command, Daniel is thrown down into a pit with lions. The king leaves Daniel with words that show his bitter awareness of his own limited power in this situation: "May your God . . . deliver you!" (6:16). This is no statement of wishful hope, however; the verb form in Aramaic indicates action that *must* or *will* happen.

Daniel 6:19-24. Despite a sleepless night of fasting, the king maintains some hope that Daniel still lives. Thus he calls out to Daniel as he approaches the pit. Daniel is indeed alive, thanks to the intervention of an angel sent by God. The irony implicit in the language is intentional: A stone shut the mouth of the pit to guarantee Daniel's death, yet an angel shut the mouths of the lions to guarantee his life; no harm came to Daniel because he had done no harm himself.

Then comes a much harsher scene. Those who accused Daniel, along with their wives and children, are thrown into the pit and are mauled before they even hit the ground. Some scholars debate whether the number of families was 122 (the presidents plus 120 satraps) or two (the presidents only), citing that a pit big enough for the former is pretty unrealistic. Others challenge us to look beyond these details, saying that revenge is not really the issue. John Calvin and others maintain that the point is to remove any

doubt concerning God's miracle. Lest we think Daniel was spared because the lions were not hungry, we see instead that they were starved enough to attack a massive amount of people while their bodies were still in the air.

Daniel 6:25-28. On the basis of a higher power—God's—Darius is now able to reverse the decree that he as king was unable to change. Instead of demanding worship of himself, he calls on the whole world to worship Daniel's God. In a nice linguistic touch that ties the story together, the word used to say that God's kingdom shall never be "destroyed" (6:26) is from the same root as the word used to say that Daniel received no "hurt" (6:22) or "harm" (6:23) from the lions. The account ends with Daniel's prosperity throughout Darius's reign and that of Cyrus the Persian.

INTERPRETING THE SCRIPTURE

Faithful God; Faithful Response

Like the story of the three men in the fiery furnace, the tale of Daniel in the lions' den affirms that the God to whom we are to be faithful is a God of wondrous power. There are many other similarities between the two stories as well:

- an accusation that arises from racism, xenophobia (fear of strangers), and/or professional jealousy.
- a king's decree that runs counter to faithful action.
- a death sentence that is invoked when faithful people refuse to follow the decree.
- a symbol of the divine presence in the midst of the punishment.
- a miraculous rescue of the faithful.
- the king's subsequent acknowledgement of the power of God.
- a new decree that honors the Jewish faith.

- and a promotion and protection for the faithful who refused the initial decree.

Of course, there are also several differences. The stories take place in two different eras under two different kings. The faithful resistance in the first account is a public one conducted by three men, while the second account concerns a private action performed by Daniel alone. In this way, the stories supplement and complement one another. They make the point that, while the details of the circumstances may vary from age to age, there is still a single call to faithful action that challenges God's people—and one single, constant, faithful God to whom we owe all our allegiance.

What Daniel Did

The chapter begins with Darius's political restructuring of the kingdom. Daniel is one of three presidents to whom the 120 satraps report, but his "excellent spirit" (6:3) soon leads the king to consider appointing Daniel to a solo position over the entire kingdom. This inevitably leads to jealousy on the part of the other presidents and the satraps, so they conspire to ruin him. Daniel's lifestyle and political dealings are so pure, however, that "they could find no grounds for complaint or any corruption" (6:4). It is at this moment that Daniel's enemies realize the only way to trap him is through his allegiance to God's law.

The rest of this passage reveals the presidents and satraps as undesirable citizens and unworthy leaders by the way they manipulate the king. They lie to him by saying that all government officials support this plan; they tell him what to do; and they even dictate the terms of the punishment for non-compliance. The unsavory nature of their characters is augmented as we see that they are not only jealous men willing to set up a rival's death but also disrespectful courtiers who see their king only as a tool to be used.

Although Daniel is aware of the law, he chooses not to change his behavior or to hide his prayers to God. He continues to pray at the same time every day, in a manner that makes his actions unmistakable, in a part of his house where he can be watched from the outside. This is the heart of Daniel's faithfulness: He does not deviate from his practice, even though Scripture itself would allow it, because that would be offering less than his full allegiance to God. If he let fear of punishment drive him to hide his prayers, even if those prayers were regularly performed, he would no longer be faithful.

Daniel is arrested and charged with ignoring the king's command. His execution is set for the following morning, when he is thrown into a pit with lions. After a stone is placed to cover the mouth of the pit, both the king and "his lords" (6:17) seal it in wax with their signet rings. The distrust of both sides is now in the open—the king wants to ensure that the officials do not

come back to guarantee Daniel's death, and the officials want to make sure that the king does not engineer a rescue. From a theological standpoint, this detail also underscores that any action taken to save Daniel will be God's, because the possibility of human intervention has been eliminated.

What Daniel Didn't Do

Clearly, Daniel did not compromise his values. This simple fact brings up the question of whether compromise matters. Would it really have hurt anything for Daniel to have prayed in secret? In fact, couldn't he do more good for God and for God's people if he stayed in a position of power and influence? Wasn't his faithfulness a bit extreme?

While these questions may have appeal from a human perspective, the text implies that they are all dangerous in God's view. Daniel's devotion to his prayer schedule was actually devotion to God. In the same way that his three friends chose death by fire to a betrayal of God, so Daniel would rather face the lion pit than dishonor his Lord even a little.

Daniel knew that our choices have consequences. When we choose to compromise spiritually, we risk our religious integrity. Every day we face the challenge anew. Will we put honoring God above all else (risking persecution at the world's hands), or will we do whatever it takes to get along (risking spiritual corruption)? The answer matters.

Strength Through Prayer

How did Daniel find the strength and courage to withstand this challenge to his faith? The answer probably lies in the very spiritual discipline that convicted him.

Today's passage provides a wonderful incentive for us to develop the spiritual discipline of prayer ourselves. If you do not have the time to pray formally at length each day, consider making a habit of breath prayers. These simple prayers allow us to connect with God no matter where we are or what we're doing. In a breath prayer, we pray to the rhythm of our own slowed breathing. The first line of the prayer is said (or thought) as you slowly breathe in, and the second line is said as you slowly breathe out.

Breath prayers can be verses from Scripture, hymns, poems, or whatever lifts your spirits. From the hymn "Spirit of the Living God," here is one example:

Line one: Spirit of the living God,
Line two: Fall afresh on me.

A lifetime of prayer helped to shape Daniel into the person he became. Just as his diet of food helped him stay true to God when he was younger (Daniel 1), a regular "diet" of prayer helped him to remain faithful under far more difficult circumstances now. Even more, his time of prayer was actually a time of preparation. Through it, he was able to withstand anything that the world threw his way.

This can—and should—be true for us as well. After all, as Christians, we pray in the name of Jesus Christ himself, who said, "If in my name you ask me for anything, I will do it" (John 14:14). His promise is that if we ask for things in prayer that are consistent with who God is and who God wants us to be, it is the same as holding a matter before God and saying, "Thy will be done." In that spirit we can be assured that we will always be granted the strength we need to stand firm in God, if we but ask for it. Through an active prayer life, we will be able to say with the author of Philippians: "I can do all things through him who strengthens me" (Philippians 4:13)!

SHARING THE SCRIPTURE

Preparing Our Hearts

Meditate on this week's devotional reading, found in Psalm 119:57-64. In this psalm of the wisdom tradition, which takes the form of an acrostic in 176 verses, the writer meditates on God. Read verses 57-64 aloud. How can you affirm what the writer of this passage has to say about God and his relationship with God?

Pray that you and the adult learners will devote significant time to studying God's word.

Preparing Our Minds

Study the background from Daniel 6 and lesson Scripture, verses 4-7, 10, 16, 19, 21, 25-26. As you prepare, think about what difference it makes if you begin to compromise your convictions even in seemingly small ways.

Write on newsprint:

❑ information for next week's lesson, found under "Continue the Journey."
❑ activities for further spiritual growth in "Continue the Journey."

LEADING THE CLASS

(1) Gather to Learn

❖ Welcome the class members and introduce any guests.

❖ Pray that all who are present today will be open to hear and respond to what God has to say to them today.

❖ Read this quotation from Dag Hammarskjöld (1905–1961): **Never, for the sake of peace and quiet, deny your own experience of convictions.**

❖ Encourage the class to respond to this quotation by citing examples of people who have held steadfastly to their convictions. Here are three examples you may wish to use.

■ Patriot Patrick Henry delivered an impassioned speech to delegates in the Virginia colony on March 23, 1775, just prior to the American Revolution in which he said, "I know not what course others may take; but as for me, give me liberty, or give me death!"

■ Alabama seamstress Rosa Parks refused to give up her seat to a white passenger in December 1955 and was arrested. By holding her ground she became known as "the mother of the civil rights movement" in the United States.

■ Standing before the Imperial Diet at Worms, Reformation leader Martin Luther refused to recant the *95 Theses* he had posted on the door of the church in Wittenberg, Germany. In response to the charges against him, Luther avowed, "Unless I am convicted by scripture and plain reason—I do not accept the authority of the popes and councils, for they have contradicted each other—my conscience is captive to the Word of God. I cannot and I will not recant anything for to go against conscience is neither right nor safe. God help me. Amen."

❖ Read aloud today's focus statement: **People may be tempted to compromise their convictions in seemingly small ways. What does it matter if you compromise your convictions? When the order was made not to pray to anyone but the king for thirty days, Daniel refused to quit his three daily times of prayer to God or to hide his actions.**

(2) Survey the Events Leading Up to and Following Daniel's Night in the Lions' Den

❖ Invite a volunteer to read Daniel 6:4-7, 10, 16, 19, 21, 25-26. Or, if time permits, have three volunteers read the entire chapter (divided verses 1-9, 10-18, 19-28) to get a

more comprehensive understanding of the story.

❖ Discuss these questions.
  (1) What observations can you make about Daniel's faith?
  (2) Why do you think he would not back down, but instead kept to his regular prayer practice? He could, for example, have been more private about his praying. Why did he risk his life?
  (3) What would you have done had you been Daniel? Would you have been willing to risk all for the sake of your convictions? Why or why not?

❖ Read or retell "Faithful God; Faithful Response" from Interpreting the Scripture to help the students compare and contrast this week's story of Daniel in the lions' den with last week's tale of the three men in the fiery furnace.

❖ Ask: **What does the book of Daniel teach us concerning faithful living in a world that is inhospitable to our beliefs and values?**

(3) Recognize That Prayer Empowers People to Withstand Challenges to Their Faith

❖ Encourage the students to tell the class or a small group about times when they found strength through prayer. What were the circumstances? How did prayer seem to help? Even if the prayer was not answered as they had hoped, what value did it have for them?

❖ Read or retell the first, second, and third paragraphs of "Strength Through Prayer." Encourage students who have used breath prayers to comment on their experiences.

❖ Distribute paper and pencils. Ask the students, individually or in groups, to write at least three breath prayers. Remember, these are two short lines that can be said as one inhales and exhales.

❖ Invite participants to read examples of their prayers.

❖ Suggest that the students try several of these breath prayers in the coming weeks to see which ones are most helpful to them.

(4) Make a Commitment to Include Prayer and Other Spiritual Disciplines as a Regular Part of Life

❖ Brainstorm with the class a list of spiritual disciplines. Your list, which you will write on newsprint, may include activities such as *prayer, Bible study, meditation, fasting, simplicity, solitude, worship, tithing, journaling, walking a labyrinth.*

❖ Ask for volunteers who have practiced any of these disciplines to talk about what they do and the impact they believe it has on their spiritual lives.

❖ Allow time for class members to question each other concerning techniques and helpful resources.

❖ Conclude this portion of the lesson by encouraging the adults to list, on the back of the papers on which they have written their breath prayers, several disciplines that they would be willing to try in the weeks ahead.

❖ If time permits, go around the room and ask each person to name aloud at least one discipline he or she will try. Perhaps students who are familiar with that discipline would be willing to offer support and encouragement to those who are just getting started.

(5) Continue the Journey

❖ Pray that the adults will hold fast to their faith and refuse to compromise on essential matters.

❖ Read aloud this preparation for next week's lesson. You may also want to post it on newsprint for the students to copy.

■ **Title: Daniel's Prayer for the People**
■ **Background Scripture: Daniel 9**
■ **Lesson Scripture: Daniel 9:1-7, 17-19**
■ **Focus of the Lesson: Some people willingly offer prayers of confession and intercession. What drives them to approach God? Daniel was so overcome by grief over the devastation of Jerusalem and exile of his people that he made intercession and confession on their behalf for their sin against God.**

❖ Challenge the students to complete one or more of these activities for further spiritual growth, which you will write on newsprint for the students to copy.

(1) Be aware of situations this week in which you may feel tempted to compromise your convictions. What strategies do you use to combat such temptation? You may wish to offer a prayer or recall some Bible verses that are meaningful to you.

(2) Try a spiritual discipline that is unfamiliar to you. Evaluate how well this works for you.

(3) Set aside extra time this week to pray.

❖ Sing or read aloud "What a Friend We Have in Jesus."

❖ Conclude today's session by leading the class in this benediction, based on 2 Chronicles 34:31: **We renew our covenant to follow the LORD, keeping his commandments, with all our heart and all our soul, to perform the words of the covenant.**

UNIT 2: THE COVENANT IN EXILE
DANIEL'S PRAYER FOR THE PEOPLE

PREVIEWING THE LESSON

Lesson Scripture: Daniel 9:1-7, 17-19
Background Scripture: Daniel 9
Key Verse: Daniel 9:17

Focus of the Lesson:
Some people willingly offer prayers of confession and intercession. What drives them to approach God? Daniel was so overcome by grief over the devastation of Jerusalem and exile of his people that he made intercession and confession on their behalf for their sin against God.

Goals for the Learners:
(1) to overhear Daniel's prayer of confession on behalf of his people.
(2) to recognize the transformational possibilities of confession and intercessory prayer.
(3) to identify contemporary situations where there is need for confession and intercessory prayer, and make the commitment to pray.

Pronunciation Guide:
Ahasuerus (uh has yoo er' uhs)   Antiochus Epiphanes (an ti' uh kuhs i pif' uh neez)
Chaldean (kal dee' uhn)   Darius (dah ri' uhs)
gāber (gheh' ber)   Onias (oh ni' uhs)
Uriel (yoor' ee uhl)   Xerxes (zuhrk' seez)
Zedekiah (zed uh ki' uh)   Zerubbabel (zuh ruhb' uh buhl)

Supplies:
Bibles, newsprint and marker, paper and pencils, hymnals

READING THE SCRIPTURE

NRSV
Daniel 9:1-7, 17-19
¹In the first year of Darius son of Ahasuerus, by birth a Mede, who became

NIV
Daniel 9:1-7, 17-19
¹In the first year of Darius son of Xerxes (a Mede by descent), who was made ruler over

king over the realm of the Chaldeans—[2]in the first year of his reign, I, Daniel, perceived in the books the number of years that, according to the word of the LORD to the prophet Jeremiah, must be fulfilled for the devastation of Jerusalem, namely, seventy years.

[3]Then I turned to the Lord God, to seek an answer by prayer and supplication with fasting and sackcloth and ashes. [4]I prayed to the LORD my God and made confession, saying,

"Ah, Lord, great and awesome God, keeping covenant and steadfast love with those who love you and keep your commandments, [5]we have sinned and done wrong, acted wickedly and rebelled, turning aside from your commandments and ordinances. [6]We have not listened to your servants the prophets, who spoke in your name to our kings, our princes, and our ancestors, and to all the people of the land.

[7]"Righteousness is on your side, O Lord, but open shame, as at this day, falls on us, the people of Judah, the inhabitants of Jerusalem, and all Israel, those who are near and those who are far away, in all the lands to which you have driven them, because of the treachery that they have committed against you.

[17]Now therefore, O our God, listen to the prayer of your servant and to his supplication, and for your own sake, Lord, let your face shine upon your desolated sanctuary. [18]Incline your ear, O my God, and hear. Open your eyes and look at our desolation and the city that bears your name. We do not present our supplication before you on the ground of our righteousness, but on the ground of your great mercies. [19]O Lord, hear; O Lord, forgive; O Lord, listen and act and do not delay! For your own sake, O my God, because your city and your people bear your name!"

the Babylonian kingdom—[2]in the first year of his reign, I, Daniel, understood from the Scriptures, according to the word of the LORD given to Jeremiah the prophet, that the desolation of Jerusalem would last seventy years. [3]So I turned to the Lord God and pleaded with him in prayer and petition, in fasting, and in sackcloth and ashes.

[4]I prayed to the LORD my God and confessed:

"O Lord, the great and awesome God, who keeps his covenant of love with all who love him and obey his commands, [5]we have sinned and done wrong. We have been wicked and have rebelled; we have turned away from your commands and laws. [6]We have not listened to your servants the prophets, who spoke in your name to our kings, our princes and our fathers, and to all the people of the land.

[7]"Lord, you are righteous, but this day we are covered with shame—the men of Judah and people of Jerusalem and all Israel, both near and far, in all the countries where you have scattered us because of our unfaithfulness to you.

[17]"Now, our God, hear the prayers and petitions of your servant. For your sake, O Lord, look with favor on your desolate sanctuary. [18]Give ear, O God, and hear; open your eyes and see the desolation of the city that bears your Name. We do not make requests of you because we are righteous, but because of your great mercy. [19]O Lord, listen! O Lord, forgive! O Lord, hear and act! For your sake, O my God, do not delay, because your city and your people bear your Name."

UNDERSTANDING THE SCRIPTURE

Overview. This chapter contains a prophecy that falls in the midst of three visions recorded in the book of Daniel. These are the Vision of the Four Beasts (7:1-28), the Vision of the Ram and the Male Goat (8:1-27), and the Vision of the Last Days (10:1–12:13). Daniel's prophecy builds on and reinterprets one made by Jeremiah, in which the Babylonian exile was predicted to last "seventy years" (Jeremiah 25:11-12; 29:10), a symbolic term for a lifetime.

The core question posed in this chapter by both the character Daniel and the author himself on behalf of their respective communities is, "How long? How long will this torment last before God saves us?"

In order to answer this question, the author does a bit of tricky juggling. He revisits a prophecy delivered by Jeremiah (25:11-12; 29:10). This prophecy, according to 25:1, came "in the fourth year of King Jehoiakim . . . [and] the first year of King Nebuchadnezzar," which according to scholars would be 605 B.C. This prophecy is then reinterpreted in the book of Daniel, ostensibly to apply to the circumstances in the book—an exile set in a time before the return to Jerusalem validated God's promise made through Jeremiah. Yet, the author is really trying to send a message to the community of his own time, which was suffering persecution centuries after Daniel's tale takes place.

The author's need to help his own community place themselves within God's timetable for salvation explains the mathematical gyrations that take place at the end of chapter 9. The author stretches Jeremiah's original seventy years so that they now encompass his own time and point to a restoration that is more cosmic than earthbound. As W. Sibley Towner puts it so well in *Daniel*, a book of the Interpretation series:

The purpose of this reapplication of the seventy-year scheme is to enable

the second century writer to point out to the contemporary reader a spot on the end-time scenario and say, "You are here!"

Daniel 9:1-2. The author puts Daniel's prophecy in the first year of Darius the Mede, which is 538 B.C. according to the book's chronology. Ahasuerus, the Hebrew name for Xerxes, is a name from history, here applied to a fictitious sire of a fictitious king (see notes on Daniel 6:1-5 in the lesson for April 20). Daniel's words relate to Jeremiah's prophecy concerning seventy years of exile (Jeremiah 25:11-12; 29:10).

Daniel 9:3-6. Daniel begins with a lengthy prayer of confession (9:4-19) that has several elements in common with other prayers in the Bible: Solomon's prayer at the dedication of the temple (1 Kings 8:23-53), the psalmist's prayer after the destruction of the temple and Jerusalem (Psalm 79), and the prayers of Ezra and Nehemiah (Ezra 9:6-15; Nehemiah 1:5-11; 9:6-37). Because of the strong linguistic similarities of these prayers, scholars think the prayer in Daniel was lifted from the community's liturgy, rather than representing an original creation of the book's author. Throughout the prayer, we see God's faithfulness set in contrast to the people's unfaithfulness.

In preparing for the prayer, Daniel turns his face toward God, which may reflect the ancient practice of facing Jerusalem during prayer (see Daniel 6:10; 1 Kings 8:35). He also fasts and puts on sackcloth and ashes. While these practices were associated with repentance, they were also signs of great desperation and earnestness on the part of the petitioner.

Daniel 9:7-14. The confessional language of the prayer continues, still setting the people's guilt in contrast to God's righteousness. Note that in verses 9-10 and verses 12-14, the language shifts from a direct address to God to a description of God that appears to address the reader directly. Perhaps this was a device intended to pull the reader more personally into the prayer itself.

The curse mentioned in verse 11 refers to Deuteronomy 28:15-45, where Moses told the people that blessing or curse would come to them depending on whether or not they chose God. Another account of this curse can be found in Leviticus 26:14-22.

Daniel 9:15-19. The "desolated sanctuary" of verse 17 anticipates the description of "an abomination that desolates" in verse 27. Most scholars think the abomination refers to the actions of Antiochus Epiphanes (see notes on 9:24-27).

Daniel 9:20-23. While Daniel is still in prayer, an answer comes in the form of the angel Gabriel. Gabriel has appeared to Daniel once before (8:15-26), in the first scriptural occurrence of a named angel. As is often the case in Hebrew, the name has meaning. The angel is said to have the appearance of a man (*gāber*). Using that same word as root, Gabriel translates as "my man is God." By the time Luke wrote his Gospel, tradition identified Gabriel as the "angel of the Lord" (Luke 1:11). Subsequent Jewish tradition would name Gabriel, Michael (see Daniel 10:13, 21; 12:1), Uriel, and Raphael as the four angels that stand at the corners of God's throne area.

Daniel 9:24-27. Gabriel announces that Jeremiah's "seventy years" actually meant seventy "weeks" of years. A week has seven days, so the math becomes seventy years times seven—or 490 years. As with any time that the number seven (or a multiple of seven) is used, however, the number is meant to be taken not literally but symbolically. It refers to the fullness of events in God's time, not ours.

This chronology then breaks down the symbolic 490 years into a series of events. After "seven weeks" (or forty-nine years), there will be an anointed prince (9:25), probably Zerubbabel or Joshua (Ezra 3:2). From this point, after "sixty-two weeks" (or 434 years), an anointed one will be "cut off" (9:26)—probably a reference to Onias III (see also Daniel 11:22; 2 Maccabees 4:34). Then a prince-to-come (Antiochus Epiphanes) will make a covenant with many for "one week" (or seven years), will stop all sacrifices and offerings for "half a week" (or three and a half years), and will desecrate the temple (9:26-27). Antiochus Epiphanes did indeed make an agreement with many of the Jews who had adopted the Greek language and culture to stop all temple worship for a period of time, and did desecrate the temple by rededicating it to Zeus Olympus and slaughtering a pig there in the Greek god's honor.

INTERPRETING THE SCRIPTURE

A Prayer from the Heart

Daniel 7–12 contains several visions designed to show that the sufferings of this world will eventually end and that God's kingdom will be established. Nestled in among these visions is Daniel's prayer, recorded in chapter 9.

The text begins by saying that Daniel's prayer was prompted by something he read in Scripture. Many of us can identify with

that: We gain new insights through the study of God's word, and that in turn prompts us to reach out to God.

In this case, what Daniel saw upset him. He was reading the prophecies of Jeremiah regarding the exile, and there he discerned that the designated time for that period of punishment was seventy years. This point in Daniel's tale is set about sixty years into the exile, so the author shows Daniel bewailing the fact that there are ten years left until the prophesied return. In distress, Daniel cries out to God and makes a passionate confession and plea for pardon on behalf of the exilic community. They know they sinned, and now they truly repent; might God relent and let them go home sooner than planned?

The structure of Daniel's prayer should look familiar—it's one that the church still follows in its prayers of confession. First, he praises God for keeping the covenant and maintaining steadfast love. All our prayers begin with an address to God and some statement of praise. After all, we are approaching the Creator and Lord of the Cosmos, so we do so with appropriate awe, honor, and respect.

Daniel's acknowledgment that God has been faithful then leads to the second part of the prayer: the confession that the people have not been faithful. You will often hear a pastor or liturgist preface the communal prayer of confession by saying something like, "Because God is faithful and loving, we dare approach God even in our sinful state." It is an important theological point. By all rights, we should expect to be denied entry into the presence of the Holy One because our sins are an affront to God's own nature. In grace and mercy, however, God lets us draw near so that all can be made right.

Finally, Daniel asks for a restoration of the relationship, in this case marked by the specific plea that Jerusalem be restored and the people allowed to return to it. Notice the motive, however: Ultimately Daniel's plea is not for the sake of the people alone; his true prayer is that God will send the people home to repair the city for God's own glory. Likewise, we end our prayers of confession by asking for something—always pardon, but often also strength, wisdom, or courage—and we ask these things, not for selfish reasons, but so that God's name can be praised.

What Can We Learn?

What can Daniel's prayer teach us? First, there can be no doubt that prayer was extremely important to Daniel and to the ancient community of faith; it was certainly central in the life of Jesus. We need to learn from that and make communication with God the foundation of all our actions.

Second, everything can be expressed in prayer: grief over a tremendous loss, longing for God, despair from seemingly endless waiting for relief, repentance from sin, deep love and concern for others, praise of the Creator. When the community of faith was suffering, Daniel (and others) reached out to God.

Daniel's prayer is full of passion. It's almost embarrassing by today's standards. The bottom line, however, is that it is honest. Perhaps we need to stop making artistic prayers and begin to pray honest prayers. We can be ourselves before God and know that God accepts us and loves us in all our brokenness. And we can know also that God's love will redeem us.

Daniel's prayer also teaches us that God is concerned about all that happens. Life is not divided into compartments. There is no area that is beyond the concern of God. Rather, God is acting at the deepest level in all of life. Everything can be brought to God in prayer, even the ugly feelings. When we acknowledge them and give them up to God, God can bring good out of our pain and brokenness.

Finally, Daniel's prayer nurtures us because it reminds us that we are not alone. Other people in other times and faraway places have stood before God in wretchedness, pain, awe, or joy. We are bound in community with them by that common experience. We are also bound to them by the ongoing practice of prayer.

Why Pray?

What drives people to pray? Sometimes we pray because that is the only way we can help. Daniel could not change the reality of the exile, but he could pray for restoration into a relationship with God and for an eventual return to the homeland.

Likewise, even when we can't do anything else, we can pray. Prayer is the one thing we can do regardless of our circumstances. We are never too busy, too financially strapped, or too young or old to offer up a prayer. One minister made a practice of calling a homebound member in his church every day and giving her a list of people or situations about which he asked her to pray. If, as we believe, God answers prayer, who is to say that this woman may not have been the most active person in that congregation? Even in the situation that imprisons us, we can pray, especially for other people.

Another reason we pray is because we recognize that God can do what we cannot. As in Daniel's case, God can meet us in our grief and help us through it. In prayers of confession, we affirm that God can remove the barrier of our sins and restore us into a right relationship with the Holy One and one another. In prayers of intercession, we show confidence that God can and will extend divine mercy and love to ourselves and others.

At the heart of all these prayers, both those of confession and those of intercession, is our longing for God to bring peace, healing, and wholeness to the broken places of human lives. We pray, in essence, for the total well-being that only God can grant and that can endure in the face of incredibly painful conditions. We pray for the peace that passes human understanding and perseveres through calamity and trial. We pray for the peace Jesus leaves with his followers to sustain them.

Thanks to the ongoing work of the Holy Spirit, we see the evidence that our prayers do make a difference. Through prayer, the Spirit is an ever-present source of encouragement and consolation for us in our times of anxiety or sorrow. The Spirit gives strength when we are weak, guidance and direction when hard decisions confront us, and an awareness of the divine presence when we are imprisoned in our human loneliness. Of course, we discover God's gift of the Spirit as we worship, study, and serve together in the community of faith—but we especially feel its presence and power when we open ourselves sincerely in prayer.

SHARING THE SCRIPTURE

Preparing Our Hearts

Meditate on this week's devotional reading, found in Psalm 130. In this short psalm we hear a penitent soul cry out to God from the depths of his heart. As the psalm ends, the writer calls all of Israel to place their hope and confidence in the loving God, for God has the power to redeem them. How does this prayer touch the wounded places of your own soul? Read it aloud several times. Which words jump out at you? Linger over these words and listen to what God wants to say to you right now.

Pray that you and the adult learners will recognize that prayer is an essential way in which we communicate with God and, therefore, is an important spiritual discipline for our lives.

Preparing Our Minds

Study the background, Daniel 9, and lesson Scripture, verses 1-7, 17-19. Consider what prompts people who offer intercessory prayers for others and confessions to approach God.

Write on newsprint:
❑ questions for "Gather to Learn."
❑ information for next week's lesson, found under "Continue the Journey."

❏ activities for further spiritual growth in "Continue the Journey."

LEADING THE CLASS

(1) Gather to Learn

❖ Welcome the class members and introduce any guests.

❖ Pray that all who have come today will be open to experiencing the power of prayer.

❖ Suggest that the students interview one another in groups of two or three to answer these questions, which you may want to list on newsprint.
  (1) Why do you pray?
  (2) What gives you confidence to believe that God hears and answers prayer?

❖ Bring the class together and invite the adults to report on highlights from their conversations. Perhaps their own viewpoints were affirmed. Possibly they heard some new ideas that they will want to ponder.

❖ Read aloud today's focus statement: **Some people willingly offer prayers of confession and intercession. What drives them to approach God? Daniel was so overcome by grief over the devastation of Jerusalem and exile of his people that he made intercession and confession on their behalf for their sin against God.**

(2) Overhear Daniel's Prayer of Confession on Behalf of His People

❖ Choose a reader for Daniel 9:1-7, 17-19.
❖ Help the class to recognize that:
  ■ Daniel was moved to prayer because of words he read in the Scriptures, specifically Jeremiah 25:11-12; 29:10, where the prophet speaks of seventy years of exile. (See the third paragraph of "A Prayer from the Heart" in Interpreting the Scripture.")
  ■ Daniel took on the stance of one who

is penitent by fasting and dressing in sackcloth, the traditional garb of persons in mourning.
  ■ The structure of his prayer is still used in the church today. (See the fourth and fifth paragraphs of "A Prayer from the Heart.")

❖ Ask: **What can we learn from Daniel's prayer?** Use information from Interpreting the Scripture to augment the discussion.

❖ Divide the class into five groups, give each group newsprint and a marker, and assign each group one of the following prayers. Challenge the students to compare their assigned prayer to Daniel 9 to see what similarities they can find. Provide time for each group to report back to the class.
  ■ 1 Kings 8:23-53 (Solomon's prayer at the dedication of the temple).
  ■ Psalm 79 (the psalmist's prayer after the destruction of the temple and Jerusalem).
  ■ Ezra 9:6-15 (Ezra's prayer).
  ■ Nehemiah 1:5-11 (a prayer of Nehemiah).
  ■ Nehemiah 9:6-37 (a prayer before renewal of the covenant).

❖ Sum up this portion of the lesson by noting common themes or structures among all of these prayers. Point out that because of these commonalities scholars believe Daniel's prayer might have been part of the liturgy of the faith community that seemed appropriate to use in this context.

(3) Recognize the Transformational Possibilities of Confession and Intercessory Prayer

❖ Select one or more volunteers to read aloud Psalm 106 (or portions you select), which, like Daniel 9, is a confession of communal sin.

❖ Ask these questions.
  (1) What do you learn from this psalm concerning how one makes confession?

(2) **What do you learn about God?**

(3) **Where in this psalm do you see possibilities for hope and transformation?**

❖ Read these words of Alphonsus Luguori: **"For a good confession three things are necessary: an examination of conscience, sorrow, and a determination to avoid sin."**

❖ Distribute paper and pencils. Encourage the students to write a confession of their own sins, keeping in mind the three necessities they just heard. Make clear that they will not be asked to read or discuss what they have written. Suggest that they look for signs of transformation in their own lives as they offer a silent prayer of confession.

(4) Identify Contemporary Situations Where There Is Need for Confession and Intercessory Prayer, and Make the Commitment to Pray

❖ Post a sheet of newsprint. Invite the students to call out situations locally and around the world that cry out for prayer.

❖ Identify, if possible, those situations where confession and repentance are needed. Sins such as racism, abuses of power, incompetence, and oppression are examples.

❖ Identify those situations where intercessory prayer is needed to lift before God those who are ill, grieving, or victims.

❖ Provide a few moments of quiet time for the students to choose one or two items from the list that they will commit to praying for in the coming weeks.

❖ Encourage the class to stand in a circle (or several circles if the group is large) and spontaneously offer prayers for the situations that have touched them.

❖ Invite the students who are willing to commit to continue in prayer during the coming week for a particular situation to raise their hands before God, as the class stands with heads bowed.

(5) Continue the Journey

❖ Pray that each of the learners will honor her or his commitment to offer intercessory prayers this week.

❖ Read aloud this preparation for next week's lesson. You may also want to post it on newsprint for the students to copy.

■ **Title: The Temple Rebuilt**

■ **Background Scripture: Haggai 1; Ezra 5**

■ **Lesson Scripture: Haggai 1:1-4, 7-10, 12-15**

■ **Focus of the Lesson: Recovery from any kind of devastation requires rebuilding. Who determines what the priorities will be in a rebuilding process? The prophet Haggai reminded the Israelites of their first priority, to keep their covenant with God and rebuild the temple in Jerusalem.**

❖ Challenge the students to complete one or more of these activities for further spiritual growth, which you will write on newsprint for the students to copy.

(1) **Offer intercessory prayers, especially for church and political leaders and volatile situations around the world.**

(2) **Be alert for people who are in crisis. Do whatever you can to assist them, including offering intercessory prayers.**

(3) **Use a concordance to locate words related to "pray" or "prayer" in your Bible. Look up some of these references to see models of how people prayed and under what circumstances.**

❖ Sing or read aloud "Lord, Speak to Me."

❖ Conclude today's session by leading the class in this benediction, based on 2 Chronicles 34:31: **We renew our covenant to follow the LORD, keeping his commandments, with all our heart and all our soul, to perform the words of the covenant.**

UNIT 3: RESTORATION AND COVENANT RENEWAL
THE TEMPLE REBUILT

PREVIEWING THE LESSON

Lesson Scripture: Haggai 1:1-4, 7-10, 12-15
Background Scripture: Haggai 1; Ezra 5
Key Verse: Haggai 1:8

Focus of the Lesson:
Recovery from any kind of devastation requires rebuilding. Who determines what the priorities will be in a rebuilding process? The prophet Haggai reminded the Israelites of their first priority, to keep their covenant with God and rebuild the temple in Jerusalem.

Goals for the Learners:
(1) to analyze God's call to the people to rebuild the temple and God's promise to be with them.
(2) to recognize that people's lives can become difficult when they ignore God's priorities.
(3) to evaluate their own priorities to determine if they are putting God first in their lives.

Pronunciation Guide:
Artaxerxes (ahr tuh zuhrk' seez)   Darius (dah ri' uhs)
Haggai (hag i')   Jehozadak (ji hoh' zuh dak)
Shealtiel (shee al' tee uhl)   Sheshbazzar (shesh baz' uhr)
Tattenai (tat' uh ni)   Zerubbabel (zuh ruhb' uh buhl)

Supplies:
Bibles, newsprint and marker, paper and pencils, hymnals, Bible commentaries and/or dictionaries

MAY 4

READING THE SCRIPTURE

NRSV
Haggai 1:1-4, 7-10, 12-15
¹In the second year of King Darius, in the sixth month, on the first day of the month,

NIV
Haggai 1:1-4, 7-10, 12-15
¹In the second year of King Darius, on the first day of the sixth month, the word of the

the word of the LORD came by the prophet Haggai to Zerubbabel son of Shealtiel, governor of Judah, and to Joshua son of Jehozadak, the high priest: ²Thus says the LORD of hosts: These people say the time has not yet come to rebuild the LORD's house. ³Then the word of the LORD came by the prophet Haggai, saying: ⁴Is it a time for you yourselves to live in your paneled houses, while this house lies in ruins?

⁷Thus says the LORD of hosts: Consider how you have fared. **⁸Go up to the hills and bring wood and build the house, so that I may take pleasure in it and be honored, says the LORD.** ⁹You have looked for much, and, lo, it came to little; and when you brought it home, I blew it away. Why? says the LORD of hosts. Because my house lies in ruins, while all of you hurry off to your own houses. ¹⁰Therefore the heavens above you have withheld the dew, and the earth has withheld its produce.

¹²Then Zerubbabel son of Shealtiel, and Joshua son of Jehozadak, the high priest, with all the remnant of the people, obeyed the voice of the LORD their God, and the words of the prophet Haggai, as the LORD their God had sent him; and the people feared the LORD. ¹³Then Haggai, the messenger of the LORD, spoke to the people with the LORD's message, saying, I am with you, says the LORD. ¹⁴And the LORD stirred up the spirit of Zerubbabel son of Shealtiel, governor of Judah, and the spirit of Joshua son of Jehozadak, the high priest, and the spirit of all the remnant of the people; and they came and worked on the house of the LORD of hosts, their God, ¹⁵on the twenty-fourth day of the month, in the sixth month.

LORD came through the prophet Haggai to Zerubbabel son of Shealtiel, governor of Judah, and to Joshua son of Jehozadak, the high priest:

²This is what the LORD Almighty says: "These people say, 'The time has not yet come for the LORD's house to be built.'"

³Then the word of the LORD came through the prophet Haggai: ⁴"Is it a time for you yourselves to be living in your paneled houses, while this house remains a ruin?"

⁷This is what the LORD Almighty says: "Give careful thought to your ways. **⁸Go up into the mountains and bring down timber and build the house, so that I may take pleasure in it and be honored," says the LORD.** ⁹"You expected much, but see, it turned out to be little. What you brought home, I blew away. Why?" declares the LORD Almighty. "Because of my house, which remains a ruin, while each of you is busy with his own house. ¹⁰Therefore, because of you the heavens have withheld their dew and the earth its crops."

¹²Then Zerubbabel son of Shealtiel, Joshua son of Jehozadak, the high priest, and the whole remnant of the people obeyed the voice of the LORD their God and the message of the prophet Haggai, because the LORD their God had sent him. And the people feared the LORD.

¹³Then Haggai, the LORD's messenger, gave this message of the LORD to the people: "I am with you," declares the LORD. ¹⁴So the LORD stirred up the spirit of Zerubbabel son of Shealtiel, governor of Judah, and the spirit of Joshua son of Jehozadak, the high priest, and the spirit of the whole remnant of the people. They came and began to work on the house of the LORD Almighty, their God, ¹⁵on the twenty-fourth day of the sixth month in the second year of King Darius.

UNDERSTANDING THE SCRIPTURE

Overview of Haggai 1. After Cyrus conquered Babylon in 538 B.C., he let the Jews return to Jerusalem and he encouraged them to rebuild the city and the temple. Haggai's story picks up eighteen years after the return. No significant progress has been made on the temple, and Haggai cannot stand any further delay. His book contains five addresses to the governor (Zerubbabel) and the high priest (Joshua), along with other leaders in the Jewish community, pressing them to begin restoring the temple and proper worship as soon as possible. The addresses all took place over a three-month period in 520 B.C.

Part of the urgency on Haggai's part is the belief that once the temple and proper worship are restored, God's promised grand new age will come to bring peace and prosperity to the people. So far, they have not fared well in terms of harvest or economics, and Haggai believes this is because they have neglected God's house while trying to establish their own physical comfort. His concern now is that if the people do not gather wood and supplies while they can, then a later drought or poor harvest might stop the project (1:7-11).

It is interesting to note that Haggai's complaints against the people are not found in the book of Ezra, although the positive results of the prophet's urging are. Neither does Ezra record a certain political hope. Both Haggai and Zechariah, who was another prophet in Jerusalem at this time, anticipated that more than the reconstruction of the temple was at hand. Both men placed great emphasis on Zerubbabel's bloodline. They hoped that the governor, as a direct descendant of David, might be the king who was to restore the monarchy and bring the nation back into glory. This aspiration is not mentioned in Ezra, however.

Haggai 1:1-6. Darius was king of Persia from 521 to 485 B.C. The date recorded in verse 1 places the text at August 29 of 520 B.C. Zerubbabel, the appointed governor of Judah, was a direct descendant of King David. He shared authority with the high priest, Joshua.

Haggai 1:7-11. The hard times of the past eighteen years are now put in a theological context. At the time of the people's return, the temple had lain plundered and burned for almost fifty years. Their first priority should have been to begin repairs on it immediately. For the next eighteen years they focused on other things, however—so for that time God did not see fit to let them prosper.

Haggai 1:12-15. Inspired by Haggai's prophetic speech, the leaders and people begin work on the temple at last. Scholars suspect a corruption in the text, however, and propose that the oracle in 2:15-19 may have come next. If that is so, then the date given in verse 15a would apply to the oracle and not to the start of work on the temple.

Overview of Ezra 5. The books of Ezra and Nehemiah were originally one scroll, a single history that some scholars think the Chronicler wrote as a follow-up to Chronicles, though some dispute that notion. The Chronicler drew on several archives and historical documents to construct this post-exilic history, including the memoirs of Ezra and Nehemiah themselves.

Based on these histories and other books from the period, such as Haggai and Zechariah, we can see at least four stages of the return. At Cyrus's original decree in 538 B.C., a group of Jews returned under the leadership of Sheshbazzar. They began construction on the temple but had to stop because of local opposition. A second wave of returnees, led by Zerubbabel and Joshua, came during the time of Darius. They also met resistance to restoring the temple, but they were subsequently inspired by Haggai and Zechariah to finish it anyway.

The history then gets a little unclear because the Hebrew text became jumbled over years of transmission. Nehemiah 8 probably belongs between Ezra 8 and 9.

One reconstruction of the history says that Ezra led a third group home during the reign of Artaxerxes I (464–424 B.C.), bringing with him a codified version of the law of Moses. Sometime during this period, Nehemiah visited to help get the walls rebuilt. There was still local opposition, so his extra encouragement was needed. Then, during the reign of Artaxerxes II (404–358 B.C.), Nehemiah returned again as a leader of another group, and he continued his efforts to purify the community and its worship practices. An alternate version of the historical reconstruction places Ezra's return after Nehemiah's, under the reign of Artaxerxes II.

The fifth chapter of the book of Ezra provides more insight into the opposition faced by Haggai and others in rebuilding the temple. Tattenai, a Persian governor of a neighboring province, questions whether this construction project is legal. Ezra 5 tells of the action he took, while Ezra 6 describes the outcome.

Ezra 5:1-2. These initial verses set the time period. Haggai and Zechariah have prophesied, and now Zerubbabel and Joshua set out to rebuild the temple.

Ezra 5:3-5. The name of Tattenai as governor of a province called "Beyond the River" appears in a cuneiform tablet dated 502 B.C. His province was west of the Euphrates River. Tattenai's investigation into the Jews' authority to rebuild the temple should not be seen as hostile, in that he did not try to stop the reconstruction. His letter to Darius was a precaution: If this work should indeed be without authorization (and therefore rebellious), Tattenai did not want to be vulnerable to an accusation of collusion by virtue of having remained silent. Just in case there is a problem, he takes the names of the men responsible for the construction.

Ezra 5:6-17. Tattenai's letter to Darius describes the construction on the temple and his exchange with the leaders there. If the account is accurate, then the men somewhat deftly avoided giving him their names. They did, however, attest to the legality of their activity and provide enough information that their claim could be substantiated by the royal archives.

INTERPRETING THE SCRIPTURE

A Difficult Homecoming

Have you ever been excited about plans you've made, only to be disappointed in how things actually worked out? That must have been the case for those who were in the first groups to return to Jerusalem. For generations, they had heard of the glorious city of God. Even though they knew, intellectually, that the city had been besieged and the temple and walls torn down, on an emotional level they thought of it as sacred ground. Even more, they thought of it as *home*.

Historians estimate that as many as 50,000 people returned to Jerusalem over time. Those who got there first would have discovered a disaster zone. The massive stones of the former wall were tumbled into the streets. Farm lands lay fallow and overgrown, yielding nothing. Local families had taken over every livable home, and these folk saw no reason to vacate. Worst of all, the temple was just a burned stone outline of a foundation, nothing more.

It's no wonder that so much time and effort went into establishing themselves. Granted, some work was done on rebuilding the walls and the temple, but this quickly ceased when local opposition arose. With so many other priorities, like food and shelter, "unnecessary" work like rebuilding the walls and the temple had to wait—especially if it was going to cause trouble that no one had the time or inclination to deal with.

Fast forward almost twenty years. The prophet Haggai began to say, "Enough is enough." The people had been living in a survivalist mentality that dictated their priorities, but the need for that had passed. Now was the time to reevaluate their priorities and to look at what God had been calling them to do all along.

Haggai's speech to the people says that they have, in fact, been suffering as a result of their bad priorities. Applying a common ancient Near Eastern theology, he identifies a recent drought and crop failure as the direct result of God's displeasure. Whereas we may or may not agree with that interpretation of the weather, we can easily recognize another truth in Haggai's message: The people have indeed cut themselves off from God's blessing by not making God's priorities their own. They live with constant insecurity and the threat of violence because they have not rebuilt the wall, and they are limited in their ability to sense God's empowering presence because they have not rebuilt the temple. This is not to say they had to have the temple for God to be with them, any more than we require a church building to feel God's presence in worship. Rather, the failure to rebuild the temple had gone on for so long that it now amounted to sin. The people's inaction had become a barrier between them and God. They needed to set new priorities, and they needed to do it with no more delay.

A Recent Parallel

As I write this, the United States is still recovering from the effects of a series of devastating hurricanes. The government is having to set priorities and make choices related to rebuilding. Where will it start? What town or region will get the most aid first? Hospitals clearly need to be on the list of structures to be restored first, but what else should be on that list? What goes on the "second priority" list? the third?

Likewise, priorities have to be set on a more personal level. Evacuated families have fled to cities across the nation: some to friends or family but most to a place where they know no one. Do they stay and build a life in their new location, or do they go home? Do they write off their home and belongings and jobs as irreparably lost, or do they try to salvage and rebuild? These decisions were just as hard to make in Ezra's day as they are in our own.

Furthermore, the people who are returning to New Orleans or the Gulf Coast at this time face a heartbreak similar to that which awaited those who returned to Jerusalem. Several homes are still standing, some even with such minimal damage that the families can easily reclaim them, but most are not. Beyond that, regardless of the state of one's personal property, the routine of day-to-day life is gone. Schools and businesses remain closed, whole neighborhoods remain empty, and most churches are incapable of housing worship. Joy at what survived has been muted by awareness of how much still has to be done—and the pressing need to set priorities yet again.

One other parallel between the two situations is worth mentioning. Both Haggai and Ezra emphasized the need to rebuild the temple after the people's basic needs for food and shelter were met. Likewise, many who returned to the areas of destruction in the southern United States have actively sought help across the nation to rebuild their houses of worship as soon as possible. In this time of grief and loss, the need to feel God's presence in the gathered community of faith is stronger than ever. We see this poignantly in the requests of the congregations trying to rebuild: In addition to carpenters, electricians, and cooks for the work teams, they consistently ask for ministers and laity gifted with pastoral skills to come be with the congregation and the surrounding community.

When disaster hits, buildings need to be reconstructed but, even more, hearts and souls need to be healed. That remains the number one priority of the Christian community—and it is comforting to know that rebuilding our places and means of worship is still such a vital part of that healing for the church and for the world.

Now Is the Time

Of course, most of us are not reconstructing houses or churches, but may be reconstructing relationships—possibly even whole lives. When we are building the structures of our lives, we quickly learn that priorities need to be set immediately. If we wait, some of our current options will no longer be available. For example, making our children a priority is a "limited-time offer." Children are young for only a few short years, and so the opportunity for a parent to be truly present with them is transient. Or there may be only a brief window of critical time for reconciliation to occur in a relationship before estrangement is irreparable. The priorities we set, or fail to set, have lasting consequences, whether they involve faith and our relationship to God or our relationship to other people.

But this still leaves the question of what priorities we are to set. Clearly worshiping God is at the top of the list, as is showing honor to God in all ways. Another is abiding in Christ and letting his Spirit work through us. Not surprisingly, Jesus said it best. What priorities are we to have in all that we do, rebuilding or otherwise? "Love the Lord your God with all your heart, and with all your soul, and with all your mind . . . [and] love your neighbor as yourself" (Matthew 22:37-39).

SHARING THE SCRIPTURE

Preparing Our Hearts

Meditate on this week's devotional reading, found in Psalm 84:1-4. This psalm extols the joy of living in God's presence. Not only we humans but also the animals God created long to live in God's home. Ponder the psalmist's words. How do you feel about living in God's presence? Think specifically about being in your house of worship. What special feelings do this building and its setting conjure up in you?

Pray that you and the adult learners will feel blessed and at home in the house of the Lord.

Preparing Our Minds

Study the background from Haggai 1 and Ezra 5. The lesson Scripture focuses on Haggai 1:1-4, 7-10, 12-15. As you prepare, think about what determines priorities in a rebuilding process.

Write on newsprint:
- ❏ words under "Evaluate the Learners' Priorities to Determine If They Are Putting God First in Their Lives."
- ❏ information for next week's lesson, found under "Continue the Journey."
- ❏ activities for further spiritual growth in "Continue the Journey."

Gather Bible dictionaries and commentaries for the activity suggested under "Analyze God's Call to the People to Rebuild the Temple and God's Promise to Be with Them." Or, prepare an optional lecture for this activity.

Recognize, as mentioned in the Understanding the Scripture portion, that scholars disagree on the timeframe of some of the events related to the return of the exiles to Jerusalem. You will likely find what appears to be conflicting information, so you may want to present more than one possible scenario.

LEADING THE CLASS

(1) Gather to Learn

❖ Welcome the class members and introduce any guests.

❖ Pray that all who have gathered today will be open to God's leading, especially as they set their priorities.

❖ Encourage the adults to imagine that they are in charge of setting priorities for recovery from a major natural disaster, such as a tsunami, tornado, or hurricane. Lead them through these steps, either as a class or in small groups.

■ List on newsprint the types of things that need to be done to help victims.

■ Prioritize the order in which these activities will be done by placing a number next to each item, with one (1) being the highest priority.

■ Conclude by discussing why class members assigned the numbers that they chose. Ask: **What criteria determined the order in which you placed these activities?**

❖ **Option:** Read "A Recent Parallel" from Interpreting the Scripture.

❖ Read aloud today's focus statement: **Recovery from any kind of devastation requires rebuilding. Who determines what the priorities will be in a rebuilding process? The prophet Haggai reminded the Israelites of their first priority, to keep their covenant with God and rebuild the temple in Jerusalem.**

(2) Analyze God's Call to the People to Rebuild the Temple and God's Promise to Be with Them

❖ Select a volunteer to read Haggai 1:1-4, 7-10, 12-15.

❖ Distribute several Bible dictionaries or commentaries and ask individuals to locate information related to the following people and report back to the class. Or, present an optional lecture to the students on informa-tion you have prepared on these people. You may wish to include other background information as well.

■ Darius I, king of Persia.

■ Zerubbabel, governor of Judah.

■ Joshua, high priest.

■ Haggai, a prophet of 520 B.C.

❖ Discuss these questions with the class.

(1) Why are the returned exiles suffering from crop failure and other problems? (Verses 2-4, 7-10 show that the people have their priorities skewed. They have been tending to their own business, living in nicely finished—paneled—houses while the temple lies in ruins.)

(2) How can these problems be resolved? (They need to rebuild God's house.)

(3) How do the people respond to Haggai? (They take action and begin to work on the temple. Note that this positive response is rather unusual. Often, people ignore the words of the prophets.)

(3) Recognize That People's Lives Can Become Difficult When They Ignore God's Priorities

❖ Point out that the lives of those who had returned from exile in Babylonia were difficult because they had ignored God's priority for their lives by allowing the temple to lie in ruins.

❖ Ask: **When have you seen people's lives become difficult because they have ignored God's priorities?** (Caution the students not to use real names or specific situations the class members could identify, unless they are speaking about well-known people whose challenges are common knowledge.)

❖ Here is an example from Larry Burkett, a well-known Christian financial counselor, who is concerned about the problems Christians face when they do not have biblical priorities on their use of money: **"Believers need to get their priorities right** if Christian households have any hope of getting on solid financial ground. . . . The giving that you have—or the lack of it—reflects the spiritual values that you have," he says. "If your priorities are right, you're going to give to God and you'll make adjustments in your spending—your living, literally—to be able to give to God's work. If that's the first priority in your life, it's going to be reflected [in your giving]."

(4) Evaluate the Learners' Priorities to Determine If They Are Putting God First in Their Lives

❖ Post a sheet of newsprint with the following words written on it. Distribute paper and pencils and ask the students to copy these words. They are then to rank these in order of priority, with one (1) being the most important priority. Urge the students to be honest. Provide a few moments for them to think about how they actually spend their time, which is the best indicator of priorities. Encourage them to be aware of conflicts in their priorities.

- Spouse
- Children
- Volunteer work
- Parents
- Work
- College/schooling
- Recreation/hobbies
- God
- Church services/events
- Home/yard maintenance

❖ Ask the adults to talk with two or three people about how they resolve conflicts in priorities. How do they determine what is most important?

❖ Encourage the groups to share any helpful ideas they gleaned regarding solving priority conflicts.

❖ Pose these questions for quiet reflection: **Do you believe that the order of your priorities is the same one God would want you to follow? If not, what changes do you need to make? What barriers have to be** overcome in order to make these changes?

(5) Continue the Journey

❖ Break the silence by praying that all who have gathered will be aware of God's priorities for them and order their lives accordingly.

❖ Read aloud this preparation for next week's lesson. You may also want to post it on newsprint for the students to copy.

- **Title: Rebuilding the Wall**
- **Background Scripture: Nehemiah 1:1–2:20**
- **Lesson Scripture: Nehemiah 2:1-8, 11, 17-18**
- **Focus of the Lesson: When a person of vision is in charge of a task, people will join in the work with a passion. How do we discern a worthy vision and recognize a visionary leader? God gave Nehemiah a vision of rebuilding the walls and the leadership ability to seek the king's favor and motivate people to work.**

❖ Challenge the students to complete one or more of these activities for further spiritual growth, which you will write on newsprint for the students to copy.

(1) **Think back on your priorities throughout life. What changes have you noticed? What are your current priorities? Are you truly keeping them in order?**

(2) **Contribute to a rebuilding project somewhere in the world.**

(3) **Do whatever you can to help someone who is spiritually adrift due to misplaced priorities.**

❖ Sing or read aloud "Breathe on Me, Breath of God."

❖ Conclude today's session by leading the class in this benediction, based on 2 Chronicles 34:31: **We renew our covenant to follow the LORD, keeping his commandments, with all our heart and all our soul, to perform the words of the covenant.**

UNIT 3: RESTORATION AND COVENANT RENEWAL
REBUILDING THE WALL

PREVIEWING THE LESSON

Lesson Scripture: Nehemiah 2:1-8, 11, 17-18
Background Scripture: Nehemiah 1:1–2:20
Key Verse: Nehemiah 2:18

Focus of the Lesson:
When a person of vision is in charge of a task, people will join in the work with a passion. How do we discern a worthy vision and recognize a visionary leader? God gave Nehemiah a vision of rebuilding the walls and the leadership ability to seek the king's favor and motivate people to work.

Goals for the Learners:
(1) to recount the story of Nehemiah's vision and strategy for rebuilding the wall of Jerusalem.
(2) to engage in dreaming about the tasks God has for them.
(3) to identify ways they can become involved in tasks for God and commit to action.

Pronunciation Guide:
Ammon (am' uhn)
Asaph (ay' saf)
Elam (ee' lhum)
Geshem (gesh' uhm)
Nisan (ni' san)
Susa (soo' suh)

Artaxerxes (ahr tuh zuhrk' seez)
Chislev (kiz' lev)
Elephantine (el uh fan ti' nee)
Kedar (kee' duhr)
Sanballat (san bal' at)
Tobiah (toh bi' uh)

Supplies:
Bibles, newsprint and marker, paper and pencils, hymnals

READING THE SCRIPTURE

NRSV
Nehemiah 2:1-8, 11, 17-18
¹In the month of Nisan, in the twentieth year of King Artaxerxes, when wine was served him, I carried the wine and gave it to

NIV
Nehemiah 2:1-8, 11, 17-18
¹In the month of Nisan in the twentieth year of King Artaxerxes, when wine was brought for him, I took the wine and gave it

the king. Now, I had never been sad in his presence before. ²So the king said to me, "Why is your face sad, since you are not sick? This can only be sadness of the heart." Then I was very much afraid. ³I said to the king, "May the king live forever! Why should my face not be sad, when the city, the place of my ancestors' graves, lies waste, and its gates have been destroyed by fire?" ⁴Then the king said to me, "What do you request?" So I prayed to the God of heaven. ⁵Then I said to the king, "If it pleases the king, and if your servant has found favor with you, I ask that you send me to Judah, to the city of my ancestors' graves, so that I may rebuild it." ⁶The king said to me (the queen also was sitting beside him), "How long will you be gone, and when will you return?" So it pleased the king to send me, and I set him a date. ⁷Then I said to the king, "If it pleases the king, let letters be given me to the governors of the province Beyond the River, that they may grant me passage until I arrive in Judah; ⁸and a letter to Asaph, the keeper of the king's forest, directing him to give me timber to make beams for the gates of the temple fortress, and for the wall of the city, and for the house that I shall occupy." And the king granted me what I asked, for the gracious hand of my God was upon me.

¹¹So I came to Jerusalem and was there for three days.

¹⁷Then I said to them, "You see the trouble we are in, how Jerusalem lies in ruins with its gates burned. Come, let us rebuild the wall of Jerusalem, so that we may no longer suffer disgrace." **¹⁸I told them that the hand of my God had been gracious upon me, and also the words that the king had spoken to me. Then they said, "Let us start building!" So they committed themselves to the common good.**

to the king. I had not been sad in his presence before; ²so the king asked me, "Why does your face look so sad when you are not ill? This can be nothing but sadness of heart."

I was very much afraid, ³but I said to the king, "May the king live forever! Why should my face not look sad when the city where my fathers are buried lies in ruins, and its gates have been destroyed by fire?"

⁴The king said to me, "What is it you want?"

Then I prayed to the God of heaven, ⁵and I answered the king, "If it pleases the king and if your servant has found favor in his sight, let him send me to the city in Judah where my fathers are buried so that I can rebuild it."

⁶Then the king, with the queen sitting beside him, asked me, "How long will your journey take, and when will you get back?" It pleased the king to send me; so I set a time.

⁷I also said to him, "If it pleases the king, may I have letters to the governors of Trans-Euphrates, so that they will provide me safe-conduct until I arrive in Judah? ⁸And may I have a letter to Asaph, keeper of the king's forest, so he will give me timber to make beams for the gates of the citadel by the temple and for the city wall and for the residence I will occupy?" And because the gracious hand of my God was upon me, the king granted my requests.

¹¹I went to Jerusalem, and after staying there three days.

¹⁷Then I said to them, "You see the trouble we are in: Jerusalem lies in ruins, and its gates have been burned with fire. Come, let us rebuild the wall of Jerusalem, and we will no longer be in disgrace." **¹⁸I also told them about the gracious hand of my God upon me and what the king had said to me.**

They replied, "Let us start rebuilding." So they began this good work.

UNDERSTANDING THE SCRIPTURE

Overview. The book of Nehemiah tells of Nehemiah's two governorships over Jerusalem. His first trip came in 445 or 444 B.C. when, distressed at the news of how little progress was being made in Jerusalem, he asked to be allowed to help. Once in Jerusalem, Nehemiah inspired the people to renew their building efforts despite the opposition, and within fifty-two days they had rebuilt the city walls (Nehemiah 6:15). Nehemiah served as governor for twelve more years and then returned to Persia.

His second trip came "after some time" (13:6). During this subsequent time as governor, Nehemiah was determined to strengthen the moral and liturgical life of the post-exilic community in Judah. To this end, he forced Jewish men to put away any local-born wives and their children (saying that marriage with these "foreign women" was a "great evil" and treacherous act against God, according to 13:27), restored the practice of tithes to the temple (13:10-14), and tightened the restrictions concerning Sabbath observance (13:15-22).

The first seven chapters of Nehemiah probably come from a personal memoir. (Note the use of "I" throughout the passages for this lesson and the next.) This means that we see everything in these chapters—from people to events—through Nehemiah's own perspective. For more history on the book of Nehemiah as a whole, see the Overview of Ezra 5 in the previous lesson.

Nehemiah 1:1-3. Nehemiah served King Artaxerxes I in the winter capital of Susa in Elam, located in what is now southwest Iran. The text says that word came to him in the month of Chislev, which corresponds to our November–December, in the twentieth year of the king's reign (445–444 B.C.). This is somewhat problematic because the date listed in 2:1, when he asks the king for permission to go to Jerusalem, is *earlier* than this. The men who bring word to Nehemiah

seem to be visitors to the capital, not folk who were there specifically to report to him.

Nehemiah 1:4-11. In learning of events back in Jerusalem, Nehemiah mourns and makes confession on the people's behalf, just as Ezra did (see Ezra 10:1-6). He recalls apparent words of Scripture in verses 8-9, but no such passage remains in the Hebrew Bible as we have it. The words do echo the sentiment found in Deuteronomy 30:1-5, however. The divine promise Nehemiah lifts up mentions a "place" where God's people will be gathered; for Nehemiah, that place is Jerusalem.

Verse 11 is a petition to God, asking that Nehemiah receive mercy from "this man." Because "this man" refers to Artaxerxes, scholars suggest that this verse has been displaced and really belongs after 2:4.

At the end of verse 11, Nehemiah explains that he was the king's cupbearer—a role we see enacted in 2:1. This was a position of great honor and trust. The cupbearer sampled wine for the king, certainly to assure the quality of its taste but perhaps also to test for poisoning, and then poured the actual wine to be drunk by the king himself. Because poison was a somewhat popular form of assassination in the ancient Near East, only the most trusted of servants handled the king's food and drink. Because Nehemiah was also allowed into the presence of the queen (2:6), he was probably a eunuch.

Nehemiah 2:1-8. The chapter begins in the month of Nisan, the equivalent of our March–April. No explanation is offered as to why this conversation between the king and Nehemiah takes place eight months prior to the events recorded in chapter 1.

When the king sees Nehemiah's sadness and asks as to the cause, Nehemiah explains (with great fear, 2:2) that his distress is over conditions in "the city, the place of my ancestors' graves" (2:3). Notice that Nehemiah does not call Jerusalem by name in the presence of the king, either here or later in verse 5. Some scholars speculate that this might be because the king thinks the city represents potential sedition or rebellion, perhaps based on reports from the "opposition" back in and near Jerusalem, and is therefore a sensitive subject to mention.

In any event, Nehemiah's language shifts the concern from the political realm to the personal one. The king agrees to his request for a trip to Judah—and then some! In 5:14 we finally learn that Nehemiah was sent as governor.

Nehemiah 2:9-10. Ezra 4:4-24 mentions that local leaders tried to interfere with the building of the walls. Apparently they rallied to marshal new resistance at the news of Nehemiah's appointment by the king and the support he was granted in the form of an army and cavalry. The Elephantine papyri mention Sanballat as a governor of Samaria, and Tobiah was probably in a similar position in Ammon. The lack of information regarding their titles in Nehemiah's memoirs may reflect a personal disinclination to record that the opposition held positions of honor and prestige.

Nehemiah 2:11-16. In verse 11, Nehemiah calls Jerusalem by name for the first time since 1:2-3. After the governor has been there three days, he makes a secret inspection of the walls at night. Beginning and ending at the Valley Gate, he covers the entire circumference of the walls. Verses 12 and 16 underscore that he is careful to let no one know what he is doing, other than the few men who accompany him, and that no one besides himself yet knows his plans for the city.

Nehemiah 2:17-20. If Nehemiah has been slow to call Jerusalem by name before, he makes up for it now. The name occurs three times in these three verses, and it is used as a powerful symbol. To the priests, nobles, officials, Jews, "and the rest that were to do the work" (2:16), the name resounds like a clarion call. Jerusalem lies in ruins and Jerusalem's gate needs rebuilding. As if hearing the name of God's holy city wakes them to their senses, all the people commit to the restoration project.

Verse 19 then reintroduces the theme of opposition. Sanballat, Tobiah, and Geshem (the king of Kedar, whose title is also omitted by Nehemiah) assume that the rebuilding of the walls is a first step leading to rebellion. In answering them, Nehemiah uses the name of Jerusalem to draw a definitive line marking them as outsiders to God's city and God's purposes.

INTERPRETING THE SCRIPTURE

Nehemiah the Leader

In today's lesson, we turn our attention to Nehemiah and the start of his ministry. The temple had been rebuilt and dedicated, but Jerusalem's walls still lay in ruins. Rebuilding the wall was an important piece of unfinished business, and Nehemiah devoted himself to that cause. It was not easy. Courageous and devoted leadership was essential to the completion of the project; Nehemiah provided that. He also provided well-developed skills in planning, organizing, and supervising—skills that his prominent position in Babylon had provided.

Nehemiah was not a trained diplomat, politician, or priest. He was a servant and a layman. He displayed a thorough knowledge of the law and the tradition of his people, however. In addition, Nehemiah was a gifted planner and an administrator. He was tactful where tact was called for, but he was firm and unyielding in the face of his opponents. He was a leader who showed great vision and who was able to inspire others to help him achieve his goals—which he knew to be God's goals.

Assessing a Leader's Vision

Most of us feel inspired by leaders who are people of vision. We are motivated by their commitment to a future goal, and we love the sense of being part of something larger than just our present circumstances. How can we recognize a truly visionary leader, though, and how can we discern if her or his vision is a worthy one?

One place to start is by seeking to know what undergirds the leader's vision. Nehemiah was guided by a genuine desire to do God's will, and his personal skills helped him get others to join his cause. John Wesley, the founder of Methodism, considered every vision—every goal—in light of Scripture, tradition, experience, and reason. All four, in tension and balance, enabled him to make faithful and responsible choices toward the future.

Another important question to ask is what, if anything, the leader has to gain by the vision that is held up. Does it consolidate that person's power? Does it give him or her more wealth or status? If so, then the vision and the leader are rightly suspect. In Nehemiah's case, he stood to lose the comfort and security of his place in the king's household. He had nothing to gain, as far as he knew, except the satisfaction and joy of helping others and pleasing God.

True visionary leaders, like Nehemiah, look to what they can do to the glory of God's name in humble service to the Lord of life. They are often called on to put themselves in dangerous situations, and many are willing to volunteer for these difficult tasks. They are frequently the ones who take an unpopular stance. Visionary leaders are people who demonstrate self-knowledge, humility, openness, and often a healthy sense of humor. They are the ones who encourage us, cajole us, yell at us, cry with us, love us, hold us, push us, pull us, walk beside us—and keep us moving deeper toward God's vision for ourselves, the church, and the world.

Following God's Call

We all have dreams, some of which may be more realistic than others. Young children dream of being astronauts or firefighters or jungle explorers, for example. While some grow up to attain those careers, most do not. As we age, we find ourselves going down other paths instead, based on interests or circumstances or, one hopes, a growing sense of vocation.

Although following a visionary leader is important, so is following our own sense of God's call. This passage challenges us to reevaluate our lives not in terms of the dreams we have held, but in terms of the dreams that God holds for us. Who is it that God wants us to be? What is it that God wants us to do? That is the vision that can open our eyes to a whole new level of understanding of our place in the church and in the world.

Of course, part of the role of visionary leaders is to help us discern God's dream for our lives. According to Ephesians 4:11–13:

The gifts [Christ] gave were that some would be apostles, some prophets, some evangelists, some pastors and teachers, to equip the saints for the work of ministry, for building up the body of Christ, until all of us come to the unity of the faith and of the knowledge of the Son of God, to maturity, to the measure of the full stature of Christ.

Notice verse 12, which says that the aim of these gifted leaders is "to equip the saints for the work of ministry." In other words, they are charged with the task of empowering all laity so that, together, God's dreams can come true through us. The writer of Ephesians knew that one of the ways God's visions are achieved is through the gifts with which we are born. Like a gifted singer or artist we hone and develop our innate skills and abilities through use and practice. We also achieve our greatest potential by working with an accomplished mentor or trainer who can teach us the finer points of our craft. Thus, the writer identified offices in the church designed to give all members the special help they need to develop and use their gifts to the fullest. These leaders are part of God's plan for seeing the divine vision come to fruition.

A Holy Yes

The theology of the empowerment of the whole community to perform ministry is central to the church's understanding of itself. Nevertheless, most of us do not think of ourselves as gifted or as leaders, much less as gifted leaders! We do affirm that the Spirit gives gifts and that all these gifts are necessary to the good of the whole. When it comes to seeing our own place in the plan, however, we often think, "Yes, but . . . not in my case."

Today is Pentecost, the key day in the Christian year when the church says back to us that there is no "yes, but." The gift of the Spirit, given in Jerusalem two thousand years ago and every moment since, is for us all. We may not all be visionary leaders in the way Nehemiah was, but we each receive the Spirit nonetheless.

Granted, we may not be as open to the control and direction of the Spirit as were the folk at that first Pentecost. Our hectic lives sometimes blind us to the vision that the Spirit provides. At work or school there is no time to be open to God. At home we are swamped by chores, bills, and over-full personal schedules. Even at church we are consumed by meetings and never-ending tasks. Sometimes there is little room left for the Spirit at all.

The good news is that, as Nehemiah declared, we too can still proclaim that the hand of our God has been gracious upon us, in that God sends the Spirit whether we feel ready for it or not. Moreover, when the Spirit comes, it comes saying a holy "Yes" that drowns out all our "buts." In that "Yes," as Nehemiah found, we also find ourselves inspired, empowered, and transformed. Thanks be to God!

SHARING THE SCRIPTURE

Preparing Our Hearts

Meditate on this week's devotional reading, found in Psalm 137:1-7 and 138:1-5. Psalm 137 is a lament written in Babylon during the exile, apparently in response to taunting by captors who want the Israelites to sing their own music. In contrast, an individual offers praise to God in Psalm 138, thanking God for help in answer to prayer. As you read aloud these psalms, imagine how you would have felt had you been the writer of either of them. Look for connections between your life at this moment and these psalms.

Pray that you and the adult learners will recognize God's presence even in extremely difficult circumstances and give thanks for God's intervention on your behalf.

Preparing Our Minds

Study the background from Nehemiah 1:1–2:20 and lesson Scripture, Nehemiah 2:1-8, 11, 17-18. As you consider this passage, think about how you discern a worthy vision and recognize a visionary leader.

Write on newsprint:
❑ information for next week's lesson, found under "Continue the Journey."
❑ activities for further spiritual growth in "Continue the Journey."

Plan a brief lecture on Nehemiah 1 for "Recount the Story of Nehemiah's Vision and Strategy for Rebuilding the Wall of Jerusalem."

LEADING THE CLASS

(1) Gather to Learn

❖ Welcome the class members and introduce any guests.

❖ Pray that all who have come together today will be led by God's Spirit to envision new possibilities in their own lives and in the life of their church.

❖ Write the word "vision" on newsprint. Invite the students to define that word and give an example of someone who had vision and acted upon it. (This person may even be someone in the congregation's history whose vision set the church on the path that it finds itself on today.)

❖ Read aloud today's focus statement: **When a person of vision is in charge of a task, people will join in the work with a passion. How do we discern a worthy vision and recognize a visionary leader? God gave Nehemiah a vision of rebuilding the walls and the leadership ability to seek the king's favor and motivate people to work.**

(2) Recount the Story of Nehemiah's Vision and Strategy for Rebuilding the Wall of Jerusalem

❖ Use information for Nehemiah 1 from Understanding the Scripture to set the stage for today's lesson.

❖ Call for three volunteers to read the parts of a narrator, Nehemiah, and King Artaxerxes as a drama from Nehemiah 2:1-8. Discuss these questions.

(1) **What did you learn about Nehemiah's vision?**

(2) **What details prompt you to believe that Nehemiah has carefully prayed and thought about what he will say to the king?**

(3) **Based on the king's response, how would you describe his relationship with Nehemiah?**

❖ Select someone to read Nehemiah 2:11, 17-18.

■ Invite the students to list on newsprint any characteristics of a visionary leader that Nehemiah seems to exhibit.

■ Note that the people committed themselves to this building project, based on Nehemiah's visionary leadership. Read or retell "Assessing a Leader's Vision" in Interpreting the Scripture.

(3) Engage the Learners in Dreaming About the Tasks God Has for Them

❖ Read or retell "Following God's Call" from Interpreting the Scripture. You may want to ask the students to turn to Ephesians 4:11-13 as you read that passage.

❖ Provide quiet time. Encourage the adults to recall some dreams from their childhood. Ask these questions, pausing after each one to allow time for the students to respond silently.

(1) **Which of your childhood dreams have you fulfilled?**

(2) **Which one do you wish you could still fulfill?**

(3) **Do any of these dreams point you toward any task(s) that God has for you to do now?**

❖ Invite volunteers to tell about their dreams. Encourage the class to affirm these visions. Also ask the students to be aware of others who have dreams that are similar to their own.

(4) Identify Ways the Learners Can Become Involved in Tasks for God and Commit to Action

❖ Distribute paper and pencils. Invite the students to create a plan of action related to the dreams they have regarding a task that God has for them to do. Read aloud these steps and ask the class to write specific ideas on their papers.

■ **Step 1: Write in one sentence what you believe your task is.** (Example: I believe God is calling me to alleviate hunger.)

■ **Step 2: Write one sentence explaining why you think this task needs to be done.** (Example: Due to the closure of a major business, many people in our community are unemployed and in need of food.)

■ **Step 3: Write one sentence detailing how and where you can accomplish this task.** (Example: I can help our church to collect food that can be delivered to the county food bank.)

■ **Step 4: Write ideas about who you need to contact, what you need to do, and any money that will be involved in accomplishing your task.** (Example: I will talk with the county food bank about the kinds of food they collect, when they accept deliveries, and how they determine who is eligible to receive food. I will present my idea to our outreach committee to enlist support and volunteer help. We may need a minimal amount of money for publicity, but everything else will be donated.)

❖ **Option:** Encourage volunteers to share the tasks to which they have been called. Students with similar callings may want to work together in fulfilling their tasks.

❖ Read aloud "A Holy Yes."

❖ Invite those who will commit themselves to becoming involved in the task(s) to which God calls them to indicate by saying "Yes, yes, yes!"

(5) Continue the Journey

❖ Pray that today's participants will catch God's vision for their lives and enact that vision, just as Nehemiah did.

❖ Read aloud this preparation for next week's lesson. You may also want to post it on newsprint for the students to copy.

■ **Title: Up Against the Wall**

■ **Background Scripture: Nehemiah 4–6**

■ **Lesson Scripture: Nehemiah 4:1-3, 6-9, 13-15; 6:15**

■ **Focus of the Lesson: With every worthy cause come detractors, those who will ridicule or work against it. How can we carry on? Nehemiah and the Israelites found God's help to counteract the plots against them and to continue the work on the wall—finishing in record time.**

❖ Challenge the students to complete one or more of these activities for further spiritual growth, which you will write on newsprint for the students to copy.

(1) Ponder the characteristics of people to whom you look for leadership: clergy, church leaders, bosses, elected officials. What common traits do you notice among those who offer vision and inspiration? What traits are common among those leaders who seem ineffective?

(2) Work with a group right now being led by someone who has vision to accomplish something for God.

(3) Research someone who has been led by God to create a visionary ministry. Consider Robert Schuller, who built the Crystal Cathedral; Nicky Cruz, a gang-member-turned-evangelist whose story is told in *Run, Baby, Run;* or Bill Wilson and Robert Smith, co-founders of Alcoholics Anonymous.

❖ Sing or read aloud "Be Thou My Vision."

❖ Conclude today's session by leading the class in this benediction, based on 2 Chronicles 34:31: **We renew our covenant to follow the LORD, keeping his commandments, with all our heart and all our soul, to perform the words of the covenant.**

UNIT 3: RESTORATION AND COVENANT RENEWAL
UP AGAINST THE WALL

PREVIEWING THE LESSON

Lesson Scripture: Nehemiah 4:1-3, 6-9, 13-15; 6:15
Background Scripture: Nehemiah 4–6
Key Verse: Nehemiah 4:6

Focus of the Lesson:
With every worthy cause come detractors, those who will ridicule or work against it. How can we carry on? Nehemiah and the Israelites found God's help to counteract the plots against them and to continue the work on the wall—finishing in record time.

Goals for the Learners:
(1) to discover the story of how the people continued the work of rebuilding the wall despite the plots of neighboring enemies.
(2) to relate the Israelites' perseverance to their own determination in the face of difficulties.
(3) to trust God to help them complete tasks even when obstacles seem insurmountable.

Pronunciation Guide:
Ammonite (am' uh nit)   Ashdodite (ash' duh dit)
Elul (ee' luhl)   Geshem (gesh' uhm)
Noadiah (noh uh di' uh)   Sanballat (san bal' at)
Shemaiah (shi may' yuh)   Tobiah (toh bi' uh)

Supplies:
Bibles, newsprint and marker, paper and pencils, hymnals

READING THE SCRIPTURE

NRSV
Nehemiah 4:1-3, 6-9, 13-15

¹Now when Sanballat heard that we were building the wall, he was angry and greatly enraged, and he mocked the Jews. ²He said in the presence of his associates and of the army of Samaria, "What are these feeble Jews doing? Will they restore things? Will

NIV
Nehemiah 4:1-3, 6-9, 13-15

¹When Sanballat heard that we were rebuilding the wall, he became angry and was greatly incensed. He ridiculed the Jews, ²and in the presence of his associates and the army of Samaria, he said, "What are those feeble Jews doing? Will they restore their

they sacrifice? Will they finish it in a day? Will they revive the stones out of the heaps of rubbish—and burned ones at that?" [3]Tobiah the Ammonite was beside him, and he said, "That stone wall they are building—any fox going up on it would break it down!"

[6]So we rebuilt the wall, and all the wall was joined together to half its height; for the people had a mind to work.

[7]But when Sanballat and Tobiah and the Arabs and the Ammonites and the Ashdodites heard that the repairing of the walls of Jerusalem was going forward and the gaps were beginning to be closed, they were very angry, [8]and all plotted together to come and fight against Jerusalem and to cause confusion in it. [9]So we prayed to our God, and set a guard as a protection against them day and night.

[13]So in the lowest parts of the space behind the wall, in open places, I stationed the people according to their families, with their swords, their spears, and their bows. [14]After I looked these things over, I stood up and said to the nobles and the officials and the rest of the people, "Do not be afraid of them. Remember the LORD, who is great and awesome, and fight for your kin, your sons, your daughters, your wives, and your homes."

[15]When our enemies heard that their plot was known to us, and that God had frustrated it, we all returned to the wall, each to his work.

Nehemiah 6:15
[15]So the wall was finished on the twenty-fifth day of the month Elul, in fifty-two days.

wall? Will they offer sacrifices? Will they finish in a day? Can they bring the stones back to life from those heaps of rubble—burned as they are?"

[3]Tobiah the Ammonite, who was at his side, said, "What they are building—if even a fox climbed up on it, he would break down their wall of stones!"

[6]So we rebuilt the wall till all of it reached half its height, for the people worked with all their heart.

[7]But when Sanballat, Tobiah, the Arabs, the Ammonites and the men of Ashdod heard that the repairs to Jerusalem's walls had gone ahead and that the gaps were being closed, they were very angry. [8]They all plotted together to come and fight against Jerusalem and stir up trouble against it. [9]But we prayed to our God and posted a guard day and night to meet this threat.

[13]Therefore I stationed some of the people behind the lowest points of the wall at the exposed places, posting them by families, with their swords, spears and bows. [14]After I looked things over, I stood up and said to the nobles, the officials and the rest of the people, "Don't be afraid of them. Remember the Lord, who is great and awesome, and fight for your brothers, your sons and your daughters, your wives and your homes."

[15]When our enemies heard that we were aware of their plot and that God had frustrated it, we all returned to the wall, each to his own work.

Nehemiah 6:15
[15]So the wall was completed on the twenty-fifth of Elul, in fifty-two days.

UNDERSTANDING THE SCRIPTURE

Overview. Chapters 4, 5, and 6 outline the problems Nehemiah faced in the reconstruction of Jerusalem. The section ends with the successful completion of the walls.

Nehemiah 4:1-5. Sanballat and his associates, mentioned in Nehemiah 2:10, 19, appear again to offer more opposition to Nehemiah's efforts. Verses 4-5 are a prayer that Nehemiah offers, asking God to bring punishment to them in accordance with the evil taunts they have made against the Jews. This concept of retribution, wherein an enemy's plans or thoughts for evil come back on them, was common in the ancient Near East.

Nehemiah 4:6-9. The people persist in rebuilding the wall anyway. This angers the foreign opposition, who then decides to cause conflict and confusion within Jerusalem— apparently by killing workers (see 4:11). Accordingly, Nehemiah leads the people in prayer and sets a guard on the walls.

Nehemiah 4:10-14. Nehemiah faces two crises. The first is that the laborers are becoming worn out by the sheer amount of work, and progress is subsequently slowed. Far worse, Jews coming into Jerusalem from the outer areas bring news of the plot hatched by Sanballat and the others. Nehemiah responds by organizing "troops" of the citizenry and stationing them behind the wall with weapons. These forces were apparently composed of adult men only, because Nehemiah urges them to fight for "your kin, your sons, your daughters, your wives, and your homes" (4:14).

Nehemiah 4:15-20. When Sanballat and the others learn that Nehemiah is aware of their plot, they apparently back off on their plans to attack. The situation changes enough that Nehemiah resumes work on the walls, albeit with caution. His own personal bodyguard ("my servants," 4:16), who are better trained and better armed than the average citizens, help in the work and in the protection of the laborers. All the laborers wear weapons, however, and Nehemiah devises a plan in case of attack.

Nehemiah 4:21-23. Nehemiah details the seriousness of the situation. The adult male populace is pressed into guard duty all night in addition to wall labor by day. Nehemiah himself is so determined to be ready in case of an attack that no one in his party ever undresses, and they carry their weapons in their hands.

Nehemiah 5:1-5. The concentration of all male labor on repairing the wall leads to an economic crisis. Farms and vineyards had not been cultivated for some time, so now there is neither grain nor money from crops. The people have been forced to borrow money, putting up their land and homes as collateral, in order to buy food and to pay their annual tax to the Persian king. The debts are now coming due, and the people are unable to pay. They have lost their farms and vineyards and are facing the worse prospect of having their children sold into slavery for partial restitution of the debt. Apparently some of the debt holders have already sought payment in the form of "ravishing" the daughters of debtors (5:5).

Nehemiah 5:6-13. When Nehemiah hears these complaints, he becomes outraged at the nobles and officials. He orders them to stop charging interest on these debts, as the law only allows taking interest from non-Jews (see Deuteronomy 23:20). The typical amount of interest was 1 percent paid monthly. Nehemiah also orders the nobles and officials to give back everything that had already been confiscated in the name of repaying a debt.

Nehemiah does not stop at political reform, however. He also calls the priests and makes them swear to uphold their promises. He then casts a form of curse on the priests, to be invoked if they break their promise. This kind of verbal curse that mirrors an action to which it is tied, such as Nehemiah shaking empty the garment fold that served as his pocket, was very typical in the ancient Near East.

Nehemiah 5:14-19. Nehemiah describes how he refused for the twelve years of his appointment to take the food ration allotted to him as governor. He also points out that he acquired no land during this time. He wants to make it clear that he did not burden the people or take advantage of them in any way.

Nehemiah 6:1-9. When Sanballat and Geshem learn that the walls are complete except for doors in the gates, they try to destroy Nehemiah's credibility as leader. Four times they ask Nehemiah to meet outside the city, but Nehemiah refuses out of distrust. Nehemiah is wise enough to know that even if bodily harm is not meant, simply going to this meeting could be used to discredit him with the Persian court.

Then Sanballat sends a letter to say that he is going to report to the Persian king that Nehemiah has not only built up the walls in preparation for a rebellion, but that prophets have already declared him to be king of Judah. (The mention of prophets would be a buzzword for the Persian king, because they were often considered the instigators of rebellion.) Nehemiah is apparently unafraid of this threat.

Nehemiah 6:10-14. The plot to discredit Nehemiah continues, this time with enemy collaborators within Jerusalem. A man named Shemaiah warns Nehemiah that his life is in danger and urges him to seek sanctuary in the temple. Nehemiah soon sees this as a trap, however—going into the temple would be a sacrilege and would thus discredit Nehemiah with the local Jewish leadership. Apparently more people than just Shemaiah tried to persuade Nehemiah to do this rash act; his prayer for retribution names "the prophetess Noadiah and the rest of the prophets who wanted to make me afraid" (6:14).

Nehemiah 6:15-19. The people finish the wall in the sixth month, Elul (August–September). Nehemiah's joy is muted, however, by the continued presence of his enemies—and one in particular. For the first time, we learn that the nobles of Judah regularly correspond with Tobiah the Ammonite (6:17) and that he even has in-laws and friends in Jerusalem (6:18). The pro-Tobiah folk openly speak on his behalf in front of Nehemiah, and they report Nehemiah's own words back to him (6:19). The chapter does not end on a note of triumph and joy, as we might expect, but with the ongoing, seemingly endless conflict: "And Tobiah sent letters to intimidate me" (6:19). One can almost hear Nehemiah sigh, "Again."

INTERPRETING THE SCRIPTURE

Confidence Busters

In the last lesson, we saw how Nehemiah became governor of Judah and began a campaign to rebuild Jerusalem's walls. This week's study highlights a major problem that Nehemiah encounters while trying to rebuild the wall of Jerusalem. Two of his foreign political counterparts, Sanballat and Tobiah, become enraged over the construction and set out to halt the project.

We are not told why Sanballat and Tobiah react as they do to the plan to rebuild the wall. Nehemiah 2:19 suggests that they believe this action is a prelude to rebelling against the king, but we are left to wonder if something else motivates them as well. The text leaves no doubt as to their determination, however—they will try anything to stop the building process. Initially, Sanballat stages a speech to his associates and army that the Jews inside the wall are supposed to overhear. Later on, we will see that he and Tobiah plan to move from words to violence.

The tactics employed by the two men are familiar ones. They look for the soft spots in the public psyche and then try to use the people's fears and insecurities against them. Many of us have seen schoolyard bullies and maladjusted adults do the same. In Nehemiah 4:1-3, Sanballat and his cronies focus on four key concerns designed to undermine the people's confidence and dedication.

First, Sanballat raises the issue of *ability*. Chapter 3 showed that Nehemiah placed each person at the job for which they were best suited. One gets a sense from that chapter of each person doing their best and feeling happy with the results. Here, however, Sanballat talks about "these feeble Jews" (4:2) and, in so doing, sets himself at a psychological advantage. The Jews have no strength compared to the army he is addressing, and everyone knows they have not been trained for the task they are doing. Sanballat plays on natural human doubt and raises the question of whether the people will have the energy and skill necessary to complete the task.

Next he questions the *quality* of their work. Will they be able to restore the wall to its former glory (4:2)? Of course not. As if this might not be demoralizing enough, Sanballat's stated question also points to an implied one: If the Jews cannot create the wall as it was, then why bother with this inferior copy? Shouldn't they all just give up this pretense at rebuilding and go back to their lives?

Third, Sanballat mentions *time*. Will the people finish the wall in a day (4:2)? Again, the answer is of course not—but the very mention of a time limit will automatically get the people thinking about just how long a project like this takes to complete. Certainly that will discourage and dissuade them, or so Sanballat hopes.

Finally, he raises up their lack of *resources*. What do the people have to work with? Just "the stones out of the heaps of rubbish— and burned ones at that" (4:2). Surely they cannot believe that such damaged building material, such trash, can build a wall that will stand, much less protect them? Again, the implication is that the people are wasting their time because they have no hope of accomplishing this goal. "You might as well quit while you're ahead," we can almost hear Sanballat say.

All too often, these same confidence busters crop up in our congregations. Members constantly doubt their ability and skills, believing that they have no gift of value to offer to the community, and they often hesitate to take on a task because they do not think they can perform it well. How many times, for example, have you heard someone say, "I don't know enough to teach the Bible"? Certainly the time factor involved in a project continues to be an issue for volunteers, and the lack of resources has kept many of our smaller churches from doing all that they would like. Yet, God's people do persevere.

More Problems

Sanballat and his associates said to the Jews, in essence, "Give up. You don't have the strength, skills, time, or resources to finish this task. Your very efforts are a joke." Yet what does Nehemiah tell us next? "So we rebuilt the wall" (4:6). Despite all the problems that Sanballat named, which were real, the people persevered at their task.

When they get the wall rebuilt about half-way up, Nehemiah and the people then face a more serious problem from their enemies. Word comes to Nehemiah that Sanballat, Tobiah, and others are through taunting and mocking. Now they intend to attack. If the people felt inadequate and insecure at being builders, imagine how they must feel at suddenly becoming a defending force!

Nehemiah and the Jews meet this latest news with piety and practicality. First they pray, then they set a twenty-four-hour guard on the wall. Their caution is rewarded when the attack is canceled.

Carrying On

In reading through the list of obstacles that Nehemiah and the others overcame, we have to wonder what gave them the strength and courage to carry on. The answer may lie in Nehemiah's speech to the people (4:14). First he exhorts the people to remember

God, "who is great and awesome." By focusing on God's nature and power, the people can see that nothing is impossible. The half-built wall before them is proof of what a people can do when they work with God and for God.

Next Nehemiah charges the makeshift army to fight for their families and homes. If this were a war movie and Nehemiah were a general making a speech to inspire the troops, we would say that he had just hit all the basics. God, family, and home—these are all worth fighting for. They are the motivations that keep us going when difficulties make it tough.

The inspiration from Nehemiah, plus whatever encouragement the Jews lend to one another while they are gathered at the wall, works. The people do not break and run from the threat, and the enemies back down. Our text ends with the joyous announcement that the wall is complete, and in only a few months' time. The Jews' persistence has created the great gift of safety for all who live in the city—a gift understood to come from the sheer grace of God.

In this second part of the story, we see how we too can carry on when problems arise. First, like the people in this text, we need to go to God in prayer. Through prayer, we remind ourselves that the Lord is indeed an awesome and great God who can work amazing things through us. On a human level, there may be plenty of reason for our personal confidence to be shaken. On a divine level, however, there is no room for doubt—God can do anything.

In addition, we can find strength to continue when we remember the people we love. The desire to provide and care for them, as well as the desire to protect them, is often a powerful motivating force. On our own, we will certainly be tempted to quit when trouble hits. When we combine our love of others with our faith in God, however, we find, "I can do all things through him [Christ] who strengthens me" (Philippians 4:13).

SHARING THE SCRIPTURE

Preparing Our Hearts

Meditate on this week's devotional reading, found in Psalm 70. We hear an individual who cries out to God for deliverance from his enemies. The psalmist clearly fears for his life, but he also trusts that God will take care of him. When have you felt that enemies were trying to make your life miserable? How did you respond? Where was God? If enemies are disturbing your peace now, write your own psalm, asking God to set you free from those persons, ideas, or memories that have bound you.

Pray that you and the adult learners will be open to God's amazing guidance and support in your life.

Preparing Our Minds

Study the background, which includes chapters 4, 5, and 6 of Nehemiah, and lesson Scripture, Nehemiah 4:1-3, 6-9, 13-15 and 6:15. How can we carry on when detractors ridicule us?

Write on newsprint:
❑ information for next week's lesson, found under "Continue the Journey."
❑ activities for further spiritual growth in "Continue the Journey."

Practice reading aloud today's Scripture passage. You are being asked to read this because it contains names that you can find in the Pronunciation Guide.

LEADING THE CLASS

(1) Gather to Learn

❖ Welcome the class members and introduce any guests.

❖ Pray that everyone who has gathered today will experience God's empowerment and encouragement.

❖ Read aloud this story: **In 2004 the Boston Red Sox overcame the eighty-six-year-old "curse of the Bambino" (Babe Ruth) to make an amazing comeback over the New York Yankees and win the American League pennant. The Red Sox had been down 3–0 games but managed to hang on as no other team in major league history had done and finally rout the Yankees in Game 7 with an incredible score of 10–3. The team went on to win the World Series over the Saint Louis Cardinals, their first Series win since 1918.**

❖ Discuss these questions.

(1) **What do you think people might have said before the pennant match about the Red Sox team's chances of beating the Yankees?**

(2) **How might such negative comments have made you feel had you been a Red Sox team member?**

(3) **Why do you suppose the Red Sox won not only the pennant but also the World Series?**

❖ Read aloud today's focus statement: **With every worthy cause come detractors, those who will ridicule or work against it. How can we carry on? Nehemiah and the Israelites found God's help to counteract the plots against them and to continue the work on the wall—finishing in record time.**

(2) Discover the Story of How the People Continued the Work of Rebuilding the Wall Despite the Plots of Neighboring Enemies

❖ Ask the students to follow along in their Bibles as you read aloud Nehemiah 4:1-3, 6-9, 13-15; 6:15.

❖ Look first at 4:1-3. Make a list of the taunts uttered by Sanballat and Tobiah. Use the comments under "Confidence Busters" in Interpreting the Scripture, paragraphs four through seven, to round out the list. Note that these taunts focus on ability, quality of work, time, and lack of resources.

❖ Direct attention to 4:7-9. Observe that the work did not stop, despite continuing harassment and threat of attack. Look at verse 9 to discern how the people were able to continue.

❖ Look at 4:13-15. Ask: **How did Nehemiah encourage the people to continue working?** You may wish to read or retell "Carrying On" in Interpreting the Scripture.

❖ Point out that Nehemiah 6:15 records that the wall was completed "in fifty-two days." Ask: **What observations can you make about the people, their leader Nehemiah, and God?**

(3) Relate the Israelites' Perseverance to the Learners' Determination in the Face of Difficulties

❖ Note that we have discussed the problems Nehemiah and the people faced as enemies taunted them and tried to destroy their confidence. Still, they persevered and completed their task.

❖ Encourage the students to talk with a partner about these questions: **Under what circumstances have you also been taunted by people who thought you could not do what you had set out to do? How did you handle the situation?**

❖ Read aloud these two verses from "Be Still, My Soul" by Katharina von Schlegel (1752), translated by Jane Borthwick (1855).

Be still, my soul: the Lord is on your side.

Bear patiently the cross of grief or pain; leave to your God to order and provide;

in every change God faithful will remain.

Be still, my soul: your best, your heavenly friend

Through thorny ways leads to a joyful end.

Be still, my soul: your God will undertake

to guide the future, as in ages past.

Your hope, your confidence let nothing shake;

all now mysterious shall be bright at last.

Be still, my soul: the waves and winds still know

the Christ who ruled them while he dwelt below.

❖ Encourage the adults to comment on how the poet's words might prompt them to persevere in the face of difficulties.

(4) Trust God to Help Complete Tasks Even When Obstacles Seem Insurmountable

❖ Read aloud this comment by Oswald Chambers (1874–1917): **"It is a great thing to see physical pluck, and greater still to see moral pluck, but the greatest to see of all is spiritual pluck, to see a man who will stand true to the integrity of Jesus Christ no matter what he is going through."**

❖ Provide quiet time for the students to ponder Chambers' words. Suggest that they think about a difficult situation in their own lives right now and consider how they are standing with the integrity of Christ.

❖ **Option:** Conclude this portion of the lesson by reading responsively Psalm 27:1-4 from the Psalter in your hymnal. Here the psalmist affirms his faith in God, even though he is surrounded by enemies.

(5) Continue the Journey

❖ Pray that the students will go forth resolved to complete whatever tasks God calls them to do, no matter what the obstacles.

❖ Read aloud this preparation for next week's lesson. You may also want to post it on newsprint for the students to copy.

■ **Title: Call to Renew the Covenant**

■ **Background Scripture: Nehemiah 8**

■ **Lesson Scripture: Nehemiah 8:1-3, 5-6, 13-14, 17-18**

■ **Focus of the Lesson: The rebuilding of life requires reestablishing right relationships. What relationships are important to reestablish? Ezra challenged the returned Israelite exiles to reestablish their covenant relationship with God and with one another.**

❖ Challenge the students to complete one or more of these activities for further spiritual growth, which you will write on newsprint for the students to copy.

(1) **Work with a child to build a wall of play blocks. What factors enabled the wall to stand? What happened that caused the wall to fall? Tell the story of Nehemiah to the child as you work.**

(2) **Locate a group, such as Habitat for Humanity or a Volunteers in Mission work team, that builds/rebuilds homes and lives. Work with this group. Consider going to an area that has experienced natural devastation.**

(3) **Bolster the confidence of someone who has been beaten down by naysayers. Help this person to know that God will empower him or her to complete the project/mission.**

❖ Sing or read aloud "How Firm a Foundation."

❖ Conclude today's session by leading the class in this benediction, based on 2 Chronicles 34:31: **We renew our covenant to follow the LORD, keeping his commandments, with all our heart and all our soul, to perform the words of the covenant.**

UNIT 3: RESTORATION AND COVENANT RENEWAL

CALL TO RENEW THE COVENANT

PREVIEWING THE LESSON

Lesson Scripture: Nehemiah 8:1-3, 5-6, 13-14, 17-18
Background Scripture: Nehemiah 8
Key Verse: Nehemiah 8:3

Focus of the Lesson:
The rebuilding of life requires reestablishing right relationships. What relationships are important to reestablish? Ezra challenged the returned Israelite exiles to reestablish their covenant relationship with God and with one another.

Goals for the Learners:
(1) to examine Ezra's challenge to the people to obey the law of the covenant.
(2) to see the relationship between worship and obedience to God.
(3) to commit to obey and worship God as a sign of renewed relationship with God and neighbor.

Pronunciation Guide:
Jeshua (jesh' oo uh)   Rosh Hashanah (rosh huh shah' nuh)
Succoth (suk'ut)   Tishri (tish' ree)
torah (toh' ruh)   Yom Kippur (yom kih poor')

Supplies:
Bibles, newsprint and marker, paper and pencils, hymnals, optional picture(s) of Succoth booths

---

READING THE SCRIPTURE

NRSV
Nehemiah 8:1-3, 5-6, 13-14, 17-18

¹All the people gathered together into the square before the Water Gate. They told the scribe Ezra to bring the book of the law of Moses, which the LORD had given to Israel. ²Accordingly, the priest Ezra brought the

NIV
Nehemiah 8:1-3, 5-6, 13-14, 17-18

¹All the people assembled as one man in the square before the Water Gate. They told Ezra the scribe to bring out the Book of the Law of Moses, which the LORD had commanded for Israel.

law before the assembly, both men and women and all who could hear with understanding. This was on the first day of the seventh month. **³He read from it facing the square before the Water Gate from early morning until midday, in the presence of the men and the women and those who could understand; and the ears of all the people were attentive to the book of the law. . . .** ⁵And Ezra opened the book in the sight of all the people, for he was standing above all the people; and when he opened it, all the people stood up. ⁶Then Ezra blessed the LORD, the great God, and all the people answered, "Amen, Amen," lifting up their hands. Then they bowed their heads and worshiped the LORD with their faces to the ground.

¹³On the second day the heads of ancestral houses of all the people, with the priests and the Levites, came together to the scribe Ezra in order to study the words of the law. ¹⁴And they found it written in the law, which the LORD had commanded by Moses, that the people of Israel should live in booths during the festival of the seventh month. . . . ¹⁷And all the assembly of those who had returned from the captivity made booths and lived in them; for from the days of Jeshua son of Nun to that day the people of Israel had not done so. And there was very great rejoicing. ¹⁸And day by day, from the first day to the last day, he read from the book of the law of God. They kept the festival seven days; and on the eighth day there was a solemn assembly, according to the ordinance.

²So on the first day of the seventh month Ezra the priest brought the Law before the assembly, which was made up of men and women and all who were able to understand. **³He read it aloud from daybreak till noon as he faced the square before the Water Gate in the presence of the men, women and others who could understand. And all the people listened attentively to the Book of the Law.**

⁵Ezra opened the book. All the people could see him because he was standing above them; and as he opened it, the people all stood up. ⁶Ezra praised the LORD, the great God; and all the people lifted their hands and responded, "Amen! Amen!" Then they bowed down and worshiped the LORD with their faces to the ground.

¹³On the second day of the month, the heads of all the families, along with the priests and the Levites, gathered around Ezra the scribe to give attention to the words of the Law. ¹⁴They found written in the Law, which the LORD had commanded through Moses, that the Israelites were to live in booths during the feast of the seventh month.

¹⁷The whole company that had returned from exile built booths and lived in them. From the days of Joshua son of Nun until that day, the Israelites had not celebrated it like this. And their joy was very great.

¹⁸Day after day, from the first day to the last, Ezra read from the Book of the Law of God. They celebrated the feast for seven days, and on the eighth day, in accordance with the regulation, there was an assembly.

UNDERSTANDING THE SCRIPTURE

Overview. Nehemiah 8 picks up Ezra's story and the reading of the book of the law. Notice that it is the people who initiate the action. They gather in Jerusalem without being summoned, and they ask Ezra to bring the book of the law and read it. Seasonally, they had come to one of the holiest periods in the Jewish calendar, and the people were hungry for Scripture and ritual to help renew their spirits and their sense of community. This chapter is the story of how their leaders—and the people themselves—responded to that need.

Nehemiah 8:1-8. The people gather in the square before the Water Gate on the first day of the seventh month, Tishri (September–October). This was Jewish New Year—Rosh Hashanah. The day was to be greeted with trumpet blasts, and it was a day for solemn convocation (Leviticus 23:23-25; Numbers 29:1). The first day of the month ushered in a period of significant worship and renewal. The tenth day of the month was the Day of Atonement, and the fifteenth marked the beginning of the Festival of Booths.

Ezra stands on a wooden platform (8:4; literally, "tower") to read from the book of the law, which is in Hebrew. Others around him translate the words into Aramaic so the people can understand (8:7-8). It is possible that they also interpret the passages theologically to help the people understand the application of the texts for their current situation.

The "book" from which Ezra read was actually a scroll, and it was probably large enough that assistants were required to hold it for the reader. The scroll most likely contained a version of the Torah (or "teaching") that now forms the first five books of our Old Testament. In Ezra's day, tradition held that Moses wrote these books.

Whereas our English Bible most often translates *torah* as "law," that gives a misconception of what these texts meant to the Jewish people. They understood these writings to be a merciful gift from God—a set of teachings and instructions for the faith community to structure their lives with God and one another in such a way as to allow them to live fully into the blessings God offered them. For the people living in the hardship of postexilic Judah, this was a powerful promise.

Nehemiah 8:9-12. After hearing the Torah read and interpreted, the people react in what seems an unusual way—they weep (8:9). The other verbs used in verses 9-11 flesh out the emotions they are feeling. The people weep because they mourn and grieve.

In Hebrew, the words "weep" and "mourn" indicate action associated with personal tragedy or national disaster. In ancient Near East, weeping and mourning were often associated with fasting, wearing sackcloth and ashes, and tearing one's clothes and/or hair. The word translated "grieve," however, is somewhat rare and occurs "when the reaction of a person is a mixture of guilt and sadness when caught in a conflict of personal loyalty," according to Johanna W. H. van Wijk-Bos, writing in *Ezra, Nehemiah, and Esther* (Westminster Bible Companion series). Thus we find the word applied to Joseph's brothers, who sold him into slavery (Genesis 45:5); Jonathan, the son of Saul, who had to choose between his father and his best friend, David (1 Samuel 20:3); and David himself at the death of his rebellious son Absalom (2 Samuel 19:2).

The people mourn and grieve because they realize that, in some ways, they have not advanced much since the time of Moses. The original wanderers in the wilderness entered the land that God promised them only after many bad choices and examples of unfaithfulness. Subsequent generations repeated that behavior and, in the end, their actions led to the nation being conquered by a foreign king. The passages that Ezra reads describe the results of such unfaithful choices very clearly. The descendants of the original exiles hear these passages and cannot help but face the guilt-laden history of their ancestors and, to some extent, themselves.

In an interesting twist, however, the leaders do not call for a public confession of communal sin. Rather, they focus on the good news of the reading and of the current situation—the fact that God has brought them home, as God once brought home the people freed from bondage in Egypt. In addition, God has restored the city. It is a time for celebration and for honoring God; the time for confession will come later (see Nehemiah 9).

Nehemiah 8:13-18. The people and Ezra study the words of the law. Ezra is apparently reading from a version that has not survived transmission intact, because the quotation we find in Nehemiah 8:15 is not part of the Hebrew Bible as it stands today. The actions described, however, fit the instructions found in Leviticus 23:33-43.

Following the law, the people celebrate the Feast of Booths (or Tabernacles; the Hebrew word is *succoth*). Theologically, this feast fits their situation beautifully, because it celebrates the exodus from Egypt and the successful wandering through the wilderness to reach the promised land. In memory of the time in the wilderness, the festival calls for all the people to build temporary shelters and to live in them for the duration of the holiday (see Exodus 23:16; 34:22; Leviticus 23:33-43; Deuteronomy 16:13-15).

Verse 17 indicates that the Feast of Booths had not been celebrated since the days of Joshua (here called "Jeshua"). That is not true in the literal sense. Several passages describe this feast being celebrated throughout Israel and Judah's history (for example, 1 Kings 8:65-66; Ezra 3:4; Hosea 12:9). The writer may have meant that this was the first time since Joshua's day that the people had celebrated the feast all together in a single location. It is more likely, however, that this was a deliberate exaggeration intended to communicate that there had never been a bigger, better, or more joyous celebration of the feast since it was first held.

INTERPRETING THE SCRIPTURE

Ezra the Priest and Scribe

At last we meet Ezra, the priest and scribe. This remarkable man stood in a line of priestly ancestors that reached back to Aaron (Ezra 7:1-5). Priests in Babylon had no real function, however, because there was no temple. Consequently, although Ezra was a priest, it was more significant that he was a scribe and was learned in the law of God. Some scholars have suggested that Ezra held the position of secretary of Jewish affairs in the Persian government. In any case, he was a scribe in the sense of being one who wrote and drafted documents, and he was also a scribe in the sense of being a student of the law and well-versed in its meaning and application. In this regard, he was admirably suited for the mission he was to undertake.

In this passage, we see Ezra lead the community in a series of rituals and celebrations that help the people restore their relationship with God and with one another. Through this historical record, we catch glimpses of the significance of such worship for our own lives as well.

An Ancient Holiday Season

While our lesson Scripture for this week only describes one festival, the events recorded in Nehemiah 8 actually encompass a season of three significant Jewish holidays. Our text begins on the first day of the month called Tishri, the traditional date for Rosh Hashanah, the celebration of the new year. On the tenth day is Yom Kippur, the Day of Atonement; the Feast of Booths comes five days after that. It is easy to see that, in terms of ritual and renewal, this is indeed a special time of year.

The theological themes of these holidays include repentance, restoration, and renewal. The sequence is not unlike what we experience during Lent, Easter, and Pentecost in the Christian calendar. We see:

- a period of self-examination and penitence (the ten days ushered in by Rosh Hashanah);

- followed by a symbolic act that reconciles the community with God (at Yom Kippur);
- culminating in the whole community gathered together to rejoice and celebrate God's presence in their midst.

Instructions for the Feast of Booths are found in Leviticus 23:33-43. It started as a festival of harvest and of ingathering. The people were to build little huts from branches and live in them for seven days as a reminder of the wilderness experience. The huts symbolized the tents, as well as the tabernacle, from that nomadic period of their history. The true source of celebration, however, was in remembering how God's presence never left the people during all their years of wandering.

The Role of Scripture

Ezra and Nehemiah both were proactive leaders, and certainly the public reading of the law was of prime importance to them. In this case, however, it is the people who call for the reading of Scripture. The first thing we notice about them is that they are eager to hear the holy word (Nehemiah 8:1). More than that, they are attentive, even though the reading took "from early morning until midday" (8:3). Finally, after hearing the book of the law read aloud, the people respond with worship and prayer.

Notice the communal aspect of hearing and responding to Scripture. When Ezra starts to read the book of the law, everyone "who could hear with understanding" (8:2) gathers as near to him as possible. This probably means that youth are present who are not yet of an age to be considered adults, but who are old enough to understand the message. Although our Scripture lesson leaves out this detail, Ezra is standing on a tall wooden platform that the people themselves had built for this occasion. No one wants to miss what he has to say.

In this scene, we find three implications for the role of God's word in the church. First, as noted above, *Scripture is to be read in community.* While private reading of Scripture is a wonderful spiritual discipline, the word of God is not meant to be read always in isolation. Our tradition affirms that the Spirit works most powerfully when the people of God are gathered together, not alone.

Second, *Scripture must be studied so that it can be understood.* Just reading or hearing the text is not enough. Verse 7 says that while Ezra read the original Hebrew text to the assembly, others then translated the text into Aramaic (which the people understood) and helped interpret the meaning of the more difficult passages. Today pastors, Christian educators, and teachers all help in that same process, as do commentaries, study Bibles, and other resources.

Third, *Scripture must be applied if it is to make a difference.* The people in this passage did not stop at hearing and studying. They took what they learned and integrated it into their lives. As a result, they were transformed as individuals and as a community. Such is the power of the Spirit working through the word!

The Importance of Rituals

The passage began with all the people gathered into the square before the Water Gate to hear the reading of the book of the law; it ends with the celebration of the Feast of Booths.

In both events, we see that rituals bring us together. Think of the rituals in your own family and congregation. Celebrations of birthdays and anniversaries, times of worship and fellowship—these are the times when being with one another gains extra meaning. In our rituals we rediscover, time and again, the depth of our bond to each other and the significance of our shared life.

Likewise, rituals add meaning to our experience of worship. There is something both comforting and sacred in saying familiar words and performing familiar actions that have been passed down through centuries of believers. For the Jews in the square before the Water Gate, the moments when they said "Amen" together or bowed their heads in unison (8:6) added to the mystical experience of entering into the divine presence as the people of God. It connected them to the generations that had gone before, as well as to those that would come after.

Finally, rituals renew us for the ongoing journey of faith. In today's text, the worship service (8:1-6) and the festival (8:13-18) required the people to step outside of their daily routine so they could experience more fully God's presence in their midst. This reminds us that we too need to set aside time

periodically to encounter God without the distractions of life interrupting us. The worship hour on Sunday or other times at church provide us one such opportunity. So do spiritual retreats, Bible studies, special calls to prayer, and other opportunities to withdraw from the world into God's presence.

As this text shows, when we routinely stop and rest in God, then we are better able to continue on the journey of our faith walk. As with Ezra and the people, these moments of true worship restore and renew us. To our delight and gratitude we find that, no matter what difficulties may have come before, we are now able to lift up our hands, bless the Lord, and say a resounding, "Amen!"

SHARING THE SCRIPTURE

Preparing Our Hearts

Meditate on this week's devotional reading, found in Psalm 27:11-14 and Psalm 19:7-14. In Psalm 27, the writer calls upon the God he trusts to teach him and protect him from his enemies. He waits with strength and courage. Psalm 19 speaks about the perfection of God's law. Those who keep the law are greatly rewarded. How do these two psalms speak to you today in whatever joys, sorrows, and challenges you are facing?

Pray that you and the adult learners will stand firm in God's teachings, knowing that all things are possible when we trust in God.

Preparing Our Minds

Study the background from Nehemiah 8 and lesson Scripture, verses 1-3, 5-6, 13-14, 17-18. Ponder which relationships are important to reestablish when it is necessary to rebuild one's life.

Write on newsprint:
❏ questions for "See the Relationship Between Worship and Obedience to God."

❏ information for next week's lesson, found under "Continue the Journey."
❏ activities for further spiritual growth in "Continue the Journey."
Option: Locate in a book or on the Internet a picture of a Succoth booth.
Option: Invite a Jewish speaker to talk briefly about the Festival of Booths (Succoth) and what it symbolizes for the Jewish people. Be sure to give clear directions and a time limit.

LEADING THE CLASS

(1) Gather to Learn

❖ Welcome the class members and introduce any guests.
❖ Pray that the adults who are present today will be open in heart, mind, and spirit to what God has to say to them today.
❖ Read aloud this information (from a September 8, 2004, article on www.unhcr.org): **According to an article by Myrna Flood on the UN Refugee Agency website, members of minority groups in Kosovo— Serbs, Roma, Ashkaelia, and Bosniaks—**

still fear the Albanian majority. In March of 2004 serious violence destroyed the peace, but afterward there was still an effort to get all groups talking to one another so that the residents could move forward. The article, written six months later, states: "There are signs that the scars may be slowly healing, judging from the friendly greetings between the Serb visitors and their former neighbours in the village. Nevertheless, as the March disturbances illustrated all too graphically, such progress is extremely fragile and can be easily overturned. But even during those terrible three days of looting and burning in the spring, there were signs that the seeds of ethnic reconciliation had taken firm root in some places. Largely unnoticed among the reports of mayhem, there were a number of occasions where local Albanians stood up strongly and courageously in defence of minority members living in their midst."

❖ Solicit comments from the class concerning the importance of rebuilding relationships in order to rebuild one's life.

❖ Read aloud today's focus statement: **The rebuilding of life requires reestablishing right relationships. What relationships are important to reestablish? Ezra challenged the returned Israelite exiles to reestablish their covenant relationship with God and with one another.**

(2) Examine Ezra's Challenge to the People to Obey the Law of the Covenant

❖ Choose a volunteer to read Nehemiah 8:1-3, 5-6.
- ■ Use information from Nehemiah 8:1-8 in Understanding the Scripture to help the class to discern the events in this story. You may also want to include "Ezra the Priest and Scribe" from Interpreting the Scripture to introduce Ezra.
- ■ Discuss these questions.
- **(1) Suppose you had been in the** crowd. Why would you have "stood" (8:5) listening "from early morning until midday" (8:3) to Ezra read from "the book of the law of Moses" (8:1)? In other words, what were you hoping to hear or learn?
- **(2) How would you describe the worship portrayed in Nehemiah 8:6?**
- **(3) How might the contemporary church be different if we took worship as seriously as the people in the days of Ezra and Nehemiah did?**

■ Conclude this section by reading or retelling "The Role of Scripture" from Interpreting the Scripture. Look especially at the three major italicized points in the third, fourth, and fifth paragraphs, and encourage the students to comment on how these points relate to beliefs and practices in your congregation.

❖ Select someone to read Nehemiah 8:13-14, 17-18.
- ■ **Option:** Show picture(s) you have been able to locate of Succoth booths.
- ■ Use "An Ancient Holiday Season" in Interpreting the Scripture to discuss the Festival of Booths and other important holidays. (Omit this activity if you have a Jewish speaker present.)
- ■ **Option:** Ask a Jewish guest speaker to talk about Succoth, particularly how and why it is celebrated. Allow time for the class to ask questions.
- ■ Talk with the class about the importance of rituals. Use information under that title in Interpreting the Scripture for a lecture or to fill in gaps in the conversation.

(3) See the Relationship Between Worship and Obedience to God

❖ Recall that the Israelites worshiped God as they heard the law of God read.

Point out (or read aloud) this Scripture, which relates to the reading of the law: Deuteronomy 31:9-13.

❖ Note as we have already seen in this lesson, "Scripture must be applied if it is to make a difference."

❖ Divide the class into groups. Post these questions on newsprint for the groups to discuss.

(1) **Is it possible for one to truly worship God and fail to obey God's word? Explain your answer.**

(2) **What strength or resources do you gain from worship that empower you to be obedient to God?**

(3) **How is your obedience to God in itself a sign of your worship?**

❖ Call the class back together and encourage each group to report on highlights of their discussion.

(4) Commit to Obey and Worship God as a Sign of Renewed Relationship with God and Neighbor

❖ Distribute paper and pencils. Encourage each student (individually or working with a partner) to write words of covenant renewal that demonstrate their willingness to obey and worship God. Suggest that they consult these biblical references for ideas.

■ Exodus 34:10, 27-28
■ Joshua 8:30-35
■ Joshua 24:14-15

❖ Invite each person to read what he or she has written. Ask the class to respond with "Amen, Amen" (Nehemiah 8:6).

❖ Challenge the students to write one step they will take this week to begin to fulfill the commitment they have just made. Perhaps they will need to be reconciled with God or neighbor. Possibly they will need to respond obediently to God's call on their lives. Whatever is needed, encourage the students to take action.

(5) Continue the Journey

❖ Pray that all who have come today will renew their covenant with God and restore their relationships with neighbors.

❖ Read aloud this preparation for next week's lesson. You may also want to post it on newsprint for the students to copy.

■ **Title: Jesus as God's Son**
■ **Background Scripture: Hebrews 1**
■ **Lesson Scripture: Hebrews 1:1-4, 8-12**
■ **Focus of the Lesson: People search for authoritative and credible voices to answer life's questions. Who can speak to us about the deeper meanings of life? God spoke to us through God's beloved Son, Jesus Christ.**

❖ Challenge the students to complete one or more of these activities for further spiritual growth, which you will write on newsprint for the students to copy.

(1) **Research the Jewish week-long Festival of Booths, also known as the Festival of Tabernacles, or Succoth.**

(2) **Talk with a young person who has been/will be confirmed this year. Discuss your understanding of how confirmation symbolizes a covenant with God.**

(3) **Volunteer to read the Scriptures aloud in your Sunday school class or, if appropriate in your church, during worship. Recognize the importance of the public reading of the Scriptures.**

❖ Sing or read aloud "Jesus, Lord, We Look to Thee."

❖ Conclude today's session by leading the class in this benediction, based on 2 Chronicles 34:31: **We renew our covenant to follow the LORD, keeping his commandments, with all our heart and all our soul, to perform the words of the covenant.**

FOURTH QUARTER
Images of Christ

JUNE 1, 2008–AUGUST 31, 2008

The summer quarter, which features fourteen lessons, examines images of Christ as found in Hebrews, the Gospels, and the Letter of James. As we will see, some of these images, particularly those highlighted in Hebrews, are unique to Christ: No one else can be intercessor or redeemer, for example. Other images, seen in the Gospels, we can emulate. We can be Christ-like teachers and servants. In the final unit, James teaches us how we can embody many images, such as "doers of the word," in our daily lives.

Unit 1, "Images of Christ in Hebrews," includes five sessions spotlighting Jesus: God's Son, intercessor, redeemer, leader, and the eternal Christ. The unit opens on June 1 with an exploration of "Jesus as God's Son," "the exact imprint of God's very being," as discussed in Hebrews 1. "Christ as Intercessor," the lesson from Hebrews 7 on June 8, considers how we can approach God through Christ, who intercedes for us. We learn that Christ takes away our guilt in "Christ as Redeemer," a study of Hebrews 9:11–10:18 on June 15. Hebrews 12:1-13, which refers to Christ as "the pioneer and perfecter of our faith," is the Scripture passage for the lesson on June 22, "Christ as Leader." To help us find stability and permanence, Hebrews 13:1-16 considers "The Eternal Christ" on June 29.

Unit 2, "Images of Christ in the Gospels," is a four-session unit that highlights Christ as teacher, healer, servant, and the Messiah. As we study Luke 4:31-37 and 20:1-8 on July 6, we find "Christ as Teacher," an authoritative educator whose teaching transforms lives. In the lesson for July 13 from Mark 1:29-45 we see Jesus in another very familiar role—"Christ as Healer." "Christ as Servant," the image from John 13:1-20 that we encounter on July 20, challenges us to be servants for others. To conclude this unit, we hear Jesus' familiar words, "But who do you say that I am?" in "Christ as Messiah," the lesson for July 27 from Matthew 16:13-23.

Unit 3, "Images of Christ in Us," illustrates in five sessions how James teaches Christians to model Christ in their lives by being doers of the word, impartial disciples, wise speakers, people of godly behavior, and a prayerful community. On August 3, James 1 challenges us to be "Doers of the Word" and not merely hearers. To be "Impartial Disciples," as the lesson from James 2 calls us to be on August 10, we need to honor all people, regardless of their station in life. James 3 admonishes us to control our tongues in the lesson for August 17 entitled "Wise Speakers." On August 24, James 4 invites us to "draw near to God" so that we may live as "People of Godly Behavior." The unit and our summer quarter draw to a close on August 31 with "Prayerful Community," a lesson rooted in James 5 that teaches us the power and effectiveness of prayer.

MEET OUR WRITER

DR. JOHN INDERMARK

John Indermark received a bachelor of arts degree in History from St. Louis University and a Master of Divinity degree from Eden Seminary. John has retired from pastoral ministry in the United Church of Christ, and lives in southwest Washington State with his wife, Judy. He writes for several Christian education curricula (*New International Lesson Annual* and *Seasons of the Spirit*, among others) and authors devotional books for Upper Room Books (*Parables and Passion*, his most recent, will be published in the fall of 2007).

THE BIG PICTURE: IMAGES OF CHRIST IN HEBREWS, THE GOSPELS, AND US

A look at the title of this quarter may lead you to suspect it will be an exploration of artistic impressions of Jesus. To be sure, there would be significant value in such a study. Jesus has been portrayed in art in many ways down through the ages, more often than not linked to where and how life was experienced in particular locale and era. But art, however, will not provide the "texts" for this quarter's exploration of images of Christ.

Rather, the "images" studied will be provided by a variety of New Testament passages and narratives: some about Jesus, some about the living of the Christian life.

Addressing "image" does require a bit of caution. Part of the caution stems from ancient prohibitions. Part of the caution stems from our (post) modern experience.

The ancient caution has to do with the creation of images of deity, expressly forbidden in the commandments of Sinai ("You shall not make for yourself an idol, whether in the form of anything that is in heaven above, or that is on the earth beneath, or that is in the water under the earth. You shall not bow down to them or worship them" Exodus 20:4-5a). The prohibition did not have to do with an aversion to artistic expression, though that clearly suffered under severe interpretations of this command. Rather, the command had to do with avoiding the pitfalls of reducing the worship of God to a veneration of images made by human hands. The problem is not in the images themselves, but in our uncanny human ability to confuse the reality to which an image would direct us with the object fashioned.

The connection to idolatry is clear. But the caution brought to this study lies in not forgetting that the images we derive from words—even holy words, even inspired words—can never be confused with the reality to which they intend to point. The images of Christ we draw from Scripture and community are impressions. They are ways that help us see more deeply into the truth of revelation, but they are not the revelation themselves. Or, to use an older analogy: The words of Scripture witness to, but do not stand as substitute for, the living Word who is Jesus Christ. So as we explore these images of Christ from Gospels and Epistles, remember it is not the image we worship, nor is the image itself the truth. Rather, the truth is the One to whom these images direct our faith, Jesus Christ.

The second caution as we approach this quarter on "images" of Christ is the way in which image gets used—and abused—among us. Consider, for example, a relatively recent development in modern advertising. In days gone by, an ad would try to give us all the facts (or at least, the arguments) for the value of this or that product. We would be besieged by words. But now, it is not unusual to see ads where not a single word is spoken. At the most, at some critical point in the succession of images that evokes confidence or success or sensuality, a brand name will simply be revealed. Such advertising is all about image, leaving us with an impression or a feeling with which we are then to associate a product. Some forms of political advertising do the same thing. Words are almost irrelevant, so long as the "image" of the candidate (wrapped in flags, seen in action, and so on) is right.

The danger of such use of images, in connection with this study, is that sometimes it seems easier to replace substance with image. As long as it looks or sounds "good," we'll go with it. Religion can find itself reduced to such image-driven expression. When we settle for vague expressions of Christianity's purpose, versus its particular calls to faith and service; when we reduce the particular and often scandalous nature of Jesus' ministry and associations to some sort of generic hero worship; when discipleship is stripped of cross-bearing; when hope is confused with optimism—then we verge on the edge of an image-only religion. That is why continually keeping our images of Christ in dialogue and tension with the actual stories of who Jesus is and what Jesus does—and what all that may mean for those who would follow—is crucial. Otherwise, our images of Jesus become benign.

Yet—and this is one of the real values of this quarter's study—image also allows our witness to be accessible to folks. There may have been a time in our culture when most were familiar with the stories of Scripture and the language of faith. No more. Like it or not, we live in an era when many are unfamiliar with even the most fundamental stories of faith. To them, our words may initially either make no sense or seem divorced from the age in which we live. But images can be universal. They may provide windows that allow others to see what words alone might not have been able to express. So, for example, the words we speak (from the session on June 8) about Jesus as high priest or intercessor might seem archaic or remote. But to use the imagery of Christ as one who speaks for us, one who takes our side, *that* is what folks inside and outside the circle of faith community can understand. That is a need they (like we) have experienced in deep ways. That image of Christ can open up talking points and connective tissue that then makes possible the understanding of all those words of priesthood and mediator and "Melchizedek" that, in and of themselves, might have held no interest.

If you have already skimmed the table of contents or thumbed through the summer section of *The New International Lesson Annual,* you will have seen that there are three units in this quarter. Each unit will derive from a different set of New Testament works that addresses the common theme of the images of Christ. Those three sets of materials are: the Letter to the Hebrews, the Gospels, and the Letter of James. What follows next is a brief exploration of each of those works, along with some general comments about the images of Christ they address.

Images of Christ in the Hebrews

The Letter to the Hebrews is a fascinating starting point. On the one hand, Hebrews may be among the least understood and least read of the New Testament epistles (along with Titus). Its language and argumentation is complex at many points. Even the title, "Hebrews," makes it sound as if this epistle is written to someone other than who we are as Christians. Ask yourself: When was the last time I spent extended time studying the Letter to the Hebrews at any length?

On the other hand, Hebrews presents an excellent starting point for a study of Christ based upon images. Why? Hebrews, perhaps more than any other New Testament writing other than John's Gospel and Revelation, trades in images. Its theology draws deeply on the sacrificial cult of first-century Judaism for bearing witness to the identity and work of Jesus. The imagery of sacrifice and priesthood plays a key role in illustrating and evoking its words.

Who wrote this epistle is a question subject to much disagreement. While some of the early church leaders attributed it to Paul, others did not. Among the suggested alternatives is Barnabas, the former traveling companion of Paul and the one who first vouched for Paul (Saul) to the apostolic community (Acts 9:27 and following). Luther suggested Apollos. Suffice it to say that no agreement exists on authorship today. The date of composition is subject to some interpretation as well. Passages from Hebrews are found in one of the patristic writings of Clement, which is believed to come from the last decade of the first century. How early to date the letter depends upon whether it is believed the temple sacrifices, so much a part of the imagery here, were still in place. The temple was destroyed by Roman forces during the Zealot uprising in A.D. 70. So any time from the late sixties until the early nineties seems to be the most likely date. The audience is Christian. The title of "Hebrews" does not mean it was written to Jews, for the sake of their conversion. Rather, it seems more to indicate a witness to the faith grounded in the writings and symbols of Judaism. Although pinning down the specific community or communities this epistle was addressed to seems unlikely, some recent suggestions have included Diaspora Jewish Christians living in Rome.

The five sessions drawn from Hebrews in this study focus on five images of Christ: God's Son, intercessor, redeemer, leader, and the eternal Christ. In each case, the background of worship practices plays a major role in developing the meaning of these images of Christ. Also, as will be noted especially in the first session, the identity of Christ will be juxtaposed with that of the angels, which posed for some people, apparently, other objects of veneration—if not in the Christian community, then at least in the culture surrounding it.

Images of Christ in the Gospels

If the first unit's exploration of Hebrews presents some unfamiliar scriptural terrain for you and/or some of those in your group, the second unit may be seen as returning to something akin to "home." For in the four sessions that make up this second unit, the source of texts will be the Gospels. In what may be seen as a balancing of story and perspective, each of the four Gospels will provide a text for one of these sessions.

As a brief reminder and refresher: Matthew, Mark, and Luke are sometimes known as the "Synoptic" (literally, "common view") Gospels. Much of the theorizing about how the Synoptics came to be so closely related at points goes beyond the scope, and need, of this introduction. A simple example of those interrelationships, however, comes in looking at the three texts used in this quarter from these three Gospels: an exorcism and then a confrontation with religious authorities about Jesus' authority (Luke 4:31-37; 20:1-8); the healings of Simon's mother-in-law, the crowds, and a leper (Mark 1:29-45); and the confession on the road to Caesarea Philippi (Matthew 16:13-23). In each case, the session uses a text from one of the three Synoptics. But, each session could also have used a parallel passage from either of the other two Gospels. Sometimes, the stories among the Synoptics are almost verbatim. At other times, there are differences that hint at different perspectives from the Gospel writers (different "images" of Jesus they would emphasize).

John differs from the Synoptics—not because it tells a different story of Jesus, but because it tells the story of Jesus *differently*. For example, the story taken from John in this quarter is the footwashing (John 13:1-8, 12-20). In John, when the disciples gather at table for the final evening before betrayal and arrest and crucifixion, the narrative is not of the meal, but of the footwashing. All four Gospels deal at this point with Jesus' service and humility. But the particular image they use to express those themes differs. It is not that one is right and one is wrong. It is not as if there is some burning question did Jesus break the bread or wash their feet. The point is that the image is Christ as servant.

So as you explore the four sessions in this unit and the images of Christ as teacher, healer, servant, and Messiah, keep those varieties of perspective in mind. Even if you do not have time with the learners to deal, for example, with the parallel passages in the Synoptics, you might spend some of your preparation time glancing at how Mark and Luke relate the story told by Matthew, and vice versa. Consider how the scene of tabled ministry in John envisions the Synoptics' scene of tabled communion. As you are able, bring the importance of perspective into play in the conversations in your study group. For, unless you have a group unlike any other, there will be difference in perspectives there as well: differences that enrich, rather than contradict, the faith we hold and the ways in which we see (image) Christ.

Images of Christ in Us

The final unit in this study has the intriguing suggestion that we may find images of Christ not simply in words of Scripture, or even out there in the world, but somehow "in us." The companion for these five sessions will be the epistle of James.

James is traditionally associated with the brother of Jesus, who became a leader in the early Jerusalem church. Although some scholars have argued recently for someone other (and later) than James as the author, that is by no means universal—and the perspective of the commentary in this resource holds with the traditional designation of James. If that is so, James would have to have been written before the year A.D. 62. That is the year, according to the historian Josephus, when James was martyred for his faith. If that is true, then the context for this letter would clearly be while the church existed as a group still within Judaism—a conflicted relationship, to be sure, but still intact. The epistle's strong emphasis on works, along with its stylistic and thematic connections with wisdom literature, grows out of that connection with Judaism.

Some have sought to draw strict and irrevocable divisions between the theology of law and the theology of grace, precisely on the point of grace and works. Rightly seen, however, James simply draws out the ethical implications of Paul's own teachings about love and conduct in explicit terms. James sounds very close to the spirit of Jesus' teachings on the Sermon on the Mount, teachings that are also highly practical and behaviorally oriented. After all, it is not originally James but Jesus who details the folly of hearing Jesus' words without acting upon them (see Matthew 7:24-27).

The images of Christ identified in this unit have to do with how Christians are to model Christ in their lives. Those images we are to exhibit include (but certainly are not limited to): doers of the Word, impartial disciples, wise speakers, people of Godly behavior, and prayerful community. Listen to the words, and images, of James on their own merit. Imagine with your group how their embodiment today by individuals and by faith communities might transform the landscape of religion. On this point, James and Paul are most closely aligned. Paul's image of the body of Christ finds clear support and encouragement in James's witness to the need for faith to take embodiment.

May this quarter's study of these images of Christ open you and your group to Christ's continuing presence and ongoing work in our midst. Thank you for offering yourself to the ministry of teaching as you lead this group. Do so prayerfully, and joyfully, as you with your participants deepen your faith and its practice through these sessions and texts . . . and the images of Christ you will find on this way.

CLOSE-UP:
JESUS IN THE VISUAL ARTS

To enhance this quarter's study, you may wish to include visual images of Jesus as imagined by people of many cultures and historical eras. Here is some information to help you locate helpful sources on the Internet.

Jesus Mafa (http://www.jesusmafa.com/index.htm) exquisitely portrays Jesus as an African. This project, which began in 1973 in the Mafa communities of Cameroon, has produced sixty-five scenes spanning the Annunciation through Pentecost. A black Christ is an evangelical tool to proclaim the universality of God's message through Jesus.

Check http://www.asianchristianart.org for information about Christian artists from a variety of Asian countries. Explore this website and locate pictures of artists whose work gives you new perspectives on Christ. Specific pictures are linked with the section on artists' profiles.

The site http://www.goarch.org/en/resources/clipart provides you with pictures of icons used by the Greek Orthodox community. You'll find icons related to this quarter's lessons under "Miracles, Parables, and Events in the Life of Christ."

Another site, http://temp.eg-Gym.dk/fagene/religion/Ortodokse%20kirke/dox.html, includes links to many sites featuring icons from the various branches of the Orthodox church. Compare, for example, some of the Greek ones with the Russian master iconographer Andrei Rublev and note the similarities and differences. Also note how different the representations of Jesus are in the Ethiopian church.

Born in 1938 in California, John August Swanson's work reflects his mother's Mexican roots and his father's Swedish background. Swanson is a master of telling stories through his art, many of which depict biblical stories. You can find this very distinctive work at http://www.johnaugustswanson.com.

Check out http://www.eskimo.com/~telical/christ-art.html, which includes numerous links (some of which are not working as of this writing) to modern Christian artists from a variety of backgrounds.

To see some images from the very early church, check http://gbgm-umc.org/umw/bible/jcart.stm. One of the most popular early images Jesus was as the good shepherd. If you search the Internet for "early Christian art" or "catacomb" art you will find a variety of shepherd images.

Saint John's College of the University of Cambridge has catalogued images from medieval manuscripts. Look at http://www.joh.cam.ac.uk/library/special_collections/manuscripts/medieval manuscripts/image index/christ images index.

The site http://biblia.com/jesusart includes links to a wide variety of images and music.

Find creative ways to use these images. Print out some of these (but not, however, if they are copyrighted). View them onscreen with the class, if possible. Or choose several that you find meaningful and give the adults the website prior to a class discussion.

However you and the students are able to glimpse these images, discuss how the artists' renderings enable the class members to see Jesus in new ways. Perhaps some of these ways will be comforting or exciting, whereas others may cause uneasiness because the image seems so different or unfamiliar. Your purpose in working with these images is not to convince everyone to see Jesus through the same lens, but rather to recognize and appreciate that in different times and places Christians have imagined the Messiah in ways that reflect who they are and what they believe.

FAITH IN ACTION: REFLECTING CHRIST'S IMAGE

As we have explored images of Jesus the Christ this quarter, we have become aware that we are to reflect those images in what we say and do. In Hebrews we saw images that describe only Christ. In the Gospels we explored images of Christ as teacher, healer, servant, and Messiah, which we can emulate to a certain degree. The Letter of James, however, offers us many specific ideas for living in the image of Christ. Note what James has to teach us.

James 1:2-4	Face trials with joy.
James 1:5-8	Ask God for wisdom.
James 1:9-11	Do not depend on wealth.
James 1:12-16	Endure temptation.
James 1:19-21	Be "quick to listen, slow to speak, slow to anger."
James 1:22-25	Be doers of God's word.
James 1:26-27	Practice true religion that cares for vulnerable people.
James 2:1-13	Do not show partiality, but treat everyone equally.
James 2:14-26	Do good works to show your faith.
James 3:1-12	Keep your tongue under control.
James 3:13-18	Live wisely and peaceably.
James 4:1-10	Humbly submit yourself to God.
James 4:11-12	Do not judge others or speak evil about them.
James 4:13-17	Do not boast about what you plan to do.
James 5:1-6	Do not exploit others.
James 5:7-12	Wait patiently for the coming of the Lord, even if you must endure suffering.
James 5:13-18	Pray in all situations: in times when you or someone else is suffering, sick, joyous, or needing to make a confession.
James 5:19-20	Bring back a believer who has wandered from the fold of God.

Help the students live according to these teachings by taking the following steps.

Step 1: List the references from James and brief descriptions on newsprint and challenge the learners to copy and/or mark them in their Bibles. Distribute paper and pencils.

Step 2: Brainstorm with the class ways that they could live out any of these specific biblical teachings. For example, you may focus on one item, such as "Keep your tongue under control." Talk about the kinds of situations in which our words can become hurtful, such as when we are angry or insisting on our own way or belittling someone else or criticizing an individual's actions. Challenge the class to think of ways that we can control our tongues, such as offering a brief silent prayer during a difficult discussion or ending a heated conversation with kind words about how we need to continue this talk when we're more settled.

Step 3: Prompt the students to make a written commitment, for their eyes only, to work on at least one of these teachings. Suggest that they indicate what they plan to do to become more in tune with this teaching.

UNIT 1: IMAGES OF CHRIST IN HEBREWS
JESUS AS GOD'S SON

PREVIEWING THE LESSON

Lesson Scripture: Hebrews 1:1-4, 8-12
Background Scripture: Hebrews 1
Key Verse: Hebrews 1:3

Focus of the Lesson:
People search for authoritative and credible voices to answer life's questions. Who can speak to us about the deeper meanings of life? God spoke to us through God's beloved Son, Jesus Christ.

Goals for the Learners:
(1) to understand that God spoke in a totally new way by sending Jesus Christ, God's Son.
(2) to experience the magnificence of God's new way of communicating with us.
(3) to respond positively by acknowledging the majesty of God's Son.

Pronunciation Guide:
Christology (kris tol' uh jee)
leitourgikos (li toorg ik os')
Septuagint (sep too' uh jint)

Supplies:
Bibles, newsprint and marker, paper and pencils, hymnals, basic art supplies

---

READING THE SCRIPTURE

NRSV
Hebrews 1:1-4, 8-12

¹Long ago God spoke to our ancestors in many and various ways by the prophets, ²but in these last days he has spoken to us by a Son, whom he appointed heir of all things, through whom he also created the worlds.

NIV
Hebrews 1:1-4, 8-12

¹In the past God spoke to our forefathers through the prophets at many times and in various ways, ²but in these last days he has spoken to us by his Son, whom he appointed heir of all things, and through whom he

³He is the reflection of God's glory and the exact imprint of God's very being, and he sustains all things by his powerful word. When he had made purification for sins, he sat down at the right hand of the Majesty on high, ⁴having become as much superior to angels as the name he has inherited is more excellent than theirs.

⁸But of the Son he says,

"Your throne, O God, is forever and ever,
    and the righteous scepter is the scepter
        of your kingdom.
⁹   You have loved righteousness and hated
        wickedness;
    therefore God, your God, has anointed
        you
    with the oil of gladness beyond your
        companions."

¹⁰And,

In the beginning, Lord, you founded the
        earth,
    and the heavens are the work of your
        hands;
¹¹   they will perish, but you remain;
    they will all wear out like clothing;
¹²   like a cloak you will roll them up,
    and like clothing they will be changed.
    But you are the same,
    and your years will never end."

made the universe. ³The Son is the radiance of God's glory and the exact representation of his being, sustaining all things by his powerful word. After he had provided purification for sins, he sat down at the right hand of the Majesty in heaven. ⁴So he became as much superior to the angels as the name he has inherited is superior to theirs.

⁸But about the Son he says,

"Your throne, O God, will last for ever
        and ever,
    and righteousness will be the scepter of
        your kingdom.
⁹You have loved righteousness and hated
        wickedness;
    therefore God, your God, has set you
        above your companions
    by anointing you with the oil of joy."

¹⁰He also says,

"In the beginning, O Lord, you laid the
        foundations of the earth,
    and the heavens are the work of your
        hands.
¹¹They will perish, but you remain;
    they will all wear out like a garment.
¹²You will roll them up like a robe;
    like a garment they will be changed.
    But you remain the same,
    and your years will never end."

UNDERSTANDING THE SCRIPTURE

Hebrews 1:1-2. God "speaks." Hebrews begins similarly to Genesis, where God's speaking results in the fashioning of creation. The opening four verses (prologue) of Hebrews are likewise sometimes compared to the opening prologue of John. There, too, the speaking of God ("in the beginning was the Word," John 1:1) introduces the redeeming of creation. The testimony of Hebrews to God's speaking bridges the past ("long ago") and the present ("in these last days"). In those times gone by, the "new thing" spoken had to do with the message of the

prophets. Now, God's speaking takes the form of a "Son." At this point, the affirmations that identify this Son have to do with his serving as heir (a theme developed repeatedly in this epistle) and God's agent in creation (similar to the "Word" in John 1 and "Wisdom" in Proverbs 8:22-31).

Hebrews 1:3-4. The terminology and imagery of Hebrews in identifying the Son takes a more philosophical tone in verse 3. "Reflection of God's glory" and "exact imprint of God's very being" suggests a mooring in Hellenistic thought that many readers find in this epistle. Yet, there is no New Testament work more deeply rooted in the traditions of Judaism than Hebrews. It should be noted, though, that the vast majority of quotations from the Hebrew Scriptures (and there are many) come from the Greek version of the Old Testament known as the Septuagint. God's "sustaining" all things balances the earlier affirmation of God's "creating the worlds." The cosmos is neither accident in its origin, nor "on its own" in its ongoing life. God creates and sustains . . . two requisites for trusting any affirmation for how and why God redeems. That redemptive purpose makes its first, but not last, appearance in Hebrews in the assertion of the Son making "purification for sins." Again, a key theme that will inform the later Christology of this letter (the Jewish temple and sacrificial system) makes an appearance. Also introduced in verse 4—what will become the focus for the remaining verses of this opening chapter—is the relationship of Jesus to the angels.

Hebrews 1:5-6. These verses contain the first three of what will be seven quotations from the Hebrew Scriptures in this chapter (five from the Psalms, one from Deuteronomy, and one from 2 Samuel). Each of the quotations in these verses, like all but the final quotation that follows, is offered with little interpretation. The question that opens verse 5 closely resembles the question that will preface the last of the quotations in verse 13: "To which of the angels did God ever say . . . ?" "Say" is highlighted, for it returns us to that important theme of God's speaking. God speaks to bestow life or standing. Here, the contrast is made by what God speaks to the Son and, by implication, what God does not speak to any angel. And here, speaking relates to the bestowal of standing: "You are my Son." The quotation is from Psalm 2:7, whose original context is a royal psalm that solidifies the relationship between Israel's king and God. The quotation in the second half of verse 5 is from 2 Samuel 7:14, where the

promise of the Davidic dynasty related originally to David's descendants. Last, the quotation in verse 6 comes from Deuteronomy 32:43. The difference between the Septuagint and Hebrew version (the Hebrew text is used for most modern Bible translations) can readily be seen here—for the Septuagint uses "angels," not present in the Hebrew text.

Hebrews 1:7-9. A pair of contrasting quotations concerning what God says of the angels and of the Son forms these three verses. The first quotation, about the angels, quotes Psalm 104:4. The usual interpretation of this verse might suggest the swift and/or unseen nature of God's angels in bearing God's messages across the earth. The contrasting quotation from Psalm 45:6-7 suggests another meaning: namely, "winds" are moving and changing, while God's throne "is forever and ever." In this interpretation of the contrast, angels are shifting while the Son is secure and solid.

Hebrews 1:10-12. Another extensive quotation from a psalm (102:25-27) follows to continue the contrast between the angels and the Son. It is a word the author of Hebrews attributes to God's speaking of the Son—and like the previous quotation from Psalm 45, it conveys a sense of anchoring ("you founded the earth") and permanency ("they will perish, but you remain"). One intriguing note on this quotation is that it comes from a psalm of lament, in which the psalmist cries for help and healing. Later passages suggest the setting of Hebrews is in a time when the church faces some degree of persecution and distress. Utilizing this psalm's affirmation of God's enduring character may serve as a quiet way of reminding the community or communities addressed by Hebrews that faithfulness to God is not dependent on outward circumstances: "But you are the same, and your years will never end" (1:12).

Hebrews 1:13-14. The last of the quotations is from Psalm 110:1, a psalm that will play a critical role in the remaining chapters of Hebrews. Indeed, as Fred Craddock notes in *The New Interpreter's Bible,* one scholar has even suggested that the whole of Hebrews is an extended commentary on Psalm 110. Psalm 110:1 uses the imagery of "sitting at the right hand." In ancient times, this was a place not only of trust but also of power. Its association with the place given Jesus by God is reflected not only in this verse but also in the Apostles' Creed. Verse 14 concludes this passage by asserting a positive role for the angels, who to this point have been seen primarily in their inferiority to Jesus. Here, the author identifies them as spirits in the divine service (*leitourgikos,* from which we get the word *liturgy,* and which literally means "work of the people"). In the ancient Greek world, the term referred to work done for the public good. The angels are spirits who do such good service . . . but the "Son" in Hebrews is more than spirit, and his service as well as identity is unique.

INTERPRETING THE SCRIPTURE

The God Who Speaks

My denomination (United Church of Christ) has capitalized on the theme "God is still speaking." That is not by any means a new idea for the church or the Jewish faith. The God who speaks is a central tenet of our faith. Yet it is more than a "thing" we say about God. The God who speaks is how we understand this world and our lives to be "under construction" and in progress.

The God who speaks will be a theme encountered time and again in this quarter. For how we come to perceive the image of Christ—in the book of Hebrews, in the Gospels, in The Letter of James—will always be a matter of listening to what God reveals in words of old. Of course, as James will remind us, words alone do not exhaust faith. The God who *speaks* is also the God who *acts.* This first chapter in Hebrews reminds us of some of those actions in creating and sustaining life. To follow this God, revealed to us in Jesus, involves not just listening to what God speaks, but to *doing* what God speaks.

To assert faith in the God who speaks challenges us to listen for voices other than our own on our religious journey. A renewed interest in spiritual practices these days reminds us that the deeper meanings of life are not self-generated. Our experiences will raise questions about matters that exceed our capability to understand, much less control. We bring those questions into our search for meaning. As we do, we are invited to listen for the voice of the God who speaks—in words of Scripture; in acts of human compassion. To believe in a God who speaks can be a radical act of faith, especially when we allow ourselves to hear words and priorities that cut against the grain of popular opinions and rival claims to power. But that is our calling as disciples of Jesus Christ: to listen for the speaking of God.

A Word on Angels

Hebrews 1 spends a lot of time talking about angels. Some have taken this interest shown at the outset to indicate that the community(ies) to whom this letter was addressed struggled with meanings of (or obsessions with!) angels. And there can be no doubt that many beliefs and opinions abounded about angels in the first century A.D. Angels were messengers. Angels were members of the heavenly court. There were fallen and rebellious angels. Some considered angels among those "powers" and "principalities" that Paul said could not separate us from God's love (Romans 8:38-39).

Similar varied opinions about angels circulate among us today. Who has not heard of guardian angels? Television shows and movies portray angels, whether as benign helpers or avenging spirits seeking justice. No less a figure than Billy Graham has written a book on angels. Angels are intriguing and fascinating because of stories and legends.

But what role do they serve in faith?

Hebrews addresses the issue of angels exclusively in relationship to their comparison with "the Son." Hebrews does not either castigate or congratulate people for their beliefs or disbeliefs about angels. The author simply, yet critically, roots the focus of this epistle, and with it the focus of faith and Christian community, on the identity and work of Jesus. This is not a book that explores angelology. It is a book that affirms Christology.

As such, it is a work that may help folks these days keep focused on what is central to faith and discipleship. It would seem that angels, at the time of this epistle's writing, may have diverted attention from the core, to which this author returns. Some today still become diverted by secondary topics. Speculation, whether about angels or rapture or the best church polity or the most effective process for calling ministers, may provide stimulating conversation. But the core of Christian faith remains today, as it was when this epistle was written, Christology. The image of Christ, and how that image affects and shapes and transforms our lives, is central to who we are as individuals and communities of faith.

Valuing Tradition

Some folks talk about valuing tradition, and leave it at that. Other folks engage and structure and interpret life with the traditions that matter most. We see the latter not only in this first chapter of Hebrews but throughout this book. In an epistle that stresses the speaking of God, the author underscores his point by constantly drawing from the words and texts of the Hebrew Scriptures to bring God's speaking in days past into the context of his work. As noted in the Understanding the Scripture portion, this chapter as a whole uses seven explicit quotations of Scripture, and in other places uses allusions to those same passages and others.

The strategy is partly tactical. A common way of bolstering one's position at that time, and one still reflected in our legal system through the importance of precedents, was to make appeals to accepted traditions. The fact that the Psalms provide the most frequent source quoted in Hebrews strongly suggests the importance of worship traditions in furthering the epistle's points.

It is an intriguing combination, worship and tradition, to hear these days. For clearly, we are in times of great transition, and not a little conflict, over the relationship of tradition and worship in our churches. Hebrews could appeal to a common "hymnal" (the Psalms) in addressing the church of that day. That common ground has largely disappeared, not simply among churches but *within* churches. Sides are chosen within congregations on the issue of contemporary versus "times gone by" worship (I use "times gone by" rather than "traditional" because traditions can be found, or lost, in both options).

Hymnals or PowerPoint screens? Organs or praise bands? Perhaps you have been part of those conversations.

Keeping faith with tradition is not necessarily doing what we did ten or twenty years ago. Valuing tradition is delving deeper, to listen for what in our resources and practices of times past still is effective, still is *needed*. Hebrews' constant use of Hebrew Scriptures reminds us that identity, tradition, and mission are part of a seamless whole.

Faithful Response

Later chapters in Hebrews explored in this quarter will bring to the forefront the importance of lives and discipleship rendered in faithful response to the example and leading of Christ. To omit that response would transform the serious theology of this epistle into head-tripping.

But at this point, at the close of the first chapter, a different sort of response is evoked. That response is wonder. That response is praise. That response is listening to this extraordinary affirmation that God's voice still rings out in creation in providential and redemptive ways—and in the One who has come to us.

Indeed, it is this first response, very much one of worship and devotion, that leads us and empowers the active life of disciples of Jesus that flows later. For in worship, our spirits find renewal, grace, and power. Renewal in the presence of the One who moved over the waters at creation. Grace from the hands of the Son who brings forgiveness. Power from having the One who came as the embodiment of love for us all sits now on the right hand of God.

And let the people of God say, Amen.

SHARING THE SCRIPTURE

Preparing Our Hearts

Meditate on this week's devotional reading, found in Proverbs 8:22-31. Here we see a description of Wisdom, personified as a female, and the role she played in creation. What do you learn about Wisdom from this passage? What else do you want to know about Wisdom? What questions does the figure of Wisdom raise for you?

Pray that you and the adult learners will continue to study and live faithfully.

Preparing Our Minds

Study the background from Hebrews 1 and lesson Scripture, verses 1-4, 8-12. As you focus on this passage consider who can speak to you about the deeper meanings of life in an authoritative and credible voice.

Write on newsprint:
❑ information for next week's lesson, found under "Continue the Journey."
❑ activities for further spiritual growth in "Continue the Journey."

Be prepared to read or retell whatever information you choose to use from Introduction to the Summer Quarter and/or "The Big Picture: Images of Christ in Hebrews, the Gospels, and Us."

Plan a brief lecture from Understanding

the Scripture for "Understand That God Spoke in a Totally New Way by Sending Jesus Christ, God's Son."

Decide which activities you will use for "Respond Positively by Acknowledging the Majesty of God's Son" and have the appropriate supplies available.

LEADING THE CLASS

(1) Gather to Learn

❖ Welcome the class members and introduce any guests.

❖ Pray that everyone who has gathered today will find new meaning in life as they consider their relationship to Jesus, God's Son.

❖ Invite the students to list specific sources they turn to for local, national, and international news. Include television, newspapers, news magazines, the Internet, and other sources. Write these names on newsprint.

❖ Discuss these questions with the class.
   (1) What prompts you to turn to the specific source(s) you have cited?
   (2) Why do you believe that this source is credible?

❖ Read aloud today's focus statement: **People search for authoritative and credible voices to answer life's questions. Who** can speak to us about the deeper meanings of life? God spoke to us through God's beloved Son, Jesus Christ.

(2) Understand That God Spoke in a Totally New Way by Sending Jesus Christ, God's Son

❖ Use the Introduction to the Summer Quarter to provide a survey of this quarter's sessions.

❖ Consider reading or commenting on selected parts of "The Big Picture: Images of Christ in Hebrews, the Gospels, and Us" article to give the students a broader base from which to study this quarter's sessions.

❖ Choose someone to read Hebrews 1:1-4.
■ Discuss these two questions. List ideas on newsprint.
   (1) What does this passage tell you about God and how God works?
   (2) What does this passage tell you about who Jesus is, what he does, and how he is related to God?
■ Convey information from Understanding the Scripture for Hebrews 1:1-2 and 1:3-4, noting especially the Hebrews writer's bridge between the past and present.
■ Invite the students to comment on how the depiction of God and Jesus in this passage supports or challenges their own beliefs.

❖ Select a volunteer to read Hebrews 1:8-12. Note that the writer had been speaking about angels, and now in verse 8 turns attention to the Son.
   ■ Provide an opportunity for the students to add to the list they made in the previous activity.
   ■ Discuss the picture that the writer paints of the Son. Given this picture, consider what the students would expect of the Son.
   ■ **Option:** Note that in verses 5-13 the writer quotes the Hebrew Bible seven times. You may wish to check these references with the class,

though some are quoted from the early Greek translation of the Hebrew Bible and will not read the same as in your Bible. Talk about why the writer seems to rely so heavily on what we would call the Old Testament. What point(s) might he be trying to make?
   • 1:5   Psalm 2:7
   • 1:5   2 Samuel 7:14
   • 1:6   Deuteronomy 32:43
   • 1:7   Psalm 104:4
   • 1:8-9   Psalm 45:6-7
   • 1:10-12 Psalm 102:25-27
   • 1:13   Psalm 110:1

(3) Experience the Magnificence of God's New Way of Communicating with Us

❖ Encourage volunteers to tell the class or a small group about how they have found deeper meaning in their lives through the Son. (Be sure to create a safe, accepting environment to do this so that people will feel free to talk and not feel judged. A former alcoholic, for example, may want to talk about how life changed as a result of finding Christ. Another person, abused as a child or spouse, might report how redemption by Christ has freed him or her for a new life.)

❖ Suggest that worship is a way to experience the Son in our lives. Work with the students to write a creed that includes what they believe about the Father and the Son. Recommend that they refer to the lists made earlier about the person and work of both God and the Son. (Note that creeds generally include the Holy Spirit as well, but you may not have time to craft a section on the Spirit.) If the class is large, divide into groups and distribute paper and pencils to do this. If the group is small, use newsprint to capture ideas as you work together.

❖ End this part of the lesson by reading the class creed in unison, or by having each group read the creed they have written.

*(4) Respond Positively by Acknowledging
the Majesty of God's Son*

❖ Read or retell "Faithful Response" from Interpreting the Scripture.

❖ Encourage the students to acknowledge and praise Christ by doing one or more of the following activities. If possible, let each student choose what he or she will do.

■ Distribute paper and pencils. Challenge the students to write a psalm or hymn of praise. If possible, provide time for the students to read aloud their work.

■ Distribute hymnals. Invite class members to select one or more hymns that portray the majesty of Christ. Sing at least one of these hymns. Or sing one verse of several hymns.

■ Distribute art supplies, such as paper and markers or colored pencils. Suggest that the adults draw a scene depicting Christ's magnificence. Or suggest that students create an abstract design or simply splash colors on the page that reflect their interpretation of Christ's majesty. If time allows, let the students show their work to the class or small group.

❖ Conclude this portion of the lesson by reading in unison today's key verse, Hebrews 1:3.

(5) Continue the Journey

❖ Pray that those who have participated today will allow the light and love of Christ to reflect in their own lives.

❖ Read aloud this preparation for next week's lesson. You may also want to post it on newsprint for the students to copy.

■ **Title: Christ as Intercessor**
■ **Background Scripture: Hebrews 7**
■ **Lesson Scripture: Hebrews 7:20-28**
■ **Focus of the Lesson: Sometimes we need someone to speak up for us, to take our side. Who speaks on our behalf? God chose Jesus to be the perfect and permanent intercessor for humanity.**

❖ Challenge the students to complete one or more of these activities for further spiritual growth, which you will write on newsprint for the students to copy.

(1) Seek out someone who gives credible witness to Christ to help you deal with a problem.

(2) Choose a prophetic book of the Bible to read this week. Compare ways in which God speaks through this prophet with ways that you understand God speaks through Christ.

(3) Research information on "angels." Many people have opinions on angels. Which ideas seem credible in light of what you know from the Bible?

❖ Sing or read aloud "Because He Lives."

❖ Conclude today's session by leading the class in this benediction, which is adapted from James 1:22, 25: **Let us now go forth as doers of the word and not merely hearers, for doers who act will be blessed in their doing.**

UNIT 1: IMAGES OF CHRIST IN HEBREWS
CHRIST AS INTERCESSOR

PREVIEWING THE LESSON

Lesson Scripture: Hebrews 7:20-28
Background Scripture: Hebrews 7
Key Verse: Hebrews 7:25

Focus of the Lesson:
Sometimes we need someone to speak up for us, to take our side. Who speaks on our behalf? God chose Jesus to be the perfect and permanent intercessor for humanity.

Goals for the Learners:
(1) to discover how they can approach God.
(2) to consider how they see themselves as part of the priesthood of all believers.
(3) to reaffirm their faith in Jesus, who intercedes for them.

Pronunciation Guide:
dunamis (doo' nam is)
Melchizedek (mel kiz' uh dek)
teleiosis (tel i' o sis)
Yom Kippur (yom kih poor')

Supplies:
Bibles, newsprint and marker, paper and pencils, hymnals

READING THE SCRIPTURE

NRSV
Hebrews 7:20-28

²⁰This was confirmed with an oath; for others who became priests took their office without an oath, ²¹but this one became a priest with an oath, because of the one who said to him,

"The Lord has sworn
and will not change his mind,
'You are a priest forever'"—

NIV
Hebrews 7:20-28

²⁰And it was not without an oath! Others became priests without any oath, ²¹but he became a priest with an oath when God said to him:

"The Lord has sworn
and will not change his mind:
'You are a priest forever.'"

²²accordingly Jesus has also become the guarantee of a better covenant.

²³Furthermore, the former priests were many in number, because they were prevented by death from continuing in office; ²⁴but he holds his priesthood permanently, because he continues forever. ²⁵Consequently he is able for all time to save those who approach God through him, since he always lives to make intercession for them. ²⁶For it was fitting that we should have such a high priest, holy, blameless, undefiled, separated from sinners, and exalted above the heavens. ²⁷Unlike the other high priests, he has no need to offer sacrifices day after day, first for his own sins, and then for those of the people; this he did once for all when he offered himself. ²⁸For the law appoints as high priests those who are subject to weakness, but the word of the oath, which came later than the law, appoints a Son who has been made perfect forever.

²²Because of this oath, Jesus has become the guarantee of a better covenant.

²³Now there have been many of those priests, since death prevented them from continuing in office; ²⁴but because Jesus lives forever, he has a permanent priesthood. ²⁵Therefore he is able to save completely those who come to God through him, because he always lives to intercede for them. ²⁶Such a high priest meets our need—one who is holy, blameless, pure, set apart from sinners, exalted above the heavens. ²⁷Unlike the other high priests, he does not need to offer sacrifices day after day, first for his own sins, and then for the sins of the people. He sacrificed for their sins once for all when he offered himself. ²⁸For the law appoints as high priests men who are weak; but the oath, which came after the law, appointed the Son, who has been made perfect forever.

UNDERSTANDING THE SCRIPTURE

Hebrews 7:1-3. "This 'King Melchizedek. . . .'" The seventh through tenth chapters of Hebrews delve into the understanding of Jesus as "high priest." To begin that exploration, the shadowy figure of Melchizedek is summoned. It is an interesting tactic. Melchizedek appears as a seemingly minor character in Genesis 14:18-20. His function in that text is to bless Abram, and to receive from Abram "one tenth of everything." But from that brief encounter, the author of Hebrews uses Melchizedek to lay the foundation of the superiority of Christ's priesthood over and above the Levitical priests descended from Aaron. In verse 3, the author reads into Genesis' silence about Melchizedek's family connections a bold assertion of one who is (as will be argued later of Christ) a "priest forever." In such details as the tithe from Abram, the resemblance to the "Son of God," and a

priesthood that extends beyond time, Hebrews provides the framework for later assertions of Christ's identity and work.

Hebrews 7:4-10. These seven verses take up the interpretation of the tithes Abraham paid to Melchizedek. In modern ears, the line of argument may seen tenuous. But the author of Hebrews meticulously constructs in the rabbinic style of his time his central point: "the inferior is blessed by the superior." For once the author can establish Melchizedek as a "superior" order of priesthood, he has set the stage for the more pressing affirmation regarding Jesus as a priest in the order of Melchizedek. One other element of this argument is worth noting: the understanding of community as bridging not only space but time. Levi, the ancestor of the Levitical priesthood, is said to be "in the loins of his ancestor" (7:10) Abram when he paid the tithe. Israel understood community across generations. Passover celebrated a redemption that invited its later observers to count themselves as those who crossed the waters and experienced God's deliverance. This is closely related to the nature of community affirmed by the church in the "communion of saints."

Hebrews 7:11-14. The next stage of the argument in Hebrews' moves to affirming the inability of the previous priestly system to fulfill its purpose: "perfection." Perfection translates the Greek *teleiosis* (the verb form of this word occurs in verses 19 and 28). As you look at that word, you may recognize a familiar prefix: tele. It literally means "at a distance" (tele-phone as "distant sound," tele-scope as "distant sight"). Perfection, while including the idea of "without flaw," more importantly connotes "completion" or "to bring something to fulfillment or its end." The Levitical priesthood system, guided by the law, had been unable to bring to fruition its core purpose: the reconciliation of humanity (and creation) to God. For that, another priestly "order" was necessary: that of Melchizedek and (still unnamed but clearly by implication) Jesus. The closing two verses here respond to the objections to Jesus as priest since he was not from the priestly line of Levi. For the author of Hebrews, that is not a problem—indeed, it is his point. Jesus' priesthood is not a matter of genealogy.

Hebrews 7:15-19. The core of this section (7:17) quotes Psalm 110:4 to hold up one who comes from another priesthood: the "order of Melchizedek." Hebrews asserts a not-so-subtle hint as to who this one is. Like the everlasting origins of Melchizedek alluded to in verse 3, the one who follows him has become a priest "through the power of an indestructible life" (7:16), a veiled reference to Jesus' resurrection. Verses 18-19 contrast the inability of the law to "make perfect" with the "better hope" that makes it possible for us to "approach God." In that line of argument, the author of

Hebrews aligns the purpose of perfection with the ability to approach God. The priest of Melchizedek's order brings God's intent to reconcile to fulfillment and completion.

Hebrews 7:20-22. For the first time in this chapter, Jesus is specifically named as the priest of Melchizedek's order. The verses now contrast the Levitical order with that of Melchizedek on the basis of oaths (and the lack thereof). The Levitical priests took no oath, as they were born into the order. The Melchizedek priesthood relies on an oath. But notice, this is not an oath that Jesus, or Melchizedek, took. The quoting of the first half of Psalm 110:4 reveals that God is the One who has taken the oath. God's word (remember last week's emphasis on God's speaking) has fashioned this new order of priesthood, and thus has fashioned a "better covenant" (7:22). Describing Jesus as the "guarantee" of this covenant uses language related in that day to someone who gave a legally binding pledge to fulfill that action, even if it involved risk to self. God's oath in word is matched by Jesus' "guarantee" of that word in his life and death and raising.

Hebrews 7:23-25. Another distinction is drawn between the Levitical priesthood and Christ's priesthood. Levites were limited in their service by their mortality. No matter how good a priest he was, no matter how effectively he led or sacrificed or enabled the faithfulness of others, each one died. Christ's identity as a priest of the order of Melchizedek ("you are a priest forever") ensures that he will always and at all times be able to intercede. Intercession means to approach someone for the sake of another. It is to place one's own self between two others. Those who seek to approach God will, in Christ, always and at all times be able to do so through him.

Hebrews 7:26-28. A final distinction in these orders of priesthood has to do not with the mortality of the human condition, but with its frailty. The Levites' sacrifices for sin were not only for the people's but also for their own. It was an act in need of daily (in the case of Yom Kippur, yearly) practice. The high priesthood of Christ, in contrast, involved a "once for all" act. Humanity's weakness finds balance and healing in the Son's perfection—perfection not merely as

one without sin, but as the One who fulfills God's purposes to restore relationship through interceding for us and thus providing us access to God.

INTERPRETING THE SCRIPTURE

Approaching God

In one sense, the fundamental purpose of all religious activity and yearning has to do with the matter of approaching God. How can it be done? What makes it possible for human beings to encounter God, much less enter into relationship with God?

In ancient Judaism, the system of ritual sacrifice, priesthood, and law aimed at that goal. The Torah and its interpretations intended to shape lives that would be acceptable in God's sight. The sacrificial system provided a means to praise God for the gifts of life and to seek forgiveness for failings within it. The priests served as those who ritually carried out the sacrifices. The high priest oversaw the entire enterprise. And once a year, on the Day of Atonement, the high priest entered the holy of holies in the temple for the sake of atonement, to seek God's forgiveness for Israel's sins. But the high priest was the only one who could make such a direct approach to God—and only once a year at that.

That is why Hebrews lingers so long in the imagery of the temple and priesthood in its affirmation of the identity and work of Jesus Christ. For that system was the fundamental way in which the approach to God was understood by the community(ies) to which this epistle was directed.

The particular imagery of this passage may seem far removed from our experience, but its underlying concern remains the same. How can we approach God today? And how does our approach continue to rely on the identity and work of Jesus Christ?

The remaining sections of Interpreting the Scripture will seek to provide some insight into those issues.

Christ-Centered

At the heart of this passage's understanding of how we approach God is the person and vocation of Jesus. Jesus is the "guarantee of a better covenant . . . a priest forever. . . ." His work of providing access to God, unlike the repeated activity of the Levitical priests, is said to be "once for all" (7:27). Jesus Christ is at the center of how (and in whom) we encounter God.

A word of caution is in order here. To be Christian is to be Christ-centered: that is part of our very naming. But to be Christ-centered is not to fall into one category of interpretation of how that "centeredness" takes place. Nor is being Christ-centered a designation of spiritual pride. Far too much rhetoric within the church today seeks to distinguish between those who are Christ-centered (namely, the ones who believe and practice the Christian life like I do) and those whose Christianity is "nominal" or "worldly" or whatever term we use to only thinly veil disdain at other views of Christ.

The author of Hebrews clearly argues for Christian faith that places Christ at the center of all things, and in particular of how we are graced to approach God. But neither Hebrews nor other New Testament works— nor Jesus himself—condones spiritual egocentricity that makes "Christ-centered" a synonym for judgmental religion. Jesus' disciples once came up to him, complaining about someone casting out demons "because he was not following us." Jesus' reply was clear and to the point: "Do not stop him. . . .Whoever is not against us is for us" (from Mark 9:38-40). To be centered in Christ is to be open to the diverse ways (and ones) in which God works, even if they do not "follow us" by conforming to all our ideas about following Jesus.

The One Who Speaks for Us

Intercession. We see it at baptism. A parent or sponsor not only names a child but also offers promises on behalf of one who cannot as yet speak for himself or herself. We see it in courtroom situations. One lawyer speaks on behalf of a client—and another on behalf of the "people." We have each likely been in other situations in our lives when we relied, and/or felt relief, when another spoke on our behalf when words either failed us or we did not have the understanding to know what to say. In all such times, we need someone to speak for us—someone whose word holds authority and sway.

Hebrews portrays Jesus as such a one. When we approach God, even in the truth of our failings, we have one who speaks for us. Intercession literally means to place oneself between two parties, to be a "go-between." The Reformation principle of the priesthood of all believers, free to approach God without any human intermediary, is premised on the intercession of Christ on our behalf.

Christ as intercessor also reminds us that Jesus is presently active. Sometimes we fall into the habit of looking at Jesus only for his life and ministry in the distant past . . . and the hope of his return and coming sovereign realm. But for now, we think, we live in his absence. Physically, that is true. But spiritually, Jesus remains present and active on our behalf through intercession on our behalf. The "habit" of ending prayers "in Jesus' name" intends to serve as a reminder that

Jesus even now is the one who intercedes for us in the community we call Trinity. As in baptism, we still have someone who names us as God's child, held in grace, loved unconditionally in this time and for all time to come. Jesus speaks for you.

"Able for All Time"

This section closes with an exploration of what lies at the heart of today's key verse: Christ "is able for all time to save those who approach God through him" (Hebrews 7:25). Our approach to God is illuminated by three assertions.

"Able." The Greek word there is the verb form of *dunamis*, from which we get the English "dynamite." It is a word associated with the power to get things done. What makes our approach to God possible is the power of Jesus' life and ministry to make it so. Our approach to God is not empowered by our piety, by our uncanny way of living a moral and good life, or by our clever understandings of the mysteries of God's purposes. Our approach to God is empowered by the person and work of Jesus Christ. Christ is able to bridge the relationship between human and divine.

"For all time." There are none "left out" or "left behind" because they were born before the time of Jesus or after his earthly life. There is no time in this earthly existence when approach to God is "disabled." Before the dust of stars congealed to make the matter that constitutes this earth and our bodies, after the sun in our solar system burns out, the foundation for approach to God remains sure and everlasting in the literal sense of that word.

"To save." Christ does not intercede on our behalf so we may be brought to judgment and destruction. God's final word to us is not spewed out in disgust so that we will pass out of being and no longer offend an indignant deity. Our approach to God in Christ is for the sake of our being saved, by the grace of God revealed in the One who speaks on our behalf. The universe does not end in a hollow cold emptiness. The universe comes to completion (*perfection*, in the language of Hebrews) in God's purpose of salvation, a purpose made incarnate in Jesus the Christ.

SHARING THE SCRIPTURE

Preparing Our Hearts

Meditate on this week's devotional reading, found in Jeremiah 31:31-34. In this familiar passage the prophet writes about a "new covenant," which will be written not on stone tablets but on the hearts of God's people. Jeremiah also writes that God "will forgive their iniquity, and remember their sin no more" (31:34). How would your life change if you took these words from verse 34 seriously? Ponder what this new covenant, which Jesus refers to as he institutes the Lord's Supper, means in your life.

Pray that you and the adult learners will be open to God's gracious covenant and ready to live according to it.

Preparing Our Minds

Study the background, found in Hebrews 7, and lesson Scripture, verses 20-28. As you prepare, identify someone who is willing and able to speak on your behalf.

Write on newsprint:
❏ information for next week's lesson, found under "Continue the Journey."
❏ activities for further spiritual growth in "Continue the Journey."

Plan to read or lecture on information found in Hebrews 7:1-19 in Understanding the Scripture to introduce "Discover How the Learners Can Approach God."

LEADING THE CLASS

(1) Gather to Learn

❖ Welcome the class members and introduce any guests.

❖ Pray that the adults who have come today will be eager to hear God's voice.

❖ Invite the students to tell stories to the class or a small group about situations in which someone spoke for them and made a difference. They may recall an incident from childhood when a friend or older sibling stood up for them. Perhaps they will remember a time when a peer or co-worker rallied to their side.

❖ Ask: **How did you feel knowing that someone was not only on your side but also willing to take a risk to speak up on your behalf?**

❖ Read aloud today's focus statement: **Sometimes we need someone to speak up for us, to take our side. Who speaks on our behalf? God chose Jesus to be the perfect and permanent intercessor for humanity.**

(2) Discover How the Learners Can Approach God

❖ Use information in Understanding the Scripture for verses 1-19 to set the stage for today's lesson. Help the students make connections between Jesus and Melchizedek, first mentioned in Genesis 14:18-20 and later referred to in Psalm 110:4, which will be cited in today's lesson in Hebrews 7:17, 21.

❖ Choose a volunteer to read Hebrews 7:20-28.

❖ Encourage the class to look at their Bibles to identify ways in which Jesus is a "one of a kind" priest. Write these ideas, which may include the following, on newsprint:

■ Jesus became a priest as a result of an oath sworn by God;

■ Jesus' priesthood continues forever, rather than ending at his death;

■ Jesus is always alive and making intercession for "those who approach God through him";

■ Jesus is "holy, blameless, undefiled, separated from sinners, and exalted about the heavens";

■ Jesus has no need to offer daily sacrifices for himself or others because his sacrifice on the cross was once and for all;

■ God's oath appointed Jesus, the Son, "who has been made perfect forever as high priest."

❖ Encourage the class to consider these questions.

(1) **Is this discussion of Jesus as priest in any way surprising or troubling to you? If so, how?** (Be aware that the notion of a priest is generally unfamiliar to most believers in Protestant traditions.)

(2) **How do you understand Jesus to be a priest in your own life? Think here about what Jesus might do for you before God.** (Be aware that the word "intercessor" may be more comfortable for some class members than "priest.")

(3) Consider How the Learners See Themselves as Part of the Priesthood of All Believers

❖ Encourage the students to turn in their Bibles to 1 Peter 2:1-10 as you read this passage aloud.

❖ Pay particular attention to verse 9 by inviting the students to state their understandings of this verse's implications for how each believer relates to the church and to other believers.

❖ Ask: **In what way are we all priests?**

❖ **Option:** Here is some information to read aloud concerning the "priesthood of all believers" that may be useful if your

students are unfamiliar with this concept. When you have finished reading, ask: **How do you see yourself in this priestly role?**

Based on 2 Peter 2:9, the concept of the "priesthood of all believers" asserts that all people of faith have equal access to God. While there is a difference between ordained clergy and laity, this distinction is rooted in church order, not in a spiritual hierarchy that perceives some persons to be closer to God than others.

The "priesthood of all believers" became an important tenet in Lutheranism and many Protestant churches. Although Martin Luther neither used the phrase "priesthood of all believers" nor denied the importance of the role of those persons educated, ordained, and duly recognized by the church to have oversight of the sacraments, he did assert that all baptized Christians shared in a "common priesthood." Throughout the years since the Reformation, churches have apparently stretched Luther's ideas beyond his original intent.

Within The United Methodist Church the notion of the "priesthood of all believers" undergirds this denomination's emphasis on the ministry of all baptized believers—a ministry that very much includes social action.

Other denominations, such as those within the Baptist movement, base their "congregational polity" on the notion of the "priesthood of all believers." In this form of church governance, individuals have a voice in decision-making for the congregation.

(4) Reaffirm Faith in Jesus, Who Intercedes for the Learners

❖ Point out that though many Christians understand themselves to be part of the "priesthood of all believers," we are aware that Christ is the one who intercedes for us before God. Therefore, faith in Christ is essential.

❖ Distribute paper and pencils. Challenge the students to write a brief statement affirming their faith in Jesus, or to sketch a picture illustrating Jesus interceding on their behalf before God.

❖ Invite volunteers to read their statements or show their drawings.

(5) Continue the Journey

❖ Pray that students will affirm Christ as intercessor, the one who speaks to God on their behalf.

❖ Read aloud this preparation for next week's lesson. You may also want to post it on newsprint for the students to copy.

- ■ **Title: Christ as Redeemer**
- ■ **Background Scripture: Hebrews 9:11–10:18**
- ■ **Lesson Scripture: Hebrews 9:11-18; 10:12-14, 17-18**
- ■ **Focus of the Lesson: People feel a need to be absolved of their wrongdoing. Who can take away our guilt? In Hebrews, we read that Jesus shed his blood for the redemption of humanity.**

❖ Challenge the students to complete one or more of these activities for further spiritual growth, which you will write on newsprint for the students to copy.

    (1) Intercede for someone who needs help. Perhaps, for example, an elderly person would appreciate your assistance in solving a problem with medical insurance.

    (2) Research Melchizedek to see what you can learn about him and his priesthood.

    (3) Write a letter to an elected official to speak as an advocate for people, such as those who are homeless or hungry, who have no voice or power.

❖ Sing or read aloud "Forgive Our Sins as We Forgive."

❖ Conclude today's session by leading the class in this benediction, which is adapted from James 1:22, 25: **Let us now go forth as doers of the word and not merely hearers, for doers who act will be blessed in their doing.**

UNIT 1: IMAGES OF CHRIST IN HEBREWS
CHRIST AS REDEEMER

PREVIEWING THE LESSON

Lesson Scripture: Hebrews 9:11-18; 10:12-14, 17-18
Background Scripture: Hebrews 9:11–10:18
Key Verse: Hebrews 9:12

Focus of the Lesson:
People feel a need to be absolved of their wrongdoing. Who can take away our guilt? In Hebrews, we read that Jesus shed his blood for the redemption of humanity.

Goals for the Learners:
(1) to explore the requirement of sacrifice for God's forgiveness of human sin.
(2) to reflect on God's forgiveness and its cost.
(3) to embrace the Redeemer and be grateful for redemption.

Pronunciation Guide:
Yom Kippur (yom kih poor')

Supplies:
Bibles, newsprint and marker, paper and pencils, hymnals, picture of Christ on the cross, CD or tape of Handel's "I Know That My Redeemer Liveth" (from the *Messiah*) and appropriate player

READING THE SCRIPTURE

NRSV
Hebrews 9:11-18

¹¹But when Christ came as a high priest of the good things that have come, then through the greater and perfect tent (not made with hands, that is, not of this creation), ¹²**he entered once for all into the Holy Place, not with the blood of goats and calves, but with his own blood, thus obtaining eternal redemption.** ¹³For if the blood of goats and bulls, with the sprinkling

NIV
Hebrews 9:11-18

¹¹When Christ came as high priest of the good things that are already here, he went through the greater and more perfect tabernacle that is not man-made, that is to say, not a part of this creation. ¹²**He did not enter by means of the blood of goats and calves; but he entered the Most Holy Place once for all by his own blood, having obtained eternal redemption.** ¹³The blood of goats and bulls

of the ashes of a heifer, sanctifies those who have been defiled so that their flesh is purified, [14]how much more will the blood of Christ, who through the eternal Spirit offered himself without blemish to God, purify our conscience from dead works to worship the living God!

[15]For this reason he is the mediator of a new covenant, so that those who are called may receive the promised eternal inheritance, because a death has occurred that redeems them from the transgressions under the first covenant. [16]Where a will is involved, the death of the one who made it must be established. [17]For a will takes effect only at death, since it is not in force as long as the one who made it is alive. [18]Hence not even the first covenant was inaugurated without blood.

Hebrews 10:12-14, 17-18

[12]But when Christ had offered for all time a single sacrifice for sins, "he sat down at the right hand of God," [13]and since then has been waiting "until his enemies would be made a footstool for his feet." [14]For by a single offering he has perfected for all time those who are sanctified.

[17][H]e also adds,

"I will remember their sins and their lawless deeds no more."

[18]Where there is forgiveness of these, there is no longer any offering for sin.

and the ashes of a heifer sprinkled on those who are ceremonially unclean sanctify them so that they are outwardly clean. [14]How much more, then, will the blood of Christ, who through the eternal Spirit offered himself unblemished to God, cleanse our consciences from acts that lead to death, so that we may serve the living God!

[15]For this reason Christ is the mediator of a new covenant, that those who are called may receive the promised eternal inheritance—now that he has died as a ransom to set them free from the sins committed under the first covenant.

[16]In the case of a will, it is necessary to prove the death of the one who made it, [17]because a will is in force only when somebody has died; it never takes effect while the one who made it is living. [18]This is why even the first covenant was not put into effect without blood.

Hebrews 10:12-14, 17-18

[12]But when this priest had offered for all time one sacrifice for sins, he sat down at the right hand of God. [13]Since that time he waits for his enemies to be made his footstool, [14]because by one sacrifice he has made perfect forever those who are being made holy. [17]Then he adds:

"Their sins and lawless acts
I will remember no more."

[18]And where these have been forgiven, there is no longer any sacrifice for sin.

UNDERSTANDING THE SCRIPTURE

Hebrews 9:11-14. The scene envisioned by the author of Hebrews is the liturgy associated with the annual Day of Atonement, Yom Kippur. "Tent" recalls the time before the building of the Jerusalem temple, when Israel's place of worship was in a tent ("tabernacle"). On the Day of Atonement, the high priest entered the innermost sanctuary (often referred to as the "holy of holies"). This was done only by the high priest once a year to offer sacrifice for the sins of the people for the previous year. Hebrews contrasts this yearly ritual with Christ's "once for all" (9:12) act involving his own sacrifice. "Blood" is a symbol for life, and its frequent use here—although perhaps foreign to modern ears—spoke clearly to those familiar with the sacrificial system of first-century Judaism and other religious traditions of that era.

Hebrews 9:15-17. "For this reason" alludes to Christ's unique embodiment of the high priesthood. Three key words are used in verse 15 to further underscore the identity and vocation of Jesus as high priest. "Mediator" illustrates the way in which Christ "goes between" (mediator as "one in the middle") the people and God. Modern understandings of mediator as negotiator do not correspond with this word's meaning and function in Hebrews. "Covenant" identifies Christ's work in God's ongoing history of entering into relationship with God's people (see comments on 10:15-18, where Jeremiah's promise of a new covenant is drawn into the thought of Hebrews). Lastly, "redeem" asserts the consequence of God's work in Jesus. The word, in its secular meaning related to a payment made to ransom a hostage or free a slave. In Paul's works, this word family takes on the meaning of what God does to release us from sin.

Hebrews 9:18-22. Recall the earlier assertion of "blood" as a symbol for life. In these verses, the author of Hebrews seeks to establish a point of contact between the former covenants and the covenant initiated in Christ through the common imagery of blood sacrifice. Although only the example of the Sinai covenant is given in Moses' act of sprinkling blood on the people, it is to be remembered that the covenants with Noah and Abraham both involved such sacrifices in ritual (Genesis 8:20-22 and 15:7-21). The key interpretive challenge with this material is finding a way to convey its message to those for whom blood sacrifice is not only a practice of the distant past but in many ways an image foreign to our understandings of God and how we approach God.

Hebrews 9:23-28. Contrasts once more come to the forefront. The sanctuary Christ enters is the real and true (that is,

"heavenly") one, not its "mere copy" (that is, Jerusalem or any other physical place of worship). Philosophical categories of "real" versus "copy" or "shadow" are employed by Hebrews. Christ's sacrifice is not the Jerusalem high priest's annual repetition ("again and again," "year after year") but "once for all." Furthermore, Jesus' sacrifice is not of other things but of self (9:26). All of these contrasts underscore the new covenant's ability in Christ to bring forgiveness of sins. Even beyond that, this new covenant has as its purpose not simply the removal of sin (which had been the function of the old sacrifices) but the *saving* of those who form the community bound in Christ (9:28).

Hebrews 10:1-4. These verses form a summary of sorts of what Hebrews has already asserted. "Shadow," "true form," "realities": Again, the line of the argument in Hebrews draws upon the philosophical language of its day. "Make perfect" recalls a word and theme explored in previous sessions that continues to assert how the covenant enacted in Christ fulfills God's purposes for human life and community. "Consciousness" is the same word used in 9:14 ("conscience"). It corresponds to the interior life of an individual, almost a synonym for what is referred to elsewhere as "mind and heart." And in a passage so taken with using the imagery of Judaism's rituals of sacrifice, it is intriguing that the author uses a word implicit in developing Christian ritual. "A *reminder* of sin year after year" translates the word Paul used in 1 Corinthians 11:24-25 to speak of the celebration of communion ("in remembrance of me").

Hebrews 10:5-10. This section opens (10:5-7) with a loose quoting of Psalm 40:6-8. Amos 5:21-24 and Isaiah 1:11-17 make similar pronouncements, declaring the emptiness of such rituals when they are not joined to acts of justice. Following the quotation, Hebrews interprets its words in explaining Christ's enacting of this covenant. Twice quoted in this passage is God "taking no pleasure." The contrast made explicit here between the old sacrifices and Christ's work may also be conveyed more subtly in this repeated verb. It is the same verb used in the accounts of Jesus' baptism (Matthew 3:17; Mark 1:11) and transfiguration (Matthew 17:5) to speak of God being "well pleased" with Jesus.

Hebrews 10:11-14. The contrast between the daily priestly activity and Christ's once and for all time offering is drawn once more. Brought into it is a quotation from Psalm 110:1, noted in the first session as a key psalm throughout Hebrews. A caution might be offered about the image of Christ "waiting until . . ." (10:13). It is not an image of inactivity. As noted in last week's session, Christ is presently engaged and active in intercession on our behalf. We are not left to

fend for ourselves until kingdom come. Christ continues to act and speak on our behalf during this "interim" time.

Hebrews 10:15-18. Hebrews 8:8-12 had quoted Jeremiah 31:31-34 at length to begin this extended commentary (chapters 8–10) on the new covenant enacted in Christ that fulfills what the old covenant had been unable to do. Now, once more in these verses that close this session, Jeremiah 31 comes to the forefront by way of summary. The new covenant in Christ as foreseen by Jeremiah is not merely the testimony of the church. Hebrews identifies it as the testimony of the Holy Spirit (10:15). The covenant resides within us, perhaps recalling earlier references to the role of conscience/consciousness. And sin will be remembered no more.

INTERPRETING THE SCRIPTURE

Ritual That Matters

Religions in general, and Christianity in particular, sometimes have "love-hate" relationships with their rituals. As noted in Understanding the Scripture, the sacrificial system of Judaism did not escape the critical eye of Israel's prophets. They clearly understood that ritual alone, if not connected to the conduct of one's daily life, had no meaning. The church, in times past and present, has also had such voices decrying the separation between liturgy and life that empties the former of meaning.

It would be a mistake, however, to take those positions and this passage to the extreme of saying that ritual does not matter and has no place in Christian faith. Quite the contrary: The seriousness and the length to which Hebrews goes in today's readings and through this epistle can be taken as an argument that ritual *is* an integral component. The issue comes in discerning those

rituals that truly matter and have consequence upon our lives and faith.

The identity and work of Jesus Christ as "high priest" brings that into clear focus. What Christ does on our behalf is of consequence to us—and to him. For both of us, it is a life-and-death matter. Thus, all the language about "blood" and "sacrifice" that may seem foreign to our understanding and experience points to a deeper truth: namely, that what God is about in the mystery of Christ's redemptive work can only be communicated to us and enacted in Jesus by life and faith made incarnate. Rituals that matter are those that communicate the truth of God's love and grace, and that then evoke our own faithful response not simply in the structuring of liturgies but in the living of lives expended in service.

Mediator and Redeemer

Last session's passage and Interpreting the Scripture explored the "Christ-centered" nature of the argument in Hebrews. In today's passage, two particular words focus our understanding of why Jesus stands at the core of our relationship with God: "mediator" and "redeem."

Hebrews explicitly identifies Jesus as "the mediator of a new covenant" (9:15). As noted in today's Understanding the Scripture, "mediator" simply and literally means "one who is in the middle." It is important not to bring modern shades of meaning to this word that were not part of the life and understanding of the author. This is not a mediator as one brought in to mediate a   dispute, whether labor or domestic or political. Jesus as mediator is not one who bargains and cajoles two opposing parties into arriving at a mutually agreeable (and mutually compromised) position. Jesus as mediator is more like the "meeting place" between God and humanity, the One in the middle whose life and work give substance to the new covenant God brings.

The other key word about Jesus' work, and its consequences for our relationship with God, is "redeem." Recall the original meaning of this word identified in Understanding the Scripture: to free a hostage or slave by payment. "Redemption" is both a metaphor and mystery for forgiveness that enables new life. A cautionary word needs to be spoken here, lest the mystery of redemption becomes compromised by trying to apply its secular meaning in ways that are not helpful. For example, some traditions stress—to the point of obsession—Jesus' "paying" for our sins with his blood. So who does he pay? If it is God, what does that make of God, who insists on the death of God's own son? And if it is not God, who else? Satan? If Satan must be "appeased," does that give too much authority to the power of evil as a rival to God? Again, redemption's gift ought not be squandered by doing away with redemption's mystery. Hebrews affirms only Christ as

the One who redeems, and does not get drawn into the blind alleys of faith bogged down in legalisms and literalisms.

Sin, Guilt, and Grace

The human problem that rests at the core of Jesus' work as high priest, as was the case with the entire sacrificial system of Judaism, is sin. One of the meanings of the word translated as sin is "to miss the mark." Sometimes, we fall into conversations that debate the nature of sin. Some Christian traditions have turned obsession with sin into a faith that is dour and sullen, devoid of joy. Other traditions, in eagerness to escape that caricature of Christian living, have swung the pendulum to an almost anything-goes attitude. Most of us likely live somewhere between those margins, understanding with various degrees of agreement with Paul that "all have sinned and fall short of the glory of God" (Romans 3:23).

Awareness of sin leads to what can be an equally disabling condition: guilt. And guilt is a problem, at least for those whose conscience admits to the truth of one's sin, especially against another. For if we are guilty, how can we move out of that paralyzing sense that our guilt will always be there to nag us and critique us until we take our last breath? Sometimes we flee guilt by denial, or by doing good in hopes that it will outweigh the wrong. But "earning" one's way out of guilt tends to produce either frustration or pride, neither of which has redemptive qualities.

Freedom from sin, and the guilt it induces, comes through the person and work of Jesus—and through our participation in that covenant made possible by God's grace. All of the sacrificial language and imagery in Hebrews points to that gift of forgiveness extended to us that makes it possible then to live with faith. (See Hebrews 11 for the lived consequences of this covenant.)

Where There Is Forgiveness

Where there is forgiveness. . . . Pause for a moment in this reading and recall such a place and time in your life. Where you received forgiveness . . . where you extended forgiveness . . . . What did you experience? How has that shaped your life and faith?

At the end of this passage, and at the end of a long section (beginning at 8:1 and concluding here) that has explored the nature of Christ's high priestly ministry in the enacting of God's new covenant, it all comes down to this: Sin will be remembered no more. "Where there is forgiveness" becomes postlude to Christ's work—and prelude to the lives we now live as God's faithful and forgiven. It is not coincidental that the letter of Hebrews now shifts from its focus on Christ to a focus upon the community addressed by it (10:19-31).

Theology, like politics, must always become "local": that is, lived out in daily conduct. And this closing word to this section reminds the Christian community, then and now, that forgiveness seeks out embodiment and incarnation as surely as Christ's ministry needed to be lived in the flesh. Jesus once made a fascinating connection with such forgiveness. To a Pharisee who looked down on a woman who anointed Jesus' feet, Jesus said: "Her sins, which were many, have been forgiven; hence she has shown great love. But the one to whom little is forgiven, loves little" (Luke 7:47). Where there is forgiveness, Jesus seems to be saying, there you will find love. And vice-versa. So it is with us.

SHARING THE SCRIPTURE

Preparing Our Hearts

Meditate on this week's devotional reading, found in John 4:21-26. As Jesus speaks with the woman of Samaria, he reveals that he is the awaited Messiah. What do you believe about Jesus of Nazareth? Is he, for you, God's Christ, God's anointed One? How does the image of Jesus as Messiah help you to know him better—and to know more fully the God who sent him?

Pray that you and the adult learners will be aware of the many images of Christ that are found in the Bible.

Preparing Our Minds

Study the background from Hebrews 9:11–10:18 and lesson Scripture, Hebrews 9:11-18 and 10:12-14, 17-18. Ponder the issue of guilt and how you can be absolved of wrongdoing.

Write on newsprint:
❏ information for next week's lesson, found under "Continue the Journey."
❏ activities for further spiritual growth in "Continue the Journey."

Locate a recording of "I Know That My Redeemer Liveth" from Handel's *Messiah*, along with an appropriate player.

Find a picture of Jesus on the cross. Check your local or church library, picture file at the church, and/or Internet sites. An especially striking picture is in Matthias Grünewald's *Isenheim Altarpiece*, which you can find at http://www.wga.hu/frames-e.html?/html/g/grunewal/2isenhei/1view1c.html.

LEADING THE CLASS

(1) Gather to Learn

❖ Welcome the class members and introduce any guests.

❖ Pray that adults who have gathered today will glean new understandings about who Jesus is and how they can relate to him.

❖ Encourage the students to recall situations when as children or teens they did something wrong, even sinful, and felt guilty about it. They need not divulge their wrongdoing, but invite the adults to say how their inappropriate actions caused them to feel.

❖ Ask: **How can we get rid of guilt when we have done something wrong— or is that guilt ever present?**

❖ Read aloud today's focus statement: **People feel a need to be absolved of their wrongdoing. Who can take away our guilt? In Hebrews, we read that Jesus shed his blood for the redemption of humanity.**

(2) Explore the Requirement of Sacrifice for God's Forgiveness of Human Sin

❖ Choose someone to read Hebrews 9:11-14.

    ■ Read information from Understanding the Scripture for these verses to help the students understand how the writer of Hebrews is comparing Jesus to the high priest of the Jerusalem temple.

    ■ Help the students to compare and contrast Jesus' sacrificial offering of himself with the high priest's offering of animal sacrifices.

❖ Ask a student to read Hebrews 9:15-18.

    ■ Read or retell "Mediator and Redeemer" from Interpreting the Scripture.

    ■ Ask: **What does it mean to you that Christ is both mediator and redeemer? What difference does that make in your life?** (You may want to discuss these questions in small groups to give more people a chance to participate.)

❖ Select a volunteer to read Hebrews 10:12-14, 17-18.

■ Note that we need to define "sin" in order to understand this portion of the text clearly. Invite the students to give their own definitions, which you will list on newsprint. Here are some musings on sin you may wish to add to the discussion.

• **"Christ's definition of sin penetrates far deeper than a list of sins on a membership card. It goes to our inner desire, motivations, and secret thoughts."** (Erwin W. Lutzer, 1941–)

• **"Disobedience and sin are the same thing, for there is no sin but disobedience."** (Theologia Germanica, about 1350)

• **"Sin has four characteristics: self-sufficiency instead of faith; self-will instead of submission; self-seeking instead of benevolence; self-righteousness instead of humility."** (E. Paul Hovey, 1908–)

• **"Sin becomes a crime, not against law, but against love; it means not breaking God's law so much as breaking God's heart."** (William Barclay, 1907–1978)

• Raise these questions for discussion. The students may want to look again in their Bibles to Hebrews 10:12-14, 17-18.

    (1) What does this passage tell you about Jesus and his work?

    (2) What does this passage tell you about sin?

    (3) What does this passage tell you about forgiveness?

■ Provide a few moments of quiet time for the students to ponder this question: **How do the teachings in Hebrews 10 help me to recognize my sin, seek forgiveness, and grow in my relationship with Jesus Christ?**

(3) Reflect on God's Forgiveness and Its Cost

❖ Distribute paper and pencils. Read aloud the first paragraph of "Where There

Is Forgiveness" in Interpreting the Scripture." Allow time for the students to think about the questions raised here and to respond, if they choose, in writing. Assure them that this activity is confidential.

❖ Show a picture of Christ on the cross. Talk with the students about how the artist has chosen to portray this event, especially in terms of colors, facial expressions, nearness or distance of characters from the cross, and so on.

❖ Explore with the students the cost of God's forgiveness in terms of Jesus' sacrificial death. Try to encourage empathy with Jesus by talking about the physical, emotional, and social pain associated with knowing an agonizing death awaits you because you have chosen to be the bearer of forgiveness.

(4) Embrace the Redeemer and Be Grateful for Redemption

❖ Read these words from Job and 1 Corinthians, which are the lyrics of George Frideric Handel's "I Know That My Redeemer Liveth," #45, air for soprano, from his *Messiah:* **"I know that my Redeemer liveth, and that he shall stand at the latter day upon the earth. And though worms destroy this body, yet in my flesh shall I see God" (from Job 19:25-26). "For now is Christ risen from the dead, the first fruits of them that sleep" (from 1 Corinthians 15:20).**

❖ Play a recording of this music. Invite the students to close their eyes and envision Christ, the living redeemer, and the benefits that his redemption have bestowed upon them.

❖ Work with the students to write on newsprint a brief prayer expressing gratitude for the redemption that they experience in Christ. Read this prayer in unison.

(5) Continue the Journey

❖ **Option:** Pray that all who have come today will recognize that in Christ the redeemer their sins are forgiven and their guilt is absolved.

❖ Read aloud this preparation for next week's lesson. You may also want to post it on newsprint for the students to copy.
■ **Title: Christ as Leader**
■ **Background Scripture: Hebrews 12:1-13**
■ **Lesson Scripture: Hebrews 12:1-13**
■ **Focus of the Lesson: People want to follow leaders who will give them direction. What makes a leader credible? By his action and godly discipline, Jesus demonstrates that he is a leader who can be trusted.**

❖ Challenge the students to complete one or more of these activities for further spiritual growth, which you will write on newsprint for the students to copy.
(1) **Think about the service of Holy Communion as it is done in your church. Write in your spiritual journal about how your practices reflect the images of sacrifice seen in Hebrews. What comparisons and contrasts can you make?**
(2) **Participate in Holy Communion. As you return to your pew, ponder how this experience of eating Christ's body and blood changes and shapes you into the likeness of Christ.**
(3) **Offer forgiveness to someone who has wronged you.**

❖ Sing or read aloud "Nothing but the Blood."

❖ Conclude today's session by leading the class in this benediction, which is adapted from James 1:22, 25: **Let us now go forth as doers of the word and not merely hearers, for doers who act will be blessed in their doing.**

UNIT 1: IMAGES OF CHRIST IN HEBREWS
CHRIST AS LEADER

PREVIEWING THE LESSON

Lesson Scripture: Hebrews 12:1-13
Background Scripture: Hebrews 12:1-13
Key Verses: Hebrews 12:1c-2a

Focus of the Lesson:
People want to follow leaders who will give them direction. What makes a leader credible? By his action and godly discipline, Jesus demonstrates that he is a leader who can be trusted.

Goals for the Learners:
(1) to consider God's plan for helping us live according to God's will.
(2) to ponder the impact on their lives of following Jesus.
(3) to commit to following Jesus.

Pronunciation Guide:
Masoretic (mas uh ret' ik)
Septuagint (sep too' uh jint)

Supplies:
Bibles, newsprint and marker, paper and pencils, hymnals

READING THE SCRIPTURE

NRSV
Hebrews 12:1-13

¹Therefore, since we are surrounded by so great a cloud of witnesses, let us also lay aside every weight and the sin that clings so closely, and **let us run with perseverance the race that is set before us, ²looking to Jesus the pioneer and perfecter of our faith,** who for the sake of the joy that was set before him endured the cross, disregarding

NIV
Hebrews 12:1-13

¹Therefore, since we are surrounded by such a great cloud of witnesses, let us throw off everything that hinders and the sin that so easily entangles, and **let us run with perseverance the race marked out for us. ²Let us fix our eyes on Jesus, the author and perfecter of our faith,** who for the joy set before him endured the cross, scorning its shame,

its shame, and has taken his seat at the right hand of the throne of God.

³Consider him who endured such hostility against himself from sinners, so that you may not grow weary or lose heart. ⁴In your struggle against sin you have not yet resisted to the point of shedding your blood. ⁵And you have forgotten the exhortation that addresses you as children—

"My child, do not regard lightly the discipline of the Lord,
  or lose heart when you are punished by him;
⁶ for the Lord disciplines those whom he loves,
  and chastises every child whom he accepts."

⁷Endure trials for the sake of discipline. God is treating you as children; for what child is there whom a parent does not discipline? ⁸If you do not have that discipline in which all children share, then you are illegitimate and not his children. ⁹Moreover, we had human parents to discipline us, and we respected them. Should we not be even more willing to be subject to the Father of spirits and live? ¹⁰For they disciplined us for a short time as seemed best to them, but he disciplines us for our good, in order that we may share his holiness. ¹¹Now, discipline always seems painful rather than pleasant at the time, but later it yields the peaceful fruit of righteousness to those who have been trained by it.

¹²Therefore lift your drooping hands and strengthen your weak knees, ¹³and make straight paths for your feet, so that what is lame may not be put out of joint, but rather be healed.

and sat down at the right hand of the throne of God. ³Consider him who endured such opposition from sinful men, so that you will not grow weary and lose heart.

⁴In your struggle against sin, you have not yet resisted to the point of shedding your blood. ⁵And you have forgotten that word of encouragement that addresses you as sons:

"My son, do not make light of the Lord's discipline,
  and do not lose heart when he rebukes you,
⁶ because the Lord disciplines those he loves,
  and he punishes everyone he accepts as a son."

⁷Endure hardship as discipline; God is treating you as sons. For what son is not disciplined by his father? ⁸If you are not disciplined (and everyone undergoes discipline), then you are illegitimate children and not true sons. ⁹Moreover, we have all had human fathers who disciplined us and we respected them for it. How much more should we submit to the Father of our spirits and live! ¹⁰Our fathers disciplined us for a little while as they thought best; but God disciplines us for our good, that we may share in his holiness. ¹¹No discipline seems pleasant at the time, but painful. Later on, however, it produces a harvest of righteousness and peace for those who have been trained by it.

¹²Therefore, strengthen your feeble arms and weak knees. ¹³"Make level paths for your feet," so that the lame may not be disabled, but rather healed.

UNDERSTANDING THE SCRIPTURE

Hebrews 12:1-3. "Therefore" serves to link this day's passage with Hebrews 11, the author's extended "homily" on faith. In that chapter, Hebrews provides a summary of individuals, both named and unnamed, whose lives embodied faithful witness to God—and those to whom God bore witness (11:39). These are the ones who form the great "cloud of witnesses." "Cloud" calls to mind the exodus story, where God led the people by day with a pillar of cloud (Exodus 13:21). Now, God's leading of the community addressed by Hebrews is exemplified by those whose lives of faith "surround" that community. Much of the imagery of this entire passage draws from the realm of athletic contests—and that imagery begins now with the life of faith compared to a race set before us. "Race" is a word that can also mean struggle or conflict, deepening the associations with a community whose faithfulness brought them into conflict with the wider culture. The key to this race, in a Greek word that will occur four times (12:1, 2, 3, 7) in this whole passage, is revealed in verse 1: "endure." Such endurance and perseverance is not limited, however, to the cloud of witnesses. In verse 2, the passage shifts to the source and model of both in Jesus. "Pioneer" is a word that elsewhere is translated as "leader" and "author." Linked here with a word we have continually encountered through these studies in Hebrews ("perfector/make perfect"), Jesus is portrayed as the one in whom we find faith's true embodiment and fulfillment. "Right hand" is a symbol for the place of power and authority. The "race that is set before us" in verse 1 finds parallel now in what had been set before Jesus: the cross, which he endured for the sake of joy. The text does not suggest that the race that is ours and Jesus' cross are identical. Rather, they each relate differing forms of (and calls to) faithfulness. The purpose of Christ's enduring seeks to encourage us to "not grow weary or lose heart."

Hebrews 12:4-6. The passage makes a definite shift in emphasis at this point. The focus upon Jesus now turns to an exploration of a theme that will dominate the central portion of this text: "discipline" as the means for enduring. The author acknowledges at the outset that such endurance, and the discipline it will require, are of a different sort than that embodied in Jesus. Verse 4

is a word of observation, not judgment, that the community has not yet been tested to the point of death (as had Jesus on the cross). There is, however, a chiding in verse 5 about forgetfulness concerning their role and vocation. Common to the author's style throughout this epistle, the core of these verses turns on a quotation from Proverbs 3:11-12 (from the Greek version, the Septuagint, which accounts for why it may sound somewhat different from those same verses in Bibles based on the Masoretic or Hebrew text). The book of Proverbs draws on Israel's wisdom tradition, and one of the chief themes in that tradition (as reflected in the passage quoted here) has to do with parent/child relationships, particularly the importance of instruction and "discipline." "Discipline" needs to be heard in that context beyond its association today with punishment. It involved the broader sense of nurture that seeks to fashion responsibility and faithfulness. "Discipline" occurs no less than nine times, both as a noun and a verb, in verses 4-11. In verses 5-6, the quotation from Proverbs seeks to establish the point to be developed later of God's discipline in our lives. It is identified as a sign of God's love for us, not rejection of us.

Hebrews 12:7-11. It is not the theme of discipline "in general," however, that interests Hebrews. Rather, the author in these verses addresses the difficult and potentially hazardous consideration of how discipline, suffering, and endurance interact to involve the activity of God in this community. Elsewhere in Hebrews, the author has relied on lines of argument that compared and contrasted the "greater" with the "lesser"— for example, Christ as the "great" high priest who fulfills the sacrificial work that had been done by the Levitical priests. Here, Hebrews lifts up the short-term discipline provided by human parents that engenders respect (12:9-10) with the discipline God provides that is "for our good." The closing verse of this section (12:11) draws out a general principle for discipline of all kinds: At the moment of experiencing it, it may be painful rather than "pleasant" (the Greek word for pleasant is the same word translated as joy in verse 2). The positive value of such discipline comes to those who have been "trained by it," where again the author draws imagery from the realm of athletic contests and training.

Hebrews 12:12-13. Two paraphrases of Old Testament verses are combined here to bring the passage to a close—and to a final encouragement. Verse 12 recalls a portion of Isaiah 35:3 to urge the community to faithful action in the face of difficulties and suffering that might otherwise be wearying. Many scholars believe Isaiah 35 comes from the time of Israel's exile. The wearying despair and grayness of captivity caused hope to disappear in part of the community—and these words, among others, sought to stir hope that in turn would prepare the people for return and restoration (that would, in turn, be difficult ventures themselves). The first half of Hebrews 12:13 alludes to Proverbs 4:26. That chapter, perhaps not coincidentally, begins with: "Listen, children, to a father's instruction. . . ." Instruction and discipline bear close resemblance, even as the imagery of "paths" in the verse is a common metaphor for the way one conducts one's life in following God. The second half of verse 13 is slightly unclear, perhaps indicating that walking in the ways (and disciplines) God provides results not so much in the immediate pain experienced in discipline but in an outcome of healing and restoration.

INTERPRETING THE SCRIPTURE

Jesus' Leadership

"Leaders lead," so one saying goes. There is a world of difference between a CEO (chief executive officer) who collects his pay and is sheltered from what happens to workers as a result of his decisions and one who is out on the front lines showing the way and sharing the consequences.

Jesus' leadership is clearly the latter form. Jesus does not "mail in" how folks should or should not live. Jesus lives the life and provides the example. When we wonder what it means to follow God faithfully, when we consider what actions and attitudes might best fit the model of grace and justice and mercy, we have the benefit of Christ's incarnation. WWJD ("what would Jesus do?") may have taken on the air of a popularized slogan of late, but it does have serious truth attached to it. And "what would Jesus do?" has as its starting point "what Jesus did."

One key element of Jesus' leadership alluded to here that cuts against the grain of far too many examples of leadership among us is this: Leadership is not defined by the prerogatives and privileges it brings. Hebrews lifts up the model of leadership that endures negative circumstances and reactions for the sake of a greater good. Leadership's true power is not in what it can get others to do but in what it can bring to others and enable them in turn to do. "Enduring the cross" rules out any perception of Jesus' leadership that links it to judging which way the wind is blowing and taking the path of least resistance. "Pioneering" leadership takes risks and breaks ground. "Perfecting" leadership is willing to see things to completion and fulfillment (the literal meaning of that word in Greek), rather than go only as far as it is of benefit to me and mine.

Such a leader as Jesus engenders trust. Such a leader as Jesus invites emulation. Such a leader as Jesus can be followed.

Running with Perseverance

As noted in the Understanding the Scripture section, the imagery of athletic competition looms large in this passage. But it is critical to note that this is not competition against others. The competition, the striving, has to do with one's own self. "Perseverance" is the quality sought. "Endurance" is the task.

To be sure, the passage identifies pressures and problems outside that evoke these qualities. There is hostility. There is sin. But these things are a given, they are part of the environment, if you will. In spite of our attempts to appease everyone, we will not. In spite of our efforts to live without sin, we will on occasion fall. The key, in those moments when appeasement fails and sin returns, is whether we will persevere in faith, whether we will endure in our remaining open to God's grace and in our striving to be faithful come what may.

At the risk of carrying the sports image too far, I think it fair to say that "running with perseverance" is less a sprint to an end line in sight and more of a marathon that keeps one moving forward, one foot at a time, one breath at a time, one act of faith and one act of justice at a time. It is not just the cross Jesus endured, that one final moment at the end of his earthly life; the "cross" of Jesus also included exchanging the intimacy of life lived within the Trinity for life among those who live indifferent to God and neighbor, those who hate another for a color of skin or lifestyle different from their own, those who share all the foibles—and graces—of the human condition, including our own. Why? "So that you may not grow weary or lose heart" (Hebrews 12:3). We find ourselves invited and enabled to run with perseverance because Christ has done so.

Discipline

The core of this passage, verses 4-11, turns on a difficult issue that may raise as many questions as it answers. The importance of discipline, in and of itself, may be granted. But how does that relate to our "punishment" by God (12:5)? Underneath this text is the issue of the "why" of suffering. While the author points out that the community addressed has not yet experienced suffering "to the point of shedding your blood" (12:4), implicit is the idea that they are experiencing difficult times. It is not indicated whether this might be persecution by the Roman authorities or conflict with the Jewish community. Although that may be of historical interest, the more pressing truth is that they are experiencing hostility. Is that an outcome of faithfulness or punishment of unfaithfulness—and is it, possibly, the working of God in their midst?

We likely sympathize with such questions, because we have asked them at one time or another. Why do we have to suffer? Why is there a beatitude that blesses us when we are cursed and reviled—why does that have to happen in the first place?

The author of Hebrews in this passage does not attempt to address such overarching questions of suffering. Rather, the interest is on the focused point: How can the community of Jesus Christ maintain faithfulness ("endure") in the midst of turmoil? Hebrews does not see God's "abandoning" the community as a viable option. While leaving the precise details of "how" a mystery, Hebrews affirms that in this particular instance there is a "disciplining" of the community at work, and God is involved for the sake of the future. The illustration of human parents and children is an imperfect one, but it is understandable.

If the passage does not answer all our questions about suffering and discipline, it is because the text never intended to. Its point is to affirm God's presence and purposes, even in the midst of "painful" experiences. And the affirmation of God's presence and purposes is to encourage endurance that is not resigned to "the way things are" but that seeks to live and transform life to the way God intends.

The Commissioning

Worship services tend to end in one of two ways. One is with a benediction, literally a "good word," that reminds us of God's grace or continuing presence. There is nothing wrong with benediction.

The second way worship services may end is with a commissioning. Often attached to the "good word" of God's presence, commissioning then says in effect: so go out and live accordingly! Commissioning implies and evokes mission.

In one sense, this whole passage opens with a commissioning to the community. "Run with perseverance . . . look to Jesus . . . consider him" (12:1, 2, 3). Basic to the mission is endurance. Christian life is not a short-timed sprint. It is a lifelong race that it is possible to run, by the grace and example of Jesus.

Then, just to make sure things are not forgotten, the passage draws to a close with another commissioning in verses 12-13. Like Israel of old in exile, like the community Hebrews addressed: Drooping hands are still to be lifted, weak knees are still to be strengthened, straight paths are still to be sought out, in our time. Why? The Christian life is not merely the claiming of a "good word" handed over to us. The Christian life is the co-missioning of life lived in the example and toward the realm of Jesus Christ.

Christ leads us to be leaders of the God movement in our day. So let the people of God say: Let's get going!

SHARING THE SCRIPTURE

Preparing Our Hearts

Meditate on this week's devotional reading, found in Proverbs 3:5-12. Here the writer cautions us to trust in God, to honor God with our material goods, and to accept God's discipline, which is given to those whom God loves. Evaluate yourself in light of these three admonitions. Do you honestly trust God to lead you in the right path? Do you honestly honor God? Do you accept— or despise—God's discipline? Ponder the difference these traits make in your life as a follower of Jesus.

Pray that you and the adult learners will be open and ready to trust God, knowing that God's treatment of us is for our own good.

Preparing Our Minds

Study the background and lesson Scripture, both of which are found in Hebrews 12:1-13. As you prepare, consider the characteristics that make a leader credible.

Write on newsprint:
❏ group discussion questions for "Consider God's Plan for Helping Us Live According to God's Will."
❏ information for next week's lesson, found under "Continue the Journey."
❏ activities for further spiritual growth in "Continue the Journey."

LEADING THE CLASS

(1) Gather to Learn

❖ Welcome the class members and introduce any guests.

❖ Pray that those who have come today will be able to trust wholeheartedly in Jesus.

❖ Read (or sing) these lyrics from Walt Disney's *Peter Pan*.

We're following the leader, the leader, the leader

We're following the leader wherever he may go.

❖ Ask these questions.

(1) Does anyone remember singing these words as you followed a playmate, perhaps around a schoolyard?

(2) Were there times when you chose not to follow a particular leader? If so, why did you refuse his or her leadership?

(3) What characteristics did a leader who you were willing to follow possess?

❖ Draw parallels, if possible, between traits of leaders the students would follow as children and characteristics of leaders they would follow now as adults.

❖ Read aloud today's focus statement: **People want to follow leaders who will give them direction. What makes a leader credible? By his action and godly discipline, Jesus demonstrates that he is a leader who can be trusted.**

(2) Consider God's Plan for Helping Us Live According to God's Will

❖ Choose someone to read Hebrews 12:1-13.

❖ Divide the class into the following groups.

■ **Group 1:** Hebrews 12:1-2.
■ **Group 2:** Hebrews 12:3-6.
■ **Group 3:** Hebrews 12:7-11.
■ **Group 4:** Hebrews 12:12-13.

❖ Ask each group to consider these questions, which you will post on newsprint. Note that not all questions may apply equally well to each group. Tell the groups that they will be asked to report their ideas to the class.

(1) What do you learn about Jesus from this passage?

(2) What do you learn about endurance and suffering?

(3) What do you learn about how to behave, even in difficult situations?

❖ Call for reports. Encourage the students to add ideas and to raise any questions that occur to them.

❖ Look closely at the image of the race being run in the presence of a "cloud of witnesses" by following these steps.

■ Note that the race referred to here is not a hundred-yard dash, but rather a marathon or bicycle tour, such as Le Tour de France. Encourage the students to talk about how one prepares for such a long-distance race. Here are some ideas to consider, which you will list on the left column of a sheet of newsprint.

• Physical exercises to improve one's endurance.

• Psychological prepping to tell yourself that you can reach the finish line, even if your body is suffering and wants you to stop.

• Selection of a coach or leader who can guide you and help you strategize how you will win.

• Decisions regarding what one will wear and carry, so as not to be burdened with unnecessary weight.

• Proper nourishment to give one's body the fuel it needs.

• Acceptance of discipline by the coach and self-discipline to achieve goals.

• Practice. Practice. Practice.

■ Try to draw parallels between race preparations and living as faithful people, who follow our leader and "coach," Jesus Christ. List the students' ideas on the right side of the newsprint.

■ **Option:** Read "Running with Perseverance" from Interpreting the Scripture.

■ Read together today's key verses, Hebrews 12:1c-2a (beginning with "let us" and ending with "our faith") to summarize this portion of the lesson.

(3) Ponder the Impact on the Learners' Lives of Following Jesus

❖ Read aloud "Jesus' Leadership" from Interpreting the Scripture. Talk with the class about how they perceive Jesus' leadership to be different from what we normally think of as leadership with all its perks and prerogatives.

❖ Ask: **What reasons can you think of for wanting to follow Jesus' leadership? What reasons can you think of for not choosing to follow him?** (Be aware that some students will find the notions of discipline and suffering and enduring trials to be more than they are willing to commit to.)

❖ Encourage the adults to tell stories, either to the class as a whole or a small group, concerning how following Jesus has had an impact on their lives. These stories may include tales of help in times of trial and suffering, and also examples of godly discipline that enabled the students to grow in their relationship with Jesus.

(4) Commit to Following Jesus

❖ Distribute paper and pencils. Invite those who are willing to make a commitment to follow Jesus as their "coach" and "leader," as the one in whom they find faith's true embodiment and fulfillment, to complete this sentence with whatever actions they are willing to take: **I have decided to follow Jesus and commit myself to running with perseverance the race that he sets before me by. . . .**

❖ Wrap up this activity by inviting volunteers to read their commitments.

(5) Continue the Journey

❖ Pray that today's participants will continue to envision themselves following Jesus in a race.

❖ Read aloud this preparation for next week's lesson. You may also want to post it on newsprint for the students to copy.

■ **Title: The Eternal Christ**
■ **Background Scripture: Hebrews 13:1-16**
■ **Lesson Scripture: Hebrews 13:1-16**
■ **Focus of the Lesson: In a world of rapid change, people seek stability and permanence. Where can we find such grounding? God gave Jesus eternal life so that humans would have a firm foundation for living in relationship to God and others.**

❖ Challenge the students to complete one or more of these activities for further spiritual growth, which you will write on newsprint for the students to copy.

(1) **Recall a time when you suffered. Ponder and/or write in your spiritual journal about how this suffering transformed your faith, positively or negatively.**

(2) **Offer whatever support and assistance you can to someone who is suffering or in the midst of a trial.**

(3) **Participate in an endurance sport, such as bicycling or running. What traits do you have to have, physically and mentally, to meet the challenge of an endurance sport? What parallels can you draw between this sport and endurance in your spiritual life?**

❖ Sing or read aloud "Lead On, O King Eternal."

❖ Conclude today's session by leading the class in this benediction, which is adapted from James 1:22, 25: **Let us now go forth as doers of the word and not merely hearers, for doers who act will be blessed in their doing.**

UNIT 1: IMAGES OF CHRIST IN HEBREWS
THE ETERNAL CHRIST

PREVIEWING THE LESSON

Lesson Scripture: Hebrews 13:1-16
Background Scripture: Hebrews 13:1-16
Key Verse: Hebrews 13:8

Focus of the Lesson:
In a world of rapid change, people seek stability and permanence. Where can we find such grounding? God gave Jesus eternal life so that humans would have a firm foundation for living in relationship to God and others.

Goals for the Learners:
(1) to examine what Hebrews says about the unchangeable nature of God and Jesus.
(2) to accept Jesus as their eternal helper.
(3) to choose to live in their community according to Christ's example.

Supplies:
Bibles, newsprint and marker, paper and pencils, hymnals

READING THE SCRIPTURE

NRSV
Hebrews 13:1-16

¹Let mutual love continue. ²Do not neglect to show hospitality to strangers, for by doing that some have entertained angels without knowing it. ³Remember those who are in prison, as though you were in prison with them; those who are being tortured, as though you yourselves were being tortured. ⁴Let marriage be held in honor by all, and let the marriage bed be kept undefiled; for God will judge fornicators and adulterers. ⁵Keep your lives free from the love of money, and be content with what you have; for he has said, "I will never leave you or forsake you."

NIV
Hebrews 13:1-16

¹Keep on loving each other as brothers. ²Do not forget to entertain strangers, for by so doing some people have entertained angels without knowing it. ³Remember those in prison as if you were their fellow prisoners, and those who are mistreated as if you yourselves were suffering.

⁴Marriage should be honored by all, and the marriage bed kept pure, for God will judge the adulterer and all the sexually immoral. ⁵Keep your lives free from the love of money and be content with what you have, because God has said,

[6]So we can say with confidence,
"The Lord is my helper;
I will not be afraid.
What can anyone do to me?"
[7]Remember your leaders, those who spoke the word of God to you; consider the outcome of their way of life, and imitate their faith. [8]**Jesus Christ is the same yesterday and today and forever.** [9]Do not be carried away by all kinds of strange teachings; for it is well for the heart to be strengthened by grace, not by regulations about food, which have not benefited those who observe them. [10]We have an altar from which those who officiate in the tent have no right to eat. [11]For the bodies of those animals whose blood is brought into the sanctuary by the high priest as a sacrifice for sin are burned outside the camp. [12]Therefore Jesus also suffered outside the city gate in order to sanctify the people by his own blood. [13]Let us then go to him outside the camp and bear the abuse he endured. [14]For here we have no lasting city, but we are looking for the city that is to come. [15]Through him, then, let us continually offer a sacrifice of praise to God, that is, the fruit of lips that confess his name. [16]Do not neglect to do good and to share what you have, for such sacrifices are pleasing to God.

"Never will I leave you;
never will I forsake you."
[6]So we say with confidence,
"The Lord is my helper; I will not be afraid.
What can man do to me?"
[7]Remember your leaders, who spoke the word of God to you. Consider the outcome of their way of life and imitate their faith. [8]**Jesus Christ is the same yesterday and today and forever.**
[9]Do not be carried away by all kinds of strange teachings. It is good for our hearts to be strengthened by grace, not by ceremonial foods, which are of no value to those who eat them. [10]We have an altar from which those who minister at the tabernacle have no right to eat.
[11]The high priest carries the blood of animals into the Most Holy Place as a sin offering, but the bodies are burned outside the camp. [12]And so Jesus also suffered outside the city gate to make the people holy through his own blood. [13]Let us, then, go to him outside the camp, bearing the disgrace he bore. [14]For here we do not have an enduring city, but we are looking for the city that is to come.
[15]Through Jesus, therefore, let us continually offer to God a sacrifice of praise—the fruit of lips that confess his name. [16]And do not forget to do good and to share with others, for with such sacrifices God is pleased.

UNDERSTANDING THE SCRIPTURE

Hebrews 13:1-2. Somewhat hidden in the translation of these verses are two parallel imperatives (in Greek) regarding "love." The first is obvious: "Let *mutual love* continue. The second is more subtle due to the translation: "Do not neglect to *show hospitality to strangers.*" As if to emphasize the importance—and difficulty—of the latter, the author uses another word in the second half of verse 2 (translated in English as "entertain") that shares the same root word as "show hospitality to strangers." The reference to "entertaining angels" likely has in mind the story of Abraham and Sarah in Genesis 18:1-15, although other passages might also be called to mind. "Do not neglect" not only contrasts with the two ensuing calls to "remember" (see 13:3, 7) but it will be repeated in the passage's closing (13:16). Thus, this whole passage is bracketed by calls to not neglect these various instructions on what it means to live in community.

Hebrews 13:3-7. A series of assertions, which might be understood as how "mutual love" is given expression, follows. "Remember" calls the community to be mindful of those who might go otherwise forgotten, whether because of removal and isolation from community (13:3) or those who have passed on (13:7). "The outcome of their way of life" is somewhat unclear. It could refer to the consequences of their leadership in the community. Or it could refer to their death, which seems in keeping with the way this word is used, for example, in other religious texts. Verse 4's issue regarding marriage does not clarify whether a specific situation of abuse is in mind or if this is simply an underscoring of the church's teaching. The Corinthian community wrestled with the issue of sexual morality (1 Corinthians 5:1-13), so it is not inconceivable that there were those whom Hebrews addresses who were in the midst of similar moral conflicts. Verses 5-6 deal with a "love" from which the community is urged to flee: love of money. The basis for doing so is not economic but covenantal, reflected in two Old Testament excerpts (Deuteronomy 31:6; Psalm 118:6) in Hebrews to assert confidence in God as the reason we need not rely on greed.

Hebrews 13:8. This verse stands at the center of the passage both structurally and thematically. As commentators such as Fred Craddock in *The New Interpreter's Bible* have noted, this verse serves as a connecting transition between what has been affirmed thus far and what will follow. The "sameness" of Jesus follows on the temporal impermanence of leaders who have passed from the scene. While their past example may be imitated, it is Jesus Christ who remains present and at the core of the church's life and vocation. Likewise, the "sameness" of Jesus contrasts with the topic of the verses immediately following: the diversity of "strange teachings." In the midst of transitory persons and ideas, the church's life finds its grounding in Jesus.

Hebrews 13:9. Hebrews 9:9-10 already addressed the secondary nature of regulations about food and drink. Now the theme is joined again. The specifics about the dietary regulations in question are not specified. We do not know if this is, for example, related to the controversy Paul dealt with in 1 Corinthians 8 and 10:23-33. In truth, the lack of naming the specifics only underscores the argument of Hebrews. Regulations about food, restrictive or inclusive, are not the point. The point is to strengthen life, whether of the individual or community, by partaking of "grace." The author does offer a parting shot at those obsessed by such regulations, noting briefly but clearly that these rules have not "benefited those who observe them." Strange teachings, be they dietary or otherwise, are not the core of Christian community and lifestyle. That core, implicit between these lines, is the affirmation of verse 8.

Hebrews 13:10-13. These verses return to one of Hebrews' most frequent settings: the cultic life of Judaism. Some hear in the reference to "altar" (13:10) an early reference to the Christian practice of communion. That is by no means clear. The altar may well be the person or cross of Jesus. The specifics of verse 11 describe in part the liturgy of the Day of Atonement—again, a liturgical setting Hebrews has addressed before in affirming a new understanding of Jesus as high priest. Here, however, the emphasis is not so much upon sacrificial imagery as it is on Jesus' suffering "outside the city gate" (13:12). The literal detail here relates to Jesus' crucifixion outside the walls of Jerusalem. The metaphor, however, has multiple levels of meaning. According to Deuteronomy 21:23, death on a tree carries the meaning of being accursed by God. Jesus' execution is seen by the authorities as vindicating their position that he had placed himself outside the circle of Judaism.

He was, in another phrase, an "outlaw." Verse 13 has this curious, and difficult, word about our following Jesus "outside the camp." For the immediate audience of this epistle, this may have been a word heard in the context of a growing separation of the Christian community from Judaism. The fact that this following of Jesus is linked to suffering abuse may also hint at persecutions or conflicts either already experienced or anticipated because of this separation. Judaism had, at various times, official standing within the empire and thus was afforded some protections. Christianity, apart from Judaism, did not.

Hebrews 13:14-16. The journey "outside the camp" is now linked to an earlier image from Hebrews 11:13-16, where the Christian community is envisioned, like the faithful before them, as strangers and sojourners in search of a "city" that comes as a gift of God. Christian life is given an unmistakable (and irrevocable) forward-looking stamp on its life. Worship, which has been such a key element of Hebrews in previous thoughts and themes, remains the church's calling. But notice in verse 16: Following the emphasis of Israel's prophets, liturgy that "pleases" God is linked with ethical behavior toward and for one another. "Doing good" and "sharing" form concrete expressions of our praise to God.

INTERPRETING THE SCRIPTURE

The Reach of Love

In an epistle that has sometimes ventured into the realm of speculative theology and symbolism somewhat removed from our religious experience, matters turn now to more familiar ground: namely, the imperative to love. And it is instructive—and challenging—to understand just how widely the author now casts the net of love.

The opening line of letting mutual love "continue" (the verb also means "dwell") ought not come as any surprise, though even this rule can be difficult to follow at times in the close quarters of living in Christian community. We understand the importance of loving those with whom we worship and serve and with whom we often share similar, if not lockstep, beliefs and values. But if love calls us only to exercise mutuality of relationship with those with whom we travel and to whom faith joins us, we might want to revisit Jesus' own words in the Sermon on the Mount: "if you love those who love you, what reward do you have?" (Matthew 5:46).

The author of Hebrews, like Jesus, understands that love surpasses a mutual admiration society. And the broad stretch of that love, in the instruction of Hebrews, comes in this exhortation: "show hospitality to strangers" (13:2). Hospitality is not mere etiquette. Hospitality is a fundamental virtue and vocation of grace. And here, it is extended to our receiving others. And who are we to receive? Look back at the Understanding the Scripture portion on verses 1-2. "Show hospitality to strangers" translates a word that literally means "love of strangers." Think of the ways in which our day and culture associate "stranger" with "fear." "Stranger danger." Society largely adopts the rationale of "xenophobia"—fear of the stranger. Like Jesus' commanding our love of enemies (Matthew 5:44), Hebrews here counsels a love and hospitality that cuts against the grain of society, now as much as then. The reach of love we are to practice is not limited to our own, however we define "own." The reach of our love's practice is enjoined to reflect the love of Christ. For only then does the community bearing Christ's name embody the love with which Christ came.

Remembrance and Action

"Remember." The verb is a critical one in Judaism. It is the verb used in liturgies that confess faith, inviting Israel's remembrance of their status as slaves and sojourners, and of God's redeeming and home-bringing acts. The verb is also a critical one in Christian liturgy. When we gather at the table, we hear the words "do this in remembrance of me" to recall not only betrayal but grace, not only dying but rising. Remember.

And here in Hebrews, "remember" is a verb that invites the church in every time to recall that its life in community with God has implications for its life in relationship to one another. "Remember" becomes a prelude to the practice of love.

Remembrance is invoked first for those whose place in the community suffers from the experience of separation. "Prison" and "torture" are the two conditions identified here of those to be remembered by those whom the author addresses. Suffering for one's faith has not always been hypothetical in the life of the church, not always limited to perceived slights or social inconveniences. Remembrance invokes solidarity with folk who truly suffer. It cements our understanding of the church as the body of Christ as more than an expression of belief, and more an act of compassion and empathy. To not remember those who are separated from community, for whatever reason, lessens our faith and participation in Christ's communion.

Remembrance is secondly asked regarding "your leaders" (13:7). Leadership in this passage is identified with those who spoke the word of God. But speaking need not exhaust the list. Who has spoken, or embodied, or provided for, the faith you and your congregation enjoy? Who are the ones who have gone on before you, who made life and community and ministry possible in this place you identify as your spiritual home and sanctuary? Remember them. What is asked is not hero worship, and certainly not placing human beings on unrealistic pedestals, into which this can sometimes degenerate. What is asked is the remembrance that we are not self-made individuals or communities in faith.

Remembrance of such persons who have shaped our lives and given us examples by which to live forms another key element of living in community. For it gives community breadth, and depth, beyond the contributions of those immediately present. Like the remembrance of those who suffer separation from community, it invites us to service and witness that goes beyond self and self-interest. For biblical remembrance is never just thinking about something or someone: Biblical remembrance takes shape in action reliant on the grace of God and the gracious witness of others.

Following Jesus

Hebrews bids us love and remember . . . and now it invites us to follow Jesus in several ways.

The first image of following Jesus asks us to go, like Jesus, "outside the camp" (3:13). Jesus' ministry often offended and challenged religious insiders because it reached to those considered religious outsiders: Samaritans, women, a thief on a cross. And largely for that reason, and the threat it posed, civil and religious authorities determined to see that Jesus died as an outsider: literally (outside the city wall) and theologically (as one who died a cursed death on a tree). And what does Hebrews do but invite us to join Jesus there?

It is an invitation that runs counter to the spirit of an age that prizes conformity and insists on the power of fear. It does so for the sake of transforming life and disarming fear. To follow Jesus there accepts risk—yet to follow Jesus there enacts hope. That is why Hebrews joins the invitation with the theme explored more extensively earlier in this image of faith as "looking for the city that is to come" (13:14). Belief in that vision, and lives lived in response to that vision, are what constitute the church's vocation and witness.

The second way in which this passage closes with an invitation to follow Jesus comes in the final verse: "Do not neglect to do good and to share what you have" (13:16). The call is simple, yet it too runs contrary to a culture ingrained with far too much looking out for number one and "he who dies with the most toys wins." Think for a moment: Is "do-gooder" a compliment these days, or an insult of naiveté? Yet the doing of good is precisely how Hebrews understands the "sacrifices pleasing to God." And it is joined to "sharing what you have." To share by necessity takes community seriously. Such sharing, as the early apostolic community practiced it, meant pooling resources not only for the good of all, but in particular for the relief of the poor and widowed and orphaned—the most vulnerable among them. Sharing is not just a matter of charity, as important as that is. Sharing is also a matter of justice. How does sharing fare these days, not just as an individual virtue but as a societal and communal "good"?

For the Letter to the Hebrews, what pleases God is the doing of good and the sharing of resources. It is not far from the prophetic tradition of Israel once heralded by Isaiah, where the sacrifices pleasing to God come in these injunctions: "Learn to do good; seek justice, rescue the oppressed" (Isaiah 1:17; see also verses 10-16).

Do good. Seek justice. Share what you have. So Hebrews understands the following of Jesus . . . and the practice of love.

SHARING THE SCRIPTURE

Preparing Our Hearts

Meditate on this week's devotional reading, found in Psalm 118:5-9. As you read these verses from this victory song, note that the psalmist perceives God as the only one on whom he can rely. Regardless of the situation, we know that with God we have no need to fear; we are never alone, for God stands ready to help us. Recall a time when you put your full faith and confidence in God. How did this situation work out for you? Even if the outcome was not what you hoped, can you still trust God?

Pray that you and the adult learners will be aware that God is eternally present with all of you giving stability to your lives in an often turbulent world.

Preparing Our Minds

Study the background and lesson Scripture, both found in Hebrews 13:1-16.

As you contemplate this passage, identify where you can find stability, permanence, and grounding in a world of rapid change.

Write on newsprint:
❑ information for next week's lesson, found under "Continue the Journey."
❑ activities for further spiritual growth in "Continue the Journey."

LEADING THE CLASS

(1) Gather to Learn

❖ Welcome the class members and introduce any guests.

❖ Pray that all who have come today will be touched by God's presence with them.

❖ Challenge the class members to make a list on newsprint of all the changes they have seen in their lifetimes. You may want to focus on inventions, but you may also want to include social/cultural, economic, and political changes.

❖ Ask these questions.
  (1) Which one of these changes has improved life?
  (2) Which one of these changes has caused your quality of life to deteriorate?
  (3) How do you feel about the fact that so much in our lives seems to change—often quickly?

❖ Read aloud today's focus statement: **In a world of rapid change, people seek stability and permanence. Where can we find such grounding? God gave Jesus eternal life so that humans would have a firm foundation for living in relationship to God and others.**

(2) Examine What Hebrews Says About the Unchangeable Nature of God and Jesus

❖ Choose a volunteer to read Hebrews 13:1-6 and another to read verses 7-13.

❖ Direct attention to Hebrews 13:8, today's key verse. Encourage the students, either together or in small groups, to talk about their understanding of this verse and the impact its meaning has on their lives.

❖ Read this quotation from *Glorify His Name!* by A. W. Tozer (1897–1963), concerning the nature of God: **"His immutability presuppose His faithfulness. If He is unchanging, it follows that He could not be unfaithful, since that would require Him to change. . . . God being who He is, cannot cease to be what He is, and being what He is, He cannot act out of character with Himself. He is at once faithful and immutable, so all His words and acts must be and remain faithful."**

❖ Ask: **Do you agree with Tozer's argument? Why or why not?**

❖ Note that because God (and Jesus) are eternally ("yesterday and today and forever") the same, that permanence gives us a firm foundation for living in relationship to God and others.

❖ Suggest that the students look at verses 1-5b to discern what this relationship

is to look like. Write their ideas on newsprint. The list might include: *mutual love, hospitality to strangers, concern for those who are imprisoned and tortured, fidelity in marriage, contentment with what one has rather than chasing after money.*

❖ **Option:** Read or retell information from verses 1-2, 3-7 in Understanding the Scripture to clarify points you have just discussed.

❖ Conclude this portion of the lesson by reading aloud the third verse of Walter Chalmers Smith's 1867 hymn "Immortal, Invisible, God Only Wise" and asking the students to ponder its meaning. Hear their ideas.

To all, life thou givest, to both great and small;
in all life thou livest, the true life of all;
we blossom and flourish as leaves on the tree,
and wither and perish, but naught changeth thee.

(3) Accept Jesus as the Learners' Eternal Helper

❖ Read aloud again Hebrews 13:5c-6. Note that verse 6 quotes Psalm 118:6, though it may sound a bit different from the translations the students have.

❖ Invite the class members to cite examples of how the Lord has been a reliable helper to them. To give everyone time to tell a brief story, suggest that they work with a partner. They might consider stories related to family crisis, war, natural disaster, death, or serious illness.

❖ **Option:** Divide the class into three groups and assign one of these verses to each group. Tell the adults to read additional verses around their assigned verse to get the context. Provide time for the groups to report on what they learned about God as helper.
  ■ Psalm 10:14
  ■ Psalm 54:4
  ■ Psalm 72:12

(4) Choose to Live in Community According to Christ's Example

❖ Read "Following Jesus" from Interpreting the Scripture.

❖ Brainstorm with the group concrete examples that demonstrate how your congregation as a community of faith is responding positively to the invitation to follow Jesus. List these ideas on newsprint.

❖ Discuss ways that your congregation could:

■ go "outside the camp" to reach religious outsiders.

■ share more of what the church has to offer. (Think here about use of your building facilities; pooling resources; helping the poor and oppressed as a matter of justice.)

❖ Distribute paper and pencils. Invite students who are willing to commit themselves more fully to living in community to write one or two actions they will take this week. Suggest that they place their commitment sheets in their Bibles where they can refer to them daily.

(5) Continue the Journey

❖ Pray that all who have come today will see the eternal Christ as their model for living within community in a loving, caring way.

❖ Read aloud this preparation for next week's lesson. You may also want to post it on newsprint for the students to copy.

■ **Title: Christ as Teacher**
■ **Background Scripture: Luke 4:31-37; 20:1-8**
■ **Lesson Scripture: Luke 4:31-37; 20:1-8**

■ **Focus of the Lesson: Many teachers bombard us with competing information. How do we discern which teachers give information of lasting value? Jesus taught as no other teacher, with the power to transform lives.**

❖ Challenge the students to complete one or more of these activities for further spiritual growth, which you will write on newsprint for the students to copy.

(1) **Read 1 Corinthians 13 and 1 John 4:7-21. Ponder how these passages might help you to love others as Christ loves them.**

(2) **Offer hospitality to someone in need, someone who cannot repay you. Consider how this hospitality enables you to conform more closely to the image of Christ.**

(3) **Use your political power to speak out against torture in any form by any government or regime. Contact elected officials and/or write letters to the editor of a newspaper. Check out organizations, such as Amnesty International, that decry inhumane treatment.**

❖ Sing or read aloud "Saranam, Saranam," based in part on Hebrews 13:8, today's key verse.

❖ Conclude today's session by leading the class in this benediction, which is adapted from James 1:22, 25: **Let us now go forth as doers of the word and not merely hearers, for doers who act will be blessed in their doing.**

UNIT 2: IMAGES OF CHRIST IN THE GOSPELS
CHRIST AS TEACHER

PREVIEWING THE LESSON

Lesson Scripture: Luke 4:31-37; 20:1-8
Background Scripture: Luke 4:31-37; 20:1-8
Key Verse: Luke 4:32

Focus of the Lesson:
Many teachers bombard us with competing information. How do we discern which teachers give information of lasting value? Jesus taught as no other teacher, with the power to transform lives.

Goals for the Learners:
(1) to examine two instances of Jesus teaching the people.
(2) to appreciate the complexity and power of Jesus' teachings.
(3) to accept Jesus' teachings as authoritative for the way they live.

Pronunciation Guide:
logos (loh' gohs)
pneuma (nyoo' muh)

Supplies:
Bibles, newsprint and marker, paper and pencils, hymnals

READING THE SCRIPTURE

NRSV
Luke 4:31-37

³¹He went down to Capernaum, a city in Galilee, and was teaching them on the sabbath. **³²They were astounded at his teaching, because he spoke with authority.** ³³In the synagogue there was a man who had the spirit of an unclean demon, and he cried out with a loud voice, ³⁴"Let us alone! What have you to do with us, Jesus of Nazareth? Have you come to destroy us? I know who

NIV
Luke 4:31-37

³¹Then he went down to Capernaum, a town in Galilee, and on the Sabbath began to teach the people. **³²They were amazed at his teaching, because his message had authority.**

³³In the synagogue there was a man possessed by a demon, an evil spirit. He cried out at the top of his voice, ³⁴"Ha! What do you want with us, Jesus of Nazareth? Have

you are, the Holy One of God." [35]But Jesus rebuked him, saying, "Be silent, and come out of him!" When the demon had thrown him down before them, he came out of him without having done him any harm. [36]They were all amazed and kept saying to one another, "What kind of utterance is this? For with authority and power he commands the unclean spirits, and out they come!" [37]And a report about him began to reach every place in the region.

Luke 20:1-8

[1]One day, as he was teaching the people in the temple and telling the good news, the chief priests and the scribes came with the elders [2]and said to him, "Tell us, by what authority are you doing these things? Who is it who gave you this authority?" [3]He answered them, "I will also ask you a question, and you tell me: [4]Did the baptism of John come from heaven, or was it of human origin?" [5]They discussed it with one another, saying, "If we say, 'From heaven,' he will say, 'Why did you not believe him?' [6]But if we say, 'Of human origin,' all the people will stone us; for they are convinced that John was a prophet." [7]So they answered that they did not know where it came from. [8]Then Jesus said to them, "Neither will I tell you by what authority I am doing these things."

you come to destroy us? I know who you are—the Holy One of God!"

[35]"Be quiet!" Jesus said sternly. "Come out of him!" Then the demon threw the man down before them all and came out without injuring him.

[36]All the people were amazed and said to each other, "What is this teaching? With authority and power he gives orders to evil spirits and they come out!" [37]And the news about him spread throughout the surrounding area.

Luke 20:1-8

[1]One day as he was teaching the people in the temple courts and preaching the gospel, the chief priests and the teachers of the law, together with the elders, came up to him. [2]"Tell us by what authority you are doing these things," they said. "Who gave you this authority?"

[3]He replied, "I will also ask you a question. Tell me, [4]John's baptism—was it from heaven, or from men?"

[5]They discussed it among themselves and said, "If we say, 'From heaven,' he will ask, 'Why didn't you believe him?' [6]But if we say, 'From men,' all the people will stone us, because they are persuaded that John was a prophet."

[7]So they answered, "We don't know where it was from."

[8]Jesus said, "Neither will I tell you by what authority I am doing these things."

UNDERSTANDING THE SCRIPTURE

Luke 4:31-32. The fourth chapter of Luke introduces the public ministry of Jesus. The opening scenes relate Jesus' temptation in the wilderness (4:1-13) and his appearance in the synagogue of his hometown of Nazareth (4:16-30). Between those scenes, Luke describes Jesus with a phrase that sets the stage for this Gospel as a whole and today's passages in particular: "filled with

the power of the Spirit" (4:14). Jesus' power is not purely his own, but that of God's Spirit. That assessment leads directly into the observation in verse 32 of this passage about Jesus' authority. The phrase translated as "he spoke with authority" literally says in the Greek "his word (logos) was with authority." The reaction of astonishment to such a word in verse 32 anticipates the amazement in verse 36 that follows the exorcism of the spirit. Capernaum, the site of this episode, is on the northwest shore of the Sea of Galilee. It is the home of Peter, and many consider it to be the "base" of Jesus' ministry in Galilee.

Luke 4:33-35. The portrayal of Jesus as one filled with the Spirit now provides the narrative with tension and action when Jesus encounters an individual in the synagogue who is reported to have the "spirit" (*pneuma*, the same word as used in describing Jesus) of an "unclean demon." Belief in demons and demonic possession was an accepted part of the first-century world, both within and outside Judaism. Whether that coincides or not with modern worldviews is not the issue of the text. The issue of the text has to do with what (who) has power over human life, to enslave or free. At the Nazareth synagogue, Jesus had read part of the Isaiah scroll, which included the call to "proclaim release to the captives" (Luke 4:18). Those words now become what is at stake, and which "spirit" has the power. As with other exorcism stories, the unclean spirits express recognition of Jesus' identity as holy or of God. The actual exorcism itself comes solely from a word spoken by Jesus. "Be silent" (4:35) uses the same verb as Mark 4:39, where Jesus stills the sea.

Luke 4:36-37. Intriguingly, the amazement of the crowd in the synagogue is identified not so much with the act of exorcism as with the word of Jesus ("utterance" translates *logos*, the same word used in verse 32). Verse 36 speaks of both Jesus' "authority" and Jesus' "power." "Authority" translates a word that has to do with the "right" or "privilege" to do something. "Power" translates a word that has do with the sheer capability to do something. Authority *allows* someone to do something. Power is the *ability* to do something. Filled with God's Spirit, Jesus possesses both. He has the right (and indeed, the calling) to set this individual free—and he has the wherewithal to do so. The passage ends, as did verse 14, with the news about Jesus spreading throughout the region (Galilee).

Luke 20:1. The setting of Jesus' ministry has changed entirely from this first passage. Galilee was approximately seventy miles to the north. Jerusalem, at the heart of Judea both geographically and theologically, is now the scene. It housed the temple of Herod. It also housed a Roman garrison in the tower known as the Antonia. This verse mentions three key sets of groups who will play critical roles not only in this passage but also in the unfolding events in Jerusalem. (This is now holy week, and but a few days from arrest and crucifixion.) The chief priests were the hereditary caretakers of the temple cult and sacrifices: in other words, the "authorities" of Judaism's rituals. The scribes were the educated interpreters of Torah and its associated traditions: the "authorities" of Judaism's laws. The elders came from the leading families of Jerusalem, mostly associated with the Herodian ruling family: the "authorities" of Judaism's society. Together, the representatives of these three groups formed the Sanhedrin, the council in Jerusalem that would later interrogate Jesus after his arrest. The conflict that arises here between them and Jesus portends what is to come.

Luke 20:2-4. And the conflict has to do with authority. The question posed to Jesus by these groups is an understandable one: By what right do you do these things? For folks who were accustomed to, and entrusted with the authority of overseeing Jewish religious and civil life, any other authority could be seen as a threat or challenge. Jesus' reply, in turn, takes the form of a related question. It is not a question that directly seeks to undermine their authority, as in "by what right do you do what you do?" Rather, it is a question about a third party: the late John the Baptizer. His baptism, as preached in Luke 3, had to do with repentance of sins and taking on a new life. It was a message that did not sit well with, among others, the Herodian ruler at that time. Those earlier stories of John, and of his eventual execution, all point toward a general excitement about John and his message among the crowds—and worry among established "authorities." Now Jesus, another outsider, asks about how these leaders view John's authority. It is a lively question, as it is clear from biblical and extra-biblical sources that John continued to have a following.

Luke 20:5-8. One commentator argues that Jesus responds to the leaders' question with a question of his own to test their openness. The remaining verses simply

report their reluctance to take a stand, for fear of the public's reaction to either answer. Interestingly, they do not take issue that there is only one of two ways to answer Jesus' question. In so doing, they allow Jesus to set the terms of the encounter. As a result, they make no commitment in order to not jeopardize their authority among the people. One wonders what Jesus' response might have been, had they taken a stand one way or another on John's authority. As it is, their avoidance of an answer provides Jesus with the means to refuse their question.

INTERPRETING THE SCRIPTURE

An Authoritative Word

Have you ever heard just the right word at just the right time? A word that spoke to you? A word that moved you? A word that changed you?

Notice in that paragraph that nothing was said about the speaker or the style of speaking. Much is made these days, and rightly so, about the "medium as the message." How you say something strongly influences how whatever you say gets heard. The best of sermons in the worst of hands can be a hardship.

But conversely, "style" sometimes gets in the way. We become so influenced by the charisma of this speaker or that leader that we become caught up in the rhetorical flourishes. And only later do we wonder why—as mesmerizing as the experience was at the time—we don't recall anything of importance really being said.

When Luke says Jesus "spoke with authority" (4:32) the focus is on "word" (as the Greek literally means). The Gospel writers do not tell us what kind of a voice Jesus possessed, or what style of speaking he projected. The focus is on the word itself. The word conveyed the

authority of one "filled with the power of the Spirit" (4:14).

It is a point worth remembering, and instilling, in an age where church and media so rely on style of communications that we sometimes neglect word. And Word. Folks in Luke 4:32 responded to Jesus because they recognized in his word "authority." That is, it was a word that carried weight and substance among them.

Whose word speaks with authority to you . . . within your congregation? That is, whose word says just the right thing at just the right time—and moves you, and changes you?

Openness to Amazement

Children can be amazed by the simplest of things for the longest of times. An ant carrying a load twice its size and weight across a sidewalk can be watched and observed while the rest of us rush by, unable to be distracted by the mundane. Growing up brings a certain ability to defer wonder for the sake of busyness.

Twice in this passage from Luke 4, the author pauses to note that those around Jesus are "astounded" or "amazed" by what he says and does. When was the last time anyone in your church was astounded or amazed by what happened there? When was the last time you were astounded or amazed?

If you are anything like me, it may have been awhile. Now, we may think about that and figure that the blame falls on the church. We (they!) need to be doing something exciting around here! Especially if numbers are stagnant or in decline, the rationale goes that it's boring—that most devastating of judgments in these days.

But I would take the matter back to the opening story about children and ants. Sometimes, the lack of astonishment and amazement in our religious life traces to our being closed to the sights and sounds around us. Age can do that. But so can cynicism. Think for a moment about some of the ways in which the Spirit of God is at work in your community: feeding the hungry, caring for persons who are hurting, celebrating the grace of God. Perhaps if we ourselves were more *open* to be amazed, we would be. And in allowing ourselves the gift of such amazement and astonishment, we might even be able to discern that even in the most ordinary and mundane of things, God's Spirit is stirring among us and inviting our recognition of the Holy in our midst. If only we would pause and see, like a child poised over an ant in wonder.

By What Authority?

"Tell us, by what authority are you doing these things?" (Luke 20:2). Deep down, we sympathize with these religious leaders in their questioning of Jesus. Here they are in Jerusalem, taking care of the business that keeps the temple running and the Torah observance going, each having a role to play that has defined them and been developed for them over long generations. And into the scene comes Jesus, something of a gatecrasher in their eyes. Who does he think he is? What makes him think he can get away

with doing these things? Whom does he answer to?

The implication of their question, of course, ought to include at least a partial "to us." The triad of priests and scribes and elders have had a long-standing tradition of authority in and over the community. Newcomers need to go through the gatekeepers, or at least acknowledge their authority.

On the one hand we sympathize with those leaders, because we know that "loose cannons" have troubled the church from time to time. People who come in out of nowhere, wanting to do this or lead that, without ever having paid the dues of time spent in community. The church has sometimes been preyed upon by folks whose sudden appearance among us has a lot to do with a flight from pasts they'd prefer not to be known.

But on the other hand, the church—like these leaders of old—sometimes wants to hold on too tightly and too exclusively to authority. And when someone comes on the scene speaking words that do not serve the status quo, the tightness and exclusivity about that authority becomes even more gripping. Prophets like Jesus or John the Baptizer do not fare well in such circumstances, for folks in authority tend to operate on the assumption that those who are not for us are automatically against us. And from that stranglehold come crucifixions, ancient and modern.

An Open Question

The leaders end up refusing to answer Jesus' question. Jesus ends up refusing to answer the leaders' question. So in a sense, if you were to punctuate the closing of Luke 20:1-8, you might want to choose an ". . . ." Because the questions are left hanging in the air. It is as if the author wants us to leave them rolling around in our minds and hearts, so that in the end we have to supply the answers:

"By what authority are you doing these things?" (20:2)

"Did the baptism of John come from heaven, or was it of human origin?" (20:4)

That leaving the questions in our hands actually is a very real function of this story, as it is of others. For in the end, it matters less what answers others provide than what answers we hold to be true, and in holding them then practicing them in our lives. It is like the ending of the story of the loving father (prodigal son): After the father assures the elder son he still loves him, it is left up in the air whether he will come inside and join the celebration or stay outside and fume. That choice is ours to make, when it comes to accepting the grace God exercises not just toward ourselves, but toward others. It is like the original ending of the gospel of Mark (16:8), where the women flee the tomb—and the question is who will go and tell the story?

Faith is not the rote memorization of someone else's answers about God. Faith is the lived practice of our trust in God. By what authority is Jesus doing these things he does? What do you say . . . and how do you live?

SHARING THE SCRIPTURE

Preparing Our Hearts

Meditate on this week's devotional reading, found in Isaiah 11:1-3. Some scholars believe that Isaiah 11:1-9 was part of the ritual used when Hezekiah was crowned king. He was of David's lineage, and Jesse was David's father. Yet, many Christians also interpret this as a description of Jesus, on whom the Spirit of the Lord would rest. What traits does this passage attribute to the one who reigns over this peaceful kingdom? How does this passage speak to you about Jesus?

Pray that you and the adult learners will be open to receiving the one who comes with wisdom and knowledge.

Preparing Our Minds

Study the background and lesson Scripture, both of which are found in Luke 4:31-37 and Luke 20:1-8. Consider this question as you read: In a world where we are constantly bombarded with information, how do you discern which teachers give information of lasting value?

Write on newsprint:

❏ questions and Scripture references for "Appreciate the Complexity and Power of Jesus' Teachings."

❏ information for next week's lesson, found under "Continue the Journey."

❏ activities for further spiritual growth in "Continue the Journey."

Option: Plan a lecture for "Examine Two Instances of Jesus Teaching the People."

LEADING THE CLASS

(1) Gather to Learn

❖ Welcome the class members and introduce any guests.

❖ Pray that all who have come will discern God's word for them today.

❖ Talk with the class about how they get their information (the Internet, print, other media, teachers, and so on). You may wish to list their ideas on newsprint.

❖ Invite them to comment on the criteria they use to determine whether or not the information they are getting is truly authoritative and worthwhile.

❖ Read aloud today's focus statement: **Many teachers bombard us with** competing information. **How do we discern which teachers give information of lasting value? Jesus taught as no other teacher, with the power to transform lives.**

(2) Examine Two Instances of Jesus Teaching the People

❖ Choose a volunteer to read Luke 4:31-33, 35-37. Ask all of the students to read verse 34 in unison. Discuss these questions. Use information from Understanding the Scripture, as needed, to augment the conversation.
(1) **How do the demons respond to Jesus?**
(2) **How do the people respond to Jesus?**
(3) **What do you learn about Jesus from this story?**
❖ Select three volunteers—one to read the part of the narrator, two to read in unison the part of the priests, elders, and scribes, and one to read the words of Jesus in Luke 20:1-8. Again, use information from Understanding the Scripture as appropriate.
(1) **What do the chief priests, scribes, and elders hope to gain by questioning Jesus?**
(2) **Why do you think Jesus responded as he did?**
(3) **What do you learn about Jesus from this story?**
❖ Look for similarities and relationships between these two stories. Either draw these ideas from the students, or present them in an optional lecture.
■ The common theme in both these stories is the matter of Jesus' authority.
■ Whereas the religious leaders raise questions about Jesus' authority, the "unclean demon" is able to recognize "the Holy One of God" (4:33-34).
■ The people in Capernaum are "astounded at his teaching" (4:32) because of his authority.
■ The people who heard Jesus in the

temple at Jerusalem must have taken his teaching as authoritative, or the religious leaders would not have felt it necessary to intervene.
■ In contrast, the religious leaders, whose authority comes by virtue of their position within the temple hierarchy, try to protect their authority by questioning Jesus' authority.

(3) Appreciate the Complexity and Power of Jesus' Teachings

❖ Prepare the class for this portion of the lesson by reading or retelling "An Authoritative Word" from Interpreting the Scripture.
❖ Divide the class into three groups. Assign one group to look through Matthew to locate other stories where Jesus' teachings, actions, and/or words witness to his authority. Assign the second group to Mark, and the third to Luke. Provide paper and pencils for each student. Here are some references if the students need help in getting started. You may want to write these on newsprint.
■ Matthew 9:6
■ Matthew 10:1
■ Matthew 28:18
■ Mark 1:27
■ Mark 2:10
■ Mark 6:7
■ Luke 5:24
■ Luke 9:1
❖ Post these questions on newsprint as a guide for discussion within the groups.
(1) **Imagine yourself present with Jesus when he taught this lesson or said these words as recorded in one of the Gospels. What would you have learned about his power and authority?**
(2) **How would you have responded to Jesus?**
(3) **How might this story transform your life right now?**
❖ **Option:** Either call time and allow the groups to report to the rest of the class, or

allow them more time to peruse the assigned Gospel, rather than call for reports.

❖ Wrap up this portion of the lesson by encouraging volunteers to comment on how these stories enable them to appreciate the complexity and power of Jesus' teachings.

(4) Accept Jesus' Teachings as Authoritative for the Way the Learners Live

❖ Read or retell "An Open Question" in Interpreting the Scripture. Focus on the last paragraph, perhaps reading it a second time.

❖ Invite the students to discuss the difference between a faith that is simply learned from someone else and left unexamined and a faith that we recognize as based on Jesus' authority and, therefore, one that we must live out in practice. Consider how persons with a faith that they have examined and made their own react in times of testing and crisis, as opposed to those who have simply memorized some stories and accepted them verbatim.

❖ Brainstorm with the adults teachings of Jesus that they believe are crucial in charting the course for how they live. List these teachings on newsprint.

❖ Distribute paper and pencils if you have not done so already. Recommend that the students write personal lists of authoritative teachings, using ideas from the class list as well as other teachings that may be important to them. Stress that these are to be teachings clearly rooted in Jesus' ministry and teachings.

❖ Challenge the students to list one or two actions they do take—or will take—to live according to each teaching they have listed.

(5) Continue the Journey

❖ Pray that today's participants will treasure the value of Jesus' teaching.

❖ Read aloud this preparation for next week's lesson. You may also want to post it on newsprint for the students to copy.

- ■ **Title: Christ as Healer**
- ■ **Background Scripture: Mark 1:29-45**
- ■ **Lesson Scripture: Mark 1:29-45**
- ■ **Focus of the Lesson: Many people are looking to be made whole. To whom can they turn for healing? Faith in the power of Jesus Christ will lead to wholeness, though not necessarily a physical cure.**

❖ Challenge the students to complete one or more of these activities for further spiritual growth, which you will write on newsprint for the students to copy.

(1) **Be aware of the "teachings" that bombard you daily from the media, family, friends, your employer, and others. What kinds of "teachings" set up a "caution" signal for you? Do you respond by clarifying (and stating) your own views, remaining quiet, or agreeing with something you do not honestly believe?**

(2) **Research "demon possession." What evidence does the Bible give concerning this phenomenon? What evidence do you find for it today? What do you think about this phenomenon?**

(3) **Thank someone whose teaching has transformed your life. Consider sending a note, making a phone call, or arranging a visit to express your appreciation.**

❖ Sing or read aloud "Silence, Frenzied, Unclean Spirit."

❖ Conclude today's session by leading the class in this benediction, which is adapted from James 1:22, 25: **Let us now go forth as doers of the word and not merely hearers, for doers who act will be blessed in their doing.**

UNIT 2: IMAGES OF CHRIST IN THE GOSPELS
CHRIST AS HEALER

PREVIEWING THE LESSON

Lesson Scripture: Mark 1:29-45
Background Scripture: Mark 1:29-45
Key Verse: Mark 1:34

Focus of the Lesson:
Many people are looking to be made whole. To whom can they turn for healing? Faith in the power of Jesus Christ will lead to wholeness, though not necessarily a physical cure.

Goals for the Learners:
(1) to examine stories of Jesus healing.
(2) to realize that faith in Jesus does not always result in physical healing.
(3) to praise Jesus for healing.

Supplies:
Bibles, newsprint and marker, paper and pencils, hymnals, optional votive candles and lighter

---

READING THE SCRIPTURE

NRSV
Mark 1:29-45

²⁹As soon as they left the synagogue, they entered the house of Simon and Andrew, with James and John. ³⁰Now Simon's mother-in-law was in bed with a fever, and they told him about her at once. ³¹He came and took her by the hand and lifted her up. Then the fever left her, and she began to serve them.

³²That evening, at sundown, they brought to him all who were sick or possessed with demons. ³³And the whole city was gathered around the door. **³⁴And he cured many who were sick with various diseases, and cast**

NIV
Mark 1:29-45

²⁹As soon as they left the synagogue, they went with James and John to the home of Simon and Andrew. ³⁰Simon's mother-in-law was in bed with a fever, and they told Jesus about her. ³¹So he went to her, took her hand and helped her up. The fever left her and she began to wait on them.

³²That evening after sunset the people brought to Jesus all the sick and demon-possessed. ³³The whole town gathered at the door, **³⁴and Jesus healed many who had various diseases. He also drove out many demons,** but he would not let the

out many demons; and he would not permit the demons to speak, because they knew him. [35]In the morning, while it was still very dark, he got up and went out to a deserted place, and there he prayed. [36]And Simon and his companions hunted for him. [37]When they found him, they said to him, "Everyone is searching for you." [38]He answered, "Let us go on to the neighboring towns, so that I may proclaim the message there also; for that is what I came out to do." [39]And he went throughout Galilee, proclaiming the message in their synagogues and casting out demons.

[40]A leper came to him begging him, and kneeling he said to him, "If you choose, you can make me clean." [41]Moved with pity, Jesus stretched out his hand and touched him, and said to him, "I do choose. Be made clean!" [42]Immediately the leprosy left him, and he was made clean. [43]After sternly warning him he sent him away at once, [44]saying to him, "See that you say nothing to anyone; but go, show yourself to the priest, and offer for your cleansing what Moses commanded, as a testimony to them." [45]But he went out and began to proclaim it freely, and to spread the word, so that Jesus could no longer go into a town openly, but stayed out in the country; and people came to him from every quarter.

demons speak because they knew who he was.

[35]Very early in the morning, while it was still dark, Jesus got up, left the house and went off to a solitary place, where he prayed. [36]Simon and his companions went to look for him, [37]and when they found him, they exclaimed: "Everyone is looking for you!" [38]Jesus replied, "Let us go somewhere else—to the nearby villages—so I can preach there also. That is why I have come." [39]So he traveled throughout Galilee, preaching in their synagogues and driving out demons.

[40]A man with leprosy came to him and begged him on his knees, "If you are willing, you can make me clean."

[41]Filled with compassion, Jesus reached out his hand and touched the man. "I am willing," he said. "Be clean!" [42]Immediately the leprosy left him and he was cured.

[43]Jesus sent him away at once with a strong warning: [44]"See that you don't tell this to anyone. But go, show yourself to the priest and offer the sacrifices that Moses commanded for your cleansing, as a testimony to them." [45]Instead he went out and began to talk freely, spreading the news. As a result, Jesus could no longer enter a town openly but stayed outside in lonely places. Yet the people still came to him from everywhere.

UNDERSTANDING THE SCRIPTURE

Mark 1:29-31. The departure from the synagogue connects this episode with Jesus' Sabbath act of exorcising a demon from a man there (Mark 1:21-28). (The parallel to this exorcism story in Mark is last week's text from Luke 4:31-37.) The singling out of the four apostles by name in verse 29 likewise links to the two call stories in Mark 1:16-20 that preceded the exorcism story. The rapid flow of events from call to exorcism and now to healing(s) is emphasized by Mark's use of the word "immediately" (the usual translation of the word here rendered "as soon as"). Such immediacy heightens the flow of action throughout the Gospel of Mark, as well as subtly emphasizes the decisive and/or authoritative nature of Jesus' words and actions. (Jesus' actions or words *immediately* lead to something or somewhere or someone.) The reference to Simon's mother-in-law reveals that at least this disciple had a family of his own that otherwise is not mentioned. The consequence of Jesus' healing comes in her "serving them." The word typically refers to acting as a table servant. More cryptically, it is the same word Jesus uses of himself in Mark 10:45 in his teaching that "the Son of Man came not to be served but to serve." Later in the history of the church, it is the verb translated as "minister."

Mark 1:32-34. "At sundown" marked the official end of Sabbath. Restrictions against work or carrying loads would have been removed, and the crowd is thus represented as bringing to Jesus those whom they would have been unable to assist under the narrow restrictions of Sabbath law—an issue which Jesus will confront in subsequent episodes. Having left the synagogue, the whole city "gathered" (a word that shares the same root in Greek with "synagogue") outside the door—apparently they are still in the house of Simon and Andrew. Verse 34 raises the issue of what has sometimes been referred to as the "messianic secret" in Mark's Gospel. That is, Jesus wishes to keep his identity hidden for the time being. Some suggest the reason has to do with a misunderstanding of the function of Messiah: The popular expectations of a military and triumphant leader would never "fit" the Messiah Jesus came to be (see, for example, the dispute with Peter in Mark 8:31-33).

Mark 1:35. "Morning" is not a function of light so much as it is time of day. Therefore, it is not a contradiction to speak of morning when "it was still very dark." Jesus' seeking of a deserted place for prayer will be repeated in the Gospel of Mark, as well as in Matthew and Luke. The word for "deserted" carries the meaning of "desolate" and "lonely." It is also the same word used in Mark 1:12 to describe the "wilderness" into which the Spirit drives Jesus. Intriguingly, the place of temptation to which Jesus had earlier been "driven" now

becomes the place that he seeks out on his own. Wilderness also echoes the experience of Israel in their sojourn after Egypt. The text makes no mention of the words of Jesus' prayer in this place.

Mark 1:36-39. "Hunted" is an accurate translation of what Simon and the others did to find Jesus. They do not indicate who the "everyone" is who is searching: whether the crowds remaining at the door, a new influx of seekers, or simply to indicate that the surrounding folks of the countryside are abuzz. Jesus' words of his intent in verse 38, and Mark's summary of his activity in verse 39, both employ the same word (translated here as "proclaim the message") that had been used in Mark 1:14 in the introduction to Jesus' public ministry: Jesus came into Galilee, *preaching* the gospel of God. Mark's summary couples this word of proclamation with Jesus' actions of exorcising demons. The latter is a sign of Jesus' power, an indication that his ministry will take on whatever powers or authorities would hold people captive. Exorcism is a prelude to confronting other oppressions of the human spirit, physical or spiritual. Acts of healing belong to that same liberating ministry.

Mark 1:40-42. Leprosy was not a single affliction, but a catchword for a variety of skin diseases that brought with them not only physical pain and disfigurement but also social ostracism. The law had clear and definite prescriptions for what was to be done . . . and should healing occur, what steps needed to be taken before society and cult could be reentered (leprosy prohibited its victims, among other things, from worshiping with the wider community). The question posed to Jesus hints at Jesus' own petition in the garden of Gethsemane: "if you *choose*" uses the same word root as "not what I *want*, but what you *want*" (14:36). There is a significant textual variant (meaning manuscripts contain different readings of words) in verse 41. One manuscript tradition has a word that means "moved with pity or compassion." The other manuscript tradition has a word that means "anger" or "indignation" on Jesus' part. Cases can be made for both traditions fitting in the context of these verses. It depends on whether the emphasis is seen falling on Jesus' compassion for the man, or his anger at the disease's debilitating effects.

Mark 1:43-45. A similar choice has to do with the translation of the opening words of verse 43. "Sternly warning" could also be accurately rendered as "snorting with anger or displeasure." Part of the interpretation traces back to the emphasis on compassion or anger. As with Jesus' earlier desire for

anonymity in verse 34, he charges this individual to not say anything to anyone. Rather, he is to go through the prescribed procedures that would lead to this man's restoration to community. But this man does more than simply what the law calls for. In verse 45, his "proclaiming" of what had happened echoes Jesus' "proclaiming" in verses 38-39 (again, the verbs are identical). The end result here is the same as what it had been in 1:28. Word spreads. But, as the end of verse 45 hints, popularity and celebrity can be hindrances to ministry.

INTERPRETING THE SCRIPTURE

Healing as Up-Lifting and Restoration

Does faith healing "work"? Is there a difference between "healing" and "curing"? We may bring many questions with us to these two accounts of healing. Some may be spurred by excesses or abuses we have seen (or experienced). Some may come in the wake of wonderings about the illness or suffering of a loved one, arising either from a remarkable experience of otherwise unexplained relief . . . or from the lack of healing. I once read an account, whose source I have long since forgotten, about an interview done with a priest at Lourdes, a Roman Catholic shrine in France where many healings have been reported. The interviewer asked the priest about the greatest miracle he had ever seen there. The response, as best I recall, went something like this: "the look of faith and peace on the faces of those who go away without a cure."

These texts from Mark, in isolation, will likely not answer all of our questions about healing in the context of faith. But they do make two affirmations worthy of exploration. In the case of Simon's mother-in-law, Mark notes that Jesus "took her by the hand and lifted her up" (1:31). On one

level, the words simply convey a physical depiction of the healing. On another level, the words are revealing of deeper meanings of healing. Healing lifts people up. Think of your own associations of what it means to be lifted up. To be supported. To be helped. To be brought to a position where more can be seen—and done. Jesus' *lifting* directly leads to this woman's *serving*. "Lifting up" reminds us that we ought to think of healing in holistic terms. Cures may be limited to the body, but healing—with or without cure—relates to the whole person. Faith heals when it lifts persons out of situations that limit or inhibit the experience of life.

And that leads directly to the second lesson in these texts about healing: It *restores*. In the story of Simon's mother-in-law, healing restores her to exercise hospitality toward guests in her home. The fact that "serve" later becomes a synonym for "minister" only heightens this sense of the value of our actions toward others. The story of the leper deals with restoration even more directly. Without healing, this individual is cut off from family, from community, even from God in the sense that he is barred from participating in community worship.

Healing for this man, besides ridding him of an awful disease, enables him to be seen by others as he has always been even in the midst of the disease: someone created in the image of God, someone valued as a beloved child of God. Neither leprosy nor anything else can reverse that truth about him (or about us)—but it can (and did) cause others and perhaps at times him (and us) to lose sight of that truth. When Jesus heals, restoration accompanies the healing.

The Community of Christ

The passage begins in verse 29 with Jesus leaving one expression of community (the synagogue), only to be confronted, in verse 32, by another expression of community (the crowds gathered outside of the door). And what a community is the latter!

Recall what your church looks like in the half hour or so leading up to worship. What do the folks there look like, and dress like? What are they talking about? Imagine, now, the scene outside the doorway of Simon's home transported to the corner streets around your church, spilling into the narthex. Wheelchairs and walkers. A few have even managed to push hospital beds that bear friends or loved ones. There are plenty of oxygen bottles with nasal cannulas attached for those with difficulty breathing. Others have the gaunt look of cancer or AIDS victims. All of these are pressing to enter the doors of your sanctuary, in order to. . . .

It is an interesting scene to consider. So often, we speak of the church needing people—in order to pay the bills, in order to have the children to return a Sunday school to its former glory, in order . . . well, for us to survive. But what if the roles are reversed? What if it is not so much the church needing people that shapes our outreach and strategies for growth? What if it is the people who need us—who need the word of hope, the experience of healing, we have found in Christ? What if that were the dominating image of what it means to be the community of Christ?

Heal Thyself

Framed within this bookend of healings is an episode of what you might call self-healing. I don't mean by that healing that I do for myself, nor even that Jesus does for himself. Rather, it is the healthy reminder that we need to avail ourselves of moments of experience and healing.

Jesus retreats to a "deserted" place. A place to himself—though not alone, for it is the company of God Jesus seeks. And please notice: The retreat does not come when Jesus has finished meeting everybody else's needs. The leper is still to be healed. And as the remainder of Mark will reveal, there is still lots to be done. Retreat comes not at work's end, but in its midst.

Overachievers, workaholics, savers of the world: take note. Unless care is taken of self, self will eventually be unable to care for others.

God's Choices

"If you choose, you can make me clean" (1:40). The statement of the leper to Jesus may well return us to some of the questions referred to in the opening paragraph of this section of interpretation. *If you choose, God, you can. . . .* How we might fill in that sentence is almost unlimited in its possibility, given our affirmation of God's omnipotence—and in its difficulty, in the face of human suffering and tragedy. A child is stricken with a brain tumor: *If you choose, God, you can. . . .* You face an unwieldy situation at work, which would be a lot easier if only: *If you choose, God, you can. . . .* Another incident of terror devastates innocent civilians, or another calculated move by a powerful nation brings suffering to those in the way of its objectives: *If you choose, God, you can. . . .*

In all sorts and times, we do wonder about the choices of God. Often it seems to us the choice is to leave us to fend for ourselves. There is a point that responsibility, of individuals and communities, needs to be learned and assumed, that God is not in the business of doing for us what we could do for ourselves. And yet, and yet, if only God, just this one time, would. . . .

The choice of Jesus regarding this leper is for his healing. We may deduce from that, and other passages, that the choice of God is for good and for life. Perhaps we need to hold such choices close to mind and heart in those times and experiences when

it does not seem so clear and explicit—when the sovereign realm of God seems a long time in coming. Mark reports at the very outset of Jesus' ministry: "the kingdom of God has come near" (1:15). The remainder of Mark's Gospel, like the remainder of our lives, becomes the site of that realm's slow unfolding. As such, it not only invites our faith in its coming, and in God's choices—but also it invites our own choosing of the good and the just in this interim time when we still pray and ask, *If you choose, God, you can. . . .*

SHARING THE SCRIPTURE

Preparing Our Hearts

Meditate on this week's devotional reading, found in Isaiah 61:1-4. Note the ways that people are healed and liberated in this familiar passage, which Jesus quotes, in part, in Luke 4:18-19. Where do you need healing and release in your own life? What good news do you need to hear today? Meditate on this passage. Listen for what God may be saying to you. Give thanks for whatever healing and liberation God provides for you.

Pray that you and the adult learners will recognize that you can find healing and wholeness in Christ the healer.

Preparing Our Minds

Study the background and lesson Scripture from Mark 1:29-45. As you ponder this passage, consider who you can turn to for healing so as to be made whole.

Write on newsprint:
❏ chart for "Examine Stories of Jesus Healing."
❏ information for next week's lesson, found under "Continue the Journey."
❏ activities for further spiritual growth in "Continue the Journey."

Option: Research the effectiveness of intercessory prayer for those who are sick. A wide variety of material is available on the Internet. Be aware that much of this research makes no distinction between praying in the name of Jesus and praying in the context of other beliefs.

Option: Gather votive candles and a lighter if you choose this option for "Praise Jesus for Healing."

LEADING THE CLASS

(1) Gather to Learn

❖ Welcome the class members and introduce any guests.

❖ Pray that each adult who has come today will be open to God's healing presence.

❖ List on newsprint the first names of people that class members know who are seeking healing. Either offer verbal prayers as a class, or provide quiet time for students to pray silently.

❖ **Option:** Discuss with the class their views on how intercessory prayer can affect someone who is ill. Much has been written on this topic, so you may wish to do some Internet research on this topic that you will share with the class at this time.

❖ Read aloud today's focus statement: **Many people are looking to be made whole. To whom can they turn for healing? Faith in the power of Jesus Christ will lead to wholeness, though not necessarily a physical cure.**

(2) Examine Stories of Jesus Healing

❖ Choose four volunteers to read Mark 1:29-45, dividing the passage as follows: verses 29-31, 32-34, 35-39, 40-45. Stop after each person has read and fill in the chart below, which you will write on newsprint prior to class.

Verses in Mark 1	Patient(s)	Illness(es)	Jesus' Action	Patient's Response
29-31				
32-34				
35-39				
40-45				

❖ Review this completed chart with the group to see if they can find similarities and differences in the way Jesus healed people.
❖ Discuss these questions.
(1) What do you learn about Peter's mother-in-law? (She did not ask for healing, but Jesus healed her. When she was well, she responded by serving Jesus and the disciples.)
(2) How does her response (rising up to serve) relate to us? (Use "Healing as Up-Lifting and Restoration" in Interpreting the Scripture to help the class answer this question.)
(3) What do you learn about the leper? (Note that he does not press Jesus, but simply says in verse 40 "If you choose, you can make me clean." You may want to use "God's Choices" in Interpreting the Scripture to discuss this idea of choice more fully. Also note that although Jesus had told him to be silent about his healing, the leper

immediately went and told so many people that Jesus no longer had free access to the neighboring communities.)
❖ Summarize this part of the lesson by inviting the students to say how the stories we have studied relate to their own lives. Perhaps some students will tell stories of healing, whereas others will indicate that they are seeking healing.

(3) Realize That Faith in Jesus Does Not Always Result in Physical Healing

❖ Read aloud these two quotations:
■ **"I have prayed hundreds, if not thousands, of times for the Lord to heal me—and he finally healed me of the need to be healed."** (Tim Hansel, whose serious fall during a climb left him in pain due to a compressed spine.)
■ **"Our Father yet heals the spirit of amputees—even when they will not grow legs. And, once the spirit is healed, the legs can be done without."** (Calvin Miller is a writer, poet, and preacher.)
❖ Invite the students to respond to these quotations, both of which focus on healings that do not include a physical cure. Also ask: **Do you believe that it is possible for people to be healed without being cured? Explain your answer.**
❖ **Option:** Encourage the students to tell to a small group stories of people who showed great courage in physical adversity, even if they died without ever being cured.

(4) Praise Jesus for Healing

❖ Distribute half sheets of paper and pencils. Suggest that each person complete this sentence: **I give praise and thanks to Jesus for healing**. . . . The sentence may refer to a healing that the student has experienced or to a healing that someone he or she knows has experienced. Remind the class members that "healing" and "cure" are not necessarily synonymous. Caution the students about medical privacy by suggesting that they use only first names and keep any descriptions of the illness rather general.

❖ Collect the papers and redistribute them. Ask whoever is holding a paper to read it aloud as a testimony of praise.

❖ **Option:** As each testimony of praise is lifted up, light a votive candle that you have placed on the class worship table.

(5) Continue the Journey

❖ Pray that all who have participated in today's lesson will recognize Christ as the One in whom they can find healing and wholeness.

❖ Read aloud this preparation for next week's lesson. You may also want to post it on newsprint for the students to copy.
- Title: **Christ as Servant**
- **Background Scripture: John 13:1-20**
- **Lesson Scripture: John 13:1-8, 12-20.**
- **Focus of the Lesson: No one is too good to serve others. How are we to know whom and when to serve? Jesus Christ demonstrated what it means to be a humble servant.**

❖ Challenge the students to complete one or more of these activities for further spiritual growth, which you will write on newsprint for the students to copy.

(1) **Research some alternative medical practices, such as herbal treatments, Reiki, massage, magnets, or acupuncture. How do you see the practice(s) you explored as being related to the healing work of Christ?**

(2) **Offer support to someone who has a chronic, perhaps terminal, illness. Help that person to do healing work necessary to restore relationships. Recognize that faith in Jesus leads to wholeness, though not necessarily to a physical cure.**

(3) **Pray for at least two people each day who seek healing. Unobtrusively find out how each one is doing.**

❖ Sing or read aloud "O Christ, the Healer."

❖ Conclude today's session by leading the class in this benediction, which is adapted from James 1:22, 25: **Let us now go forth as doers of the word and not merely hearers, for doers who act will be blessed in their doing.**

UNIT 2: IMAGES OF CHRIST IN THE GOSPELS
CHRIST AS SERVANT

PREVIEWING THE LESSON

Lesson Scripture: John 13:1-8, 12-20
Background Scripture: John 13:1-20
Key Verse: John 13:15

Focus of the Lesson:
No one is too good to serve others. How are we to know whom and when to serve? Jesus Christ demonstrated what it means to be a humble servant.

Goals for the Learners:
(1) to unpack the implications of Jesus washing the disciples' feet.
(2) to explore the limits of their willingness to serve.
(3) to identify service opportunities that stretch their limits and then to commit themselves to action.

Supplies:
Bibles, newsprint and marker, paper and pencils, hymnals, picture of Jesus washing the disciples' feet

---

READING THE SCRIPTURE

NRSV
John 13:1-8, 12-20

¹Now before the festival of the Passover, Jesus knew that his hour had come to depart from this world and go to the Father. Having loved his own who were in the world, he loved them to the end. ²The devil had already put it into the heart of Judas son of Simon Iscariot to betray him. And during supper ³Jesus, knowing that the Father had given all things into his hands, and that he had come from God and was going to God, ⁴got up from the table, took off his outer robe, and tied a towel around himself.

NIV
John 13:1-8, 12-20

¹It was just before the Passover Feast. Jesus knew that the time had come for him to leave this world and go to the Father. Having loved his own who were in the world, he now showed them the full extent of his love.

²The evening meal was being served, and the devil had already prompted Judas Iscariot, son of Simon, to betray Jesus. ³Jesus knew that the Father had put all things under his power, and that he had come from God and was returning to God; ⁴so he got

⁵Then he poured water into a basin and began to wash the disciples' feet and to wipe them with the towel that was tied around him. ⁶He came to Simon Peter, who said to him, "Lord, are you going to wash my feet?" ⁷Jesus answered, "You do not know now what I am doing, but later you will understand." ⁸Peter said to him, "You will never wash my feet." Jesus answered, "Unless I wash you, you have no share with me."

¹²After he had washed their feet, had put on his robe, and had returned to the table, he said to them, "Do you know what I have done to you? ¹³You call me Teacher and Lord—and you are right, for that is what I am. ¹⁴So if I, your Lord and Teacher, have washed your feet, you also ought to wash one another's feet. **¹⁵For I have set you an example, that you also should do as I have done to you.** ¹⁶Very truly, I tell you, servants are not greater than their master, nor are messengers greater than the one who sent them. ¹⁷If you know these things, you are blessed if you do them. ¹⁸I am not speaking of all of you; I know whom I have chosen. But it is to fulfill the scripture, 'The one who ate my bread has lifted his heel against me.' ¹⁹I tell you this now, before it occurs, so that when it does occur, you may believe that I am he. ²⁰Very truly, I tell you, whoever receives one whom I send receives me; and whoever receives me receives him who sent me."

up from the meal, took off his outer clothing, and wrapped a towel around his waist. ⁵After that, he poured water into a basin and began to wash his disciples' feet, drying them with the towel that was wrapped around him.

⁶He came to Simon Peter, who said to him, "Lord, are you going to wash my feet?"

⁷Jesus replied, "You do not realize now what I am doing, but later you will understand."

⁸"No," said Peter, "you shall never wash my feet."

Jesus answered, "Unless I wash you, you have no part with me."

¹²When he had finished washing their feet, he put on his clothes and returned to his place. "Do you understand what I have done for you?" he asked them. ¹³"You call me 'Teacher' and 'Lord,' and rightly so, for that is what I am. ¹⁴Now that I, your Lord and Teacher, have washed your feet, you also should wash one another's feet. **¹⁵I have set you an example that you should do as I have done for you.** ¹⁶I tell you the truth, no servant is greater than his master, nor is a messenger greater than the one who sent him. ¹⁷Now that you know these things, you will be blessed if you do them.

¹⁸"I am not referring to all of you; I know those I have chosen. But this is to fulfill the scripture: 'He who shares my bread has lifted up his heel against me.'

¹⁹"I am telling you now before it happens, so that when it does happen you will believe that I am He. ²⁰I tell you the truth, whoever accepts anyone I send accepts me; and whoever accepts me accepts the one who sent me."

UNDERSTANDING THE SCRIPTURE

John 13:1-2. In the Gospel of John, Jesus observes three Passovers in Jerusalem (see also 2:13 and 6:4). Passover commemorated God's deliverance of Israel from Egypt. At the time of Jesus, Passover was one of three festivals (Weeks and Booths were the others) associated with pilgrimage to Jerusalem. Some estimates run as high as

125,000 pilgrims coming to Jerusalem for the festival. The core of the Passover celebration, outside of the temple rituals, was a meal celebrated with either family or friends. In the Synoptic Gospels (Matthew, Mark, and Luke), the table gathering for Passover is associated with Jesus' last meal with his disciples. In John, the table gathering for Passover is related in the story of footwashing. The first indication that Jesus' "hour" had come is 12:23, when disciples relate to Jesus that some Greek pilgrims wish to meet him. Earlier in the Gospel, the "hour" had been a recurring symbol framed in terms of "is coming" or "not yet." The betrayal by Judas is not newly revealed here, as Jesus' awareness of this goes back in John's telling all the way to 6:71. The repetition of this knowledge here introduces the ongoing tension between community and betrayal that will color this entire chapter, culminating in the prediction of Peter's denial (13:36-38).

John 13:3-5. "During supper" (13:2) heightens the surprise of this action. "During" suggests this footwashing ritual interrupts the meal itself, adding to the shock of Jesus being the one to do the washing. Footwashing would have normally occurred when guests arrived at the home of the host, before any food would have been served. Typically, the host would either have provided water for the guests to wash themselves, or designated one of the lower-ranking house servants to do the washing. The washing of feet in an age of sandals, when long walks on dusty roads was the norm, made it one of the lowliest of tasks. Earlier, Mary had anointed Jesus' feet at a dinner in the home of her brother Lazarus (12:3). It is a ritual of hospitality with ancient roots (see also 1 Samuel 25:40-41).

John 13:6-11. John does not clarify whether Jesus goes to Peter first, or if not, whether those whose feet Jesus washed before said nothing. John is not interested in providing accounts of how every individual disciple responded. Rather, as is the case elsewhere, it seems more likely that Peter speaks here as representative of the other disciples. The scene here anticipates and even sets up the scene that closes this chapter (13:36-38). Peter's bravado dominates here and later: "You will never wash my feet. . . . I will lay down my life for you." The word for "share" in verse 8 carries the sense of a place or portion with something or someone else. It is a community word, and the scene of footwashing is all about the nature of community shared with Christ and with one another. In some ways, it echoes the teaching of Mark 10:35-45, where requests by and bickering among the disciples for "greatness" find answer in Jesus' example of (and calling the disciples to) servanthood. The text for the second time references the theme of betrayal in verses 10b-11, though without naming Judas. The image of "clean" plays upon understandings related not only immediately to the footwashing but also to more ancient connections of "clean" as ritually fit to stand in the presence of God.

John 13:12-15. Earlier in the Gospel of John, the miracles or "signs" of Jesus were followed by extended teachings. Here, the experience of footwashing is followed by Jesus' interpreting its meaning—and evoking its practice. That the early church heard this command in literal ways finds evidence in 1 Timothy 5:10. There, footwashing is identified as one of the good works practiced by widows in the community ("shown hospitality, washed the saints' feet"). "That you also should do as I have done to you" (John 13:15) parallels an earlier teaching of Jesus (Matthew 7:12; Luke 6:31). The difference, however, is that here the measure is "as I have done to you" instead of "as you would have them do to you."

John 13:16-20. The word for "servant" used here is the same word used of a slave, while "master" translates the same word elsewhere rendered as "Lord" (as in 13:13). The symbolism of a "messenger" and the "one who sends" recalls an important tradition of this era. Namely, the one who is sent is to be treated with the same authority and dignity as the one who sends. In other words, an emissary of a king was to be treated with the same respect as if the king himself were present. Elsewhere in John, this symbolism is joined to the relationship between Jesus and God, and the acceptance (and often rejection) of Jesus is in effect the acceptance or rejection of God (5:23). In John 13:16-19, however, the emphasis is not on the shared authority of sender and one who is sent, but rather the reminder that as servants the disciples do not rise above the level of the one who sends them (Jesus). The servanthood Jesus has exemplified in the footwashing is, therefore, the servanthood that disciples cannot set aside as "beneath" them. For a third time, the theme of betrayal is raised (13:18) in the ironic image of one who "lifted his heel" (foot) against Jesus. The Scripture this is identified as fulfilling is Psalm 41:9. The context of that verse ("even my bosom friend in whom I trusted") accentuates the breach of trust and relationship involved in betrayal. Likewise, the importance and almost sacred nature of table fellowship makes the pairing of betrayal with the act of breaking bread an even greater affront. The passage closes with verse 20's affirmation about receiving and sending begun in verse 16b. Only now, the disciples come into the formula of faith's hospitality. Those who receive one whom Jesus sends receive Jesus, even as those who receive Jesus receive God. The text prepares for this chapter's later revelation that Jesus will be among the disciples "only a little longer" (13:33). Soon, disciples ("taught ones") will become apostles ("sent ones").

INTERPRETING THE SCRIPTURE

Washing Feet

I recently read a paper written by a woman who serves in a hospice ministry. As she described the variety of functions she has been called upon to do from time to time, she recounted experiences of washing some of her hospice "parishioners." Her descriptions of those very humble acts were almost sacramental in nature. For as I recall, she described them in terms connected far less to the humility it certainly required of her, and far more to an experience of community shared in the presence of the Holy.

As commentators like Gail O'Day in *The New Interpreter's Bible* help us to see, John 13 and Jesus' footwashing is not simply about humility. The passage's interpretation does not solely hang on trying to find some action or gesture in our own experience that would require what footwashing required of Jesus, and then going out and doing it.

Beyond that, the passage has to do with intimacy of relationship and participation in community with Jesus. That is part of the underlying meaning of Jesus' words in verse 8, "you have no share with me," if the washing is refused. What we share of ourselves in relationship with Christ involves opening the whole of our lives to Jesus' presence and transformation.

"Do you know what I have done?" (13:12) pushes us to search deeper in this passage—and in turn, to search deeper in our lives. It invites us to see not only Jesus' actions but also our responses as something more than merely duplicating what was once done long ago. It invites us to practice the kind of community—the kind of love—that is willing to take on the humblest of tasks for the sake of another. It invites us to servanthood that is not imposed, but exemplified.

Servanthood

Servanthood: Words of caution need to be uttered here. Part of the caution stems from the experiences of groups who have suffered oppression. Servant and slave are interchangeable terms in Greek—and too often, servanthood and servitude have been applied in terribly one-sided ways in society. "Behind every great man stands a woman . . ." with the inescapable emphasis on "behind." The church has likewise, in subtle and obvious ways, let the weight of servanthood fall on some more than others. My home church in which I grew up readily praised the work of its very large and very active Women's Fellowship. Most of my teachers in Sunday school were women. Most of the workers in the kitchen at church suppers (with a few notable exceptions) were women. But never was a woman entrusted with service on the Church Council as long as I was there.

"Servant" can be a demeaning term and experience. That is a terrible misfortune, because service as practiced and invoked by Jesus was not meant to be demeaning. Rather, its intent was the building of community. And in truth, Jesus' own practice of servanthood was intended to reverse the very types of role stereotypes that afflict church and society. When Jesus as "Teacher and Lord" (13:13) took up the towel and basin to wash the feet of those who would shortly use those feet to flee from his side, Jesus intended to establish a countercultural example of servanthood and leadership that we have still not gotten right today. This servanthood is the kind of example that those who would aspire to leadership must first (and continually!) practice. As previously noted, Jesus' footwashing puts into practice the teaching about greatness in Mark 10:35-45. Servanthood is not about keeping folks in vulnerable positions vulnerable. That is oppression. Servanthood is about revealing power in acts of love freely chosen.

Testing Our Limits

The interchange in the text between Jesus and Peter in verse 8 turns on the disciple's sense of limits: "You will never. . . ." How might you complete that sentence? What would it be that you would never allow Jesus to do for you, and why?

Some might say, with good reason, that Jesus pushes Peter on the issue of limits ("Unless I wash you . . ." 13:8) because of a deeper matter than whether Peter's feet get washed. For when we are talking about limits, we are talking about the edge of what we are willing to do—and what we are not. And in Peter's case, it may well have been that the refusal to accept such humble service from Jesus stemmed from Peter's own resistance to do such things for another himself. In other words: As long as I don't let you do that for me, then I won't feel obligated to do that for another.

Note the term there: *obligated.* What Jesus does for the disciples is not an act of obligation on his part. It is an act of love, of community so deeply valued that he takes on this service as an expression of that love. It is an act of grace. Grace is not obligation. Grace is invitation.

And that is what makes the limits being tested here—the limits of Peter, of you, of me—so extraordinary. For the limits of love and community are not drawn in tight lines around whether or not you or I or Peter will or will not literally wash someone's feet—or allow our own to be washed. For as we are all sometimes loath to admit, it is easier to give than to receive. It can be easier to minister to than to be ministered to. Why? Because we then face the *limits* of our own self-reliance. We face the truth that our needs go beyond our capabilities. And we face, and find, the grace of discovering that in Christ and in one another, we receive life.

Do Unto Others

We've all heard it, perhaps from childhood. "Do unto others what you would have them do unto you." This teaching of Jesus, this "golden rule," has close parallels in many religious traditions. Its ethical stance helps us avoid the tit-for-tat cycle of what Proverbs 24:29 counsels against: "Do not say, 'I will do to others as they have done to me.'" In his record of this teaching by Jesus, Matthew notes that Jesus follows it by saying, "for this is the law and the prophets" (Matthew 7:12).

"Do unto others what you would have them do unto you." The words are indeed a valuable guide for ethical conduct. But I would add that John 13:15b may be even more valuable . . . and more challenging: "You also should do as I have done to you." The immediate context, of course, is foot-washing, and Jesus' commanding ("ought") to wash one another's feet. But consider it as a corollary, and deepening, of the golden rule. Now, it is not just what we would want done in return to us that measures our code of conduct—it is what Christ has done.

Consider the kinds of things Christ has done for us, in the stories told of his actions. He has healed. He has forgiven. He has broken bread with outcasts. He has spoken truth to power. He has sought the good of others, even when it meant ill for him. He has served, in the best and highest sense of that word.

Do unto others . . . as Christ has done for you.

SHARING THE SCRIPTURE

Preparing Our Hearts

Meditate on this week's devotional reading, found in Isaiah 53:4-6, which is an excerpt from the Fourth Servant Song of Isaiah. What do you suppose motivated the servant to suffer on behalf of others? Many people assume that when someone is having great difficulties he or she has been "struck down by God" (53:4). Do you think that someone who willingly serves interprets the situation this way? Why or why not? What are you willing to do to serve others? What is your motivation for doing so?

Pray that you and the adult learners will follow God's leading and serve wherever called to do so.

Preparing Our Minds

Study the background from John 13:1-20 and lesson Scripture, verses 1-8, 12-20. Consider your own attitudes toward servanthood and ponder how you can know whom and when to serve.

Write on newsprint:
❑ information for next week's lesson, found under "Continue the Journey."
❑ activities for further spiritual growth in "Continue the Journey."

Locate a picture, either online or in a book, of Jesus washing the disciples' feet. Make sure it is large enough for the students to see, or bring several copies.

Be sensitive to how members of the class will react to the idea of servanthood. Some ethnic groups feel they have always been in servant roles in society and may object to the term "servant." Women traditionally have been servants in the home, church, and community.

LEADING THE CLASS

(1) Gather to Learn

❖ Welcome the class members and introduce any guests.

❖ Pray that each person who participates in today's class will recognize the image of Christ as servant within himself or herself.

❖ Invite the students to list on newsprint occupations that are basically service oriented, such as restaurant servers, delivery persons, parking attendants, salespersons, and cashiers.

❖ Ask: **What observations can you make about how people we have listed are treated by the public?** Some students may wish to share brief stories. Remember that some class members may be employed in the service sector and will have personal stories to share.

❖ **Option:** Ask, if appropriate based on answers you have heard: **Why do you think that people in service-oriented positions are often treated shabbily by others?**

❖ Read aloud today's focus statement: **No one is too good to serve others. How are we to know whom and when to serve? Jesus Christ demonstrated what it means to be a humble servant.**

2) Unpack the Implications of Jesus Washing the Disciples' Feet

❖ Engage the class with the story of Jesus washing the disciples' feet, which is unique to the Gospel of John, by asking volunteers to read John 13:1-8, 12-20. Select readers for the roles of the narrator, Jesus, and Peter.

❖ Show a picture or icon of Jesus washing the disciples' feet. Ask these questions.

    (1) **Which characters do you recognize?**

    (2) **Judging by the expressions on their faces, what do Jesus and each of the disciples seem to be thinking?**

    (3) **What meaning might the disciples have discerned as Jesus washed their feet?**

    (4) **How do you think you might have reacted had you been in this scene?**

❖ Read in unison today's key verse, John 13:15.

❖ Invite the class to comment on how they understand Jesus' washing of his disciples' feet to be an example or role model for them.

❖ Wrap up this portion of the lesson by reading or retelling "Servanthood" in Interpreting the Scripture.

(3) Explore the Limits of the Learners' Willingness to Serve

❖ Refer to "Gather to Learn" and the discussion about how people in service-oriented occupations are treated.

❖ Distribute paper and pencils. Encourage the students to draw several concentric circles, that is, circles within one another centered on the same point. Suggest that the adults list in each circle service jobs they do, with those in the ring closest to the center being ones they do willingly. As they move out from the center, the jobs become less desirable, even though the student performs the task. Recommend that they mark their own limits on doing certain service-oriented tasks, perhaps around the second or third ring, or wherever appropriate.

❖ Invite the learners to talk with the class or a small group about why they placed certain tasks where they did, and where they "drew the line" on doing certain things.

❖ Provide meditation time for the class to consider these questions: **What do the limits you have identified say about your willingness to serve? Can you identify certain jobs you should be more open to doing or people you need to be more open to helping?**

❖ Break the silence by reading this excerpt from a poem by Annie Johnson Flint (1862–1932), which may be familiar to some class members.

    Christ has no hands but our hands
    To do his work today;
    He has no feet but our feet
    To lead men in his way.

❖ Ask: **When you are reminded that Christ is not only our example but is also depending on us to do his work here on** earth, would you still limit your willingness to serve? Why or why not?

(4) Identify Service Opportunities That Stretch the Learners' Limits and Then Commit to Action

❖ Brainstorm and place on newsprint a list of tasks that need to be done within the church and community.

❖ Challenge each student to choose at least one task that he or she could do but has never volunteered to do, perhaps because the work seemed too menial.

❖ Ask the adults to each list on the back of their papers this one task and any steps he or she will take to do the task.

(5) Continue the Journey

❖ Pray this prayer of the sixteenth-century Spanish saint Ignatius of Loyola:

Teach us, good Lord, to serve you as you deserve; to give and not to count the cost; to fight and not to heed the wounds; to toil and not to seek for rest; to labor and not to ask for any reward, except that of knowing that we do your will; through Jesus Christ our Lord. Amen.

❖ Read aloud this preparation for next week's lesson. You may also want to post it on newsprint for the students to copy.

■ **Title: Christ as Messiah**
■ **Background Scripture: Matthew 16:13-23**
■ **Lesson Scripture: Matthew 16:13-23**
■ **Focus of the Lesson: We come to know people not by what others**

say about them but by a personal relationship with them. How well do we ever really know somebody? Peter's confession of Jesus was a milestone in his understanding of Jesus as the Messiah.

❖ Challenge the students to complete one or more of these activities for further spiritual growth, which you will write on newsprint for the students to copy.

(1) **Identify the people in your congregation who are truly the servants—the ones who do jobs, big and small, without thought of reward or recognition. Talk to a few of these folks to find out what motivates them to serve.**

(2) **Plan to serve a stranger you can help through a local agency, such as a nursing home, soup kitchen, or shelter. Be alert for opportunities to offer a low-key witness as to why you serve.**

(3) **Look up serve in a computer concordance. You will find nearly 1300 references in the NRSV, referring to words such as** *"serve"* **and "servant." Review selected references to discern what the Bible says about service.**

❖ Sing or read aloud "Jesu, Jesu."

❖ Conclude today's session by leading the class in this benediction, which is adapted from James 1:22, 25: **Let us now go forth as doers of the word and not merely hearers, for doers who act will be blessed in their doing.**

UNIT 2: IMAGES OF CHRIST IN THE GOSPELS
CHRIST AS MESSIAH

PREVIEWING THE LESSON

Lesson Scripture: Matthew 16:13-23
Background Scripture: Matthew 16:13-23
Key Verse: Matthew 16:15

Focus of the Lesson:
We come to know people not by what others say about them but by a personal relationship with them. How well do we ever really know somebody? Peter's confession of Jesus was a milestone in his understanding of Jesus as the Messiah.

Goals for the Learners:
(1) to retell the conversation between Peter and Jesus in which Jesus acknowledges that he is the Messiah.
(2) to explore their understanding of Messiah.
(3) to publicly confess their faith as a new or renewed commitment to Jesus as the Messiah.

Pronunciation Guide:
Caesarea Philippi (ses uh ree' uh fil' i pi)
Herod Antipas (her' uhd an' tee puhs)
Petrine (pee' trin)
Sheol (shee' ohl)
skandalon (scan' dal on)

Supplies:
Bibles, newsprint and markers, paper and pencils, hymnals, optional recording of meditative music and appropriate player

JULY 27

READING THE SCRIPTURE

NRSV

Matthew 16:13-23

¹³Now when Jesus came into the district of Caesarea Philippi, he asked his disciples, "Who do people say that the Son of Man is?"

NIV

Matthew 16:13-23

¹³When Jesus came to the region of Caesarea Philippi, he asked his disciples, "Who do people say the Son of Man is?"

¹⁴And they said, "Some say John the Baptist, but others Elijah, and still others Jeremiah or one of the prophets." **¹⁵He said to them, "But who do you say that I am?"** ¹⁶Simon Peter answered, "You are the Messiah, the Son of the living God." ¹⁷And Jesus answered him, "Blessed are you, Simon son of Jonah! For flesh and blood has not revealed this to you, but my Father in heaven. ¹⁸And I tell you, you are Peter, and on this rock I will build my church, and the gates of Hades will not prevail against it. ¹⁹I will give you the keys of the kingdom of heaven, and whatever you bind on earth will be bound in heaven, and whatever you loose on earth will be loosed in heaven." ²⁰Then he sternly ordered the disciples not to tell anyone that he was the Messiah.

²¹From that time on, Jesus began to show his disciples that he must go to Jerusalem and undergo great suffering at the hands of the elders and chief priests and scribes, and be killed, and on the third day be raised. ²²And Peter took him aside and began to rebuke him, saying, "God forbid it, Lord! This must never happen to you." ²³But he turned and said to Peter, "Get behind me, Satan! You are a stumbling block to me; for you are setting your mind not on divine things but on human things."

¹⁴They replied, "Some say John the Baptist; others say Elijah; and still others, Jeremiah or one of the prophets." **¹⁵"But what about you?" he asked. "Who do you say I am?"** ¹⁶Simon Peter answered, "You are the Christ, the Son of the living God." ¹⁷Jesus replied, "Blessed are you, Simon son of Jonah, for this was not revealed to you by man, but by my Father in heaven. ¹⁸And I tell you that you are Peter, and on this rock I will build my church, and the gates of Hades will not overcome it. ¹⁹I will give you the keys of the kingdom of heaven; whatever you bind on earth will be bound in heaven, and whatever you loose on earth will be loosed in heaven." ²⁰Then he warned his disciples not to tell anyone that he was the Christ.

²¹From that time on Jesus began to explain to his disciples that he must go to Jerusalem and suffer many things at the hands of the elders, chief priests and teachers of the law, and that he must be killed and on the third day be raised to life. ²²Peter took him aside and began to rebuke him. "Never, Lord!" he said. "This shall never happen to you!" ²³Jesus turned and said to Peter, "Get behind me, Satan! You are a stumbling block to me; you do not have in mind the things of God, but the things of men."

UNDERSTANDING THE SCRIPTURE

Matthew 16:13-14. Caesarea Philippi was twenty or so miles north of the Sea of Galilee. Located at the base of Mount Hermon, Caesarea Philippi was the site of a spring whose waters formed one of the chief sources of the Jordan River. The spring and cave (grotto) from which it came formed a popular site of earlier religious traditions: first of Baal, then of Pan. The city's location also made it a strategic stronghold for the region. The son of Herod the Great, Philip, had rebuilt it as his capital and renamed it to honor the emperor ("Caesarea") and himself ("Philippi"). The initial question posed by Jesus in this text asked about popular opinions as to his identity ("Son of Man" was Jesus' frequent self-designation). The setting of the question at Caesarea Philippi may have subtly drawn on those older associations of this place as a crossroads of religious beliefs. The common thread among those whom the disciples identify in response to Jesus' question is that they are all prophets. John the Baptizer had only recently been executed by the brother of Philip, Herod Antipas (see Matthew 14:1-12). The naming of Elijah is significant. Some rabbinic traditions indicated that Elijah, who had been taken up into heaven without having died (2 Kings 2:1-12), would return to herald the coming of Messiah. Less clear is the significance of Jeremiah's naming: perhaps in recollection of his proclaiming of a "new covenant" (Jeremiah 31:31-34).

Matthew 16:15-16. The question Jesus now poses to the disciples is aimed not at the speculation of others, but at their own grasp of his identity. It is a question directed to them as a whole: the "you" in verse 15 is in the plural form. As elsewhere, Simon speaks up as a representative of the group. The two titles Simon uses to peg Jesus' identity are "Messiah" and "Son of the Living God." "Messiah" is from a Hebrew word that means "anointed." (The word in Greek is *christos,* from which we get "Christ.") Anointing was originally associated with kingship (see, for example, 1 Samuel 16:1-13, the story of David). Thus, Jewish messianic ideas formed primarily around the notion of dominion. In the time of Jesus, when there was no Jewish monarchy and Judea and Galilee were under Roman rule, the promise of God's Messiah largely was understood in terms of a restoration of some form of Davidic rule and an independent Jewish state. "Son of God" is not a new term in Matthew's Gospel. It is the identity of Jesus revealed by the voice from heaven at the time of his baptism (Matthew 3:17). It is also the confession of the disciples in the boat on the Sea of Galilee (14:22-33). Later, it will be the word pronounced by the centurion on duty at the crucifixion at the time of Jesus' death (27:54).

Matthew 16:17-19. The story of Simon's name change to Peter parallels other stories: for example, Abram to Abraham, and later Saul to Paul. In each case, the new identity comes linked to a new vocation. In the case of Simon-now-Peter, the vocation has to do with serving as the "rock" on which Christ would build his church. There is a clear wordplay in this exchange. Peter is the anglicized form of *petros,* which means "rock." So the "rock" (*petra*) on which Christ builds his church is Petros. Dealing with the word play in this text is far simpler than dealing with two underlying, and controversial, associations made here with Peter. First is the way in which this text has served as a battleground between Roman Catholic, Orthodox, and Protestant views of the papacy and "Petrine supremacy." Clearly from the text, Peter's role is unique and critical. The question is: Does Peter's unique role continue in the office of the papacy for Peter's successors? The second issue this text raises is the meaning of the "keys of the kingdom," and the ensuing words about binding and loosing. Traditionally, the words have been used, for example, to justify both the church's practice of absolution of sins and to levy the judgment of excommunication.

One final note: "Hades" in this time period is not a place of punishment, but a more shadowy realm of the dead (parallel to the Jewish "Sheol").

Matthew 16:20-21. In Understanding the Scripture for the session on July 13, comments were made under Mark 1:32-34 to explain or at least suggest possibilities for understanding the so-called "messianic secret" theme there. Please refer to those comments as you consider the meaning and role of verse 20 in today's passage. Verse 21 consists of the first passion (suffering) prediction in Matthew's Gospel. As in Mark (8:27-33), this first declaration of what would come to pass in Jerusalem takes place immediately after this exchange outside of Caesarea Philippi. "From that time on" (Matthew 16:21) does not only emphasize the importance this revelation will have for the journey ahead. But also, more immediately, it stresses the change in the focus of the audience in Matthew from crowds to the disciples that will dominate the next several chapters. Caesarea Philippi, though distant in miles from Jerusalem, now finds itself joined to that destination, geographically and theologically. The suffering is attributed in this text not to the whole Jewish people, but rather to their dominant leadership groups ("elders and chief priests and scribes"). For more details about the significance of each of these groups in the power structure of that day, review the material for Luke 20:1 in Understanding the Scripture on July 6.

Matthew 16:22-23. Having confessed Jesus as Messiah, Peter now rejects the suffering messianic role as Jesus has described it. "Rebuke" is the same word Matthew uses to describe Jesus' stilling of the sea (8:26) and the disciples barring of those bringing children to Jesus (19:13). "Get behind" invites Peter to resume the role of a disciple, and not one who dictates to Messiah what Messiah will or will not do. The use of "Satan" recalls the temptation story (4:1-11). The temptation here, as in the wilderness, is to set aside following the path of God for one of "least resistance." The wordplay on Peter and rock at the core of this passage subtly concludes with Peter, who is to be the rock, now identified in this resistance as a "stumbling block" (*skandalon* in Greek).

INTERPRETING THE SCRIPTURE

Questions of Identity

That many names are associated by the crowds with Jesus ought not to be surprising. We are, each of us, something different to various persons. I am son, and brother, and father, and friend. Who I am to you depends upon the relationship we have. Some of those relationships are given. I could not cease to be the son of my parents. But some of those relationships are chosen; they are matters of will and decision and insight born out of experience. To some, I have become friend—and likely foe to others.

Jesus tests the waters concerning the opinions about him as the text opens. Not surprisingly, all the names come from the past. Whenever we encounter someone new, or different, we try to pin that individual down on the basis of one who is known. *Oh, John, he is just like my cousin Fred.* Or, *Every time I look at Susan, I see my sister.* There is nothing wrong with that . . . to a point. And that point is this: Do we allow that individual to be uniquely who she or he is, or do we eventually constrict the person into the role of someone already known? Jesus may just be testing the waters with his first question of "Who do people say I am?" But the conversation suddenly turns serious and becomes definitive and filled with the possibility of commitment in the second question: "Who do you say that I am?" (16:15).

Questions of identity always, eventually, get personal. "Who I am" in your life is finally not a matter of testing public opinion or putting a finger in the wind to see what the polls are saying: "Who I am" comes down to "Who do you decide I will be?" Religious identity always, eventually, takes this direction. Who God is in my life is not just what the creeds say, or the preacher preaches, or the hymns sing: Who God is comes down to the decision I make about how I name, and follow, that relationship . . . and how I accept the name offered to me. For the gospel names us in our baptism, as it named Christ in his, graced by God—and gives us the vocation that comes with it of gracing others. For you see, identity always, eventually, leads to more than who we are. Identity always, eventually, leads to what we do. For in Jesus Christ, who we are and what we do are expected to be a seamless whole. Our calling is our identity.

Identity Crisis

Usually this term is reserved for, and applied to, that peculiar developmental stage when we find ourselves wrestling with matters of self-identification. Am I to simply be my parent's child, or am I also to be my own person?

In our passage from Matthew, there is a very stark and conflicted identity crisis. Only here, the leading issue is not one's own identity (although that ends up being wrapped up in it if you read on to verses 24-25). Rather, it is at least initially the crisis of the identity Jesus avows. At first, there is agreement on Jesus' identity. Peter says, *"You are the Messiah (Christ)."* Peter has the name and identity of "Messiah" correct. The crisis comes when Jesus' portrayal of who Messiah is and what Messiah will experience (in Jerusalem) does not coincide with Peter's understanding of the identity of Messiah.

The popular identity of Messiah, which likely underlies Peter's ensuing rebuke of Jesus, is of a triumphant military and political leader. Messiah will be the one who will inflict suffering on the enemies of Judaism. Messiah will be the one who will put to death Rome's oppression of the land and its people.

But that is not the identity of Messiah Jesus portrays—and as a result, Peter can only say to Jesus: "God forbid it!" (16:22). That is, of course, one of the choices always faced in crises of identity—whether of children or workers or spouses—the choice to forbid the unacceptable identity (of self or other). The choice to rule out change from the status quo, and what everyone knows to be true or right (we sometimes call that "conventional wisdom").

The face-off between Peter and Jesus in Caesarea Philippi is not an isolated incident on the road of faith, but a recurring theme. It recurs whenever the grace of God freshly understood seeks to shed new light on a new identity—and new calling—of the church. It happened during the civil rights movement in the United States. Some saw Jesus beckoning the faithful to a renewed vision of Galatians 3—in Christ there is neither slave nor free—some said "God forbid" to any mixing of race, be it in church or culture.

Does it still happen now? I invite you to be the judge of that in your own community, in your own denomination, in your own congregation. But if matters of identity and vocation are up for grabs, if words about suffering or any breaching of the customary powers that be still evoke dissent and conflict, you may want to take to heart the clear possibility of another identity crisis playing itself out. And where, in that crisis, do you hear and see the grace and call of Jesus Christ lived out . . . and making demands of a costly discipleship?

Stumbling Blocks and Building Blocks

The opening paragraph in this section explored how one person can be many things to many people. We do not find that difficult to understand when it comes to identities that are not exclusive of one another. *Yes, I can see how Sheila can be wife and mother and daughter and sister and friend and pastor all at once.* The difficulty comes in matters of identity, and in the vocations that follow, when those names or titles seem contradictory. For illustration of that, we have Peter.

Peter is, at first, the very rock upon which Christ will build holy community. Peter is foundation, blessed of God. Yet in a matter of a few breaths, Peter the blessed rock has become the stumbling rock compared to Satan.

So, which one is he?

Both.

For Peter is, in a way we may not like to admit in front of others, like us. On the best of our days, we may be building blocks of and for community—in our families, in our churches, in our communities. Folks may call us blessed, with good reason.

And on other days, we are more like *Petros* the stumbling block. We find ourselves, consciously or unconsciously, blocking the way of grace toward others . . . not to mention ourselves.

So, which one are we?

Both.

Which is why the church of Jesus Christ is constantly being re-formed and re-shaped by the grace of God, with or without our consent. We have within us the capability to be building blocks, rocks of foundation upon which others can stand and hold on and find their way. We have within us the capability to be stumbling blocks (remember: that word in Greek is *skandalon*), rocks that occasionally get in the way of ("scandalize") God's purposes. But notice this: Jesus does not give up on Peter. God does not give up on you. God in Christ builds the church now, as God in Christ built the church then, with very human building blocks.

With the likes of Peter. With the likes of you and me. Perhaps that is why grace is such a scandal—and such a gift!

SHARING THE SCRIPTURE

Preparing Our Hearts

Meditate on this week's devotional reading, found in Isaiah 43:1-7. What do you find in this passage about God's identity? What do you find about your own identity? What difference does it make in your life to know who you are and whose you are? Ponder your relationship with God as expressed in these words of Isaiah.

Pray that you and the adult learners will be aware of who God is, who you are, and how you and God are related.

Preparing Our Minds

Study the background and lesson Scripture, found in Matthew 16:13-23. Consider this idea: We know people not by what others say but by our own relationship with them. Do you agree?

Write on newsprint:

❑ affirmation of faith for "Publicly Confess Faith as a New or Renewed Commitment to Jesus as the Messiah."
❑ information for next week's lesson, found under "Continue the Journey."
❑ activities for further spiritual growth in "Continue the Journey."

Choose some meditative music for an optional activity under "Explore the Learners' Understandings of Messiah."

LEADING THE CLASS

(1) Gather to Learn

❖ Welcome the class members and introduce any guests.

❖ Pray that all who have come today will be open to a relationship with the living Christ.

❖ Divide the class into groups of two or three. Set a time limit and ask each person to answer these two questions: **What is one of your greatest achievements as a young person that most people do not know anything about? Why is this achievement special to you?**

❖ Gather the group together and ask: **What benefit is there in knowing something that happened, perhaps decades ago, to a class member?** (Help the students see the value of knowing information in order to grow in a relationship.)

❖ Read aloud today's focus statement: **We come to know people not by what others say about them but by a personal** relationship with them. **How well do we ever really know somebody? Peter's confession of Jesus was a milestone in his understanding of Jesus as the Messiah.**

(2) Retell the Conversation Between Peter and Jesus in which Jesus Acknowledges That He Is the Messiah

❖ Choose three volunteers to read the parts of the narrator, Peter, and Jesus in Matthew 16:13-23. Ask the class to join in reading verse 14.

❖ Use information from Matthew 16:13-14 in Understanding the Scripture to set the stage for Peter's confession.

❖ Look at verses 15-19, where Jesus calls for a personal response to his identity, Peter responds, and Jesus commends him. Ask: **In what ways does Peter seem to be right about Jesus' identity?**

❖ Note that after verse 21, when Jesus declared that he would suffer and be raised on the third day, we get another glimpse of Peter's understanding of Messiah in verse 22. Ask: **Based on these comments, what kind of Messiah do you think Peter thought Jesus was?**

❖ Read or retell "Identity Crisis" in Interpreting the Scripture.

❖ Suggest, as described in Interpreting the Scripture, that Peter is both a stumbling block and a building block. Invite the students to comment on how they see him as both of these kinds of rocks.

❖ Ask: **How can we as Christians be both stumbling blocks and building blocks in our churches?** (Focus on generic examples here, such as the person who tries to block any new initiatives versus the one who goes the extra mile to make a project work. Avoid mention of specific individuals.)

(3) Explore the Learners' Understandings of Messiah

❖ Divide the class into groups and give each group a sheet of newsprint and a marker. Challenge them to look through the New Testament to locate images of Jesus as the Messiah. They are to record these images and references on newsprint. Images of teacher, healer, deliverer, and servant will be easy to find. Suggest that they recall images from previous lessons to see how they inform the students' understandings of Messiah.

❖ Call time and post the newsprint around the room. If possible, allow the students to circulate to read what others have written. If that cannot be done, ask each group to give a brief report of its findings.

❖ Distribute paper and pencils. Encourage each student to express in writing a personal understanding of what it means to say, "You are the Messiah." Suggest that students use any images the groups have discerned, plus other images that are important to them.

❖ **Option:** Play some meditative music as the students write. This should be soft, instrumental music that aids the adults in focusing.

(4) Publicly Confess Faith as a New or Renewed Commitment to Jesus as the Messiah

❖ Read in unison today's key verse, Matthew 16:15.

❖ Invite each class member to read or state his or her personal beliefs about who Jesus the Messiah is. Do not press anyone who chooses not to participate. Be aware that some students may not, for a variety of reasons, be able to state their beliefs.

❖ Conclude this portion of the lesson by asking the students to read this affirmation of faith based on the Gospel of John, which you will have written on newsprint prior to class, as a sign of their commitment to Christ.

I believe in the Word, who from the beginning was with God and was God.

I believe that all things came into being through the Word.

I believe this Word, who I know as Jesus the Messiah, became flesh and dwelled among us. Through him, I see the grace and truth of God the Father, for in Jesus, God is made known.

I believe that the Father, who disclosed to Moses the divine name "I AM," is revealed through Jesus, who said to his followers:

I AM the Bread of Life;

I AM the Light of the World;

I AM the Door of the Sheepfold;

I AM the Good Shepherd;

I AM the Resurrection and the Life;

I AM the Way, the Truth, and the Life;

I AM the True Vine.

I believe Jesus fulfilled his promise to send an Advocate, divinity who dwells in me as the Holy Spirit.

I believe Jesus was crucified, buried, and resurrected from the dead and reigns with God the Father and the Holy Spirit, now and forevermore.

(5) Continue the Journey

❖ Pray that today's participants will continue to get to know Christ as Messiah.

❖ Read aloud this preparation for next week's lesson. You may also want to post it on newsprint for the students to copy.

■ Title: Doers of the Word

■ Background Scripture: James 1

■ Lesson Scripture: James 1:17-27

■ Focus of the Lesson: Some people have abundant knowledge, but it does not necessarily motivate their behavior. What is the appropriate relationship between knowing what to do and acting on that knowledge? James tells us that as God's people we must not only hear the word of God but also respond to it with transforming action.

❖ Challenge the students to complete one or more of these activities for further spiritual growth, which you will write on newsprint for the students to copy.

(1) Use a study Bible to identify Old Testament prophecies that seem to be fulfilled in Jesus. Remember that the Old Testament is a sacred canon unto itself and prophecies may refer to multiple people.

(2) Spend time getting to know a new church member or neighbor. How does this person seem similar to and different from how you imagined him or her to be, based on initial impressions?

(3) Talk with someone about what you know about Jesus and who you believe him to be. Listen to what this person has to say about his or her beliefs about Jesus.

❖ Sing or read aloud "Lord, I Want to Be a Christian."

❖ Conclude today's session by leading the class in this benediction, which is adapted from James 1:22, 25: **Let us now go forth as doers of the word and not merely hearers, for doers who act will be blessed in their doing.**

UNIT 3: IMAGES OF CHRIST IN US
DOERS OF THE WORD

PREVIEWING THE LESSON

Lesson Scripture: James 1:17-27
Background Scripture: James 1
Key Verse: James 1:22

Focus of the Lesson:
Some people have abundant knowledge, but it does not necessarily motivate their behavior. What is the appropriate relationship between knowing what to do and acting on that knowledge? James tells us that as God's people we must not only hear the word of God but also respond to it with transforming action.

Goals for the Learners:
(1) to study God's plan for faithful and active discipleship rooted in God's word.
(2) to recognize that as people of the word they must allow that word to transform the way they live.
(3) to identify ways to integrate Bible study with the rest of life and make a commitment to study.

Pronunciation Guide:
Diaspora (di as' puh ruh)

Supplies:
Bibles, newsprint and marker, paper and pencils, hymnals

READING THE SCRIPTURE

NRSV
James 1:17-27

[17]Every generous act of giving, with every perfect gift, is from above, coming down from the Father of lights, with whom there is no variation or shadow due to change. [18]In fulfillment of his own purpose he gave us birth by the word of truth, so that we would become a kind of first fruits of his creatures.

NIV
James 1:17-27

[17]Every good and perfect gift is from above, coming down from the Father of the heavenly lights, who does not change like shifting shadows. [18]He chose to give us birth through the word of truth, that we might be a kind of firstfruits of all he created.

¹⁹You must understand this, my beloved: let everyone be quick to listen, slow to speak, slow to anger; ²⁰for your anger does not produce God's righteousness. ²¹Therefore rid yourselves of all sordidness and rank growth of wickedness, and welcome with meekness the implanted word that has the power to save your souls.

²²But be doers of the word, and not merely hearers who deceive themselves. ²³For if any are hearers of the word and not doers, they are like those who look at themselves in a mirror; ²⁴for they look at themselves and, on going away, immediately forget what they were like. ²⁵But those who look into the perfect law, the law of liberty, and persevere, being not hearers who forget but doers who act—they will be blessed in their doing.

²⁶If any think they are religious, and do not bridle their tongues but deceive their hearts, their religion is worthless. ²⁷Religion that is pure and undefiled before God, the Father, is this: to care for orphans and widows in their distress, and to keep oneself unstained by the world.

¹⁹My dear brothers, take note of this: Everyone should be quick to listen, slow to speak and slow to become angry, ²⁰for man's anger does not bring about the righteous life that God desires. ²¹Therefore, get rid of all moral filth and the evil that is so prevalent and humbly accept the word planted in you, which can save you.

²²Do not merely listen to the word, and so deceive yourselves. Do what it says. ²³Anyone who listens to the word but does not do what it says is like a man who looks at his face in a mirror ²⁴and, after looking at himself, goes away and immediately forgets what he looks like. ²⁵But the man who looks intently into the perfect law that gives freedom, and continues to do this, not forgetting what he has heard, but doing it—he will be blessed in what he does.

²⁶If anyone considers himself religious and yet does not keep a tight rein on his tongue, he deceives himself and his religion is worthless. ²⁷Religion that God our Father accepts as pure and faultless is this: to look after orphans and widows in their distress and to keep oneself from being polluted by the world.

UNDERSTANDING THE SCRIPTURE

James 1:1. Tradition attributes this epistle to James the brother of Jesus, a leader in the church at Jerusalem. The past century has brought questions to that attribution. Among the reasons cited is the epistle's sophisticated style of Greek language that one would not expect from a Galilean Jew. Even so, James is still considered by many as author. If so, the writing dates from before A.D. 62, the date Josephus gives for the martyrdom of James. If the epistle is not from James, it likely dates to the latter part of the first century. The other question of identity raised here concerns the "tribes" in the Dispersion (in Greek, *diaspora*).

Traditionally, *Diaspora* referred to Jews living outside of Palestine. The Letter of James, as a Jewish Christian document, may have in mind Jewish Christians who live outside the bounds of Judea. Diaspora may also have in mind the more theologically-minded expression of all Christians who live in a state of "exile" from their true home in the presence of God.

James 1:2-4. The word for "trials" in verse 2 is the same word translated as "temptation" in verse 12—and in the prayer Jesus teaches in Matthew 6:13. In a letter that will take "works" as one of its key themes later, the author uses two different words in verses 3 and 4 ("produces," "effect") that share the same root of "act" in verse 25. "Endurance" suggests a virtue shared in common with the wider (and secular) world, where character is built by the experiences one endures (see a more developed expression of this thought in Romans 5:3-5). The epistle of James is considered to be in the genre of wisdom writing. Some have even ventured that parts of the letter came from non-Christian wisdom sources that the author borrowed. More likely is that the author (especially if it is James) grew up in a culture instilled with Hebrew wisdom traditions, and writing of the Christian faith in wisdom categories and ideas is simply a natural development.

James 1:5-8. In the background of verse 5 may be the request of Solomon for wisdom (1 Kings 3). The wider context of asking God who gives generously sounds a similar note to that of Jesus' teachings in Matthew 21:22: "Whatever you ask for in prayer with faith, you will receive." Likewise, the negative view of doubt parallels Mark 11:23, where Jesus invites prayer that does not doubt but believes. The image in verse 6 of being driven by wind will be returned to by James when he speaks of the power of the tongue (3:4-5). As Jesus often taught in parables drawn from nature, so the author of James here and elsewhere wraps wisdom teaching in experiences within creation and human affairs.

James 1:9-11. Rich and poor will play key roles later in this epistle. The presumption of the rich as blessed of God, as one element of wisdom tradition teaches, is confronted by the author here. Themes of exaltation and humiliation are introduced—and again, imagery for illustration comes from the created order, an order that will outlive any economic orders not driven by justice and care for the vulnerable.

James 1:12-16. The theme of "testing"/"trials" introduced in verses 2-4 takes a different direction. Those temptations are attributed not to God, but rather to the makeup of our lives. Verses 14-15 in

particular portray a deadly cycle begun by "desire." Later in this epistle (4:1 and following), the same cycle is shown at work on a wider scale, the result of "cravings." The author uses the imagery of birth and growth in this first chapter to depict this pernicious cycle whose end is death.

James 1:17-18. In contrast, birth imagery is employed in these verses to depict our calling to a new way of living grounded in openness to the goodness of God's gifts. The opening line of verse 17 celebrates God as the source of every good and perfect gift. It parallels that section in the Sermon on the Mount where Jesus remarks that, if imperfect parents can provide good gifts for their children, "how much more will your Father in heaven give good things to those who ask him!" (Matthew 7:11b). "Father of lights" (James 1:17) calls to mind the fourth day of the creation story, where God fashioned the sources of light in the sky (Genesis 1:14-19). The absence of "variation or shadow due to change" affirms God's dependability. "Shadow" may reflect a Platonic ideal current in that day's philosophies contrasting the "real" with the "shadow" world. In James, however, philosophy always serves practical wisdom.

James 1:19-21. The first of the "practical" lessons of this epistle focuses on listening, speaking—and anger. The word for "anger" in Greek is the root for the English word "orgy." In that sense, anger is an all-consuming and boundary-breaking expression of emotion. Righteous anger and indignation over injustice is not the subject at hand. As the epistle makes clearer in verse 21, what is at stake is the kind of outburst that takes us and others on a downward track. The rejection of such anger on the basis of God's righteousness is key. Righteousness will elsewhere play a leading role in this epistle (2:23; 3:18). It is a word that grows out of the legal tradition, referring to one who is adjudicated innocent. In religious terms, it has come to mean one who has been given such standing by God.

James 1:22-25. The epistle does not break new ground with these words. Jesus concluded his Sermon on the Mount with a parable that opened by saying: "Everyone then who hears these words of mine and acts on them will be like a wise man who built his house on rock" (Matthew 7:24). Jewish wisdom as a whole grounded itself not merely in knowledge of God but in right action based upon that knowledge and experience. So in that sense, Jesus and now James simply bring that older tradition to bear upon the gospel's proclamation.

James 1:26-27. The power and use of tongues will gain further attention in James 3:1 and following, as hinted above. Perhaps that flows from this epistle's concern that words (the product of tongues) cannot be thought to exhaust faith's call. Such "religion," as James speaks of it here and will develop it in more detail in chapter 2, has to do with treatment of the vulnerable in our midst and our own integrity. The urging to keep oneself "unstained" likely has in view the earlier warnings against the cycle born purely of desire (1:15) and the later illustration of this world's preference for the rich (2:2-4).

INTERPRETING THE SCRIPTURE

All Good Gifts

Gratitude is an amazing power in human life and community. With it, individuals and groups can live freely toward others and themselves and all of creation, knowing its deepest gifts come as grace. Without gratitude, individuals and groups endure a kind of slavery—where everything to be had involves a struggle and a grasping, where nothing is given, where life is constantly mine to take or lose.

James throws in his lot with religion that is of the first sort mentioned above. He asserts that all good gifts come from God. He goes on to say that even our very birthing in creation traces to God's purposes for us to be "first fruits" (1:18) of God's creatures—which I take to mean, among other things, that we are created with the possibility of gratitude for the gift of life, a sort of harbinger of that potential to all creation.

So says James. But what say you? Gratitude is an easy mark in easy and prosperous times—though not completely so. For even as the Deuteronomist warned centuries before James and millennia before us, prosperity makes it easy to forget life as gift and fashion it as an idol of our own creation (Deuteronomy 8:11-17). And when hard times settle in, a grateful word in the midst of pain or struggle might not be the first thought considered.

Gratitude is, in the end, an act of faith. It is an assertion of God's grace and providence. To say, with James, that "every generous act of giving" (1:17) comes from God can be a powerful witness in the face of a culture that celebrates the pulling of one's own bootstraps and sleeping in the bed one makes. And James will certainly speak of responsibilities in words to come. But all those words, and all their faith, begin with gratitude.

Do we?

Quick and Slow

A philosophy current in the time of this epistle—and not unknown in our own—urges moderation in all things. It has much to commend it as a wisdom by which to live. But it also has its limitations. Some things deserve more attention in our lives than others. Some things need more control and less free rein.

James urges a wisdom that is "immoderate" in its devotion to and practice of listening. "Quick to listen" (1:19) reminds us that, in the midst of community, only one voice can be heard at a time. And unless the exchange is simply between two persons, the balance of speaking and listening will require more of the latter unless we seek a Babel of voices sounding all at once.

"Slow to speak" (1:19) offers the hinge point of this concern. Notice, James does not say "be unwilling" to speak. He does not say "refrain" from speaking. The wisdom is found in slowness. It infers the choosing of times and moments when the word you bring needs to be sounded. To be muted is no Christian virtue—in fact, it is a denial of participation in community. But to always be mouthing one's thoughts and opinions destroys community just the same.

"Slow to anger" (1:19) offers James's third piece of wisdom here. It is easy to be offended. It is easy to take issue. And sometimes, sometimes, it is right to be offended and take issue. Jesus likely did not overturn the tables of moneychangers or speak of some religious leaders as "whitewashed tombs" without a sense of anger evoked by injustice. But neither did Jesus' entire ministry consist of overturning and accusing. One could easily make a case that Jesus' ministry of compassion and healing and forgiveness exhibits exactly the slowness to anger—and the quickness to love—that James has in mind here for his community . . . and for all Christian communities to follow.

Integrity

Context is everything. "Doers of the word, and not merely hearers" (1:22) is offered in the midst of much religious hearing in James's day. Rituals abounded. Readings and interpretations flourished. Zealots and Pharisees, Herodians and Sadducees, and now these Jews who followed the way of Jesus: Many philosophies and words could be heard and considered and weighed and debated. The question is: Would they be done?

"Doers of the word, and not merely hearers" speaks of the need for integrity in religious life—both for individuals and for communities. And still, context is critical. Some traditions deemed activist may be immersed in the doing of good deeds, sometimes to the neglect of the words or the One that would guide or measure those activities. Perhaps those traditions need to remember the grounding of James and his community deep in the word of tradition and the Living Word whom they had encountered. Perhaps there is a case to be made that such traditions, which may strike close to home for some of you who read this, may need to hear this proverb inverted: "Be hearers of the word and not doers only."

Integrity between word and deed is the point and issue, then and now. Faith resides in the holding of those two together in dynamic tension and fruitful interplay. And then as now, the proverb as James spoke it bears repeating in lives and traditions today that are good at talking and listening to the word of faith—but leave it there. Or those who think that faith is exhausted in its reception by us, rather than its expression. The actions do not generate the grace of which we speak; they merely, and profoundly, testify to its life, for us and others.

Doers of the word and not hearers only. Hold the two together. One cannot do what one has not heard or experienced. And one ought not hear and experience what one is not then committed to do.

Got Religion?

You may have seen the ad campaign: "Got milk?" It suggests that this or that experience of eating is not complete unless accompanied by a tall glass of milk.

Got religion? The experience of faith may not be complete without a "full" version of religion. And what does religion truly consist of? Micah once said: Do justice, love kindness, walk humbly with God. Jesus once taught: Love God, love neighbor as self.

And now James adds his own summary of the essence of religion: Care for the vulnerable, live "unstained by the world" (1:27).

I take the latter to mean: Live a life that is distinctive in contrast to how the wider world or culture dictates life. Live a life that dwells on the qualities and characteristics invoked by God's coming reign and evidenced in Jesus' own life.

And in both cases, such a life points us back to James' first dictum: Care for the vulnerable. Not because it is the socially correct thing to do. Not because it is the politically expedient thing to do. No, do it because it is God's way of doing things in the person of Jesus.

Got religion? Micah and Jesus and James all point us to the same basic compass to measure our take on that question. It is a compass whose "magnetic north" is care for others as God cares for us. The rituals, the prayers, the creeds, are all well and good . . . so long as they help us maintain that orientation that is God-ward in source and Christ-ward in example. So long as they do not confuse themselves with what God ultimately seeks from those whom James earlier identified as "a kind of first fruits of [God's] creatures" (1:18).

Got religion?

SHARING THE SCRIPTURE

Preparing Our Hearts

Meditate on this week's devotional reading, found in Psalm 92:1-8. In this wisdom psalm, the writer offers a song of thanksgiving, which is meant to be sung on the Sabbath. The psalmist is especially grateful for God's steadfast love, faithfulness, and works. Sing a song of praise or write your own psalm, giving thanks to God for whatever is on your heart today.

Pray that you and the adult learners will continually praise God.

Preparing Our Minds

Study the background in James 1 and lesson Scripture, verses 17-27. Think about the appropriate relationship between knowing what to do and acting on that knowledge.

Write on newsprint:
❑ information for next week's lesson, found under "Continue the Journey."
❑ activities for further spiritual growth in "Continue the Journey."

Decide if (and how) you will use the suggested class activities option under "Study

God's Plan for Faithful and Active Discipleship Rooted in God's Word."

LEADING THE CLASS

(1) Gather to Learn

❖ Welcome the class members and introduce any guests.

❖ Pray that today's participants will open their hearts and minds to receive the word that God has for them today.

❖ Choose several modern situations in which knowledge is well known, but people often choose not to act on that knowledge. Here are some examples, but ask the class for additional ones.
■ Smoking is a major risk factor for lung cancer, but many people continue to smoke.
■ Obesity and inactivity are major risk factors for heart disease, but obesity is rampant in the United States and far more people talk about exercise than actually do anything.
■ Wearing seatbelts reduces serious injury and fatalities, but some states

have had to legislate seatbelt use because people will not buckle up. The same is true of helmet use for motorcyclists.

❖ Ask: **Why do you think people are not motivated to act on the knowledge they have?**

❖ Read aloud today's focus statement: **Some people have abundant knowledge, but it does not necessarily motivate their behavior. What is the appropriate relationship between knowing what to do and acting on that knowledge? James tells us that as God's people we must not only hear the word of God but also respond to it with transforming action.**

(2) Study God's Plan for Faithful and Active Discipleship Rooted in God's Word

❖ Choose four volunteers to read James 1:17-27, divided as follows: verses 17-18, 19-21, 22-25, 26-27.

❖ **Option:** Read or retell each of these portions of Interpreting the Scripture after the appropriate segment is read. You may also wish to add information from Understanding the Scripture.

■ 1:17-18—"All Good Gifts"
■ 1:19-21—"Quick and Slow"
■ 1:22-25—"Integrity"
■ 1:26-27—"Got Religion?"

❖ Encourage the students to call out specific actions that disciples are to take, according to the passage from James. List these ideas on newsprint.

❖ Flesh out this list by brainstorming ways that one can, for example, be a doer of the word or control one's tongue or care for vulnerable members of society. Here are some ideas to "prime the pump": speak only well of other people; control anger until you can find a constructive way to deal with it; volunteer with church and non-profit groups that assist vulnerable people; prompt elected officials to enact legislation that will protect and aid vulnerable people. Refer to "Faith in Action: Reflecting Christ's

Image" at the beginning of this quarter's study for additional ideas.

❖ **Option:** Identify activities that the class can do together. Choose a task force to arrange for one or more of these activities to occur.

(3) Recognize That as People of the Word the Learners Must Allow That Word to Transform the Way They Live

❖ Point out that some very diligent Bible students know their Bibles well in an academic sense but do not allow God's word to transform the way they live. James states that hearing the word is not enough; one must act on it.

❖ Distribute paper and pencils. Provide quiet time for the adults to assess their way of living in light of James's teachings. Suggest that they slowly and silently reread James 1:17-27, lingering over words and ideas that speak to them. Suggest that they ask: **What is God trying to say to me about how I am to live my life? In what ways do I need to be transformed?** Some students may wish to jot down any ideas that come to mind.

❖ Break the silence by inviting volunteers to state any insights they have gleaned and choose to share.

(4) Identify Ways to Integrate Bible Study with the Rest of Life and Make a Commitment to Study

❖ Read these words: **For many people, finding time to study the Bible is difficult. So many people, projects, and plans clamor for attention. Yet, James reminds us that we cannot live as committed disciples unless we both know and act on God's word. What strategies have worked for you in making regular Bible study a priority in your busy life? How can you organize yourself to study productively?** If the class is large, you may want to divide into groups to discuss these questions. Here are some possible strategies to fit in time for study and organize your study: *get up earlier or go to bed later; study as you eat lunch; join a mid-week study group; use a pre-printed list of readings to guide your study; choose a biblical book and devote time to it; choose a topic and find concordance references to study it; write a question you want to explore and do some research to find possible answers; select a biblical theme, such as covenant or atonement, and study it.*

❖ Distribute paper and pencils if you have not already done so, or if students need additional paper. Challenge each participant to write a commitment stating (a) at least one step he or she will take to find time in his or her schedule to devote to Bible study, and (b) at least one idea for a particular study he or she would like to undertake.

❖ Suggest that the students hold these papers as you pray the closing prayer, and then place them in their Bibles as a reminder of what they plan to do.

(5) Continue the Journey

❖ Pray that all who have come today will delve more intentionally into the Bible and commit themselves to live holy lives that are continually being transformed by the word of God.

❖ Read aloud this preparation for next week's lesson. You may also want to post it on newsprint for the students to copy.
- **Title: Impartial Disciples**
- **Background Scripture: James 2**
- **Lesson Scripture: James 2:1-13**
- **Focus of the Lesson: People often**

value people in relation to material wealth. By what criteria do we determine our values? James teaches that Christians should make no distinctions in their treatment of people based on their material wealth.

❖ Challenge the students to complete one or more of these activities for further spiritual growth, which you will write on newsprint for the students to copy.

(1) **Make a conscious effort to be "quick to listen, slow to speak, slow to anger" (1:19). Notice how such behaviors improve relationships with other people. Also note how these behaviors make you feel.**

(2) **Do whatever you can this week to care for vulnerable members of society. James referred to orphans and widows, but look around to see who else needs care and take appropriate action.**

(3) **Spend extra time this week encountering God in the Scriptures. "Hearing" the word in this way will empower you to "do" the word more faithfully.**

❖ Sing or read aloud "Thy Word Is a Lamp."

❖ Conclude today's session by leading the class in this benediction, which is adapted from James 1:22, 25: **Let us now go forth as doers of the word and not merely hearers, for doers who act will be blessed in their doing.**

UNIT 3: IMAGES OF CHRIST IN US
IMPARTIAL DISCIPLES

PREVIEWING THE LESSON

Lesson Scripture: James 2:1-13
Background Scripture: James 2
Key Verse: James 2:5b

Focus of the Lesson:
People often value people in relation to material wealth. By what criteria do we determine our values? James teaches that Christians should make no distinctions in their treatment of people based on their material wealth.

Goals for the Learners:
(1) to examine what James wrote to fellow Christians about the requirement of impartiality in valuing other people.
(2) to explore their own treatment of others according to material wealth.
(3) to discern what they need to change in order to treat others impartially.

Pronunciation Guide:
Rahab (ray' hab)
Shema (shuh mah')

Supplies:
Bibles, newsprint and marker, paper and pencils, hymnals, pictures showing people of different socioeconomic positions

---

READING THE SCRIPTURE

NRSV
James 2:1-13

¹My brothers and sisters, do you with your acts of favoritism really believe in our glorious Lord Jesus Christ? ²For if a person with gold rings and in fine clothes comes into your assembly, and if a poor person in dirty clothes also comes in, ³and if you take notice of the one wearing the fine clothes

NIV
James 2:1-13

¹My brothers, as believers in our glorious Lord Jesus Christ, don't show favoritism. ²Suppose a man comes into your meeting wearing a gold ring and fine clothes, and a poor man in shabby clothes also comes in. ³If you show special attention to the man wearing fine clothes and say, "Here's a good

and say, "Have a seat here, please," while to the one who is poor you say, "Stand there," or, "Sit at my feet," [4]have you not made distinctions among yourselves, and become judges with evil thoughts? [5]Listen, my beloved brothers and sisters. **Has not God chosen the poor in the world to be rich in faith** and to be heirs of the kingdom that he has promised to those who love him? [6]But you have dishonored the poor. Is it not the rich who oppress you? Is it not they who drag you into court? [7]Is it not they who blaspheme the excellent name that was invoked over you?

[8]You do well if you really fulfill the royal law according to the scripture, "You shall love your neighbor as yourself." [9]But if you show partiality, you commit sin and are convicted by the law as transgressors. [10]For whoever keeps the whole law but fails in one point has become accountable for all of it. [11]For the one who said, "You shall not commit adultery," also said, "You shall not murder." Now if you do not commit adultery but if you murder, you have become a transgressor of the law. [12]So speak and so act as those who are to be judged by the law of liberty. [13]For judgment will be without mercy to anyone who has shown no mercy; mercy triumphs over judgment.

seat for you," but say to the poor man, "You stand there" or "Sit on the floor by my feet," [4]have you not discriminated among yourselves and become judges with evil thoughts?

[5]Listen, my dear brothers: **Has not God chosen those who are poor in the eyes of the world to be rich in faith** and to inherit the kingdom he promised those who love him? [6]But you have insulted the poor. Is it not the rich who are exploiting you? Are they not the ones who are dragging you into court? [7]Are they not the ones who are slandering the noble name of him to whom you belong?

[8]If you really keep the royal law found in Scripture, "Love your neighbor as yourself," you are doing right. [9]But if you show favoritism, you sin and are convicted by the law as lawbreakers. [10]For whoever keeps the whole law and yet stumbles at just one point is guilty of breaking all of it. [11]For he who said, "Do not commit adultery," also said, "Do not murder." If you do not commit adultery but do commit murder, you have become a lawbreaker.

[12]Speak and act as those who are going to be judged by the law that gives freedom, [13]because judgment without mercy will be shown to anyone who has not been merciful. Mercy triumphs over judgment!

UNDERSTANDING THE SCRIPTURE

James 2:1-7. The word translated as "favoritism" is a compound word in Greek that literally means "to take/receive the face." This entire chapter deals with the meaning of faith, introduced here in verse 1 with the issue of how favoritism "really believes." The example of rich and poor entering the assembly ("synagogue") is likely not imaginary but actual. Paul's correspondence (for example, 1 Corinthians 11:21) suggests clear economic divisions within the Christian community. The

offering Paul solicited from Corinth and Galatia was specifically for the relief of the poor in the Jerusalem church (Galatians 2:10). The response to the rich and poor is not simply in the tone taken (the rich receive an invitation, "please," while the poor are given directives). "Sit at my feet" speaks of assuming a position of submission. "Made distinctions" (2:4) uses the same verb as in Acts 11:12 and 15:9, where the divisions in mind had to do with the separation of Jew and Gentile. The "excellent name that was invoked over you" (2:7, a reference to baptism and/or benediction) links back to verse 1's "our glorious Lord Jesus Christ." It is not just that social favoritisms are bad manners: They are denials of the faith taught and practiced by Jesus.

James 2:8-13. "Royal" law suggests sovereignty, and sovereignty in the New Testament belongs to the kingdom of Jesus, which he came pronouncing. At the core of that proclamation is the verse quoted here from Leviticus 19:18 (and from Jesus' own teaching): "You shall love your neighbor as yourself." Partiality (a variation on the same word translated earlier as "favoritism") is, again, not just poor etiquette: It is sin. Beginning at verse 10, James argues that offense at one point of the law (and clearly in the background is the command to love neighbor) is to fail in it all. In one sense, it parallels Jesus' line of argument in the Sermon on the Mount. There, for example, it was not simply the commission of adultery that brings on its judgment, but the very thought of adultery (Matthew 5:27-28). Neither James nor Jesus engages in legalism. Rather, they seek to put a practical spin on the calling of faith. In the context of this passage, it is not enough to claim the faith of Jesus and then practice favoritism that runs counter to Jesus' way and command to love. The reference to "law of liberty" in verse 12 hearkens back to James 1:25, where the emphasis is on hearing as well as doing. That emphasis remains in place here. Only now, the importance of integrity between "hearing and doing" now is framed (and will be argued in the second half of the chapter) in the integrity between "faith and works." The concluding word in verse 13 on judgment and mercy echoes Jesus' teachings on forgiveness (see Matthew 6:14-15).

James 2:14-17. "Faith and works" comes to the forefront of James's epistle and remains there throughout the rest of this chapter. "What good is it" is very close to the same phrase used by Jesus when his first passion prediction leads to the teaching of

discipleship: *"For what will it profit them to gain the whole world and forfeit their life?"* (Mark 8:36, italics added). James gives the example of one in dire straits for whom faith's works are needed. To be without clothing or food reflects extreme vulnerability, expressive of the type of need James earlier identified as the focus of true religion (1:27). Verse 16's benediction (which means "good word") is not good enough; the repetition of the previous "what is the good of that" only underscores the irony and incompleteness. Separation of good wishes from supplying bodily needs does not cut it. Such "faith," James declares, is dead on arrival.

James 2:18-19. Who the "someone" is who interrupts the line of thought in verse 18 is not identified. Whether James lifts this from some ongoing dialogue within the community or invents it as a rhetorical device to further develop his point is uncertain. What is clear, however, is James's next direction. The issue at hand is a contest of "showing." It is a one-sided dialogue. The text offers no voicing of what faith apart from works would look like. In a sense, that is because James has already done that in the preceding empty benediction and even in the assembly gathered in Jesus' name that falls all over itself fawning over the rich. While the examples James will produce of works that demonstrate faith appear in the concluding verses (2:21-26), in verse 19 James does make one introductory argument. The belief that "God is one" sounds very close to the confession of the *Shema* of Judaism, found in Deuteronomy 6:4: "Hear O Israel: the LORD is our God, the LORD alone" (which can also be translated, "The LORD our God, the LORD is one"). A Jewish Christian community like that of James' community would have confessed that as well. But James then makes the point: Even that confession does not exhaust faith, for "even the demons believe—and shudder." Believing is not a matter of words alone; it is a matter of living.

James 2:21-26. James offer two examples

of works that show faith. No other figure save Moses rivaled the figure of Abraham in Judaism. And Abraham, for James, proves to be the father of faith in works when he offers Isaac on the altar. "You see" (2:22) goes back to the "showing" promised in verse 18. But James adds another example: Rahab. Jewish tradition celebrates Rahab not only for her confession of faith (Joshua 2:11) but also for her hospitality to the spies sent by Joshua (see the rest of that chapter for the full story). That connection with hospitality may also provide a subtle link in this text between her and Abraham. For Abraham, too, was remembered for his practice of hospitality to strangers, one of whom was none other than God (Genesis 18:1 and following). Such hospitality forms an eloquent tie with this entire chapter in James and its call to love neighbor and welcome the poor. One final point worth noting: The last verse speaks of faith without works as the body without spirit. One might have expected the pairing to suggest spirit and faith, and body and works. But it is the other way around. In the language of James, works are the "spirit" of faith—they are faith's expression and empowering.

INTERPRETING THE SCRIPTURE

Playing Favorites

Years ago, the Smothers Brothers comedy duo capitalized on a running gag about "Mom always liked you best." Playing favorites is a very old, and not always humorous, game. We read in Genesis 25:28: "Isaac loved Esau . . . Rebekah loved Jacob." The favoritism there led to deceit and years of estrangement.

But playing favorites within families does not exhaust its devastating potential. Does the phrase "teacher's pet" ring a bell? Other phrases, less suited for publication, might be called to mind in terms of favorites played (and favoritism sought) at work.

The epistle of James exposes the pernicious playing of favorites within the body of Christ. It is cast in uncomfortably familiar terms of "whom would we prefer to have as members?" The ones who will be strong contributors and magnets of folk similarly situated in the ranks of economy and prestige? Or the ones who will likely, initially, require our assistance and not glean popular acceptance of the kind of people we let in the door (or in the pulpit).

Part of the problem with playing favorites in the church goes deeper than superficial longings for the right kind of people. You see, when we prefer the company of these over those, there is the subtle temptation to presume God does the same. It is not so great a jump from playing favorites to, say, the racism that counts one group as "nearer" to the image of God than others. James casts the issue in economic and class terms. Peter and Paul weighed in on this in the issue of whether Gentiles would be included or excluded.

And what of us? Where do we find ourselves drawn to play favorites in the church—and on what basis? Who do we fall all over ourselves to make room for—and who do we barely have time to address with today's equivalent of "sit at my feet"? James's opening question bears repeating: "Do you with your acts of favoritism really believe in our glorious Lord Jesus Christ?" (2:1).

The Ungospel of Materialism

The epistle of James has always had a difficult time of it in the church. Martin Luther took a dim view of its (alleged) favoring works over faith (more on that later). He called it an "epistle of straw" and wondered if it should not be deleted from the canon of Scripture.

I suspect James would be found wanting in our day, though not for Luther's reasons. James is not the sort of work to be appreciated by individuals and a society for whom materialism and the possession of wealth are taken as hallmarks of God's blessings.

The view of the rich in James is not unlike what we hear in the teachings of Jesus, who at one point offers the observation: "How hard it is for those who have wealth to enter the kingdom of God!" (Luke 18:24). Our passage from James portrays the irony of playing favorites with the very ones who oppress. And if that were not enough, the opening of James 5 offers an even starker indictment of all those for whom wealth is synonymous with power and its corruption.

So what do we do with James? Do we, like Luther, attack it as an "epistle of straw" that misses the gospel's point? Or do we take a deep breath and allow its framing of faith to address (or confront, as the case may be) our view of and participation in the world and its structures?

In one sense, the title given above of "The Ungospel of Materialism" is misleading. James is very concerned with the material world and bodily existence. Indeed, he castigates prayers that speak soothing words and leave pained and deprived bodies untouched. James simply practices the materialism of human dignity in opposition to human greed. Wealth is not the sign and seal of God's favor. At best, it may become a means to tend to others in the name of God. But that takes us next into the core concern of James: the relationship between faith, works, and love.

Faith, Works, and Love

Luther's primary objection to James came precisely on the nature of faith and works. He perceived James to elevate works above faith, even to exclude it. After all, James avows not just once but twice that

faith without works is dead (2:17, 26).

But the words of James that Luther took as a contradiction of faith by works can also be understood as the complementary nature of faith and works. They are not "either/or" propositions. They certainly are not in this passage. "Works" occurs twelve times in James 2:14-26—and in all but two of those times, it occurs in conjunction with faith. The two belong together. All that James seeks to say, and with good reason if you accept his argument in verses 1-13, is that you cannot speak of faith separated from the works faith evokes. It would be like, as he uses for an illustration, the "faith" of demons (2:19). If having the right words and concepts alone was all that was necessary, the demons would be fine because they believe in God. Faith, however, has to do with responsiveness to God. Responsiveness that not only forms in an internal attitude and trust but also takes shape in outward actions that embody trust.

And the most critical of all of faith's works is love. It is, as James speaks of it, the "royal" command. It is the teaching of Jesus as well as of Leviticus 19. Ironically, given the tendency to make Paul and James opposites, it is also Paul's message: "Owe no one anything, except to love one another; for the one who loves another has fulfilled the law" (Romans 13:8). Love negates favoritism. Love surpasses materialism. Love fulfills the command Jesus gives, and embodies faith in God even as God's love for us came embodied in Jesus.

Mercy

Mercy can be a peculiar word. It may be used today of a plea that seeks reprieve from some power wielded over us. In that sense, it is the religious version of the cry of "uncle" in children's games. In the Old Testament, the most common word for mercy had largely to do with the covenant relationship between God and Israel. Its connotations ranged from loyalty to kindness to pity, but usually, whatever the connotation, it had to do with a situation of helping one in need. So the "mercy" of God related to the ways in which God helped Israel, deserved or not, simply because of God's covenanting commitment. In the New Testament, mercy often came linked with a plea to be healed ("have mercy on me"). As such, mercy still had to do with that foundational understanding of God's mercy as God's activity on our behalf that helps us in time of need, apart from our ability to help ourselves.

Here in James 2:13, though, the intended subject of mercy (that is, the one called on to show it) is not God (at least at first) but us. We are commanded to act with mercy. For if we do not show mercy, well, what goes around comes around. It is like the story Jesus told of the unforgiving servant (Matthew 18:23-35). It is like the way Jesus teaches us to pray ("forgive us our debts *as we also have forgiven our debtors*," Matthew 6:12, italics added).

Like love, mercy embodies faith. Like the absence of love, the absence of mercy betrays faith.

SHARING THE SCRIPTURE

Preparing Our Hearts

Meditate on this week's devotional reading, found in Matthew 25:31-46. In Jesus' discourse about how we will be judged when he comes again, note the criteria for determining who will be rewarded and who will be punished. Neither right belief nor knowledge is even mentioned. What's important is how one has treated those in need. Examine your own behavior. Would you be sent to Christ's right hand—or his left? What action do you need to take now?

Pray that you and the adult learners will be aware of needs and do whatever is in your power to meet those needs.

Preparing Our Minds

Study the background from James 2 and lesson Scripture, verses 1-13. Ponder the criteria you use to determine how you value other people.

Write on newsprint:
❏ information for next week's lesson, found under "Continue the Journey."
❏ activities for further spiritual growth in "Continue the Journey."

Locate in magazines, in books, or on the Internet pictures depicting people from a variety of socioeconomic stations. Be careful about stereotyping any group of people. Mark the pages or cut out the photos you plan to use.

Create the suggested lecture for "Examine What James Wrote to Fellow Christians About the Requirement of Impartiality in Valuing Other People."

LEADING THE CLASS

(1) Gather to Learn

❖ Welcome the class members and introduce any guests.
❖ Pray that all who have come today will feel welcomed and cherished in the midst of the group.
❖ Distribute paper and pencils. Direct the students to write the following information, adding a letter (and numbers 1 through 4) for each picture you have.

A	1	2	3	4
B	1	2	3	4

❖ Hold up, one at a time, at least five pictures of people in various socio-economic positions. Say "A," "B," and so on as you show each picture.

❖ Ask the students to circle the number that best corresponds to how likely they would be to want to get to know this person and treat him or her as an equal, with "1" being "No Way" and "4" being "Absolutely."

❖ Divide the students into groups and have them talk about what number they assigned to each person's picture and why that number was selected.

❖ Read aloud today's focus statement: **People often value people in relation to material wealth. By what criteria do we determine our values? James teaches that Christians should make no distinctions in their treatment of people based on their material wealth.**

(2) Examine What James Wrote to Fellow Christians About the Requirement of Impartiality in Valuing Other People

❖ Select a volunteer to read James 2:1-13.

❖ Present a lecture, based on Understanding the Scripture, to familiarize the class with James's teachings in verses 1-13. Note that James's particular concern here is the church's partiality in favor of the rich.

❖ Ask: **In what ways, if any, do churches show partiality toward the rich? Why?**

❖ Distribute additional paper. Challenge the students to read verses 1-13 silently and then write in their own words what James might say to the modern church in general on this issue of treating wealthy people with greater respect than those who are poor. Suggest that the adults consider these questions: **Why does this happen? How can it be stopped? Why would impartial treatment be better for both those who are poor and those who are rich?**

❖ Encourage the students to read to a partner what they have written.

❖ Bring the class back together. Invite comments from the adults, including ideas for making your congregation more welcoming to all.

(3) Explore the Learners' Treatment of Others According to Material Wealth

❖ Read aloud this story and ask the students to finish it as honestly as possible: **A new neighbor has just moved in across the street. You notice that the moving truck is there all day, carrying in very nice furniture and box after box of "stuff." The new owner arrives in a late-model Mercedes. You decide to go over and introduce yourself. [Tell us how you will dress for the occasion and what you will take. What is your attitude toward the new neighbors, based solely on your first impression? Why would you hope to become friends with these folks—or wouldn't you?]**

❖ Read aloud this story and ask the students to finish it as honestly as possible: **A new neighbor has just moved in across the street. You notice that the family arrives with a small U-Haul trailer, not much furniture, and an old car that needs a paint job. You decide to go over and introduce yourself. [Tell us how you will dress for the occasion and what you will take. What is your attitude toward the new neighbors, based solely on your first impression? Why would you hope to become friends with these folks—or wouldn't you?]**

❖ Encourage the students to compare and contrast their attitudes toward these two new families, which, in this case, are based solely on what can be observed about their material goods. (Acknowledge that attitudes may change once the students get to know these families personally.)

❖ Ask: **What would James say about our responses to these two new neighbors?**

(4) Discern What the Learners Need to Change in Order to Treat Others Impartially

❖ Post the pictures you used for "Gather to Learn" where everyone can see them.

❖ Ask the students to turn over the papers they used for that activity and list any attitudes that they need to change in order to act impartially. Next to each attitude, encourage them to write one step they can take to begin to change.

❖ Conclude the session by asking the learners to read in unison today's key verse, James 2:5b. Then add, **"And the people of the Lord said Amen."**

(5) Continue the Journey

❖ Pray that all who have come today will go forth ready to act impartially toward all people.

❖ Read aloud this preparation for next week's lesson. You may also want to post it on newsprint for the students to copy.

- ■ Title: Wise Speakers
- ■ Background Scripture: James 3
- ■ Lesson Scripture: James 3:1-10, 13-18
- ■ Focus of the Lesson: People often say unwise and harmful things to and about others. How can people become kinder in their speech? James exhorts people to discipline their tongues by accepting the wisdom and peace that come from above.
- ■ Challenge the students to complete one or more of these activities for further spiritual growth, which you will write on newsprint for the students to copy.

(1) Think objectively about your own congregation. How would someone of a different socio-economic group be treated as a visitor in your church? What would James say about your response in light of his teachings?

(2) Look again at your congregation. Do you feel that certain individuals, who may have more of this world's goods, try to lord their wealth over others by insisting that things be done their way? How do you and other members of the congregation respond?

(3) Research disparities between the rich and poor in first-century Palestine. How does your research support or refute what James was saying about the rich oppressing the poor? How are these disparities still present today? Are James's words equally applicable to today's church? Why or why not?

❖ Sing or read aloud "O God of Every Nation."

❖ Conclude today's session by leading the class in this benediction, which is adapted from James 1:22, 25: **Let us now go forth as doers of the word and not merely hearers, for doers who act will be blessed in their doing.**

UNIT 3: IMAGES OF CHRIST IN US

WISE SPEAKERS

PREVIEWING THE LESSON

Lesson Scripture: James 3:1-10, 13-18
Background Scripture: James 3
Key Verse: James 3:10

Focus of the Lesson:
People often say unwise and harmful things to and about others. How can people become kinder in their speech? James exhorts people to discipline their tongues by accepting the wisdom and peace that come from above.

Goals for the Learners:
(1) to discover James's advice about using the tongue wisely.
(2) to examine their speaking habits.
(3) to resolve to discipline their speech.

Pronunciation Guide:
shalom (shah lohm')

Supplies:
Bibles, newsprint and marker, paper and pencils, hymnals, recording of a news or talk show and appropriate player

---

READING THE SCRIPTURE

NRSV
James 3:1-10, 13-18

¹Not many of you should become teachers, my brothers and sisters, for you know that we who teach will be judged with greater strictness. ²For all of us make many mistakes. Anyone who makes no mistakes in speaking is perfect, able to keep the whole body in check with a bridle. ³If we put bits into the mouths of horses to make them obey us, we guide their whole bodies. ⁴Or

NIV
James 3:1-10, 13-18

¹Not many of you should presume to be teachers, my brothers, because you know that we who teach will be judged more strictly. ²We all stumble in many ways. If anyone is never at fault in what he says, he is a perfect man, able to keep his whole body in check.

³When we put bits into the mouths of horses to make them obey us, we can turn

look at ships: though they are so large that it takes strong winds to drive them, yet they are guided by a very small rudder wherever the will of the pilot directs. [5]So also the tongue is a small member, yet it boasts of great exploits.

How great a forest is set ablaze by a small fire! [6]And the tongue is a fire. The tongue is placed among our members as a world of iniquity; it stains the whole body, sets on fire the cycle of nature, and is itself set on fire by hell. [7]For every species of beast and bird, of reptile and sea creature, can be tamed and has been tamed by the human species, [8]but no one can tame the tongue—a restless evil, full of deadly poison. [9]With it we bless the Lord and Father, and with it we curse those who are made in the likeness of God. [10]**From the same mouth come blessing and cursing. My brothers and sisters, this ought not to be so.**

[13]Who is wise and understanding among you? Show by your good life that your works are done with gentleness born of wisdom. [14]But if you have bitter envy and selfish ambition in your hearts, do not be boastful and false to the truth. [15]Such wisdom does not come down from above, but is earthly, unspiritual, devilish. [16]For where there is envy and selfish ambition, there will also be disorder and wickedness of every kind. [17]But the wisdom from above is first pure, then peaceable, gentle, willing to yield, full of mercy and good fruits, without a trace of partiality or hypocrisy. [18]And a harvest of righteousness is sown in peace for those who make peace.

the whole animal. [4]Or take ships as an example. Although they are so large and are driven by strong winds, they are steered by a very small rudder wherever the pilot wants to go. [5]Likewise the tongue is a small part of the body, but it makes great boasts. Consider what a great forest is set on fire by a small spark. [6]The tongue also is a fire, a world of evil among the parts of the body. It corrupts the whole person, sets the whole course of his life on fire, and is itself set on fire by hell.

[7]All kinds of animals, birds, reptiles and creatures of the sea are being tamed and have been tamed by man, [8]but no man can tame the tongue. It is a restless evil, full of deadly poison.

[9]With the tongue we praise our Lord and Father, and with it we curse men, who have been made in God's likeness. [10]**Out of the same mouth come praise and cursing. My brothers, this should not be.**

[13]Who is wise and understanding among you? Let him show it by his good life, by deeds done in the humility that comes from wisdom. [14]But if you harbor bitter envy and selfish ambition in your hearts, do not boast about it or deny the truth. [15]Such "wisdom" does not come down from heaven but is earthly, unspiritual, of the devil. [16]For where you have envy and selfish ambition, there you find disorder and every evil practice. [17]But the wisdom that comes from heaven is first of all pure; then peace-loving, considerate, submissive, full of mercy and good fruit, impartial and sincere. [18]Peacemakers who sow in peace raise a harvest of righteousness.

UNDERSTANDING THE SCRIPTURE

James 3:1-2. James has long been identified with the Hebrew wisdom tradition brought to bear on Christian community. That identification finds in these opening verses a caution: "Teaching," which may be seen as the developing of wisdom within community, is not a vocation open to any and all comers. Precisely because of the importance of wisdom, those entrusted with this office in the community bear special responsibilities. The focus of those responsibilities has to do with "speaking" (3:2). In a letter sometimes portrayed as exclusively focusing on works and action, here begins an extended treatment (through the end of this chapter) on the importance of words. The theme of works does not deny the importance of words; it only insists that the two be joined with integrity. A key theme that will be followed and developed in a variety of images is offered now in verse 2: the "bridling" of speech for the good of the "whole body."

James 3:3-8. That theme of "bridling" speech, and in particular the tongue, is explored in these verses through several distinct images: horses, ships, fire, and the taming of wild animals. It should be noted that secular writings of those times dealing with the importance of speech (and its control) use all of these images as well. James thus uses terms and arguments familiar both to his immediate audience in the Christian community and to the surrounding culture. Much of this passage focuses on the contrasts. On the one hand, it is between the tongue as such a small "member" of the body and the effect it can have. On the other hand, it is the way in which such a limited tool as a bridle or rudder can have such power in terms of steering in a positive direction. It is to be noted that James strongly underscores the negative influence of the tongue. He does so not on the basis of social etiquette (better to listen than to speak) but on religious grounds (the tongue as a "world of iniquity" and "a restless evil"). The epistle's words here strike a consistent chord with the author's direct connection in 1:26 between an unbridled tongue and worthless religion.

James 3:9-12. The religious nature of James's comments on speech comes to the forefront in verse 9. Speech can be both gift and threat: The same tongue may bless God and curse others. The cursing of others,

again, is not just poor manners. It is sin against God, for the ones being cursed "are made in the likeness of God" (3:9). The previous passage repeated the phrase "whole body" (3:6), an image Paul used (body of Christ) of Christian community; like Paul, James places a premium on community. The bonds between us in community are not merely social in nature, and as this epistle has clearly argued, the way we treat and act toward others reveals the truth of our religion. Even so does James now argue that our words are equally revealing. The contradiction between a tongue that at once blesses and curses summons the epistle's imperative voice in verse 10: "this ought not to be so." The nature of that contradiction is given illustration in the examples of a spring, a fig tree, and salt water. One thing in nature cannot produce two different results. Blessing and cursing denies the integrity of our faith, just as much as offering a pious benediction but offering no action to back up the words (2:16).

James 3:13. Whereas the epistle focuses on speech and tongue in this chapter, it does not do so at the expense of works. "Show by your good life" keeps that core theme of the entire letter alive and clear in this exploration into the power of words. The word translated "life" in verse 13 is not the word typically used in the New Testament, but one whose connotation has to do with "conduct" or "lifestyle." "Wise" and "understanding" in verse 13a underscore the broader meanings of the wisdom tradition that go beyond the ability of one word to express. Remember, too, that wisdom in James as in the Hebrew tradition was not limited to measures of intelligence or even years of experience. Rather, it had to do with the ability to live one's life in a way congruent with what is "true" in the world and "true" to God's purposes. In other words, wisdom was knowing not just what was what, but what to do in faithful response.

James 3:14-18. Sometimes, an idea or

truth can be more clearly seen by describing its opposite or absence. That approach is taken by James in verses 14-16. Here, the opposite of wisdom is depicted. The emphasis has shifted now away from the connection between words and actions to attitudes and actions. The two opposites of wisdom that draw special focus are "envy" and "selfish ambition"—a word that is elsewhere translated as "partisanship" and "factious." The danger of those attitudes is not simply an individual matter. Wanting what is another's and the tendency to split up into rival sides threaten the well-being of community. Such attitudes foster divisions and resentments, a theme that will be developed even more extensively in the next chapter. Following the style of contrasts used earlier in the images about the tongue, the epistle now moves into a positive statement of what wisdom will consist of. The list found in verse 17 parallels other such lists in New Testament writings (Galatians 5:22-23; Colossians 3:12-14). They in turn resemble lists of virtues current in the wider culture. Notice, in James's list, the singling out of "good fruits." Attitudes alone do not suffice. Wisdom involves action. Wisdom seeks integrity between word and deed and attitude, an attribute underscored by the final quality in that list: the absence of "hypocrisy." In verse 18 is a benediction of sorts. In the exhibition of these attitudes and actions born of wisdom, a "harvest of righteousness" is sown. And its sowing is "in peace" for those who "make peace." Clearly, wisdom aims at the establishment of peace in the community. As James writes from the Hebrew tradition of wisdom, it is to be remembered that "peace" (*shalom*) in Hebrew is not simply the absence of conflict, but the presence and abundance of all that makes for life.

INTERPRETING THE SCRIPTURE

Word Power

Church nominating committees occasionally go about their jobs by confiding in would-be candidates for this office or that committee: "Don't worry. It doesn't require much." A wink and a nod later, a slate is full. But has calling been clarified?

Imagine James standing before the congregation two weeks before the start of Sunday school, with several teaching positions still unfilled: "Not many of you should become teachers, my brothers and sisters, for you know that we who teach will be judged with greater strictness" (3:1). Can you imagine the superintendent's eyes rolling backward?

Sometimes, we do take ourselves and our callings lightly. Sometimes, we may take our words and those of others lightly. They are, after all, just words. And didn't James just say during the last couple of sessions that works, not faith, is the key? Do not mishear James. Words are critical. The supposedly modern discovery that the way we talk about others (or ourselves) forms the way we think about and act toward them (or ourselves) is as ancient as this epistle, and older. Words have extraordinary power. Talk to a child who receives a steady diet of blame at home. Think of the times when you have been moved by a sermon or angered by a remark.

James stresses active faith—not because words are unimportant but because of the actions that words can set loose! Consider your congregation. Do the words spoken about what you do and who you are ring consistent? Consider your family life. Do the words routinely passed among those with whom you are in relationship nurture and support or critique and undermine? At times we neglect words, rationalizing that as long as we get the actions right all will be well. But we forget that words, like thoughts, can dictate the directions we take, almost without our thinking. Words have power, for they have potential.

The Potential of Words

Already in the previous section, this theme has been opened. Words have all the potential in the world—for good and for ill. That is not merely a linguistic truth. That is a religious truth that goes to the core of our identity as followers of Christ.

The God-given potential of words comes revealed in one of the images with which the New Testament speaks of Jesus: the Word of God. "In the beginning was the Word" the Gospel of John commences. And from that beginning, from that Word, comes all that we hope and trust in the way of love and grace. Think, too, of how the Christian community has tragically turned that Word of life and grace into a Word that bludgeons. If you do not believe as I do, you do not belong. The church down through our history has spoken some very ungracious words in the name of the Word. We understand from the inside out what James reminds us of in verse 9 about blessing and cursing with the same mouth. And that is a situation James confronts with a clear "this ought not to be so" (3:10, today's key verse).

The gift of the Word to us underscores that care needs to be taken with our words. Much has been made of late with the expression "What Would Jesus Do (WWJD)?" James reminds us that the equally pertinent calling is "What Would Jesus Say?" What would Jesus say through my words to one with whom I disagree? *You are gay (or straight), so you can burn in hell. . . .* What are the words Jesus would speak through your community of faith . . . and what actions would best accompany those words?

Words can build community or destroy it. Words can nurture fragile individuals or send them crashing down into despair. Words have all the potential in the world— and our choice of words reveals whether the potential we choose is for good or for ill. So the next time you find yourself wondering what to say or wondering what the church should say, ask: What would Jesus say? For in truth, Jesus is waiting to speak through you . . . to and on behalf of "those who are made in the likeness of God" (3:9).

The Good Life

"The Good Life." In the ears, and eyes, of many, that phrase likely evokes thoughts of leisure filled with (over)abundance. "The good life" is often the driving image of advertising, to sell this or that product . . . with always, always, a new addition to the allure every time satisfaction seems close at hand. Such a "good life" centers on self.

James writes of "the good life." It is not, however, a life relieved of responsibility, but one where responsibilities and actions have found peaceful co-existence. Adjectives like *gentleness* and *purity* describe both its gift to us and its expression by us. It is a life full of mercy and "willing to yield."

So: Which good life would you rather have?

It is not a rhetorical question. The church, too, is in the advertising business—we simply give it the religious-sounding name of evangelism. We are in the business of purveying a vision of life blessed by God. How does it compare with the visions of blessed lives elsewhere on today's market? Sometimes, for the life of me, I find it difficult to tell the difference. Some folks will tell you that to be blessed of God is to have all the good stuff that the "world" gets to enjoy. Indeed, God wants to bless us if we only ask—and only make that donation that will "prove" our faith. The fact that donations tend to enrich their coffers is, well, part of the cycle.

Does that cycle jibe with what James suggests about the good life born of wisdom? Of gentleness and a willingness to yield? Of mercy and a lack of hypocrisy?

It is not a rhetorical question. The vision we offer is the news we bring. Is it good news, or just more of the same you can see on all the other channels?

Sowing and Reaping Peace

Earlier in the epistle, James wrote that "anger does not produce God's righteousness" (1:20). What does produce righteousness, that state of experiencing God's acceptance and grace, comes in the gift— and vocation—of peace. In the comments on James 3:18 in Understanding the Scripture, the point was made of the Hebrew tradition surrounding *shalom*. Peace not just as "absence" of bad things but also as "presence" of life-giving things is critical in hearing this text . . . and in understanding our lives. Peace exists not simply when the community is not fighting. Peace is experienced when the community understands with gratitude and lives with obedience toward the One who is life's source.

It is not anger or stridency that enables us to accept, and then live on the basis of, God's righteousness that is God's gracious acceptance. It is a spirit of peace that moves us into genuine relationship with God and neighbor. And more than just spirit, it is our actions of peace-making that respond to God's movement toward us. We do not make our own peace with God. Righteousness is not our work to do. But God's gracious acceptance of us is a gift for us to respond to and extend toward others. God's peace is not just for individuals. This passage and chapter has consistently dealt with the exercise of wisdom in the context of Christian community. Peace comes to the community in its exercise of peace-making in the name of and for the sake of God with those made in God's likeness. We have reaped the harvest of God's peace. So wisdom now is lived in the vocation of sowing that peace.

SHARING THE SCRIPTURE

Preparing Our Hearts

Meditate on this week's devotional reading, found in Proverbs 15:1-4 and Proverbs 16:21-24. Most of these proverbs relate to how one uses language. Do you agree with these sayings? Why or why not? Do you watch your own tongue so as to live according to these sayings? What evidence can you give to support your answer?

Pray that you and the adult learners will be aware of how your words have the potential to heal or hurt others.

Preparing Our Minds

Study the background, which includes all of James 3, and lesson Scripture, James 3:1-10, 13-18. Consider your own speech. How can you become kinder with your words?

Write on newsprint:
❑ sentence for "Examine the Learners' Speaking Habits."
❑ information for next week's lesson, found under "Continue the Journey."
❑ activities for further spiritual growth in "Continue the Journey."

Make an audio and/or video recording of a news or talk show that you can play back to the class. Select a two- or three-minute segment of this recording in which the speakers demonstrate James's idea of the destructive power of speech for use with "Examine the Learners' Speaking Habits."

LEADING THE CLASS

(1) Gather to Learn

❖ Welcome the class members and introduce any guests.

❖ Pray that those who have come today will be careful about how they talk to and about others.

❖ Read these two Chinese proverbs:

■ **A word rashly spoken cannot be brought back by a chariot and four horses.**

■ **Mischief all comes from much opening of the mouth.**

❖ Ask: **Without disclosing specifics, can you recall a time when you wanted to take back words you had spoken? Why did you feel that way? What were you able to do to resolve or reconcile this difficult situation?**

❖ Read aloud today's focus statement: **People often say unwise and harmful things to and about others. How can people become kinder in their speech? James exhorts people to discipline their tongues by accepting the wisdom and peace that come from above.**

(2) Discover James's Advice About Using the Tongue Wisely

❖ Choose a volunteer to read James 3:1-10.

■ List the images that James uses to make his points about speech: *horses, ships, fire.* Make sure that the class understands that a small, seemingly insignificant thing—such as a bridle, rudder, or small flame—is able to direct a large "object" or cause massive destruction. Note that James contrasts the control of the tongue with the taming of wild animals, claiming that the latter is far easier than the former. Ask: **What other images can you think of to illustrate James's teachings?** List these on newsprint. Possibilities include:

steering wheel guiding a vehicle, mouse controlling a computer, and laser directing powerful light.

■ Read or retell "The Potential of Words" in Interpreting the Scripture.

❖ Select a student to read James 3:13-18.

■ Divide a sheet of newsprint into two columns. On the left side list the characteristics of godly wisdom, as found in these verses. On the right side, list the traits of earthly wisdom.

■ Use entries for James 3:13 and 14-18 in Understanding the Scripture to flesh out the contrasts between these two kinds of wisdom and their effects.

(3) Examine the Learners' Speaking Habits

❖ Play an excerpt from an audio or video recording of a news or talk show.

❖ Discuss these questions with the class.

(1) **How would you describe the speaker's attitude toward his or her subject?**

(2) **What words or tone of voice (or body language) conveyed this attitude to you?**

(3) **Do you think the speakers' words were fair, even if they were offering criticism? Why or why not?**

❖ Post this sentence on newsprint: **I can't imagine you said that.** Invite volunteers to read the sentence with as many changes in inflection of voice as possible. The easiest way to do this is to stress the first word "I" and then talk about what the emphasis there means. Next, emphasize "can't imagine" and consider what that means, and so on. Some tones of voice will come across as highly judgmental, whereas others may be funny. The class may want to "play" with this sentence in small groups.

❖ Conclude this portion of the lesson by drawing everyone together and asking them to consider these questions silently.

(1) **What would you say about the way your own words come across to others?**

(2) **What do you think others would say about the way they hear your words?**

❖ Break the silence by encouraging volunteers to summarize ideas they have gleaned so far.

(4) Resolve to Discipline Speech

❖ Point out that often in life we have "alarms" that notify or warn us. For example, a buzzer may go off when it's time to get up; a teakettle whistles when the water is hot; the computer signals when a new e-mail has arrived; and the car warns us that we've left our lights on. Ask: **What kinds of "alarms" go off when our tongue is out of control?** (Examples include: *The body language of the person to whom we are speaking changes; the conversation ends abruptly; we feel stung in our hearts because we know we've hurt someone; someone else registers disapproval.*)

❖ Distribute paper and pencils. Encourage the students to draw a buzzer (a circle will do), siren, or some other warning device. Suggest that they write or sketch within their "alarm" any "triggers" that make them aware their speech is unbecoming. Recommend that underneath their "alarm" they write a sentence or two expressing their resolve to be alert to these "alarms" so as to discipline their speech.

(5) Continue the Journey

❖ Pray that today's participants will be thoughtful, well disciplined speakers.

❖ Read aloud this preparation for next week's lesson. You may also want to post it on newsprint for the students to copy.
- **Title: People of Godly Behavior**
- **Background Scripture: James 4**

- **Lesson Scripture: James 4:1-12**
- **Focus of the Lesson: Many people act greedily, engage in disputes, or judge others in order to obtain something they want. What alternatives exist to such behavior? James says that people must submit themselves to God, who frees them from behaving in ungodly ways.**

❖ Challenge the students to complete one or more of these activities for further spiritual growth, which you will write on newsprint for the students to copy.

(1) **Ask someone for permission to tape-record a conversation between the two of you. Analyze your voice. How do you sound: friendly, open, warm, angry, aloof? Do you tend to overuse certain words? Do you say what you mean, or might your words be misconstrued? How would James evaluate your speech?**

(2) **Be aware of the way speech as it is used in the media sways your opinions. How do advertisers in particular try to convince you to buy their products?**

(3) **Listen to your own words. Sometimes what we mean is not clearly articulated in our speech. Ask forgiveness, if necessary, if you realize that your words have hurt, perhaps inadvertently, someone else.**

❖ Sing or read aloud "Open My Eyes, That I May See."

❖ Conclude today's session by leading the class in this benediction, which is adapted from James 1:22, 25: **Let us now go forth as doers of the word and not merely hearers, for doers who act will be blessed in their doing.**

UNIT 3: IMAGES OF CHRIST IN US
PEOPLE OF
GODLY BEHAVIOR

PREVIEWING THE LESSON

Lesson Scripture: James 4:1-12
Background Scripture: James 4
Key Verse: James 4:8

Focus of the Lesson:
Many people act greedily, engage in disputes, or judge others in order to obtain something they want. What alternatives exist to such behavior? James says that people must submit themselves to God, who frees them from behaving in ungodly ways.

Goals for the Learners:
(1) to consider what James wrote about humbling ourselves before God in order to become more Christ-like.
(2) to identify greed, disputations, and judgments in their own behavior.
(3) to commit to improving their behavior and to work toward healing the injuries they have caused others.

Pronunciation Guide:
hedone (hay don ay')

Supplies:
Bibles, newsprint and marker, paper and pencils, hymnals, optional recording of meditative music and appropriate player

---

READING THE SCRIPTURE

NRSV
James 4:1-12

¹Those conflicts and disputes among you, where do they come from? Do they not come from your cravings that are at war within

NIV
James 4:1-12

¹What causes fights and quarrels among you? Don't they come from your desires that battle within you? ²You want something but

you? ²You want something and do not have it; so you commit murder. And you covet something and cannot obtain it; so you engage in disputes and conflicts. You do not have, because you do not ask. ³You ask and do not receive, because you ask wrongly, in order to spend what you get on your pleasures. ⁴Adulterers! Do you not know that friendship with the world is enmity with God? Therefore whoever wishes to be a friend of the world becomes an enemy of God. ⁵Or do you suppose that it is for nothing that the scripture says, "God yearns jealously for the spirit that he has made to dwell in us"? ⁶But he gives all the more grace; therefore it says,

"God opposes the proud,
but gives grace to the humble."

⁷Submit yourselves therefore to God. Resist the devil, and he will flee from you. **⁸Draw near to God, and he will draw near to you.** Cleanse your hands, you sinners, and purify your hearts, you double-minded. ⁹Lament and mourn and weep. Let your laughter be turned into mourning and your joy into dejection. ¹⁰Humble yourselves before the Lord, and he will exalt you.

¹¹Do not speak evil against one another, brothers and sisters. Whoever speaks evil against another or judges another, speaks evil against the law and judges the law; but if you judge the law, you are not a doer of the law but a judge. ¹²There is one lawgiver and judge who is able to save and to destroy. So who, then, are you to judge your neighbor?

don't get it. You kill and covet, but you cannot have what you want. You quarrel and fight. You do not have, because you do not ask God. ³When you ask, you do not receive, because you ask with wrong motives, that you may spend what you get on your pleasures.

⁴You adulterous people, don't you know that friendship with the world is hatred toward God? Anyone who chooses to be a friend of the world becomes an enemy of God. ⁵Or do you think Scripture says without reason that the spirit he caused to live in us envies intensely? ⁶But he gives us more grace. That is why Scripture says:

"God opposes the proud
but gives grace to the humble."

⁷Submit yourselves, then, to God. Resist the devil, and he will flee from you. **⁸Come near to God and he will come near to you.** Wash your hands, you sinners, and purify your hearts, you double-minded. ⁹Grieve, mourn and wail. Change your laughter to mourning and your joy to gloom. ¹⁰Humble yourselves before the Lord, and he will lift you up.

¹¹Brothers, do not slander one another. Anyone who speaks against his brother or judges him speaks against the law and judges it. When you judge the law, you are not keeping it, but sitting in judgment on it. ¹²There is only one Lawgiver and Judge, the one who is able to save and destroy. But you—who are you to judge your neighbor?

UNDERSTANDING THE SCRIPTURE

James 4:1-3. The theme explored in these verses traces directly to the preceding verses (3:13-18). There, James contrasted the wisdom from above with its opposite, seen in actions of jealousy and ambition. James closed that passage with the affirmation of the wisdom from above generating peace. Now, in verses 1-3, the epistle takes up the

results when such wisdom and peace are set aside for the sake of greed. Peace gives way in verse 1 to two terms related to war; ("conflicts and disputes" are, if anything, mild translations of the Greek words). The word translated as *cravings* in verse 1 and "pleasures" in verse 3, is *hedone*: the root for the English word *hedonism*. Verse 3 provides an ironic counterstatement to the promise of Jesus to "ask, and it will be given you" (Matthew 7:7). That promise breaks down in "wrong" asking that restricts itself to seeking one's own pleasures.

James 4:4-6. "Adulterers" may sound somewhat out of context, if it is heard strictly as unfaithfulness in marital covenant. James has not raised that issue. Partially, it connects to the cravings that lead persons to desire beyond that which is good. Even more relevant is adultery's use in the Old Testament as a metaphor for idolatry. James's critique of envy grows out of his recognition that it leads persons to other allegiances than God (see comments on "double-minded" in verse 8). James has already used "world" in the pejorative sense as that which is opposed to God (1:27). What James means by "world" in 4:4 can be seen in the system or cycle he describes in verses 1-3. Verse 5 poses a peculiar problem, as it corresponds to no Old Testament passage. In addition, it is very difficult to translate (for example, it is unclear in Greek whether the subject of the verb "desire" is God or Spirit). Verse 6 quotes Proverbs 3:34, which is also quoted by 1 Peter 5:5.

James 4:7-10. The chief verbs in this section are all in imperative form. They summon the reader or listener to engage in particular actions, for example: submit, resist, draw near. There is a clearly parallel structure in verses 7b-8a. There, movement away from the devil and his subsequent withdrawal from you is contrasted with the opposites of drawing near to God and God's subsequent drawing near to you. The language of 8b comes from the cultic language of Judaism of cleansing and purification (literally, "make holy"). "Double-minded" calls to mind the previous addressing of "adulterers" in verse 4. Two minds result from trying to live according to the wisdom of God while still holding on to, and being swept up in, the "wisdom" of getting and grasping detailed in verses

1-3. The threefold summons to "grieve" in verse 9a employs language reminiscent of Jesus' words in Luke's account of the Sermon on the Mount ("Woe to you who are laughing now, for you will mourn and weep," Luke 6:25b). The concluding imperative to "humble yourselves" (James 4:10) connects back to verse 6's declaration that God "gives grace to the humble."

James 4:11-12. Some commentators hold that these two verses introduce a new section in James's epistle related to arrogance and the abuse of wealth. The abuse confronted in these verses is "speaking evil." There is no attempt to distinguish any shades of meaning here: Anything from public slander to malicious private gossip falls under the indictment. James uses a sophisticated argument here that equates such speech not simply with bad manners, but with a religious crisis borne of inflated ego that presumes to take the role of God in levying judgment upon others. Such presumption in judgment contradicts one of this epistle's most fundamental teachings: It leaves one "not a doer of the law" (4:11). The statement in verse 12 that "there is [only] one lawgiver" (God) may reflect a slight departure of the Jewish Christian community from the synagogue's view of Moses as lawgiver. The closing challenge of "who are you" to judge neighbor sets up an interesting parallel with James's earlier assertion in 2:8 of the royal law being observed in love of neighbor.

James 4:13-16. This section echoes several teachings of Old Testament wisdom, and of Jesus' own teachings. The transitory nature of life asserted in verse 14 resembles Psalm 90's sobering perspective that our days "are like a dream" and "they are soon gone" (Psalm 90:5, 10). Such a perspective can be easily forgotten by those who so struggle and strive to get what they can by whatever means necessary (James 4:1-3). In the forgetting of that truth comes the loss of perspective on life and God. The plans laid in verse 13 of "today or tomorrow" sound also a bit like the parable Jesus tells of the rich fool who planned the tearing down of old barns and building up of new ones to house all he had—only to discover he had run out of the one true treasure given to him, his time (Luke 12:13-21). James returns to the theme of his earlier assertion of God's opposition to the proud (4:6) by now critiquing the boastful arrogance of those who think they own time as well as everything else. This tie between arrogance and riches will be confronted even more sternly in the next chapter (especially 5:1-6).

James 4:17. This final verse in the passage stands on its own as a proverbial-style wisdom saying. Its connection to the previous material and the following is tenuous, except in that they all consistently declare James's theme of the importance of faith expressed in works. Here in this verse, the sin of omission takes center stage. Sin is not simply in the actions that hurt and destroy, the actions strongly implied in the cycle depicted in the chapter's opening (4:1-3). Sin also comes through inaction. Whenever the right is known but ignored, sin has been committed. The wisdom James teaches is one in which knowledge of the "right things" is not enough; such knowledge must find its way into practice.

INTERPRETING THE SCRIPTURE

Mired in the Cycle

It does not take a degree in religion or psychology to recognize the cycle James portrays here. It is the pernicious drive to have more, of never being satisfied with the good one has. "Keeping up with the Joneses" is an innocent but cogent parallel to this in our everyday lives. We see what another has, and soon what had been a "want" becomes a "need." We lose our sense of perspective.

In extreme cases, that loss leads to a willingness to "do whatever it takes" to achieve the desired object. In personal relationships, fidelity gets broken to indulge in exciting but ultimately empty experiences of sexuality. Among nations, the desire to attain this piece of land or that prized resource leads to skulduggery at best and violence at worst. Within nations, political campaigns degenerate into extended smear campaigns, with the attitude "I don't care so long as my side comes out the winner." Even religion finds an Achilles heel, when we spend our prayers and efforts not for the sake of the poor and vulnerable, but for seeking the "good life" as the world speaks of it for ourselves.

James offers a potent critique of what ails us, not simply in understanding the first-century Jewish-Christian community but also in grappling with what still threatens to undo us as individuals and communities today. Such cycles that confuse wants with needs create prime fields for abuse. Why? Attending first to me and mine by definition leaves God either out of the picture or simply as a prop to our self-centered grasping. Religion that is sidelined to spiritual pursuits while we recklessly pursue our wants, regardless of consequence to others or future generations, is no religion at all. It is a cycle that can continue to drag us down, if we do not bring to bear against it the grace of God linked strongly with the acts of faith James consistently seeks.

God's Preferences

Elsewhere, James urges our impartiality (2:9). The attitude he addresses there is the very human tendency to be attracted to things, and persons, of wealth and power to the exclusion of those without. Peter, in the sermon to Cornelius and his household, asserts that God shows no partiality (Acts

10:34 and following), a remarkable assertion of God's freedom to embrace Gentiles as well as Jews.

But did you know God does have preferences? "God opposes the proud, but gives grace to the humble" (James 4:6). Generally, we don't like to think of God *opposed* to anyone, at least when we are talking around the children. Although, come to think of it, we occasionally do have those moments when we may tip our hand and secretly hope God has it in for those who are on the other side of some fence from us. And down through history, we have some very clear—and awful—examples of folks (including Christians) who wagered quite heavily on the presumption that God sided against the enemy. "God with us" has emblazoned the attitude of more than one nation . . . and more than one arrogance.

Ironically, when God gets around to stating preferences, the words have less to do with warning others than they do with warning us. *God opposes the proud*—think, for a moment, about the meaning of pride. Doesn't pride, by definition, presume the rightness of one's side or cause? So one way of understanding God's preferences is that God does not look kindly on the self-righteous or the self-assured or those who think they and they alone are the chosen ones (or real Christians, or whatever phrase you would like to substitute there).

God does have preferences. It is just that as soon as we think God prefers us because of who we are, we need to do some humble soul-searching, lest we come to a rude awakening.

Taking Responsibility

We fail to see it in English translations, but the word for "opposes" in verse 6 and "submit" in verse 7 share the same root in Greek. To avoid finding ourselves *opposed* by God requires the taking of certain actions. Submit. Resist. Draw near. Cleanse. Purify. Lament. Humble yourself.

These are stern words. But they are necessary words. They are the kind of words that are likely to be associated with discipline, or with setting aside something we have gotten used to. That is exactly their point. What we have gotten used to, in the argument of this epistle, is the cycle earlier depicted in verses 1-3. And that is a cycle not easily broken without clear and decisive action. The confusion of wants with needs will not be given up, unless there is clarity about what makes for life—and who makes for life.

The responsibility to which James calls individuals and communities in these verses begins in action that returns them to primary allegiance and trust in God. Taking responsibility in these verses recognizes that another has a claim upon us. The cycle we have let ourselves be fooled by pride into assuming leaves out God, for all that matters there is what we covet. The changing of that cycle requires a return to responsibility to the One from whom all things come. The language about lament and mourning and weeping is not there because God is without joy. Rather, it is because we need to grieve an old way of life before we can lay it to rest and move on to the new. The closing call to humble ourselves (4:10) balances with the disclosure that God's grace is given to the humble (4:6).

The way is clear, even if not easy. The cycle can be broken, though not without change. Responsibility can be taken for our actions and for seeking new actions in and by the grace of God.

The Power of Words—and Word

James returns to the power of words in 4:11-12, which he had first discussed in chapter 3 concerning the power of the tongue. Not once or twice but three times, the author censures "speaking evil."

Earlier (2:8), James had referred to Leviticus 19:18 as exemplifying the "royal law" ("you shall love your neighbor as yourself"). Leviticus 19 seems a favorite passage of this epistle, for Leviticus 19:16 offers this command: "you shall not go around as a slanderer among your people." "Slanderer" and "speaking evil" are a close match.

For an epistle that preaches the importance of action, James knows all too well the power of words. He shares that assessment with none other than Jesus. In the Sermon on the Mount, Jesus connected the sin of murder with a verbal insult (Matthew 5:21-22).

Sometimes, the rightful stress on the importance of works has been used to undermine the power of words. So, we rea-

son, it's not what a person says but what a person does that counts. But the devaluing of words does more than make absurd the quadrennial offering of political campaign promises too soon linked with their forgetting. Devaluing words devalues the communities and relationships that form them. Speaking evil is not simply as bad as doing evil: Speaking evil is doing evil. The moment we forget that is the moment we lose integrity between word and deed, between promise and commitment. And in a faith whose central tenet involves the Word made flesh, the neglect of the power and potential of our words breeds hypocrisy.

SHARING THE SCRIPTURE

Preparing Our Hearts

Meditate on this week's devotional reading, found in Proverbs 3:13-18. Wisdom, personified as a woman, is discussed in these verses. Wisdom is seen as true wealth for those who find her—far more valuable than precious metals and gems. What are you seeking? How might wisdom empower you to live as a godly person? Write a prayer or meditation asking God to give you wisdom.

Pray that you and the adult learners will allow people to be aware of your Christian behavior by living wisely with integrity.

Preparing Our Minds

Study the background, James 4, and lesson Scripture, James 4:1-12. As you prepare, consider alternatives to acting greedily, engaging in disputes, or judging others in order to obtain something that you want.

Write on newsprint:

❑ information for next week's lesson, found under "Continue the Journey."
❑ activities for further spiritual growth in "Continue the Journey."

Choose optional meditative music and an appropriate player.

LEADING THE CLASS

(1) Gather to Learn

❖ Welcome the class members and introduce any guests.

❖ Pray that those who have gathered today will experience God's presence in their midst.

❖ Read this information gleaned from an Associated Press story: **The North American Securities Administrators Association reports that religion-related fraud has netted billions of dollars in recent years, and the scope of the problem is only increasing. Often, a clever scam artist will ingratiate himself or herself with the pastor by making a generous donation to the church and encouraging the pastor to invest in a legitimate-sounding business or real estate deal. Parishioners follow suit, and before anyone understands what has happened church buildings are lost, investors are bilked out of thousands of** dollars, or projects for the church the scammer has promised never materialize because the money is gone. The system works, in part, because Christians do not like to speak against other Christians, even if they are skeptical of the purportedly wonderful deal. It also works because the "prosperity gospel," which asserts that faith in God leads to financial rewards in this life, is increasingly taught in churches, including mainstream ones. Even when the perpetrator is caught, church members are often reluctant to speak against someone they have perceived to be a good Christian.

❖ Discus these questions.

(1) **What motivates people to present a pious front while bilking a congregation and/or its members?**

(2) **Why do you think Christians are so willing to invest in schemes that prove to be fraudulent?**

(3) **What can churches do to prevent these frauds?**

❖ Read aloud today's focus statement: **Many people act greedily, engage in disputes, or judge others in order to obtain something they want. What alternatives exist to such behavior? James says that people must submit themselves to God, who frees them from behaving in ungodly ways.**

(2) Consider What James Wrote About Humbling Ourselves Before God in Order to Become More Christ-like

❖ Encourage a volunteer to read James 4:1-12.

❖ Read or retell "Mired in the Cycle" from Interpreting the Scripture to get a modern view of the kinds of problems James intends to address.

❖ Draw a circle in the center of a sheet of newsprint. In the center of the circle write "friendship with the world." Add "spokes" to the circle, as on a bicycle wheel. Ask the students to call out behaviors and attitudes that constitute friendship with the world. Write each idea on a separate "spoke."

❖ Ask: **From what you know about Jesus, his teachings, and his expectations of us as disciples, why would he find each of these "spokes" to be a barrier to friendship with God?** If the class is large, consider discussing this question in small groups.

❖ Suggest that the antidote to "friendship with the world" is humility before God. Assign volunteers to look up and read aloud the following references to humility. (You may wish to add others if time permits.)

■ Proverbs 3:34
■ Proverbs 15:33
■ Proverbs 18:12
■ Proverbs 22:4
■ Zephaniah 2:3
■ Ephesians 4:1-3
■ Philippians 2:1-11
■ Colossians 3:12
■ 1 Peter 5:5-6

❖ Wrap up this portion of the lesson by asking the students to summarize their understanding of what it means to be humble before God.

(3) Identify Greed, Disputations, and Judgments in the Learners' Behavior

❖ Recall the story of the fraudulent scammers presented in "Gather to Learn." Note that although the vast majority of Christians are not engaged in illegal activities, we can still be greedy, argumentative, and judgmental.

❖ Divide the class into groups of three or four. Challenge each group to identify some common situations that show forth greed, disputes, and judgments. Ask each group to prepare to role-play one situation they have selected. Situations may include problems that most churches encounter, such as a dispute at a meeting or criticism of a member, but they may also include ungodly behaviors of individual Christians at home, work, or the community.

❖ Call on each group (or as many as possible) to present their role-play to the class.

❖ Debrief each role-play by asking these questions.

(1) How was this role-play in tension with the godly behavior to which James calls us?

(2) What changes would one or more of the characters need to make in order to reflect the image of Christ?

❖ Provide a few moments for quiet reflection, asking the students to recognize themselves in at least one of these situations and ask God's forgiveness.

(4) Commit to Improving Behavior and Work Toward Healing the Injuries the Learners Have Caused Others

❖ Note that when we behave in the conflict-producing ways seen in James 4:1-12, we can and do cause injuries to ourselves and others. Hurt feelings, damaged self-esteem, and doubts about why one would want to be a Christian when behavior seems so at odds with Jesus' behavior are examples of injuries that need to be healed. We need to take responsibility for our actions.

❖ Read or retell "Taking Responsibility" from Interpreting the Scripture.

❖ Distribute paper and pencils. Encourage the adults to list steps/actions they need to take in order to humble themselves before God and set things right with someone whom they have harmed as a result of their ungodly behavior. Ask the adults to work in silence, or you may choose to play softly some meditative background music.

(5) Continue the Journey

❖ Bring the class together by praying that today's participants will go forth committed to living a godly life that clearly reflects the image of Christ.

❖ Read aloud this preparation for next week's lesson. You may also want to post it on newsprint for the students to copy.

■ Title: Prayerful Community
■ Background Scripture: James 5
■ Lesson Scripture: James 5:13-18
■ Focus of the Lesson: People's attitudes toward life shape the way they respond with joy or concern to circumstances and events. How can we achieve a positive attitude that leads to powerful and effective living? James teaches that our lifestyle is to be shaped by an attitude of prayer.

❖ Challenge the students to complete one or more of these activities for further spiritual growth, which you will write on newsprint for the students to copy.

(1) Devote prayer time this week to confession, asking God to empower you to live a responsible, godly life.

(2) Guide a young person who is apparently choosing friendship with the world over friendship with God. Help this person understand that although we need some material goods to live, an over-emphasis on them leads us away from God. Share your own experiences.

(3) Look through your belongings. How much "clutter" and unneeded "stuff" do you have? What can you give away, recycle, or discard? Try to pare down and simplify your life as a means of freeing yourself from the things of the world.

❖ Sing or read aloud "I Am Thine, O Lord."

❖ Conclude today's session by leading the class in this benediction, which is adapted from James 1:22, 25: **Let us now go forth as doers of the word and not merely hearers, for doers who act will be blessed in their doing.**

UNIT 3: IMAGES OF CHRIST IN US
PRAYERFUL COMMUNITY

PREVIEWING THE LESSON

Lesson Scripture: James 5:13-18
Background Scripture: James 5
Key Verse: James 5:13

Focus of the Lesson:
People's attitudes toward life shape the way they respond with joy or concern to circumstances and events. How can we achieve a positive attitude that leads to powerful and effective living? James teaches that our lifestyle is to be shaped by an attitude of prayer.

Goals for the Learners:
(1) to explore James's teachings on personal and community prayer.
(2) to identify different reasons for them to pray and ways they pray.
(3) to take steps to pray with increasing frequency each day.

Pronunciation Guide:
kakopatheo (kak o path eh' o)

Supplies:
Bibles, newsprint and marker, paper and pencils, hymnals

READING THE SCRIPTURE

NRSV
James 5:13-18

¹³Are any among you suffering? They should pray. Are any cheerful? They should sing songs of praise. ¹⁴Are any among you sick? They should call for the elders of the church and have them pray over them, anointing them with oil in the name of the Lord. ¹⁵The prayer of faith will save the sick, and the Lord will raise them up; and anyone who has committed sins will be forgiven. ¹⁶Therefore confess your sins to

NIV
James 5:13-18

¹³Is any one of you in trouble? He should pray. Is anyone happy? Let him sing songs of praise. ¹⁴Is any one of you sick? He should call the elders of the church to pray over him and anoint him with oil in the name of the Lord. ¹⁵And the prayer offered in faith will make the sick person well; the Lord will raise him up. If he has sinned, he will be forgiven. ¹⁶Therefore confess your sins to each other and pray for

AUGUST 31

one another, and pray for one another, so that you may be healed. The prayer of the righteous is powerful and effective. [17]Elijah was a human being like us, and he prayed fervently that it might not rain, and for three years and six months it did not rain on the earth. [18]Then he prayed again, and the heaven gave rain and the earth yielded its harvest.

each other so that you may be healed. The prayer of a righteous man is powerful and effective.

[17]Elijah was a man just like us. He prayed earnestly that it would not rain, and it did not rain on the land for three and a half years. [18]Again he prayed, and the heavens gave rain, and the earth produced its crops.

UNDERSTANDING THE SCRIPTURE

James 5:1-4. James' earlier words concerning the abuses of the rich against community (2:6-7) now come to a head in this description of the end of such arrogance and greed. The objects of desire (riches, clothes, gold, silver) that have obsessively dictated a life of "possessing" prove themselves to be of no lasting value. "Laid up treasure" (5:3) uses the same verb as Luke 12:21, the ending of Jesus' parable about the rich fool. There, too, the collision of this world's mortality with the coming age's arrival portends a sad end for those who have expended their lives in the pursuit of materialism.

James 5:4-6. In verses 4-6, the words of James take on the tone of Old Testament prophets who took the wealthy and powerful of Israel to task for injustices against the poor and common laborers (see, for example, Amos 8:4-6). The voices of the laborers crying out resembles both the blood of Abel crying from the ground (Genesis 4:10) and Israel's cries out of Egypt (Exodus 2:23-24). In both cases, God heard those cries and acted. On page 217 of Volume 12 of *The New Interpreter's Bible*, Luke Timothy Johnson states that the final clause of verse 6 can be interpreted as a question with God as the subject: "Does he [God] not oppose you?" That translation would make a compelling parallel to James 4:6, which quotes Proverbs 3:34 to make exactly that point.

James 5:7-9. Underlying these words of James that counsel forbearance (another

translation of the word rendered in the NRSV as "patience") is the twice-stated affirmation of Jesus' coming. The patience or forbearance is not set in the context of interminable waiting, much less an inability to do anything about this world or the conditions in it (on that point, James has given already plentiful advice and wisdom on living out the faith in action). Rather, patience is given the assurance of fulfillment by the Lord's coming. It is not in vain. The imagery of the farmer is one used by Jesus several times in parables told of the kingdom. In later Jewish tradition, "early and the later rains" took on the meaning of the day of God's coming when God's Spirit would be poured out (see Joel 2:23-29). The directive "do not grumble against one another" (James 5:9) serves to incorporate the practice of patience into the life of the community. "Grumbling" parallels the murmuring of Israel in the wilderness. Far more valuable is raising one's voice and condition to God, as already indicated in God's hearing the cries of the poor (5:4) and in anticipation of the impending section on the importance of prayer (5:13-18). The final sentence of verse 9 calls to mind the image in Revelation 3:20, of Jesus (in James identified as Judge) standing at the door and knocking.

James 5:10-12. Earlier in this epistle, James appealed to the examples of Abraham (2:21-23) and then Rahab (2:25) for illustration of his point about works as central to faith. Now, in seeking to give example of patience and "suffering" (see comments on this word under 5:13-18), James invokes the memory of the prophets. In particular, he points to Job. Job is not usually counted among Israel's prophets. However, one of the functions of a prophet is not only to speak God's word to the people but also to bring the people's need to God. Job certainly accomplishes that function, in voicing both lament and trust in the face of innocent suffering. The word James uses to speak of the prophets and Job is "endurance." It is the same word used at the beginning of this epistle (1:12). There, it had been used to encourage faithfulness in times of testing. Here, endurance is the quality that enables a life of faithful patience. The description of God in verse 11 as "compassionate and merciful" mirrors the words God used to reveal God's self to Moses on Mount Sinai (Exodus 34:6). Verse 12 concludes this section with a teaching on not swearing that parallels Jesus' teaching in the Sermon on the Mount (Matthew 5:33-37). The point of swearing is to invoke a higher authority for the truthfulness of one's words. The words of both James and Jesus suggest our words should be trustworthy enough, with the implication that our actions in living out those words produce such reliability.

James 5:13-18. The first "condition" identified and connected to the need for prayer in these verses is: "suffering" (NRSV) or being "in trouble" (NIV). Neither of those translations catches the full meaning of this word in Greek. *Kakopatheo* (another form of the word used in verse 10) is a compound word that literally means "evil suffering." In Interpreting the Scripture we will explore the connotations of this meaning in greater depth. The

mention of "elders" and "church" (the only time either of these words is used in James) leads to conjecture about the degree to which the Christian community had developed as a separate institution outside of Judaism. More clear is the emphasis these words lend to prayer as engaging the whole community. Another element linking community and prayer is the confession of sins "to one another" (5:16). The Greek word is not the usual one for sins; its meaning is closer to "fallings" or "mishaps." In other words, members of the community are to be honest about themselves, and in that shared honesty comes healing. The example James appeals to for prayer from the Hebrew writings is Elijah. The affirmation in verse 17 that Elijah was "a human being like us" conveys the sense that prayer does not belong to the spiritually elite.

James 5:19-20. The final two verses of this chapter—and the epistle itself—encourage the practice of mutual correction. "Wandering from the truth" is not portrayed to be an act from which there is no return. Indeed, the one who brings the wanderer back into community serves a Christ-like function of "saving" that individual. The exact meaning of the "multitude of sins" that go covered is unclear. It could be interpreted as the sins of the one who does the correcting. It could be interpreted as the sins that would otherwise have been committed by the wanderer. Or, perhaps, it is both. In any case, James ends on the uplifting note of reconciliation. The wisdom of this epistle aims at life lived in community with God and one another, where forgiveness renews even those who wander. And who among us has not?

INTERPRETING THE SCRIPTURE

Pray for One Another

Prayer presumes community. Community weaves its way through every sec-

tion of James's teaching on prayer. "Are any among you" (5:13) implies we live our faith in the midst of others. "To one another" and "for one another" (5:16) presume we have others to whom we are connected and for whom we are concerned.

Too often, prayer has been seen as the bailiwick of the "spiritual" among us, and more often than not, that assessment has swayed based on whether one has a seminary degree or not. How many times have you been in a gathering of your faith community and when it came time for a prayer to be offered, all eyes (and expectations!) turned to the pastor alone? In my own early years of ministry, it seemed my invitation to Kiwanis or Chamber meetings hinged on my agreeability to offer the mealtime prayer. And I did. But have you ever had the experience in one of those settings of hearing a minister, having been asked, saying: "Actually, no, why don't you pray?"

In truth, prayer belongs to the whole community. In a lecture to a group of Christian clergy, I once heard a rabbi tell us that is why, in his understanding of the Jewish ritual, the sermon always preceded the prayers. Why? The sermon was to enable the people to pray—rather than the other way around.

It is a lesson well worth heeding. Prayer is a practice of the community, not the elite few with theological degrees or outgoing personalities or religious-sounding voices. Prayer is the activity (and James is the epistle of action!) of the whole people of God: in conversation with God for the sake of one another and for this God-beloved world. Prayer takes seriously the condition and need of individuals in the community (see 5:13-14). Prayer trusts the grace and purpose of God who will hear us as God has always heard human need and cries (see 5:4). So we pray: out of a history that teaches trust; out of present experience that offers crisis and opportunity; out of the hope that, even though we cannot really explain how, prayer truly is effective and powerful.

Prayer is not a spectator sport. Prayer is participation with one another, and with God, in active speaking and active listening and, above all else, active trusting that God hears, and from that hearing can come life and transformation.

Powerful and Effective Prayer

How is prayer powerful and effective? Doesn't God already know the need before we speak? And if prayer is badgering God into action, what does that make of God—or us?

All sorts of opinions float around these days, as they have for generations, about whether or how prayer *works*. It would seem the more we try to pin down the explanations in logical fashion, the deeper we find ourselves in paradox or further questions.

For example, recent studies have been made about the effects of prayer on healing. And, it would seem, there does seem to be a positive effect. My understanding is that at least some of these studies have not sought to make any distinction about the type of prayer employed, or the tradition out of which it comes. The medical community's interest is in the healing process, not the efficacy of one religious tradition over another. So is it simply a matter of the relaxation of the mind associated with prayer or meditation, or is something "spiritual" happening? I am not aware of medical tests capable of discerning the difference there. All that they appear to indicate is some positive impact on those who combine traditional medical treatment with a practice related to prayer.

Anecdotal stories of individuals—perhaps your own stories—may witness to stronger links between prayer and healing. We may not share the same perspective of those who encourage viewers to place their hands on the television set for a prayer of healing to come through, but we may have experienced for ourselves something of prayer's healing gift in our lives. Words and touch can convey the grace of God. We base our worship, and our sacramental life, on those understandings. Why not, then, in the realm of prayer and healing?

James confesses prayer to be powerful and effective, capable of healing. We may differ on exactly how that is, or why that is, but unanimity is not the point. The point is the practice of prayer, the holding up of others and ourselves to the transforming power of God. God remains free to work outside of our words and gestures and presence. But we also confess God in incarnational ways, which means, among other things, we confess God works through the words and actions of others. Even ourselves. Even through our prayers. Even for healing. Do you believe that . . . and if so, do you practice that?

Prayer and the Opposing of Evil

Take another look at verse 13a, based on the comments in Understanding the Scripture. "Are any of you *suffering evil* [my translation]? They should pray" (5:13a). James is not talking about the kind of suffering one has with a head cold. Or, to follow this word's translation in the NIV, it is not the sort of "trouble" one gets into because of some momentary lapse in personal judgment. The suffering here has to do with the kind of suffering and injustice and indignity that can result when evil holds an upper hand. The church had already experienced something of this during Saul's murderous persecution of the Way (Acts 8:1-3; 9:1). James, the brother of Jesus to whom this epistle is traditionally attributed, would himself be martyred for the faith.

And that is just the beginning of the collision between the faith community and the forces of evil. Apartheid. Holocaust. Ethnic cleansing. In every generation, the church and all creation has never lacked for evil to make its presence known.

One might think, especially given James's "activist" bent (faith without works is dead), that the invitation to pray in the face of suffering produced by evil is, well, weak. Shouldn't we be out there taking action? Absolutely! But the insistence on prayer underscores powerful lessons.

Partly, it is the lesson of remembering that the combating of evil is not carried out by doing evil in return. "Do not be overcome by evil, but overcome evil with good" (Romans 12:21) reminds us that evil's seductive power lies precisely in its ability to lure us into its ways even in the name of combating it. And partly, the insistence on prayer in the face of evil reinforces the teaching that vengeance belongs not to us, but to God. By centering ourselves and our resistance and our witness against evil in the context of relationship with God we let go of the need to "get even" or "settle the score." The lament psalms of Israel often did this in powerful ways.

Pray then in the face of suffering brought on by evil. Not because it is the only way we can resist evil, for James remains an epistle of action, but because prayer will temper our action, and deliver us (hopefully) from becoming no different than the very ones whom we oppose.

SHARING THE SCRIPTURE

Preparing Our Hearts

Meditate on this week's devotional reading, found in 1 Thessalonians 5:16-22. Here we are told to rejoice, pray, and give thanks. Although these are three distinct activities, ponder how they mesh together. How are our lives different when we approach all circumstances with joy, prayer, and thanksgiving, even if the situations are challenging for us? What clues can this passage give you as to how to live a more Christ-centered life?

You may want to record your thoughts in a spiritual journal.

Pray that you and the adult learners will "pray without ceasing" so as to build up the community of faith and walk faithfully with God.

Preparing Our Minds

Study the background found in James 5 and lesson Scripture, verses 13-18. As you read consider how you can achieve a positive attitude that leads to powerful and effective living.

Write on newsprint:

❑ information for next week's lesson, found under "Continue the Journey."

❑ activities for further spiritual growth in "Continue the Journey."

Consider researching types of prayer to augment the discussion under "Identify Different Reasons for the Learners to Pray and Ways They Pray."

LEADING THE CLASS

(1) Gather to Learn

❖ Welcome the class members and introduce any guests.

❖ Pray that today's participants will sense the presence of God among them.

❖ Point out that many people throughout history have made the claim that our attitude, not our outward circumstances, is what causes us to react positively or negatively. Read aloud these quotations.

■ **"At any moment in life we have the option to choose an attitude of gratitude, a posture of grace, a commitment to joy."** (Tim Hansel)

■ **"Attitudes are capable of making the same experience either pleasant or painful."** (John Powell)

■ **"It all depends on how we look at things, and not how they are in themselves."** (Carl Jung, 1875–1961)

■ **"It isn't your problems that are bothering you. It is the way you are looking at them."** (Epictetus, about A.D. 55– about 135)

■ **"It's not what happens to me that matters most; it's how I react to what happens to me."** (Robert Schuller, 1926–)

■ **"People can alter their lives by altering their attitudes."** (William James, 1842–1910)

■ **"The mind is its own place, and in itself can make a heaven of hell, a hell of heaven."** (John Milton, 1608–1674)

❖ Ask these questions.

(1) **Without mentioning names, what examples can you cite of people who had reason to be despondent but who exuded joy?**

(2) **Similarly, what examples can you give of people whose circumstances seemed good but who focused on the negatives of life?**

(3) **What made the difference as to how these people reacted?**

❖ Read aloud today's focus statement: **People's attitudes toward life shape the way they respond with joy or concern to circumstances and events. How can we achieve a positive attitude that leads to powerful and effective living? James teaches that our lifestyle is to be shaped by an attitude of prayer.**

(2) Explore James's Teachings on Personal and Community Prayer

❖ Select a volunteer to read James 5:13-18.

❖ List on newsprint reasons why believers should pray, according to James 5. Leave this newsprint posted throughout the session.

❖ Add information from James 5:13-18 in Understanding the Scripture as appropriate.

❖ Read or retell "Powerful and Effective Prayer" from Interpreting the Scripture and then discuss these questions.

(1) If you were asked, "Doesn't God already know what we need, why should we pray?" how would you respond?

(2) What examples can you give about the effectiveness of prayer? (You may want to focus on prayers for healing.)

(3) What can you say to someone who believes that prayer has not been heard and/or answered?

❖ Discuss with the class ways that they see "powerful and effective prayer" being practiced in their own congregation.

❖ **Option:** Talk about ways that the congregation can strengthen its prayer life, especially if the students feel it is weak. Could you hold regularly scheduled prayer services? Could you offer classes on prayer? Could you create a telephone chain/tree with designated leaders so that people can call or e-mail their prayer requests and know that a specific group in the church is praying for them? Whatever you decide is appropriate, consider steps that you need to take to turn these ideas into reality within the structure of your church.

(3) Identify Different Reasons for the Learners to Pray and Ways They Pray

❖ Refer to the list of reasons James gives for praying that you wrote on newsprint earlier in the session. Invite the students to add other reasons for prayer.

❖ Try to identify and describe several types of prayer. Here are some examples, but encourage the class to add others. Write your list on another sheet of newsprint, and leave it posted throughout the session. (Recognize that there may be overlap between the previous activity and this one.)

■ *Thanksgiving*—These prayers show gratitude to God for who God is and what God has done.

■ *Petition*—When we ask God for something for ourselves, we are offering prayers of petition.

■ *Intercession*—When we lift up people or situations we are interceding in prayer for them.

■ *Confession*—We acknowledge our guilt and seek God's forgiveness when we confess our sins in prayer.

❖ **Option:** Augment this discussion by adding biblical examples of types of prayer that you have researched prior to class.

❖ Encourage the students to talk about ways that they pray. They may talk about different positions that they find helpful (such as *kneeling, standing with arms upraised, sitting, lying prostrate on the floor, or walking*), or they may name places they prefer to pray (such as *in a quiet space at home, in church, in a garden or other natural setting, in the car, while waiting in line somewhere, sitting at a desk writing a prayer journal entry*). They may speak about breath prayers, or state that they are constantly in communication with God. Note that there is no one "correct" way to pray; we all have ways that work for us.

(4) Take Steps to Pray with Increasing Frequency Each Day

❖ Distribute paper and pencils. Direct the students to look again at the list of reasons to pray that James propounds, as well as the types of prayers they have identified.

❖ Suggest that the adults identify those types of prayers and positions that are most familiar and comfortable for them, and write these on their papers.

❖ Ask them to select a type of prayer and/or a position that is unfamiliar but that they would like to try.

❖ Recommend that they write a commitment stating what they will try to do and how often they plan to do it.

❖ Break the silence by asking the class to form a circle. Provide time for volunteers to offer a brief prayer about anything that is on their hearts. Conclude the community prayer by adding the prayer suggestion under "Continue the Journey."

(5) Continue the Journey

❖ Pray that all who have come today will feel surrounded by the prayers of the faithful.

❖ Read aloud this preparation for next week's lesson. You may also want to post it on newsprint for the students to copy.

■ Title: A New Community

■ Background Scripture: Mark 1:1-8; Matthew 3:1-12

■ Lesson Scripture: Mark 1:1-8; Matthew 3:1-3

■ Focus of the Lesson: People look for a place where they can belong. What kind of community fosters a sense of belonging? The new community about which John talked and to which Jesus called people was a community of love, acceptance, repentance, and forgiveness.

❖ Challenge the students to complete one or more of these activities for further spiritual growth, which you will write on newsprint for the students to copy.

(1) Pray for several people in need this week, especially those who are sick.

(2) Use a concordance to find references to "pray" or "prayer" in the New Testament. What do you learn about how Jesus prayed? What do you learn about how the members of the early church prayed? Which lessons can you apply to your own prayer life?

(3) Talk with other Christians concerning their experiences with prayer. Based on their experiences and your own, do you believe prayer is effective? Why or why not?

❖ Sing or read aloud "Prayer Is the Soul's Sincere Desire."

❖ Conclude today's session by leading the class in this benediction, which is adapted from James 1:22, 25: **Let us now go forth as doers of the word and not merely hearers, for doers who act will be blessed in their doing.**